T0297986

Lecture Notes in Artificial Intelligence (LNAI)

Lecture Notes in Artificial Intelligence

Subseries of Lecture Notes in Computer Science
Edited by J. Siekmann

Lecture Notes in Computer Science

Edited by G. Goos and J. Hartmanis

Editorial

Artificial Intelligence has become a major discipline under the roof of Computer Science. This is also reflected by a growing number of titles devoted to this fast developing field to be published in our Lecture Notes in Computer Science. To make these volumes immediately visible we have decided to distinguish them by a special cover as Lecture Notes in Artificial Intelligence, constituting a subseries of the Lecture Notes in Computer Science. This subseries is edited by an Editorial Board of experts from all areas of AI, chaired by Jörg Siekmann, who are looking forward to consider further AI monographs and proceedings of high scientific quality for publication.

We hope that the constitution of this subseries will be well accepted by the audience of the Lecture Notes in Computer Science, and we feel confident that the subseries will be recognized as an outstanding opportunity for publication by authors and editors of the AI community.

Editors and publisher

Lecture Notes in Artificial Intelligence

Edited by J. Siekmann

Subseries of Lecture Notes in Computer Science

444

S. Ramani   R. Chandrasekar
K.S.R. Anjaneyulu   (Eds.)

Knowledge Based Computer Systems

International Conference KBCS '89
Bombay, India, December 11–13, 1989
Proceedings

Springer-Verlag

Berlin Heidelberg New York London
Paris Tokyo Hong Kong Barcelona

Editors

S. Ramani
R. Chandrasekar
K. S. R. Anjaneyulu
National Centre for Software Technology
Gulmohar Cross Road No. 9
Juhu, Bombay 400 049, India

CR Subject Classification (1987): I.2

ISBN 3-540-52850-4 Springer-Verlag Berlin Heidelberg New York
ISBN 0-387-52850-4 Springer-Verlag New York Berlin Heidelberg

© Springer-Verlag Berlin Heidelberg 1990
Printed in Germany

Printing and binding: Druckhaus Beltz, Hemsbach/Bergstr.
2145/3140-543210 – Printed on acid-free paper

Preface

The area of Knowledge Based Computer Systems (KBCS) is becoming increasingly popular for intellectual endeavor, and for commercially viable enterprise. The past few years have seen a number of practical applications of AI technology coming out of the laboratories. We are now on the threshold of major advances in KBCS.

This volume consists of forty-seven papers covering a broad spectrum of areas in Knowledge Based Computer Systems, both theoretical and practical. This volume will give readers an insight into developments in the rapidly growing area of Artificial Intelligence and will also give a feel for practical applications that are possible with the state of the art.

These papers were selected by an international team of referees for presentation at the Conference on Knowledge Based Computer Systems - KBCS '89. This is the second in a series of annual conferences hosted by the Knowledge Based Computer Systems Project. This project is funded by the Government of India and is assisted by the United Nations Development Programme. This volume also contains papers describing research and development at the nodal centres of the KBCS project.

We thank the sponsors and the members of the advisory committee and the program committee for their support and suggestions in arranging the conference. We also thank the referees (listed on page 543) who played a major role in helping the program committee select the papers in this volume from the one hundred and forty-one received. The intellectual capital for the conference was contributed by the invited speakers, authors, tutorial speakers and authors of poster papers. We thank them all.

Mr Sasikumar contributed substantially to the planning of the conference, coordination and communication with the referees, and the production of this volume. Mr Srinivas lent us his expertise with TeX, in typesetting parts of this volume. Every member of the KBCS group at NCST contributed to the organisation of the conference. Colleagues at NCST helped in a variety of ways. Colleagues in the ERNET Project provided us with excellent e-mail facilities. Mr NK Mehra of Narosa Publishing House helped us plan the publication of this volume, and organised remarkably fast printing of the participants' edition. We are grateful to all of them.

S Ramani
R Chandrasekar
KSR Anjaneyulu

Bombay, March 1990

Conference Committees

International Advisory Committee

K Apt, Centrum voor Wiskunde en Informatica, Amsterdam
Arvind, Massachusetts Institute of Technology, USA
M Boden, University of Sussex, UK
A Joshi, University of Pennsylvania, USA
R Kowalski, Imperial College, UK
CJP Lucena, Pontifficia Universidade Catoilica do Rio de Janeiro, Brazil
P Saint-Dizier, Université Paul Sabatier, France
A Togashi, Tohoku University, Japan

Programme Committee

S Ramani, National Centre for Software Technology, Bombay *(Chairman)*
S Arun Kumar, Indian Institute of Technology, Bombay
KK Bajaj, Department of Electronics, Delhi
VP Bhatkar, Centre for Development of Advanced Computing, Pune
PCP Bhatt, Indian Institute of Technology, Delhi
D Dutta Majumder, Indian Statistical Institute, Calcutta
HN Mahabala, Indian Institute of Technology, Madras
V Rajaraman, Indian Institute of Science, Bangalore
PVS Rao, Tata Institute Fundamental Research, Bombay
R Sangal, Indian Institute of Technology, Kanpur

Contents

AI Applications

Computer Architecture and Parallel Processing

Expert Systems

Intelligent Tutoring Systems

Knowledge Representation

Logic Programming

Natural Language Understanding

Pattern Recognition and Vision

Reasoning

Search

Speech

Activities at the KBCS Nodal Centres

AI Applications

A Computational Architecture for Co-operative Systems

David Allport

Hewlett Packard Laboratories
Bristol
dea@hplb.hpl.hp.com

Abstract

This paper argues that computer systems can be classified according to the relative amounts of cognitive processing that are required from the human user and the system software, and that co-operativity takes different forms in these different classes of systems. It proposes a generic architecture for the class of systems in which cognitive processing is interactively shared between computer and user, and argues that in an important sub-class of systems, much of what is normally understood by "user-modelling" is unnecessary to provide co-operative responses to questions.

1 Introduction

This paper proposes a computational architecture that will be appropriate for co-operative computer programs in any application domain. This generic architecture is derived from a consideration of the types of functionality that might be necessary in order to provide co-operativity in a problem-solving program. We identify reasoning about participants, dialogues, tasks and applications as being the four major components of a generic co-operative architecture, and note that some domains require sophisticated kinds of reasoning in all of these components.

However, in well-structured problem-solving domains, there are definite practical limits to the complexity of reasoning that is required in order to produce co-operative responses to user inputs. Thus even though we believe that the theoretical problems of reasoning about dialogues, participants and tasks are far from being solved in the general case, we do not believe that it is premature to begin building truly co-operative problem-solving systems.

We are currently developing P R O C O D E, a P R O totype C O onfiguration Dialogue Environment, at Hewlett Packard Laboratories, Bristol. This program takes advantage of the structure of the computer configuration domain to derive limitations upon the functionality that we need to provide, and in particular eliminates all explicit reasoning about participants. We argue below that the characteristics of the configuration domain that enable our program to successfully generate co-operative responses are in fact shared by many other domains. We therefore suggest that for a large and important class of domains, the four-fold generic architecture is unnecessary, and co-operativity can be adequately realised with the limited three-fold architecture used in PROCODE.

Our argument begins with a discussion of the different forms that co-operativity takes in different kinds of computer system, depending upon the relative sophistication of the reasoning done by the user and the program. We stress that our main concern is with the type of co-operativity relevant in systems where "cognitive processing" is shared between the user and the computer system. We then discuss in turn the reasoning that is necessary about dialogues, participants, tasks and applications in order to provide this kind of co-operativity in the general case, and note the characteristics of some domains that put greater or lesser emphasis on each kind of functionality. This four-fold functional distinction is the basis of what we propose as the most *generic* co-operative architecture. However, we do not propose this as the most *generally necessary* architecture. In particular, we note that the traditional notion of "user modelling" conflates several different kinds of functionality, and that it is possible to provide co-operativity in a large class of domains without the need for explicit reasoning about particular users. We conclude with a discussion of the more limited three-fold architecture used in PROCODE.

2   Co-operativity and the cognitive processing spectrum

Co-operation between humans and computer systems takes on differing forms, depending on the extent to which the computer's software is sophisticated enough to be able to perform what we might call "cognitive processing". Any system which enables a real-world problem to be solved jointly by a human and computer may be said to lie at some point along a "cognitive processing spectrum", according to how much of the cognitive processing required to solve the problem is performed by the human user, and how much by the software.

At one end of this cognitive processing spectrum are systems in which the human does almost all of the work, with the computer simply doing "cognitively menial" tasks. For example, in most document preparation systems, the human does all the difficult work of composition, with the computer merely doing helpful chores like spelling correction and facilitating operations like textual re-organisation, cross-referencing, page layout etc. Co-operativity in this kind of system means providing facilities of a type and granularity that most closely reflects the structure of the human cognitive processes. For example, having document processing facilities for producing diagrams in which shapes can be specified directly as shapes, and not as sequences of numbers; where there are systematic relations between the means for achieving functions that are related in the human cognitive model (eg moving up vs. moving down, inserting vs. deleting etc). Co-operativity in systems where the human does most of the cognitive processing also depends upon having a maximally transparent interface, where for any given operation that a user would like to perform, the interface and/or help system makes it obvious how the user can achieve it.

At the other end of the spectrum are systems in which the computer does most of the cognitive processing. Here the intended human user might not be capable of the cognitive processing performed by the computer software, but may simply supply input data as and when called upon to do so. Many of the current "expert system" designs are of this type. At this end of the cognitive processing spectrum, co-operativity depends upon the software being able to *simulate* the human processing that *would have occurred* if the user had solved the problem, and being able to communicate with the human user about aspects of this problem-solving process. This means having good models of how humans solve the problem, and having good strategies for explanation and/or tuition.

In the middle of the cognitive processing spectrum are systems in which the problem-solving activity is shared dynamically between the user and system. There are at least two different reasons to be interested in designing systems of this type.

The first reason is pragmatic, in that the sheer difficulty of the cognitive processing functions involved may make it impossible to provide software to solve the problems without human involvement. A clear example is machine translation, where the failure of centuries of person-effort has convinced even the most optimistic researchers in the field that fully automatic high-quality translation is an impossible goal, and work is now focussed upon interactive systems.

The second reason is more fundamental, in that systems in which cognitive processing is shared dynamically between human and computer may be intrinsically more useful. A good example here is medical diagnosis systems. It has been shown that some forms of medical diagnosis are indeed possible using computer cognitive processing alone, but a problem then arises in the *use* of the diagnoses that have been produced by this method. Interactions with human experts more often take the form of joint discussions of possible solutions, with incremental problem formulation and solution specification [Kidd, 1985]. We therefore argue that a more natural approach to providing expert consultancy by computers is to design systems for co-operative problem-solving.

In an important sense, the kind of co-operativity appropriate to systems in the middle of the cognitive processing spectrum subsumes the other two, since it requires a system which has all the features of co-operativity found at the two ends of the spectrum, but *in addition* requires that there be some mechanism for allowing each partner in the interaction to take turns at having the initiative at appropriate stages. Here we need a system that (a) allows the human to drive the computer, (b) allows the computer to drive the human and (c) enables negotiation to take place for freely swapping between these modes. In the rest of this paper, we shall be considering the functionality and architectural components that are required in order to produce co-operativity of this kind.

3   Four kinds of functionality in co-operative systems

We have defined the general type of co-operative system we are interested in, as being one in which the user and system work together to incrementally develop an appropriate solution to the user's problem. It will usually be the case that the communication language used in the interface between user and system will use terms that are different from those that the system uses in reasoning about the underlying application domain (eg. natural language or graphics vs. logical predicates or analogical process models).

We can therefore identify four distinctly different kinds of functionality that must be provided in such systems, in order to successfully translate between the terms used in the interface, and the terms used in the system's representation of the application domain, such that the system (a) gains sufficient "insight" into the user's problem, and (b) provides the user with a sufficiently "insightful" understanding of the solution(s).

The following subsections discuss the functional requirements for reasoning about dialogues, participants, tasks and applications. These requirements specify the *contents* of search spaces that the system must reason over in providing co-operative problem-solving behaviour. In a separate paper [Allport and Kidd, forthcoming] we discuss in more detail the *structure* of these search spaces. There we argue that from a computational point of view, co-operativity can be measured along three orthogonal dimensions according to the greater or lesser sophistication involved in meta-level reasoning about the structure of these spaces.

It is important to bear in mind that although we discuss reasoning in these four areas of functionality separately, the actual knowledge represented in each functional component for any given domain will not in general be independent of the knowledge represented in the other components. The interdependence between functional components will be of two types:

1. The scope of the components may co-vary in different domains (for example, the structure of dialogue that needs to be modelled may be different for diagnostic applications and database query applications).

2. In any particular domain, each component may reference the knowledge represented in others (for example, a dialogue component might have rules for interpreting a *"reset"* command from the user in different ways for different applications).

3.1   Reasoning about dialogues

The notion of "dialogue" in interactive problem-solving systems can involve much more than natural language processing issues. Regardless of communication medium, (natural language, menu input, direct manipulation, etc), there is a need to control how turn-taking should proceed (e.g. does the user have to wait for the system to finish doing what it is doing, or are there mechanisms for generating interrupts?). There is also a need to specify what types of responses are allowed and appropriate for each kind of "utterance".[1] Can questions (from user or system) be met with counter-questions?, can commands or assertions by either participant be challenged by the other? etc. What we mean by "dialogue" in what follows is therefore something which includes the interpretation of user utterances, the control of turn-taking and the packaging of system output.

The poverty of current theories of dialogue management is a reflection of the inherent difficulty of the problems involved, but promising work within a fairly limited scope is reported in [Robinson et al, 1988; Frohlich and Luff, forthcoming]. Our overall approach follows that of [Cohen and Levesque, 1987], which attempts to analyse dialogue as a special case of rational interaction, although a great deal more work needs to be done before that theoretical insight can be adequately expressed computationally. Nevertheless, some work relevant to dialogue management by programs has been done from the perspective of natural language processing (see eg. Kaplan's work on correcting false pre-suppositions [Kaplan, 1982]).

Even the simplest interfaces involve some notion of reasoning about dialogue, although this is not always made explicit. For example, for a computer configuration application in which the underlying domain representation specifies how to add individual devices (such as discs, printers, tape drives), it might be possible to ask, via a menu interface, how many devices could be added to a particular configuration. This would involve some form of reasoning to the effect that a question about the class of "devices" should be interpreted as a series of questions about each of the individual devices known to the system.[2]

3.2 Reasoning about participants

Some co-operative systems will need to do some form of explicit reasoning about the individual participants[3] in the problem-solving process. There are two situations that require this kind of functionality:

1. When the participants themselves are part of the application domain.

---

[1] The notion of "utterance" here includes for example, the user clicking on a menu selection, the system displaying a graph, etc. etc.

[2] Note that the reasoning about each question in this series will not in general be independent of the reasoning about the others. For example, answers to questions about devices could take the form: "You can add:

    3 of \<device a\> **OR** 2 of \<device b\> **OR** 4 of \<device c\>
    OR 1 of \<device a\> **AND** 1 of \<device b\> **AND** 2 of \<device c\>."

[3] We use the term "participant" so as to be neutral about whether the problem-solving activity involves multiple numbers of intelligent machines or human users, each of whom might be modelled as a different participant in the interaction.

2. When there is significant variation in the knowledge and interests of different participants.

The first situation occurs, for example, in tutoring systems. Here the goal of the system is to improve the user's understanding of the course material, and hence the user can be said to form part of the application. The system should therefore have a model of the current understanding of the individual being instructed. A simple approach is to assume that the user's understanding of the domain will always be a subset of the system's understanding [Brown and Burton, 1975]. A more complex approach involves the dynamic generation of a model which may also include user misconceptions, based upon evidence from the user's verbal or other behaviour [Sleeman, 1982].

An example of the second situation occurs in the co-operative robot planning domain discussed in [Power, 1979]. Here the two co-operating robots have different knowledge and opportunities (eg. one is inside a locked room and can unlock the door, the other is outside and cannot unlock it), and each must reason about the knowledge and skills of the other in order to achieve their mutual goal.

Both the above situations occur, in part, when the aim of the system is to provide helpful information within a programming environment [Allport, 1983]. If a user asks *"How does <COMMAND X> work?"*, the question may mean very different things if asked by a novice user (who may simply wish to know the number and type of arguments that <COMMAND X> takes) or by an experienced user (who may wish to know how <COMMAND X> is implemented).

3.3 Reasoning about tasks

The third kind of functionality required for co-operative problem-solving involves knowledge about how different sub-tasks in the application domain are related to each other. Reasoning about these relationships allows a system to perform goal substitution or goal refinement where necessary. To take a very simple example from the configuration domain, a user may ask (via menu, formal query language, or natural language) *"Can I add 5 discs?"*. Simple systems might respond to this questions with just a yes or no. However, a co-operative system might, in cases of failure, give some information about a different but closely related task, for example: *"No, but you can add (up to) 3 discs."*.

Co-operative systems need to reason about what related goals it is useful to consider in such cases. Allen & Perrault's work on plan recognition [Allen and Perrault, 1980], Pollack and Hirschberg's work on types of relation between goals [Pollack, 1984], [Hirschberg, 1986], and Motro's work on query generalisation [Motro, 1986] all address issues of reasoning about problems other than those explicitly stated by the user. We discuss elsewhere [Allport and Kidd, forthcoming] how reasoning about the space of related problems constitutes one of the three dimensions of co-operativity.

Along a different dimension of co-operativity, there is the problem of how, given a specification of a task in general terms, the system can co-operate in defining it in terms of (sequences of) specific actions. This requires knowledge about strategies for ordering sets of tasks. Some good examples of the latter are given in [Finin and Morris, 1988], where Finin discusses a variety of strategies used in diagnostic systems for deciding, when there are multiple competing diagnostic hypotheses, which hypotheses to try to refute or confirm, and in what order.

3.4 Reasoning about applications

It is obvious that any co-operative problem-solving system will need to reason about a target domain. We merely note here that in many cases the application-level reasoning will be done by a "back end" system which has a very limited representation of (one aspect of) the domain. In order to use the application-level knowledge co-operatively, some form of meta-level reasoning is required for mapping to and from the user's perspective on the application domain. These mappings are provided by the other functions of reasoning about dialogues, participants and tasks (we discuss the task/application distinction further in § 6.3).

4 Why participant functionality can be ignored

An important principle of good program design is that major functional distinctions should be represented by different components in a program's architecture, because typically this leads to programs which are clearer, more modular, and hence more maintainable, portable and upgradable. So far we have identified four different kinds of functionality that will, in the general case, be required in order to produce co-operative interactive problem-solving. However, when we come to consider systems designed for particular domains, it is by no means always the case that sophisticated implementations of each type of functionality are required.

In particular, we argue in this section of the paper that in a large class of domains, the functionality of reasoning about participants is unnecessary, and that therefore co-operative programs for these domains do not need to have a participant component in their architecture.

It has become common to discuss many issues in the field of human computer interfaces in terms of some kind of "user modelling". However, it is important to note that much of the work which talks about user modelling is not primarily concerned with reasoning about participants in a given human-machine interaction. Indeed, we would argue that the extent to which it has been found to be possible to formulate general theories about building models of the user, is exactly the extent to which these theories are in fact about dialogues or tasks *irrespective of the participants involved.*

To put it simply, most inferences which are said to concern "user models" are in fact made upon the basis of what is *said* or the stated *goal*, and not upon the basis of *who* the user is. As we saw above, it is only necessary to reason about *who the user is*, ie. to have an explicit representation of individual participants, in very limited cases.

There is a striking lack of theoretical understanding of how to reason about individual participants, and this is no doubt because of the practical difficulty of acquiring knowledge about individuals. There are two possible approaches here. One is to give each individual user a "questionnaire" at the beginning of each session, to establish the individual's profile, and then to use this as the basis of subsequent reasoning about that individual participant (eg. the system might classify the participant along some spectrum from "novice" to "expert" in a programming domain). Alternatively, the system might attempt to infer information about the individual's beliefs, knowledge, skills etc. *indirectly,* from statements made during a particular interaction. However, this latter approach presupposes that we have good theories about how to reliably make inferences from statements, and hence depends fundamentally upon success in reasoning about dialogues and tasks. It also depends upon prior success in solving the problems of machine learning.

It is therefore unsurprising that much of the actual work on "user modelling" is in fact primarily concerned with the functionality of reasoning about dialogues and tasks. We mentioned Kaplan's work [Kaplan, 1982] in §3.1 above. This suggests that we should use facts about the semantics of natural language to derive co-operative responses, in order to correct false pre-suppositions. It might well be a fact that, because a user says "p" we can infer that the user believes that "q". But in formulating a principle of co-operativity, this is far more importantly a fact about natural language than a fact about a particular user. It is therefore possible to have a co-operative system which uses the same dialogue principles *without* ever doing any explicit reasoning about *who* has said that "p".[4]

Similar arguments apply to the work on reasoning about tasks that we mentioned in §3.3. For example, Allen & Perrault's work [Allen and Perrault, 1980] discusses plan recognition in terms of inferring user's goals. We regard this work as providing useful theoretical insights into how to reason about tasks, but not as being inherently concerned with reasoning about individual participants. For example, for the domain of train-timetable consultancy, it may be true in general that, as Allen & Perrault suggest, if someone asks about the time of a train, they may also be interested in knowing which platform that train departs from, because they have the goal of catching the train. However, if this is indeed a valid inference, then the co-operative response including platform information can be generated just by reasoning about the relationships between the tasks of acquiring information about train times, catching trains, and knowing platform numbers. There is no need to do any explicit reasoning here about *who* wants to know the information, catch the train, etc, in order to provide the co-operative response.

The redundancy of explicit reasoning about participants is even clearer when we consider reasoning about applications. To take an example from the configuration domain, we might have a simple direct-manipulation system for adding components, in which the user could click on an icon meaning "add a disc drive". It would obviously be *possible* for such a system to build an explicit model of the user participating in this

---

[4]There will, of course, in general be a need for "indexical" knowledge about participants: we need to know that P_1 *asserted "p"'* and P_1 *asserted "not-p"'* in order to know that P_1 *has contradicted himself'*. The point is that we don't need to know anything *else* about P_1 other than what he has said, nor do we need to make any inferences from what he has said to what kind of person he (or she) is.

interaction, to attribute to that participant the desire to add a disc drive, and for the system to then reason that because the user had this desire, the system should add a disc drive. But it would also be, equally obviously, entirely superfluous for the system to reason in this way.

We noted in §3.2 that reasoning about participants may be necessary when there is significant variation in the knowledge and interests of different participants in the problem-solving process. It will often be the case that systems for co-operative problem-solving are designed to have only two participants: the computer program, and the user. Of course, these two will in general have differing knowledge and interests. But if it is unnecessary to distinguish between different users of the same program, there is no need for the program to explicitly model the difference between itself and the user. It is perfectly reasonable for that difference to be an implicit assumption of the program design.

We may conclude, therefore, that co-operative systems for a wide variety of domains can be provided without ever reasoning about explicit models of participants, as long as the system provides adequate functionality in reasoning about dialogues and tasks.

5 Why task functionality cannot be ignored

It has often been assumed that one must have some kind of reasoning about participants in order to provide co-operativity. We have argued that this is not so. Conversely, the distinction between reasoning about tasks and reasoning about applications has not generally been made,[5] but we would argue that it is important to make it in order to provide co-operativity in systems for interactive problem-solving.

We discuss below (§6.3) *how* the distinction between task component and application component should be made for a given domain. But first we need to motivate this distinction by arguing *why* it is useful in general to distinguish domain knowledge (or application-level reasoning), from knowledge about how to use domain knowledge (or task-level reasoning). There are at least three reasons for providing a co-operative system with explicit reasoning about tasks.

- Many of the arguments we gave in §4 for *not* requiring explicit reasoning about participants are also arguments for requiring explicit reasoning about tasks instead.

- In many domains it might be advantageous to have the ability to perform multiple different tasks co-operatively using the same object-level domain knowledge. For example, the application could be a large relational database, and different co-operative systems could reason over this same database to perform different co-

---

[5]The SOPHIE system [Brown and Burton, 1975] is an exception, in that an explicit distinction was made between the representation of knowledge about electronics and the representation of knowledge concerning reasoning about electronics. However, this particular system was primarily designed for tutoring, and as we argued in §3.2, an explicit distinction between individual participants was also appropriate here.

operative tasks of database query (for normal users) and database update (for system maintainers).

- Most importantly, the distinctive feature of the kind of co-operativity necessary for systems in the middle of the cognitive processing spectrum is that it involves dynamically sharing the task between user and system (cf. §2). One cannot have a generic solution to this problem of *interactive* task-sharing, without having an explicit model of the task to reason about.

We note, however, that explicit representations of tasks are not necessary for providing co-operativity in systems at the two limits of the cognitive processing spectrum. Where the distribution of problem-solving activities between user and system is fixed, a model of the problem-solving task can be implicitly "hard-wired" into the dialogue and/or application components of the system.

6 A generic co-operative architecture for P R O C O D E

We are currently developing a P R Ototype C Oonfiguration Dialogue Environment, which will provide co-operative responses to queries and commands in the configuration domain. The design constraints on our architecture for P R O C O D E are that it should:

1. Have distinctions between components which reflect the functional distinctions that are necessary to provide co-operativity during "shared cognitive processing".

2. Be as generic as possible, i.e. appropriate for a large class of domains.

3. Avoid redundancy: if functionality is irrelevant for the class of domains we are considering, then we should not have a component for it.

4. Allow for an explicit, declarative representation of the knowledge necessary to provide each kind of functionality.

5. Allow for non-monotonicity in each area of the system's reasoning.

Regarding constraint 1: this means that the distinctions between our system components must be based upon the four-fold distinction of functionality outlined in §3. The most general form of this co-operative architecture will be as in fig.1. We describe actual distinctions made in our PROCODE architecture in §§6.1–6.3.

Constraint 2 implies both that the functional distinctions we make should be applicable across domains (we have argued this in §3), and that the individual components should be implemented in a domain-independent way wherever possible (we discuss the latter in §6.4).

The main significance of constraint 3 for us is that we do not need to have a participant component in our architecture. This class of domains we are interested in are those in which the participant is not part of the domain itself, and where there is a

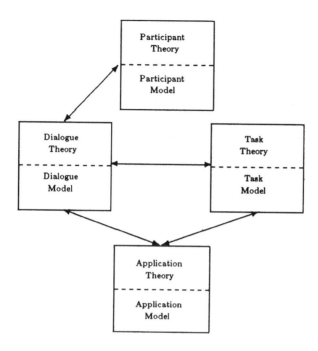

Fig. 1: The most general case: an architecture with all four functional components

similarity in the knowledge and interests of all the anticipated users of the system (for our configuration domain, all the users will be salespeople with similar training). As we argued in §4, for this class of domains explicit reasoning about participants is unnecessary for providing co-operativity. Our PROCODE architecture therefore differs from that shown in fig.1 only in the omission of the participant theory and model.

Constraints 4 & 5 upon our architectural design account for the distinction in each functional component shown in fig.1 between a theory and a model. In each case the theory consists of a set of declarative axioms that are true in all possible instantiations of the system behaviour. The models function like "state variables", representing what is true at a particular time during a particular instantiation of the system behaviour, ie the attributes of the current participants, the history of the dialogue so far, the current state of progress on the task, and the currently relevant state of the application world. It is therefore possible to have declarative theories which reason over non-monotonically changing models, so that, for example, the user is allowed to "change his mind" at various stages of an interaction, or explore alternative (mutually inconsistent) "possible worlds" (models).

6.1 The dialogue component

Some features of the PROCODE dialogue component are derivable directly from the functional considerations mentioned in §3.1 (eg. its lack of dependence upon a particular communication medium). Other features of this component are not quite so obvious, such as the translations it specifies between the user's expression of a problem and the application-level interpretation of it. The application component in P R O C O D E will be similar to that in many other domains, in that it will specify:

1. How to test for attributes of the current application model.

2. How to take actions to change the current application model (including mechanisms for backtracking through previous changes that have been made).

The axioms that constitute the theory in our dialogue component must specify input interpretation, control, and output packaging (cf. §3.1). An example of input interpretation would be the following translations from user queries about configuration actions into application level actions:

User utterance	Application level interpretation
"Can I do <action>?"	Take <action>, (report success or failure), backtrack through <action>
"If I do <action>, will <predicate> be true?"	Take <action>, test for <predicate>, (report result of test), backtrack through <action>.

Our task component will specify what the *content* of the indicated reports should be, given the conditions at the application level (this might involve referring to other possible actions and predicates at the application level). The dialogue component will specify what the *form* of the reports should be. Alternative dialogue theories allow for different kinds of co-operative response based upon inferences about what was implied in the user's question. For example, a different translation rule for the second question above might also include a test for the truth of the predicate in the *current* state also. If the task theory indicated that the predicate in question was one that was typically false initially, and that the user would typically try and make this predicate true, the system might give a response of the form *"(Yes/no, but) <predicate> is already true"*.

The dialogue component should indicate how the same semantic content can be presented differently through different media (natural language, pop-up windows, diagrams etc.). But it should also indicate how the same semantic content can be presented differently through the same medium at different times, according to the particular dialogue history as recorded in the dialogue model, for example in making the natural language distinction between "P is true" and "P is still true".

6.2   The task component

We discussed in §3.3 and §5 above the type of reasoning done in a task component, and why it is useful to make this reasoning explicit. We gave an example from the configuration domain of reasoning about the relatedness of goals such as adding n of some item and adding n-k of that item (or some other number of "equivalent" items). The task component provides an explicit meta-level representation of the application-level search space; this also allows another type of co-operative reasoning, namely about the best strategies for achieving typical tasks in a given application domain.

In a variety of domains such as design, assembly and configuration, application rules may determine the set of objects it is possible to build, but not the sort of objects a user might typically wish to build, or the way one might typically go about building them. The latter kind of information is best represented in a task theory, and can then be used to give co-operative feedback about actions whose consequences might typically be interesting to a user. For example, a user might make some decision that was perfectly acceptable according to application rules, but by using its task theory and model a system could determine that this decision now ruled out the possibility of extending the object in a typical way to arrive at the sort of object that was typically required. In this case the system could give a response of the form "Yes, but note that ...".

The task component is thus important for enabling the system to give co-operative responses to the user, but it can also be used to indicate to the system where it might be able to get co-operative information from the user. With a meta-level representation of the application search space, the system can have an explicit representation of the characteristics of states in the space at which it is appropriate to ask for help from the user.

6.3 The application component

We are using the architecture of fig. 1, minus the participant component, as the basis for a co-operative system in the configuration domain. More specifically, we are using it to produce a computational model of co-operative responses actually given by human "experts" in experimental situations [Kidd, forthcoming], where the co-operativity is defined computationally as in [Allport and Kidd, forthcoming].

For the architecture of fig. 1 to be useful in building co-operative systems in any domain, it is necessary to be clear about how the application component and task component should be distinguished; i.e. given a piece of knowledge that seems relevant in constructing a co-operative system in a particular domain, what is the key criterion for choosing whether that knowledge should be represented in the task theory or the application theory?

We can answer this question using an analogy with game-playing: the application theory corresponds to the rules of the game, and the task theory corresponds to knowledge about strategies for playing the game. The application model then corresponds to a description of the current state of the board (or whatever the game is being played over), and the task model corresponds to a description of the relevance of current strategies to the current state of the board (for example, in chess one might be following a standard opening, with the task model indicating how far in the standard series of moves the game has progressed so far).

To pursue the example of chess for a moment, let us assume that we are designing an interactive cognitive processing system in which the user and the computer are trying to co-operate in playing together against a third person. The third person is an advanced chess player, and neither the computer nor the human user are capable of winning alone against her. However, by combining the memory and processing abilities of the computer with the pattern-recognition and heuristic strategies of the system user, it is possible for the human/computer team to win. At any point in the game after the human opponent has made her move, our co-operative system must come up with its next move. Due to the *ex hypothesis* interactive nature of the co-operative processing involved, there must be a dialogue between human user and computer about what the best move would be. Here the user might suggest a line of attack, which the system could critique, showing it either to be reasonable or flawed because of some possibility not computed by the user, and vice versa.

In this situation, the axioms of the dialogue theory would dictate the form of the debate between user and system about the next best move (and hence the contents of possible dialogue models). The semantic content of this debate would make reference to the application model (the board), the application theory (the rules stating allowable moves) and the task theory and model (which state how series of moves are strategically interrelated). This is why the application, task and dialogue components are shown as interconnected in fig. 1.

6.4 Domain independence

We have noted the design criterion for our architecture that it should be as domain-independent as possible. We have argued that the four-fold functional distinction is domain-independent, but the question then arises as to what extent should we expect the four functional components themselves to be domain-independent?

We would expect that within the theories of each component, there will be considerable variation in the degree of "domain-dependence" embodied in the different axioms. Nevertheless, we would still try to express domain-dependent axioms in the most general terms possible. We can illustrate this design principle by considering an example from the tutoring domain. Here the participant theory, if expressed declaratively, might contain many axioms that are applicable across domains (e.g. "If the user is a novice, explanations should use simple concepts"), and others that are domain-specific (e.g. "If the user has taken the PROLOG course, the user may understand graph unification by comparing it with PROLOG's term unification"). But even these more domain-specific axioms can be expressed in a more general way in the participant theory, such as:

(1) $\forall x, y, z \left[taken\_course\,(x,y) \quad \wedge \quad explained\_in\_course\,(z,y) \quad \supset \quad understands\,(x,z) \right.$
(2) $\forall x, y, z \left[understands\,(x,y) \quad \wedge \quad related\_concept\,(z,y) \quad \supset \right.$
$$may\_understand\_with\_reference\_to\,(x,z) \left. \right]$$

The latter formulation of such rules could then leave it to the application theory to specify the axioms for *related_concept* and *explained_in_course*. The participant model would contain statements about *taken_course* for each participant. The task theory would contain axioms specifying teaching strategies that might be appropriate for an arbitrary participant, if *may_understand_with_reference_to* applied for that participant and an arbitrary pair of concepts. Formulating the participant theory in this way would make it far easier to adapt a system to different, though related domains (eg. teaching concepts vs. teaching manual skills [6]). This representation also makes explicit the assumptions which the system is making about the user. When stated explicitly, it is much clearer that axioms such as (1) above might well be false for many real users.

7 Conclusion

Our short term goal is to implement a co-operative configuration system. But our long term goal is to understand the fundamental principles of co-operativity in its various manifestations, so as to be able to design co-operativity into systems for any domain. We have identified four kinds of functionality in co-operative systems for interactive problem-solving, and proposed a corresponding generic computational architecture for such systems. However, we have also argued that for a large class of domains, of which configuration is just one example, co-operativity can be provided just by reasoning about dialogues, tasks and applications. Hence in our PROCODE architecture, we only have functional components for dialogue, task and application. Occam's razor cuts out the participant.

References

[Allen and Perrault, 1980]
   Allen J and Perrault PC. *Analysing intention in utterances.* Artificial Intelligence, 15, pp. 143-178, 1980.

[Allport, 1983]
   Allport D, A Parser for "Help File English". MSc Thesis, Sussex University, 1983.

[Allport and Kidd, forthcoming]
   Allport D and Kidd A. *Using Knowledge about Search Space to Give Co-operative Responses.* Paper submitted to Theoretical Aspects of Reasoning about Knowledge Conference 1990 (forthcoming).

[Burton and Brown, 1975]
   Burton RR and Brown JS. *Multiple Representations of Knowledge for Tutorial Reasoning.* In Bobrow DG and Collins A (eds), Representation and Understanding. Academic Press, New York, 1975.

[Cohen and Levesque, 1987]
   Cohen PR and Levesque HJ. *Persistence, Intention and Commitment.* Technical Note 415, SRI International, 1987.

[Finin and Morris, 1988]
   Finin T and Morris G. *Abductive Reasoning in Multiple Fault Diagnosis.* Technical Report, Unisys, Paoli PA, 1988.

---

[6]This is not quite as far-fetched as it might seem. Work is currently in progress in several U.S. centers on tutoring systems for piano playing [Sanchez and Joseph, 1988].

[Frohlich and Luff, forthcoming]
Frohlich DM and Luff P. *Conversational Resources for Situated Action*, Paper submitted to CHI 90 (forthcoming).

[Hirchberg, 1986]
Hirschberg J. *Anticipating False Implicatures: Co-operative Responses in Question-answering System*. In Kerschberg L (ed), Expert Database Systems. Benjamin Cummings Publishing Co Inc, 1986.

[Kaplan, 1982]
Kaplan SJ. *Co-operative Responses from Portable Natural Language Database Query System*. In Brady M (ed), Computational Models of Discourse. MIT Press, 1982.

[Kidd, 1985]
Kidd AL. *What do Users Ask? Some Thoughts on Diagnostic Advice*. In Merry M (ed), Expert Systems '85. Cambridge University Press, 1985.

[Motro, 1986]
Motro A. *Query Generalisation: a Method for Interpreting Null Answers*. In Kerschberg L (ed), Expert Database Systems. Benjamin Cummings Publishing Co Inc, 1986.

[Pollack, 1984]
Pollack ME. *Good Answers to Bad Questions: Goal Inference in Expert Advice-giving*. In Proceedings of the Fifth Biennial Conference of the Canadian Society for Computational Studies of Intelligence, London, Ontario, 1984.

[Power, 1979]
Power R. *The Organisation of Purposeful Dialogues*. Linguistics, 17, pp. 107-152, 1979.

[Robinson et al, 1988]
Robinson P, Luff P and Jirotka M, Hardey M, Gilbert GN, Frohlich DM, Cording-ley B and Buckland S. *Functional Specification for the Advice System*. University of Surrey, 1988. Technical Report, Alvey DHSS Demonstrator Project.

[Sanchez and Joseph, 1988]
Sanchez M and Joseph A. *Piano Tutor Project: a State-of-the-art Approach to Piano Teaching*. In Proceedings of the Computers in Music Research Conference. University of Lancaster, 1988.

[Sleeman, 1988]
Sleeman D. *Assessing Aspects of Competence in Basic Algebra*. In Sleeman D and Brown JS (Eds) Intelligent Tutoring Systems, Academic Press, 1982.

CENTRAL GOVERNMENT PENSION RULES AS A LOGIC PROGRAM
*

K.K. BAJAJ, R.K. DUBASH
KBCS NODAL CENTRE, DEPARTMENT OF ELECTRONICS,
LODI ROAD,A BLOCK, CGO COMPLEX,NEW DELHI
E-MAIL : +uunet!shakti!vikram!kbcs
AND
ROBERT KOWALSKI
DEPARTMENT OF COMPUTING, IMPERIAL COLLEGE OF
SCIENCE & TECHNOLOGY, UNIVERSITY OF LONDON, LONDON, ENGLAND
E-MAIL : shakti!uunet!NSFNET-RELAY.AC.UK!doc.imperial.ac.uk!rak

Abstract

An automated legal reasoning system for the Central
Civil Services (CCS) Pension Rules is under development.
This paper discusses the use of logic programming for
representing the knowledge contained in the rules and how
the logic program can be used as an expert system. The
emphasis of the paper is in the use of temporal reasoning in
the laws under consideration, the separation of the logic
part of the program from the user data interface and the
interaction of the user through forms with the knowledge
base. The importance of the interplay of the propositional
logic analysis of the rules with the entity-relationship
analysis for the determinmation of predicates and parameters
is also discused.

1.   Introduction

Logic programming is one of the knowledge
representation paradigms. Although it has received
considerable attention as a basic pillar for fifth
generation computer system ever since the Japanese project
was launched almost a decade ago, it is only recently that
application development has picked up using logic
programming for representing knowledge. In the area of
automated legal reasoning systems, one of the first
applications of logic programming was for the British
Nationality Act (1). The group at Imperial College has used
logic programming for other applications such as the social
security disbursements under the Department of Health and
social Security (DHSS) Program (2). Logic programming has
been found to be an effective scheme for representing legal
knowledge.

Logic programs represent knowledge in the form of
statements

$$A \text{ if } B_1 \text{ and } \ldots B_n , \quad n \geq o$$

---

* Any correspondence may be addressed to K.K. Bajaj.

Where A and B are all atomic formulae. The conditions
B can also be negative atomic formulae.   Most knowledge
 i
can be represented in the form of such statements and hence
by logic programs.

In this paper we present the use of logic programming
for representing the knowledge contained in Central Civil
Services (CCS) Pension Rules and how the logic program can
be used as an expert system.   A similar automated reasoning
system for import policy legislation is also   under
development and has been reported elsewhere (3). The two
applications present technical challenges in logic
programming which are quite diverse in nature.   While the
latter has comparatively shallow reasoning power, wider
breadth of data, larger data base, more complex user

interface, relatively simpler English with fewer ambiguities
in language, the former offers the possibilities of deeper
reasoning, more complex English language, complex temporal
reasoning.   The applications demonstrate the power of logic
programming in different domains of reasoning in law.

The CCS Pension Rules are applicable to most government
employees.   These rules determine the number of years which
qualify for pension, regulate the amounts of pensions,
decide on the classes of pensions and conditions governing
their grant. Determination and authorisation of the amounts
of pension and gratuity, of family pension and death-cum-
retirement gratuity in respect of government servants dying
while in service are also as per the rules laid down in the
CCS pension rules.   In addition, the rules also deal with
sanction of family pension and residuary gratuity in respect
of deceased pensioners, commutation of pension etc.   There
are 89 pension rules which are sub-divided into 252 sub-
rules.   Over and above these, there are 338 Govt. of India
decisions in the form of Office Memoranda and Circulars
which are in the form of case laws or new rules. These
decisions have been announced from time to time taking into
account the problems and hardships caused to a section of
employees, by the main rules. The rules, sub-rules and govt.
decisions for Commutation Rules are 34,73 and 23 whereas in
the case of Extraordinary Pension Rules the numbers are
13,29 and 23 respectively.

We are at present writing the section on Qualifying
Service as a logic program.   This is the largest of the
sections and relatively more complex in the formulation of
the statutory laws.   It contains 20 rules, 45 sub-rules and
95 Govt. of India decisions as case laws and/or new rules.

The main emphasis of this paper is in the use of temporal reasoning in the laws under consideration, the separation of the logic part of the program from the user data interface, the interaction of the user through forms with the knowledge base, the interplay of the propositional logic analysis of the rules with the entity-relationship analysis for the determination of predicates, parameters and conditions.

2. Logic Program Implementation Methodology

The program was first implemented in PROLOG without any considerations of logic and data interface problems. This mixing of user interface with knowledge representation led to complications in data management and logic management. At times for certain data values one could not be sure of the results of the program. It was difficult to ensure the correctness of the logic with data capture from the user and data manipulation interspersed all over the program.

The problem was then analysed de novo with Logic first. During the propositional logic analysis of the rules a strict discipline was maintained in keeping away from PROLOG and implementation problems. The idea was to identify appropriate propositional logic predicates. Soon it was discovered, that while one could identify the predicates to a reasonable degree of accuracy, the same was not true of conditions and parameters. In fact the choice of parameters seemed to affect clarity in so far as conditions were concerned.

We then tried the entity-relationship analysis of the variables involved to identify simple relations in the form of tables. The interplay of entity-relationship analysis with the propositional logic analysis led to the identification of minimum predicates with appropriate conditions and parameters. The logic of the problem could thus be completed. This is elaborated in the next section.

The analysis of the problem thus far was carried out without any worry of user interface with respect to data input. The program could be tested by supplying the required data as prolog facts. The user data interface (UDI) was designed separately so as to keep the logic of rules totally independent. A similar approach has been followed in the work on import export policy as well. It is proposed to develop a general shell as a user data interface for this class of problems.

The UDI captures the data at the start of the session. Simple forms have been designed for this purpose, which are similar to the manual forms being used by the offices. Necessary details concerning qualifying service, emoluments etc. are obtained through the filling of these soft forms.

Consultation with the knowledge base or the rules base begins at this stage and the program returns the results of consultation.

Finally, it is proposed to add a simple Explanation Module to the program. This will refer back to the logic program to pick up the applicable clauses and subclauses for a given situation and provide structured English of the clause as an explanation. We also propose to keep the English text of the corresponding clause verbatim from the book of rules. A prolog subprogram containing rule numbers and titles forms the simplest explanation module. There is thus a three stage approach to the automated reasoning system.

It may be noted here that unlike APES, the data is not being captured from the user interactively. The data is captured at the initial stage and then consulting with the logic begins. Thus this approach is an alternative to APES architecture. It is a general architecture applicable to a large body of problems. It is being used in the Import Policy problem referred to above. The main body of rules is a clean logic program free from user/data interaction. UDI, Logic and Explanation modules are three independent but interacting subprograms of the logic program.

3. Analysis of the Logic Problem

The rules on qualifying service relate to commencement of qualifying service, conditions subject to which service qualifies etc. The pension rules clearly specify how to treat the time spent on probation, whether pre-retirement civil service in the case of re-employed government servants counts and if so, under what conditions. Like this all aspects of service (leave, suspension, removal, reinstatement, resignation etc.) are covered in the section on qualifying service. It is obvious that the basic idea is to establish the initial date from which service should be counted in a given case. The uninterrupted service time period is expected as a result of application of this set of rules. Thus the concept of time is very crucial to this problem. The first-order logic makes it possible to take care of time explicitly thereby making temporal reasoning practical in a real life knowledge and inferencing problem.

As with a problem of this kind, we took the rules as laid down in the book in sequence and analysed with respect to logic. The entity relationship analysis was carried out subsequently which showed that the formulation of predicates was not entirely correct. This is best illustrated through an example. Rule 13 on qualifying service is as follows :

13. " Subject to the provisions of these rules, qualifying service of a Government servant shall commence from the date he takes charge of the post to which he is first

appointed either substantively or in an officiating or temporary capacity :

Provided that officiating or temporary service is followed without interruption by substantive appointment in the same or another service or post:

Provided further that -

(a) in the case of a Government servant in a Group 'D' service or post who held a lien or a suspended lien on a permanent pensionable post prior to the 17th April, 1950, service rendered before attaining the age of sixteen years shall not count for any purpose, and

(b) in the case of a Government servant not covered by clause (a), service rendered before attaining the age of eighteen years shall not count, except for compensation gratuity."

Predicates formulated for "commencement of qualifying service" included :

```
start-of-service (rule-no,Post,T1)
end-of-service(rule-no,Post,T2)
```

The entity relationship analysis and the need for reapplicability of predicates to later rules, however, led us to replace the "end-of-service(rule-no,Post,T)" predicate by "follows (Post, Post1)"

This was due to the fact that end of one service means start of another. With the former predicate we are storing redundant information and have to use 'start-of-service' after 'every end-of-service'. The 'follows' predicate, however, makes explicit the fact that the time of occurrence of the post corresponding to the second parameter is immediately after the post represented by the first parameter.

Direct representation of the text of rule 13 with respect to time using propositional logic analysis gave a representation such as

```
qual-serv(13,T1,T2) :-

(type(Post,officiating);type(Post,temporary) ),
start-of-service(T1),
end-of-service(T2).
```

However, with entity relationship analysis we handled the
minimum age limitation in the predicate through the
formulation given below :

```
real-start(13,Post,T1,T2) : -

service (Post,T1,T2),
start-qual-service(Post,T0),
(T0<T1, T=T1) or (T0>T1, T=T0)
```

The predicate start-qual-serv(13,Post,T) initially
incorporating information regarding actual start of service
so as not to count service before minimum age was also
suitably amended as follows, owing to formulation of the
generally applicable predicate real-start(13,Post,T) as
defined previously. The entire rule 13 is formulated as
follows :

```
start-qual-serv (13,Post,T) :-
    (type(Post,officiating);/*or*/type(Post,temporary),
    follows (Post, Post1), type (Post1, substantive),
    service (Post, T1,T2),
    (exception-a(Post,Age,T1),age-check(Age,16,T,T1);/*or*/
    exception-b(Post, Age,T1),age-check (Age,18,T,T1) ).

exception-a(Post,A,T1) :-
    group(Post,D),lien(Post,17-apr-1950)
    service (Post,T1,T2),age (T1,A).

exception-b(Post,A,T1) :-

    not  exception-a(Post,Age,T1),
    service(Post,T1,T2),age(T1,Age).

age-check(Age,Threshold-age,T,T1) :-

    (  (Age < Threshold-age,T is T1 + Threshold-age - Age);
    (Age>=Threshold-age,T = T1)
```

The entity relating to 'Post' of an employee was
initially to be a predicate allowing access to details such
as group (A,B,C,D), organisation, type (apprentice,
probationary, etc.). It was subsequently decided on the
basis of simplicity and usability to make Post a structured
term with all these attributes and have three predicates to
access the components of this term given the post as a
parameter. These three predicates would then be group,
type, organisation, each taking as input the Post and giving
as output the appropriate result. The structured term Post
has been defined as

Post (Group, Title, Type, Organisation, Pay-scale, T1,T2)

We will consider one more rule and its formulation in
Prolog before we leave this subject to discuss the more

specific and interesting aspects of CCS Pension Rules. Rule 14.1 alongwith its Logic is given below :

14.1   "The service of a Government servant shall not qualify unless his duties and pay are regulated by the Government, or under conditions determined by the Government."

qual-serv (14.1,Post,T1,T2) :-

    (regulated-by-govt   (Post)   ;/*or*/conditions-of-post (Post)),
    (paid (Post,T1,T2,consolidated-fund);/*or*/
    paid (Post,T1,T2,local-fund)),
    not(non-pensionable   (Post,T1,T2),not   qual-serV(_,Post,T1,T2)),
    real-start (Post,T1).

There   are several pension rules which are in the form of negative conclusions, which is like any other piece of legislation. Logic programs are known to represent knowledge in the form of implications

$$A \text{ if } B_i \text{ and } ...B_n \text{ , } n \geq o$$

Negative conclusions have been shown to be represented as implications by adding extra conditions or transforming some of the existing conditions (4). A negated condition is deemed to hold if the corresponding positive condition can be shown to fail to hold - this is negation by failure (NBF). Negative statements are handled through NBF in the condition. We will examine some of the rules with negative conclusions.

16.   "Service as an apprentive **shall not qualify,** except in the case of S.A.S. apprentice in the Indian Audit and Accounts Department or the Defence Accounts Department"

This statement is handled through suitable transformation of the conditions. The equivalent statement is, "service as an apprentice shall qualify, only in the case of S.A.S. apprentice in the Indian Audit and Accounts Department or the Defence Accounts Department. After the transformation this becomes

qual-serv (16,Post,T1,T2) :-

    type   (Post,apprentice),(organisation   (Post,
    Indian-audit-and-account);organisation
    (Post,defence-accounts))

Another   rule with a negative conclusion is   rule

25.2 "The period of interruption in service between date of dismissal, removal or compulsory retirement, as the case may be, and the date of reinstatement, and the period of suspension, if any, shall not count as qualifying service unless regularised as duty or leave by a specific order of the authority which passed the reinstatement."

This can also be transformed to fit in logic programming. The equivalent statement is :

"The period of interruption in service between the date of dismissal, removal or compulsory retirement, as the case may be, and the date of reinstatment, and the period of suspension, if any, shall count as qualifying service if regularised as duty or leave by a specific order of the authority which passed the order of reinstatement." This gets easily translated into
predicate logic as :

```
qual-serv (25.2,Post,T1, T2) :-
    date-of-dismissal (Post,T1),
    date-of-reinstatement (Post,T2)
    suspension-period-regularised (Post,T1,T2)
```

We may also note here that rule 14.1 above is also an example of a negative conclusion and it has been represented through appropriate transformation of the conditions. We can safely conclude that the treatment of negative conclusions in logic programs for representing legislation as pioneered by Kowalski and others (4) is found to be adequate for this problem. We have had similar experience while representing the Indian import policy as a logic program.

We will now briefly consider the examples of those rules which exhibit dependence on time and/or result in computation of elapsed time as a result of the occurrence of certain events as laid down in the rules. This will illustrate the power of first-order logic in temporal reasoning.

The entire rule 13 as explained earlier in the context of the formulation of predicates is an example of temporal reasoning. The date of commencement of service is to be counted from the date of joining subject to an arbitrary date 17 April 1950 and the condition of whether the employee was under 18 or 16 years age depending upon his category. The age of the employee can be explicitly handled and checked against 18 or 16 years with respect to the date 17 April 1950 and a date arrived at unambiguously from where the service is to be counted. This rule has already been shown in its proper formulation in this section.

Similarly, the predicate 'follows (Post 1, Post 2)' also captures the movement of time in conjunction with other predicates. The rules applicable to an employee who works in a post Post1 from time T1 to T2 and in any break can be well represented through follows (Post1, Post2) :-

service (Post1,T1,T2),service (Post2,T2,T3)

4. User Data Interface

The data capture from the user is completed before consultation begins with the expert system. This is in contrast to the APES architecture (5) where data is captured interactively as consultation proceeds. In standard expert system shells also the data is obtained interactively from the user while the rules are tested by the expert-system.

The UDI has been developed based on forms approach which tries to present the users with forms on the screen. The entire information that needs to be collected from the user for computing pension, has been divided into a number of forms which are displayed on demand through a menu. The information relates to employee's personal details, retirement details, military service etc. The manual form has been categorised into the following screens which are shown as options to choose from a menu. The screens which must necessarily be filled by the user are shown with an asterisk.

1.   Personal Details   *
2.   Retirment Details *
3.   Military Service
4.   Autonomous Organisation Service
5.   Qualifying Service *
6.   Govt. Dues and NOC action *
7.   Commutation option

The requisite information is thus supplied by the user through these forms. After consultation with the Pension Rules knowledge base appropriate results are displayed on the screen.

5. Explanation Subsystem

The user can ask for explanation in which case the Explanation Subsystem is consulted by the expert system. The explanation part reconsults the knowledge base for the rules applicable to the case under consideration which have been saved after the initial consultation.

For the present only a simplified treatment of explanation is envisaged. The rule numbers alongwith their english text are stored which can be reproduced as part of explanation. The explanation subsystem can also interact with the knowledge base in which case structured text of the rule can be presented which will be based on the way the rule has been written in propositional logic.

This portion of the expert system is still in preliminary stages.

6. Conclusion

We have presented the development of the CCS Pension Rules as a logic proram. The formulation of the rules in logic has clearly shown the need for interaction of propositional logic analysis with entity relationship analysis. The three stage approach of data capture through a UDI, knowledge base in the form of rules represented in logic, and explanation subsystem has been seen to be extremely efficient and useful from the viewpoint of practical development. The logic part of rules and the user interaction can be kept separately, which makes it easier to maintain the knowledge base. The UDI with its provision to capture the entire data from the user through screens at the initial stage has been shown to be a general architecture which is an alternative to APES. We hope this formulation will help us to show that the subsequent legislation can be framed without any ambiguities and in simple English.

REFERENCES

1. Sergot MT, Sadri F, Kowalski RA, Krivaczek F, Hammond P and Cory H T (1986) ; 'The British' Nationality Act as a Logiç Program" CACM Vol 29 No. 5, pp 370-386

2. Bench-Capon J.J.M., Robinson G.O., Routen T.W., Sergot M.J. (May, 1989),"Large Scale Applications in Law : A formalism for Supplementary Benefit Legislation", Proceedings of the First International Conference on AI and Law, Boston, pp 190-198.

3. Bajaj K.K., Dubash R.K., Kamble A.S., Kowalski R A, Murthy B K, Rajgopalan D. (September 1989) : "Indian Import Policy and Procedures as a Logic Program" KBCS Nodal Centre, Department of Electronics, Govt. of India, New Delhi

4. Kowalski R.A. (June 1989) : "The treatment of negation in logic programs for representing legislation" Second International Conference on AI and law Vancouver, Canada

5. Hammond P., Sergot M.J. (1984), APES Reference Manual. Logic Based Systems Ltd., Richmond, Surrey, England, 1984

Solving the Generalized Job Shop Scheduling Problem via Temporal Constraint Propagation

Wesley W. Chu   Patrick H. Ngai

Computer Science Department
University of California, Los Angeles
Los Angeles, California 90024, USA

Abstract

A *Scheduling* Algorithm with *Temporal Constraint Propagation* (STCP) is proposed to solve the generalized job shop scheduling problem. STCP propagates the precedence constraints and machine interference constraints to reduce the search space of the active schedules. Further, by making use of the temporal nature of the job shop scheduling, efficient algorithms to propagate precedence constraints and machine interference constraints are developed. Experimental results reveal that constraint propagation significantly reduces the computation time for scheduling. Further, the proposed temporal constraint propagation algorithms provide an order of magnitude improvement on the computation time over the conventional constraint propagation algorithm.

1. Introduction

The classical job shop scheduling problem [MUT 63, CAR 89] is to find a schedule for processing j distinct jobs by m machines. Each job consists of a sequence of *operations* which may have different processing times. Operations in a job must be processed in a specified order (precedence constraint), and each machine can process one operation at a time (machine interference constraint). The objective of the classical job shop scheduling is to find the minimum time to complete all the jobs. The classical job shop scheduling problem is proven to be NP-complete in the strong sense [GAR 79].

In the classical job shop scheduling, the precedence relationship between operations in a job is assumed to be sequential. However, oftentimes, operations in a job can be processed in parallel. Scheduling these operations using complete sequential ordering could result in an inefficient schedule. Most job shop scheduling research assumes that different operations from the same job cannot use the same machine more than once [ADA 88, CAR 89], which is not the case in many applications. Another common assumption is that all jobs are ready to be processed at the same time. The time a job is ready to be processed is called its release time. In practice, different jobs may have different release times and deadlines. To remedy these shortcomings, we generalize the classical job shop scheduling problem so that operations in a job can be processed in parallel. Different operations in a job can use a machine more than once and different jobs may have different release times and deadlines. Since the release time and deadlines of the jobs could be different, finding the minimum time in which all the jobs are completed may not be meaningful. Therefore, the objective of a generalized job shop scheduling problem is to find a schedule for all the jobs such that the precedence constraints, machine interference constraints, the release time constraints, and the deadline constraints are satisfied.

A simple generalized job shop scheduling problem with two jobs is shown in Table 1. Each job has a different release time and deadline. There are four operations in each job. The jth operation of the ith job is denoted as O_{ij}. O_{11} has to be processed before other operations in job 1 can be processed. However, O_{12} and O_{13} can be processed in parallel. Different operations from job 1 (O_{11} and O_{14}) use machine 1 twice. The objective of the problem is to find a schedule so that both job 1 and job 2 start after the release time and finish before the deadline, and have operations processed in the order specified with no two operations scheduled to use a machine at the same time.

job	release time	deadline	operations	process time	machine used	preceding operations
1	1	11	O_{11}	1	1	none
			O_{12}	2	2	O_{11}
			O_{13}	3	3	O_{11}
			O_{14}	4	1	O_{12}, O_{13}
2	2	12	O_{21}	1	1	none
			O_{22}	2	2	O_{21}
			O_{23}	4	2	O_{21}
			O_{24}	4	3	O_{22}, O_{23}

Table 1   A simple generalized job shop scheduling problem

We shall first discuss the *Scheduling Algorithm with Temporal Constraint Propagation* (STCP) to solve the generalized job shop scheduling problem. Based on the temporal nature of the job shop scheduling, algorithms for propagating the precedence constraint (PCP) and machine interference constraint (MICP) are developed. Finally, three types of generalized job shop scheduling problems are used to compare the performance of STCP with Backtracking on Active Schedules (BAS) and that of the PCP-MICP algorithm with the revise procedure.

2. The Scheduling with Temporal Constraint Propagation Algorithm

In a given schedule, if no operation can be started earlier than as specified in this schedule without delaying other operations, or violating the precedence constraint or the machine interference constraint, then it is an active schedule [GIF 60]. The execution time of an active schedule is shorter than that of a non-active schedule. Therefore, if the optimal schedule exists, then it must be an active schedule. The generalized job shop scheduling problem can be solved by using the active schedules technique. However, the active schedules technique is not efficient enough to solve even a moderate size problem within a few hours of computation time. We propose to embed temporal constraint propagations in the active schedules technique to form the Scheduling Algorithm with Temporal Constraint Propagation (STCP). The constraint propagation technique detects deadends and eliminates infeasible schedules in the early stage of the search tree to reduce the search time.

Let us use the example in Table 1 to illustrate how to use temporal constraint propagation to eliminate the infeasible schedules. The start time window of an operation is the set of all the feasible start times of that operation. A start time window with feasible start times from 1 through 3 is represented as {[1-3]}. After O_{11} is scheduled to be processed at time unit 1, its start time window becomes {[1]}. Initially O_{21} have the start time window of {[1-3]}. When the start time window constraint of O_{11} is propagated to O_{21}, the new start time window of O_{21} become {[2-3]}. This is because O_{11} and O_{21} have to be processed by the same machine, and it takes one time unit to process O_{11}. Therefore, the earliest possible time O_{21} can start is at time unit 2.

In essence, STCP repeatedly chooses the next operation to be scheduled from the active schedules, assigns a start time to it, and then propagates the precedence constraints and machine interference constraints to eliminate the infeasible time in the start time windows of the other unscheduled operations. If an empty start time window of any unscheduled operation is formed as the result of constraint propagation, then the partially committed schedule is infeasible. This process of assigning start times and propagating temporal constraint terminates when either all operations of all the jobs are scheduled successfully without resulting in any empty start time windows, or when all the possible schedules are searched to verify that there is no feasible schedule. The flowchart of STCP is shown in Figure 1 and the detail STCP algorithm is presented in the Appendix.

3. Temporal Constraint Propagation

Both the precedence constraints and machine interference constraints can be propagated from operation X to operation Y by using the *revise* procedure [MAC 85] to eliminate the start times from different operations that do not satisfy the constraint. The revise procedure does not make use of the temporal relationship between the possible start times. For operations that contain k (discrete) possible start times in the start time window, the time complexity of the revise procedure is $O(k^2)$. By analyzing the temporal relationship among the start times in the start time window of an operation, more efficient algorithms are developed to propagate precedence constraints and machine interference constraints.

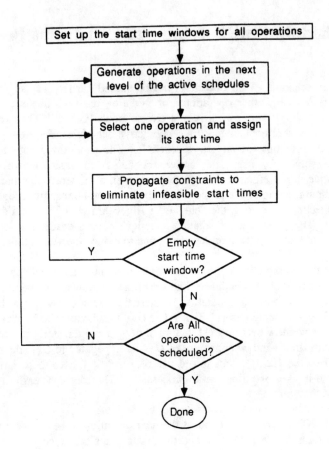

Figure 1   The flowchart of STCP

3.1. The Precedence Constraint Propagation (PCP) Algorithm

Let $ST_e(X)$, $ST_l(X)$ and $ST_i(X)$ be the earliest start time, the latest start time, and any given start time in the start time window of operation X respectively. Let $FT_e(X)$ be the earliest possible finish time of operation X and let T_x be the processing time of operation X.

Theorem 1

Given that X is an immediate preceding operation of operation Y. If $ST_i(Y) > ST_e(X) + T_x$, then $ST_i(Y)$ satisfies the precedence constraint between X and Y.

Proof:
The earliest start time in the start time window of operation X is $ST_e(X)$. By definition, the earliest finish time of X is $FT_e(X) = ST_e(X) + T_x$. Since X is an immediate preceding operation of Y, according to the precedence constraint, Y can start right after X is completed. There-

fore, all $ST_i(Y) > FT_e(X)$ (or $ST_i(Y) > ST_e(X) + T_x$) satisfies the precedence constraint.

Corollary 1

Given that X is an immediately preceding operation of operation Y. If $ST_e(X)$ does not satisfy the precedence constraint with a given $ST_i(Y)$, then no $ST_i(X)$ satisfies the precedence constraint with $ST_i(Y)$. Therefore, the precedence constraint propagation depends only on $ST_e(X)$.

Corollary 2

Given that X is an immediately preceding operation of operation Y. If $ST_i(Y)$ satisfies the precedence constraint between X and Y, then all the other possible start times of Y that are greater than $ST_i(Y)$ also satisfies the precedence constraint.

Based on Corollaries 1 and 2, the revised procedure can be reduced to the following PCP algorithm for propagating the precedence constraint from operation X to Y. Let $ST_{ep}(Y)$ be the earliest start time of operation Y after propagating the precedence constraint from X to Y.

Algorithm PCP
1. Calculate $ST_{ep}(Y) = ST_e(X) + T_x$
2. Eliminate all start times in Y that are less than $ST_{ep}(Y)$

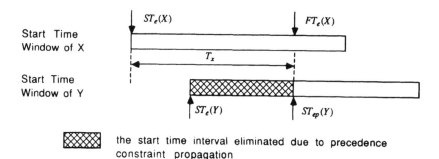

▨▨▨ the start time interval eliminated due to precedence constraint propagation

Figure 2   The start time window of Y after propagating the precedence constraint from X to Y

34

3.2. The Machine Interference Constraint Propagation (MICP) Algorithm

Theorem 2

Given that operations X and Y must be processed by the same machine. If $ST_i(Y) > ST_e(X) + T_x$ or $ST_i(Y) < ST_l(X) - T_y$, then $ST_i(Y)$ satisfies the machine interference constraint between X and Y.

Proof:
In order for operations X and Y to satisfy the machine interference constraint between them, either X has to be processed before or after Y. $ST_i(Y) > ST_e(X) + T_x$ implies operation Y can be processed after operation X, thus satisfying the machine interference constraint. $ST_i(Y) < ST_l(X) - T_y$ implies operation X can be processed after operation Y, hence satisfying the machine interference constraint.

Based on Theorem 2, the revise procedure can be reduced to the MICP algorithm to propagate the machine interference constraint from X to Y. Let $ST_{lp}(Y|Y \rightarrow X)$ be the latest start time of operation Y after propagating the machine interference constraint given that Y is processed before X. Let $ST_{ep}(Y|X \rightarrow Y)$ be the earliest start time of operation Y after propagating the machine interference constraint given that X is processed before Y.

Procedure MICP
1.   Compute $ST_{lp}(Y|Y \rightarrow X) = ST_l(X) - T_y$
2.   Compute $ST_{ep}(Y|X \rightarrow Y) = ST_e(X) + T_x$
3.   Eliminate the start time interval of Y that is larger than $ST_{lp}(Y|Y \rightarrow X)$ and less than $ST_{ep}(Y|X \rightarrow Y)$

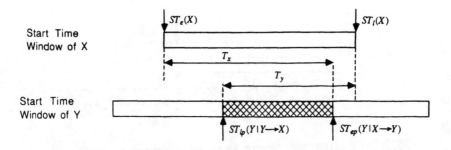

the start time interval eliminated due to machine interference constraint propagation

Figure 3   The start time window of Y after propagating the machine interference constraint from X to Y

The time complexity of the PCP and MICP algorithms depend on the number of disjointed time intervals, n, in the start time window of an operation. Initially, every operation has only one single interval in its start time window. As a result of the machine interference constraint propagation, an interval could be partitioned into smaller intervals (see Figure 3).

The computation of step 1 of the PCP algorithm takes constant time. In the worst case, step 2 of the PCP algorithm needs to examine all the n disjointed time intervals in the start time window of an operation. Therefore, the time complexity of of the PCP algorithm is $O(n)$. Note that n is usually much smaller than k, where k is the number of possible (discrete) start times in the start time window. The time complexity for the MICP algorithm can be shown to be $O(n)$ in a similar manner.

4. Experimental Results

The complexity of a generalized job shop scheduling problem depends on the the number of jobs involved, the total number of operations in the jobs, the processing time of the operations, the number of machines, and the deadlines. Three types of generalized job shop scheduling problems was used to test the performance of STCP. Problem 1 was adopted from a job shop scheduling problem in [MUT 63] with the extra feature that each job has an individual deadline. Problem 1 consists of 6 jobs and 6 machines with a total of 36 operations. The processing time of the operations ranges from 1 to 10 time units.

Problem 2 had the extra feature over the Problem 1 that different operations in a job could use a machine more than once. Problem 2 consists of 6 jobs and 11 machines with a total of 59 operations. The processing time of the operations ranges from 1 to 28 time units. Problem 3, in addition to the aforementioned features, allowed operations to be processed in parallel. Problem 3 consists of 6 jobs, 11 machine with a total of 59 operations. The processing time of the operations ranges from 1 to 15 time units. Both problems 2 and 3 were based on the job shop scheduling environment in the manufacturing division of an aerospace company. It can be shown that the number of possible schedules for these 3 problems is in the order of 10^8.

We assigned three different deadlines to each of these three problems, resulting in 12 test problems. The deadline' of a job was computed by summing the processing times of the operations in that job and multiplying it by a slack factor. The different deadlines were generated using different slack factors. Some test problems might not have feasible schedules because the deadline was set too tight. For each test problem, the scheduling algorithm would terminate when it found the first feasible schedule, or search through all the possible schedules to verify that there was no feasible schedule.

The performance comparison between *Backtracking on Active Schedules* (BAS), STCP using the Revise procedure and STCP using PCP-MICP was shown in Table 2. n_{bt} represented the number of backtrackings required to find the first feasible schedule or to verify that there was no feasible schedule. n_{op} had different meanings for different algorithms. For BAS, n_{op} represented the number of times the deadline constraint checks were performed to verify that the partially committed schedule had not violated the deadline constraints. For STCP using the revised procedure, n_{op} represented the number of times consistency checks were performed to verify if the given start times from two different operations satisfied the precedence constraint. For STCP using PCP-MICP, n_{op} represented the total number of disjoint intervals in the start time windows that were checked. Since the n_{op} operations for these algorithms consisted of a sequence of read, comparison and write operations without loops, the execution time of performing a n_{op} operation for them was comparable. The entry "sol" indicated whether a feasible schedule was found. "nc" meant non-conclusive; that is, after performing the indicated number of backtrackings, the algorithm was still unable to find a feasible schedule or verify that there was no feasible schedule. "*no*" meant that the algorithm verified that there was no solution after the indicated number of backtrackings. "*1st*" meant that the first solution was found after the indicated number of backtrackings.

problem number	slack factor		BAS	STCP with	
				Revise Procedure	PCP-MICP
1	1.375	n_{bt}	50000	5	5
		n_{op}	127570	10127	480
		sol	nc	no	no
	1.5	n_{bt}	50000	23	23
		n_{op}	129819	60477	2700
		sol	nc	no	no
	1.625	n_{bt}	50000	191	191
		n_{op}	142530	369873	18125
		sol	nc	1st	1st
2	1.25	n_{bt}	734	1	1
		n_{op}	5934	1945	74
		sol	ns	ns	ns
	1.375	n_{bt}	1431	4	4
		n_{op}	12264	12990	370
		sol	ns	ns	ns
	1.5	n_{bt}	1	1	1
		n_{op}	63	16590	397
		sol	1st	1st	1st
3	1.5	n_{bt}	50000	166	166
		n_{op}	251523	210384	8628
		sol	nc	no	no
	1.625	n_{bt}	50000	19	19
		n_{op}	275973	38031	1426
		sol	nc	1st	1st
	1.75	n_{bt}	957	19	19
		n_{op}	6181	30210	1335
		sol	nc	1st	1st

Table 2   Performance comparison between BAS and STCP

For problem 1 with a slack factor of 1.375, STCP only took 5 backtrackings to verify that there was no feasible schedule while BAS could not verify that even after 50,000 backtrackings. Based on n_{op}, the execution time of STCP using the revised procedure was at least 12 times smaller than that of BAS, and the execution time of STCP using PCP-MICP was at least 250 times smaller than that of BAS for this problem. Similar performance improvements of STCP over BAS was noted in problems 2 and 3. Since STCP was basically the BAS algorithm with temporal constraint propagation, the above results revealed that temporal constraint propagation in STCP provided significant reduction in the computation time for solving the generalized job shop scheduling problems.

To compare the performance of constraint propagation, we noted that the n_{op} for the PCP-MICP algorithm were much smaller than that for the revised procedure in the corresponding problem. Based on n_{op}, the execution time for the PCP-MICP algorithm was about 15 to 30 times less than that of the revised procedure.

5. Conclusion

We have proposed a *Scheduling Algorithm with Temporal Constraint Propagation* (STCP) for solving the generalized job shop scheduling problem. STCP propagates precedence constraints and machine interference constraints to eliminate the infeasible schedules. Since STCP is basically BAS with temporal constraint propagation, the significant improvement in computation time between the two algorithms is due to the temporal constraint propagation.

By analyzing the temporal relationship among the possible start times between operations, it is noted that the constraint propagation from operation X to operation Y depends only on the earliest start time in the start time window of X, and if a given start time of Y satisfies the temporal constraint between X and Y, any larger start time of Y will also satisfy the temporal constraint. Based on the above properties, PCP-MICP reduces the time complexity for propagating constraints to $O(n)$, where n are the disjointed time intervals in the start time windows of the operations. For the job shop scheduling problems, our experimental results reveal that using the PCP-MICP algorithm for propagating constraints yields an order of magnitude improvement in computation time over that of the revised procedure.

Appendix

Let us define the following terms used in STCP:

$T_m(X)$ = the start time when the required machine is available for processing operation X

$$T_p(X) = \begin{cases} \text{release time of X} & \text{if X is the first operation} \\ \text{finish time of the preceding operation of X} & \text{otherwise} \end{cases}$$

$EST(X) = max(T_m(X), T_p(X))$

$EFT(X) = EST(X) + \text{processing time of X}$

LST(X) = the deadline of the job that consists X minus the minimum amount of time needed to process X and its subsequent operations

The procedure of the *Scheduling Algorithm with Temporal Constraint Propagation* (STCP):

1. Compute the initial start time windows for all operations in each job. The initial start time window of an operation X consists of the time interval between its earliest possible start time, $EST(X)$, and its latest possible start time to meet the job deadline, $LST(X)$.
2. Identify the operation Y with the smallest earliest possible finish time in the set of the first unscheduled operations of each job. Identify the machine M that processes operation Y.
3. From the set of the first unscheduled operations of each job, find the operations that need to be processed by machine M and have an earliest possible start time less than

the *EFT*(Y) identified in step 2. Store these operations in the set *C*.

4. Let N_C be the number of operations in *C*. If $N_C = 0$, then remove the most recently scheduled operation from the partially committed schedule list. Backtrack to the immediately preceding search level. If the partially committed schedule list does not contain any scheduled operation, then there exists no feasible schedule. Therefore, terminate the scheduling process. If $N_C \geq 1$, then find the operation *Z* with the smallest earliest possible finish time among *C*.

5. Compute the *EST*(Z) of operation *Z*. Assign it as the only feasible start time in the start time window of operation *Z*.

6. Propagate the precedence constraints and machine interference constraints to other unscheduled operations to eliminate the infeasible start times.

7. If an empty start time window is formed during constraint propagation, then the current schedule for processing *Z* by machine *M* is infeasible. Therefore, delete operation *Z* from *C* and go to step 4.

8. Add *Z*, the most recently scheduled operation, to the partially committed schedule. If all operations are scheduled, a feasible schedule is found; otherwise, go to step 2 and continue the scheduling process at the next search level.

References

[ADA 88]
> Adams, J., Balas, E. and Zawack D., "The Shifting Bottleneck Procedure for Job Shop Scheduling", Management Science, Vol. 34, No. 3, March 1988, 391-401.

[CAR 89]
> Carlier, J. and Pinson, E., "An Algorithm for Solving the Job Shop Problem", Management Science, Vol. 35, No. 2, February 1989, 164-176.

[GAR 79]
> Garvey, M.R. and Johnson, D.S., "Computers and Intractability. A Guide to the Theory of NP-Completeness", W. H. Freeman and Co., 1979.

[GIF 60]
> Giffler, B. and Thompson, G., "Algorithms for solving Production Scheduling Problems", Operations Research, 12, 1960, 305-324.

[MAC 85]
> Mackworth, A.K. and Freuder, E.C., "The Complexity of Some Polynomial Network Consistency Algorithms for Constraint Satisfaction Problems", Artificial Intelligence 25, 1985, 65-74.

[MUT 63]
> Muth, J. and Thompson, G., eds., "Industrial Scheduling", Pretice-Hall, Englewood Cliffs, N.J., 1963, pp. 236.

Computer Architecture
and Parallel Processing

Automatic Test Pattern Generation on Multiprocessors: a summary of results[*][†]

Sunil Arvindam[§] Vipin Kumar[¶] V. Nageshwara Rao[†] Vineet Singh[§]

[†]Department of Computer Sciences
University of Texas at Austin
Austin, Texas 78712

[¶]Computer Science Department
University of Minnesota
Minneapolis, MN 55455

[§]MCC
3500 West Balcones Center Drive
Austin, Texas 78759

Abstract

Test generation of combinational circuits is an important step in the VLSI design process. Unfortunately, the problem is highly computation-intensive and, for circuits encountered in practice, test generation time can often be enormous. In this paper, we present a parallel formulation of a backtrack search algorithm called PODEM, which has been the most successful algorithm for this problem. The sequential PODEM algorithm consumes most of its execution time in generating a test for "hard-to-detect" (HTD) faults and is often unable to detect them even after a large number of backtracks. Our parallel formulation attempts to overcome these limitations by partitioning the search space in order to search it concurrently using multiple processors.

We present speedup results and performance analyses of our formulation on a 128 processor Symult s2010 multicomputer. Our results show that parallel search techniques provide good speedups (45-106 on 128 processors) as well as high fault coverage of the HTD faults in reasonable time as compared to the uniprocessor implementation.

Tree search is an integral part of several AI systems. Effective parallel processing of search problems is important in developing high performance knowledge-based systems. Results from this paper show that tree search can be effectively parallelized on large scale parallel processors in the context of practical problems.

---

[*]This work was partially supported by Army Research Office grant # DAAG29-84-K-0060 to the Artificial Intelligence Laboratory, Office of Naval Research Grant N00014-86-K-0763 to the Computer Science Department, at the University of Texas at Austin.

[†]A large part of this research was performed while the first and second authors were at the University of Texas at Austin.

1 Introduction

The problem of Automatic Test Pattern Generation (ATPG) [Goel 1981] is to obtain a set of logical assignments to the inputs of an integrated circuit that will distinguish between a faulty and fault-free circuit in the presence of a set of faults. In this paper, we consider *stuck-at* faults that force a signal line to remain stuck at a logical value of 0 or 1 independent of the logical values in the rest of the circuit. An input pattern is said to be a test for a given fault if, in the presence of the fault, it produces an output that is different for the faulty and fault-free circuits.

VLSI circuits are characterized by their high gate count ($> 10^5$ gates) and it is imperative to develop fast algorithms that will generate tests for the various faults relatively quickly. However, the problem is NP-Complete for both combinational and sequential circuits [Goel 1981] and is therefore computationally intractable in the worst case. It has been found that the average-case complexity for combinational circuits is polynomial, perhaps as low as the cube of circuit size [Goel 1980]. However, even this is very time consuming for most circuits encountered in practice. The quality of any algorithm for the ATPG problem is measured by its *fault coverage*, which is the percentage of faults for which tests were generated relative to the total number of faults. A test generation algorithm is defined to be *complete* if it is guaranteed to find a test for a fault, if one exists.

In this paper, we study sequential and parallel implementations of a backtracking algorithm called PODEM (Path-Oriented Decision Making [Goel 1981]) used for combinational circuits (and for sequential circuits based on the level-sensitive scan design approach). This is the most successful algorithm for the problem. We find that the sequential algorithm is able to generate tests for more than 90% of the faults in reasonable time but spends an enormous amount of time trying to generate tests for the remaining faults. As a result, the execution of the algorithm is terminated when it fails to generate a test after a pre-defined number of backtracks. We define those faults that cannot be solved in reasonable time by the serial algorithm as being *hard-to-detect* (HTD) faults. As we discuss later, large-scale parallel processing is effective for this problem only when searching for these HTD faults. The easier faults can be found in reasonable time even by the sequential algorithm. But, since the ultimate goal of any test generation algorithm is high fault coverage, using parallel techniques does seem like a highly feasible option. We have thus confined our attention to the HTD faults.

The techniques we use to parallelize the PODEM algorithm were originally developed and studied in [Kumar and Rao 1988,Rao and Kumar 1988,Kumar and Rao 1989] by Kumar and Rao, in the context of pure depth-first search (DFS). In this paper, we have applied these techniques to the ATPG problem.

The domain of ATPG is particularly interesting, as PODEM is a DFS algorithm augmented with some powerful heuristics. The original parallel formulation of DFS (PDFS) of Kumar and Rao was tested on problems such as the 15-puzzle for which such powerful heuristics are not available. It was not clear whether their parallel formulation of DFS would provide good speedup on problems for which sequential DFS uses strong heuristics. We find that their techniques are highly effective even in the context of such problems.

Among the central contributions of this paper are extensive speedup results and performance analyses of our parallel formulation of ATPG on a 128 processor Symult s2010 multicomputer. In Section 2, we analyze the speedup curves obtained and characterize the scalability of our work-distribution strategy. We discuss why our approach scales better than the ones presented in [Motohara et al. 1986,Patil and Banerjee 1989] for the same problem. We then study the superlinear speedups that are encountered while attempting to solve the more complex faults. Our results show that tests for HTD faults may be cost-effectively generated using parallel processing techniques. Due to space limitations, we do not discuss the sequential PODEM algorithm and how it may be viewed as a state-space search problem. We refer the reader to [Goel 1981] for these details. Similarly, we also refer the reader to [Arvindam et al. 1989] for details regarding our parallel formulation of the PODEM algorithm as well as for more extensive speedup results. In Section 3, we present a summary of our results.

2   Results

We implemented the parallel PODEM algorithm on a 128 processor Symult s2010 multicomputer, a MIMD machine with a 2-D mesh topology. In this section, we present results characterizing the performance of parallel PODEM. In all the results presented here, the heuristic used was the Fanout/Distance method [Bennetts 1984]. All experiments described in this section were performed using the following seven files from the ISCAS benchmark set [Brglez and Fujiwara 1985]: c1355, c1908, c2670, c3540, c432, c499, and c5315. The number in the name of the file corresponds to the number of signal lines between the gates in the circuit. As discussed later, this number is not necessarily a good measure of the complexity of test pattern generation for the circuit.

Our experiments were conducted as follows. HTD faults were first filtered out by picking those faults from the seven files whose test patterns could not be found within 25 backtracks using the sequential algorithm. The serial and parallel PODEM algorithms were both used to find test patterns for these HTD faults. Since some of these HTD faults may not be solvable (by the sequential and/or parallel PODEM algorithm) in a reasonable time, an upper limit was imposed on the total number of backtracks that a sequential or parallel algorithm could make. If the sequential or parallel algorithm exceeded this limit (the sum of backtracks made by all processors being counted in the parallel case), then the algorithm was aborted, and the fault was classified as undetectable (for that backtrack limit)[1]. In our experiments, the upper limit on the backtracks was varied between 1600 and 25600.

Table 1 summarizes the results obtained. Faults found to be redundant were considered covered in the data shown. The time shown is the time taken to search through

---

[1]Actually, the number of backtracks in the parallel case may be slightly higher than the specified limit since the distributed termination-detection algorithm's global information is always somewhat out of date. However, this is not significant enough to change the results.

File	HTD Flts	Procs	Time (secs) for 25600 backtracks	Speedup for 25600 backtracks	HTD Cvrg backtracks = 1600; 6400; 25600			Total Cvrg for 25600 backtracks
c432	11	1	2885	–	0.0;	9.0;	18.0	98.95
		16	233	12.38	9.0;	9.0;	9.0	98.84
		32	123	23.45	9.0;	9.0;	9.0	98.84
		64	66	43.71	9.0;	9.0;	9.0	98.84
		128	42	68.69	9.0;	9.0;	9.0	98.84
c499	26	1	15964	–	52.0;	52.0;	69.0	99.19
		16	945	16.89	62.0;	69.0;	69.0	99.19
		32	516	30.93	69.0;	69.0;	69.0	99.19
		64	308	51.83	69.0;	69.0;	69.0	99.19
		128	245	65.16	69.0;	69.0;	69.0	99.19
c1355	90	1	44942	–	38.0;	42.0;	54.0	98.47
		16	1423	38.58	91.0;	90.0;	90.0	99.66
		32	811	55.42	91.0;	91.0;	91.0	99.70
		64	550	81.71	91.0;	91.0;	91.0	99.70
		128	450	99.87	91.0;	91.0;	91.0	99.70
c1908	48	1	15623	–	42.0;	52.0;	69.0	99.61
		16	516	30.27	88.0;	90.0;	90.0	99.87
		32	279	55.99	90.0;	90.0;	90.0	99.87
		64	186	83.99	90.0;	90.0;	90.0	99.87
		128	147	106.27	90.0;	90.0;	90.0	99.87
c2670	356	1	109929	–	59.0;	76.0;	92.0	99.45
		16	8499	12.93	72.0;	81.0;	91.0	99.38
		32	4739	23.20	70.0;	78.0;	91.0	99.38
		64	3188	34.49	71.0;	78.0;	91.0	99.45
		128	2421	45.41	71.0;	77.0;	92.0	99.45
c3540	857	1	363793	–	—;	—;	85.0	98.18
		16	16822	21.63	—;	—;	89.0	98.67
		32	9497	38.31	—;	—;	90.0	98.79
		64	6165	59.01	—;	—;	90.0	98.79
		128	4650	78.24	—;	—;	90.0	98.79
c5315	87	1	29934	–	81.0;	91.0;	94.0	99.95
		16	1791	16.71	87.0;	93.0;	95.0	99.95
		32	1100	27.21	85.0;	93.0;	95.0	99.95
		64	753	39.75	87.0;	93.0;	95.0	99.95
		128	602	49.72	91.0;	93.0;	95.0	99.95

Table 1: Summary of Speedup and Coverage Results on the Symult s2010

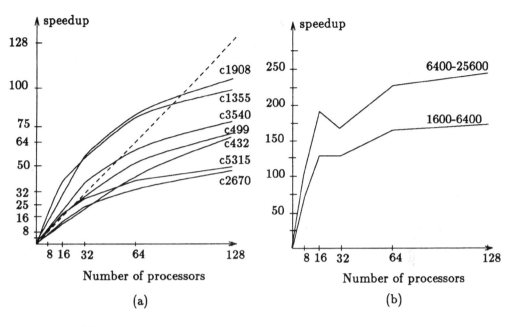

Figure 1: (a) Speedup Curves for 1 Through 128 Processors using 25600 total back-tracks, (b) Superlinear Speedups on Harder Faults

the entire HTD list. Speedup is computed as the ratio of time taken by the sequential algorithm to process all the HTD faults and the time taken by the parallel algorithm to process the same faults. The run-times, speedups and total fault coverage shown correspond to 25600 backtracks. For reasons discussed later, the sequential and parallel algorithms can have different fault coverages for the same limit on backtracks. Also, the fault coverage and the time taken in different runs of the parallel algorithm for the same circuit and backtrack limit can be different. Figure 1 (a) plots speedup curves for all seven files based on data given in Table 1, for 25600 backtracks. The results shown in Table 1 are taken from exactly one run of the parallel algorithm for each case, because we had limited access to a large parallel processor. For the same reason, we were not able to obtain HTD coverage readings for file c3540 for 1600 and 6400 backtracks.

The motivation for this experiment was two-fold. First, to study the amount of speedup obtainble from the search trees encountered in realistic instances of the ATPG problem. From Table 1 and Figure 1 (a), it is clear that very good speedups can be obtained even on 128 processors when the upper limit on the backtracks in 25600. Second, to study how coverage varied with increasing backtrack limit. It is clear from Table 1 that HTD coverage does increase by a large factor (13-33%) for the serial algorithm as the backtrack limit is increased from 1600 through 25600. The parallel algorithm shows the same trend although the improvement is not so marked (0-21%). But, it should be noted that the parallel algorithm obtains high coverage even with lower backtrack limits. Observe that the fault coverage for c432 by the parallel algorithm was slightly less than that by the sequential algorithm.

A number of factors affect the speedup:

First, speedup depends upon the work distribution scheme used in the parallel formulation. Since at any time, a processor is either searching a part of the tree or looking for work (and thus not doing useful work), the efficiency of the parallel formulation depends upon the fraction of the time the processors are doing useful work. A better work distribution scheme will keep the processors busy doing useful work for a greater fraction of the total time. This is discussed in more detail in Section 2.1.

Second, the speedup obtained for a particular fault depends upon the size of the tree searched by sequential PODEM for that fault. A given fault is easy to detect for the sequential algorithm if a solution lies in the left part of the tree. The sequential algorithm finds a solution to such faults after a small amount of search. For such faults, the parallel algorithm cannot provide much speedup, as the part of the tree to be searched to find a solution is small and thus cannot support much concurrency. If the fault is hard to detect (i.e., no solution lies in the left part of the tree), then good speedup can be obtained because the search tree is larger and therefore has more concurrency. (This is discussed in more detail in Section 2.1.) If the fault happens to be redundant, then the search tree is normally very large. Of course, for HTD faults, the size of the tree actually searched is bounded from above by the backtrack limit. Hence, the overall speedup obtained on a circuit depends upon the mix of the faults in the set (i.e., how many faults in the set are easy and how many are hard), and on the backtrack limit chosen. Clearly, if a circuit has more hard faults, then we should get more speedup. This explains the difference in speedup obtained for different circuits as reported in Table 1. Note that the files having a large number of gates do not necessarily yield higher concurrency. Also, as the backtrack limit is increased, the search space searched for the hard faults increases, which increases the overall speedup.

Third, solutions in the search space are randomly distributed and experiments with different numbers of processors lead to different parts of the search space being explored. Also, the work distribution strategy is itself non-deterministic. Different runs under the same experimental conditions may also lead to different parts of the search space being explored. Hence, in any given run, parallel search may do less work (or more work) than sequential search to find a solution for a fault resulting in superlinear (or sublinear) speedup. Superlinear speedups in isolated runs of parallel ATPG algorithms have been reported by Patil and Banerjee [Patil and Banerjee 1989], and have also been observed in our experiments as shown in Figure 1 (a). Although this might seem counter-intuitive, there is even a possibility that superlinear speedup can be obtained on the average. This is discussed in more detail in Section 2.3. The fact that sequential and parallel PODEM search different subsets of nodes also explains why the fault coverage may be different even if they are run with the same backtrack limit.

Fourth, the speedup also depends upon the shape of the tree, and on the amount of work done in each node expansion. If a tree has a smaller branching factor than another tree with the same number of nodes, then the first tree will have greater depth. This means that the communication overhead for transferring the same amount of work will be greater. If the amount of work done in each node expansion is greater, then the communication overhead becomes proportionally less significant for the same number of nodes transferred. Since (1) the trees generated by different circuits are different and (2) the work done for each node expansion is different, speedups can be somewhat different for different trees even if the total number of nodes expanded (i.e., the number of backtracks) in each case is the same.

2.1 Efficiency of the Work Distribution Strategy

In our next experiment, we measured speedups for all seven files with backtrack limit ranging from 1600 through 102400 and number of processors equal to 32, 64, and 128. Two or three faults from each circuit were chosen such that a test pattern was not found for these faults over the backtrack range described above; for these faults the sequential and parallel search performed the same number of backtracks. The motivation was to isolate the impact of the work distribution strategy on the speedup from other factors.

We plotted the efficiency obtained using 64 and 128 processors with respect to 32 processors (not shown here due to space limitations). We present two observations we made from these curves. First, higher backtrack limits lead to higher efficiencies for both 64 and 128 processors. This happens because communication overhead becomes a smaller fraction of the total work as the amount of useful work increases. A high enough backtrack limit leads to efficiencies approaching 100%. Second, efficiencies are clearly higher for 64 processors compared to 128 processors. This is because using a higher number of processors leads to more overhead to distribute the computation evenly. Larger overhead for the same amount of useful work leads to lower efficiency.

2.2 Scalability of the Work Distribution Strategy

Let W be the sequential execution time for a problem instance (also called problem size here) and N be the number of processors used. As is clear from the above results, we get higher speedups on bigger problem sizes. The reason is that Kumar and Rao's parallel formulation of DFS (PDFS) belongs to the general class of parallel algorithms for which it is possible to obtain an efficiency (defined as speedup/number of processors) arbitrarily close to 1 on any number of processors by simply increasing the problem size. The required rate of growth of W w.r.t. N (to keep the efficiency fixed) essentially determines the scalability of these parallel algorithms (for a specific architecture). For example, if W is required to grow exponentially w.r.t. N, then it would be difficult to utilize the architecture for a large number of processors. On the other hand, if W needs to grow only linearly w.r.t. N, then the parallel algorithm can easily deliver linear speedup for arbitrarily large N (provided a large enough architecture can be constructed). Since most problems have a sequential component (taken to be one node expansion in this paper), W must asymptotically grow at least linearly w.r.t. N to maintain a given efficiency. If W needs to grow as $f(N)$ to maintain an efficiency E, then $f(N)$ is the isoefficiency function and the plot of $f(N)$ w.r.t. N is the isoefficiency curve.

The isoefficiency function of the PDFS algorithm discussed here should be similar to the one for pure PDFS (presented in [Kumar and Rao 1988,Rao and Kumar 1988]) provided we assume that the sequential and parallel algorithms do the same amount of work. As discussed in [Kumar and Rao 1988], the isoefficiency function of PDFS depends upon the work-distribution scheme as well as the target architecture. As shown in [Kumar and Rao 1988,Rao and Kumar 1988], for a hypercube or shared-memory architecture, the isoefficiency function of a good work-distribution scheme (e.g., **random**) is fairly close to linear. This means that machines based on these architectures can provide linear speedup for reasonable problem instances even on a very large number of processors. On a mesh architecture, theoretically the best obtainable isoefficiency function is $O(N^{1.5})$. This is achieved by the **random** work-distribution scheme used in our implementation. Due to large message start-up time and worm-hole routing in the Symult 2010 multicomputer, the time for sending a message from one node to another does not vary much with the distance between source and destination of the message and is dominated by the message start-up time. Hence, for all practical purposes, a 128-node Symult multicomputer can be considered a fully connected multicomputer (i.e., a system in which each node can send messages to any other node in unit time, although this unit is relatively large). For fully connected multicomputers, the **random** strategy has an isoefficiency of $O(NlogN)$.

On the contrary, the work distribution schemes used in [Patil and Banerjee 1989] by Patil and Banerjee and by Motohara et al. [Motohara et al. 1986] have an isoefficiency function of $O(N^2logN)$, which is much worse than our **random** strategy. The reason is that in their scheme, the sharing of work is done through a centralized scheduler. In [Patil and Banerjee 1989], Patil and Banerjee incorrectly hypothesized, after looking at their results that were up to 16 processors only, that the speedup in their scheme will saturate for a larger number of processors. As discussed in [Kumar et al. 1989], even their scheme will provide efficiency arbitrarily close to 1 for increased problem size (and any given number of processors). But since its isoefficiency is worse that the **random** scheme, it is not as scalable as the **random** strategy, and will provide less speedup for most of the interesting problem instances and parallel processors.

2.3 Superlinear Speedups on Harder Faults

In this section, we study the superlinear speedups that may be obtained while solving some of the harder faults in parallel. The experiment was performed over two selected sets of faults. The first set consisted of those faults that the serial algorithm was able to solve after executing a total number of backtracks in the range 1600-6400. Similarly, the second set of faults was solved by the serial algorithm in the backtrack range 6400-25600. The faults in the second set were thus harder to solve for the serial algorithm. Two of the seven files, namely c499 and c1355, did not yield any faults for either of the two sets. We executed the parallel algorithm for 16 to 128 processors and averaged the speedups obtained for a given number of procesors separately for the two sets of faults. The run-time for each fault was itself the average obtained over 10 runs. These results are shown in Figure 1 (b). The mere presence of superlinear speedup is not surprising, as the sequential and parallel versions of PODEM expand different sets of nodes. (Actually, different executions of the parallel PODEM expand different sets of nodes for the same fault of a given circuit.) An important question is whether superlinear speedup is possible on the average. In other words, is parallel PODEM running on 1 processor in a time-sliced fashion better than the sequential PODEM? If the answer to this question is yes, then it is rather surprising, as the sequential algorithm (PODEM) is currently the best known algorithm for the ATPG problem.

Rao and Kumar [Rao and Kumar 1988] studied the phenomenon of superlinear speedup in PDFS in the context of an abstract model and showed that if there are many solutions and if they are non-uniformly distributed in the search space, then parallel DFS can obtain superlinear speedup over sequential DFS on the average (i.e., in such cases, parallel DFS running on 1 processor in a time-sliced fashion will perform better than sequential DFS) [Rao and Kumar 1988]. They used this model to explain superlinear speedup in PDFS for a variety of problems such as the 15-puzzle, Hamiltonian cycle, Hackers, and N-Queens problems. Clearly, in the ATPG problem, many faults have several solutions. If they are not uniformly distributed in the search space (which appears highly likely), then Rao and Kumar's model [Rao and Kumar 1988] explains the presence of superlinear speedup.

¿From Figure 1 (b), we see that as the complexity of the faults increases, the degree of superlinearity increases. This happens because for difficult faults, the efficiency of our PDFS algorithm (i.e., parallel PODEM) is higher. From the figure, it is also clear that the superlinearity factor becomes smaller as the number of processors increases. Some of the loss in superlinearity can be explained by the model and analysis of Rao and Kumar [Rao and Kumar 1988]. In addition, some loss in superlinearity may be attributed to a decrease in the efficiency of the work distribution strategy as the number of processors is increased for the same problem size (discussed earlier in Section 2.1).

3 Conclusions

As we see from the above experiments, search-level parallelism is effective only for HTD faults (the ones that need parallel processing most). Hence, a good strategy is to perform fault-level parallelism to filter out easy faults, and then use search-level parallelism on the HTD faults. On HTD faults, search-level parallelism yields two advantages: (1) increased available CPU power, as the work of tree search is shared by many processors; and (2) superlinear speedup. The first one implies that solutions for the faults can be found much more quickly on a parallel processor than on a sequential processor. The second one implies that even in the absence of a parallel processor, HTD faults should be solved on a sequential processor by simulating a parallel processor using time-slicing.

Note that the parallel PODEM algorithm finds a very large fraction (such as 99.5%) of the fault set after a moderate amount of search effort, and provides a substantial speedup over the sequential algorithm. Once this large fraction is found, progress (towards achieving 100% coverage) becomes very slow either because the remaining faults are redundant (in which case, the state-space has to be searched exhaustively) or they require enormous search before a solution for them can be found. Normally, since enough CPU power is not available, the designer has to stop and categorize these faults as undetectable. With the availability of massively parallel processors, it appears possible that the search trees of many practical circuits can be searched to completion to generate tests for all the faults (or to determine that they are redundant). Even today, the second generation of the NCUBE multicomputer offers up to 8192 nodes, each with roughly 10 MIPS performance, giving a total power of roughly 10^5 MIPS which is about 4 to 5 orders of magnitude more than what is available in a high-performance workstation today. This substantial CPU power can bring the time of performing exhaustive search for redundant faults down from years to hours.

Acknowledgements: We thank Brian Kennedy for allowing us to borrow parts of his code for PODEM. We thank Dr. Jacob Abraham for many helpful discussions. We also thank Yacoub El-ziq for his comments, MCC for financial support and the use of its facilities, and Symult Corporation for providing access to its 128 processor machine.

References

[Arvindam et al. 1989] S. Arvindam, V. Kumar, V.N. Rao and V. Singh. Automatic Test Pattern Generation on Multiprocessors. MCC Tech Report ACT-OODS-240-89, 1989.

[Bennetts 1984] R.G. Bennetts. *Design of Testable Logic Circuits*. Addison-Wesley, Reading, Massachusetts, 1984.

[Brglez and Fujiwara 1985] F. Brglez and H. Fujiwara. Neutral Netlist of Ten Combinational Benchmark Circuits and a Target Translator in Fortran. In *Special Session on ATPG and Fault Simulation, Proceedings of IEEE International Symposium on Circuits and Systems*, July 1985.

[Goel 1980] P. Goel. Test Generation Cost Analysis and Projections. In *Proceedings, 17th Design Automation Conference*, June 1980.

[Goel 1981] P. Goel. An Implicit Enumeration Algorithm to Generate Tests for Combinational Logic Circuits. *IEEE Trans. on Computers*, C-30:215–222, March 1981.

[Kumar and Rao 1988] V. Kumar and V. N. Rao. Parallel Depth-First Search, Part II: Analysis. *International Journal of Parallel Programming*, 16 (6):501–519, 1987.

[Kumar and Rao 1989] V. Kumar and V. N. Rao. Load balancing on the Hypercube Architecture. In *Proceedings, Fourth Conf. on Hypercubes, Concurrent Computers and Applications*, March 1989.

[Kumar et al. 1989] V. Kumar et al.. *Working Manuscript.*

[Motohara et al. 1986] A. Motohara, K. Nishimura, H. Fujiwara and I. Shirakawa. A Parallel Scheme for Test Pattern Generation. In *Proceedings, Intl. Conference on Computer-Aided Design*, 1986, pages 156-159.

[Patil and Banerjee 1989] S. Patil and P. Banerjee. A Parallel Branch-and-Bound Algorithm for Test Generation. *Proceedings of the 26th ACM/IEEE Design Automation Conference*, 1989.

[Rao and Kumar 1988] V.N. Rao and V. Kumar. Parallel Depth-First Search, Part I: Implementation. *International Journal of Parallel Programming*, 16 (6):479-499, 1987.

[Rao and Kumar 1988] V.N. Rao and V. Kumar. Superlinear Speedup in State-Space Search. In *Proceedings, Conference on Foundations of Software Technology and Theoretical Computer Science* , December 1988.

Design and Implementation of a Broadcast Cube Multiprocessor

Rajat Moona   V. Rajaraman

Supercomputer Education and Research Centre

Indian Institute of Science

Bangalore 560 012 INDIA

uunet!shakti!turing!vidya!moona

uunet!shakti!turing!vidya!rajaram

Abstract

In this paper, we describe a Broadcast Cube System [BCS] architecture for high speed scientific computation and logic programming. The architecture is based on multiple fully connected broadcast networks connected in cube topology. We also present the software environment for the above architecture which supports multiprocessing in a way which is very similar to the multiprocessing in UNIX operating system. A numerical integration program is also given in this paper which uses the subroutine calls from the software environment and runs on BCS architecture.

1   Introduction

During the past few years, advances in computer technology have spurred a renewed interest in architectures using small, inexpensive microprocessors as building blocks.

The goal of the architecture described here is to develop an inexpensive microprocesor based, high performance multiprocessor system suited for a class of problems that have an inherent parallelism in their data processing such as numerical weather modelling [Williamson and Swarztraber, 1984; Dennis et al, 1984; Webster, 1983], image processing [Hwang and Briggs, 1984] fluid flow analysis, molecular research etc. An architecture to perform such computation should support asynchronous operation of the nodes, *i.e.*, each node in the system with its local memory may perform any arithmetic operation at any time, and different nodes may perform different operations at the same time.

In the architecture described in this paper, the nodes are organised in a cube topology [Murthy et al, 1987; Moona 1989] in which each node is connected to d independent fully connected broadcast networks. The structure has many interesting properties. The connectivity of this structure is very high and many architectures can be emulated and studied on this structure. Architecture is highly scalable and extra processing nodes can be added in the system very easily. The software environment described in this paper allows programmers to code their applications independent of BCS configuration.

Secondly, the cubed-network topology has the following advantages over other interconnection techniques even though the queueing delays involved may be worse. This is mainly because

1. The delay encountered in terms of the switching delays a message undergoes before reaching the destination node that is connected to the source node, is zero as there are no intermediate nodes involved in the transmission. The maximum delay between any pair of nodes is $d - 1$ for a d dimensional BCS.

2. The links are passive and therefore interconnection network is highly reliable.

In section 2 of the paper, we describe the architecture. In section 3, we describe the software environment which could be used for multiprocessing. In section 4 we describe the implementation of numrical integration problem on the BCS architecture. Finally in section 5 we conclude the paper.

2 Basic architecture

2.1 Overall configuration

The Broadcast Cube System (BCS) consists of identical nodes connected by a d-dimensional network. The system is parameterized by two parameters. In a d–dimensional system, each node is connected to d fully connected broadcast networks. In a p–drop system, each fully connected network connects p nodes. The nodes are addressed with d p–radix digits as follows :

$$Nodeaddress = \overbrace{n_0, n_1, \cdots, n_{d-1}}^{d-digits};\ \ 0 \leq n_i < p$$

The communication in the system [Moona, 1989] can be done in "one to many write" and "read from one" mode. This is done by the use of a mask pattern. A node can broadcast a message to one or more nodes in the system which are connected to the source node through any of the fully connected networks. A broadcast to all the nodes in a d-dimensional system takes d steps. The most important aspect of a broadcast network is the arbitration scheme which controls the access to the network. In BCS implementation, all nodes in a dimension are arranged in a fully connected network as shown in Figure 1. In such a scheme, all nodes get the access to the communication media without any delay. BCS allows a broadcast in a single instruction on all the links emerging from a node. This structure has been implemented using the IBM-PC compatible motherboards and the communication links designed for this application. MSDOS[1] has been the underlying operating system which is available on IBM-PC.

2.1.1 Node

All the nodes in the BCS architecture are identical and are responsible for both computation and communication. In a d dimensional system, each node consists of one Arithmatic

---

[1] MSDOS is the operating system developed by Microsoft USA for IBM-PC

54

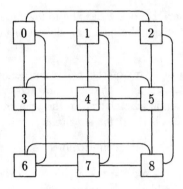

Figure 1: Implementation of a $p = 3, d = 2$ BCS

$\mathcal{P}$rocessing $\mathcal{U}$nit (APU) and $d(p-1)$ $\mathcal{C}$ommunication $\mathcal{L}$inks (CLs). The APU is capable of doing all floating point computation and implements the scientific functions in the instruction set. It is also capable of performing string operations, block operations, variable bit shift and rotate operations and various other primitive operations. All tasks are executed by the APU with the communication controlled by the CLs under its supervision. The structure of a node is shown in Figure 2. Separate modules for computation and communication enable the node to perform both operations in parallel.

2.1.2 Host

The host (node with nodeaddress = 0) handles all input and output of the system and compiles the programs for BCS which are written in a high level language like Pascal, C, FORTRAN or PROLOG. The compiler translates the program to a task graph consisting of multiple interacting tasks and statically maps on the tasks onto the nodes. Once the program is mapped, the system operates asynchronously.

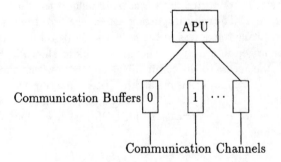

Figure 2: Structure of a node

3 Software environment

Software instructions in this architecture are divided into three subgroups. This environment is a language independent software environment for the BCS architecture. Various language interfaces have been developed for the BCS architecture. We provide here the PASCAL interface to the software environment.

3.1 Data communication

These calls constitute the interprocessor communication ensemble. Communication among nodes may be in blocked or unblocked mode. In blocked mode, the executing CPU is blocked till the requested transfer is over. In an unblocked mode, the CPU can resume other operations while the CL is not available for communication.

Procedure **BWRITE**(Mask:integer; Dataptr:↑anytype; Len:integer);

A node writes Len number of bytes from the memory address Dataptr to a number of nodes specified in Mask. This procedure is a blocked write procedure. In a normal error free execution, control is returned only after all the bytes specified by Len are written. The routine may return an error if any one of the parameters is illegal in which case no data is written. A global variable ComError is set to contain the error code. Details about Mask and error codes are given at the end of this section.

Function **UBWRITE**(Mask:integer; Dataptr:↑anytype; Len:integer):integer;

The node writes Len number of bytes from the memory address Dataptr to all the nodes specified in Mask. This function, however, does not block the CPU if at any time any of the requested channel is unable to accept the data being written. In a normal error free execution, this function returns the number of bytes not yet written. A return value of 0 means success in full transmission. An error code is returned in a global variable ComError.

Procedure **BREAD**(Mask:integer; Dataptr:↑anytype; Len:integer);

A node reads, in blocked mode, Len number of bytes into memory address Dataptr from the channel specified by Mask. The routine may return an error in the global variable ComError.

Function **UBREAD**(Mask:integer; Dataptr:↑anytype; Len:integer):integer;

A processing node reads Len number of bytes from the processing node specified by Mask in unblocked mode. The CPU does not wait for the complete data transfer to be over. If during the execution of this instruction, the communication buffer becomes empty, control is returned back to the calling process with the return value indicating the number of bytes not read. A return value of 0 means success in reception of the data. Any other return value gives the number of bytes yet to be read. This number is always less than or equal to Len. Error codes are returned in a variable ComError.

3.2 Process creation and termination

The calls described in this section enable a node, or APU to fork a remote process in way very similar to that used in process creation in UNIX operating system. A process has three sections namely Code, Data and Stack. For 8088 processor in IBM PC, each of these sections may be as long as 1MBytes and as short as 0 Byte. For a newly created remote process, code, data and stack sections are copied at the remote node from the source node. At the termination of a process, all the allocated memory to the process is returned to the operating system kernel and the process is terminated. Following are the calls in this catagory.

```
Type
   ParamType=record
      CStart:integer; { Code section start segment address }
      CSlen:integer; { Code section length in paragraphs }
      DStart:integer; { Data section start segment address }
      DSlen:integer; { Data section length in paragraphs }
      SSlen:integer; { Stack section length in paragraphs }
   end;
```

Function **FORK**(Mask:integer; var ForkParam:ParamType):integer;

This call creates a number of remote processes at the nodes specified by the Mask. In case of a normal error free execution, the function returns 1 to the children processes and 0 to the parent process. In case of an error, no process is created and the error code is returned in the global variable ComError. The execution at the remote processes starts immediately after the fork call.

Procedure **TERMINATE**;

This call terminates the process executing this call. Control is returned back to the operating system kernel and the code, data and stack sections pertaining to the process are deallocated. This call does not return any error and is always successful.

3.3 General instructions

These instructions are used for getting the address of a node, and various system configuration parameters. The following calls are available in this category.

Function **NODEID**:integer;

This function returns the address of the node on which it is executed. This call does not cause any error and returns the global variable ComError as 0.

Procedure **SYSPARAM**(var p,d:integer);

This procedure returns "drop" and "dimension" parameters of the BCS architecture. A program may use these values to configure itself so that it can be run independent of the system configuration.

3.4   Error codes

In case of an error, the routine performs a return without any effect. All the above routines return the error code in a global variable `ComError` which is accessible to the program.

3.5   Mask generation

The mask is used by a processing node in the interprocess communication and process creation subroutines to communicate to one or more of the processing nodes which are connected through one of the d buses. It is a data structure which has at least $d * (p-1)$ bits, one bit for each connected processing node. In a p drop, d dimension BCS, as there are $d * (p-1)$ neighbors of a processing node, the mask has a unique bit-field for each neighbor. Setting a bit to 1 in the mask enables communication with the processing node which corresponds to the set bit. We now define the bit mapping of the processing nodes and the mask.

The mask can be thought of d blocks of $(p-1)$ bits each as shown in Figure 3.

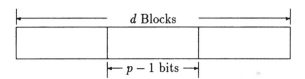

Figure 3: Mask bit pattern

Two processing nodes A $(= a_{d-1}a_{d-2}\ldots a_0)$ and B $(= b_{d-1}b_{d-2}\ldots b_0)$ are connected

$$iff \exists j \ni a_j <> b_j, 0 \le j \le (d-1), \text{ and,}$$

$$a_i = b_i \ \forall i <> j, 0 \le i \le (d-1).$$

The processing nodes are then said to be connected in dimension j.

The algorithm to generate the mask from processing node A to processing node B is given below.

> if $a_j > b_j$ then
>   set b_j bit in block j
> else if $a_j < b_j$ then
>   set $(b_j - 1)$ bit in block j

The above algorithm ensures a unique bit position for each of the neighboring processing nodes. For enabling multiple processing nodes, more than one bit can be set in **mask**. Mask for communication from one processing node to more than one processing node can be found by ORing the mask for each of them.

The following algorithm reproduced in TURBO Pascal[2] is used for generation of the mask from the list of processing node addresses. The subroutine takes as input number of processing nodes whose node identifiers are specified in the array list having minimum n entries. A *mask* is returned as per the algorithm described above.

Function get_mask(n:**integer**; **var** list):**integer**;
    var
        i, mask, peid, dim_conctd, dimen_indA, dimen_indB:**integer**;
    begin
        peid := *nodeid*;
        mask := 0;
        for i:=0 **to** n−1 **do**
            begin
                if *connected*(peid, list[i]) **then**
                    begin
                        dim_conctd := *get_dim*(peid, list[i]);
                        (∗ dimension along which two nodes are connected ∗)
                        dimen_indA := *get_digit*(peid, dim_conctd);
                        dimen_indB := *get_digit*(list[i], dim_conctd);
                        /∗ a_j and b_j ∗/
                        if (dimen_indA > dimen_indB) **then**
                            mask := mask **or**
                                (1 **shl** (dimen_indB + dim_conctd ∗$(p-1)$));
                        else if (dimen_indA < dimen_indB) **then**
                            mask := mask **or**
                                (1 **shl** (dimen_indB − 1 + dim_conctd ∗$(p-1)$));
                  end
                else
                    begin
                        get_mask:= −1;
                        exit
                    end
        end;
        get_mask := mask;
    end;

The function *connected* takes the addresses of two processing nodes and returns a value TRUE if two nodes are connected. A FALSE values is returned otherwise. Function *dim_conctd* takes the addresses of two processing nodes which are connected and returns the dimension in which they are connected. Function *get_digit* takes the address of a node and an index i as input. It returns ith digit in the radix p representation of node address.

---

[2]TURBO Pascal is a version of Pascal available on MSDOS and implemented by BORLAND INTERNATIONAL USA

4 Numerical Integration

We use a finite difference scheme for the integration. For this problem, the BCS structure is decomposed in a p-ary tree of depth d. Each processing node in the system integrates the function over a specific subrange of the integration interval and sends the results to the parent processing node. A processing node receives integrated values from all of its children processing nodes and adds them. This process is repeated till all the values are received by the apex of the tree.

4.1 Mapping of the problem

We consider a BCS architecture with p drop and d dimension. If the function f is to be integrated over the range (σ, σ'), then this range is divided into p^d equal subranges. As there are p^d processing nodes in the system, each processing node gets one such subrange for the integration. The subrange (μ_i, μ_i') for a processing node with $nodeid = i$ can be found by the following formula.

$$\mu_i = \sigma + i * \frac{\sigma' - \sigma}{p^d}, \quad \forall i = 0 \ldots p^d - 1, \text{ and,}$$

$$\mu_i' = \mu_i + \frac{\sigma' - \sigma}{p^d}.$$

A processing node i integrates the function f over the range (μ_i, μ_i'). After this local integration is over, the results are sent to processing node 0. For this purpose, BCS structure is configured in a tree structure with arity p and depth d as shown in Figure 4 for a 4 processing node machine $(p = 2, d = 2)$. The p^d processing nodes at the leafnode level

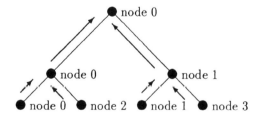

Figure 4: Tree structure organization of BCS(p=2, d=2)

compute the integration over the subrange specified. After computation, these processing nodes send results to their parent processing nodes which are at the next higher level. At this level there are p^{d-1} processing nodes each of which collects results from its p children nodes. All the p intermediate results are then added by these processing nodes. This process continues till the processing node 0 gets results from p processing nodes at level 1. The flow of these results is also shown in Figure 4 by arrows.

4.2 Algorithm and Implementation

We chose the trapezoidal method for numerical integration. The integral of a function $f(x)$ of an independent variable x can be written as

$$S = \int_{\sigma}^{\sigma'} f(x)dx = \sum_{i=0}^{n-1} f(x_i + h/2) * h$$

$$x_0 = \sigma \ and \ x_n = \sigma'$$

$$= \sum_{i=0}^{m-1} f(x_i + h/2) * h + \sum_{i=m}^{2m-1} f(x_i + h/2) * h +$$

$$\cdots + \sum_{i=n-m}^{n-1} f(x_i + h/2) * h$$

$$where \ n = p^d * m$$

We now give the TURBO Pascal implementation of the above algorithm to run in parallel.

4.3 Program

```
Program Numerical_integration;
{$I COMM.H}
var
    peid, p, d, x, PEs:integer;
    min, max:real; (*μ, μ'*)
    peid_radixp:array [1..10] of integer;
    gmax, gmin:real; (*σ', σ*)
    localrange:real; (*μ' − μ*)
    i, time, Steps, mask, it, k:integer;
    integloc, readint:real;
    done:boolean;
    ForkParam:array [1..5] of integer;
Function integ:real;
    var
        i:integer;
        total, halfstep, step:real;
    begin
        step:=(max-min)/60;
        halfstep:=0.5*step;
        for i:=0 to 59 do
            begin
                total := total + step*func(min+halfstep);
                min := min + step;
            end
        integ:=total;
    end;
Function func(x:real):real;
```

```
    begin
        func := exp(-x));
    end;
Procedure max_min(peid:integer);
    begin
        min := gmin + peid * localrange;
        max := min + localrange;
    end;
Procedure get_digits;
    var
        i, j:integer;
    begin
        j:=peid;
        for i:=0 to d - 1 do
            begin
                peid_radixp[i]:=j mod p;
                j:=j div p;
            end
    end;
begin
    sysparam(p,d);
    set_forkparam; (* sets the fork parameters *)
    PEs := 1;
    for i:=1 to d do
        PEs := PEs * p;
    (* PEs = p^d, Number of processing nodes *)
    if (p <> 1) then
        begin
            mask := (1 shl (p - 1)) - 1;
            for i:=0 to d - 1 do
                begin
                    k := fork(mask, ForkParam);
                    mask := mask shl (p - 1)
                end
        end;
    if (PEs <> 1) then peid := nodeid
    else peid := 0;
    get_digits;
    max_min(peid);
    time := timetick; (* function to note the time *)
    integloc := integ;
    done := false;
    for it := d - 1 downto 0 do
        if (peid_radixp[it])
            begin
                bwrite(1 shl ((p - 1)*it), integloc, sizeof(integloc));
```

```
                done := true;
          end
      else if not done then
          begin
              for k:=0 to p − 2 do
                  begin
                      bread(1 shl (k + (p − 1)*it), readint, sizeof(readint));
                      integloc := integloc + readint ;
                  end
          end
      writeln('integral = ', integloc, ' Time = ', (timetick − time));
      terminate;
  end.
```

5   Conclusion

In this paper, we presented the BCS architecture and provided a software environment
for BCS. Two different version of this structure with 4 processing nodes (1 dimension, 4
drops), 8 processing nodes (3 dimension and 2 drops) and 9 processing nodes (2 dimension, 3 drops) have been implemented with IBM-PC motherboards as the APUs at every
node. Many scientific application programs like numerical integration, solution of linear
equations, simplex method of linear programming etc. have also been implemented and
show a speedup merit factor (speedup/no. of nodes) between (0.7 to almost 1). Through
simulation and implementation, it is found that BCS performs much better than many
other popular topologies like Hypercube and mesh [Moona, 1989].

References

[Williamson and Swarztraber, 1984]
> D.L. Williamson and P.N. Swarztraber, "A Numerical Weather Prediction
> Model - Computational aspects on the CRAY-1", *Proc. IEEE*, vol. 72, no.1,
> pp. 56-67, 1984.

[Dennis et al, 1984]
> J.B. Dennis, G.R. Gao and K.W. Todd, "Modelling the Weather with a Data
> Flow Supercomputer", *IEEE Trans. Comp.*, vol. C-33, no.7, pp.592-603, 1984.

[Webster, 1983]
> P.J. Webster, "Mechanisms of Monsoon Low-Frequency Variability", *J. At-
> mos. Sci.*, vol. 40, no. 9, pp. 2110-2124, 1983.

[Hwang and Briggs, 1984]
> K. Hwang and F.A. Briggs, "Computer Architecture and Parallel Processing",
> McGraw-Hill Book Company, 1984.

[Murthy et al, 1987]

C.Siva Ram Murthy, Rajat Moona and V. Rajaraman, "A Multiprocessor Architecture for Weather Modelling", *Proc. Second Intl. Conf. on Supercomputing*, Santa Clara, CA, 1987.

[Moona and Rajaraman, 1988]

Rajat Moona and V. Rajaraman, "Broadcast Cube Multiprocessor System–Architecture and Programming", *KBCS Project Document*, SERC, IISc. Bangalore, 1988.

[Moona, 1989]

Rajat Moona, "Design and Implementation of a Multidimensional Multilink Multicomputer Hardware and Software", Ph.D. thesis, IISc. Bangalore, 1989.

Expert Systems

INTELLIGENT ONBOARD TELEMETRY SYSTEM -A DESIGN APPROACH

P Anguswamy   M Krishna Kumar   V Mala

Abstract

Intelligent onboard telemetry monitoring based on expert system techniques can provide many conceptual advantages compared to conventional telemetry monitoring. However, realisation of such a system calls for systematic design approach. In this paper a layered telemetry system architecture - which has many advantages - is described. Taking into account the recent developments in micro electronics and software techniques, a system architecture which can fit with various missions is described. A low cost ground simulation test bed can be configured using high performance multiple personal computers. It is concluded that the successful realisation of an onboard intelligent telemetry system may lead to the application of expert system techniques to many other critical systems.

1. INTRODUCTION

Telemetry monitoring is a vital and essential function in any space mission. In conventional telemetry systems (Fig 1a) large number of onboard parameters are measured, digitized and transmitted to ground as telemetry frames. On the ground, various parameters are decommutated and analysed using ground decommutators/data processing computers. However, inferences are usually drawn by human experts (may be mission controllers) by analysing the various parameters in addition to applying their knowledge (rules of thumb) on any specific problem domain. In an effort to minimise the number of experts required for a particular mission (especially long duration missions), telemetry monitoring function has been automated using ground based computers and expert system techniques (ref 1). However, if we can port the inference capability of the human experts on to an intelligent onboard telemetry system, we can foresee many conceptual advantages. The design and realisation of such a complex onboard intelligent system calls for a systematic design approach at all levels. A layered design approach is one of the possible solutions for realising such a complex system.

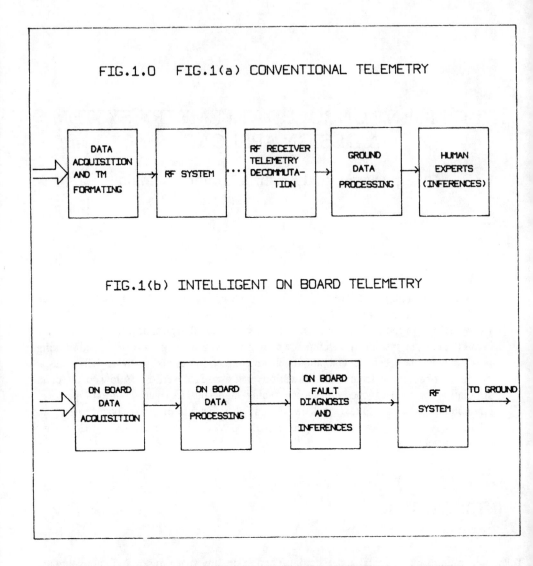

FIG.1.0 FIG.1(a) CONVENTIONAL TELEMETRY

FIG.1(b) INTELLIGENT ON BOARD TELEMETRY

2. INTELLIGENT TELEMETRY - FUNCTIONAL MODEL

A high level functional model of the proposed onboard intelligent telemetry system (Fig 1b) consists of the following basic functions.

- Onboard Data Acquisition
- Onboard Data Processing
- Onboard Inferencing (based on expert system techniques)

The advantages of the above system are described below.

a) Most of the time, inferences will be transmitted instead of bulky raw data. Because of this, there will be substantial savings in the realtime bit rate which can be judiciously utilised to reduce the onboard transmitted power.

b) We can have access to more data (as much data as necessary) without bothering much about the RF bandwidth constraints. Space availability for instrumentation may be the only constraint.

c) In conventional telemetry systems, the measurement plan is usually predefined assuming a normal flight. But many times when there is an abnormal flight it is felt that some more information on a particular subsystem may be useful and relevant. If there is intelligence onboard, it is possible to choose an appropriate monitoring strategy (adaptive monitoring) depending on the flight conditions. For example, in case of a malfunction, the associated subsystems can be given more attention (by way of increased sampling rate etc) and unrelated subsystems can be ignored or given less attention.

d) Depending on the flight conditions, some of the relevant data can be transmitted by the most reliable transmission mode (by repeated transmission of same data, application of rigorous error control techniques selectively on a certain set of data etc.).

e) In future space missions, time will be a very critical factor due to increasing frequency and complexity of the missions. Intelligent monitoring can enhance the post flight analysis by giving more "focussed", fast and reliable information.

f) In case of manned space missions, intelligent telemetry monitoring can relieve the crew from the routine monitoring functions and provide them the "expert assistance".

The following functional capabilities are desired to be built into the intelligent monitor.

- Capability to assess the global mission/vehicle status.
- In case of observed anomaly, characterise the anomaly in the order of criticality and priority.
- Provide more information on relevant subsystems.
- Trace the root cause of the anomalous behaviour.
- Predict probable causes of failure.
- Raise alarm flags whenever there is a malfunction.
- Explain reasons for the predictions or conclusions.
- Predict the mission impact.
- Adopt suitable monitoring / transmission strategy.
- Generate telemetry information packets.
- Provide intelligent assistance during preflight checkout operations.

A layered concept model and a hardware system architecture capable of realising the above mentioned functional capabilities are described in the following sections.

3. INTELLIGENT TELEMETRY - A LAYERED CONCEPT MODEL

A layered concept model of the intelligent telemetry system is shown in Fig 2.0. It consists of 4 layers and the functions of each layer is described below.

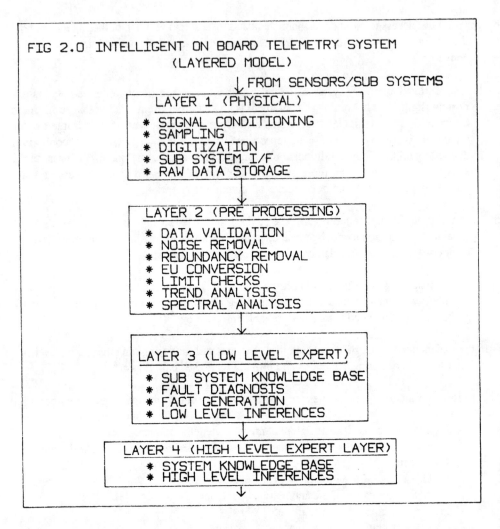

FIG 2.0 INTELLIGENT ON BOARD TELEMETRY SYSTEM
(LAYERED MODEL)

↓ FROM SENSORS/SUB SYSTEMS

LAYER 1 (PHYSICAL)
* SIGNAL CONDITIONING
* SAMPLING
* DIGITIZATION
* SUB SYSTEM I/F
* RAW DATA STORAGE

LAYER 2 (PRE PROCESSING)
* DATA VALIDATION
* NOISE REMOVAL
* REDUNDANCY REMOVAL
* EU CONVERSION
* LIMIT CHECKS
* TREND ANALYSIS
* SPECTRAL ANALYSIS

LAYER 3 (LOW LEVEL EXPERT)
* SUB SYSTEM KNOWLEDGE BASE
* FAULT DIAGNOSIS
* FACT GENERATION
* LOW LEVEL INFERENCES

LAYER 4 (HIGH LEVEL EXPERT LAYER)
* SYSTEM KNOWLEDGE BASE
* HIGH LEVEL INFERENCES

3.1 Layer 1 (Physical Layer)

The major functions to be realised at this layer are signal conditioning, data acquisition, sampling, digitisation, subsystem and / or telemetry physical interface and raw data storage.

3.2 Layer 2 (Preprocessing Layer)

This layer consists of two levels of preprocessing. The first level performs functions such as noise removal, redundancy removal (sample size reduction), data validation and engineering unit conversion. The second level processing consists of functions such as limit checks, trend analysis, digital filtering, spectral analysis, etc. This layer requires intensive mathematical computational capability.

3.3 Layer 3 (Low level Expert Layer)

This layer is the true knowledge based layer, but is limited in scope to certain specified subsystems only. Layer 3 has a detailed knowledge base on the specified subsystem and a moderate inference engine. Fault diagnosis, at subsystem level is done in this layer. This layer is responsible for feeding facts, about specified subsystems, to the next layer.

3.4 Layer 4 (High level Expert Layer)

This layer consists of a global knowledge base (dealing with the entire vehicle / mission) and a high level inference engine. Rules handled at this layer are complex and may involve a lot of heuristics. Inferences drawn at layer 3 are used as facts for this layer.

4. HARDWARE ARCHITECTURE

4.1 System Configuration

The hardware architecture of the intelligent telemetry system is shown in Fig 3.0. It consists of multiple Intelligent Remote Units (IRU) and one Intelligent Control Unit (ICU). The IRUs are to be housed nearer the signal sources (ie sensors or subsystems) and the ICU nearer the RF transmitter. The IRUs are connected to the ICU over a high speed optical bus (10 mbps or faster). The IRUs perform the functions of the first three layers and the ICU performs the functions of layer 4 and that of telemetry frame generation. Other subsystems such as the Onboard Computer and Checkout interfaces can also be connected onto the same optical bus and they can have concurrent access to all the layers of IRU and ICU, provided they can simulate an IRU in terms of hardware as well as software protocols. The ICU can command any one of the IRUs and demand either raw data, processed data, low level inferences (facts) or all the three together. Such a demand is made dynamically depending on the flight phase and flight conditions.

4.2 Intelligent Remote Unit (IRU)

The block diagram of the IRU is shown in Fig.4. It consists of four independent stand alone modules interconnected by high speed transputer links (Transputer (ref 2&3) is a high-speed single chip computer system with multiple high speed communication links. It provides many levels of concurrency and high speed computational capabilities (10 MIPS)). Transputer ideally fits into our model where the transputer links can be utilised for inter-layer communication).

The module 1 which performs the layer 1 functions consists of data acquisition ICs, data communication peripherals such as multi protocol serial communication controllers, single chip microcontrollers with built-in DMA, First-In-First-Out (FIFO) memory for raw data storage, special Application Specific Integrated Circuits (ASICs) and transputer link interfaces.

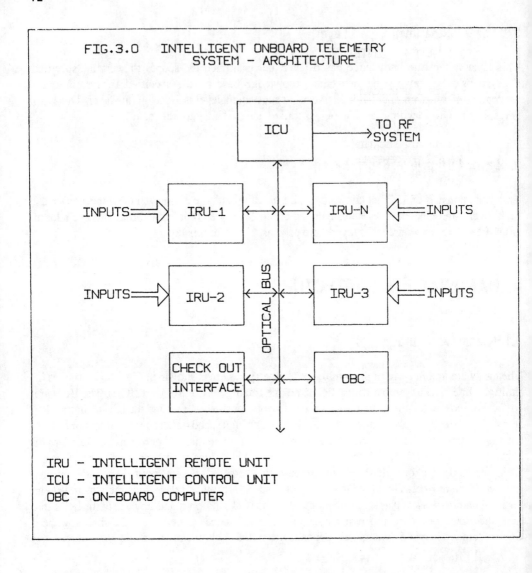

FIG.3.0   INTELLIGENT ONBOARD TELEMETRY
SYSTEM - ARCHITECTURE

IRU - INTELLIGENT REMOTE UNIT
ICU - INTELLIGENT CONTROL UNIT
OBC - ON-BOARD COMPUTER

The second module performs all the functions specified in the preprocessing layer (Layer 2). This module can be built using an array of transputers and advanced VLSI Digital Signal Processors (DSP). The transputer can perform highly mathematical intensive computations and the DSPs can be used to implement the signal processing functions such as spectral analysis, digital filtering etc. The Module 3 performs the functions as defined in Layer 3. It consists of high performance microprocessors, symbolic processors such as LISP Processor (ref4), single chip expert system etc., and a transputer for inter layer communication. IRU will require high capacity memory for storing subsystem level knowledge base in the form of production rules and frames. The Module 4 is a communication manager which can route the outputs of all layers or any one of the layers as demanded by the ICU. It can be built around a high performance microcontroller with a transputer link interface and high speed optical bus controller.

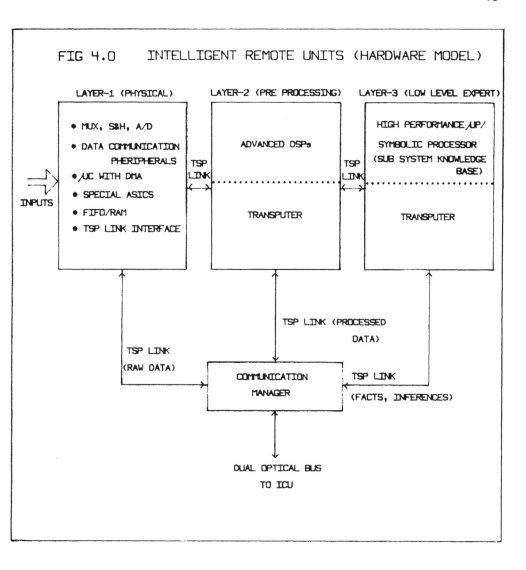

FIG 4.0   INTELLIGENT REMOTE UNITS (HARDWARE MODEL)

LAYER-1 (PHYSICAL)   LAYER-2 (PRE PROCESSING)   LAYER-3 (LOW LEVEL EXPERT)

- MUX, S&H, A/D
- DATA COMMUNICATION
  PHERIPHERALS
- /UC WITH DMA
- SPECIAL ASICS
- FIFO/RAM
- TSP LINK INTERFACE

ADVANCED DSPs

TRANSPUTER

HIGH PERFORMANCE /UP/
SYMBOLIC PROCESSOR
(SUB SYSTEM KNOWLEDGE
BASE)

TRANSPUTER

TSP LINK   TSP LINK

INPUTS

TSP LINK (PROCESSED DATA)

TSP LINK
(RAW DATA)

COMMUNICATION
MANAGER

TSP LINK
(FACTS, INFERENCES)

DUAL OPTICAL BUS
TO ICU

4.3 Intelligent Control Unit (ICU)

The block schematic of the ICU is shown in Fig.5. It consists of a high-level (system level) knowledge base and an inference engine, a communication interface, a telemetry frame generator and an RF interace. The inference mechanism can be realised using either high performance microprocessors or single chip LISP processors or with a combination of both. The knowledge base consists of high level production rules related to the global vehicle / mission configuration and performance analysis. The telemetry frame generator can be realised using a single chip microcontroller and FIFOs. The telemetry frame consists of information and data packets generated by the ICU and the IRUs. The recommendations of CCSDS (Consultative Committee on Space Data Systems) (ref 5) on packet telemetry can be adapted for generating the telemetry frame and packets.

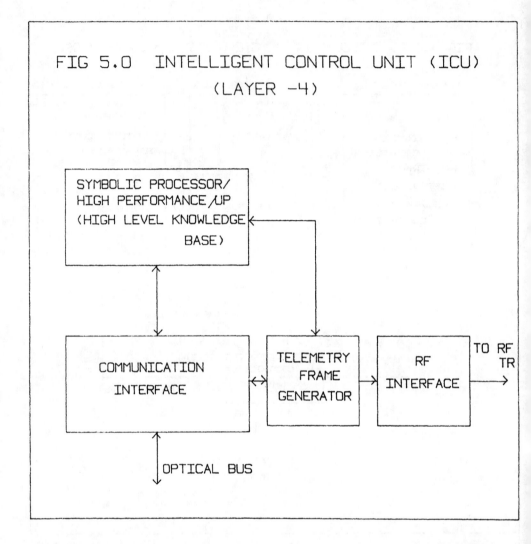

FIG 5.0   INTELLIGENT CONTROL UNIT (ICU)
(LAYER -4)

4.4 Software

Various software techniques can be used in different layers. The use of assembly language may be the most appropriate choice for the layer 1, considering the real time throughput requirements and the small volume of code at this layer. In layer 2 we can use the assembly language of the DSPs and languages such as C. The transputer code can be developed using OCCAM (assembly language of the transputer). At the same time, existing algorithms on FORTRAN can also be directly cross compiled and run on the transputer. In Layer 3&4, if a symbolic processor such as LISP processor is chosen as the target hardware, then it may be preferable to code it in LISP.

5. GROUND SIMULATION

5.1 Test Bed

Extensive ground simulations have to be carried out to validate the system concept and various

hardware and software components, before we can port them to an onboard target hardware. A
low cost test bed can be configured using multiple high performance personal computers as shown
in Fig.6.

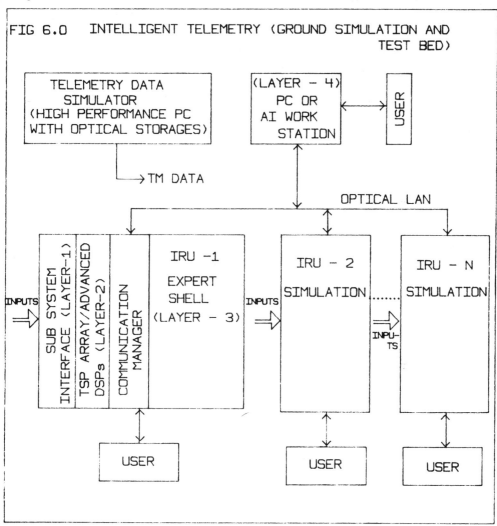

FIG 6.0   INTELLIGENT TELEMETRY (GROUND SIMULATION AND TEST BED)

The IRU can be simulated by interfacing off the shelf available data acquisition boards,
signal processing boards and transputer array boards to a PC. In the initial phase, commercial
expert system shells can be used to validate the rule set and the inference process. The ICU
simulation can be done on a high performance PC with PC compatible expert system shells or
a high performance AI work station. The input simulators for the IRU should be able to provide
continuous real time telemetry data with a provision for fault simulation at any time on any of the
parameters. A high performance PC with a built-in optical storage device is an ideal low cost
solution for realising the simulator (one 5.25" optical disc can store upto 600 MB of data).

76

5.2 Sample Studies

The development of intelligent onboard telemetry system is being pursued as an R&D activity at Vikram Sarabhai Space Centre (VSSC), Trivandrum, India. A PC based expert system workstation has been installed with expert system shells like Personal Consultant Plus, PC IMAGES and PC ONLINE (from Texas Instruments Inc. USA) which run on a dialect of LISP, called SCHEME. The hardware interfaces such as telemetry data acquisition board and transputer board have been interfaced with the IBM PC. A telemetry bit stream simulator has also been constructed for initial system level feasibility studies. A sample knowledge base (app. 50 rules) on the power system monitoring for the Polar Satellite Launch Vehicle (PSLV) has been developed. The configuration of the power system, the number and classification of batteries and the critical failure mode analysis of the power system have been encoded with a set of production rules. The system is able to identify faulty batteries, resolve measurement anamolies and predict mission impacts. Some of the sample conclusions with graphical response are shown in figures 7a, 7b, 7c and 7d.

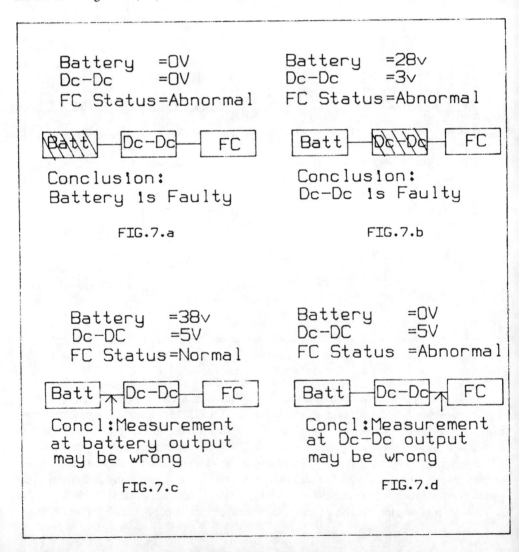

6. CONCLUSION

The development of onboard intelligent monitoring system and successful realisation will lead to the application of expert system techniques to many other critical onboard functions. Hence this development is considered to be very important and a forerunner to many other similar projects.

Acknowledgement

The authors wish to thank Dr.SC Gupta, Director, Vikram Sarabhai Space Centre (VSSC), Trivandrum, INDIA, Shri RM Vasagam, Deputy Director, VSSC/AVMD , Shri P Radhakrishnan, Group Director ELG / AVMD / VSSC for their keen interest, encouragement and support for carrying out this activity in the Baseband and Low Frequency Division (BLD), VSSC.

REFERENCES

1. [J.F.Muratore, 1987]
John F.Muratore. *Space Shuttle Telemetry Analysis By A Real Time Expert System.* AIAA Computers in Aerospace VI Conference. AIAA 87-2799, pp 165-171

2. [INMOS, 1987]
INMOS *Product information,The Transputer family.* 1987

3. [INMOS, 1987]
INMOS *Product Overview,IMS T800 Transputer.*

4. [Gene Matthews et al, 1987]
Gene Matthews, Robert Hewes and Steve Krueger. *Single Chip Processor Runs Lisp Environments.* Computer Design. May 1,1987 pp 69.

5. [CCSDS, 1986]
CCSDS. *Recommendations on "Packet Telemetry"' Blue book.* Consultative Committee for Space Data Systems, 1986

INTERPRETATION AND RULE PACKET IN EXPERT SYSTEMS. APPLICATION TO THE SEPT EXPERT SYSTEM

Patrick BREZILLON

CNRS URA 410, L.R.I. Bât. 490
Université de PARIS XI
91405 ORSAY CEDEX FRANCE
brezil@sun6.lri.fr

ABSTRACT
We have developed an expert system called SEPT which provides an assistance to the operator in his diagnosis of the equipment in French EHV (Extra High Voltage) substation. After a synthetic presentation of the final result, SEPT proposes various presentations of the diagnosis steps. To include an explicative dimension in SEPT, we have had to enrich the representational language which has been used, with the notion of interpretation. This notion permits the concept . and the deep knowledge on which the concept is based to meet in a rule. This facilitates an explanation with various levels of details. In the new version of SEPT, it is possible to propose different possibilities on the representation of the reasoning: a synthetic result, a trace, details at a chosen step, different levels of details of explanations.

1   Introduction

Beyond the event itself, one knows that the observer plays a role in the recognition of the event too: his behavior is not so much dictated by the event as by the echoes that this event awakes in him (by the intermediation of some preconceived ideas, or of already-established opinions, for instance). Ferber [Ferber, 1987] distinguishes two approaches with respect to this statement: the realist approach and the conceptualist approach.

In a realist approach, the observer is interested in a partial representation of the event, thus, keeping only one objective aspect of the event, he chooses a **viewpoint**. For example, a robot can be considered as an electric machine or a mechanical machine. Different viewpoints on a given event are complementary, an observer can even have several viewpoints [Hayes, 1981; Clayton, 1985; Bobrow and Winograd, 1977]. This notion has been employed in some applications [Elio and de Haan, 1986] .

In a conceptualist approach, the observer has a global representation of the event and there are as many representations as observers, each representation resulting from the observers interpretation of the event. Thus, a mechanic and a driver have two different representations of a car. This interpretation, which is independent of the event, characterizes a meaning that the observer ascribes to the event.

In this paper, we give the following meaning to the viewpoint and interpretation notions: the viewpoint concerns the definition of a concept (an event), while the interpretation concerns the deductions made from this concept. We discuss the interpretation notion in the context of the SEPT explicative-expert system. We show that its association with the rule-packet notion leads to a more efficient management of shallow and deep knowledge when several different users of the same expert system are involved.

2   The Notion of Interpretation

2.1   Field of the Study

To explain his reasoning, the expert splits it into a sequence of steps. At a given step, the explanation is based on two kinds of knowledge: the available knowledge at this step and the knowledge based on the structure and the functioning of the system. The second kind of knowledge is generally used to structure the first one.

The two kinds of knowledge must both be present in a knowledge base, but their particular exploitation depends on whether the user is an expert or a novice [Hasling et al, 1984; Neches et al, 1985]. In the approach adopted in this paper, the interpretation notion acts as a filter in the reasoning description in a similar way of the model of the user.

2.2   Presentation

Our application has been written in the Alouette language which was developed by Electricité de France [Mulet-Marquis and

Gondran, 1985] and used in several applications [Ancellin and Legaud, 1986; Cadalen et al, 1986]. The language is based on the first-order predicate logic. The fact-base syntax is a set of triplets (object, attribute, value) which allows a representation of the descriptive knowledge as objects.

The inference engine had to be modified to take into account the particular knowledge structure. These modifications concern the notion of rule packet and of interpretation. This new version of the inference engine will be called METAL.

The *rule packet notion* is not new [Davis and Buchanan, 1985; Clancey, 1986]. In METAL, the rule packets communicate together directly as in object-oriented languages. A metarule calls a rule packet when a particular action associated to the packet name is executed. Eventually, specification of some instantiations can be assigned in this rule packet at this level:

> *IF*   the equipment X is a circuit breaker,
> *THEN*   check the rule packet called "circuit breaker checking"
> with the given instantiation of the variable X.

The use of rule packets explicitly introduces metarules into the knowledge base. These metarules represent not only strategies or meta-knowledge, which are based on the structure and the functioning of the studied system, but also on the expert experience which can help to focus the expert-system search. Another benefit of rule packaging is the higher level of abstraction obtained in the resolution tree than one based on rules. However, the essential point to note in the following is that a call to a rule-packet is made from the action of a rule (several rules can call the same rule packet).

2.3   The Notion of Interpretation in an Expert System

As discussed in the introduction, the interpretation notion can take into account factors in the representation which influence the reasoning description but which are not actually involved in the reasoning. A request for an explanation on a diagnosis is such an example.

A rule consists of two parts: a *conditions* part and an *actions* part. The conditions part describes a concept through a set of characteristics. This concept is generally acquired during past experiences [Bobrow and Winograd, 1977] and corresponds to a given viewpoint. On recognition of the concept, the rule fires and the inference engine executes all the actions in the actions part of the rule. For example, the appraisal of a circuit-breaker is represented in a rule with the following actions:

A1) generate the expertise on the recognized equipment;

A2) announce that the circuit breaker X is going to be checked;
A3) explain the link between the concept recognition and the deductions;
A4) present the characteristics of the circuit breaker X.
Clearly, all these actions need not to be executed for every user (an expert, for example, already knows the characteristics of a circuit breaker). Thus, it is necessary to select the set of pertinent actions for a given request noting that an action can be evoked in different requests.

The usual approach is to make as many copies of the rule as there are requests to represent. In each copy, the conditions part contains the key clauses which characterize the concept. They also contain control clauses (screening and/or contextual clauses as in [Clancey, 1986]). These control clauses direct the exploitation of the rules by the inference engine.

This approach presents three serious inconveniences in our opinion:
- a decrease in the legibility of rules (key and control clauses are mixed);
- a difficulty in managing knowledge base (dilution of concepts in rules);
- a complexity of the knowledge base (management of control clauses).

In our system, the user request is considered as the choice of an interpretation of the expert-system reasoning, the set of valid interpretations being defined by the expert according to the different degrees of importance attached to each step of the reasoning. This interpretation allows the selection of a subset of actions which can be executed directly in the actions part of the rule. The expert defines a set of elementary interpretations as:

I_1 = execute the deductions from the recognized concept;
I_2 = describe the deductions which are made;
I_3 = explain the meaning of the concept;
I_4 = present the chosen instantiations.

He can combine these elementary interpretations, each combination increasing the total number of interpretations proposed to the user. For example, the interpretation $I_5 = I_1 + I_2$, gives a clear trace of the reasoning, while the interpretation $I_6 = I_1 + I_3 + I_4$, gives a more specific explanation than I_3 alone.

2.4   The Implementation

In practice, the list of valid interpretations (elementary and compound) is provided with the rule base. Each action must be associated to one of these interpretations. METAL includes also the classical form of rules with no interpretation associated with actions: the inference engine executes systematically these actions. METAL works under the current interpretation which is defined initially by the user.
The form of a rule can be thus be considered as:

IF   (conditions)
THEN

          action 1 : executes (for all interpretations) the deductions ;

I_5 action 2 : indicates the recognition of the concept;

I_2 action 3 : indicates what must be done after;

I_4 action 4 : presents the instantiations and the results;

I_6 action 5 : explains the concept from deep knowledge.

          Note that the diagnosis expertise does not require access to the knowledge in action 5 which is taken into account only if an explanation is requested. The interpretation is actually similar to the definition of the knowledge state of the user as discussed in [Wallis and Shortliffe, 1985]: the diagnosis must be remade each time the user wants to change the current interpretation. However, a dynamic management of the interpretations is foreseen (by considering the interpretation as a variable whose value can be modified by a particular action and/or by the call of a rule packet).

3   Application to SEPT Expert System

3.1   The Problem under Consideration

          In the French energy network, all lines are connected together at substation level. An EHV substation is composed of several busbars which are linked together by cut-off systems. The lines are also connected to the busbars by other cut-off systems. Each cut-off system is composed of several pieces of equipment, for example, a protective relay and a circuit breaker, the first being responsible for detecting and eliminating a fault rapidly by sending an *open* command to the second.

          The equipment acts only if an incident occurs on the network. Change of state of any equipment is recorded on a centralized printer, as a signal which is composed of three pieces of information: its nature, its origin (the name of the cut-off system), and the time of its appearance.

          If a fault occurs, a modification of the topology of the network is necessary to isolate rapidly that part of the network. This operation is done by a topology change of the substations concerned.

3.2   The Diagnosis

          The operator who is in charge an EHV substation analyzes the incident on the network by a sequence of logical deductions based on experience. The expertise is made to insure this progression and concerns the logical and temporal coherence of signals (the expertise is largely based upon signal redundancy). This is established on five successive levels: the signals, the equipments, the cut-off systems, the busbars and the substation. At each level, a synthetic information represents the status signals of the lower level. These successive aggregations lead to the localization of the fault and, later, to the determination of the faulty equipment at the substation level.

Note that status signal can be judged correct at one level but not at a higher level. For example, if at the equipment level, a circuit breaker can open on one phase, at higher cut-off system level, this opening must be coherent with the one-phase tripping order emitted by the protective relay.

Among the heuristics, some are used to "jump" a part of the reasoning at a given level if all conditions for a normal functioning are present. The expert system can return later to this part if unexpected behavior is found at an upper level or if it is necessary to determine why such a status signal was recorded (several reasons are possible).

3.3   Knowledge Representation

The fact base contains the descriptive part of the knowledge which consists of the topology of the substation and the status signals recorded after an incident. There is a natural structure to this knowledge: from the substation, which forms the root class, to the status signals, which form the leave classes. For simplicity, we relate the elements of the substation to objects (for example, a cut-off system is an object with two characteristics which are the protective relay and the circuit breaker). However, we do not consider the inheritance notion in this representation. This notion would have to be considered in order to provide explanations (for example, a protective relay is a special equipment).

The rule base contains the operational knowledge of the diagnosis system described by the production rules. The functioning of each entity in the substation is translated into sets of rules which form specific tasks. With this kind of representation, it is possible to build up the rule base progressively.

3.4   Conclusion of the First Version of SEPT

Since the first version of SEPT has been described elsewhere [Brézillon and Fauquembergue, 1988], we discuss here only the points which concern the introduction of the notion of interpretation. The expert system SEPT had two main objectives:
1)   to provide the final result as quickly as possible;

2)   to detail and to explain the result later.

Initially our approach led us to decompose the expert system with screening clauses into two parts (of about 300 rules each). The first part provides the diagnosis, and the second presents to the user various analyses of the diagnostic steps. Thus, the first part deduces a set of facts which can eventually be used by the second part.

SEPT has proved the benefit of an expert-system approach for this kind of problem. Electricité de France is now developing a prototype for testing *in situ*. But, whatever its benefits, this first version has some limitations as a consequence of the representation employed:
1) maintenance of the two parts is difficult: concepts are diluted in rules;
2) representation must be remade to include an explanation part;
3) all deduced facts must be kept in the fact base.

In order to remove these limitations, we have taken into account the strongest constraint: the rapid providing of the final result. Our objective was to reuse the same set of rules for the diagnosis as for the description of results, remaking the diagnosis in order to answer the user questions.

3.5   SEPT Expert System with the Interpretation Notion

Actually, SEPT simulates the expert's reasoning during the diagnosis for a given interpretation. If the user wants to change the current interpretation, it is necessary to make a new simulation of the diagnosis. This approach seems to be justified in our problem for three reasons:
- the final result of the diagnosis is rapidly obtained (initial constraint);
- the intermediate results need not be kept (onerous operation);
- the dialogue with the user is the most time consuming.

The introduction of the interpretation notion in SEPT has lead us to define some elementary   interpretations as follows (except for the actions which are always executed):

I_1 = indicate the anomalies of functioning;

I_2 = print instantiations and deductions;

I_3 = print the information on a specific step of the diagnosis.

Various combinations of these elementary interpretations are also proposed to the user.

SEPT can respond to requests: from the synthetic result of the diagnosis to a detailed presentation (presentation of the state of all the entities of the substation at a given step of the diagnosis, presentation of the whole reasoning on a particular entity).

Varying amounts of detail are provided, on the one hand, by the decomposition of the rule base into rule packets, and, on the other hand, by the use of valid interpretations. With the introduction of the interpretation notion, it is only necessary to keep the diagnosis rules of the first version of SEPT (about 320 rules). Another important consequence is that the interpretation notion permits the knowledge which was at the implementation level, to be brought back to the representation level. For example, the screening clauses were an indirect way to represent a part of the knowledge structure at the implementation level in the first version of SEPT. This knowledge structure now appears explicitly.

Explanations can be introduced in a natural way: deep knowledge is called from an action which is associated with an "explicative" interpretation. For example, we have had to represent the tripping order which is emitted by a protective relay. In the first version of SEPT, the corresponding rule (in the diagnosis part) was:

IF   *the tripping order of a protective relay is emitted in two phases,*
THEN
    action 1: conclude an abnormal functioning of the protective relay;

Using different interpretations, this rule has been implemented in the actual version of SEPT with the following actions:

action 2: sends a warning message;
action 3: presents the instantiated premisses;
action 4:   explanation level 1 :
        An opening on two phases means probably that the fault concerns three phases and that therefore the protective relay is faulty on one phase.
action 5: explanation level 2 :
        Opening of a circuit breaker can be only on 1 or 3 phases
action 6: explanation level 3 :
        Opening on 1 phase preserves the actual state of the network, whereas the opening on 3 phases isolates the faulty line.

The explanation in actions 5 and 6 supposes that the explanations of the lower levels are known. It is possible to express this implicit knowledge with a compound interpretation.

4   Discussion

In the first version of SEPT, the knowledge structure was taken into account by the screening clauses which were not really manageable. Thus, it was not possible to base the explanations on the knowledge structure: these explanations were only "shallow explanations".

The rule packet notion represents already some more "deep explanations" because it permits the representation of a part of the knowledge on the functioning principles and on the organization of the equipment in an EHV substation. Thus, knowledge structure, as represented by the rule packets, can lead to structure the explanation: the information contained in a metarule is at an higher level of abstraction than the information in the rules of the packet which it calls. It is a first hierarchical organization.

The interpretation notion authorizes an explicit representation of the explanation structure at the rule level. Indeed, the concept described in a rule is based on an implicit knowledge of some underlying principles. This deep knowledge is directly introduced inside the rule by the means of an action (a call to a rule packet which contains the deep knowledge, for example) which can be controlled by an "explicative" interpretation. Putting together the shallow and deep knowledge leads to a possible establishment of a hierarchy in the detail of the explanations.

The notions of rule packet and of interpretation have been implemented in the inference engine METAL. Their benefit is illustrated in the SEPT application. We are now studying the ways to completely integrate these notions in METAL in order to propose dynamic user management of the facilities provided. We hope in this way to give an explicative dimension to our expert system SEPT.

References

[Ancellin and Legaud, 1986]
Ancellin J and Legaud P. *Un système expert pour le traitement des alarmes d'un réacteur nucléaire.* Proceedings of the 6th Int. Workshop on Expert Systems and Their Applications, Avignon, France, 1986.

[Bobrow and Winograd, 1977]
Bobrow DG and Winograd T. *An overview of KRL, a Knowledge Representation Language.* Cognitive Science, 1(1), 1977.

[Brézillon and Fauquembergue, 1988]
Brézillon P and Fauquembergue P. *SEPT: un système expert pour la Surveillance d'Equipements dans un Poste à très haute Tension.* EDF Bull. de la Direction des Etudes et Recherches, Série B (3), 1988.

[Cadalen et al., 1986]
Cadalen H, Mulet-Marquis D and Benhamou P. *MIRIAM: système expert dans la conception et la mise en oeuvre d'une gestion prévisionnelle de personnel supporté par l'environnement ALOUETTE.*

Proceedings of the 6th Int. Workshop on Expert Systems and Their Applications, Volume 2, Avignon, France, 1986.

[Clancey, 1986]
Clancey WJ. *From GUIDON to NEOMYCIN and HERACLES in twenty short lessons: ORN Final Report 1979-1985.* The AI Magazine, 7(3), 1986.

[Clayton, 1985]
Clayton BD. Inference ART, Programming Tutorial", Inference Corporation, Los Angeles (CA), 1985.

[Davis and Buchanan, 1985]
Davis R and Buchanan BG. *Meta-level knowledge: overview and applications.* Readings in Knowledge Representation, Morgan Kaufman Publishers Inc., 1985.

[Elio and de Haan, 1986]
Elio R and de Haan J. *Representing quantitative and qualitative knowledge in a knowledge-based storm-forecasting system.* Int. J. Man-Machine Studies, 25, 1986.

[Ferber, 1987]
Ferber J. *Approches réflexives en informatique.* Cognitiva 87/ Electronic Image Electronique, CESTA, Paris, 1987.

[Hasling et al., 1984]
Hasling DW, Clancey WJ and Rennels G. *Strategic explanations for a diagnostic consultation system.* Int. J. Man-Machine Studies, 20, 1984.

[Mulet-Marquis and Gondran, 1985]
MULET - MARQUIS D., GONDRAN M., *Un langage pour les systèmes experts: ALOUETTE.* Bulletin de la Direction des Etudes et Recherches d'EDF, Série C(3/4), 1985.

[Neches et al., 1985]
Neches R, Swartout WR and Moore J. *Explainable (and maintainable) expert systems.* Proceedings of the 7th IJCAI, 1985.

[Wallis and Shortliffe, 1985]
Wallis JW and Shotliffe EH. *Customized explanations using causal knowledge.* Rule-Based Expert Systems, Addison-Wesley Publishing Co., Reading (MA), 1985.

An Expert System Framework For
The Preliminary Design Of Process Flowsheets

M. S. Gandikota and J. F. Davis
Artificial Intelligence Applications Group
Department of Chemical Engineering
Ohio State University
Columbus, OH-43210

ABSTRACT

Process design is a complex and ill-defined activity whose structure has largely been unexplored. An information processing analysis of process design suggests two distinct problem spaces called Design Conception and Design Refinement. Within each, several generically defined design tasks that transform design inputs into desired products can be identified. Integration of the tasks gives rise to a supervisory framework that has the necessary functionality for carrying out the information processing in process design. The framework has been illustrated in the paper using an industrial standard design problem for producing ethanol using molasses and bio-reactions. Using the framework as a basis, an architecture for a design expert system is developed.

1. INTRODUCTION

Design is a distinct and complex problem-solving activity which can be open-ended. A simple problem statement like "design a reactor" gives rise to many different possible reactors. The final reactor design will depend upon the initial design specifications and the assumptions made. In many instances, the design problem becomes one of searching through a space of design solutions. An experienced engineer applies many different types of knowledge and strategies for conducting the search. The availability or lack of design knowledge determines the necessary strategies for search. In domains where systematic knowledge for design is available, strategies like problem decomposition, design plans and failure handling can be used. Such design problems have been defined as routine [Brown and Chandrasekaran, 1986; Myers et al., 1988].

Process design has been in existence for many decades and computer-aided process design has been in practice for two decades. Before AI paved the way for expert systems, computer aids for process design had been developed. One of the earliest computer aided design systems, AIDES, was implemented for selection and sequencing of separation schemes [Siirola and Rudd, 1971]. The system functioned as an aid to a design engineer. The BALTAZAR system used resolution based theorem proving and depth-first heuristic search for generating optimal designs [Mahalec and Motard, 1977a; Mahalec and Motard, 1977b]. The Process Invention Procedure (PIP) uses a set of hierarchical procedures and design decisions in each level in the hierarchy for process design [Kirkwood, 1987]. The design methodology involves hierarchical planning with heuristic evolutionary search.

In this paper, an analysis of information processing in process design is presented. Process design is characterized as a coordinated activity taking place in two distinct problem spaces [Newell, 1980] called *Design Conception* and *Design Refinement*. Within these problem spaces, several generically defined tasks that transform design inputs into desired products are identified. An integration of these tasks gives rise to a supervisory framework. Using this as a basis, an architecture for a design expert system is described.

2. PROCESS DESIGN

Process design can be described as the development of a flowsheet for the commercialization of a process based on chemical reactions which link readily available raw materials to more valuable products [Siirola and Rudd, 1971]. A flowsheet is an optimal interconnection of processing systems as well as the optimal type and design of the units within a process system. The activity of process design is to select a particular interconnection of processing systems which meet certain constraints out of a large number of alternatives [Nishida et al., 1981]. It has been estimated that the search space involves as many as $10**4$ to $10**9$ possible design solutions [Douglas, 1988]. The various constraints imposed on the design task include: economic and operational objectives, product specifications, operating restrictions determined by the processing units, safety codes and environmental regulations [Stephanopoulos, 1981]. These constraints can be generalized into two types referred to as supremal and infemal. A supremal constraint is one that must be satisfied by the design solution, whereas the infemal constraint should be considered but is not absolute. The implication is that during the search an alternative is rejected as a design solution if a supremal constraint cannot be satisfied. If an infemal constraint cannot be met by an alternative, it is still acceptable as a design solution.

3. EXAMPLE INDUSTRIAL DESIGN PROBLEM

In this section, a chemical process design problem is described [Naser et al., 1988]. This problem is used both to elucidate and illustrate the details of the framework. The problem is stated as:

The objective is to design a chemical plant that produces 50 million liters/year of 95 wt% azeotropic ethanol (EtOH) using molasses as the raw material. The plant is to be on-line 330 days per year, 24 hours per day. Steam at 600 lbs/square inch and 150 lbs/square inch, and cooling water at 20 degree C and 30 degree C are available as utilities. The bio-reaction to produce ethanol from molasses is given as:

$$\text{YEAST}$$
$$\text{GLUCOSE + NUTRIENTS} \dashrightarrow \text{ETHANOL + CARBON-DIOXIDE + YEAST}$$
$$\text{+BY-PRODUCTS + ENERGY}$$

The problem stated in this form contains information about the starting point for the design as raw materials (molasses) and chemical reaction, and goal state as ethanol product specification. The design process that will be described in this paper is one of synthesizing a preliminary flowsheet to produce ethanol from molasses.

4. FRAMEWORK FOR PROCESS DESIGN

The process design framework is a collection of tasks which do the problem solving under the various contexts of design conception and design refinement problem spaces. Figure 1 shows the problem spaces, contexts and goals in the framework. Goals are achieved by the application of tasks. Each task is characterized in terms of the necessary knowledge and inferencing strategy for achieving a goal.

4.1 Design Conception

Design conception involves identification of various chemical processes or functions in order to transform raw materials into products, i.e. a chemical reaction. Additionally, it involves selection of physical components or process equipment for realizing the functions. Finally, the physical components have to be inter-connected to generate a flowsheet for the process.

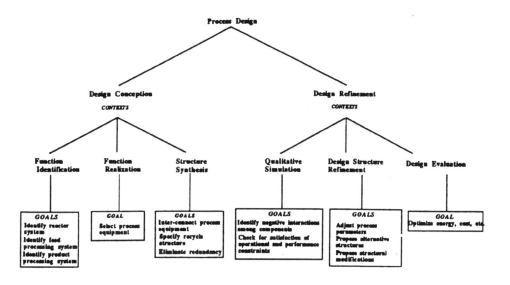

Figure 1: Framework for process design

4.1.1 Function Identification

The goals of function identification are:

1. Reactor identification: To implement the chemical reaction in a reactor

2. Reactor feed processing identification: To process the raw materials into desired inputs for the reactor. Example process operations include heat exchange, dilution, separation, etc.

3. Reactor product processing identification: To process the reactor outputs into the desired products. Example operations include separation of phases, distillation, heat exchange, etc.

These general goals are further decomposed into subgoals to identify more specific functions within the reactor, reactor feed processing and reactor product processing systems as shown in Figures 2, 3 and 4. The decomposition is carried out until a subgoal reduces to an equipment selection problem. Alternatively, if a subgoal corresponds to a desired product or a by-product then it is not decomposed any further.

The knowledge for solving subgoals essentially constitutes the knowledge about inferring the functional decomposition, i.e. functions and subfunctions from the input-output specification of the design. For example, as shown in Figure 3, if the input for reactor feed processing system design is "concentrated feed" and the required output is "dilute sterilized feed" for Glucose, the inference identifies "dilution" and 'sterilization" as the necessary functions.

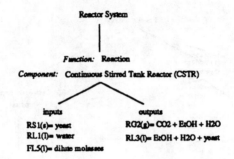

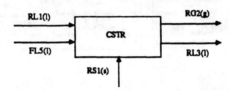

Figure 2: Design conception of reactor system

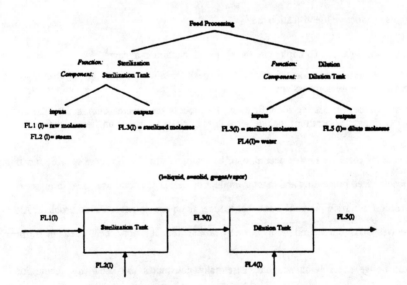

Figure 3: Design conception of feed processing system

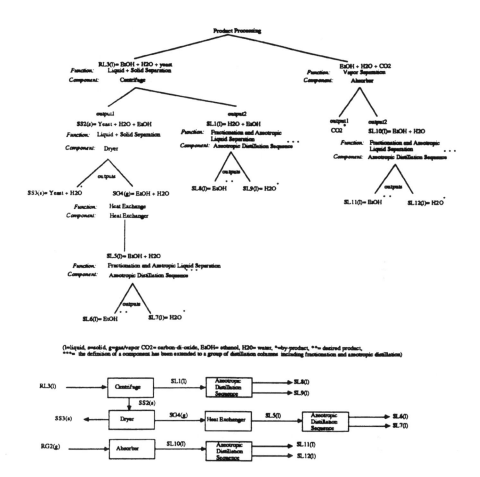

Figure 4: Design conception of separation system

4.1.2 Function Realization

Function realization is the second context of the design conception problem space. The main goal in this context is selection of process equipment to realize the functions identified in the previous context. The various tasks solve the selection problem using classification and critiquing as shown in Figure 5 [Chandrasekaran, 1986; Gandikota, 1988]. Classification here involves organizing all the processes and components that can deliver a function in a hierarchical manner and selecting feasible alternatives based upon component-specific knowledge. After classification, typically, a set of two or more feasible processes results and several components for a given function may be generated. In such cases, critiquing is done. During critiquing the selections generated by the classification are subjected to more critical evaluation by

94

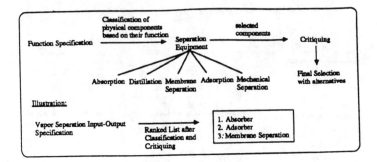

Figure 5: Function realization by classification and critiquing

a critic to determine the "best" process and its alternatives [Gandikota, 1988]. To illustrate, a "vapor separation" function could be realized by several processes like absorption, adsorption, membrane separation and distillation, which give rise to a classification hierarchy of components. After performing classification and critiquing with specifications from a design case (e.g., separation input specifications: chemical composition and their phase, separation output specification: output composition, phase, etc.), the selected separation processes could be "continuous adiabatic separation" with "adsorption" and "membrane separation" as alternatives.

In practice the function identification and function realization contexts have to be carried out alternatively. Referring to Figure 4 again, a functional analysis of the reactor products in the vapor phase shows that a vapor separation is required. So an absorber is selected with the vapor reactor product as input. Further analysis of the absorber output reveals that it needs a liquid phase separation to obtain the desired product (EtOH). So a distillation column is selected. A similar analysis for the liquid and solid phase product separation design gives rise to the selection of various components like centrifuge, dryer, heat exchanger, etc.

4.1.3 Structure Synthesis

The third context of design conception is structure synthesis. The goals of structure synthesis include:

1. Specifying the inter-connections among process equipment
2. Specifying recycle structures among reactor, feed processing and product processing systems
3. Elimination of redundant processes

During the structure synthesis the results of previous contexts are combined to generate a preliminary flowsheet which contains all the selected functions, components and their interconnections. This requires knowledge about establishing physical connections among components, to combine the solutions obtained for the subgoals after function identification and function realization.

A particular type of synthesis problem occurs if two subgoal solutions A and B, where outputs of A are inputs to B, may be combined only when A's outputs are modified by some process P in order to satisfy the constraints on B's inputs. Suppose the temperature of the output FL5 from the dilution tank (in Figure 3) is higher than the temperature specification for the reactor inputs (in Figure 2). In order to combine the two, a heat exchange process, for cooling the tank outputs to the specified temperature for reactor input, has to be included (see Figure 6).

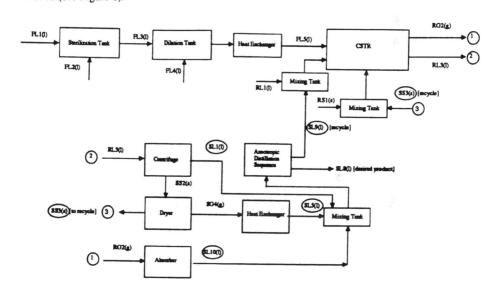

Figure 6: Preliminary flowsheet for ethanol process

Other types of synthesis problems arise due to the underlying philosophy of optimization in design: *to eliminate redundant processes and components, and conserve material by recycling of by-products.* This is shown in Figure 6 where three liquid streams of same chemical composition SL10, SL5 and SL1 are combined in a mixing tank and the output from the mixing tank is fed to a distillation process. This step effectively eliminates two redundant distillation operations associated with streams SL10 and SL5. The synthesis of recycling is done on streams SL9 and SS3 after noting that their respective chemical species H2O and Yeast are also inputs to the reactor.

4.2 Design Refinement

The result of design conception is the generation of a process flowsheet (see Figure 6) which constitutes a conceptual design. More detail is added to the conceptual design by the various contexts during design refinement as described in the following sections:

4.2.1 Qualitative Simulation

The goals of qualitative simulation are:

1. To identify negative interactions among process equipment in the flowsheet
2. To check for operational and performance constraint satisfaction

The conceptual design may not be a feasible structure from the process operation and performance point of view. In order to determine the feasibility of the conceptual design for operation and detect any negative interactions among components qualitative simulation is useful. During qualitative simulation, using the flowsheet structure, connections between functional models of the respective process equipment in the flowsheet are established. A functional model is the specification of various functions of an equipment and the underlying behavior [Sembugamoorthy and Chandrasekaran, 1986]. A state transition graph is generated by simulating the various functional models in the flowsheet. By tracing through the different paths in the graph, states which violate operational and performance constraints are detected. Suppose, from a state transition graph it is found that the concentration of EtOH in the CSTR products is too low. This violates a performance constraint upon the product concentration of CSTR. Similarly, an operational constraint violation is detected when the distillation column for separation of EtOH + H2O mixture can provide the desired state of pure EtOH by requiring a very high number of trays.

4.2.2 Design Refinement

The goals of flowsheet refinement are:

1. To adjust process parameters for better operation and performance
2. To propose structural modifications and
3. To propose alternative structures in case of functional failures

The various tasks of design refinement context take the results of simulation and try making improvements to the flowsheet. For example, increasing the concentration of molasses to the reactor decreases the net water flowrate in the reactor products. This in turn reduces the mass load on separation resulting in a smaller diameter column and reduced use of utilities. Similarly, increasing the inlet concentration of yeast improves the productivity of EtOH.

In case of functional failures, the process parameters suggested by their behavioral models are adjusted. In some cases, structural modifications in a design by reconfiguring components or even by replacing components with alternatives may be necessary for better operation and performance. For instance, if a single reactor cannot produce the desired concentration of ethanol, a sequence of reactors with the output of one as input to the next one is necessary. Similarly, a process operation can be replaced with an alternative, such as absorption replaced by the more efficient but expensive membrane separation, if there is an overall operational or economic benefit.

4.2.3 Design Evaluation

The task of design evaluation tests a design for the realization of process and economic objectives, and to determine the "goodness" of a design. Such analysis includes preliminary optimization at various levels by eliminating redundancy, exploring recycle options (elimination of material waste) and ensuring desired performance from the processes. For example, separation mass load affects the distillation column and dryer energy needs; the maximum temperature and pressure assumed in the design affect the manufacturing cost of process equipment; by-products that violate environmental protection regulations seriously undermine the goodness of a design. This kind of evaluation is entirely qualitative in nature. Semi-quantitative evaluation techniques like sensitivity analysis help in optimizing energy costs and improving productivity by quantifying their sensitivity with respect to independent parameters like reflux ratios in distillation columns, feed concentrations and feed flowrates to reactors. Systematic quantitative evaluation methods like linear and non-linear optimization can be employed for operating cost minimization, profit maximization and determining the economic potential of the plant.

5. THE ARCHITECTURE OF THE EXPERT SYSTEM FOR FLOWSHEET DESIGN

In the previous sections an information processing analysis of process design has been presented. This will be used as the basis for the algorithm underlying the expert system for process design. So in this section we will describe the architecture for implementing an expert system for carrying out process design automatically. As shown in Figure 7, the architecture contains the following components:

5.1 Context Stack

A context stack keeps track of the six contexts of the design problem which are previously analyzed as:

1. Function Identification
2. Function Realization
3. Structure Synthesis
4. Qualitative Simulation
5. Structure Refinement
6. Optimization

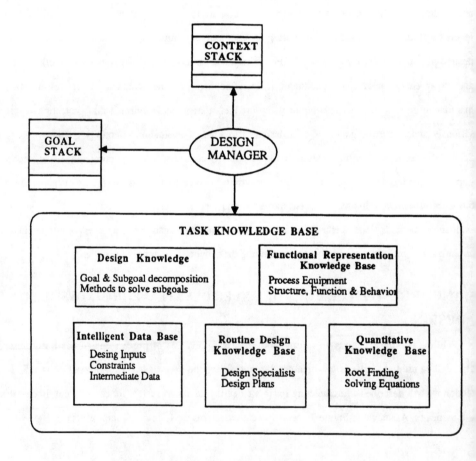

Figure 7: Design expert system architecture

At the beginning of the problem solving the stack is initialized with these six contexts. As the problem solving proceeds the stack reflects the changes in the contexts. The current context of the problem solving is reflected by the top of the stack. A context is deleted from the stack if all the goals and subgoals of a context have been achieved. The end of problem solving is reached when the stack is empty.

5.2 Goal Stack

The goal stack contains the various goals and subgoals to be achieved in the current context. The goals are entered into the stack by the Design Manager based on the current context. The top of the stack is the current goal or subgoal of the problem solving. A subgoal is deleted from the stack when it has been achieved by a task.

5.3 Design Manager

The Design Manager brings about changes in the context and goal stacks during the course of problem solving. As a context becomes current the Design Manager enters into the goal stack the goals corresponding to that context. In addition it also schedules tasks to achieve the goals. The tasks may further decompose a goal into a number of subgoals, which are again entered into the goal stack by the Design Manager. The Design Manager also deletes entries from goal and context stacks when all the subgoals of a goal and all the goals of a context are achieved, respectively.

5.4 Task Knowledge Base

The task knowledge base is a collection of rules that specify:

1. The goals a particular task can achieve
2. The subgoal decomposition of a goal
3. The method to achieve a subgoal

The methods can be in the form of design plans, procedures, etc., which are applied to solve subgoals of a design problem. In addition, the knowledge base contains routine design problem-solvers, functional models of process equipment for simulation and quantitative routines for optimization.

5.4.1 Routine Design Knowledge Base

The process design problem being described in this paper falls in the category of creative design where a prior knowledge of how the final design will look and operate is lacking, even for a human designer. Within this creative design activity, there are subgoals corresponding to design subproblems for which a designer knows a priori, from past experience, what choices to make for the design attributes using systematic design procedures. Such design subproblems have been described as *routine design problems* [Brown and Chandrasekaran, 1986; Myers et al., 1988]. The design knowledge for a routine design task chiefly constitutes, i) knowledge about how to decompose a design problem into a hierarchy of manageable subproblems which have minimal design interactions, ii) procedural knowledge in the form of design plans which consist of individual design steps and constraint testing, iii) knowledge about the selection of appropriate design plans, and iv) knowledge for adjusting the design in the event that a constraint is not satisfied.

Several routine design problem-solvers are used for the specification of CSTR size, distillation column trays, and heat exchanger areas during the design refinement context. They are incorporated in the task knowledge base and are invoked as and when necessary by the Design Manager. Design Specialists and Plans Language (DSPL), a generic task-based high level programming language for routine design problem-solving, is used for the implementation of routine design problem-solvers.

5.4.2 Functional Representation Knowledge Base

The functional representation knowledge base, used for qualitative simulation, contains the following aspects of understanding about process equipment: i) Structure: this specifies the relationships among components within a process equipment, ii) Function: this captures the intended purpose of a process equipment, specified as *what* the response is to an input, useful for generating states during qualitative simulation, and iii) Behavior: this specifies *how*, given an input, the output is accomplished, useful for providing explanations about state transitions. Functional representations of various process equipment proposed in the conceptual design, like heat exchanger, CSTR, and distillation column, are specified in a programming language called FUNC (Keuneke and Allemang, 1988; Sembugamoorthy and Chandrasekaran, 1986). FUNC is invoked by the Design Manager during the qualitative simulation context.

5.4.3 Quantitative Knowledge Base

The quantitative knowledge base is a collection of numerical routines for solving equations and finding roots. The Design Manager employs the routines during the optimization context. The quantitative knowledge base is supported mainly by FORTRAN and ACSL, where routines for engineering calculations are largely available.

101

5.4.4 Intelligent Data Base

The intelligent data base contains the various design input specifications, material balance and energy balance constraints, performance and operational constraints, and data generated during the design problem solving. The data base is also equipped with inferencing methods which can obtain unknown or unspecified data by inferencing from known data, and default values [Bhatnagar et al., 1988]. If necessary, the data base methods perform data abstraction on numerical data to obtain qualitative values for the design problem solving.

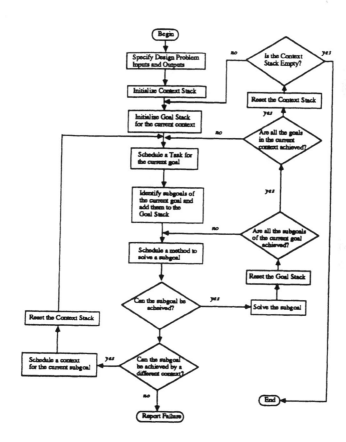

Figure 8: Flow of control in the design expert system

6. FLOW OF CONTROL IN THE EXPERT SYSTEM

The control flow among the various components of the architecture for design problem solving is shown in Figure 8. The control flow allows flexibility in the form of switching from one context to another, when necessary, to solve a subgoal. Since tasks are specified locally within a context, it may not be possible to achieve a subgoal using the tasks local to a context. In such case, the Design Manager searches the task knowledge base and selects a task from a different context to achieve the subgoal. Accordingly, a change of context is made with the current context being the one which has the task selected for achieving the current subgoal (this corresponds to the left hand side loop in Figure 8). Once the subgoal is solved, the current context is deleted and the problem solving returns to the context that has originally set up the subgoal.

7. IMPLEMENTATION

Work is in progress to implement this expert system framework. The work has been proceeding in Xerox LOOPS, DSPL and FUNC (the latter two languages are developed at Laboratory for AI Research at Ohio State University). However, SOAR is now being strongly considered because of its functionalities like universal subgoaling and chunking for the implementation of stacks and portions of task knowledge base dealing with subgoaling.

8. ACKNOWLEDGMENT

We would like to extend special thanks to Hari Narayanan and Jean Maroldt for their involvement during the initial stages of this project. We also appreciate the help of Douglas Myers and James McDowell in writing this paper.

REFERENCES

1. [Bhatnagar et al., 1988]
Bhatnagar, R., M.S. Gandikota, J.F. Davis, B.K. Hajek, D.W. Miller
and J.E. Stasenko, "An Intelligent Database for Process Plant Expert
Systems," Proceedings of ISA Conference, Houston, Texas, October, 1988.

2. [Brown and Chandrasekaran, 1986]
Brown, D. C., and B. Chandrasekaran, "Knowledge and Control for a
Mechanical Design Expert System," *Computer*, 19, 7, pp.92-100,
July, 1986.

3. [Chandrasekaran, 1986]
Chandrasekaran, B., "Generic Tasks in Knowledge-Based Reasoning: High
Level Building Blocks for Expert System Design," *IEEE Expert*, 1,
23, 1986.

4. [Douglas, 1988]
Douglas, J.M., *Conceptual Design of Chemical Processes*,
McGraw-Hill, 1988.

5. [Gandikota, 1988]
Gandikota, M.S., "Expert Systems for Selection Problem Solving
Using Classification and Critiquing," M.S. Thesis, Department of
Chemical Engineering, Ohio State University, 1988.

6. [Keuneke and Allemang, 1988]
Keuneke, A. and Allemang, D., "Understanding Devices: Representing
Dynamic States," Technical Report, Dept. of Computer and Information
Science, Ohio State University, Columbus, OH-43210, U.S.A., 1988.

7. [Kirkwood, 1987]
Kirkwood, R. L., "PIP-Process Invention Procedure a Prototype Expert
System for Synthesizing Chemical Process Flowsheets," Ph.D. Thesis,
Department of Chemical Engineering, University of Massachusetts,
May, 1987.

8. [Mahalec and Motard, 1977a]
Mahalec, V. and R.L. Motard, "Procedure for the Initial Design of
Chemical Processing Synthesis," *Computers and Chem. Eng.*, 1, pp.57,
1977.

9. [Mahalec and Motard, 1977b]
Mahalec V. and R.L. Motard, "Evolutionary Search for an Optimal
Limiting Process Flowsheet," *Computers and Chem. Eng.*, 1, pp.149,
1977.

10. [Myers et al., 1988]
Myers, D.R., D.J. Herman and J.F. Davis, "A Task-Oriented Approach to
Knowledge-Based Systems for Process Engineering Design," *Computers
and Chem. Eng.*, 12, pp.959, 1988.

11. [Naser et al., 1988]
Naser, S. F., R. L. Fournier and S. E. LeBlanc, "Alternative
Fermentation Processes for Ethanol Production- Preliminary Design and
Economic Analysis with FLOWTRAN Simulation," CACHE Process Design
Case Study Series, April, 1988.

12. [Newell, 1980]
Newell, A., "Problem Solving and Decision Processes: The
Problem Space Fundamental Category," in *Attention
and Performance VIII*, ed. R.Nickerson, Erlbaum, Hillsdale, NJ, 1980.

13. [Nishida and Stephanopoulos, 1981]
Nishida, N., G. Stephanopoulos and A.W. Westerberg, "A Review of
Process Synthesis," *AIChE J.*, 27, (3), pp.321-351, 1981.

14. [Reitman, 1964]
Reitman, W.R., "Heuristic Design Procedures, Open Constraints and the
Structure of Ill-Defined Problems," in *Human Judgments and
Optimality*. eds. M.W. Shelly II and G.L. Bryan, New York: Wiley,
1964.

15. [Sembugamoorthy and Chandrasekaran, 1986]
Sembugamoorthy, V. and B. Chandrasekaran, "Functional Representation
of Devices and Compilation of Diagnostic Problem Solving Systems,"
Experience Memory and Reasoning, J.L. Kolodner and C.K. Riesbeck,
eds., Lawrence Erlbaum Associates 1986.

16. [Siirola and Rudd, 1971]
Siirola, J.J. and D.F.Rudd, "Computer Aided Synthesis of Chemical
Process Design," *Ind. Eng. Chem. Fundam.*, 10, (3), pp.353-362,
1971.

17. [Stephanopoulos, 1981]
Stephanopoulos, G., "Synthesis of Process Flowsheets- An Adventure in
Heuristic Design or A Utopia of Mathematical Programming," Foundations
on Computer-Aided Chemical Process Design, Engineering Foundation, 1981.

The Platypus Expert System Shell

Bill Havens[1]

Expert Systems Laboratory
Centre for Systems Science
Simon Fraser University
Burnaby, British Columbia, Canada V5A 1S6
havens@cs.sfu.ca

Abstract

Platypus is a constraint-based expert system shell for diagnosis, synthesis and other recognition tasks. Next-generation expert systems will augment the rule-based approach with more powerful knowledge representations and more efficient search mechanisms. In Platypus, a object-centered knowledge representation produces explicit descriptions of the entities recognized in the task domain, their identifying parameters and the semantic constraints that exist among the entities. Constraint propagation is used to refine these descriptions dynamically during recognition, thereby limiting search. A truth maintenance subsystem supports the dependency directed backtracking of the reasoning process. Platypus is implemented as an extension to the Scheme programming language. This paper outlines some of the programming aspects of Platypus. The classic n-queens problem is used to explain the reasoning architecture and its programming language.

1. Introduction

Rule-based inference engines have seen wide application in expert systems. The methodology is natural and appealing. Expert knowledge is coded as sets of rules which collectively solve problems in the task domain. However successful, the methodology is now mature and its limitations increasingly apparent. Next-generation expert systems will augment the rule-based approach with more powerful knowledge representations and more efficient search mechanisms. Already, the newer expert systems shells offer frame-based knowledge representations, inexact reasoning calculii, truth maintenance mechanisms, as well as other capabilities [Gevarter,1987]. These new shells are much more powerful and considerably easier to use than their simpler rule-based predecessors. However, the addition of lots of new features is a "kitchen sink" approach to developing expert systems technology.

For those expert systems problems which are inherently recognition tasks, a more coherent reasoning architecture can be elucidated. Interestingly, this class encompasses many diagnostic and synthesis tasks which are prevalent in expert systems applications. This report describes a new constraint-based reasoning system called Platypus which embodies this new architecture.

---

[1]This research was conducted while the author was at Tektronix Laboratories, Beaverton, Oregon, USA 97077.

Platypus has been implemented as an extension to the Scheme [Rees *et.al.*, 1986] programming language. The implementation is portable and efficient. Most Platypus constructs are compiled into native Scheme code. Platypus is mutually recursive with Scheme allowing Platypus rules to make convenient use of recursive Scheme functions and allowing Scheme functions to access freely the Platypus rule language, knowledge base and network description. This report describes the current state of the Platypus programming shell. An application expert system for interactively configuring Tektronix 4300-series graphics workstations is being implemented in Platypus [Havens & Rehfuss, 1989].

2. System Overview

The Platypus architecture is based on the following common structure of recognition tasks. See also [Havens, 1985].

• *Many diagnosis and synthesis problems are recognition tasks.* A generative knowledge base is used to construct a structural description of the input data. The description produced is object-centered. It makes explicit the objects recognized in the input data, their internal states and the semantic relationships that exist among objects. For diagnosis tasks, the composed description represents the components, faults, conditions, exceptions and their relationships inferred from the input measurements. For synthesis tasks, the output description represents a structural solution to the design problem. The description is composed of an organized set of solution steps or components known in the synthesis domain.

• *The knowledge is object-centered.* Our knowledge of the task is organized around models of the conceptual entities or objects in the domain. The models represent classes of individuals of a particular type which share common identifying characteristics. Individual differences are represented parametrically.

• *The process of recognition is rule-driven.* Our knowledge about a class is expressed in generative rules which hold for every member. The purpose of the rules is to account for some portion of the input data by adding new instances of the model to the output description.

• *The composed description must satisfy domain constraints.* Part of our knowledge about a domain specifies the allowed relationships among objects in the domain. These relationships are manifest as constraints over the parameters of objects in the description. An object is a valid component of the output description if it is derived from the input data by the rules and its parameters are consistent with those of other objects under the constraints.

• *The search process is hypothesis-based.* Construction of the output description is a non-deterministic process requiring search. Reasoning proceeds by making hypotheses, deriving their consequences and recursively searching the remaining space. Partial solutions which are found inconsistent with the data need to be discarded and alternative search paths explored.

From these principles, the Platypus architecture has been developed. The reasoning system contains four major components: a *rule processor*, a *knowledge base*, a *constraint propagator*, and an embedded *truth maintenance system*. An overview of this architecture is illustrated in Figure 1. The rule processor is the heart of the reasoning engine and drives the reasoning process. Its task is to interpret the input data in terms of the rules in the knowledge base provided. The result of rule invocation is the construction of the network description which is the output of the system.

The actual form of the input will vary according to the recognition task. For typical diagnosis tasks it will be evidential data such as symptoms from the device under test (DUT) or answers to queries from the servicing technician. In a general purpose automated test environment, the input data may be digitized signals acquired automatically over a GPIB interface from the DUT. For synthesis problems, the input data will take the form of design choices and specifications.

The semantics of the rule language should be familiar to expert systems developers and logic programmers. In Platypus, rule language is chosen to be a conventional horn clause logic similar to Prolog. The semantics of the rule language necessarily differ in some respects since the system is embedded within (and corecursive with) Scheme.

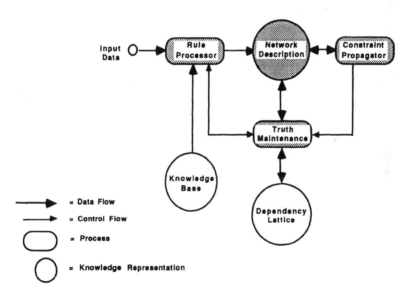

Figure 1: Playtpus Overview

The knowledge base represents models of the entities in the task domain. We are currently experimenting with implementing models using the AMOS portable object system developed by Adams and Rees [1988]. This version of Platypus does not support a specific datatype for models but relies on a traditional rule database. All rules are stored and retrieved associatively by their consequent pattern in a single global rule database.

A major component of the reasoning engine in Platypus is the constraint propagator. Constraint propagation is seen as a mechanism in advanced reasoning systems for avoiding search. In traditional rule-based systems, search creates hypotheses and then attempts to verify these choices as part of a global solution. An alternative view for reasoning is that search creates hypotheses which provide constraints on search process itself. Search and constraint propagation are characterized as mutually supportive processes. They form a positive feedback system. The choice of an hypothesis provides constraints on the search space which helps choose another hypothesis and so on, repeating the feeback cycle.

The description produced as output by Platypus is a constraint network. The network provides a persistent intensional representation for the search space. The network consists of nodes which represent parameters or state variables and a set of k-ary constraints over the possible values for the parameters. This representation is natural. To.the rule processor, the network represents instances of domain objects recognized in the input data. The arcs between instances are the semantic relationships among objects known in the knowledge base. The parameters of the instances represent the possible identities of the instance. To the constraint propagator, the network represents a set of state variables, their variable domains and a set of k-ary relations over those domains. The constraint propagator can be viewed as an independent process which is applied to the network description as it is composed incrementally by the rule processor. The constraint propagator refines the domains of the state variables under the constraints thereby refining the descriptions of the instances in the network.

The constraint propagation algorithm used in Platypus is a variation of hierarchical arc consistency [Mackworth, Mulder & Havens, 1985]. The algorithm provides pairwise consistency for k-ary relations in hierarchically organized variable domains. Other stronger forms of consistency could be applied. See Mackworth [1987] for a review.

The Platypus contains an embedded truth maintenance subsystem called the Constraint Maintenance System (CMS). The CMS currently implemented is based on a simple *justification-based truth maintenance system* as originally developed by Doyle [1979]. A more elaborate *assumption-based* ATMS [deKleer, 1986] could be fitted if necessary. The CMS includes both the TMS and constraint propagator. Their interaction is used to maintain the consistency of the network description composed by the rule processor. A data structure, called the dependency làttice, is maintained as the historical record of the side effects made to the constraint network. The CMS interacts with the rule processor by analysing inconsistencies and failures and then proposing a dependency backtrack point to the rule processor. The dependency lattice allows the backtrack of both the constraint network and the rule processor as necessary.

3. Constraint-Based Reasoning

The traditional expert systems approach relies predominantly on rule matching and invocation to search for a solution to the given problem. Whether the rule engine invokes its rules using forward-chaining or backward-chaining, search is required. Search is always inefficient and the pathological behaviour of backtrack search algorithms is well known [Haralick & Elliott, 1980]. Constraint-based reasoning can ameliorate the search problem by avoiding search whenever possible. As mentioned before, we assume reasoning is a process of making hypotheses, deriving constraints and elaborating their consequences. Specifically, rule invocations are hypotheses about the sought after solution to the input problem. From these hypotheses, the network description can be augmented to contain new nodes and/or new constraints. From these additions to the network, consistency can be propagated and the domain of possible values to consider further reduced or eliminated. This process forms a feedback cycle which can converge efficiently to a solution while avoiding large sections of the problem search space. The advantages of combining constraint propagation and logic programming into *constraint logic programming* [Jaffar & Lassez, 1987] is being actively investigated. VanHentenryck [1989] has recently added constraint handling to Prolog.

To illustrate combined constraint propagation and rule-based systems, we consider the classic *nQueens* problem. Simply stated, the problem is to populate an n-by-n chessboard with n queens, one to each column, such that no two queens can attack each other. None can share a common row or diagonal on the chessboard. The size of the search space for this problem grows exponentially with n and consequently so does the running times of backtrack solutions to the problem. For n = 8, the number of possible board configurations to consider is

$$n^n = 8^8 = 16,777,216.$$

A better methodology is to use constraint-based reasoning to significantly reduce the size of the search space. Consider the series of chessboards given in Figure 2 below[2]. The series progresses (n = 1, 2,..., 8) as more queens are added to the chessboard. The figure legend indicates that as queens are successfully placed, some of the remaining squares on the chessboard are then eliminated from consideration. Clearly, as a queen is place on some square in a particular column, the remaining squares in that same column are eliminated (since only a single queen can reside in any particular column in a correct solution). These eliminated squares are indicated in light gray. Note in a chronological backtrack solution that every square for the remaining columns on the chessboard must remain in the search space. Only by later proposing a queen for one of these squares, can the square be either rejected or confirmed (perhaps only temporarily). This is clearly inefficient. For n = 1, there remains after placing this first queen a total of 2,097,152 positions for the remaining 7 queens.

However, in a constraint-based dependency backtrack solution to the nQueens problem, large subspaces of the search space can be deleted from consideration. The result is a much faster search process. After placing the first queen (n = 1), the constraint-based approach can eliminate not only the other squares in the first column but every other square on the chessboard on a common row or diagonal (indicated by dark crosshatching in Figure 2). By so doing, the size of the remaining search space is reduced to only 257,250 possible positions for the remaining 7 queens. This is an efficiency improvement of more than 8 times. As more queens are added to the chessboard (n = 2, 3, ...), the improvement of constraint-based search over chronological backtracking is even more apparent. Note in Figure 2 that by n = 4, there are very few squares left using constraints while the backtracking solution still has half of the board to consider. At this point, the improvement seen by constraint-based reasoning is over 200 times - a worthwhile improvement that argues well for the integrated rule and constraint-based approach.

The nQueens problem is revisited later in this paper. Two solutions are given coded in Platypus. The first uses rules to implement a chronological backtrack solution; the second implements the constraint-based approach.

---

[2]Von Hentenryck [1989] provides a similar example using nQueens.

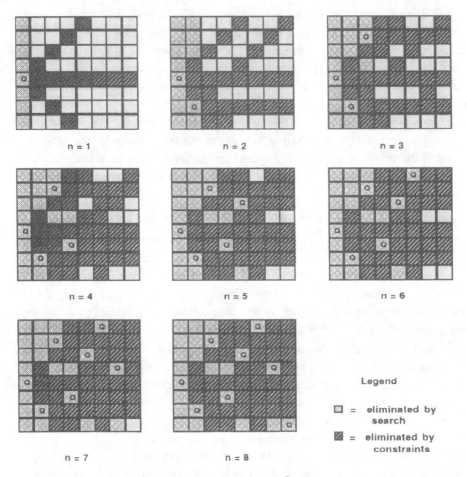

Figure 2: 8-Queens Search Space

4. Platypus Programming

This section presents an overview of the programming language constructs of Platypus. A more detailed programming specification is given in [Havens, 1988].

4.1. Rule Engine

The rule processor is the major addition to the host Scheme language. The approach has been to augment Scheme by the addition of logical variables, rules and dependency backtracking control structures while letting the Scheme compiler and run-time environment remain in control. Indeed, Platypus expressions are all compiled into normal Scheme functions.

The syntax of logical variables in Platypus is "xx" where "x" is a symbol. Logical variables obey the lexical scoping rules of Scheme and references to them can appear freely in both rules and lambda expressions. Note that a Scheme variable "x" and the logical variable

"$x" are distinct entities even though they share the same root identifier. Logical variables have the essential property that their values may be assigned by rule unification and backtracked by the CMS.

Goal expressions are the basic method for retrieving facts and invoking rules in Platypus. A unification pattern matcher is used for matching goal patterns with rule patterns. The form of a goal expression is:

(Goal <pattern> <target>*)

where <pattern> is a list of constants, variables, logical variables and nested patterns. Each <target> is either a candidate rule or a database of rules to be matched. The search of the targets proceeds left-to-right. If no target is specified then the global default database is searched alone for matching rules. On success, the logical variables appearing in the goal pattern are bound to their unifying values and the expression returns true. On backtrack, the search of targets is resumed for subsequent matches. On failure, the goal expression returns false.

Platypus adds two control primitives to Scheme for controlling search. The conjunctive backtrack operator is written:

$$(<=> <E_1> \ldots <E_n>)$$

where <E1> ... <En> are Scheme and Platypus expressions which are evaluated in left-to-right order with dependency backtrack on failure. If all expressions succeed, then <=> returns true. Otherwise, <=> captures the final failure and returns false. The disjunctive version:

(<or> <E1> ... <En>)

is analogous, returning true on the first successful expression but retaining a failpoint for backtracking to try the remaining expressions in its body on failure. If every expresson has failed, then <or> returns false.

These operators are corecursive with Scheme. For example, the top-level program for solving nQueens could be the following Scheme function. It uses the backtrack operator to implement a failure driven search. The goal of placing n queens on a chessboard of size n is represented by the pattern: (Place $n $n $Answer). If the goal can be satisfied by using the PlaceQueens rule, then $Answer contains the solution and is displayed. If the flag oneSolution? is false, then the function backtracks to find the remaining solutions.

```
(define (nQueens $n oneSolution?)
    (let ($Answer)
        (<=> (Goal (Place $n $n $Answer) PlaceQueens)
            (display* "Solution  = " $Answer)
            oneSolution?)))
```

In Platypus, rules are represented in horn clause form, a single consequent at the head of the clause followed by a conjunction of zero or more antecedent predicates as follows:

(Rule <pattern> <foo>* <E>*)

where **<pattern>** represents the consequent term and each predicate, **<E>**, is an antecedent of the rule. Rules are evaluated using back-chaining control only. The antecedents **<E>**, which may be either goal expressions or Scheme predicates. are evaluated left-to-right. A rule succeeds if every antecedent succeeds and fails otherwise. A failure causes both the control state of the rule and its logical variable assignments to be retracted by the CMS. Rules also may have defined internal Scheme functions. Each such definition **<foo>** can freely refer to the pattern variables of the rule since they are lexically contained within the rule environment. Rules are compiled into scheme code for efficiency.

Consider the following implementation of the Platypus **PlaceQueens** rule as part of a solution to the nQueens problem using chronological backtracking:

```
(define PlaceQueens
  (Rule (Place $col $n $Answer)
    (> $col 0)
    (let ($D $row ($mcol (1- $col)))
      (<=> (Goal (Place $mcol $n $Answer)        ;place n-1 queens using...
                 (Rule (Place 0 $n ()))          ;terminating clause
                 PlaceQueens)                     ;otherwise recurse
           (set! $D (MakeIndex $n))              ;make domain of rows
           (Goal (Member $D $row))               ;generate candidate rows
           (set! $pair (cons $col $row))         ;try a board coordinate
           (Satisfies? Peace $pair $Answer)      ;queens at peace?
           (set! $Answer (cons $pair $Answer))))))) ;construct solution
```

In this example, the rule **PlaceQueens** is called on its pattern where **$col** is the column of the current queen being placed; **$n** is the size of the chessboard; and **$Answer** is a list of coordinate pairs (column and row) for the queens already placed successfully. The current queen is consistently placed if its coordinate satisfies the **Peace** predicate with every other pair in **$Answer**. The predicate holds between two distinct queens if their respective coordinates do not share a common row or diagonal.

When called, **PlaceQueens** proceeds by creating new logical variables using a Scheme **let** expression and then using the backtrack operator, **<=>**, to search for a consistent board solution. The rule recursively issues the same subgoal with the pattern **(Place $mcol $n $Answer)** where **$mcol** evaluates to a reduced value for **$col**. Eventually the recursion reaches the unit clause **(Rule (Place 0 $n ()))** coded as a target in the goal expression which bottoms the recursion.

After each successful recursive return, a domain of possible rows for the current queen is constructed and bound to **$D**. Next the **Member** predicate is used to backtrack through the values in **$D**. Each of these values is used in a board coordinate pair and assigned to the variable **$pair**. The Scheme operator **Satisfies?** then applies the predicate **Peace** between $pair and every existing coordinate in **$Answer**. On success, **$pair** is added to this list thus representing one more queen being placed on the chessboard. The rule recursion then ascends another level. Otherwise, **Satisfies?** returns false and failure is signaled to the CMS for backtracking.

This example illustrates the convenience of interspersing Platypus and Scheme expressions. Normal variable assignment can be used with both logical and regular variables. Rule invocation and backtracking operate within the Scheme environment without restriction.

4.2 Knowledge Base

Pattern databases provide a convenient associative storage and retrieval mechanism for rules and facts. Hewitt [1972] introduced the idea of indexing rules in the database by their consequent pattern. In a backward deduction system, this association provides a simple *call-by-need* rule invocation scheme.

Platypus supports both a default global database and the ability to create local rule databases as Scheme objects which can be associated with models and their instances. The function: (**Database** [<size>]) returns a new empty database. The number of hash buckets in the new database is given by <size> which defaults to a reasonable value. The form (**Assert** <rule> [<db>]) adds a new <rule> to the specified database <db> under the consequent pattern of the rule. If no database is specified then the default global database is used. Like its Prolog counterpart, this operator is not backtrackable. If a rule or Scheme procedure containing an **Assert** expression is backtracked, the changes to the database will remain unaffected. The reasoning is as follows: The current state of the inference process is to be represented in the transient state of rule invocations and preferably the structural state of the constraint network. Both of these are backtrackable.

The operator (**Retract** <pattern> [<db>]) is backtrackable, however. **Retract** removes the first rule in <db> which unifies with <pattern> and saves a failpoint for finding and removing additonal rules on failure.

Given these definitions, an example of the non-deterministic invocation of rules from databases can be shown. In the previous **nQueens** example, the predicate **Member** was called to generate successively all the possible rows for a particular queen to occupy. A definition of this predicate coded as two rules in the default pattern database is:

```
(Assert (Rule (Member ($a . $rest) $a)))
(Assert (Rule (Member ($a . $rest) $b)
            (Goal (Member $rest $b)))))
```

4.3 Constraint Propagation

Constraint propagation techniques require some persistent representation for the search space. Typically, the representation is a state variable network. Nodes in the network represent possible states for some parameter of interest in the search problem. Associated with each node must be an explicit representation for the domain of the parameter which supports explicit manipulation of the set of values in the domain. Candidate representations are discrete sets and real intervals [Davis, 1987]. Hierarchical labelsets can efficiently represent even infinite domains if they can be organized as taxonomies and their subdomains manipulated symbolically [Mackworth, Mulder & Havens, 1985].

The constraint network is constructed incrementally by the rule engine. The constraint propagator is responsible for keeping the growing (or shrinking) network consistent. If the network becomes unsatisfiable (inconsistent) for some particular configuration, then the CMS subsystem is responsible for backtracking the rule engine to remove the inconsistency. The approach is to retract as little of the composed network description of the input data as possible and then proceed forward again.

The constraint network primitives defined in Platypus are the following. The function **(newNode <d>)** adds a new node to the constraint network with domain **<d>** and records the side effect in the CMS. There are no constraints applied to the new node and hence it will not enter into the constraint propagation process. Support for the new node in the CMS is the process in which the form appears. If the process is backtracked, the variable and all its side effects will be removed from the network. Conversely **(deleteNode <x>)** removes node **<x>** from the network then the CMS undoes all side effects dependent on **<x>**.

Constraints are implemented as set functions of relations over the domains of the nodes in the network. Every mathematical relation has a corresponding set function for each of its argument positions. Let R be a k-ary relation over domains $D_1,..., D_k$, then the jth set function of R is: $F_j(R) = \{ a_j \mid (a_1 ,..., a_j ,..., a_k) \in R, a_1 \in D_1,..., a_j \in D_j , ,..., a_k \in D_k \}$

Graphically, the constraints are directed arcs. Each constraint has k argument nodes and a distinguished member of the arguments called the target node. The set function is applied to the argument domains yielding a new domain for the target. In Platypus, we define a compiler for set functions which produces a Scheme function that can be applied to the domains of nodes X1 ,..., Xj ,..., Xk yielding a new domain for Xj. The expression **(SetFunction <j> <R> <k>)** constructs the **<j>**th set function of a relation **<R>** of cardinality **<k>**. Relations are just ordinary Scheme predicates.

Given the following definition of **Peace** as a Scheme predicate, we can construct two distinct set functions from it (one for each of its two argument positions):

```
(define Peace
    (lambda (Bi Bj)
        (nor    (eqv? (Qrow Bi)(Qrow Bj))
                (eqv?   (- (Qrow Bj)(Qrow Bi))
                        (- (Qcol Bi)(Qcol Bj)))
                (eqv?   (- (Qrow Bi)(Qrow Bj))
                        (- (Qcol Bi)(Qcol Bj))))))


(define F1-Peace (SetFunction 1 Peace 2))


(define F2-Peace (SetFunction 2 Peace 2))
```

Constraints are made from a specified set function **<SetFn>**, a target **<targetNode>** and a set of arguments **<argNode>*** using the operator:

(addConstraint <targetNode> <SetFn> (<argNode>*))

When a new constraint is added to the network, the constraint propagator immediately enforces the constraint on the state of the network and all its consequences are recorded by the CMS. In contrast, the expression **(deleteConstraint <x>)** removes the constraint **<x>** from the network which causes the CMS to undo all side effects dependent on **<x>**.

Given these operations, we can construct the complete constraint graph for the nQueens problem. Below is a Scheme procedure called **makeNetwork** which builds a network of size n nodes. To make the network for 8 queens, we evaluate **(makeNetwork 8 8 nil)**. The constructed network is shown in Figure 3.

```
(define (makeNetwork i domainSize nodes)
  (if (zero? i)
    nodes
    (let ((M (newNode (makeBoardDomain i domainSize))))
      (for-each
        (lambda (N) (newConstraint M F1-Peace (list M N))
                    (newConstraint N F2-Peace (list M N)))
        nodes)
      (makeNetwork (1- i) domainSize (cons M nodes))))))
```

Constraints are propagated using a form of k-ary arc consistency [Mackworth, 1987]. The function **(Propagate <c>)** propagates consistency beginning with constraint **<c>**. Let X be the target node of **<c>**. The consistency of the domain of X is tested against the domains of the argument nodes of **<c>** using the specified set function. The domain of X is updated accordingly. If it is empty then failure is signaled to the CMS. If there is no change to the domain then propagation halts. Otherwise, consistency is propagated to every other constraint for which X is an argument node. Each change to the binding of a network node by **Propagate** is recorded by the CMS as a new event. On failure, the side effects caused by constraint propagation can be backtracked by the CMS. A companion function is **(Consistent? <x>)** which checks the consistency of node **<x>** under every constraint whose target is **<x>**. It calls **Propagate** on each such constraint. If **<x>** is consistent already or can be made consistent then true is returned. Otherwise, false is returned.

Combining search with constraint propagation can yield a much faster solution to problems which can be expressed as constraint satisfactions problems. See Von Hentenryck [1989] for some impressive comparisons. For example, a constraint propagation approach to the nQueens problem can avoid a large portion of the search space considered by the simple chronological backtracking approach already presented. Here is such an improved constraint-based solution:

116

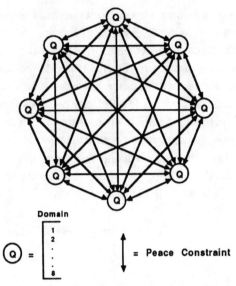

Figure 3: The Constraint Network for 8-Queens

```
(define (ConstraintNQueens $n oneSolution?)
  (let (($Queens (makeNetwork $n $n ())))
    (<=> (Goal (PlaceRest $Queens)
               ConstraintPlaceQueens)
         (display* "Solution = " $Queens)
         oneSolution?))))

(define ConstraintPlaceQueens
  (Rule (PlaceRest $Queens)
    (not (null? $Queens))
    (let* ($pair
           ($Qi (1st $Queens))
           ($QRest (rest $Queens))
           ($Di (domain $Qi)))
      (<=> (Goal (member $Di $pair))
           (newConstraint
             $Qi
             (SetFunction 1 (make-fixrow $pair) 1)
             (list $Qi))
           (Goal (PlaceRest $QRest)
                 (Rule (PlaceRest ()))
                 Self)))))
```

```
(define (make-fixrow pair)
  (lambda (x) (equal? x pair)))
```

Initially the complete constraint graph is constructed by the function **makeNetwork** (as described above). Next the algorithm evaluates the expression:

(Goal (PlaceRest $Queens) ConstraintPlaceQueens)

which recursively attempts to place each queen in the network. Note that backtracking will necessitate reversing some of the side effects made to the network by constraint propagation.

The algorithm used by the rule **PlaceRest** differs from the previous **PlaceQueens** rule because it propagates consistency throughout the network whenever a new hypothesis is made. In this problem, new hypotheses correspond to assigning a particular row as the singleton domain for a queen. This assignment is achieved by adding a new constraint to the current queen $Qi forcing its domain to be a singleton square $pair as generated by the **Member** predicate. This square is used to curry a new predicate by **make-fixrow** which forces the queen to that square. The new predicate is then used by **SetFunction** to construct a new set function which is applied by **newConstraint** as a new unary constraint to its target node $Qi and its single argument node, also $Qi. Consistency is automatically applied with the addition of the new constraint thereby reducing the domain of $Qi and by propagation some of the other queens in the network. Finally, the rule attempts the goal **(PlaceRest $QRest)** on the rest of the queens $QRest by first matching the unit clause **(Rule (PlaceRest ()))** and otherwise itself **Self**. The unit clause will only match when $QRest = () thereby successfully terminating the recursion. Otherwise, during the search some constraint will have caused the domain for some queen to become empty. This eventuality automatically signals failure to the CMS which proceeds to backtrack the search process to the last failpoint. For this simple example, these failpoints will be the calls to the **Member** predicate used to generate candidate squares.

4.4 Constraint Maintenance

The CMS constructs the dependency lattice to record all rule invocations and all changes to the constraint network. Each such change is called an *event*. The ordering relation in the lattice is support between events. One event supports another if the change recorded as the first event was used to compute the second event. A partial list of event types include:

•*UserEvent* - user has evaluated a Platypus expression causing some effect on the network.
•*RuleChoice*- the rule processor has chosen a particular rule among multiple possible choices in the knowledge base.
•*Propagate*- the constraint propagator has reduced a logic variable domain or assigned a hypothetical value to some variable.

The CMS implements simple dependency backtracking on failure. The dependency lattice provides sufficient history of the rule processor's activity to backtrack the consequences of any derivation (including all propagated constraints). Failure is signaled two ways; by the constraint propagator if the network becomes inconsistent or by the user evaluating the primitive **(Fail)**. In either case the CMS begins a straightforward analysis of the failure based on a priority of event types. The CMS must chose a most likely candidate RuleChoice or UserEvent and mark it as the culprit.[3] The choice is necessarily heuristic and Platypus uses the following simple strategy: UserEvents are considered more inviolate than RuleChoices since they require interaction with the user to select an alternative choice. Most recent RuleChoices are preferred over earlier choices since they typically will involve fewer dependencies. More sophisticated strategies are needed. Once the culprit is identified, the CMS undoes the constraint network to its previous state and restarts the rule processor from that point.

5. Conclusion

An overview of an architecture for constraint-based reasoning was introduced. The architecture was justified by considering some of the structural aspects of recognition tasks as applied to expert systems. From this development, a few programming aspects of a new expert system shell called Platypus were introduced. The famous nQueens problem was used for illustration throughout.

References

[Adams&Rees, 1988]

N. Adams & J. Rees, *Object-Oriented Programming in Scheme*, Proc. 1988 ACM Conf. on Lisp and Functional Programming, Snowbird, Utah, July 1988, pp.277-288.

[Davis, 1987]

E. Davis, *Constraint Propagation with Interval Labels*, Artificial Intelligence 32, 1987, pp.281-331.

[deKleer, 1986]

J. deKleer, *An Assumption-based TMS*, Artificial Intelligence 28, 2, 1986, pp.127-162.

[Doyle, 1979]

J. Doyle, *A Truth Maintenance System*, Artificial Intelligence 12, 1979, pp.231-272.

[Gevarter, 1987]

W. B. Gevarter, *The Nature and Evaluation of Commercial Expert Systems Building Tools*, IEEE Computer 20, 5, pp.24-41, May 1987.

[Haralick&Elliott, 1980]

R. M. Haralick & G. L. Elliott, *Increasing Tree Search Efficiency for Constraint Satisfaction Problems*, Artificial Intelligence 14, 1980, p.263-313.

[Havens, 1985]

W. Havens, *A Theory of Schema Labelling,* Computational Intelligence 1, 4, National Research Council of Canada, Ottawa, 1985.

[Havens, 1988]

W.S. Havens, *Platypus Programming Description*, Technical Report 88-12, Computer Research Lab, Tektronix Laboratories, Beaverton, Oregon, USA, 1988.

---

[3]Propagate events are not candidates since they are direct consequences of other events and offer no alternatives.

[Havens&Rehfuss, 1989]

W.S. Havens & P.S. Rehfuss, *Platypus: a Constraint-Based Reasoning System*, Proc. 1989 Int. Joint Conf. on Artificial Intelligence, Detroit, Mich., August, 1989.

[Hewitt, 1972]

C. Hewitt, *Description and Theoretical Analysis (using Schemata) of PLANNER: a Language for Proving Theorems and Manipulating Models in a Robot*, Ph.D. thesis, AI-TR-258, MIT AI Lab, Cambridge, Mass., 1972.

[Jaffar&Lassez, 1987]

J. Jaffar & J-L. Lassez, *Constraint Logic Programming*, in POPL-87, Munich, January 1987.

[Macworth, Mulder&Havens, 1985]

A. Mackworth, J. Mulder & W. Havens, *Hierarchical Arc Consistency: Exploiting Structured Domains in Constraint Satisfaction Problems*, Computational Intelligence 1, 4, National Research Council of Canada, Ottawa, 1985.

[Mackworth, 1987]

A. Mackworth, *Constraint Satisfaction*, in S. C. Shapiro (ed.) Encyclopedia of Artificial Intelligence, vol.1, Wiley, 1987, p.205.

[Rees *et.al.*, 1986]

J. A. Rees *et. al.*, *Revised Report on the Algorithmic Language Scheme*, SIGPLAN Notices 21, 12, 1986.

[Van Hentenryck, 1989]

P. Van Hentenryck, *Constraint Satisfaction in Logic Programming,* MIT Press, Cambridge, Mass., 1989.

Modelling Exceptions in Semantic Database and Knowledge-based Systems

P.L. Tan   T.S. Dillon   J. Zeleznikow

La Trobe University
Bundoora, Victoria 3083, Australia
tanp@latcs1.oz   tharam@latcs1.oz   johnz@latcs1.oz

Abstract

Exception handling has received much attention in several areas recently. In this paper, we accomodate exceptions in a semantic network model using an object-oriented approach. First, the semantic model is adequately described to allow the introduction of exceptions. Then the categories of exceptions in the model are examined. An Object-Property diagram is introduced to model the exceptions. This paper attempts to provide an alternative and better approach in handling exceptions for semantic network models. Specifically, we describe previous work done on exception handling on semantic models and introduce our proposed approach. We show how our model addresses the limitations of the previous approach as well as providing more leverage to the system.

1. Introduction

Database and Knowledge bases are generally stored in two levels: Schema or meta-level knowledge describes the constraints and invariant information of knowledge base. The facts level (facts base or database) describes the instances or data conforming to the constraints specified in the schema level.

In this irregular and changing world, the knowledge which attempts to model a portion of the world constantly changes. New information which does not conform to the constraint in the schema level is omitted from the fact base. The schema may be too restricted for the variability of information. As a consequence of the prevalence of such events, it is trivial that most systems require the facts base to be updated or augmented as the environment changes. However, this updating step is normally performed by the database administrator (or knowledge base engineer) at the time of creation of the facts base without provision for dynamic accomodation for exceptions at runtime. Without an adequate mechanism to represent exceptions in the knowledge base, the system is denied any ability to learn when exceptions are encountered. Not being able to cope with this situation results in incorrect representation of the modelled world, thus defeating the primary purpose of having schema or meta-knowledge.

Knowledge is stored in various forms: rule-based, semantic networks, frames and logic. Similarly, data can be stored in records (in Classical data models), or entities in semantic networks (Semantic data models). In this paper, we concentrate on data or knowledge stored in semantic network, focussing, on accomodating exceptions at run time.

The pioneering work on exceptions in databases was presented in [Borgida and Williamson, 1985] and [Borgida et al, 1986]. Here, we extend their work using an object-oriented approach. This approach stems primarily from the implementation of a semantic model in an object-oriented environment. A uniform framework is provided to facilitate the storage and manipulation of exceptions.

The paper is organised as follows. In the next section, we provide an insight on previous work done about exceptions and the limitations which are the motivation of this work. Section 3 presents a semantic network model and its associated concepts. Types of exceptions encountered in the semantic model are listed in Section 4. In section 5, an Object-Property diagram is introduced to incorporate the exceptions in the design stage. Following that, we give a brief description on the implementation with emphasis on the representation of the exceptions in section 6. Section 7 compares our proposal with the previous approach with respect to the problems addressed earlier. Finally, section 8 presents our conclusion.

2. Previous Work on exceptions

The problem of exceptions is recognised in knowledge-based systems. [Borgida and Williamson, 1985] and [Borgida et al, 1986] presented an approach to accomodate exceptions in a semantic data model (which is a variant of semantic network). We briefly discuss the approach used in [Borgida and Williamson, 1985] in order to facilitate a comparison with our approach.

2.1 An approach in semantic models

In knowledge base management systems, there is a set of operators to store and retrieve knowledge. When an exception is encountered, [Borgida and Williamson, 1985] provides another set of operators to handle the exception facts. Whenever a violation of constraints in an update operation is signalled, an object in a class VIOLATION is created to store the violated information. If the signal uncovers an error, the user will rectify the mistake. However, if it represents a real fact, the exception operator is used to store the object as an exceptional object. This exceptional object is an instance of class EXCEPTIONAL which has the following definition:

```
EXCEPTIONAL with
      [prop:  PropertyIdentifier]
      [obj:  AnyObject]
      [class:  ClassIdentifier]
      [withRespectTo:  AssertionIdentifier]
```

Figure 1: Definition of properties pertaining to an exception

Using the same example in [Borgida and Williamson, 1985], an employee John with degree
'Bac' violated the range for degree: [BS, MS Phd] is stored as an instance of EXCEPTIONAL
class.

```
EXCEPTIONAL with
      [prop = degree]
      [obj = John]
      [class = EMPLOYEE]
      [withRespectTo: (EMPLOYEE, degree)]
```

To retrieve an exception object, the query

```
EXCEPTIONAL <e1> ^ x.prop ^ x.class=EMPLOYEE
```

displays all employees with exceptional degree.

2.2 Limitations

Given this approach of handling exceptions, we make the following observations and note some
limitations (marked by *):

1. The user uses the normal operators (getValue, modify, createObject) to retrieve and
   manipulate only non-exceptional data. Another set of operators (exnal_getValue,
   exnal_modify, exnal_createObject) are provided for exceptional data.

* The formulation of the query is fairly limited. Because of separate operators for exceptions,
  the exception objects can only be retrieved separately. Therefore, if the user wants to retrieve
  all employees, the exception object may not be included unless a separate query is formed
  for exception EMPLOYEES.

* The user needs to know the properties of exceptions. In the query above, it is assumed that
  the user knows that class EMPLOYEE has exceptions and the violated property is degree.

2. The exception objects are stored as instances of class EXCEPTIONAL by exnal operators.
   In addition to storing the exception object as an instance of the common class
   EXCEPTIONAL, it is not clear in the approach [Borgida and Williamson, 1985] that the
   exnal operators store the object as instances of its own class (EMPLOYEE). Either appraoch
   has its limitations :

* If the exception object is stored as instance of EMPLOYEE as well as instance of

EXCEPTIONAL, this will result in two instances referring to the same object. The first problem that arises is redundancy (waste of storage). Secondly, additional mechanisms are required to prevent inconsistency during the update of the exception object.

* On the other hand, if the exception object is not stored as an instance of its class, the semantics are incomplete. The fact that it is an exceptional instance justifies the instance of EXCEPTIONAL, but it does not justify the omission of being an instance of its own class.

* There is no further information as to why and how the object is treated as an exception. As data is stored to be accessed at a later time, objects which are treated as exceptions at a time for a special reason may not be understood fully in the future, by the same user, let alone by other users. Some information related to the exception object should be kept. For instance, the employee's degree ('Bac') is treated as exception object:

     (how ?) : by violating the property range
     (why ?) : because it is a French degree

* There is no mention of instances which violate more than one property. For example, an object violates the following two properties, degree and salary range. One of two possible approaches can be adopted:

1) Additional instances of class EXCEPTIONAL are created for each violation of property. This is an apparent waste of storage and may lead to problems of inconsistency.

2) Alternatively, the 'prop' slot in Figure 2 can be extended to represent more than one property of an instance of EXCEPTIONAL.

* This approach does not cater for the situation where the exceptional instances have the additional property which is not specified in the schema.

* In our opinion, storing exception objects as instances of a separate class EXCEPTIONAL is not a natural representation. When one thinks of exceptions, we normally associate them with a violated entity. In the above example, the exception of a degree is associated with an Employee. As the purpose of database and knowledge bases is to model the world as closely as possible, we believe it is natural to store exceptions by associating them with their own class.

These limitations have motivated us to use an object-oriented approach in handling exceptions in semantic networks. We attempt to solve these limitations and provide additional leverage to the system using this approach. In the next section, a uniform framework is provided to manipulate the non-exceptional data.

3. Knowledge in Semantic models

Knowledge appears in two variants: *Stereotyped knowledge is* knowledge of only a few types and a very large number of instances for each type. This is similar to a database. *Non-stereotyped knowledge* is where a knowledge base consists of many types and a few instances per type. Stereotyped knowledge is normally represented by frames and non-stereotyped knowledge is normally represented by semantic networks. On the other hand, database models which represent stereotyped knowledge use semantic networks (called Semantic data models). In this section, a semantic model that models the knowledge and database is sufficiently presented to permit us to introduce exceptions in such an approach as detailed in section 4.

3.1 The Semantic Model

In this semantic model, the knowledge base consists of a hierarchical collection of *objects* and *classes*. An *object* is an instance of a class, and has zero or more properties. The properties of an object are *attributes* which describe the property of itself and *relationships* which relate to other objects. One example is John who is a Manager (class) has salary (attribute) of $30,000 and manages (relationship) project DV which is an instance of class Project. Diagramatically, it is shown below:

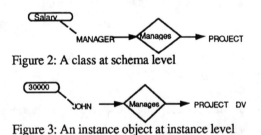

Figure 2: A class at schema level

Figure 3: An instance object at instance level

Object and Class

The unit of encapsulation provided by object-oriented programming is a class, which represents a meaningful collection of objects. Objects which have similar properties are grouped into a class. Classes are distinguished into two types:

* A *primitive class* is simple data type such as INTEGER, BOOLEAN or STRING. The instances of such type do not have any properties, for example, 2, True and "Mary" respectively. This class forms the domain of attributes and has the instances as the values.

* An *abstract class*, on the other hand consists of non-atomic objects represented in terms of property values. For example, EMPLOYEE and MANAGER with properties of name, salary and address. These properties have values of objects belonging to a primitive class or an abstract class.

As in many hierarchical knowledge-based systems, a subclass inherits the properties from its superclass. For example, Manager is a subclass of superclass EMPLOYEE and it inherits the attributes and relationships of EMPLOYEE.

Attribute

Attribute is a property that gives value(s) which is (are) instance(s) of primitive class(es). A distinction is made between instance attribute (IA) and class attribute (CA). IA decribes a property of each instance of a class. Name and address of EMPLOYEE are examples of IA which gives values "Tom" and "5 High St., Preston". A CA, on the other hand, is a property of a class on the whole. For instance, average salary is a CA of class EMPLOYEE which gives the value of $30000.

Relationship

Objects are related to other objects via relationships. Unlike an attribute which gives a value (or multi-value) of primitive object, a relationship returns a related object or a set of related objects from abstract classes. Object-relationship mappings are 1-1, 1-M, M-1 and M-N. This means an object can have the same relationship with more than one object of any class.

Operation

An operation or function can be defined for a particular class. This operation may be applied to the attributes of the class. For example, IncreaseSalary operation is associated with class EMPLOYEE to increase the salary by a ratio. Like properties, operations are localised to their applicable classes, and can be inherited or refined at the subclass levels.

4. Incorporation of exceptions

In this section, exceptions are incorporated into the semantic networks, The basic exception ideas are mentioned in [Borgida and Williamson, 1985] and [Borgida, 1988] by way of examples. We extend these exceptions and group them into several categories.

Exceptions may occur at two levels: *instance* and *schema* level.
At the instance level, an object violates the constraint specified in the schema for its class. This particular case is an *exceptional object*. At the schema level, a class may violate some of the properties it inherits from its superclass [Borgida, 1988]. This class is called *exceptional class*. In this model, there are three types of exceptions. The exceptions are incorporated at both instance and schema level as explained below:

4.1 Attribute Exceptions

At instance level, an exceptional object violates the attribute constraint specified at its class. Violated constraints could be of the following types:

a) *Irrelevant attribute:* The exceptional object does not have the attribute of its class. For example, Employee Mary does not have a salary attribute because she is a volunteer. This should be treated as exceptional object by deleting that attribute rather than storing it as a null value.

b) *Violated range:* The value of exceptional the object is not in the range of the attribute. The first example, of John having a French degree 'Bac', is not in the range of [BS, MS, Phd], is of this exception type.

c) *Violated type:* The value of the exceptional object is not the type specified in the schema. Instead of salary in dollars, the salary of an employee in Italy could be in Lira.

d) *New Attribute:* An exception instance may have extra information to be stored, however, the information does not fit any attribute specified in its class. In this case, a new attribute is created for this exceptional object.

At the schema level, exceptions that may occur including inherited attributes from the superclass chain, may be irrelevant to the exceptional class, or the range of the inherited attribute is too narrow, or too broad, or there is an extra attribute that is relevant but is unspecified. Although the refinement at exceptional class may solve the last two problems, it does not reject the inherited attribute which is irrelevant.

4.2 Relationship exceptions

Exceptions on relationships may occur in two ways: Inherited but irrelevant relationships, and inherited Relationships but with different related classes.

At instance level, an exceptional object may not have the relationship specified for instances of the class. Even if the relationship is relevant, it may not be linked to the related object of a specified class. For example, instead of having Project XG managed by a manager, it may be managed by an outside contractor. Furthermore, this instance may have an additional relationship which is not specified in its class.

At schema level, an exceptional class may reject an inherited relationship. Alternatively, it may inherit the relationship but with a different related class. The latter is solved by rejecting the inherited relationship and refining the same relationship with a different related class, at the class level.

We like to point out that, unlike attributes which override the inherited attribute from superclass, refinement of a relationship of subclass level refines or augments the inherited relationship. In addition, the exceptional class may inherit relationships as well as extend the set of related classes via the relationship. For instance, BUILDING-PROJECT is managed by MANAGER as well as CONTRACTORS. This is solved using refinement at BUILDING- PROJECT level

4.3 Operation exceptions

An operation is applied to its local class or inherited from the superclass. However, it may not be applied to certain instances of the class. In the earlier example, increaseSalary operation is applied to all instances of EMPLOYEE, except those who have salary over $80,000 p.a. Like the attributes and relationships, an inherited operation may be refined at the level of subclasses .

5. Object-Property Diagram

An Object-Property diagram is introduced to model the objects, attributes and relationships at schema level. Exceptions at the instance level cannot be modelled since instances are not determined before run-time. Classes are represented by circles, relationships by diamonds and attributes by the oval shape. The is-a hierarchy is a link using a solid bar. The diagram is influenced by the ER model [Chen, 1979], except for some modifications to model the exceptional classes. Classes which are linked by a relationship are located along the axis with respect to the relationship. One skeleton diagram is as shown in figure 4.

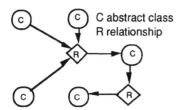

Figure 4: A skeleton Object-Property diagram

An *exceptional class* with a relationship exception is represented as a circle with a pointing octagon within the circle. The direction of the colored angle of the octagon indicates the rejected relationship with respect to the class. The number n in square bracket indicates the rejected relationship was defined at upper nth level from the level of the exceptional class. Thus, figure 5 represents that exceptional class rejecting the east relationships which are defined at first level and second level above its level.

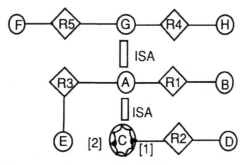

Figure 5: An skeleton Object-Property diagram with an exceptional class

128

A further example is shown in figure 5. The relationships to be inherited by class C are R1, R3, R4 and R5, but class C is an exceptional class. It rejects R1 (first level at east direction) and R5 (second level at west direction).Thus, R3, R4 (inherited) and R2 (defined) are the relationships applicable in class C.

Attribute exceptions are modelled by double circles, the attribute with a slash link at the exception class level is shown in figure 6, where attribute 2 inherited from class A is inapplicable for class B.

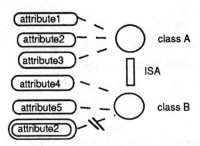

Figure 6: Illustration of an attribute exception

An example of incorporation of exceptions in the object-property diagram is shown in figure 9.

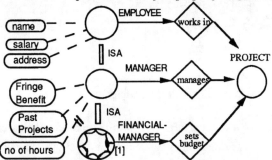

Figure 7: An example of Object-Property diagram

This diagram shows that MANAGERs do not have the attribute noOfHours, and FINANCIAL-MANAGERs do not manage PROJECT, instead they set-budget for PROJECTs.

6. Exception Handling Mechanism

A knowledge-based system based on the specified model is built on object-oriented environment using Smalltalk [Digitalk, 1986]. Thus methods for schema definition such as addition or deletion of a class are provided. This task is done by data administrators. We have built a system that is used by the end-user on top of this environment.

In Smalltalk, there are two types of variables attached to a class. An *instance variable* belongs to an instance. It has a value for each instance and can be accessed by the instance. A *class variable* belongs to a class. It has a value for the class and can be accessed by all instances of the class. In this system, the *attributes* of a class are implemented as *instance variables* local to the class. All instances of the class have a value associated with the attributes. The constraints however are stored in a ConstraintDictionary, as a class variable. All instances access the ConstraintDictionary for constraints associated with the attributes. The relationships associated with the class are specified in RelationDictionary as a class variable. Each instance accesses the RelationDictionary to determine the class to which is related. The instances have their instance variable structure to store the related objects via different relationships.

The object manipulation provided includes addition, deletion and modification of objects subject to the schema constraints. Whenever an instance of a class is added, all the properties associated with the class are displayed to allow the user to enter values of the instance. This ensures that the user enters all the required properties. Constraints applicable to the attributes are displayed to help the user in inputting the correct formatted data. An error is signalled if the data is in incorrect format. The user will be required to rectify the mistake or be forced to save it by selecting a *Save-Exception* option. This triggers the exception handler which will ask for the reason as to why the particular instance should be treated as an exception.

Exceptions are implemented at instance level and schema level. This means that an exceptional instance has an instance variable **exception** to store the constraints violated and exceptional class has a class variable (**ExceptionDictionary**) to store the exception imposed onto the class. Each time an exceptional class is accessed, a mechanism will access the **ExceptionDictionary**, if there is any, to overide the normal properties. The instance variable **exception** represents all exceptions associated with the instance. The structures of both **exception** and **ExceptionDictionary** are shown in figure 8.

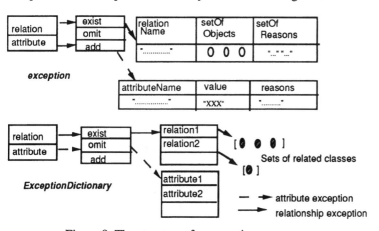

Figure 8: The structures for exceptions

When the exception handler is triggered to save an instance **exception**, it will first display the violated constraint of the property for confirmation. If it is confirmed, it will access and augment the **exception** structure, if any, with the violated constraint. If there is no exception associated with this instance before, the *exception* structure will be created.

With the structure, the violated constraints (delete/omit/modify) associated with the property (attribute/relationship) are stored locally to the instance. The relation name and all the related objects together with respective reasons are stored. Automatically, the related objects will have their *exception* structures to store this relation name and the associated information too. Note that the attribute exception does not have the set of related objects, but take the value of the attribute.

The construction above is explained for exceptional objects at instance level. The *ExceptionDictionary* structure can be used for class exceptions at schema level as shown in Figure 8. Note that at instance level, the set of related objects slot of relationship exceptions consists of the *set of instances* of various classes. At the schema level, this set consists *the set of related class names*. Furthermore, for attribute exceptions at schema level, there are slots for values of attributes. Also we wish to point out that the addition exception on attributes and relationships at schema level can be omitted, since they can be specified by refinements of the class. Despite this, the *addition* option is provided for the situation where the user would like to mark it as an exception class, because refinement is normally applied for normal classes.

Queries can be formed to retrieve exceptions. A menu is provided to retrieve the attribute, and relationships including the exceptions. The reasons and the constraints violated are displayed with each exception retrieved by the structure.

Efficiency is not our main concern at this stage. Retrieving and manipulatiing exceptions takes some overhead, since pointers are used to access the exception structure. Despite this overhead, the ability to localise the properties and exceptions is useful in providing expressiveness and understanding the adopted model.

7. Comparisons with other work

This semantic model represents an extension of ideas drawn from a number of semantic models (O2, Cactis, EXODUS). The concepts of object, attribute and relationship are common in these models. However, our model goes beyond these implemented systems. Most systems distinguish attributes and relationships at the design stage, but not in the implementation. Both concepts are mixed in that relationships are normally implemented as attributes. This has a main disadvantage in that the mechanism has to read the value of attribute before deciding if it is primitive or abstract object. In our model, when an attribute is read, the definite value is a primitive object; likewise, when a relationship is read, the definite value is an abstract object. Besides providing an advance knowledge of the value, this framework provides a better perception of data for the user. In retrieving the relationship, the user knows that there are knows that retrieving an attribute will return a value.

In addition, we like to compare our exception handling mechanism with the approach used by Borgida for semantic models. The limitations of the Borgida approach were outlined in section 2. The structure discussed in section 5 solves these limitations. To reiterate,

* This framework allows every exception object to be treated in the same manner as any other object.

* A menu-interface is provided to list the relevant attributes and relationships, including the operations for retrieval and manipulation of exceptions.

* The exception structure is localised to the object or class at instance or schema respectively. This solves the problems raised in section 2.

* It provides additional information as to why and how the object is treated as an exception. The additional information is stored in the exception structures.

* The exception structures allow the violation of more than one property.

* The object-oriented approach provides a more natural way of representing the data. It is also useful for extending types of exceptions without affecting other exceptional objects.

* An object-property diagram is used to model exceptions.

* Although the exception on operation is not discussed much, we allow exception conditions to be imposed on operations.

The assumption here is that the schema is properly designed and the exceptions are not due to erroneous schema design. If the exceptions encountered have common properties, we leave the responsibility to the knowledge base engineer to modify the schema.

8. Conclusion

In this paper, we have presented a semantic model suitable for databases and knowledge bases. Only the concepts of the model which are relevant to exceptions are discussed. Previous work done on exceptions in semantic networks is reviewed and further extended. The exceptions are grouped into a few categories for better understanding. An object-property diagram is used to model the exceptions. A prototype system has been developed based on this models with the view of providing a more complete set of operations for exception handling. Whilst there are differences between databases and knowledge bases, the proposed approach can be employed to accomodate the exceptions of the respective applications.

References

[Borgida, 1984]
Borgida,A., Generalization/Specialization as a Basis for Software Specification, On Conceptual Modelling, ed. Mylopoulos,J., Brodie,M. and Schmidt,J., Springer-Verlag, Virginia, pp. 87-114, 1984.

[Borgida and Williamson, 1985]
Borgida,A. and Williamson,K., Accomodating Exceptions in Database and Refining the Schema by learning from them, Proceedings of 11th Int'l Conference on Very Large Data Bases, Stockholm, pp. 72-81, 1985.

[Borgida et al, 1986]
Borgida,A, Mitchell,T and Williamson,K, Learning Integrity Constraint in Databases and Knowledge Bases, On Knowledge Base Management Systems, ed. Brodie,M. and Mylopoulos,J, Springer-Verlag, Virginia, pp.259-286, 1986.

[Borgida, 1988]
Borgida,A., Modelling Class Hierarchies with Contradictions, Proceedings of SIGMOD Conference, Chicago, pp. 434-443, 1988.

[Carey et al, 1988]
Carey,M., DeWitt,D. and Vandenberg,S., *A Data Model and Query Language for EXODUS*, Proceedings of SIGMOD Conference, Chicago, pp. 413-423, 1988.

[Chen, 1976]
Chen,P.P., The Entity-Relationship model:Toward a unified view of data, ACM Transactions on Database System, March, pp. 9-37, 1976.

[Digitalk, 1986]
Digitalk Inc Corporation, Smalltalk/V Tutorial and Programming Handbook, 1986.

[Hudson and King, 1987]
Hudson,S. and King,R., Object-oriented Data Support for Software Environment, Proceedings of SIGMOD Conference, Chicago, pp. 491-503, 1988.

[Lecluse et al, 1988]
Lecluse,C., Richard,P. and Valez,P., O2, An Object-oriented Data Model, Proceedings of SIGMOD Conference, Chicago, pp. 424-433, 1988.

Intelligent Tutoring Systems

Mental Models of Recursion and Their Use in the SCENT Programming Advisor

SH Bhuiyan   JE Greer   GI McCalla

ARIES Laboratory
Department of Computational Science
University of Saskatchewan
Saskatoon, SK S7N 0W0, Canada
aries@skorpio.usask.ca

Abstract

Mental modeling techniques are used to describe human understanding of the world, and to derive cognitive explanations of problem-solving behaviour. This paper identifies mental models of recursion through an investigation conducted among novice programmers. The necessity of using these mental models in diagnosis, pedagogy, and student modeling in an intelligent tutoring system is illustrated with the aid of a case study. The evolutionary and possible revolutionary development of mental models, coexistence of multiple models, and representation of these models are also discussed.

1   Introduction

The goal of an intelligent tutoring system (ITS) is to assist students on an individual basis with diagnostic and pedagogic capabilities approaching that of a human tutor. Such tutoring can be effective because the tutor can respond to the specific needs of a student, can guide slow learners, can challenge rapid learners, and can monitor the progress of each student over time. Effective tutoring is based on the tutor's ability to interpret a student's current knowledge state and behaviour, which are represented in the student model component of the ITS. Thus, student modeling is fundamental to the design of an ITS.

Although the student model may represent what the student knows, does not know, and the misconceptions he/she may have about the domain, usually it does not consider cognitive capabilities explicitly. If the tutor knows what *deep conceptual models* the student possesses about the concepts of the tutoring domain, tutoring can be planned accordingly and presumably the student will learn better.

A *deep conceptual model*, in other words a *mental model,* is a coherent collection of knowledge held by a person about some aspect, entity or concept of the world. People use mental models to interpret the world, and therefore aspects of human behaviour can be explained through these models [Conant and Ashby, 1979; Gentner and Stevens 1983]. The fundamental relationship between mental model research and epistemology underlies the importance of mental models for ITS research.

Since mental models reflect people's knowledge about entities around them, knowing and understanding mental models can help in understanding cognitive issues in instruction such as "why" a student takes a certain approach or applies a particular strategy to solve a problem, "why" the student makes mistakes, or "why" and "how" misconceptions are developed. Finally, if the mental models of a student are understood, a tutor can provide more appropriate pedagogical guidance.

In most cases, current ITSs lack cognitive capabilities that are presumably natural for human tutors. Therefore, we believe that mental model research can help to bridge this gap - at least from a pedagogical and diagnostic point of view. A good testbed for our research into mental models is the LISP programming advisor in the Student Computing ENvironmenT (SCENT) project, an ongoing ITS project at the University of Saskatchewan [McCalla *et al*, 1988].

A considerable amount of SCENT research has been devoted to the diagnostic capability of the advisor. Strategy judges and diagnosticians recognize domain specific strategies and misconceptions in students solutions to programming tasks. Strategy judges attempt to determine whether student responses exhibit strategies consistent with predetermined "ideal" strategies, which are stored in a granularity hierarchy [Greer & McCalla, 1989]. Diagnosticians assist the strategy judges when strategies cannot be identified at the finest possible grain size.

SCENT's approach to representing and recognizing strategies is quite novel, but it does not directly consider the cognitive state of the student solving a programming problem. Moreover, the cognitive analyst component, one of the six components of the SCENT architecture, is not yet developed. To look into this issue, Escott [1988] studied novice students' cognitive strategies, in particular analogy, in LISP programming. Her study confirms the use of analogy by students, and links errors in students' programs to misuse of analogy. Escott suggests that recognizing incorrect analogies is an important aid to tutoring. Although analogy is an important method for learning and problem solving, there are many other cognitive methods available to students such as generalization, specialization, refinement, and pattern matching.

This paper describes mental models of recursion, their growth and development, and their use in ITS based on a recent empirical investigation [Bhuiyan, 1989]. Recursion is a core concept in programming, and is also a rather abstract and difficult concept for novice programmers.

2   Mental Models of Recursion

2.1   The Investigation

We carried out an investigation [Bhuiyan, 1989] to understand the kinds of mental models of recursion that students possess, as well as the evolution and development of the models as the students learn a programming language. The investigation involved interviewing six students (randomly selected from a group of 19 volunteers) on a weekly basis to monitor their knowledge of recursion. The students were registered in a second-semester-level programming course in PASCAL at the University of Saskatchewan for non-majors in computer science. They had no prior experience with recursion or recursive programming. Each interview consisted of questions such as *"what are the differences between a procedure and a function"*, *"what are the properties of recursive functions/procedures"*, and *"what are the mental images or pictures that you can have for recursive functions/procedures"*. These kinds of questions were necessary to determine the students' declarative knowledge related to programming in general and to recursion in particular. In each interview, the students were also asked to trace one or two recursive programs, and to write recursive solutions for one or two problems. They were asked to think aloud and to write all versions of their solutions on paper. These interview sessions were audio-taped and in some cases video-taped.

The course content involved recursion with integer, real, array and list data structures. For list data structures, which are not supported by PASCAL, a pseudo-LISP package had been developed which supported various LISP functions. A graphics package which supported the students writing programs to draw recursive graphic patterns also had been developed.

The students attended regular classes, and therefore, every student in the class received the same treatment from their instructor. During the four weeks of lectures on recursion, each of the six students was interviewed for one hour per week. Three weeks later, toward the end of the semester, a final interview was conducted to determine the retention and development of knowledge of recursion. As the students solved class assignments using the computer system, every version of their programs was automatically collected. While data from the interviews has been analyzed to some extent, the program versions await further analysis.

2.2 Models of Recursion

People learn recursive programming over a period of time. Therefore, it is likely that they have more than one mental model of recursion. From the literature [Anzai and Uesato, 1982; Kahney, 1982; Kessler and Anderson, 1986; Pirolli, 1986; Greer, 1987] and from the results of the investigation, there seems to exist at least four different mental models of recursion: *loop model, stack model, template model* and *problem reduction model*.

2.2.1 Loop Model

Many people develop the *loop model* of recursion because they are introduced to iteration prior to recursion [Anzai and Uesato, 1982; Kessler and Anderson, 1986; Kahney, 1982]. By the time a person is introduced to recursion he/she may possess models of loop structures, and is likely to view recursion in terms of these models. Kessler and Anderson [1986] claim that learning iteration helps in learning recursion. But, it was observed in our investigation that the loop model didn't help students in understanding recursion; rather they got confused as they tried to apply their loop models in defining recursive solutions. This is because there is little pedagogical correspondence between loops and recursion.

A loop model has three basic components - *initialization, test and termination,* and *block of code*. In a loop, a block of code is executed only if the test is successful. Analogously, in a *loop model* of recursion, the base-case test to stop the recursion is mapped onto the termination test, and the recursive action corresponds to the code block. In the investigation, it was observed that the compactness of the recursive actions often puzzled the students. They apparently expected to encounter a more substantial block of code in recursive actions. During the first week, two misconceptions were observed in students' program tracing behaviour: 1) they frequently took only a single return from the many successive calls to a recursive function or procedure; and 2) they tended to restart the function or procedure from the first statement of the function or procedure body rather than from the header, which led them to neglect to reinstantiate the variables, thus overwriting those variables. These misconceptions can be attributed to their use of the *loop model*, because there is only one exit from a loop structure, and also the body of the loop is repeatedly executed as long as the test is satisfied.

Two weeks after the investigation started, the students, who were initially using loop models, seemed to have abandoned the loop models. Greer [1987] also made a similar observation in his experiment.

2.2.2   Stack Model

Unlike iterative code, recursive code cannot stand alone; rather each segment of the code is encapsulated in a function or a procedure. From the principles of function or procedure execution, a person may view the execution of recursive functions as stacks of worlds or boxes. This will be called the *stack model*. Traditionally, programming textbooks adopt the *stack model* to describe recursion.

The *stack model* is mainly useful for tracing a recursive function or procedure to separate the variables into different worlds so that they are properly reinstantiated and are not overwritten. Each call to the recursive function or procedure can be viewed as the opening of a new world or box and the prior world is stacked until a base case is reached. The corresponding returns from the function or procedure calls are closures of worlds on a last-in-first-out basis. The *stack model* is also useful for explaining how a recursion unravels, especially in constructing a desired result on the return path.

The limitation of the *stack model* is that it explains nothing about how to derive the base cases and recursive cases. Therefore, it seems that there is limited use of this model in formulating a recursive solution. In our investigation, no one was found to directly use this model in formulating a recursive solution, but many used it extensively for tracing.

2.2.3   Template Model

Students tend to acquire the *template model* of recursion by abstracting the structural features of recursion. Every recursive construct must have at least one base case and one recursive case. When a student begins constructing recursive solutions for simple problems, these two features tend to be abstracted into a *recursion template*, which can also be considered as a schema with slots for tests and actions as shown in Figure 1.

Recursive Template		
Base case	Test:	Action:
Recursive case	Test:	Action:

Figure 1: A basic schema for the *template model* of recursion

A basic recursive template might look like:

```
IF <base test> THEN <base action>
ELSE <recursive action>
```

In this template, the recursive test is a default negation of the base test. It was observed that some students started with this simple template, and later on, as they discovered multiple base cases and multiple recursive cases, they usually modified their template to additional base and recursive cases.

This recursion template is similar to the template that the LISP Tutor [Anderson and Reiser, 1985] uses to teach recursion to students. However, in the LISP Tutor students are not allowed to use their own templates; rather the tutor provides "ideal" templates [Pirolli, 1986]. We observed that students tend to try to fill template slots on a trial and error basis. Escott [1988] also made a similar observation.

The *template model* is obviously better than the *loop model*, but it does not explain a student's understanding of recursion, because most recursive solutions have multiple base cases and/or multiple recursive cases and the model does not assist the student in determining these cases. Furthermore, there seems to be no obvious template for embedded recursion, and templates may not be suitable for representing nested conditions and corresponding actions.

The advantage of using the *template model*, from a student's point of view, is that for many problems there are few choices for conditions and actions. For example, for list recursive problems, often one of the base cases is a null list test and the corresponding action is either to return a *false* value or an empty list. In a recursive action, usually the function is called with the rest of the list.

One obvious problem is that students may try to memorize these different situations without much deeper understanding, and therefore, may develop a large repertoire of possible slots and fillers which unnecessarily burdens memory [Chi et al, 1982]. They may also over-generalize the models of a one-argument recursive function or procedure to a multiple-argument recursive function or procedure. These behaviours were observed in our investigation.

The investigation has suggested that many students acquired the *template model* at an early stage and retained the model until the end of the course. This model is used during formulation of solutions to problems. It has also been observed that these students' problem solving behaviour was dominated by slot-filling on a trial and error basis. This behaviour was quite evident from their successive versions of programs, where each version was typically a minor variation of the previous one, no matter how ill-formed. Many of the surface analogies discovered by Escott [1988] might be best explained by students' use of a template model.

2.2.4 Problem Reduction Model

The *problem reduction model* is the most general and abstract model of recursion. This model arises from the problem reduction feature of recursion where every recursive problem is defined in terms of a simpler version of itself, until a base case is reached. This model captures both structural and functional properties of recursion, and is suitable for all kinds of recursion.

The *problem reduction model* is used by expert programmers during the solution formulation of a problem. For example, the *flatten* problem, to remove the inner parentheses from a nested list, can be viewed as - flatten the first element of the list, flatten the rest of the list, and combine both into the required new list. Obviously, this is a high level solution to the problem. For a detailed solution plan the programmer has to further determine the constraints, the conditions, and the corresponding actions.

Expert programmers seem to possess a *problem reduction model* of recursion; novice programmers usually do not. Throughout our investigation, only one student showed evidence of developing this model. This model does not help directly in tracing, but provides a solid

140

foundation for building recursive solutions to problems and offers evidence of correctness that can obviate the need for tracing.

2.2.5 Coexistence of Different Models

From the above description, although it may seem that the four models are quite different, there are some interactions among them. The *loop model* may be considered as a special case of the *stack model*, and similarly, the *template model* is a special case of the *problem reduction model*. Refining a *problem reduction model* gives rise to templates, but these templates, in contrast to the *template model*, are less rigid and can easily be generated. It was observed in our investigation that students more frequently used the *template model* for generating solutions (programs), and they frequently tested these programs using the *stack model*.

3 Mental Models and ITS Issues

Mental models reflect a person's understanding about an entity. In a programming language context a person has mental models about many concepts. The collection of these models can represent a total understanding of the language and of programming in general. The question remains how to use the existence of these mental models in the design of an ITS.

After presenting a case study of a student, whom we will call K, the use of mental models in an ITS for diagnosis, pedagogy, and student modeling is discussed in this section. At the same time, directions for current and further research are identified.

3.1 Case study

We conducted our first interview after the students had their first lecture on recursion. One of the problems was to *write a recursive function, SUM, to sum the integers from 1 to N*. While solving this problem, K showed strong evidence of having the *loop model* of recursion. His algorithm for SUM was as follows:

> ".. You gonna ask the user to enter the number N, which is the maximum number.
>
> Then you are gonna .. start with that number .. and assign a variable to that number.
>
> And then subtract 1 from the number and add that until you hit 0. ...."

From this iterative algorithm, he attempted to write a recursive solution as shown in Figure 2a. The statement *(N - 1)*, an attempted decrement to a loop index, provides evidence for his *loop model* of recursion. When he was unsuccessful in writing a correct recursive function, he opted to write an iterative program segment with the intention to translate to a recursive function. His correct iterative solution is shown in Figure 2b.

Although there are a lot of syntactic mistakes in K's programs, we are concerned with his strategic misconceptions only. Analysing his interview, it is clear that he thought that every program had to have at least one 'read' statement to get input(s) from the terminal, and therefore, so must a function as it is a "mini program". This misconception can be attributed to his inappropriate model of functions.

FUNCTION SUM (N: INTEGER);
VAR
    NUM : INTEGER;
BEGIN
    READ(N);
    (N - 1);
    SUM (N -1);
	READ(N);
	NUM := N;
	WHILE N >= 0 DO
	BEGIN
	    N := N - 1;
	    NUM := NUM + N;
	END;

2a: K's initial recursive solution to SUM	2b: K's iterative solution to SUM

Figure 2: K's solutions for the problem SUM

When someone learns a new concept his model about the concept is not immediately formed; rather it takes time. Moreover, different models may also interact. For example, K's thinking, shown below, reflects the use of a template model, but he did not seem to use the model in writing the code:

K: ..... I don't remember the format that goes here (that) you showed a couple of minutes ago.

Inter: Why do you have to see a format?

(He had been previously shown a recursive solution to another problem)

K: Well, the base case and the recursive case - how they are set up, I forgot.

Even after showing the recursive program that K wanted to see, he could not write a correct recursive function for SUM, preferring instead to write the iterative solution. From the second interview, K abandoned the *loop model*, and seemed to adopt the *template model* which he retained throughout the investigation.

3.2 Use of mental models

Determining what mental model(s) a student possesses can be useful to an ITS. From someone's problem solving behaviour, it may be reasonably easy to determine his/her mental models, as is shown in K's behaviour. But the question remains how to determine the student's mental model(s) looking only at at his/her program (for example, K's recursive solution to SUM). This is a very important issue for the SCENT advisor, as SCENT diagnoses students' mistakes and misconceptions solely by analyzing their program code. One possible way is by determining the kinds of strategies and misconceptions manifested for each different mental model. For example, the statement *(N - 1)* in K's recursive solution (Figure 2a) is evidence of the *loop model*. More of these pieces of evidence need to be cataloged over a student population. Research is now underway to attribute classes of errors to different models; but this job may not be easy, because a mistake may be attributed to different mental models and an inappropriate model may give rise to several mistakes.

Mental models can help in anticipating the next possible behaviour of the student. By "running" the mental models that the student is hypothesized to possess, anticipated behaviour can be inferred and actual behaviour can validate these hypotheses. Similarly, confidence and reliability of diagnosis can be enhanced by being able to explain specific student behaviour in terms of a particular mental model.

Pedagogy, in ITS, deals with teaching students individually. For individualized teaching it is necessary to know the cognitive states of every student. Students' mental models reveal their level of conceptualization of any concept within a domain. For example, since the *loop model* is inappropriate for learning recursion, an ITS should help K to develop a better model, ultimately the *problem reduction model*, an ideal model of recursion.

The student model component of SCENT will also benefit from these mental models. It appears that the student model may be represented as a subset of the union of all the mental models the student has about LISP concepts. This means the student model may be represented in terms of instantiations of all the mental models the student currently manifests.

4   Discussion

In this section, issues related to the development of mental models, the influence of mental models in learning, and the representation of mental models are discussed.

Since a mental model is an internal representation of an entity or concept, it is finite, and any new knowledge acquired by a person about the entity or the concept will reflect on, and possibly add to the model. Being finite, a mental model cannot grow in an unlimited way; i.e, after a certain point, adding new information to the model does not increase its usefulness. For example, the *stack model* of recursion, which is mainly useful for tracing recursive functions or procedures, cannot accommodate structural knowledge of the base case(s) and the recursive case(s).

The development of a mental model may be *evolutionary* or *revolutionary* in nature. Evolution of a mental model occurs as information is gradually added to an existing model. For example adding cases to the basic template in Figure 1 results in a more elaborate mental model. A mental model also may evolve through refinement. For example, the simple *stack model* is not suitable for tracing multiple recursions because multiple stacks need to be activated for multiple recursive calls. It was observed in our investigation that a few students refined the *stack model* to a *tree model,* which involves simultaneous instantiation of multiple stacks each separately maintained.

When a mental model cannot further explain the behaviour or functioning of an entity, a student may develop a revolutionary new mental model. This has been called a *conceptual shift* by Rouse & Morris [1985]. A *conceptual shift* takes place when an existing mental model cannot explain certain features of the concept no matter how the model is enhanced or refined, thus a new model is created with an underlying structure different from the existing one(s). For example, developing the *template model* for constructing recursive functions requires a conceptual shift by the student who possesses only the *loop model.* Two types of conceptual shifts have been identified in our investigation - *pattern abstraction* and *principle abstraction.* The template model of recursion is acquired through abstracting a pattern from the surface features of recursive functions, whereas the *problem reduction model* is acquired by abstracting the principles of recursion. Experts are capable of abstracting underlying principles of entities or concepts, an ability which novices tend not to possess. In fact, once someone achieves this ability he/she is no longer a novice.

Much research is still needed into the coexistence of multiple mental models and the interaction among the models. For example, during the first week of introduction to recursion, K showed evidence of having the *loop model* and at the same time some primitive form of the *template model* of recursion. Research is also needed to find out how and when a student stops using a particular mental model and embraces another one, i.e, when a *conceptual shift* takes place. Sometimes an old model stays as it is, and is used for its purposes. For example, the *stack model* seems to co-exist with the *template model* or the *problem reduction model,* and is used for tracing programs, although not for design.

Mental models influence learning. A good mental model positively influences learning, whereas an inappropriate mental model may obstruct learning. For example, when a person has a suitable *stack model* of recursion he/she should be able to trace embedded recursive programs correctly. This observation was positively verified during the third and the fourth weeks of our investigation when the students began to acquire suitable *stack models*. The *loop model* is pedagogically inappropriate for recursion. As long as students have this model, deve'opment of a better understanding of the concept of recursion is inhibited.

We believe that the outcome of this research will improve ITSs, by guiding students to gradually acquire appropriate mental models of programming concepts. For example, it would be eventually desirable that students acquire the *problem reduction model* of recursion. Such a model may not be suitably introduced early, because at that time the students may not have developed the required cognitive state to conceptualize the underlying principles of recursion. As a matter of fact, they may need to be guided through an initial understanding of the *stack model* and the *template model* before being ready to grasp the *problem reduction model*.

Since our goal is to make use of mental models in ITS, it is necessary to discover a suitable representation for these models. Any approach to representation has to deal with the contents of the models, the development (*evolution* and *conceptual shifts*) of the models, interactions among different models, and problem solving using the models. Our work in representing mental models is still preliminary at this time.

5 Conclusion

The major contribution of our research is in understanding the nature of mental models of recursion and how these models might affect the design of an ITS. We have identified four different mental models of recursion, namely the *loop, stack, template* and *problem reduction* models. There is a possibility that analysis of the data and further investigation may add more models. We have also looked into the contents of these models, coexistence and development of the models, and students' use of the models in different problem-solving situations.

We have been investigating the use of these mental models for diagnosis, pedagogy and student modeling in an ITS, and we emphasize the need for further research in this area. A thorough understanding of students' mental models is necessary if we hope to achieve truly intelligent tutoring.

References

[Anderson and Reiser, 1986]
  Anderson, JR and Reiser, B. *The LISP Tutor*, Byte, pp. 159-175, April, 1986.

[Anzai and Uesato, 1982]
  Anzai, Y and Uesato, Y. *Learning Recursive Procedures by Middle School Children.* Proceedings of the Fourth Annual Conference of the Cognitive Science Society, pp. 100-102, Ann Arbor, Michigan, USA, 1982.

[Bhuiyan, 1989]

Bhuiyan, SH. *Mental Models of Recursion in Computer Programming*. Proceedings of the First Annual Graduate Symposium on Computational Science, pp. 286-313, Dept of Computational Science, University of Saskatchewan, Canada, 1989.

[Chi et al, 1982]

Chi MTH, Feltovich PJ and Glaser R. *Categorization and Representation of Physics Problems by Experts and Novices*. Cognitive Science, 5, pp. 121-152, 1982.

[Conant and Ashby, 1970]

Conant RC and Ashby S. *Every Good Regulator of a System Must be a Good Model of the System*. International Journal of System Science, 1, pp. 89-97, 1970.

[Escott, 1988]

Escott J. *Problem Solving by Analogy in Novice Programming*. ARIES LAB Research Report 88-3. Dept of Computational Science, University of Saskatchewan, Canada, 1988.

[Gantner and Stevens, 1983]

Gentner D and Stevens A. (Eds). *Mental Models*. Hillside, NJ: Lawrence Erlbaum, 1983.

[Greer, 1987]

Greer JE. *Empirical Comparison of Techniques for Teaching Recursion in Introductory Computer Science*. Ph.D. Thesis. The University of Texas at Austin, 1987.

[Greer and McCalla, 1989]

Greer JE and McCalla GI. *A Computational Framework for Granularity and its Application to Educational Diagnosis*. Proceedings of International Joint Conference on Artificial Intelligence (IJCAI), pp. 477-482, Detroit, August, 1989.

[Kahney 1982]

Kahney H. *An In-depth Study of the Cognitive Behaviour of Novice Programmers*. Tech. Report No. 5. Milton-Keynes, England: The Open University, 1982.

[Kessler and Anderson, 1986]

Kessler CM and Anderson JR. *Learning Flow of Control: Iterative and Recursive Procedures*. Human-Computer Interaction, Volume 2, Hillside, NJ: Lawrence Erlbaum, pp. 135-166, 1986.

[McCalla et al, 1988]

McCalla GI, Greer JE and the SCENT Research Team . *Intelligent Advising in Problem Solving Domains: The SCENT-3 Architecture*. Proceedings of Intelligent Tutoring Systems, Montreal, Canada, pp. 124-131, 1988.

[Pirolli, 1986]

Pirolli PA. *A Cognitive Model of Computer Tutor for Programming Recursion*. Human-Computer Interaction, Volume 2, Hillside, NJ: Lawrence Erlbaum, pp. 329-355, 1988.

[Rouse and Morris, 1985]

Rouse WB and Morris NM. *On Looking into the Black Box: Prospects and Limits in the Search of Mental Models*. Technical Report, 85-2. Center for Man-Machine Systems Research, GIT, Atlanta, USA.

EXPLANATION OF ALGEBRAIC REASONING :
THE *APLUSIX* SYSTEM

J. F. NICAUD   M. SAIDI

L.R.I. Bât 490
CNRS UA 410
Université de PARIS XI
91405 ORSAY CEDEX, FRANCE
e-mail : jfn@frlri61.bitnet
e-mail : saidi@frlri61.bitnet

Abstract

Strategic knowledge is fundamental in order to become adaptive. Though it is crucial in factorization of polynomials and polynomial-equation solving, it is hardly ever taught in school. *Aplusix*, an ICAI system, tries to deal with this aspect. *Aplusix* can be either example-driven or reasoning driven. In the first case the problem is solved by the system. However, the student may ask for explanation concerning facts or strategic knowledge. In the second case, the problem is solved by the student. He chooses among the possible transformations and the system performs the necessary computations. The goal of *Aplusix* is to help the student to discover how to perform the necessary matching operations and to develop efficient strategies. In order to do so, the system shows all the operations performed, including backtracking, when presenting the examples. When solving the equations with the help of the system, the student is relieved of the burden of computation. He can therefore use all his resources on the task of reasoning. This paper describes the problem-solving component of *Aplusix* and its explanation module.

1 Introduction

Factorization of polynomials and polynomial-equation solving require different kinds of knowledge :
- transformation rules,
- pattern-matching,
- knowledge of calculus in order to apply the transformations,
- strategies in order to choose the adequate transformation.

All but the last type of knowledge are generally taught in school. However, strategic knowledge becomes necessary, whenever one is confronted with a new situation. As it is impossible to provide exercises for all possible situations where the known rules apply, one has to learn how to cope with new situations. In other words, one has to learn how to develop efficient strategies. Factorization of polynomials and polynomial-equation solving provide a rich domain of observation in this respect : one can follow the problem-solving process and infer different levels of expertise, by observing the success and failure, the moments where a hypothesis is abandoned (backtracking) or confirmed, etc.

The danger of not teaching strategic knowledge is that the student tends to believe that the basic mechanism of solving algebraic problems resides in discovering which transformation applies to what form and thus reaching the solution after a series of reductions. Under such circumstances it is impossible for the student to imagine that :
- a given transformation may lead to a dead-end,
- he should try to build and explore a search-space by applying a set of heuristics in order to determine which transformation rule applies,
- he has to determine whether to pursue or to abandon a given line of reasoning (backtrack).

One type of teaching consists in providing the student with the solution of the problem. Obviously, this has to be complemented with practicing how to reach the solution. Good teachers take into account the student's knowledge. This means in our case, that they use only those transformations that are known by the student, and that the steps applied are a function of the student's actual knowledge state. In order to be both motivating and clear, one has to ensure that the necessary operations (matching and calculus) are at the right level and that they are neither too elementary, nor too complex. Once this goal is achieved, the search-space can be considered as a form of explanation, containing factual and strategic information (the transformations used, backtracking, etc.). However, this kind of information is not sufficient, generally other knowledge sources are necessary :

• with respect to the calculus the problem-solving component exhibits the different steps a student is supposed to know (the program behaves as a good student at the required level) ; a particular student may need further explanations for a given transformation, matching or computation.

• given the fact that strategic knowledge is implicitly contained in the search-space, it becomes important to make it obvious by explaining the choices and the heuristics used.

Aplusix is a project in ICAI in the domain of algebraic calculus (factorization of polynomials and polynomial-equation solving). The system can be either example-driven or reasoning-driven. In the first case the problem is solved by the system, the latter explains its line of reasoning, in the second case the problem is solved by the student. He chooses among the possible transformations and the system performs the necessary computation. The goal of *Aplusix* is to help the student to discover how to perform the necessary matching operations and to develop efficient strategies. In order to do so, the system shows all the operations performed, including backtracking, when presenting the examples. When solving the equations with the help of the system, the student is relieved of the burden of computation. He can therefore use all his resources on the task of reasoning.

The problem-solving component of *Aplusix* is an expert system that uses explicitly encoded (declaratively) strategic knowledge. It attempts to simulate the way humans reason, by adapting the level of reasoning according to the needs. The system is capable providing explanations concerning the transformations, as well as concerning the strategies used. In the remainder of this paper we will present the problem-solving component of *Aplusix* as well as as its explanation component. For a more complete description of the system see [Nicaud 87, 89].

2 *Aplusix's* problem-solving component

Aplusix's problem-solving component develops a search-space whose nodes are the problems. It goes through the following cycle :
- establish the transformations applicable for the problem under study,
- choose among the possible transformations the best candidate,
- apply the transformation.

The transformations are implemented in the form of production-rules. The strategies are composed of heuristics which are implemented in the form of meta-rules. They label the transformations as well as the problems in terms of interest to allow for choosing the best problem-transformation pair. This reasoning process is composed of three components :
 • qualification of each transformation of the current problem (by taking into account the operations performed in the past, the actual context and problems of the near future),
 • an updating of the attributes of the remaining applicable transformations in order to account for the actions performed,
 • a labelling of each problem in terms of interest and choice of the most promising candidate.

Several heuristics can be applied in each sub-task. Their effect can be cumulative.

In order to factorize polynomials and to solve polynomial equations *Aplusix* takes into account different levels of knowledge :
 • beginners (13-14 years),
 • average (15 years),
 • good (16-17 years),
 • experts

These categories will be used as reference when determining the level of reasoning, or the type of explanation to be given. Each level is specified in terms of skills, or knowledge available :
 • the transformations known by the student,
 • the kind of heuristics and matching operations that the student is supposed to be able to use or understand during the learning phase[1].

Figure 1 illustrates a difficult problem for experts.

Let us try to explain parts of the meta-reasoning. At the beginning the following transformations are applicable for the problem at hand :
 $(5-2X)(X^2-4)+8(2-X)+4X^2-12X+9$

T1 : factorization of X^2-4
T2 : factorization of $4X^2-12X+9$
T3 : development of $(5-2X)(X^2-4)$
T4 : development of $8(2-X)$

The first two transformations (T1, T2) score high (good), because they allow for factorization. T1 produces a new expression $X-2$ which is contained in its neighbor term $8(2-X)$. That is why T1 scores higher than T2 : T1 receives the label "very good". On the other hand, T2 scores less well (fairly good), as the new factor $(2X-3)$ it produces is contained in none of the neighboring terms.

T3 qualifies "low" (development), while T4 receives "fairly good" (distribution of a number over a sum). The score of T4 is increased because the operation "development" could be followed by a reduction.

In sum, we have the following pairs : T1-very well, T2-fairly good, T3-low, T4-good. This explains the choice of T1. Given that T1 later leads to a mediocre result *Aplusix* backtracks. The problem chosen after the backtrack is the initial problem ; T4 becomes the next candidate as possible transformation.

---

[1] These levels have been determined with the help of C. Aubertin and P. Wach, teaching at a high-school in France.

148

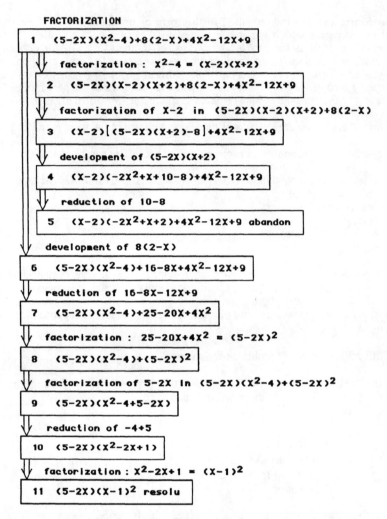

FACTORIZATION

1   (5-2X)(X²-4)+8(2-X)+4X²-12X+9

    factorization : X²-4 = (X-2)(X+2)

2   (5-2X)(X-2)(X+2)+8(2-X)+4X²-12X+9

    factorization of X-2 in (5-2X)(X-2)(X+2)+8(2-X)

3   (X-2)[(5-2X)(X+2)-8]+4X²-12X+9

    development of (5-2X)(X+2)

4   (X-2)(-2X²+X+10-8)+4X²-12X+9

    reduction of 10-8

5   (X-2)(-2X²+X+2)+4X²-12X+9 abandon

    development of 8(2-X)

6   (5-2X)(X²-4)+16-8X+4X²-12X+9

    reduction of 16-8X-12X+9

7   (5-2X)(X²-4)+25-20X+4X²

    factorization : 25-20X+4X² = (5-2X)²

8   (5-2X)(X²-4)+(5-2X)²

    factorization of 5-2X in (5-2X)(X²-4)+(5-2X)²

9   (5-2X)(X²-4+5-2X)

    reduction of -4+5

10 (5-2X)(X²-2X+1)

    factorization : X²-2X+1 = (X-1)²

11 (5-2X)(X-1)² resolu

figure 1

The problem-solving component of *Aplusix* has been designed to try to model human reasoning : it does not pose artificial sub-problems as is the case for Camélia [Vivet 84], or Tango [Faller 83, Pottier 84] ; it separates factual knowledge from strategic knowledge. The strategies used attempt to take into account the entire problem. For example, unlike Camélia, it does not exhaust all possible strategies in one direction before considering a new one. *Aplusix's* meta-rules allow to solve problems far more complex than those implemented in PRESS [Borning & Bundy 81][1].

---

[1] Bundy & Sylver signal in their paper [Bundy & Sylver 81] concerning the change of variable in equations, that PRESS is able to solve only 50% of the equations obtained after change of variable.

3 Explanations concerning the transformation applied

In order to obtain the adequate grain-size of reasoning, it is necessary to take into account the student's level of knowledge. That is to say, the system must be able to determine the size and the nature of the steps it presents to the student. These steps are part of the student's ultimate learning task. Whenever the student finds these operations non-obvious, or too complex, he may ask for help. The help is given in form of an explanation.

A knowledge base of about 50 rules allows one to decompose the process into a set of sub-tasks when necessary. These rules imply simple matching as well as computational operations.

For example, let us assume that having performed the following operation :

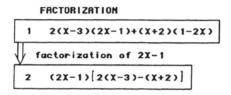

the student asks for more details. In this case, Aplusix decomposes this operation into two steps. The first one having as objective to make the factor 2X-1 explicit :

```
FACTORIZATION
┌─────────────────────────────────────┐
│ 1    2(X-3)(2X-1)+(X+2)(1-2X)        │
└─────────────────────────────────────┘
  ↓  normalization of (X+2)(1-2X)
┌─────────────────────────────────────┐
│ 2    2(X-3)(2X-1)-(X+2)(2X-1)        │
└─────────────────────────────────────┘
  ↓  factorization of 2X-1
┌─────────────────────────────────────┐
│ 3    (2X-1)[2(X-3)-(X+2)]            │
└─────────────────────────────────────┘
```

The problem solver and the explanation component measure the degree of correspondence between two expressions (complexity of different patterns). Thus 2X-1 is a possible factor :

- in 2(X-3)(2X-1)+(X+2)(1-2X)   : it scores average,
- in 2(X-3)(2X-1)-(X+2)(2X-1)   : it scores high (obvious).

Whenever a given feature is not obvious with respect to a given student's level, it is ignored by the system. On the other hand, when a feature is considered as obvious by the system, but the user asks for additional information, the explanation component performs the necessary transformation in order to increase the feature's visibility.

4 Explanation of the strategies used

The goal of this component is to explain a given strategy and to answer the following questions :
- why was / was not the transformation T applied ?
- why did one / did not one backtrack ?

The status of each transformation is determined by meta-rules. A transformation may be :
- chosen and applied,
- kept in memory, to be applied in case of backtracking,
- discarded.

As we have seen in figure 1, several meta-rules may be applied in order to determine the status of an applicable transformation. The trace of the rules used to solve a given problem are not necessarily the best way of explaining how one has reached the solution, even if the meta-rules are based upon heuristics used by a human. This problem arises for most expert systems on the factual level [Kassel 86, Safar 85]. In *Aplusix* it concerns basically the strategic level : explanations are produced by extracting the most significant information from the reasoning process.

Explanations are based (a) on a reasoning process which operates on a knowledge base of 90 rules, and (b) on the trace of the meta-reasoning.

4.1 Examples of positive explanations

4.1.1 Why was transformation T applied ?

In order to answer this question, *Aplusix* presents the major arguments that lead to the choice of transformation T.

Example 1 :
Aplusix>   prob1> solve $2(X^2-1)+2X^2-X+1-X^2-X=0$
            reduction of $2X^2-X+1-X^2-X$
Student>   why this particular transformation ?
Aplusix>   the reduced form of an expression is generally more
            interesting

Example 2 :
Aplusix>   prob1> factorize $(5-2X)(X^2-4)+8(2-X)+4X^2-12X+9$
            factorization of X^2-4
Student>   why this particular transformation ?
Aplusix>   factorization of X^2-4 is very interesting.
            factorization of X^2-4 produces the new factor X-2 .
            X-2 is also a factor in 8(2-X) .

4.1.2 Why did one backtrack ?

The system has decided to tackle another problem. In this case, two decisions are taken simultaneously : the choice of the problem and the choice of the transformation. The answer takes into account the number of factors of the problems P and PA on one hand, and the interest of their transformations on the other hand. As mentionned here above, *Aplusix* produces only the main arguments.

Example 3 :

Aplusix>   prob5> factorize $(X-2)(-2X^2+X+2)+4X^2-12X+9$
             BACKTRACK : prob1> factorize $(5-2X)(X^2-4)+8(2-X)+4X^2-12X+9$
             development of $8(2-X)$
Student>   *why this particular transformation ?*
Aplusix>   prob1 and prob2 have the same number of factors.
             The development of $8(2-X)$ in prob1 will be followed by a reduction.
             This transformation seems better than those of prob5.

4.2 Examples of negative explanations

4.2.1 Why wasn't transformation T applied ?

According to the status of T (kept in memory or discarded), we may encounter the following two cases :

a) The transformation is discarded.

When a transformation is dicarded by one heuristic, the answer is built on the basis of this rule, for example :

Example 4 :

Aplusix>   prob2> solve $(X-1)^2+2(X+1)-3=0$
           development of $(X-1)^2$
           prob3> solve $X^2-2X+1+2(X+1)-3=0$
           development of $2(X+1)$
Student>   *why doesn't one factorize X^2-2X+1 ?*
Aplusix>   we just obtained X^2-2X+1 by developing $(X-1)^2$

When a transformation has been discarded by several heuristics, it is necessary to show the student the most significant one. For that purpose, we have classified the heuristics that discard transformations hierarchically.

b) The transformation is kept in memory.

In that case, the transformation T is not applied. It is kept in memory for eventual backtracking. When T seems to be of little interest compared to TA, the transformation chosen, the system shows the interest of TA.

Example 5 :

Aplusix>   prob1> solve $(X+2)^2-8X+(X-2)(X-5)=0$
           development of $(X+2)^2$
Student>   *why doesn't one develop $(X-2)(X-5)$?*
Aplusix>   the development of $(X-2)(X-5)$ is of little interest.
           the development of $(X+2)^2$ will be followed by a reduction
           which will produce a remarkable identity.

When there is no significant difference between T and TA, *Aplusix* signals that the choice was arbitrary.

4.2.2 Why didn't one backtrack to problem P ?

The student may ask this kind of question when the system pursues the current direction, or when it backtracks to another problem PA. The answer is given on the basis of the comparison of P and PA, as this has been the case in 4.1.2 where the question was : *Why did one backtrack ?*

4.3   Implementation of the explanations of a strategy

The major problem one is faced with when giving an explanation for a strategy chosen is to extract the most relevant points. Sometimes, this consists in choosing the main heuristics applied, and to present it with its associated comment. Most of the time, the answer is composed of several sentences. These sentences are comments associated with heuristics or explanatory rules. For example, in example 2 the explanatory rule used is :

```
IF  the applied transformation T is of high interest
&   the interest of T was increased by the heuristic H
&   the effect of T is F
&   the sub-expression of T is E
THEN   tell :  F "of" E "is very interesting"
               send the comment of H
```

The heuristic H reads like follows :

```
IF  T is a transformation that can be applied to P
&   T factorizes the sub-expression E
&   T produces the new factor A
&   E is contained in E1
&   E contains another term E2
&   A is a factor of E2
THEN         increase the interest of T (2 points)
COMMENT   "factorization of" E "produces the new factor" A
             A "is also a factor in" E2
```

The transformational rule T is :

```
IF   E is a sub-expression of P
&    E matches A²-B²
THEN         replace E by (A-B)(A+B)
COMMENT   E "is a difference between two squares"
EFFECT       factorization
```

and the explanation obtained is :

factorization of X^2-4 is very interesting.
factorization of X^2-4 produces the new factor X-2 .
X-2 is also a factor in 8(2-X).

5 Experimentation

The first prototype of *Aplusix* has been implemented on a Macintosh. It has the following modes :
• the example mode (the system solves the problem) with explanation of transformations but without explanation of the strategies,
• the reasoning mode (the student solves the problem).

Experiments have been done with students of the age 15-17. The experimentation began with a familiarization phase, during which simple exercises were solved. Later, students were asked to do exercises that contained difficulties at the reasoning level and that required backtracking.
The fact that the students were generally surprised by this kind of exercise shows, that they are not familiar with this meta-heuristic : *build and reduce intelligently a search space*. Most students succeeded fairly well in elaborating heuristics. However, some of them couldn't find any one, and developed the search-space only by chance.

The explanation of the strategies has been implemented on a Sun [Saïdi 88]. This module will be transferred onto a Macintosh during the next few months, and more experiments will be done with this new prototype.

6 Conclusion

A fundamental goal of education is *to prepare people to be adaptive to the various settings they may encounter over the course of their working lives* [Resnick 87]. Learning how to develop efficient strategies is a good way to reach this end. Experimentation is very important for the student : he can build his own search-space and draw conclusions on the basis of success and failure. However, examples are needed in order to structure knowledge and to speed up the learning process. The possibility to ask for explanations both at the factual and strategic level is particularly efficient for this kind of learning. Both learning modes are implemented in our system.
The factorization of polynomials and polynomial-equation solving are in this respect a rich domain of experimentation, provided that adequate problems are chosen. In *Aplusix* particular emphasis has been laid on the explanation component, in order to enhance the student's capacity to organize the newly acquainted knowledge.

7 References

[Borning & Bundy 81]
Borning A. & Bundy A. : *Using matching in algebraic equation solving.* IJCAI7, 1981.

[Bundy 83]
Bundy A. : *The computer modeling of mathematical reasoning.* Academic Press, New York, 1983.

[Bundy & Sylver 81]
Bundy A. & Sylver B. : *Homogenization : preparing equations for change of unknown.* In proceeding of IJCAI7, 1981, p 551-553.

[Dede 86]
Dede C. : *A revue and synthesis of recent research in intelligent computer-assisted instruction.* International Journal of Man-Machine Studies, 24, 1986.

[Faller 83]
Faller B. : *Une application de TANGO au calcul des primitives.* Rapport de DEA, LRI, ParisXI, 1983.

[Ferret & Jimenez 87]
Ferret E., Jimenez C. : *A la découverte des méthodes algébriques.* Proceeding of EAO87, Cap d'Agde, France, Mars 1987, 389-398.

[Kassel 86]
Kassel G. : *Le système d'explications CQFE: une forme de méta-raisonnement intégrant règles et objets.* Thèse d'Université, Paris XI, 1986.

[Nicaud 87]
Nicaud J.F. : *Aplusix: un système expert en résolution pédagogique d'exercices d'algèbre.* Thèse d'Université, Paris XI, 1987.

[Nicaud & Vivet 88]
Nicaud J.F., Vivet M. : *Les tuteurs intelligents: réalisations et tendances de recherches.* Technique et Science Informatique, vol 7 n°1, 1988, p 22-45.

[Nicaud 89]
Nicaud J.F.: *APLUSIX un système expert pédagogique et un environnement d'apprentissage dans le domaine du raisonnement algébrique.* Technique et Science Informatique, vol 8 n°2, 1989, p 145-155.

[Pottier 84]
Pottier L. : *Une application de Tango à l'integration formelle, une solution pour le pilotage des sous-problèmes.* rapport de DEA, LRI, Paris XI, 1984.

[Resnick 87]
Resnick L. : *Learning in school and out.* Educational Researcher, 16 (9), p 13-19.

[Safar 85]
Safar B. : *Explication dans les systèmes experts, Proceeding of les systèmes experts et leurs applications.* Avigon, France, May 1985, vol 1, 585-599.

[Saïdi 88]
Saïdi M. : *Système expert d'explication des heuristiques pour Aplusix.* Rapport de DEA, Université de Paris XI, 1988.

[Vivet 84]
Vivet M. : *Expertise mathématique et informatique : CAMELIA, un logiciel pour raisonner et calculer.* Thèse d'état, Paris VI, 1984.

[Vivet 87]
Vivet M.: *reasoned explanations need reasoning on reasoning and reasoning on the student.* IFIP TC3, Frascati R Lewis & P Ercoli eds, North Holland, 1987.

The Trigonometry Tutor

Parvati Rajan   Pramod Patil   KSR Anjaneyulu   P Srinivas

National Centre for Software Technology
Gulmohar Cross Road No. 9, Juhu
Bombay 400 049
Email: {parvati,spramod,anji,srinivas}@shakti.uu.net

Abstract

This paper describes a tutor which teaches students trigonometric problem solving. We first discuss approaches others have adopted for teaching mathematics and comment on their usefulness in trigonometry. We later present a task analysis of trigonometry, based on an experiment we conducted. We then present our approach to teach different categories of problems in trigonometry.

1   Introduction

The field of Intelligent Tutoring Systems (ITS) attempts to construct systems with 'human-like' tutoring capabilities. ITS tend to be more sophisticated than conventional CAI, and offer more initiative to the student. A number of ITS have been developed for mathematics. In addition to providing powerful systems, the field also has helped researchers to get a better understanding of the problem solving process, pedagogical principles, structure of the domain, student misconceptions etc.

Trigonometry problem solving involves knowledge of prerequisites like algebra (including general arithmetic skills) and geometry (such as concept of angles, triangles, Pythagoras theorem etc.). In addition the students have to learn trigonometric ratios, relationships, and application of these to word problems.

We are developing a trigonometry tutor to help students improve their skills in solving trigonometry problems. This tutor is aimed at helping students strengthen their understanding of the various fundamental ideas such as concepts of angles and triangles, properties of right-angled triangles, as well as the concepts covered in trigonometry.

The approach we have adopted involves emphasis on problem solving and remedial instruction. We assume that the student is taught trigonometry in a normal classroom environment. The tutor attempts to reinforce his learning by providing the right type of exercises and when necessary, helping the student solve them. The tutor drives the instruction, but the student is allowed to get help, and ask for explanations when required. In this sense, the tutor fits better into a guided learning system paradigm, like the LISP tutor [Anderson and Reiser, 1985], Geometry tutor [Anderson et al, 1985] etc, than into that of a discovery learning system paradigm.

The trigonometry tutor attempts:

- To present appropriate problems and guide the student solving it

- To provide students help or advice (possibly on request), depending on the difficulty encountered by them at that point in time

- To provide a learning environment that is individualised to the needs of the student, depending on the his level of understanding

The strong points of the tutor are the provision of a user friendly interface, bug identification and providing appropriate remedial instruction. The tutor uses a black-box expert to solve problems and the student has the option to ask the system to solve a problem.

The structure of this paper is as follows. In section 2, we briefly describe two other tutors in the domain of mathematics. In section 3, we describe the domain of trigonometry in terms of the concepts and procedures which a student needs to know. Section 4 describes our tutor and our approach to teach different categories of trigonometry problems.

2 Intelligent Tutors in Mathematics

Mathematics has been a major area for which a number of intelligent tutors have been developed. In this section we briefly describe two such tutors.

[Nathan et al, 1989] in their description of their Algebra Word Problem tutor, present a model for word problem comprehension. The approach they use is based on:

a) organizing the information contained in the problem into a schema

b) relating this to the situation visualized by the student according to his interpretation of the problem.

Although the tutor does not have any knowledge of the problems being considered and no model of the student using it, it is able to help students understand and solve algebra word problems. In the tutor, a student creates an algebraic network to represent the problem. After the student has completed the network, he can run an animation to see whether the problem specification is correct or not. The tutor does not tell the student whether it is correct or not; the student has to infer this from the animation. Figure 1 illustrates a typical situation, where the student is expected to recognize an error. A positive point of the tutor is the use of graphical schemata (algebraic networks) to represent problems. The authors claim that students found it easier to solve word problems using these schemata. The tutor acts more like a discovery learning system and allows the students to find errors themselves by observing the animation.

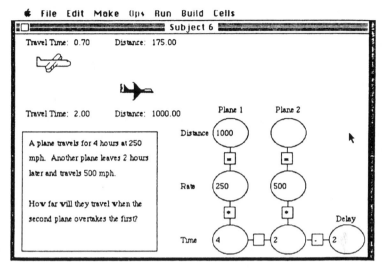

Figure 1: Improper performance of the animation suggests a conceptual error. The plane with the faster rate leaves first and cannot be passed by the slower one. (reprinted with permission from [Nathan et al, 1989])

On the other hand, the approach is based on the use of of animation and so its scope may be limited to classes of word problems like time and distance problems. It is not clear how far this approach will transfer to other categories of problems. In particular, this approach is not appropriate for trigonometry.

[Singley et al, 1989] describe an algebra word problem tutor that provides mathematical modelling tools, corrective help and feedback on errors. The tutor uses the model tracing paradigm, similar to that used in the LISP tutor [Anderson and Reiser, 1985].

The design of the tutor incorporates the following steps that a student has to take to solve a word problem:

1. Define the problem situation
2. Map the known quantities onto the problem situation
3. Generate constraints
4. Combine constraints
5. Solve the final equation

Defining the problem situation involves the representation of the qualitative relationships (referred to as the problem situation) between the various elements that constitute the problem. The next step is to map the known quantities onto elements of the problem situation. In the case of a diagrammatic representation, this would imply mapping the quantities with the corresponding constituents of the diagram and mapping the quantity to be identified or evaluated with a variable. Certain constraints, though not explicitly stated in the text of the problem, can be concluded as a consequence of information provided in the statement of the problem. In order to find the solution, an equation containing the goal variable is formed. Any unknown quantities contained in this equation are evaluated by generating additional constraints. The final solution to the problem is obtained when a relationship of the goal variable is created in terms of known quantities.

The approach the tutor uses is appropriate, in that it tries to break down the problem-solving process into different stages and guides the student through each one of these. The use of a menu of diagrams make the tutor recognition-based. We have used a similar approach, for teaching trigonometry word problems as described in section 4.2.3.

3 The Domain of Trigonometry

Students usually encounter difficulties in understanding trigonometry and solving problems in it. One of the reasons for this seems to be that trigonometry requires them to apply many of the geometrical and algebraic concepts they have learnt before. Secondly, they have to learn about a number of trigonometric ratios and their relationships. Lastly, they have to apply these concepts to a large variety of problems pertaining to various application areas. In many cases, for example in trigonometry word problems, they have to visualize the situation involved and create appropriate diagrammatic representations, map quantities on to the elements of the diagram and then solve the problem using various trigonometric relationships.

[Matz, 1982] points out that common errors in high school algebra usually arise because of one of the following two reasons:

- Inappropriate use of a known rule, for example in a new situation
- Incorrect adaptation of a known rule to solve a problem

Further she categorizes commonly observed errors as:

a) Errors generated by an incorrect choice of a technique
b) Errors reflecting impoverished (but correct) knowledge
c) Errors arising during the execution of a procedure

Similarly, errors and inefficient performance (not necessarily wrong) while solving a problem in trigonometry could arise because of:

- Incorrect choice of a trigonometric relation
- Insufficient application of knowledge of relationships
- Error in the execution of a procedure

For example, in the simplification of the expression

$$sin^2 30 + sin45/cos45 + cos^2 30$$

1. The term $(sin45/cos45)$ may be wrongly substituted as $cot45$ instead of $tan45$. Although both $tan45$ and $cot45$ have equal numerical values and may not affect

the final answer, such a substitution would be inconsistent with the relationships in trigonometry. In this case, the system would point out that $cot45$ would be an incorrect substitution for $(sin45/cos45)$

2. Actual substitution of values for $sin^2 30$ and $cos^2 30$ in the expression given above seems to indicate an inadequate knowledge of relationships. The value 1 could have been directly substituted for $sin^2 30 + cos^2 30$. In this case the system would give the student a hint saying that a trigonometric relation could have been made use of, instead of actually substituting values for sin and cos.

In addition, the following types of errors may also occur in trigonometry.

- Visualization of an incorrect diagram
- Incorrect mapping of information in the problem to the diagram

The reason for these errors, which occur typically in word problems, is normally due to a misunderstanding of the statement of the problem.

3.1 Task Analysis of Trigonometry

Learning trigonometry involves learning the following:

a) Definitions of the ratios - sin, cos, tan, cot, sec, cosec.
b) Relationship between trigonometric ratios.
c) Trigonometric ratios for 0, 30, 45, 60, 90 degrees.
d) Simplification of trigonometric expressions.
e) Solution of diagram problems and
f) Solution of trigonometric word problems.

In order to find out how students typically solve trigonometry problems and the types of errors they make, protocols of students who had just appeared for the ninth and tenth class examinations were recorded. The tenth class students had already learnt trigonometry in school, whereas the ninth class students had not. The ninth class students were, therefore, taught trigonometry before the experiment. These students were administered a test consisting of a set of problems and a think-aloud protocol analysis of their problem-solving was recorded.

The test consisted mainly of questions where the students had to use their knowledge of trigonometric ratios and the relationships between them, covering ideas a) and b) listed above. In general we found that,

a) The students tended to draw diagrams wherever possible and use them to help get the desired answer. For instance, in a problem where sin A was 5/13, most students would make the opposite side equal to 5 units, hypotenuse equal to 13 units and then compute the adjacent side. They would then use this side to compute cos A. None of them tried to use the relationship $sin^2 A + cos^2 A = 1$.

b) Most students would substitute the values for ratios and then simplify expressions instead of using relationships. For example, when they had to simplify sin A * cosec A they would not use the relationship cosec A = 1 / sin A, but instead would substitute the values for sin A and cosec A.

c) The other point we noticed was that students tended to use the relationships exactly in the form they had learnt them. None of them tried to symbolically manipulate the relationships. For example, if they had to simplify $1 - cos^2 A$, they would substitute $sin^2 A + cos^2 A$ for 1, instead of just writing $sin^2 A$. This may perhaps be due to inadequate practice in algebra. One student knew that $sin^2 A + cos^2 A = 1$, but did not quite understand why this was so. He said " I do not think it is correct " when asked about this relationship. Some of the problems we noticed may be because students do not understand the basis for the relationships they are using.

In addition, one or two candidates had problems in understanding notions like adjacent side and opposite side and seemed to confuse the two.

4 Details of the Tutor

In this section we briefly describe the various aspects of our tutor.

4.1 The User Interface

The system provides a menu-driven interface. In order to simplify interaction and reduce the number of errors, the student is provided with a trigonometric keypad for giving input. The keypad has an easy to use iconic interface and a display window in which the inputs selected by the user are displayed. The keypad consists of keys labeled with all basic trigonometric ratios, numbers and arithmetic operators. Using a mouse, a user can easily create any required trigonometric expression, in much the same way as one would use a calculator. The keypad also allows a user to modify expressions or erase what has been created so far. All interaction of the student with the tutor takes place through another window which serves as an interaction window. This window can be used to display messages from the system to the user and to obtain responses from the user (see Figure 2 for a sample display of the tutor).

4.2 Teaching Strategy

The tutor forces a student to solve a problem in stages and allows the student to ask for help whenever required. When the student is solving the problem, his input is evaluated at each stage. If the student makes an error, the mistake is pointed out and the student is allowed to modify his input or seek assistance from the system. When the student asks for help, the tutor responds from its own knowledge of how to solve the problem. The system can give various levels of help. The first level of help gives a student a hint on what he should do next in order to get closer to the solution. The next level of help would provide the student with a number of possibilities (for the next step) and allow the student to choose one. If the student still needs help, the system would specify

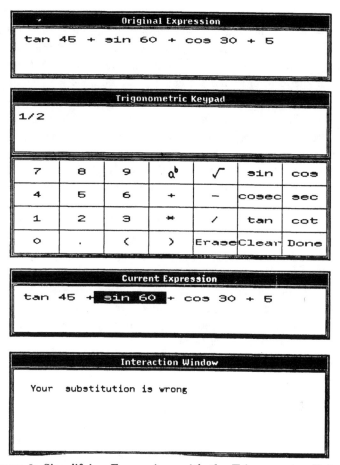

Figure 2: Simplifying Expressions with the Trigonometry Tutor

the exact relationship a student should use. If further help is sought the system would apply the correct relationship to the problem.

The tutor uses three different approaches for the three different categories of problems viz. simplification of trigonometric expressions, diagram problems and word problems. Each of these approaches are briefly described below.

4.2.1 Simplifying Trigonometric Expressions

When the student wants to simplify expressions, the tutor displays an expression in the display window of the keypad. The actual problem displayed will depend on the student's level of knowledge and the trigonometric relationships which are yet to be learnt. The user has the option to simplify the expression and/or substitute values for one or more terms in the expression. He can select the terms using the mouse and specify the substitution he wishes to make. The system checks the validity and correctness of the input and in case there are errors, the system displays a message in the interaction window.

When the student is selecting terms, the system has to check whether the terms which are selected are compatible (i.e. whether they can be combined together). For example, if the expression is $sin^2 30 + sin45/cos45 * cos^2 30$, and the user selects $sin^2 30$ and $cos^2 30$, they are not compatible. The representation that the tutor uses for expressions (which is in the form of a binary tree), allows us to check for compatibility fairly easily.

If the terms are compatible, the system asks the user what he wants to substitute for the set of terms selected. When the user specifies the value, the system first makes sure that none of the trigonometric relations are violated. For example, he is not allowed to substitute $sin45/cos45$ by $cot45$. If a relationship is violated, the tutor tells the student what is wrong with the substitution. Otherwise, it checks that the value substituted is equivalent to the value of the expression formed by the terms the user selected. If the value substituted is wrong, the system tries to determine possible mistakes a user could have made.

At any stage, the student can ask the tutor for help or ask it to complete the solution. The tutor will then solve the problem in a way similar to that of an ideal student. In this case the system uses one of the many alternate solution paths and solves the problem one step at a time. While simplifying the expression the tutor tries to come out with the most efficient solution, by trying to apply the trigonometric relationships before actually substituting values for each term.

4.2.2 Trigonometry Diagram Problems

In our tutor, there is a class of problems in which a diagram is displayed and typically one unknown quantity has to be computed. We call these *diagram problems*. The user has to apply trigonometric relationships and determine the value of the unknown. As far as the level of difficulty is concerned, diagram problems normally lie between simplification of expressions described earlier, and word problems which will be described in the next section. A sample diagram problem is shown in Figure 3.

Diagram problems are easier than word problems, because the user does not have to create a diagram or map quantities onto components in the diagram. However, the user has to determine the right relationship or set of relationships which have to be applied. These problems also form a stepping stone for the more complex word problems they will encounter later.

While solving diagram problems, the tutor can provide hints to enable the student to find the solution. Also, as in the simplification of expressions, the tutor can provide a step-by-step solution to the problem. An example of a diagram problem and the tutor's feedback is given in Figure 3. In this case,

- If the student asks for help, the tutor would provide the expression for the sine of an angle in a right-angled triangle

- If the student again asks for help, the tutor would give the statement of the

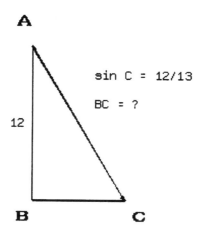

A

sin C = 12/13

BC = ?

12

B   C

Figure 3: An Example of a Diagram Problem

Pythagoras Theorem

- In case the student gives an incorrect answer, the tutor would indicate this and allow the student to try again or seek help

- If the student is still unable to give the answer, the tutor would give the appropriate answer.

4.2.3 Trigonometry Word Problems

Word problems are a major area where students have difficulties. It is often found that when students are given a set of equations or relationships, they are able to solve them in order to determine an unknown. However, if the same set of equations are camouflaged in the 'English' of a word problem, it is much harder to solve. In essence, it looks as if the most difficult part of solving a word problem is comprehending the problem, and determining which trigonometric relationships should be used. The trigonometry tutor tries to help the student comprehend problems by helping them recognize and use the correct graphical representation corresponding to the problem. The approach we use is similar to the Algebra Word Problem Tutor [Singley et al, 1989] described earlier.

The student is provided a few plausible diagrams out of which only one diagram is correct. The diagrams which are not correct are 'near misses' of the correct diagram and may correspond to the most common mistaken diagrams that students tend to use. Attached to each of the mistaken diagrams is a message which indicates why the diagram is wrong. Some of this information can be obtained from the protocol analysis of students.

Based on the analysis of mistakes generally made by students, the near-miss diagrams can be created by varying the correct diagram. This can be done by either changing the mapping of quantities to elements of the diagram or by perturbing the correct

Diagram 1

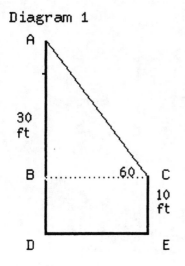

Diagram 2

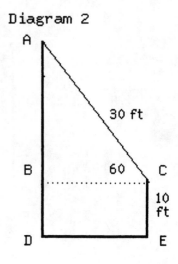

Diagram 3

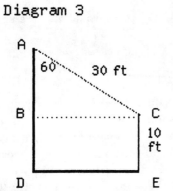

Diagram 4

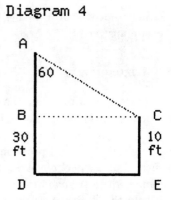

Figure 4: Diagrams Displayed for a Typical Word Problem

diagram. For example, in a triangle, the three angles and the three sides constitute the elements of the diagram. Mapping the quantities given in the word problem wrongly onto the corresponding elements would generate incorrect diagrams which are only slight variations of the correct diagram.

This method of providing diagrams with slight variations simplifies the problem as far as the student is concerned; the student just has to recognize the correct diagram, instead of having to create it. However, the student has still to determine what the unknown in the problem is and determine how to compute it.

After the student selects the right diagram, the tutor lets the student type a series of relationships which can be used to compute the unknown quantity in the problem. At each stage the tutor checks to make sure that the student is getting closer to the solution, and if not gives appropriate feedback. For example, consider the following word problem:

The angle of elevation of a tower 30 feet high from the top of another tower 10 feet high is 60 degrees. Find the distance between the towers.

The system displays the diagrams as shown in Figure 4 and asks the student to select the correct one.

If the student selects diagram 1 which is the correct diagram, the tutor indicates that his choice is correct and asks him to proceed with the computation of the unknown quantity. In the case of an incorrect diagram, a message is flashed indicating why the choice is incorrect. For example, if he selects diagram 3, the tutor would indicate that the angle of elevation is the angle ACB and that the height of the tower should be the length represented by the side AD of the triangle.

The procedure followed by the student after the selection of the correct diagram is then similar to the method used for trigonometry diagram problems.

5 Conclusions

We have described a tutor to teach trigonometry. We have presented a task analysis of trigonometry and described our approach to teach different classes of problems. At present, our tutor handles simplification of trigonometric expressions. We are in the process of implementing the other stages of the tutor (for diagram and word problems). After we complete that, we propose to conduct an experiment to evaluate the effectiveness of the tutor.

Acknowledgements

We are grateful to our colleague Mr KN Prakash, for his support during the initial stages of this work and his comments on an earlier draft of this paper. We would also like to thank Dr S Ramani for his comments and suggestions. We are thankful to Mr R Chandrasekar for his comments on the draft of the paper.

6 References

[Anderson, 1983]

Anderson, JR. *The Architecture of Cognition*. Harvard University Press, Cambridge, 1983.

[Anderson et al,1985]

Anderson, JR, Boyle, CF, and Yost, G. *The Geometry Tutor*. In Joshi, A (ed), *Proceedings of the Ninth International Conference on Artificial Intelligence*. Morgan Kaufmann Publishers, Los Altos, pp.1-7, 1985.

[Matz, 1982]

Matz, M. *Towards a Process Model for High School Algebra Errors*. In Sleeman, D and Brown, JS (eds), *Intelligent Tutoring Systems*, Academic Press, London, pp. 25-50, 1982.

[Nathan, Kintsch and Lewis, 1988]

Nathan, MJ, Kintsch, W, and Lewis, C. *Tutoring Word Algebra*. Technical Report No. 88-12, University of Colorado, Institute of Cognitive Science, 1988.

[Nathan et al, 1989]

Nathan, MJ, Johl, P, Kintsch, W, and Lewis, C. *An Unintelligent Tutoring System for Solving Word Algebra Problems*. In Bierman, D, Breuker, J, Sandberg, J (eds), *Artificial Intelligence and Education: Proceedings of the 4th International Conference on AI and Education, Amsterdam, Netherlands*, IOS Amsterdam, Netherlands, 1989.

[Anderson and Reiser, 1985]

Anderson, JR, Reiser, BJ. *The LISP tutor*. Byte, 4(10), pp. 159-175.

[Singley et al, 1989]

Singley, MK, Anderson, JR, Gevins, JS and Hoffmann, D. *The Algebra Word Problem Tutor*. In Bierman, D, Breuker, J, Sandberg, J (eds), *Artificial Intelligence and Education: Proceedings of the 4th International Conference on AI and Education, Amsterdam, Netherlands*, IOS Publishers, 1989.

[Weaver and Kintsch, 1988]

Weaver, CA, and Kintsch, W. *The Conceptual Structure of Word Algebra Problems*. Technical Report No. 88-11, Institute of Cognitive Science. University of Colorado, USA.

Knowledge Representation

Four General Representations and Processes for Use in Problem Solving

Dan Fass

Centre for Systems Science
Simon Fraser University
Burnaby, British Columbia, Canada V5A 1S6.
CSNET: fass@cs.sfu.ca

Abstract

It is argued that "knowledge representation" as normally understood is one of four very general constructs - two representations and two processes – which are commonly used in artificial intelligence (AI) research yet are largely unrecognised. These constructs mirror much of the "generate-and-test" strategy for problem solving in AI where competing solutions are generated and then tested to select the best one – except that one of the constructs, "coherence representation," is not present in the strategy. Examples of various problems are given that show uses of the constructs. Some implications for artificial intelligence research of the constructs, especially coherence representation, are discussed.

1 Introduction

A useful way to view artificial intelligence (AI) is that the central problem it addresses is problem solving [cf. Amarel, 1987], assuming the notion of "problem" is understood in broad terms as including planning, learning, reasoning – indeed, all the aspects of cognition addressed in AI. A common strategy for problem solving in AI is "generate-and-test" in which competing solutions (or part-solutions) are produced, the solutions are compared, and the best one is chosen. Knowledge representation is a major topic of study in AI [see, e.g., Barr and Feigenbaum, 1981; Cercone and McCalla, 1987; Mylopoulos and Levesque, 1983] and a good knowledge representation is generally regarded as vital to tackling any problem. I do not disagree with the importance of knowledge representation; however, it is my contention that "knowledge representation" is only one of four "constructs" of equal generality used in AI. An advantage of seeing AI through the four constructs is that, when compared to the generate-and-test strategy, three of the constructs match with explicit parts of the strategy (e.g., "generate") but a fourth construct does not. That construct is "coherence representation." Section 2 compares the generate-and-test strategy with the constructs.

In section 3, some examples are given of the uses of the four constructs, especially coherence representation. Three simple, common instances of problem solving are described – finding the shortest route between two places, determining the relatedness of pairs of concepts, and resolving lexical ambiguity in a sentence – and then the presence of the four constructs is shown in the problems. In section 4, the relationship of the four constructs to other work in AI is discussed

2 Generate-and-Test and the Constructs

To see why there are four constructs, let us inspect in more detail the generate-and-test strategy for problem solving mentioned in section 1. Like Amarel [1987, p. 767], let us assume a statement of a problem presented to an AI system as follows:

"Given a domain specification *D*, find a solution *x* such that *x* is a member of a set of possible solutions *X* and it satisfies the problem conditions *C*."

The generate-and-test strategy solves the problem statement *(D, X, C)* with the following entities:

"**1.** a domain database that implements *D*;

2. a generator based on some grammar *G(X)*;

3. a controller governed by control knowledge *CK* (which may depend on *C*);

4. a procedure *PRIOR(C)* for using the problem conditions *C* in an a priori mode to control *G(X)* and *CK*;

5. a procedure *POST(C)* for using *C* in an a posteriori mode to test and/or evaluate generated solution candidates; and

6. a working database where a record of solution construction activities is kept" [Amarel, 1987, p. 769].

The basic operation of generate-and-test consists of two main processes, *generate* and *test*:

"*Initialize.* Set the characteristics of *G(X)* and *CK* that depend on *PRIOR(C)*; direct *G(X)* to perform an initial solution-construction action.

Test. Examine, via *POST(C)*, whether the working database contains a desired solution; if yes, exit with success; otherwise, continue.

Generate. Direct *G(X)* to perform a solution-construction action based on the current state of the working database and in view of *CK*; if no action is possible ..., exit with failure; else, go back to the test step" (Ibid., pp. 769-770).

The role of knowledge representation in this strategy is to provide **1.** The knowledge representation supplies knowledge that is acted upon by the *generate* process that produces each competing solution to the problem. Then what happens in order to compare the solutions and select the best one? The generate-and-test strategy states that comparison and selection is the responsibility of just a *test* process, but I will attempt to show below that in case after case what looks like a single process is actually *a second representation* followed by *another process* so there are four basic representations and processes. To put this another way, knowledge representation is processed which results in competing solutions; this is *generate*, which I call "processing knowledge representation" because it is at least as self-explanatory, if not more so. To decide between the solutions, some value is produced for each solution which represents that solution. This second representation is what I call "coherence representation." Then those values are processed by comparing them and by using some metric to choose among these values and hence among the competing solutions; this is *test* or what I call "processing coherence representation."

3 Examples Using the Constructs

Let us now consider solving a simple problem in which the four constructs are used. The problem is to find the shortest route by road from Vancouver to Edmonton in Western Canada. A common form of knowledge representation in AI is a graph or network. Figure 1 is a network of some roads between Vancouver, Banff, Jasper, Calgary, and Edmonton. The node labels are the names of the towns and the arc labels are the distances in miles between them.

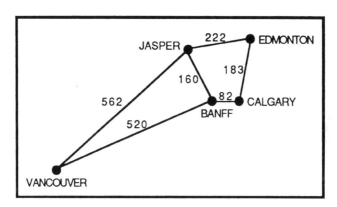

Figure 1. The constructs in solving a travel problem

An obvious way to solve the problem is to construct different routes from Vancouver to Edmonton, then compare the routes, and find the shortest one. If Figure 1 is used, the network is processed and competing solutions are generated. Each competing solution is a network path representing a route. These must be tested; that is, they must be compared and the "best" solution – the "shortest" network path – chosen. How are the alternatives compared? The answer is that the distance is found for each route and the route with the shortest distance is selected. Each distance is a value that represents its route; the value is the coherence representation for the route. When distances are compared – i.e., coherence representations are processed – the lowest distance is sought, hence the smallest value is chosen. The route represented by that value is the one selected.

Let us consider a second example of problem solving in which the constructs appear. The problem is to find which pair of a set of concepts are the most closely related. For this problem, the knowledge representation I will use is the frame, in which objects are described in terms of their properties. Frames are matched together using frame-matching algorithms which match together the properties represented in those frames. Frame-matching approaches have been used to handle problems such as learning [e.g., Winston, 1978], story understanding [e.g., Schank and Abelson, 1977] and other cognitive phenomena.

Figure 2 shows some simple frames for sharks, whales, tunas, and horses described in terms of their habitat and blood temperature. The problem to be solved is finding which two animals are the most similar. To solve this, comparisons need to be generated and tested between the animals in terms of similarities and differences in their habitat and blood temperature.

172

In Figure 2, each of the four constructs has a different graphical form. Knowledge representation is depicted by the chunky J-shapes, each shape indicating a frame. The diagram shows that every frame has an "arcs" section containing genus information about the concept being defined and a "node" section containing differentia information about the concept (in this case, the habitat and blood temperature). The two-element lists will be called "cells."

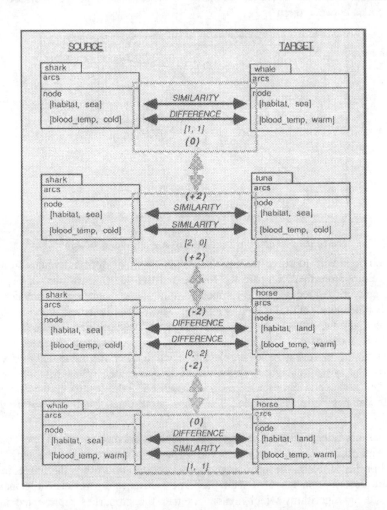

Figure 2. The constructs used in determining conceptual relatedness

Processing over a knowledge representation is indicated by the black horizontal arrows. When two frames are matched together, a conceptual relationship is generated between the pair of animals represented by those frames. When the cells from two frames are matched together in Figure 2, the match is categorised as either "same" or "different," indicated by the upper case words 'similarity' and 'difference' above the arrows.

Figure 2 shows two alternative forms of coherence representation. Both representations indicate the strength of conceptual relatedness between the animals being compared. In the two-element lists, the first number is the number of similarities found; the second is the number of differences. The bracketted numbers are the number of similarities less the number of differences found for each match. So, for example, the strength of relationship between 'shark' and 'tuna' is +2 whereas the strength of relationship between 'shark' and 'horse' is -2.

The processing of coherence representation is indicated by vertical grey arrows. Look closely at how the *test* process, as described by Amarel above, takes place in Figure 2. The conceptual relationships that have been generated – each one a comparison of two frames – are themselves compared *via their coherence representations*. Each coherence representation indicates the conceptual relatedness between two animals; the processing of two coherence representations compares their *relative* conceptual relatedness: two animals are more related than two others if the number indicating their strength of relatedness is compared and found to be higher than the number for the strength of relatedness of the others. Judging from the comparison of coherence representations in Figure 2, sharks and tunas are the most conceptually related.

For a third illustration of the four constructs and their use, let us consider how they can be used in solving the problem of resolving lexical ambiguity, a major problem in natural language understanding [see, e.g., Small et al, 1988]. Lexical ambiguity is a property of words that they can have multiple meanings or senses. For example, the word 'crook' has several different senses including a sense meaning "thief" and another meaning "shepherd's stick." Lexical ambiguity resolution is the problem of selecting the correct meaning of a word when that word occurs in a linguistic string (a clause, a sentence, etc.). Rather than construct a solution to the problem as in the previous examples, we shall examine how lexical ambiguity is resolved in Preference Semantics [Wilks, 1975a, 1975b, 1978], a pioneering theory in natural language understanding, and show how the four constructs underlie the theory.

The central idea of Preference Semantics is that of "preference" – choosing between rival, competing readings using a semantic density measure [see Fass and Wilks, 1983] – a kind of *test*. In Preference Semantics, preference is used to tackle a number of problems in language, including the resolution of lexical ambiguity, the resolution of anaphora, and the recognition of metaphor.

(1) "The crook ate the sandwich."

Let us suppose that 'crook' has the two senses given above, one meaning "a thief," the other meaning "a shepherd's stick," and then examine how Preference Semantics selects the correct sense of 'crook' in (1). All other words have a single sense, thus two readings are generated for (1): reading 1 contains crook1 (the thief) and reading 2 contains crook2 (the stick). Figure 3 shows the two readings and the tests – four semantic matches – that Preference Semantics performs to resolve the lexical ambiguity in (1). In each match there is a "source" which originates the matching process and a "target" to which the source is matched.

There are two sets of matches. One set of matches is between the verb stem 'eat' and senses of the noun 'crook'. The left hand side of Figure 3 shows the agent preference of 'eat', which is for 'animal', paired against the two senses of 'crook'. The preference 'animal' acts as the "source" of the semantic match and 'crook' is the "target" of the match. The second set of matches is between 'eat' and 'sandwich'. The right hand side of Figure 3 shows 'food', the object preference of 'eat', matched against 'sandwich'. Again the preference, 'food', acts as source and the target is 'sandwich'.

The graphical conventions in Figure 3 are the same as for Figure 2. Knowledge representation is again depicted by the chunky L-shapes, each shape indicating a frame. Processing over a knowledge representation is indicated by the black horizontal arrows. The upper case words above the arrows indicate three satisfied preferences and one preference violation found. In Preference Semantics, "satisfied" and "violated" preferences are found using a graph search algorithm that seeks paths on a hierarchically organised semantic network. Figure 3 shows that a graph search algorithm has performed the processing because the black arrows are between the arcs sections of two frames (semantic networks are commonly hierarchies of genus terms, and hence can be constructed from the genus terms in frames).

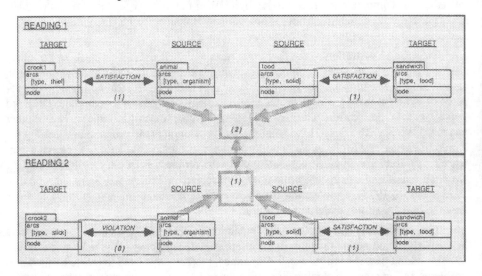

Figure 3. The constructs in resolving lexical ambiguity within Preference Semantics

Let us consider just the evaluation of those preferences that involve the two senses of 'crook', beginning with the satisfied preference of reading 1. There is a satisfied preference between the source 'animal' and the target 'crook1' (the thief sense) because in the semantic network of animals used by Preference Semantics, the network path found between 'animal' and 'thief', the genus term of 'crook1', indicates that 'animal' is the genus of 'thief'. The violated preference in reading 2 is because the path found between 'animal' and 'stick', the genus term of 'crook2', indicates that 'animal' is not a genus of 'stick'.

Coherence representation is indicated by the grey partitions in Figure 3. The numbers in brackets are how "satisfied" and "violated" preferences are signified in Preference Semantics: a one indicates a case of satisfaction and a zero indicates a violation. These numbers comprise a very simple coherence representation scheme.

Processing of coherence representation is indicated by the grey non-horizontal (i.e., angled and vertical) arrows. Of those arrows that indicate the processing of coherence representation, the grey two-headed arrows signify comparison between coherence representations, while the grey one-headed arrows indicate the input of information from one coherence representation into another. Note that in Figure 3 the way the two readings are tested is by comparing them *via their coherence representations*, as in Figure 2. To repeat, it is the processing of the coherence representations that enables the different semantic readings to be compared. Reading 1 has a score or "semantic density" of 2 and is preferred over reading 2, which has a semantic density of only 1, and hence resolves the lexical ambiguity in (1).

4 Discussion

With the three examples in the previous section, I have attempted to show that for a variety of problems tackled in AI, some kind of symbolic representation (i.e., coherence representation) is attached to each and every competing interpretation and then those symbolic representations are compared using some decision metric (i.e., processing coherence representation) in order to *test the interpretations*.

It is worth noting that, like *generate* and *test*, processing knowledge representation and processing coherence representation are in a kind of opposition because processing knowledge representation *creates* alternative solutions while processing coherence representation *eliminates* possible solutions. The opposition between the two kinds of processing is especially notable when the problem tackled is the resolution of ambiguity, e.g., the resolution of lexical ambiguity observed in Figure 3: processing knowledge representation creates the two readings while processing coherence representation chooses in favour of reading 1.

Something else worth remarking upon is that coherence representation is not the same as knowledge representation. The two kinds of representation contain different forms of information used in different ways for different purposes. Coherence representation contains information about how some solution "hangs together," "makes sense," or is "meaningful" as a result of the relationships between its constituent parts. Moreover, coherence representation has uses other than being part of some means of choosing between competing interpretations: it can be used to represent cognitive phenomena such as anomaly and metaphor, as we shall see shortly. Not much can be done with the "shallow" coherence representations used in AI theories such as Preference Semantics which uses single numbers (as we saw in Figure 3), but some other AI theories give an idea of the potential in deeper coherence representations.

One such theory is Gentner's [1983] structure-mapping theory which has been implemented in the structure-mapping engine [Falkenhainer et al, 1986]. The structure-mapping theory addresses what Gentner refers to as four "kinds of comparison." The kinds are literal similarity, analogy, abstraction and anomaly. In the structure-mapping theory, a frame-matching algorithm compares the information from two concepts represented as sets of properties in frame-like structures. Properties are either "attributes," one-place predicates like LARGE(x), or "relations," two-place predicates such as COLLIDE(x,y). The four kinds of comparison are distinguished by the relative proportions of attributes and relations that are matched, and the kinds of matches (i.e., structure mappings) established between them. This is perhaps the most novel aspect of the structure-mapping theory and the one that has drawn the most attention. In my view, the numbers of matched attributes and relations and the kinds of matches constitute the coherence between two concepts and could be readily described in a coherence representation, perhaps a more complex version of the two-element list structures shown in Figure 2. Such a coherence representation would then *represent* the four kinds of comparison.

Another theory which is already actively using deeper coherence representations is Collative Semantics (CS), implemented in a computer program called meta5 [see, e.g., Fass 1987, 1988a]. The main problems addressed by CS are lexical ambiguity and what I call "semantic relations." Seven kinds of semantic relation are distinguished: literal, metonymic, metaphorical, anomalous, novel, inconsistent and redundant relations. Meta5 analyses short sentences, discriminates the seven kinds of semantic relation between pairs of word senses in those sentences, and resolves any lexical ambiguity.

CS contains four components, two representations and two processes. The four components are instances of the four theoretical constructs. The coherence representation is called the "semantic vector." Figure 4 shows two semantic vectors produced by meta5 during sentence analysis. Basically, the vectors are like the simple coherence representations discussed in Figures 2 and 3 except that they contain more information. The array columns of the vectors represent various kinds of semantic matches found between pairs of sense-frames, the knowledge representation used in CS. Incidentally, the semantic vector to the left represents a metaphorical relation analysed by meta5 whereas the semantic vector to the right records a combination of literal and inconsistent semantic relations [see Fass, 1988b, 1988c].

```
[preference,                          [[preference,
   [[network_path,                        [[network_path,
      [0, 0, 0, 0, 1]],                      [1, 0, 0, 0, 0]],
   [cell_match,                           [cell_match,
      [[relevant,                            [1, 7, 0, 0, 0, 0, 7]]]],
         [0, 0, 1, 0, 0, 0, 10]],      [assertion,
      [non_relevant,                       [cell_match,
         [0,  3,  2, 0, 0, 2,  5]]]]]]]      [0, 0, 1, 0, 0, 0, 14]]]]
```

Figure 4. Two semantic vectors

5 Summary

The four constructs described in this paper are in effect the core of a general problem solving strategy applicable to a variety of problems in AI. The constructs include "coherence representation," a form of representation that differs from knowledge representation (as normally understood) and offers opportunities for modelling cognitive phenomena that have not proved amenable to description using conventional forms of knowledge representation. The four constructs, especially coherence representation, help in understanding better how the generate-and-test problem solving strategy works. The constructs also illuminate the operation of common mechanisms like that of Preference Semantics when tackling problems such as resolving lexical ambiguity, and hence throw light on how some quite general AI theories work.

6 Acknowledgement

This paper was written while on a postdoctoral fellowship sponsored by the Advanced Systems Institute of British Columbia and the Centre for Systems Science, Simon Fraser Univerity.

7 References

Amarel, Saul. Problem Solving. In Stuart C. Shapiro (Ed.) *Encyclopaedia of Artificial Intelligence*. New York, NY: John Wiley & Sons, pp. 767-779, 1987.

Barr, Avron, and Edward A. Feigenbaum. Knowledge Representation. *Handbook of Artificial Intelligence, Volume I*. Los Altos, CA: William Kaufman. Chap. III, pp. 141-222, 1981.

Cercone, Nicholas J., and Gordon McCalla (Eds.). *The Knowledge Frontier: Essays in the Representation of Knowledge*. New York, NY: Springer Verlag, 1987.

Fass, Dan C. Semantic Relations, Metonymy, and Lexical Ambiguity Resolution: A Coherence-Based Account. In *Proceedings of the 9th Annual Cognitive Science Society Conference*. University of Washington, Seattle, WA, pp. 575-586, 1987.

Falkenhainer, Brian, Kenneth D. Forbus, and Dedre Gentner. The Structure-Mapping Engine. In *Proceedings of the 5th National Conference on Artificial Intelligence (AAAI-86)*. Philadelphia, PA, pp. 272-277, 1986.

Fass, Dan C. An Account of Coherence, Semantic Relations, Metonymy, and Lexical Ambiguity Resolution. In Steven L. Small, Gary W. Cottrell, and Michael K. Tanenhaus (Eds.). *Lexical Ambiguity Resolution: Perspectives from Psycholinguistics, Neuropsychology, and Artificial Intelligence*. Los Altos, CA: Morgan Kaufmann, pp. 151-178, 1988a.

Fass, Dan C. Collative Semantics: A Semantics for Natural Language Processing. (PhD thesis.) Memorandum MCCS-88-118, Computing Research Laboratory, New Mexico State University, NM, 1988b.

Fass, Dan C. Collative Semantics: A Study in the Discrimination of Meaning. Technical Report CSS/LCCR TR 88-24, Centre for Systems Science, Simon Fraser University, Burnaby, BC, Canada, 1988c.

Fass, Dan C., and Yorick A. Wilks. Preference Semantics, Ill-Formedness and Metaphor. *American Journal of Computational Linguistics*, Special Issue on Ill-Formed Input, 9, (3-4), pp. 178-187, 1983.

Gentner, Dedre. Structure Mapping: A Theoretical Framework for Analogy. *Cognitive Science*, 7, pp. 155-170, 1983.

Mylopoulos, John, and Hector Levesque. An Overview of Knowledge Representation. In Bernd Neumann (Ed.). *Proceedings of the 7th German Workshop on Artificial Intelligence, Dassel/Solling, September 1983*. New York, NY: Springer Verlag, pp. 143-157, 1983.

Schank, Roger C., and Robert P. Abelson. *Scripts, Plans, Goals and Understanding*. Hillsdale, NJ: Lawrence Erlbaum Associates, 1977.

Small, Steven L., Gary W. Cottrell, and Michael K. Tanenhaus (Eds.). *Lexical Ambiguity Resolution: Perspectives from Psycholinguistics, Neuropsychology, and Artificial Intelligence*. Los Altos, CA: Morgan Kaufmann, 1988.

Wilks, Yorick A. A Preferential Pattern-Seeking Semantics for Natural Language Inference. *Artificial Intelligence*, 6, pp. 53-74, 1975a.

Wilks, Yorick A. An Intelligent Analyser and Understander for English. *Communications of the ACM*, 18, pp. 264-274, 1975b.

Wilks, Yorick A. Making Preferences More Active. *Artificial Intelligence*, 11, pp. 197-223, 1978. Reprinted in In Nicholas V. Findler (Ed.). *Associative Networks: Representation and Use of Knowledge By Computers*. New York, NY: Academic Press, pp. 239-266, 1979.

Winston, Patrick H. Learning by Creatifying Transfer Frames. *Artificial Intelligence*, 10, pp. 147-172, 1978.

Integrated Actor Paradigm
for
Knowledge Based Systems

BJ Garner   D Lukose

Department of Computing and Mathematics
School of Sciences, Deakin University
Geelong, Victoria,
Australia 3217

UUCP : {uunet,ukc,mcvax}!munnari!aragorn.cm.deakin.oz!{brian,lukose}
ARPA : {brian,lukose}%aragorn.cm.deakin.oz@uunet.uu.net

Abstract

The apparent lack of suitable active agent paradigms for Canonical Graph Models motivated the development of an integrated actor paradigm for the representation and manipulation of various types of knowledge. An actor paradigm called "Intelligent Control Script" has been designed and implemented for the representation and manipulation of both domain dependent and domain independent knowledge, including reasoning knowledge, strategic and control knowledge, and planning knowledge. The incorporation of semantic networks as the message carrier for the message passing mechanism extends the actor paradigm to complex knowledge processing. Complex control transfer mechanisms enable the actor paradigm to take full advantage of static schemes such as frames and Canonical Graph Models. Models exhibiting novel (dynamic) character have now been enabled and complex abstractions actualised for problem solving.

1 Introduction

The Artificial Intelligence (AI) community uses the term "ACTOR" while the term "OBJECT" is used by the Smalltalk [Goldberg and Robson, 1983; Tesler, 1981] community to describe a software engineering paradigm known as "anthropomorphic programming" [Pugh, 1984]. Object-oriented programming can be traced back to Simula [Dahl and Nygoard, 1966]. Substantial work on this paradigm was conducted by Carl Hewitt et al [Greif and Hewitt, 1975; Hewitt, 1969; Hewitt et al, 1973a; 1973b] in the early 1970's at MIT. Evolution towards a true actor model of computation comes mainly, however, from the development of Smalltalk by the Learning Research Group at Xerox PARC [Goldberg and Robson, 1983] and the ACT family of languages by Carl Hewitt and colleagues at MIT [Theriault, 1983].

More recently, research has been undertaken into an actor model of computation, mainly due to the inadequacy encountered in existing software engineering paradigms in A.I. research. The motivation for the development of an actor model or similar model of computation is to integrate various different types of knowledge encoded with different knowledge representation techniques. The requirement to represent factual, procedural and reasoning knowledge for "current value" programming for complex problems has been the principal motivation for the development of Intelligent Control Scripts at Deakin University [Lukose, 1987a; 1987c; 1987d; 1988].

The application and development of an active agent paradigm based on Intelligent Control Scripts (ICS) at Deakin University has enabled the representation and manipulation of meta-level knowledge for knowledge acquisition. The Conceptual Graph formalism [Sowa, 1984] offers a unifying knowledge representation scheme for AI applications. This is evident in the Canonical Graph Model (CGM) [Garner and Tsui, 1986; Tsui, 1988]. With the incorporation of an active agent paradigm to complement the CGM, both "current value" programming as well as "expectation driven" and "functional" reasoning for the knowledge acquisition process can be performed.

2 Actor Formalism

Various definitions of "**actor**" are encountered in the literature. A few of the definitions listed below outline the functions, characteristics and the knowledge represented by actors and their role in the knowledge engineering paradigm. John Sowa [Sowa, 1984] defines an actor as a "**process**" that responds to messages by performing some service and then generating messages that it passes to other actors. Timothy E. Nagle [Nagle, 1986] defines an active agent to be a "**capsule**" of knowledge with behaviour including self invocation, reproduction, self introduction and communication. John R. Puge [Puge, 1984] states that an actor or an object oriented system takes a view of a "**single entity**", and the actor or object is used to represent both data and procedures, while Hewitt et al [Hewitt et al, 1973b] states that an actor is an "**active agent**" which plays a role on cue according to a script.

One can answer a novice's question "**What is an actor ?**", by describing an actor as a small processor, defined solely by its behaviour, and characterised by its response to messages. The behaviour of an Actor System highlights its capabilities as well as the level of its implementation. The complexity involved in the implementation of such systems varies from simple objects with message passing capabilities to very complex objects with the ability to dynamically modify their methods without altering the generic functionality of the actors [Nagle, 1986]. The behaviour of an actor will include:-
 • self introduction;
 • posting a need for a service;
 • posting a response to a need;
 • posting a general notice;
 • behaviour locking mechanism (to manage its behaviour in a temporal domain).

Actors are entities that combine the properties of procedures and data (ie. knowledge) since they perform computations and save local state information. Communication between actors is through "**message passing**". All actions in an active agent paradigm are the result of message transfer between actors. Message passing is a form of indirect procedure call. Instead of naming a procedure to perform an operation on an object, a message is sent to an object. When an actor receives a message, it will first determine if it recognises the message for response purpose and if it does, the associated script, method or procedure is evaluated, and a response is relayed back to the sender of the original request (ie. only if necessary).

An important programming principle supported by "message passing" is data abstraction, which makes it possible to change the underlying implementation without changing the calling program. The active agent paradigm supports data abstraction because it has the mechanism for bundling together all procedures for a data type. An actor might respond to a set of messages to provide a certain facility. This set of related messages is called a "**protocol**". Protocol extends the notion of modularity (ie. reusable & modifiable as enabled by data abstraction subroutines) to polymorphism (ie. interchangeable pieces as enabled by message passing).

In an actor model of computation, actors are divided into two major categories: classes and instances. A class is analogous to type in procedural language. An instance is an actor that is not a class. The method and structure of an instance is determined by its class. For example, "John" is an instance of "person". Variables are used for storing state information. Most of the actor systems support two types of variables: **class variables** and **instance variables**. Class variables are used to hold information shared by all instances of the class, while instance variables contain information specific to a particular instance.

In the various knowledge representation formalisms, information is often represented redundantly with different uses of the same knowledge appearing in several places. Knowledge may consist of procedures, state change information and data together with its associated data structures. Substantial difficulty is encountered in representation and manipulation of procedural knowledge. An actor formalism provides both an encapsulation of declarative and procedural knowledge while enabling a unifying modularity through the use of the "**inheritance**" principle, which is highlighted in the frame system [Minsky, 1975]. In an actor model of computation, knowledge and behaviour can be acquired through inheritance (ie. objects defined in an "**isa**" hierarchy or "**class**" system). Objects can inherit "**scripts**" or "**methods**" or "**procedural knowledge**" or "**declarative knowledge**" from their parent object.

Inheritance enables specialisation. Specialisation uses class inheritance to elide information. Actors may be created dynamically for various functions without the need to store an impossibly large number. Polymorphism extends downwards in the inheritance network because subclasses inherit protocols from parent actors. In general terms, the main characteristics of an actor include:-

- the maintenance of a local body of knowledge;
- it can provide operations which allow other actors to interrogate and/or update its local body of knowledge;
- it owns its own local body of knowledge;
- it decides if and when other actors can access it;
- it decides when other actors should know of its existence.

3 Related Work

Active research (conducted by Carl Hewitt) for more than a decade to provide a concrete foundation for actor formalisms, actor semantics, actor induction and meta evaluation. Several actor based programming languages and reasoning systems have resulted from this pioneering work, including the ACT family of languages [Theriault, 1983] , the PLANNER system [Hewitt, 1969] and, the famous SMALLTALK programming language [Goldberg and Robson, 1983] from Xerox PARC. Our review of contemporary actor systems is biased towards the knowledge based formalism rather than an actor based programming paradigm.

The CONGENT system by Nagel et al [Nagle, 1986] provides a flexible invocation, self manipulation as well as reproductive behaviour and uses conceptual graphs [Sowa, 1984] for representing factual knowledge. They also serve as active templates to generate interpretation graphs of the data. Information and communication management is through the use of "basket", information blackboard and system level blackboard. The pragmatic, semantic and syntactic description of the actors is embedded in the actor using the three components listed below:-

- **knower** - pragmatic knowledge such as intention and focus of attention;
  - conceptual graph;
  - identifies agent to system;
  - specifies what agent can do;
  - specifies what agent is interested in hearing about.
- **knowing** - syntactics of knowledge such as form and structure expectations;
  - collection of knowledge;
  - specifies what to do, given conditions present when agent invoked.
- **known** - semantics or content of knowledge such as context and intentions of the knowledge;
  - collection of procedures;
  - to carry out the specific tasks outlined in the "Knowing".

Figure 1 depicts the conceptual framework of CONGENT. It utilises three related knowledge components (listed above) for reasoning. Apart from the flexible behaviour obtained from an actor paradigm, CONGENT also includes a robust algebra and a rich knowledge representation formalism based on conceptual graph theory [Sowa, 1984].

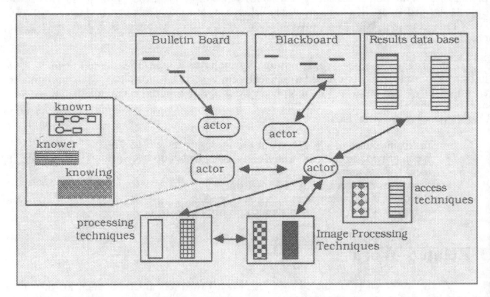

Figure 1: Conceptual Framework of CONGENT

John Sowa designed a network of actors to form "**dataflow graphs**" (DFG), which are finite, connected, directed, bipartite graphs with one set of nodes called "**concepts**"and the other set called "**actors**" as shown in Figure 2. "**Control marks**" on the graph are used to trigger the actors and compute referents for generic concepts (ie. direct the flow of computation). Control marks are drawn in the referent field after the colon. "**Assertion marks**" initiate a computation that starts at the input, while "**request marks**" initiate a goal-directed computation that starts from the outputs.

Roger Hartley [Hartley, 1985; 1986] attempted to elevate procedural knowledge to the same level as declarative knowledge. He defined actor type in the same way as concept type and relation type. Actors are used to compute referents or produce state change. An assertion mechanism is utilised to activate the actors. An example of an actor in this formalism is given in Figure 3.

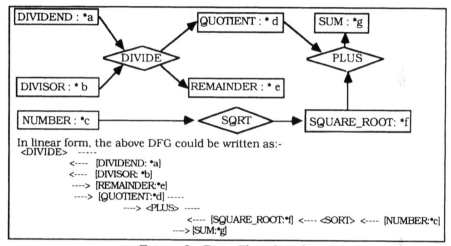

Figure 2: Data Flow Graph

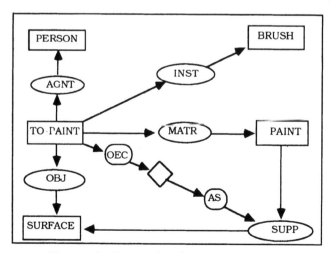

Figure 3: Example of Hartley's Actor

184

4 Alternative Approaches Considered

The main motivation for implementing an active agent (ie. actor) paradigm at Deakin University is the need to transform the static reasoning paradigm of the Canonical Graph Model (CGM) into a dynamic paradigm to enable **"current-value programming"** for the reasoning and planning process. Among others, the characteristics established now for the actor paradigm are **"reusability"**, **"extendibility"** and **"portability"**. Thus the main thrust is the development of an actor paradigm that can be utilised to implement many different problem solving applications as well as the integration of knowledge encoded in diverse knowledge representation schemes for the implementation of complex dynamic abstractions, similar to the **"Problem Map"** [Garner and Lukose, 1989].

There are two main approaches to the implementation of an active agent paradigm, in which the theory of conceptual graphs can be incorporated and utilised to its fullest advantage. The first framework involves embedding actors in conceptual graphs, similar to the approach taken by John Sowa [Sowa, 1984] and Roger Hartley [Hartley, 1985; 1986]. The second approach utilises conceptual graphs as the knowledge representation formalism, while adopting an object oriented method to implement the "actor" paradigm. This latter approach was adopted by Timothy E. Nagel [Nagle, 1986].

Both approaches have been reviewed at Deakin University for our purposes. In fact, we tested three different prototypes . The first system incorporated the procedural component of the actor into the conceptual graph formalism. This approach also involved the extension of the Canonical Graph Processor (CGP) [Garner and Tsui, 1986] to include two new functions called **"scan"** and **"execute"** [Lukose, 1987b]. These additional functions have the capability to perform a scanning process followed by the execution of the conceptual graph, if the graph is an actor. Within this approach, the method or the procedural knowledge is made up of various Canonical Graph Processor (CGP) and Knowledge Base Editor (KBE) scripts. It is similar to procedural attachment, but various limitations were identified, resulting in the abandonment of this approach. The principal limitations encountered were:-

- the underlying data structure for representing conceptual graphs is limited for the incorporation of procedural knowledge;
- considerable overhead is involved in preprocessing the actor before execution;
- the variables used in the script are fixed, thus there is no flexibility to allow the manipulation of a dynamically changing conceptual graph.

An alternative approach was thus considered. This approach defines a "procedural attachment" for each of a selected subset of type labels in the knowledge base [Garner et al, 1987]. The procedural attachment represents the control knowledge associated with a type (ie. class) and can be triggered to perform reasoning on graph(s) when required. This approach involves the maintenance of a **"status table"** concerning the actors, to represent the generic and specific information about the status of all actors. The complex processing involved and the difficulty in maintaining the "current-values" associated with each actor are the main limitations of this approach.

Using the experience gained in the above experiments, a third approach has been developed. It incorporates many of the techniques identified in the above two approachs, but is based on the conceptual graph as the knowledge representation and manipulation formalism without restriction on the object-oriented design for the actor paradigm. This unifying actor paradigm is known as Intelligent Control Script (ICS).

5 Intelligent Control Script System

The Intelligent Control Script (ICS) incorporates the benefits from the conceptual graph formalism of John Sowa as well as the actor formalism of Carl Hewitt. Conceptual graphs, particularly Canonical Graph Models, provide a rich knowledge representation and manipulation paradigm, while actor formalism provides modularity, knowledge and method inheritance, together with the capability to dynamically create and destroy actors.

A unifying data structure has been designed for the actors. An improved message carrying capability, mainly for knowledge passing has been developed, and complex control transfer mechanisms provided to enable the actor to manipulate and evaluate knowledge structures using the existing Canonical Graph Models. ICS has been implemented in Melbourne University Prolog.

5.1 Actor Data Structure

The proposed data structure for representing the actors has to be able to represent state change information, methods, and be able to handle incoming and outgoing messages, together with the capability to transfer control to various components of the Canonical Graph Model. In general , the data structure should enable the representation and manipulation of both procedural and declarative knowledge , while dealing with the idiosyncrasyies of an actor paradigm.

The adopted data structure consists of three sub-structures known as "**nomenclature**", "**basic structure**" and "**extension structure**". Figure 4 depicts an actor, while Figure 5 depicts the associated data structure. The "**nomenclature**" sub-structure is basically used as an actor identification sub-structure. The "**basic structure**" is utilised for storing information (ie. knowledge) which does not alter throughout the life of the actor, while the "**extension structure**" is used to store the methods and information that alters when the actor is activated. This component will also handle the incoming and outgoing messages.

The "**nomenclature**" is made up of "**actor name**" and "**actor identifier**". We define both the "**actor identifier**" and "**actor name**" to distinguish actors with the same name, since every actor will have a unique "**actor identifier**".

The "**basic structure**" consists of "**long term memory**" and "**default routine location**". The "**long term memory**" is used to represent various information which does not alter during the life of the actor. This information is usually in the form of expertise (ie. expert knowledge) available to the actor. The "**default routine location**" is a memory space where default procedural knowledge is stored. These routines are automatically executed when the actor is invoked. These routines are beyond the control of the actor's message handler.

The "**extension structure**" is made up of three sub-structures called "**message handler**", "**short term memory**" and "**method location**". Each actor may have more than one method associated with it. Each method is invoked by a different message. The "**message handler**" has the task of associating the incoming messages to the methods in the actor. Thus the "**message handler**" consists of a set of messages (ie. protocol) and pointers to the associated methods. Actor model of computation is also known as current value computation. The values of its variables alter throughout its life. The variables are stored in the "**short term memory**". The "**method location**" is where all the methods associated with the actor are

186

stored. The **methods** in ICS are encoded either as a "**prolog function**", "**script**" made up of CGP or KBE scripts, or a combination of both.

The ICS paradigm is based on class - subclass hierarchy. There are two types of actors. One is called the class actor and the other is the instance actor. The class actor has a data structure shown in Figure 5, while the instance actor has a data structure as in Figure 6.

5.2 Instance Actor Data Structure

As with every actor paradigm, ICS can handle instances of classes. An example of a class actor is "**person**". "**john**" is an instance of class "**person**". Here "**john**" will have all characteristics of "**person**", with some additional information which is particular to "**john**". In the ICS paradigm, there is no limit to the number of instances which may exist for a particular class.

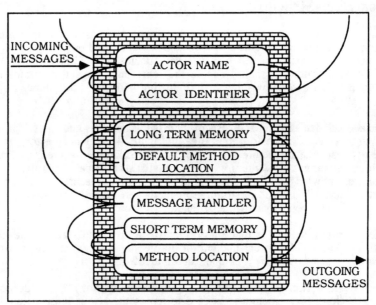

Figure 4: Structure of an Actor

```
icsobject( <ics name>,
            basic_structure( long_term_memory([ ], <LTM identifier>),
                             defaultrtn([ ])
                           ),
            extension_structure( message_handler([<message pattern>,......]),
                                 short_term_memory([ ]),
                                 methods([<method>,.......])
                               ),
            <icsidentifier>
          ).
```

Figure 5: Data Structure of a Class Actor

The data structure for an instance actor differs considerably to that of the class actor, because the instance actors need only maintain the information that is particular to it. There is no need to replicate the generic information about its class in each of the instances. The instance data structure is made up of two sub-structures called the "**nomenclature**" and "**subextension structure**", as depicted in Figure 6.

The "**nomenclature**" consist of "**instance name**", "**instance identifier**" and "**instance-class link**". The "**instance-class link**" contains information which links an instance to a class. The "**subextension structure**" consist of the "**short term memory**" which is a copy of the "**short term memory**" of its class. Only the names of the variables are obtained, not the values of the variables.

```
instance( isa_instance ( <instance name>,
                         <classname>,
                         <instance identifier>,
                         <localreg([ ], <local reg identifier>)>
                       ),
          short_term_memory([ ], <stm identifier> )
        ).
```

Figure 6: Data Structure of an Instance Actor

5.3 Control Transfer Mechanisms

The control transfer mechanism has been implemented to enhance the capability of the ICS. This mechanism complements the flexibility of the method to take full advantage of the various components of the CGM. Five different sub-mechanisms make up the whole control transfer mechanism. They are the CGP Control Transfer, KBE Control Transfer, GPIE Control Transfer, and QG Control Transfer. QG (ie. Question Generator) is a new addition to the CGM. A description of QG is beyond the scope of this paper.

These mechanisms allow the transfer of control between various different components of CGM to enable the reasoning and problem solving process to take place. Control Transfer Mechanisms have enabled the construction of complex scripts (ie. methods in the actors).

5.4 Message Passing Mechanism

The nerve system of the ICS is the Message Passing Mechanism. The message packet is made up of two components. The first is the name of the actor that is going to receive the message, while the second component is the message itself.

As the whole system is written in Prolog, the message carriers are "prolog facts". The message carrying capability of ICS has been enhanced by the incorporation of a semantic network as the message carrier. Thus, one can represent the message as a conceptual graph [Sowa, 1984], and transmit it to the destination actor.

6 Application Paradigm

The overall conceptual framework for ICS is depicted in Figure 7. This paradigm was constructed to aid my research work on "Goal Interpretation" [Lukose, 1989] and Knowledge Acquisition [Garner and Lukose, 1989].

ICS is utilised to construct dynamic abstractions, one of which is the "**Problem Map**" [Garner and Lukose, 1989]. ICS is the underlying tool for the work on "Goal Interpretation as a mechanism for Knowledge Acquisition". "Problem Maps" are made up of various actors representing "goals". Each actor contains both the declarative and procedural knowledge related to the "goal" which it is representing. Strategic knowledge is utilised to determine which of the actors in the "problem map" should be executed. The execution of the actors, guided by the strategic knowledge, will attempt to solve problems within the scope of the "Problem Map". The case study in knowledge acquisition is concerned with "The Selection of Candidates by Deakin University College".

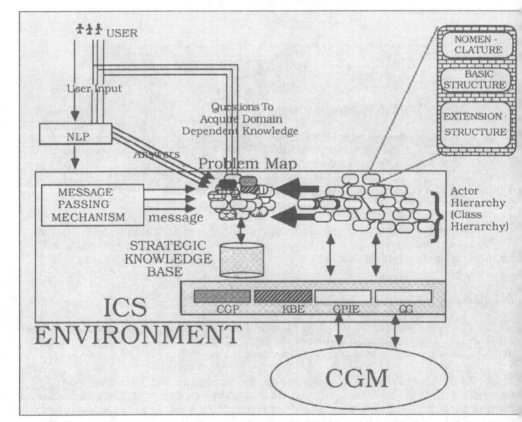

Figure 7: The Overall Structure of the "Knowledge Acquisition System"

7 Conclusion

The development of a computational paradigm such as the Intelligent Control Script (ICS) permits the manipulation of both declarative and procedural knowledge dynamically. The actor paradigm and associated control transfer mechanisms, when complemented with sophisticated message carrying capabilities, have permitted the construction of novel models (e.g. PROBLEM MAPS) for the solution of appropriate applications. The significance of this research lies not only in the paradigm for constructing complex abstractions for problem solving, but also in the generic characteristics of these complex models and the consequential insights into knowledge representation issues for knowledge engineering.

Acknowledgement

D. Lukose is supported by CRS Scholarship in Artificial Intelligence.

References

[Dahl and Nygoard, 1966]
Dahl O-J., & K. Nygoard, SIMULA - An Algol-based Simulation Language, CACM, Vol 9, No 9, pp 671-678, 1966.

[Garner et al, 1987]
B.J. Garner, C. Chong, A. Jiramahasuwan, D. Lui, D. Lukose & E. Tsui, Actor Implementations in Cybernetic Reasoning Systems, 2nd Annual Conference on Conceptual Graphs, IBM Paris Scientific Center, Paris, September 2-4, 1987.

[Garner and Lukose, 1989]
B.J. Garner & D. Lukose, Goal Interpretation as a Knowledge Acquisition Mechanism, to be presented at the International Conference on AI in Industry and Government, Hyderabad, India, November 23-25, 1989.

[Garner and Tsui, 1986]
B.J. Garner & E. Tsui, An Extendible Graph Processor for Knowledge Engineering, Applications of AI III, John F. Gilmore, Editor, Proc. SPIE 635, pp 415-33 (1986).

[Greif and Hewitt, 1975]
I. Greif & C. Hewitt, Actor Semantics of PLANNER-73, 2nd. ACM Symposium on Principles of Programming Languages, pp 67-77, 1975, Palo Alto, Calif., USA.

[Goldberg and Robson, 1983]
A. Goldberg & D. Robson, Smalltalk-80, The Language and its Implementation, Addison-Wesley, 1983.

[Hartley, 1985]
R.H. Hartley, Representation of Procedural Knowledge for Expert Systems, Proceedings of the IEEE Conference on Artificial Intelligence Applications, December 11-13, 1985, Miami Beach, Florida.

[Hartley, 1986]
   R.H. Hartley, The Foundations of Conceptual Programming, First Annual Rocky Mountain Conference on Artificial Intelligence, Boulder, Colorado, 1986.

[Hewitt, 1969]
   C. Hewitt, PLANNER: A Language for Proving Theorems in Robots, IJCAI-69, Washington D. C., May 1969.

[Hewitt et al, 1973]
   C. Hewitt, P. Bishop, I. Greif, B. Smith, T. Matson, R. Steiger, Actor Induction and Meta-Evaluation, paper presented at the ACM Symposium on Principles of Programming Languages, Boston, Massachusetts, October 1-3, 1973, pp 153-168

[Hewitt, Bishop and Steiger, 1973]
   C. Hewitt, P. Bishop, R. Steiger, A Universal Modular ACTOR Formalism for Artificial Intelligence, IJCAI-73, Stanford, August 1973.

[Hewitt and Lieberman, 1984]
   C. Hewitt, H. Lieberman, Design Issues in Parallel Architectures for Artificial Intelligence , Digest of Papers Compcon Spring '84, 28th IEEE Computer Society International Conference, pp 418-423EEE Comput. Soc. Press, Silver spring, MD, USA, 1984.

[Lukose, 1987a]
   D. Lukose, Active Agent Paradigm, Internal Report 87/1, Department of Computing and Mathematics, School of Sciences, Deakin University, Geelong, Victoria, Australia, 3217, May 1987

[Lukose, 1987b]
   D. Lukose, CGP Command "Scan" and "Execute", Internal Report 87/2, Department of Computing and Mathematics, School of Sciences, Deakin University, Geelong, Victoria, Australia, 3217, May 1987

[Lukose, 1987c]
   D. Lukose, Intelligent Control Script, Internal Report 87/3, Department of Computing and Mathematics, School of Sciences, Deakin University, Geelong, Victoria, Australia, 3217, May 1987

[Lukose, 1987d]
   D. Lukose, Active-Agent Paradigm for Conceptual Structures, Internal Report 87/5, Department of Computing and Mathematics, School of Sciences, Deakin University, Geelong, Victoria, Australia, 3217, Sept 1987.

[Lukose, 1988]
   D. Lukose, Set Script for the Manipulation of Conceptual Structures, Internal Report 88/3,Department of Computing and Mathematics, School of Sciences, Deakin University, Geelong, Victoria, Australia, 3217, Aug. 1988.

[Lukose, 1989]
   D. Lukose, Some Goal Interpretation Issues, Presented at the Workshop on "Creativity in Knowledge Acquisition", 13th July, 1989, Melbourne, Australia.

[Minsky, 1975]
   M. Minsky, A Framework for Representing Knowledge, in The Psychology of Computer Vision, edited by Patrick Henry Winston, McGraw-Hill, New York, 1975.

191

[Nagle, 1986]
T.E. Nagle, Conceptual Graphs in nn Active Agent Paradigm, paper presented at the IBM Workshop on Conceptual Graphs, 18-20th August, 1986, Tornwood.

[Pugh, 1984]
J. R. Pugh, Actors - The Stage is Set, SIGPLAN Notices, v19 #13, March 1984, pp 61-65.

[Sowa, 1984]
J. F. Sowa, Conceptual Structures - Information Processing in Mind and Machine, Addison Wesley, Reading, 1984.

[Tesler, 1981]
L. Tesler, The Smalltalk Environment, BYTE, August 1981, pp 90-147.

[Theriault, 1983]
D. Theriault, Issues in the Design and Implementation of ACT2, Technical Report 728, MIT AI Lab., June 1983.

[Tsui, 1988]
E. Tsui, Canonical graph Model, Phd Thesis, Department of Computing and Mathematics, School of Sciences, Deakin University, Geelong, Victoria, Australia, 3217, 1988.

A representation for modeling functional knowledge in geometric structures

Amitabha Mukerjee

Department of Computer Science
Texas A&M University

Abstract

Most geometric models are quantitative (half-spaces and transformations), making it difficult to perform the kind of abstraction needed to model the underlying functional knowledge. Typically, users have used ad hoc subjective notions to perform this abstraction, which we call the "get-beneath-the-geometry" syndrome.

In this work we describe a systematic representation scheme that builds spatial maps based on local relations between objects. It derives relations that are more "functionally relevant" - i.e. those that involve accidental alignments, or can be described based on such alignments. The principal advantages of this representation in building functional descriptions is that

    a) it is free of subjective bias,
    b) it is complete in the qualitative sense of distinguishing all overlap/ tangency/no-contact geometries.

In addition, the model is capable of handling uncertainty in the initial system (e.g. "the fuse box is somewhere behind the compressor") by constructing bounded inferences from disjunctive input data. Two kinds of uncertainty can be handled - those arising from deliberate imprecision in the interest of compactness ("down the road from"), or those caused by an inadequacy of data (sensors, spatial descriptions, or maps).

The representation is an extension to two and higher dimensions of the one-dimensional interval logic [Allen 83]. In orthogonal domains, this extension is straightforward, but a new non-commutative algebra has been developed for handling angular relations.

Keywords: Spatial reasoning, path planning, knowledge representation, natural language generation.

1. INTRODUCTION

In this paper, we present a systematic method for extracting meaningful symbolic descriptions from geometric data. For example, in order to analyze the flow behavior in a pipe system, it is first necessary to establish the interconnections between various pipes and valves, their relative height, inclination, and flow directions. Conventional geometric modeling systems can represent this information with great precision, but the problem of reasoning requires a measure of abstraction which is difficult to obtain from these large databases of geometric coordinates.

Very often, one assumes that this problem can be solved somehow, and the input to the model is a list of carefully chosen symbolic descriptors. The difficulty of this problem has long been known [McCarthy 77, epistemological problem 4]:

> "A robot must be able to express knowledge about space, and the locations, shapes and layouts of objects in space. Present programs treat only very special cases. Usually locations are discrete - block A may be on block B but the formalisms do not allow anything to be said about where block on B it is, and what shape space is left on block B...A formalism capable of representing the geometric information that people get from seeing and handling objects has not, to my knowledge, been approached."

While we have moved some distance away from the traditional blocks world ON(A,B), the basic issue addressed in this excerpt still remains a fundamental problem. In practice, the descriptive vocabulary is usually chosen using some insights into the particular process, and often involves some trial-and-error.

1.1 What is functionally important?

This paper is concerned mostly with spatial representation itself, rather than with any particular application. A new and powerful representation is developed that can be used to describe and infer geometric relations under conditions of complete or partial information. The principal thrust is to describe positions relative to other objects, as opposed to descriptions in terms of global coordinates. Such descriptions arise naturally in human spatial reasoning, and many cognitive models are based on some particular orientation of the viewer [Shepard 80] or in relation to other objects (e.g. "behind the tree") [Dennett 75].

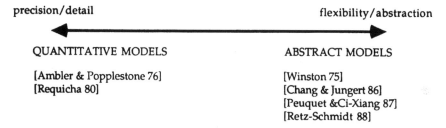

precision/detail   flexibility/abstraction

QUANTITATIVE MODELS   ABSTRACT MODELS

[Ambler & Popplestone 76]   [Winston 75]
[Requicha 80]   [Chang & Jungert 86]
                                       [Peuquet &Ci-Xiang 87]
                                       [Retz-Schmidt 88]

Figure 1. Given two objects, their position and orientation with respect to each other can be described either in terms of a series of numbers (coordinates), or in terms of some less quantitative measure (e.g. "cross the Safeway store and veer right at the fork"). The two descriptions involve a tradeoff between precision/detail and flexibility/abstraction.

The formal representation developed here can describe one, two, and three-dimensional models, involving orthogonal or angular relations. In the past, abstract spatial relations in orthogonal domains have been considered in the blocks world [Winston 75], in geographic data systems [Chang and Jungert 86], and in natural-language generation [Retz-Schmidt 88]. In all these instances a vocabulary has been selected carefully so as to be able to describe the relevant issues for the problem at hand; little attention has focused on the issue of vocabulary generality.

Our approach differs from these prior attempts in that we obtain the set of spatial primitives based on a categorization of all possible configurations that are qualitatively distinct; this is the sense in which it is *complete*. The concepts that we focus on involve tangency - Are the given objects are aligned at some face, line, or point? If not, then where is one object with respect to the other? At the same time, there are spatially relevant concepts such as "near" and "far" which we cannot model, since these are both in the same qualitative category (no-contact). Figure 2 shows some examples to illustrate the importance of this kind of reasoning in human thinking.

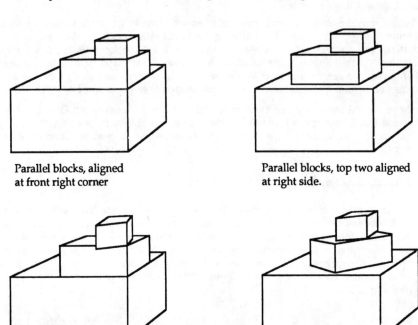

Parallel blocks, aligned
at front right corner

Parallel blocks, top two aligned
at right side.

Top block not parallel, but
aligned at front right corner

No parallel blocks, no alignment

Figure 2a: These arrangements of blocks are distinguished by the accidental alignments between face, edge, and vertices. Usually, such alignments indicate a functional aspect: either the alignment was artificially created, or it is the result of some physical process in accordance with physical laws. For example, along the z-axis, all the objects shown have a face tangency relation, indicating the physical reality of support. In addition to alignments, the other issue that is immediately apparent is that of size - in all three images, the blocks are graded in size.

Figure 2b: A number of psychological tests bear witness to the fact that the human cognitive process emphasizes accidental alignments. A well known example is that of the hexagonal cube, where the accidental alignment precludes us from seeing the three-dimensional shape.

One of the more useful aspects of this representation is the ability to model uncertainties in the description of the model - situations where the spatial knowledge is not precise enough to quantify through coordinates. Two kinds of uncertainty can be handled - those arising from deliberate imprecision in the interest of compactness ("down the road from the laundry"), or those caused by the inadequacy of data (resolution or storage limits in sensors, spatial descriptions, or maps). In most of these instances, bounded inferences can be made despite the uncertainty involved.

Another significant motivation behind a formal theory of spatial relations is to provide an objective set of spatial primitives, so that one can remove the influence associated with selecting the predicates used in a spatial inference system (e.g., in learning arches, "touches" is more important than "overlaps"). At the same time, a formal representation, by providing a known domain over which it is complete, unburdens the designer of many of the problems involved in ensuring that his/her vocabulary is powerful enough to describe all the possible descriptions that can arise. We present an example later of machine learning based on this representation.

In order to define a systematic approach towards this abstract yet comprehensive representation, we begin by identifying the qualitatively different aspects of the relative positions of two objects in space, i.e. the basic vocabulary of binary spatial relations.

2. ONE-DIMENSIONAL RELATIONS : INTERVAL LOGIC

Let us first consider objects along a single dimension. This case has been investigated in depth in the study of time. We consider here only one of the formalisms proposed, the interval logic model [Allen 83] in which relations are typically defined only between locally related events.

The description predicates are chosen by a simple, comprehensive process. To start with, we realize that objects in one-dimension can be either points or intervals. Also, we assume that the points are ordered along some direction, which may be due to a physical fact (e.g. time), due to some abstract notion (e.g.positive numbers), or some object feature (e.g.direction of motion). There are three possible cases for relations between two objects A and B:

   i) *Both A and B are points.* In this case there can be only three relations - A can be behind B (-), it can be the same point as B (=), or it is ahead of B (+).

   ii) *A is a point and B is an interval.* In this case, there are five qualitatively distinct cases: A is behind B (-), A is at the same point as the back of B (b), A is inside B (i), A is at the front of B (f), and A is ahead of B (+).

   iii) *Both A and B are intervals.* This is the most interesting case, and has been dealt with in some detail in the study of temporal events [Allen 83]. In general thirteen relations are possible. These are discussed below.

In the two-interval case, if we consider the front boundary of an interval C (the front boundary is a point), then this point can be either before, inside or after B. In addition, there are two more cases of interest - coincidence with either the front or the back boundary of B. So there are 5 regions of interest for the front of C, which can be labeled as above: +, f, i, b, - (ahead, front, interior, back, and behind respectively). Corresponding to these five, there are a total of thirteen (5+3+3+1+1) positions for the back boundary of C. The relation between two intervals C and B can then be expressed for example, as C (++) B, which would mean that C is *after* B. These relations are shown along the left hand margin of Figure 3.

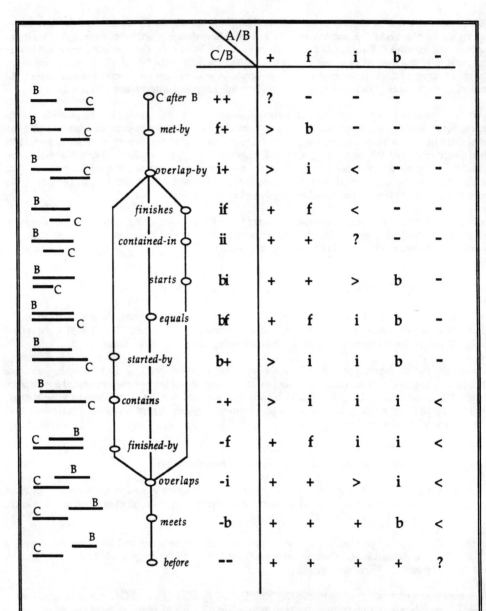

C/B	A/B	+	f	i	b	-
C after B	++	?	-	-	-	-
met-by	f+	>	b	-	-	-
overlap-by	i+	>	i	<	-	-
finishes	if	+	f	<	-	-
contained-in	ii	+	+	?	-	-
starts	bi	+	+	>	b	-
equals	bf	+	f	i	b	-
started-by	b+	>	i	i	b	-
contains	-+	>	i	i	i	<
finished-by	-f	+	f	i	i	<
overlaps	-i	+	+	>	i	<
meets	-b	+	+	+	b	<
before	--	+	+	+	+	?

Figure 3. One-dimensional interval relations and the transitive inference table. The diagrams on the left show the relations between the intervals C and B as C moves leftwards from "after" B to "before" B. The graph next to it shows the progression of relations during the movement; the three branches in the continuum represent the cases where C is longer than, equal to, or shorter than B. The table on the right shows the relationship of the point A with respect to the interval C if the relations of both A and C are known with respect to another interval B. The symbol ? denotes that the relation A/C can be any of the five possible relations, > implies that A/C can be one of {i,f,+}, and < implies that the relation is in {-,b,i}.

Given the local relations between "neighboring" intervals [Allen 83] shows that transitive relations can be used to derive indirect relations that are often disjunctive. The inference relations shown above are more compact than Allen's (5x13 instead of 13x13) since they exploit the independence between the two ends of an interval. For example if A was an interval and we knew that A was *overlap-by* B (A/B = i+) and that C *starts* B, (C/B = bi) then we can conclude based on the table above that with respect to C, the rear end of A is > or {i,f,+} and the front end of A is +. Therefore the relation A/C is either i+ (*overlap-by*), f+ (*met-by*), or ++ (*after*). This establishes a constraint in the possible positions of A with respect to C, which can be exploited, for example, in the map direction generator applications shown below.

Another benefit of this decomposition is the ability to clearly identify the continuum that exists between relations. This is shown in the elongated vertical graph in the figure. C is initially ahead of B (++), and as it moves towards B, it intersects B, and can have relations along one of three branches, e.g., if C is smaller than B, then only the relations {if, ii, bi} are possible. This notion allows us to compare and represent the relative size of objects, which is an important qualitative distinction. Thus if we define a flush-translation operator ϕ for moving A until it is flush with B, then by observing the relation between ϕA and B one can determine whether A is longer, equal or shorter than B.   Another benefit of the continuum concept is that it lets us define a measure for inductive bias in learning (see section 5).

3. MULTI-DIMENSIONAL SPACES : ORTHOGONAL DOMAINS

One-dimensional interval logic can be easily extended to multi-dimensional cases where each object is either oriented with the axes, or is enclosed in a box which is so oriented (if the axes are orthogonal, then the box becomes a cuboid). Now we represent the relations along each of N axes as one element in a N-dimensional relation. For objects that are not rectangular, one can associate a "front" direction, which can be used to determine the enclosing rectangle.

In this logic, the "atomic element" is the triple (X,Y,reln), where X and Y are objects with finite extent in each dimension and reln is a n-vector each element of which is in the set of one-dimensional relations outlined above. The "disjunctive element" is the triple (X,Y,complex-reln), where complex-reln is an n-vector where each element is a disjunction from the same relation-set. The interpretation for this syntax is fairly straightforward. Figure 3 shows an example of a transitive inference.

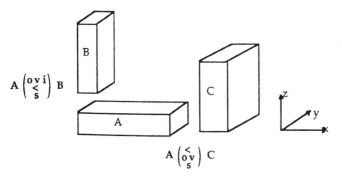

Orthogonal Relations in three dimensions. From the position shown, one can infer that

$$B \begin{pmatrix} c,f,o\,v\,i,m\,i,\overset{<}{>} \\ s,=,si \end{pmatrix} C$$

This inference can be reached by independently applying the interval logic rules to each dimension.

Figure 4. Given the three-dimensional atomic relations (A,B) and (A,C), we can transitively obtain the disjunctive relation (B,C). Here we have used a more compact notation due to Allen; e.g. ovi is overlap-by, < is before, mi is met-by, etc. Note that in the orthogonal domain, the relation (A,B) has clearly defined inverses: e.g. if A (ovi) B, then B (ov) A. The lack of such an inverse in the angular case implies that it is necessary to use both the forward and inverse relation in making inferences.

Orthogonality arises quite "naturally" in human thought (e.g. left, right, front, back, east, north). One problem is that each object often has a different "natural" orthogonal system, so that no one representation can model all of them. Another significant problem is that for non-aligned objects, the rectangular enclosures often overlap when the actual objects are disjoint.

The system is actually more powerful than appears at first. By adding operators into our system, many qualitatively interesting questions can be answered. For example, let us consider a reflection operator ρ which reflects the object about a +45 degree line through its bottom left corner. Now, by comparing ρA with A, one can answer a query of the form "Is it a square?". Earlier we introduced a flush-translation operator; by repeating translations equal to an object's own dimensions, we can define a "integer-multiple" vector operator λ; e.g. $\begin{pmatrix} 2\lambda \\ 3\lambda \end{pmatrix}$ A would imply a rectangle twice as large as A in x and thrice as large in y, and with the same bottom left corner. This can be used, along with the flush-translate operator described earlier to compare the relative sizes of two objects: "A is three times as large as B in x". Even more complex questions can be answered. For example, we can compare A with $\rho \begin{pmatrix} 2\lambda \\ \lambda \end{pmatrix}$ A to establish if "the aspect ratio for A is greater than 2 or less than 1" (this compares the x-dimension against both the y-dimension and its double). It is clear that even concepts such as near and far can be actually represented in terms of this language.

4. OBJECTS WITH ARBITRARY ANGLES

When objects are not oriented orthogonally, relationships become more complex. One of the primary problems is that the relationships are no longer meaningful with respect to some absolute coordinate frame but must be expressed in terms of one object or the other. ("The road veered to the left". It did not "make an angle of 25.77 degrees to the 59th parallel of longitude"). Unfortunately space does not permit a detailed discussion of the issues here; somewhat more detail is available in [Mukerjee and Joe 89]. We limit ourselves to a brief sketch of the basic structure.

In the past, [Peuquet and Ci-Xiang] have considered a similar problem for map-based query systems. A notion of 45 degree cones is used to analyze verbal relationships. The representation is somewhat ad hoc, and chosen with a very specific function in mind. Our model on the other hand, is a comprehensive mapping of the relations between two objects at an angle, in the qualitative contact sense. Since angular relations of B w.r.t A are dependent on A's direction, which is generally not related to B's direction, the operators in this formalism are non-commutative and do not have well-defined inverses, i.e., given the relation (A,B), the (B,A) relation cannot be determined.

Let us consider the relations with respect to a single object A, which has a designated front. This defines four angular quadrants with respect to A, and the "front" for the other object may be oriented in any of these quadrants. It turns out that relations between objects in certain quadrants are interdependent so we need to model the algebra for two quadrants only. Using the fact that the lines of support of B divide those of A into several "zones" (-,b,i,f and +), we have developed the complete transitivity relations for each of the cases for both the distinct quadrants. Unfortunately the limited space in this paper precludes further discussion of this topic; the interested reader is referred to the technical report cited above. Let us now flesh out the concepts developed with two application descriptions.

5. SAMPLE APPLICATIONS

5.1. Application one: Path Planning / Process Flow

Path planning involves some level of abstraction from the underlying geometry. The key element in this abstraction involves preserving the connectivity relations between features such as roads and buildings. We assume that roads and buildings are approximated as orthogonal segments. Connectivities between neighboring features are extracted from natural language queries or from quantitative data. These are then used to construct a set of binary spatial relations between neighboring objects which constitutes the search space, and contains all the access information embedded in the original map. Note that the paths found will be minimal in terms of the number of roads, but cannot be minimal in terms of path length since the planner has no information about path lengths. A similar effort is the CITYTOUR project [Retz-Schmidt 88], which is a natural language query handler for spatial maps, but makes no attempt to plan paths.

Roads can have properties associated with it (express-way,.., dirt-road) which modulate the search process. Given a graphical representation of a map as shown in Figure 5, two-dimensional binary relations are created between all adjacent objects as well as some neighboring ones (e.g. two side roads from the same main road). Since all features in the model is orthogonal, it suffices to maintain two orthogonal relations - a X component and a Y component.

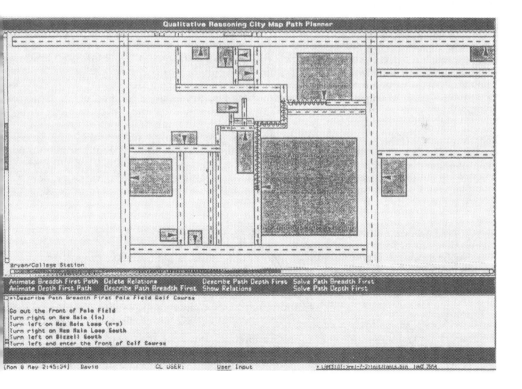

Figure 5. A screen from the City Map path planner with a part of the Texas A&M University campus and showing a path found between two locations. The lower window contains some natural-language like directions.

Before a model that has been derived from a quantitative city map can be used for path planning, the spatial relations must be checked for validity. In our domain, one precondition for validity is that no building can intersect another building or a road. The following predicate formulation in this logic can be used to ensure that every relationship in the model passes the no-intersection condition:

no-intersection rule: $(\forall x)(\forall y)\{ \sim x \begin{pmatrix} INT \\ INT \end{pmatrix} y \}$

where INT = {-i, bi, ii, -f, bf, if, -+, b+, i+}, and implies a degree of overlap.

The no-intersection rule prohibits two objects from overlapping in both axes. Note that the INT relation is like a hierarchical abstraction for the nine relations it represents - a generalized overlap. Such relation clusters can be used to create hierarchical concepts for higher level abstractions.

The path planning paradigm can be extended to pipe flow, circuits and similar flow systems. In the more general case we would consider the same map as before with directionality attached to the paths. In one application, this allows us to determine all possible flow paths between any two elements and enables us to determine suitable locations for valve positioning, for example.

5.2. Application two: Spatial Learning

The vocabulary developed above provides a powerful tool for acquiring concepts about spatial structures since it can describe *all* the qualitatively different combinations for any spatial structure. This capability has been demonstrated in a robot/teach pendant setup for recognizing the structure of geometric assemblies (with a overhead camera to obtain the part geometry information). Three-dimensional structures are created using the teach pendant and these are identified by the user as positive or negative examples. The system then obtains the underlying concept behind the examples shown.

For structures that have only geometric attributes (e.g. blocks world arches and tables, alphabet characters), it is possible to acquire the concepts from a set of positive examples alone. In our implementation we used a modified version space algorithm for very cautious learning, which required a number of negative examples also. Since this algorithm is well known to be slow but methodical, the concept was acquired but only after a large number of examples (approx. 60 for the arch concept).

Using this vocabulary for acquiring spatial concepts raises two important issues. First, since the vocabulary is comprehensive in the qualitative sense, the programmer is assured that all concepts that can be defined in such a domain can indeed be expressed in the language. In other words, the system has little or no representation bias. Thus the program will work for a wide range of concepts, and is less brittle than representations such as [Winston 75].

The second issue, which is really the other side of the same coin, is that because there is so little representation bias, the hypothesis space (the number of possible concepts) is very large indeed - for n objects, $O(13^n)$ relations are possible. This manifests itself in the large number of examples needed to learn a concept. Thus, again for the arch concept, many fewer examples are needed if one uses the notation of [Winston 75].

There is, however, a unifying approach. Due to the great expressiveness of the representation, it is possible to formulate powerful "inductive bias"es for learning. Inductive bias can be thought of as the "leaps of faith" that enables quick, but possibly incorrect learning. Typically, inductive bias is controlled by expectations for the behavior of the system. Thus here one could use inductive bias to conclude, for example for the arch, that if A *overlap* B and A *contained-in* B are both valid rules, then the in-between relation (see fig.2) is also a valid rule: A(-i, bi, ii)B are all valid constructs, and A(bf, -f, -+, b+)B, etc., are invalid rules (since A is on the smaller-than-B branch of the continuum).

Another capability inherent in the system is building commonsense theories for explanation-based learning. The representation allows one to define "naive" notions such as the need for support against gravity, and that solids cannot physically intersect (see the no-intersection rule above).

$$\text{gravity rule:} \qquad (\forall x) \{ \ \sim\text{Lies-on-floor}\ (x) \ => \ (\exists y)\ y \begin{pmatrix} \text{INT} \\ \text{INT} \\ \text{meets} \end{pmatrix} x \}$$

In essence, the gravity rule states that if an object A is not lying on the floor, then there must be some other object such that it overlaps A in the x and y directions, and meets it in z. Similarly the no-intersection rule stated earlier (extended to three dimensions) prohibits two objects from overlapping in all three axes. Note that the INT relation {-i, bi, ii, -f, bf, if, -+, b+, i+} is a hierarchical abstraction for the nine relations contained in it. As an illustration of the power in the representation, we note that many similar conceptual clusterings are possible, for example: A smaller-than B = {bi,ii,fi}; touch-contact = {-b, +f}; no-contact= {++, --}; flush-overlap = {-f, b+, bi, if}, etc. Such clusters can be used to constrain the hypothesis space for learning.

Rules like gravity and no-intersection allow for easy acquisition of concepts such as that of the arch, staircase, T-shapes, etc. In the case of non-physical structures, such as alphabet recognition, heuristic notions such as spatial domain for each alphabet can also be defined using similar predicates.

6. CONCLUSION

In this paper we have presented a spatial representation scenario that is useful for extracting symbolic representations from geometric models. It can be used to represent relations in any dimensions for objects that are aligned to the reference frame. For objects at arbitrary angles, the methodology has been developed for two dimensions, and higher dimensions appear to be possible but have not been investigated in full yet.

The essence of this logic is that it preserves the information of contact, no-contact and tangency. Given two objects, one can determine if they are flush along some face or line, and this contains all the information required to identify accidental alignments and relative positions of objects. Such relations, which describe the properties at the boundaries of an object, are critical in the analysis of many systems such as VLSI, circuits, mechanisms, structures - indeed almost anywhere geometrical relations are important. The representation has been applied to a model for city maps, and also to a concept learning scenario. It is capable of learning a large variety of spatial structures, modeling inductive bias, and generating representing powerful commonsense notions for building explanations.

At this point it would be appropriate to note that clearly there are a number of spatial relations of interest that cannot be represented well using this mechanism. One such instance is that of "near" or "large", which require some degree of quantitative information which this model does not provide for, although one can extend the logic with the notion of operators that would permit one to model such attributes also. However, it must be realized that for these two predicates at least, there is considerable ambiguity involved in the semantics, and to model these may introduce a degree of arbitrariness that would defeat one of the principal objectives of this work. More precise definitions can be obtained by representing concepts such as these as a predicate in terms of the translation and rotation operators, which are mentioned briefly above.

In conclusion, we have discussed a simple yet powerful mechanism for representing the spatial relations between objects. This technique offers expressive power and logical transitivity, and is capable of dealing with imprecision in the spatial knowledge.

References

[Allen 83]

Allen, James F., Maintaining knowledge about temporal intervals, Communications of the ACM, vol.26(11), November 1983, pp.832-843.

[Ambler and Popplestone 75]

Ambler, A.P., and R.J. Popplestone, Inferring the positions of bodies from specified spatial relations, Artificial Intelligence, v.6:129-156.

[Chang and Jungert 86]

Chang, S.K., and Jungert E., A spatial knowledge structure for image information systems using symbolic projections, IEEE Fall Joint Computer Conference, 1986, pp. 79-86.

[Dennett 75]

Dennett, David C., Spatial and temporal uses of english prepositions - an essay in stratificational semantics, Longman Group, London 1975.

[Peuquet and Ci-Xiang 87]

Peuquet, Donna J., and Zhan Ci-Xiang, An algorithm to determine the directional relationship between arbitrarily-shaped polygons in the plane, Pattern Recognition, v.20(1):65-74, 1987.

[Mukerjee and Joe 89]

Mukerjee, Amitabha, and Joe, Gene, Representing spatial relations between arbitrarily oriented objects, Proceedings of the Second International Conference on Machine Intelligence and Vision (MIV-89), Tokyo, April 1989, p. 288-291. (also available TR 89-017 from Texas A&M University, Department of Computer Science).

[McCarthy 77]

McCarthy, John, Epistemological problems of artificial intelligence, Proceedings IJCAI-77, Cambridge MA, 1977, p.1038-1044.

[Retz-S chmidt 88]

Retz-Schmidt, Gudula, 1988. Various views on spatial prepositions, AI Magazine, Summer 1988, p. 95-105.

[Winston 75]

Winston, Patrick Henry, 1975. Learning structural descriptions from examples, The Psychology of Computer Vision, ed. Patrick Henry Winston, McGrawHill, 1975, p.157-209. (Also reprinted in "Readings in knowledge representation", ed. Ronald J. Brachman and Hector J. Levesque, Morgan Kaufman, 1985).

[Requicha 80]

Requicha, A.A.G., Representation for Rigid solids: Theory, methods, and systems, ACM Computer Surveys, Dec. 1980.

[Shepard 80]

Shepard, R.N., Multidimensional scaling, tree-fitting and clustering, Science, vol.230, pp.390-398.

Differing Perspectives of Knowledge Representation in Artificial Intelligence and Discrete Event Modeling

*Ashvin Radiya**   *Robert G. Sargent***

*School of Computer and Information Science
**Simulation Research Group
Syracuse University
Syracuse, NY 13244, USA
radiya@top.cis.syr.edu   rsargent@top.cis.syr.edu

Abstract

In several subfields of Artificial Intelligence (AI) and in Discrete Event Modeling (DEM) there is a need to represent temporal and causal relationships in a problem domain. Some of these formalisms of AI and DEM are presented and compared. Most of the AI formalisms are beset by the frame, qualification, and/or ramification problems. DEM formalisms which can be viewed as formalisms for temporal and causal reasoning are not beset by these problems. They, however, in general, lack a formal theory. The Propositional Discrete Event Logic L_{PDE} which avoids the characteristic problems of AI formalisms and which also gives a formal theory to DEM is briefly discussed. Examples illustrating the use of this logic are given.

1 Introduction

Temporal and causal reasoning plays an important role in knowledge representation formalisms for dynamic systems. The need to represent temporal and causal relationships in a problem domain arises in several subfields of Artificial Intelligence (AI) such as expert systems, planning, prediction tasks, and qualitative reasoning, and in Discrete Event Modeling (DEM). In this paper, we restrict our discussion to the discrete event models commonly known as discrete event simulation models and refer to the languages used to express them as DEM languages which are commonly known as discrete event simulation languages. The existing formalisms in both fields are inadequate on several accounts. Most of the formalisms in AI for expressing temporal and causal reasoning are beset by the frame, qualification, and/or ramification problems [MH69, Sh86, GS88, AI84] which are defined below. Most of the these formalisms are some type of logics which are frequently computationally intractable. Their effectiveness has yet to be well established. On the other hand, DEM has been widely used for analyzing and understanding complex problems; particularly in the field of operations research. The infamous frame, qualification, and ramification problems do not exist in DEM formalisms. Most of the DEM languages for representing (discrete event) models are developed by extending existing procedural programming languages. They lack formal semantics and only a few have a formal syntax.

Although, the origins, approaches, and nature of temporal and causal knowledge representation formalisms of AI and DEM are different, the tasks are very related. Both fields can benefit from a critical comparison of the knowledge representation formalisms used in them. One of the problems in comparing concepts developed in disjoint fields is the multiplicity of terminology emanating from quite different application contexts. In the following, while discussing a formalism in a particular field, the definitions of different terms that seems to be the most acceptable in that field are used. In section 4, new terminology is defined and the relationship among various definitions introduced earlier is established.

The rest of the paper is organized as follows. In section 2, some of the temporal and causal reasoning formalisms in AI are discussed. In section 3, the essential temporal and causal elements implicit in the DEM formalisms are discussed. In section 4, the logic L_{PDE} [Ra90] is briefly discussed. In section 5, it is demonstrated that the characteristic problems of AI formalisms do not occur in the logic L_{PDE}. In section 6, examples illustrating the use of this logic are given. Section 7 is the summary.

2 Temporal and causal reasoning in AI

Most of the formalisms for temporal and causal reasoning in AI are related to either situation calculus [MH69] or temporal logics. These formalisms are beset by the frame, qualification, and/or ramification problems. As will be shown below, these problems exist because of the particular concepts of state and action used in these formalisms. In AI, other formalisms have been developed to overcome some of these problems (see, for example, [GS88, Mc86, Sh86]); they are not considered, here, because (1) our interest is in showing why these problems exist in the first place, (2) these new formalisms are still deficient in some ways such as computational intractability, and (3) the essential concepts in these new formalisms are similar to those in situation calculus. These problems are first discussed with reference to situation calculus. Then it is demonstrated that they also occur in temporal and causal reasoning formalisms based on temporal logics.

Situation calculus [MH69] is one of the earliest formalisms for representing and reasoning about actions and causality in a problem domain. The concepts of situation, condition (also called propositional fluent), and action are central to situation calculus. A *situation* is the complete state of the universe at an instant of time [MH69]. It is assumed that the world is in one of the situations at a particular instant in time. Let *Sit* be the set of all possible situations. A condition is a formula in a suitable logic that can be evaluated to truth or falsity with respect to a given situation. Actions are essentially viewed as functions from *Sit* to *Sit*. However, an action is not specified by giving a particular function from *Sit* to *Sit* but it is characterized by giving axioms of the form: $f_1 \supset f_2 \, (result(\alpha))$. This axiom asserts that the condition f_2 is **t** in the resulting situation of an action α occurring in a situation in which the condition f_1 is **t**. The conditions f_1

and f_2 are also called precondition and postcondition of an axiom, respectively. Note that an action can occur over a time interval. An example of an action is *a–bookcase–is–moved–from–one–location–to–another* [GS88] and of an axiom characterizing this action is – clear(x) $\supset$ in(bookcase, x) (*result*(move(bookcase, x))) – which asserts that if the position x is clear in situation s then bookcase is in the position x in the resulting situation of the action of moving the bookcase to x occurring in the situation s. In this approach, causality in a problem domain must be specified by giving axioms characterizing the effect of every possible action occurring in every possible situation. There are numerous difficulties that arise when one considers the task of expressing causality in situation calculus and the related formalisms.

To specify axioms characterizing an action, it is necessary to have axioms for not only what has changed but also for what has remained the same in the resulting situation. This has been referred to as the *frame problem* – that is the problem of specifying not only what is different but what is similar in the resulting situation. For example, a separate axiom characterizing the action move(bookcase, x) is necessary to infer that if in(vacuum_cleaner, y) is t in situation s then it is also t in the situation *result*(move(bookcase, x))(s). Also, the axioms of an action must completely characterize the resulting situation. This leads to what is called the *ramification problem* [Fi87] – that is one has to specify all the possible consequences of an action. For example, if a table is moved from location A to another location B then one needs to assert that after the completion of the action, every book on the table is at location B, every page of all the books on the table is at location B, and so on.

Another problem is that one has to check infinitely many preconditions if one wants to claim logically the conditions that are true in the resulting situation of an action. This is called the *qualification problem*. For example, to logically assert the postconditions of the action move(bookcase, x), one must examine the preconditions such as who is attempting to execute the action, how heavy is the bookcase, etc. Also, conditions such as a bomb is not going explode next to the book case while the action move(bookcase, x) is being carried out have to be examined in order to assert the postconditions of the action. Situation calculus is also deficient in that simultaneous actions cannot be directly modeled. One cannot describe the result produced by two actions initiated in the same situation because each axiom's postcondition characterize the resulting situation due to an occurrence of a single action (see, however, Gregoff [Ge86] who extends situation calculus so this can be done).

Several interval–based temporal logics have been developed to avoid some of the problems in situation calculus. E.g., Allen [Al84] and McDermott [MD82] have put forth logics that can represent simultaneous actions, also, called events. However, the frame problem still persists as one cannot describe that an action does not affect some property or another action; e.g., it is not possible to state that moving a table does not affect the property that a vaccum cleaner is in the corner. The ramification problem also persists if the effects of actions are to be described in utmost detail. The qualification problem is not relevant in these formalisms as one cannot represent that an action can occur only under certain conditions. Some logics have been developed to overcome the deficiencies in these interval–based formalisms, e.g., [Sh86]. Others have been developed to make an existing logic more expressive in the sense that in the proposed logic the truth of a formula can be asserted at different temporal elements like intervals (e.g., [Mo83]) and moments (e.g., [AH87]). These formalisms will not be considered here for the reasons similar to those mentioned earlier for not considering other formalisms developed to overcome problems in situation calculus.

3 Temporal and causal reasoning in DEM

DEM and simulation are considered to be practitioners' tools. For a general introduction see, e.g., [Kr86]. Formal logics have not been developed for expressing discrete event models. The only major theoretical work in DEM is that of Zeigler [Ze76] which uses the general system theoretic approach. The existing approach to defining a DEM language is to specify the syntax and the algorithm, called the time flow mechanism, for interpreting simulation programs to advance simulation along the simulation clock time. Most DEM languages are developed by extending an existing procedural programming language. Additional features are contained in them to aid in representing models of real systems. Real systems are characterized by being intrinsically concurrent and by the fact that real clock time can be associated with their activities. The DEM languages have a simulation clock time and contrary to real systems DEM languages are sequential in nature.

The commonly accepted view is – "A model an 'appropriate' representation of structures and processes of a miniworld, ... [Kr86]." It is claimed here that (representations of) models are theories for specifying (partial) causality in a problem entity. The idea that one is identifying and defining causality in a problem domain when one is constructing a (discrete event) model of a system is not wide spread. In DEM, causality is defined in terms of state, state–changes, events, and actions. A *state* is a collection of variables, which will be called state variables, and their values representing the relevant information about the system. A *state–change* is a subset of state variables and their values. An *event* is a fundamental entity which can be said to occur or not occur at a point in time. The events are grouped into a finite number of *event types*. The concept of action is not explicitly defined in DEM world views. The implicit concept of *action* is a function from states to states. Actions can be specified by giving algorithms or programs in a procedural programming language. Unlike the actions in AI formalisms, the actions in DEM occur only at points in time and are represented by giving functions on states. A *model* consists of a set of causal rules.

Different forms of causal rules specify different ways in which state, state–changes, events, and actions must be related. A particular way in which these entities are to be related provides a strategy which can be employed to think about a problem entity and to organize modeler's knowledge of the problem entity's essential features. This is what is known as a world view. The three major world views of DEM are event scheduling, activity scanning, and process interaction world views. Overstreet [Ov82] has analyzed these world views and identified time, state, and object–centered localities. In the following we first present the common DEM semantic assumption and then the essential temporal and causal elements of different world views.

DEM makes numerous assumptions at the semantic level and about the nature of a system that can be modeled. The implicit assumptions of DEM includes (1) the number of event types is finite, (2) the number of event occurrences of an event type over a bounded time interval are finite, (3) the state of a model which consists of variables and their values is finite, (4) the state of a model can change only at finitely many time points in any bounded time interval, and (5) a condition (as defined in section 2) for the occurrences of a sequence of actions is finite.

In event scheduling world view (ESWV), the causal rules are called event routines which specify causal effects of every possible event occurrence of the event routine's event type. One event routine is defined for every event type. Causal effect of an event occurrence must consist of state–changes to be made at the time of the event occurrence and a set of (possible) future event occurrences caused by it. The future event occurrences that are caused by an event must be determined by referring to simulation clock time. It is further assumed that the causal effect of any event occurrence depends only on the state at the time of the event occurrence. Thus, an event routine is specified by giving a function which returns state–changes and a set of (possible) future event occurrences given a state (at the time of an event occurrence).

In activity scanning world view (ASWV), the causal rules are called activity routines which specify causality by relating events, conditions on state, and actions. An activity rule specifies a sequence of (instantaneous) actions in the future, referred to by simulation clock time, that occurs whenever the condition of the rule is satisfied. This is somewhat similar to causal rules in situation calculus. Due to the finiteness assumptions of DEM, the problems of situation calculus do not arise in ASWV formalism. Activity routines may also refer to event occurrences.

In Process interaction world view (PIWV), the causal rules are called process routines which specify causality by relating events, conditions on state, and actions in a different way than that of ASWV. The general form of the causal rules is that a sequence of (instantaneous) actions is associated with event occurrences. Unlike ASWV and ESWV, the sequence of actions associated with an event type can refer to the future either by referring to simulation clock time or by referring to a condition on state. Process routines can be thought of as specification of processes. The PIWV is basically a combination of ESWV and ASWV formalisms.

Two other relevant issues in DEM are event canceling and the stochastic nature of models. In DEM, there is a need to cancel a previously scheduled event occurrences because it is required that the finitely many future event occurrences or actions that are caused by an event occurrence must be determined from the state at the time of the event occurrence. This may not always be possible. For the stochastic nature of models, there are two major reasons as follows. First, it is not always possible or desirable to determine the causality of event occurrences of certain event types. Second, for certain event occurrences it may be possible to identify other causally related event occurrences but it may not be desirable to model the "exact" time interval between the event occurrences. In such cases the time interval between two causally related event occurrences is modeled by a probability distribution. See [RS89] for examples.

4 The Propositional Discrete Event Logic L_{PDE}

As shown in the sections 2 and 3, the concepts of state, action, event, and causality are different in AI and DEM formalisms. A new logic called Propositional Discrete Event Logic L_{PDE} is defined in [Ra90] for the primary purpose of formalizing DEM. The approach to designing the logic L_{PDE} has been developed by analyzing some of the logics in philosophy and AI and the underlying semantic assumptions and semantic theory have been developed by analyzing the essential temporal and causal elements of DEM. Causality in a problem entity can be expressed in the logic L_{PDE} using the concepts of snapshot, action, instantaneous description, and static description.

4.1 Semantic concepts

DEF: A *snapshot* is a description of some of the nontemporal aspects of a problem entity at a time point.

What is to be included in a snapshot depends on the purpose for which the knowledge base about the problem entity is being created. Here we consider only the propositional case. Let P be the set of propositions. A snapshot is a finite theory, i.e., a finite set of formulas in the classical propositional logic on the set of propositions P. From the analysis of DEM formalisms it follows that the set of propositions P must be partitioned into the two disjoint set of propositions, $\dot{P}$ and $\overline{P}$. The set $\dot{P}$ is the set of instantaneous propositions and $\overline{P}$ is the set of static propositions.

DEF: A proposition p is a *static (instantaneous) proposition* iff p can be associated with a truth value at different points in time and (not) over different time intervals.

An example of instantaneous proposition is *a–customer–arrives–at–the–bank*. Instantaneous propositions correspond to events in DEM. The view of events as instantaneous propositions allows one to combine events in a logical manner which is not possible with the ESWV introduced in section 3. An example of static proposition is *length–of–the–queue–is–five*. A *static (instantaneous) description* is a finite theory in the classical propositional logic on the set of propositions $\overline{P}$ ($\dot{P}$).

Intuitively, a *static–description–change* describes changes that are to be made in a static description. A new static description can be obtained from a given static description by making changes specified in a static–description–change. As an example of static–description–change, consider – {*length–of–the–queue–is–four*/**false**, *length–of–the–queue–is–five*/**true**}; this static–description–change asserts that the truth value associated with the propositions *length–of–the–queue–is–four* and *length–of–the–queue–is–five* must be changed to **false** and **true**, respectively. Actions occur instantaneously. An action is a function from static descriptions to static–description–changes, i.e., given an action α and a static description s, α specifies the changes to be made in the given static description s (may be dependent on s). This view of actions allows one to neatly capture simultaneous actions. Simultaneous actions must be specified in such a way that they do not specify conflicting static–description–changes.

The underlying semantic assumptions of the logic L_{PDE} are derived from the analysis of DEM formalisms. The semantic assumptions can be explained by considering the concept of scenario.

DEF: A *scenario* is a partial description of a problem entity over a time interval using instantaneous and static descriptions.

The following semantic assumptions of L_{PDE} (and DEM formalisms) are such that finiteness of a scenario can be achieved.

For any bounded interval I of time (represented by real numbers):
(1) All the instantaneous (static) formulas known to be true at a time point can be represented by a finite theory, called instantaneous (static) description, in classical propositional logic on $\dot{P}$ ($\bar{F}$).
(2) There are only finitely many time points in I at which instantaneous descriptions need to be asserted.
(3) There are only finitely many time points in I at which a static description is different from a static description just prior to that time point.

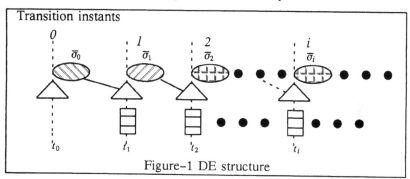

Figure–1 DE structure

Under the above semantic assumptions a scenario is called a *Discrete Event (DE) structure*. The generic pictorial representation of a DE structure is shown in the Figure–1. In the generic pictorial representation of a DE structure, triangles, divided boxes, and ovals represent instantaneous descriptions, simultaneous actions, and static descriptions, respectively.

4.2 Causality

Causality in a problem entity is to be expressed by relating instantaneous description formulas, static description formulas, and actions. These can be related by using quantified formulas of the logic L_{PDE}. In [Ra90], the complete syntax of the logic L_{PDE} is defined and its model theoretic semantics is specified with respect to DE structures. Here, we consider only some of the formulas and their usage for specifying temporal and causal relationships. A quantified formula has the general form of $F \equiv \{(C \ W) \ f\}$, where F is the quantified formula and it has has three subexpressions – a quantifier C,

210

a set–term *W*, and a formula *f*. The following is the intuitive meaning of different syntactic expressions.

Set–terms – Set–terms are either instantaneous description formulas, static description formulas, or formulas involving simulation clock time. A set term provides a means to refer to a set of future time points in a DE structure.

Quantifiers – Quantifiers denote functions of a special type. The role of quantifiers is to provide a mechanism to construct other related sets from a given set. The set of quantifiers include **while, until, whenever, when,** and **at**.

Transition instant terms – Transition instant (t–i) terms denote functions from static descriptions to static–description–changes.

Formulas – Formulas assert the truth of instantaneous description formulas and other formulas at the future time points. A formula can be viewed as a rule for describing causal relationships in terms of instantaneous descriptions, static descriptions, clock time, and (instantaneous) actions.

Theories – Theories are a finite set of formulas.

The logic *L$_{PDE}$* provides means to refer to the set of future time points using set–terms, to obtain other sets from a given set by applying quantifiers, and, then, to assert the truth of other formulas at the set of referred time points. The logic *L$_{PDE}$* also allows formulas of the forms – { <formula> **&** <formula> }, { <formula> **xor** <formula> }, and { <formula> **followed-by** <formula>}. These forms can be used to represent simultaneous actions and action sequences.

5 Avoiding the problems of AI formalisms

Unlike AI formalisms, the logic *L$_{PDE}$* is not beset by the frame, ramification, and qualification problems because of the semantic assumptions and the particular concepts of static description, action, and instantaneous description used. The concept of static description is similar to the concept of situation in situation calculus and to the concept of state in DEM formalisms. A static description, like a state in DEM formalisms but unlike a situation in AI formalisms, can be represented in a computer as it is a finite theory. Unlike DEM and AI formalisms, in the logic *L$_{PDE}$* actions are not modeled as functions from states to states but are modeled as functions from static descriptions to static–description–changes. An action, as in DEM formalisms, must occur instantaneously. The concept of instantaneous description in *L$_{PDE}$* does not have any direct counterpart in situation calculus and it is similar to the concept of events (as defined in section 3) in DEM formalisms.

The frame problem does not exist in the logic *L$_{PDE}$* because actions are modeled as functions from state descriptions to state–description–changes. In the resulting static description of an action, the formulas not changed by its static–description–change have the same truth values. The ramification problem is avoided due to the semantic assumptions (1) in section 4.1. The finiteness of static descriptions guarantees that changes in a static description at any point in time are finite; this avoids the ramification problem. The qualification problem does not arise because the semantic assumptions (1), (2), and (3) in section 4.1 guarantee that the occurrences of an action sequence depends only on finitely many conditions and the concept of action asserts that actions must occur instantaneously.

6 Examples

Several simple examples for expressing different types of causality are considered. In the following, the `typewriter` fonts, *italic fonts*, **bold fonts**, and <u>under-lined fonts</u> are used for instantaneous description formulas, transition instant terms, quantifiers and sentential connectives, and static description formulas, respectively.

Problem description : For a teller in a bank, service begin event causes service end event after certain service time.
> (**whenever** `service-begins`)
> > {(**at** t=current-time+service-time) `service-ends`}

This example illustrates a form of causal rules that are typical of ESWV; where causality is expressed by relating events (instantaneous description formulas) along the axis of simulation clock time.

Problem description : For a teller in a bank, service begin event is caused whenever there is at least one customer in the queue and the server is free.
> (**whenever** <u>queue-length-is > 0</u> **&** `server-is-free`)
> > {*server-is-free-is-false* **&** *decrement queue-length-by-1*
> > > **&** {(**at** t=current-time+service-time) *server-is-free-is-true*}}

This example illustrates a form of causal rules that are typical of ASWV; where causality is expressed by relating a sequence of actions along a simulation clock time to a formula on static and instantaneous descriptions.

Problem description : If manager steps out before 11:00 am then the first customer to arrive in the bank after manager has stepped out receives a gift of $2.
> {(**whenever** `manager-steps-out` **&** @t<11am)
> > {(**when** `customer-arrives`) {[*customer-gets-a-gift-of-$-2*]} } }

This example illustrates the usage of the **when** operator and causal relationship involving transition instant terms. The **when** operator is used in PIWV.

Problem description : If a customer arrives when the manager is out of the bank then the customer gets a flower.
> {(**whenever** `manager-steps-out`)
> > {(**until** `manager-comes-back`)
> > > {(**if** `customer-arrives`) **then** {[*customer-gets-a-flower*]} } } }

This example illustrates the usage of **until** operator which is not available in DEM. The causality expressed by the above formula can be expressed in any of the ESWV, ASWV, or PIWV using different forms of causal rules than the one given above.

7 Summary

In this paper, the AI and DEM formalisms for expressing the temporal and causal relationships are critically compared. The particular concepts of situation and action accepted by AI researchers are shown to be at the root of the characteristic problems in AI formalisms. The implicit concepts of action, event, and causality and semantic assumptions in different DEM formalisms are explicitly stated. A new logic L_{PDE} which avoids the characteristic problems of AI formalisms is briefly described. The semantic assumptions and the semantic theory of the logic L_{PDE} have been developed by analyzing the temporal and causal elements of DEM formalisms. The logic L_{PDE} overcomes the deficiency of DEM formalisms in that it is a formal logic amalgamating and extending their essentials. The expanded version of this paper is [RS89].

References

[Al84] J. F. Allen. Towards a general theory of action and time. *Artificial Intelligence*, 23, 2, 1984, 123–154.

[AH87] J. F. Allen and P. J. Hayes. Moments and points in an interval–based temporal logic. TR80, Department of Computer Science and Philosophy, The University of Rochester, Rochester, NY 14627, December 1987.

[Ge86] M. Georgeff. The representation of events in multiagent domains. *Proc. of the National Conference on Artificial Intelligence*, Philadelphia, PA, 1986, 70–75.

[GS88] M. L. Ginsberg and D. E. Smith. Reasoning about Action 1: A possible world approach. *Artificial Intelligence*, 35, 1988, 165–195.

[Fi87] J. J. Finger. Exploiting constraints in design synthesis. *PhD Thesis*, Stanford University, 1987.

[Kr86] W. Kreutzer. *System Simulation: Programming Styles and Languages*. Addison-Wesley, Reading, Mass., 1986.

[Mc86] J. McCarthy. Applications of circumscription to formalizing common–sense knowledge. *Artificial Intelligencce*, 28, 1986, 89–116.

[MD82] D. V. McDermott. A temporal logic for reasoning about processes and plans. *Cognitive Science*, 6, 1982, 101–155.

[MH69] J. M. McCarthy and P. J. Hayes. Some philosophical problems from the standpoint of artificial intelligence. *Readings in Artificial Intelligence*, Tioga Publishing Co., Palo Alto, CA, 1981, 431–450 (originally appeared in 1969).

[Mo83] B. C. Moszkowski. Reasoning about Digital Circuits. *PhD Thesis*, Stanford University, 1983.

[Ov82] C. M. Overstreet. *Model specification and analysis for discrete event simulation*, *PhD Thesis*, Virginia Polytechnic Institute and State University, 1982.

[Ra90] A. Radiya. A Logical approach to discrete event modeling and simulation. *PhD Thesis*, School of Computer and Information Science, Syracuse University, 1990 (Forthcoming).

[RS89] A. Radiya and R. G. Sargent. Differing perspectives of knowledge representation in Artificial Intelligence and Discrete Event Modeling, Technical Report 89-1, Simulation Research Group, Syracuse University, 1989.

[Sh86] Y. Shoham. Reasoning about change: Time and causation from the standpoint of artificial intelligence. *PhD Thesis*, Yale University, 1986.

[Ze76] Bernard P. Zeigler. *Theory of modelling and simulation*. John Wiley, 1976.

IMPLEMENTATION OF CONCEPTUAL GRAPHS

USING FRAMES IN LEAD

K.C. REDDY, C.S. REDDY K. and P.G. REDDY

School of Mathematics and Computer/Information Sciences
University of Hyderabad
Hyderabad - 500 134
A.P., INDIA

Telex: 425-2050 UHYD-IN
Tel. No.: 253901,253902. Ext. 218.

Abstract

This paper chiefly discusses the implementation of Sowa's Conceptual Graph notation using a frame-like data structure. Conceptual graphs serve as the basis for knowledge representation in our two systems, LEAD (Learning Expert system for Agricultural Domain) and XLAR (Universal Learning ARchitecture). The importance of conceptual graphs in knowledge representation is also briefly accounted for. Rationale for choosing frames for conceptual graph implementation is presented. Comparison of this implementation with other extant implementations is made.

Key Words: Knowledge Representation, Conceptual Graphs, Frames, Semantic Nets, Rules, Learning Expert system.

0. INTRODUCTION

The issue of selection of a knowledge representation scheme is sine qua non in the development of knowledge based systems. The problem of selection of a knowledge representation scheme is of vital importance as good representation can ease the encoding of knowledge, reasoning from that knowledge and modification of that knowledge. A hybrid knowledge representation scheme combining both conceptual graphs (CGs) and rules is chosen for our Learning Expert system for Agricultural Domain (LEAD) [CSReddy, 1989]. CGs and rules play complementary roles, because rules lend themselves to a natural representation of diagnostic knowledge whereas CGs can take care of the structure and the function of the domain. Hence, we use rules to capture shallow knowledge and CGs to capture deep knowledge. Moreover CGs conduce building a natural language interface to help the user/expert by obviating the necessity to deal with arcane and baroque programming languages in the process of developing and using the system.

In this paper we describe the conceptual graphs part of the knowledge representation scheme, the rationale for choosing CG notation, implementation of CGs using a frame-like data structure and criteria for selecting such a data structure for implementing CGs along with the comparison of this implementation vis a vis other implementations.

1. Why Conceptual Graphs ?

The conceptual graphs representation is a graph-based notation for knowledge representation. It was first proposed by Sowa in [Sowa, 1976], and later developed and formalized by Sowa in his encyclopaedic work [Sowa, 1984]. [Sowa and Way, 1986], [Fargues, et al., 1986] and [Garner and Tsui, 1986] are some noted applications of CGs for building a semantic interpreter, knowledge processing and knowledge engineering respectively. CG representation is a more flexible and more precisely defined knowledge representation system than any of its precursors (network-based representations) from which many ideas have been taken and integrated to form CG representation [Jackman and Pavelin, 1988]. CG notation fully satisfies Woods' two aspects of knowledge representation systems - expressive adequacy and notational efficacy [Woods, 1987]. Expressive adequacy is the ability to make important distinctions and the ability to avoid undesirable distinctions. The taxonomic structure provided by the organization of concepts in a hierarchical structure in the semantic network of the CG base enables CG notation to demonstrate expressive adequacy. For example subtle distinctions between 'work', 'run', 'amble', 'drive' and 'fly' are easily expressed in CG notation as each of them is expressed as a concept. Each of these concepts has a definition. These definitions bring out the distinctions between them. The taxonomic structure of concepts provided by the semantic network of the knowledge base also facilitates notational efficacy. Conceptual graphs are usually more concise than logical formulas because arcs on the graphs show the connections more directly than variable symbols [Sowa, 1984]. The first order rules of inference given in [Sowa, 1984] facilitate proofs which are short, simple and easy to understand (since they are graphical).

Clancey in [Clancey, 1985] says: "the CG notation encourages clear thinking by forcing us to unbundle domain terminology into defined or schematically described terms and constant vocabulary of relations (restricted in the types of concepts each can link)". This understanding of the domain is very essential in building an expert system especially, a learning expert system.

The implementation of CGs in LEAD is unlike other implementations which use records [Sowa and Way, 1986] or

Prolog predicates [Garner and Tsui, 1986]. Here CGs are implemented making use of a frame-like data structure.

2. CG Implementation

Before CGs can be mapped into frames, we need to identify the basic objects of CG notation using which other objects can be represented. These basic objects are:

1. Conceptual graphs,
2. Contexts,
3. Lambda Abstractions,
4. Concept Types and
5. Relation Types.

The remaining CG objects could be represented in terms of these basic objects in the following way:

. a Type Definition using a lambda abstraction,
. a Canonical Graph using a conceptual graph and
. a Schema using a lambda abstraction.

Hence, it is sufficient if we map the above mentioned basic objects into frames.

2.1. Mapping of objects into frames

Since frames are used for implementing CGs, the structure of frames has to be described first. This description is necessary, for there is no single commonly accepted (or used) structure for frames.

2.1.1. Structure of frames

Each frame implemented here has a unique name and a number of slots specifying various aspects of the objects being represented. Each slot has a number of facets. These facets normally hold values. A facet can hold no value or a single value or more than one value. Values can be of any type - ranging from numbers, symbols, lists to frame names themselves. A frame structure can be specified more precisely and formally by the regular expression:

(<frame-name> (<slot-name> (<facet-name> <value>*)*)*)

For example, the chair, 3-leg chair, which has three legs, a round back and two arms can be represented as a frame as:

```
(3-leg-chair
    (legs (value 3))
    (back (type round))
    (arms (value 2))
)
```

2.1.2. Mapping into frames

A frame is the basic data structure chosen for implementing menting the objects of CG. Different kinds of frames are used for the implementation of these objects. They are as follows:

. CG frames : To represent conceptual graphs,
. CO frames : To represent concepts,
. LA frames : To represent lambda abstractions,
. Concept type frames : To represent concept types in the semantic network along with the background knowledge of the domain it possesses,
. Relation type frames : To represent relation types.

The subsequent sections describe each of these frames along with examples.

2.1.3. CG frames

A conceptual graph is a connected, finite, bipartite graph formed from concept and relation nodes. Each relation is linked only to its requisite number of concepts, each concept to one or more relations - apart from the special use of a graph consisting of a single concept. Each conceptual graph which asserts some information is represented using a single frame.

The various slots and their facets, in a CG frame are:
. Type slot: Value facet indicates whether it represents a conceptual graph or a canonical graph.
. There is a single slot for each of the concepts, regardless of the number of times it occurs in the graph. For each such slot there is 1) a facet to count the number of occurrences of that concept in that graph and 2) an occurrences facet which contains information about each occurrence as a separate value (each facet can have more than one value as there can be more than one occurrence of the same concept).

Further, each value has
1. a referent of the concept in that occurrence,
2. a list of incoming relations to that concept,
3. a list of outgoing relations from that concept.
Referent: A referent of a concept denotes the extension of that concept. The referent field is necessary to refer to specific individuals. The CAR (of LISP) of the referent field gives the type of referent and CDR the referent itself. The following are the various types of referents:

Individual: An individual concept is indicated by having a unique tag after the colon field in the concept. An individual concept corresponds to a particular and unique instance of a modelled entity. Sowa's notation of an individual concept may have a unique number as the referent. This type is denoted by 'i'.

Empty set: This is denoted by having an '{}' in the refer ent field. It specifies that there does not exist any instance of the concept. This is denoted by 'es'.

Generic set: This is denoted by '{*}' in the referent field. It specifies that there exists a set of unidentified elements as the referent of the concept. Note that the notion of a generic set specifies the existence of a set of elements for the concept, but gives no information about the elements in the set. This is denoted by 'gs'.

Individual set: This is denoted by having a set of individual referents as the referent field. It specifies that there exists a fifnite set of individual referents as the referent of the concept. This is denoted by 'is'.

Partially specified set: This is denoted by placing the result of the union of an individual set and a generic set as the referent. It specifies a set of identified elements and some unidentified elements. This is denoted by 'ps'. Variable: This is denoted by having a '*x' where x can be any symbolic tag. It specifies that the referent is a variable to be filled in later. When used in a rule, identical variables share a common value.

Nested graph: A graph can itself be a referent of a concept. This is useful for contexts. This is denoted by 'g'.

The lists given by 2 and 3 (incoming and outgoing relations) are complex lists. The first element of these lists is an atom giving the name of an incoming or outgoing relation as the case may be. Second and third elements are lists giving incoming concepts into that relation and outgoing concepts from that relation along with their occurrence numbers in that graph. All this is essential to ensure strong connectivity at the cost of less space which is in contrast to [Sowa and Way, 1986] which uses a record for each concept and each relation to ensure strong connectivity at the expense of space. The following simple example illustrates this mapping.

220

The natural language sentence, "Leaves have spindle shaped spots", can be represented as the conceptual graph,

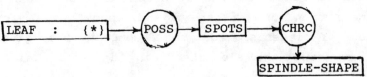

This CG can be mapped to the following frame (underlined words are key words for the CG frame).

```
(CG01
   (type (value  graph))
   (LEAF
     (no-of-occurrences 1)
     (occurrences
       ((referent  'gs') ;gs denotes generic set
       ()                ;no relations coming in
       ((POSS  (in) (out (SPOTS 1))))   ;outgoing relation
     )
    )
  )


 (SPOTS
       (no-of-occurrences 1)
     (occurrences
         ((referent)  ;no referent
         ((POSS    (in (LEAF 1)) (out)))
         ((CHRC (in) (out (SPINDLE-SHAPE 1))))
        )
     )
  )
```

```
(SPINDLE-SHAPE
        (no-of-occurrences  1)
      (occurrences
            ((referent)      ;no referent
             ((CHRC (in (SPOTS 1)) (out)))
             ()    ;no out going relations
            )
      )
   )
 )   ;end of CG01
```

Actors which relate schemata to external procedures for computations and database access, are implemented using if-needed daemons attached to the concepts whose referents are to be determined.

2.1.4. Contexts

All graph notations represent the conjunction operator by simply drawing the operand graphs on a sheet of paper. But, for representing other operators like disjunction, negation, implication, etc., [Sowa, 1984] makes use of Pierce's contexts. Each context is a group of propositions. To represent contexts, we make use of the following slots:

   . type whose value facet is propositions,

   . referent whose value facet gives the set of propositions being asserted in the context.

   . Relation list: a list of relations by which the present context is connected to other contexts.

   . Individuals: a list of individuals which are existentially quantified in the present context.

   . Environment: gives the name of the outer context in which the present one is embedded.

2.1.5. Lambda Abstractions

Lambda abstractions are useful in representing definitions, schemata, aggregations and prototypes. They are conceptual graphs with one or more concepts as formal parameters. Because of these parameters these abstractions have to be used differently.

The following are the various slots:

. Type : whose value facet is the name of that abstraction, if any.

. No-of-parameters : whose value facet gives the number of concepts which are formal parameters.

. Parameters : whose value facet is a list of concepts which are acting as formal parameters.

. Body : whose value facet gives the canonical graph which is the body of the lambda abstraction. A canonical graph is a conceptual graph that specifies selectional constraints on possible combinations of concepts that could be linked to the present concept through some particular relations.

Example

relation QOH(x,y) is

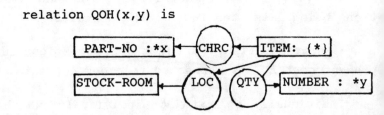

The above relation QOH could be mapped to the following frame:

```
(LA01
 (type    (value    QOH))
 (no-of-parameters    (value  2))
 (parameters (value (PARTNO : *x NUMBER : *y)))
 (body (value CG02))
 )
```

Here, CG02 is the graph containing the body of the relation.

2.1.6 Concept and relation types

The concept types are organized into a semantic network to show their type hierarchy. These concept types should be predefined in any CG system.

The hierarchy thus formed should be a lattice as a consequence of which any two types have only one maximal common subtype and only one minimal common supertype. 'T' is the supermost type and 'F' is the submost type. For a concept type, the following slots have to be defined:

. Canonical graph . Schemata - some concepts can not be defined by a single definition, for example, the concept GAME. But this can be specified as a group of schemata - each one for a different game. So, schemata help in defining some not-so-easy-to- define concepts like GAME, ENERGY, etc..

. Prototypes - these specify some prototypical objects typifying that concept.

Relation types need only their definition and canonical graphs to be specified. Also, the number of incoming and outgoing arcs are to be noted for each relation type. This will be useful while performing operations on CGs.

Examples

Concept type: ACT

```
(ACT
 (type  (value concept-type))
 (definition (value )) ;no definitions
 (canonical-graph (value CG03))
 (super-types (value (EVENT)))
 (sub-types (value (ARRIVE, GIVE, CUT, PLAY..)))
 (schemata (value))
 (prototypes (value))
)
```

Relation Type: (DEST)

```
(DEST
      (type  (value      rel-type))
      (definition   (value))
      (canonical-graph  (value CG03))
      (inarcs (value 1))
      (outarcs (value 1))
)
```

CG03, CG04 are canonical graphs for concept type ACT and relation type DEST respectively.

3. Criteria for choosing frames

A frame representation is chosen for mapping CGs so as to exploit frames' innate features. These features are:

1. Inheritance: Inheritance of frames is used directly to implement inheritance in CGs - i.e., a concept acquires canonical graphs, prototypes, etc. from its super types.

2. Daemon: If-needed daemon is used for implementing actors, which may involve some minor calculation or processing using other concepts in the graph. If-needed daemon

comes into effect when a value has to be determined for that concept.

3.Dynamic structure: In frames the number of slots or facets can vary and they can be deleted or inserted at any time. Frames have a flexible structure unlike the Procrustean structure of records, Prolog predicates, etc. This flexible structure enables us to incorporate changes necessary due to future exten^ions. For instance, prototypes for concept-type frames not yet incorporated, can easily be added in future.

4. Comparisons with other implementations

Efficient implementation of the chosen representation is as crucial as the representation itself. There are other existing implementations of CGs, by Sowa, et al. 1986 and Garner, et al. 1986.

[Sowa and Way, 1986] uses records for representing concepts and relations, and uses two-way pointers to maintain strong connectivity. As mentioned earlier, they do not take care of multiple occurrences of a concept in a graph. Actors are not implemented (probably because, actors are not needed for the purpose of implementing a semantic interpreter, for which the CGs have been used). This implementation of CGs implements a conceptual graph as a linked list of nodes where each node is either a concept record or a relation record. This sort of implementation of graphs leads to inefficient traversal of the graph. The adjacency list representation of graphs is efficient for both faster traversal of the graph and reduction in space complexity. The implementation presented here by us conforms to this adjacency list method of representing a graph.

Projection, join and maximal join are frequently-used operations on CGs. These operations are seriously affected by the implementation used. For instance, the projection operation requires spotting a part of the graph in a bigger graph. The linked list [Sowa and Way, 1986] implementation of graphs is inefficient as compared to the adjacency list method in doing this.

[Garner and Tsui, 1988] uses prolog facts of different types - one type for each graph, concept and relation. As in the earlier case this implementation also does not take care of multiple occurrences of a concept and actors. Moreover, this implementation does not consider the case of relations which are n-adic where n>2. But, this implementation can make use of backtracking and unification algorithms in Prolog to simplify their operations.

5. Conclusions

An advantage of conceptual graphs over other kinds of knowledge representation is that CG notation embodies the salient features of network based representations. The theory of CG notation due to Sowa in [Sowa, 1984] formalizes CG notation which is found wanting in other network based representations such as frames or semantic nets. CG implementation in LEAD which is presented here is advantageous over other CG implementations as discussed in this paper. This aspect of knowledge representation - implementation of the chosen representation - is as important as choosing a notation for knowledge representation itself. In this implementation of CGs, features of frames such as inheritance, flexible structure and the daemon procedural attachment facility, are exploited. At present frames play a secondary role in the implementation. As a part of the further work in this direction, avenues for giving frames a primary role - e.g., making schema and prototypes of CG notation do reasoning with frames, etc. - are being explored. This implementation is done in Common LISP on Texas Instruments Explorer at the University of Hyderabad, Hyderabad.

REFERENCES

[Barr, 1981]

Barr, A., Feigenbaum, E.A., The Handbook of AI, vol.1, William Kaufmann Inc., 1981.

[Barr and Feigenbaum, 1982]

Barr, A., Feigenbaum, E.A., The Handbook of AI, vol.2, Addison Wesley, Reading, 1982.

[Carbonnel et al., 1983]

Carbonnel, J., Michalski, R. and Mitchell, T., Machine Learning: An AI Approach, ed. by R.Michalski, J.Carbonnel, T.Mitchell, Tioga Press, Palo Alto, CA, 1983.

[Cersone and McCalla, 1983]

Cersone, N., and McCalla, G., The Knowledge Frontier, ed. by Cercone, N., McCalla, G., Springer Verlag,NY,1983.

[Chan et al., 1988]

Chan, Garner, B.J. and Tsui, E., Recursive Modal Unification for Reasoning with Knowledge using a Graph Representation, in Knowledge Base Systems, March,1988.

[Clancey, 1985]

Clancey, W.J., Heuristics Classification, Artificial Intelligence Intelligence, 27, 1985, pp. 289-350.

[Cohen and Feigenbaum, 1982]

Cohen, P.R., Feigenbaum, E.A., The Handbook of AI, vol.3, Addison Wesley, 1982.

[CSReddy, 1989]

C. S. Reddy. K., LEAD-1: Design and Implementation of a Knowledge Representation Scheme and a Proposal for a Learning Paradigm, M. Tech. Thesis, Univ. of Hyd., 1989

[Duda et al., 1978]

Duda, R.O., Hart, P.E., Nilson, N.J., Sutherland, G.L., Semantic Network Representation in Rule-based Inference Systems, in Pattern Directed Inference Systems, ed. by Waterman, D.A., Hayes-Roth, F., Academic Press,1978.

[Fargues et al., 1986]

Fargues, J., Landau, M.C., Dugourd, A., Catach, L., Conceptual Graphs for Semantics and Knowledge Processing, IBM Jr. of Research and Development 30, No.1, Jan. 1986.

[Garner, 1985]

Garner, B.J., Knowledge Representation for An Audit Office, Australian Computer Journal 17, No.3, Aug.1985.

[Garner and Tsui, 1986]

Garner, B.J., Tsui, E., An Extendible Graph Processor for Knowledge Engineering, SPIE Proceedings, vol.635, Application of AI III, Corlando, Florida, April, 1986.

[Garner and Tsui, 1988]

Garner, B.J., Tsui,E., General Purpose Inference Engine for Canonical Graph Models, Knowledge Based Systems, Dec.1988.

[Jackman and Pavelin, 1988]

Jackman, M., Pavelin, C., Conceptual Graphs, in Approaches to Knowledge Representation - An Introduction, ed. by Ringland, G.A., Duce,D.A., John Wiley & Sons Inc., NY,1988.

[Minsky, 1975]

Minski, M., A Framework for Representing Knowledge, in The Psychology of Computer Vision, ed. by P.H. Winston, McGraw-Hill, NY, 1975, pp.211-277.

[Rangaswamy, 1984]

Rangaswamy, G., Disease of Crop Plants in India, 2nd. ed., Prentice-Hall of India Pvt. Ltd. New Delhi,1984.

[Rao and Foo, 1987]

Rao, A.S. and Foo, N.Y., Congres: Conceptual graph reasoning system, Proc. IEEE, 1987, pp.87-92.

[Reddy and Reddy, 1986a]

Reddy, K.C., Reddy, K.R.C., Advisory Expert systems in Plant Disease Diagnosis and Control, All India Seminar on Computer as a Tool for improving Agricultural Productivity, Hyderabad, India,1986.

[Reddy et al., 1986b]

Reddy, P.G., Reddy, K.C., Reddy, Y.B., Artificial Intelligence: Expert Systems Research: Adapting Technical Knowledge for Computer Based Agricultural Consultancy Systems, All India Seminar on Computer as a Tool for Improving Agricultural Productivity, Hyderabad, 1986.

[Reddy, 1987]

Reddy, K. C.; Ph. D. Thesis Proposal, University of Hyderabad, Hyderabad, 1987.

[Reddy et al., 1989]

Reddy, K.C., C.S.Reddy.K, Reddy, P.G., LEAD: A Learning Expert System for Agricultural Diseases - Rice Diseases, accepted for International Conference on Applications of AI in Govt. and Industry, Hyderabad, 1989.

[Sowa, 1976]

Sowa, J.F., Conceptual Graphs for a Data Base Interface, IBM Jr. of Research and Dev. July 1976.

[Sowa, 1984]

Sowa, J.F., Conceptual Structures: Inf. Processing in Mind and Machine, Addison-Wesley, Reading, 1984.

[Sowa and Way, 1986]

Sowa, J.F. and Way, E., Implementing a Semantic Interpreter using Conceptual Graphs, IBM Jr. of Research and Dev., Jan. 1986.

[Steel, 1984]

Steele Jr., G.L., Common LISP, The Language, Digital Press, 1984.

[Winston and Horn, 1981]

Winston, P.H., Horn, B., LISP, Addison-Wesley, Reading, 1981.

[Woods, 1987]

Woods, W. A., What's Important About Knowledge Representation, in Knowledge Frontier, ed. Cercone, N., McCalla, G., Springer Verlag, NY 1987.

Knowledge Representation in Distributed Blackboard Architecture - Some Issues

Manoj K. Saxena

C.M.C. Ltd. , A-5 Ring Road
N.D.S.E.-I , New Delhi - 110049
India

K.K. Biswas   P.C.P. Bhatt

uunet!shakti!vikram!netearth!PCP

Computer Science and Engineering Department
Indian Institute of Technology
New Delhi - 110016

Abstract

This paper discusses some issues and problems in knowledge representation(KR) in systems employing blackboard problem solving paradigm. In particular it focusses on concurrency and consistancy in the context of distributing the blackboard in a multicomputer environment required for event recognition and recording. The paper describes how DKRL - A Distributed Knowledge Representation Language developed for DISPROS - a Distributed Blackboard Architecture, handles these issues.

1 Introduction

The choice of knowledge representation becomes very crucial for the states of reasoning for large and distributed system. In the absence of a good representation scheme , systems become progressively more difficult to construct, extend and maintain.

There are two major aspects of KR to be considered. The **expressive adequacy** and **notational efficacy.** The expressive adequacy has to do with the expressive power of the representation. It can be further broken down into **representational and inferential adequacies.** Representational adequacy deals with the representation of the knowledge that is needed in a particular domain where as inferential adequacy deals with the ability to manipulate the representation to derive new inferences. The **notational efficacy** concerns with the actual shape and structure of the representation as well as the impact this structure has on the system's operations. This further breaks down into such components as **computational efficiency** for various kinds of inferences, conciseness of representation, inferential efficiency to focus the attention of inference mechanism, and **acquisitional efficiency** to acquire new information easily.

The blackboard problem-solving paradigm was first developed for the HEARSAY - II [Erman et al 80]. Because of its advantages of modularity, flexibility, extensibility and generality in problem solving, it has been used for many applications [Nii 86]. Briefly stated, in blackboard systems, the total solution is obtained by combining several parts of solution that emerge in different structural partitions of the blackboard. This suggests that built-in concurrency in problems can be exploited, but so far very few attempts have been made in this direction. Distributing the blackboard on a computer network adds issues like how to capture knowledge at each site and still maintain the consistency of the knowledge base.

In this paper we consider the representational issues related to a distributed blackboard system. While in section 2 we introduce the blackboard architecture and the associated knowledge representation scheme; section 3 describes **DISPROS** - the **DIS**tributed blackboard architecture for **PRO**blem Solving. Section 4 describes **DKRL** - the KR scheme for DISPROS and how the various representational issues have been handled in DISPROS. The final section notes the conclusions.

2 Knowledge Representation and Blackboard Architecture

The blackboard problem-solving metaphor is very simple. It entails a collection of cooperating experts gathered around a shared data structure, called Blackboard. The experts react to partial solutions with a view to build a total solution. The blackboard architecture has the following four definitive elements [Hayes-Roth 83] :

i) **Entries** : which are intermediate results generated during problem solving. They may include both elements of problem solution and information necessary for generating future solutions.

ii) **Knowledge Sources** : which are independent, event driven processes generating or modifying blackboard entries. They contain knowledge employed by the system to progressively solve problems.

iii) **Blackboard** : which is a structured global database which mediates knowledge source interactions and organises entries; and

iv) **Intelligent Control Mechanism** : which decides if and when particular knowledge sources should generate entries and record them on the blackboard.

The knowledge representation is the most important aspect of any blackboard system as all co-operating experts use the blackboard for interacting with each other. The overall efficiency of the system depends on the notational efficacy and expressive adequacy of the KR scheme. To simplify the task of organising entries on blackboard, most BB system consider it as a two dimensional structure with vertical, and horizontal dimensions.

The vertical dimension separates and distinguishes entries at different levels of abstraction. These may elaborate or support entries at the next level or at some other level in the hierarchy. Typically the information is stored at its most general level of applicability and indirectly accessed by more specific concepts, using the inheritance mechanism. The horizontal dimension essentially captures the notion of an interval in the solution.

Conventional BB systems adapt following repsentational and problem solving strategy to take care of issuses stated in section 1 .

- **Declarative Knowledge** is encoded in rules, which exist within knowledge sources, knowledge sources bind knowledge about a subject/aspect together into one unit. The implementors of blackboard systems often think of knowledge sources as scheduling units and thus design their scheduling strategies around the idea of the invocation of knowledge sources.

- **Procedural Knowledge** is an all encompassing term usually used to describe both knowledge about the relationships between values (functions) and the mechanisms for performing side-effects and for sequencing events (procedures). It is encoded in procedures as part of knowledge source.

- **The Sequencing of Activities** in most blackboard systems is encoded in the scheduling mechanism. Knowledge of the required sequencing of events at a macroscopic level is expressed by the implementation of the system's scheduler.

- **The Structure of the Solution Space** plays a very important role in the problem solving process in the blackboard system, because the complete solution is obtained by combining several partial solutions that emerge in different structural partitions of the blackboard. This knowledge is encoded in the definition of the structure of the blackboard. The representation scheme should be computationally efficient and adequate to represent the complex objects/entities of various types and draw inferences from them.

- **Knowledge about Relationship** between entities in blackboard systems are often expressed by a form of link mechanism, which conserves memory and maintains consistency of the knowledge base.

3   DISPROS - Distributed Blackboard Architecture

The blackboard framework offers natural exploitation of concurrency, some of the possible parallelism can be ; **Knowledge Parallelism** : KSs and rules within each KS running concurrently. **Pipeline Parallelism** : As many KSs are working concurrently on partial data; transfer of information from one abstract level to another can be pipelined. **Data Parallelism** : Blackboard can be partitioned into solution components that can be operated on concurrently.

The distribution of blackboard leads to the problem of consistenancy in recording the events because causally related events occuring in various parts of the blackboard are to be observed in real-time through out the distributed BB system. Very few attempts have been made for exploiting the concurrency [Aiello 86, Corkill 88]. DISPROS [Saxena et al 89a] is one other such attempt. It retains the concept of KS and BB level of a conventional blackboard architecture. However, each level is considered to be an independent unit and is contained in a Level Manager(LM). LMs are active structures and consist of the following components (Figure -1) :

i) **Local Database**: It is a working memory purely local to the LM. All BB objects are stored in it. The objects are represented as frames with a slot-and-filler representation structure. Links, which are special purpose slots, are used to store relationship between various objects. The objects get defined as follows :

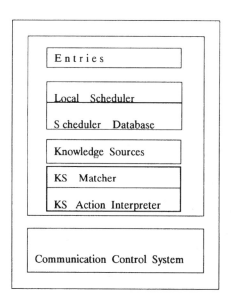

Figure -1   Structure of a typical Level Manager

```
( DEFINE-OBJECT ( object-name :CONSTRUCTOR level-name
{ object-option object-option-value }*)        ["Documentation"]
( :SLOTS {(slot-name [initial value] {slot-option-name  slot-option-value}*)}+)
[( :LINKS {(link-name  object-name {link-option-name  link-option-value}*)}+)]
```

DEFINE-OBJECT not only defines a new object type but also defines functions to create and delete instances of the object, and accessor functions for its slots and links. :CONSTRUCTOR keyword indicates the abstraction level of the object in structured taxonomy of the BB. Object-option argument is used to define various attributes of the object. The :SLOTS argument contains a list of slot-descriptions which is used to define the slot and the characteristics of the filler which can fill the slot. The :LINKS argument is a list of link-descriptions which define additional slots holding inter object links.   An access function is automatically defined for each link in the same way that access functions are defined for the slots.   The slot and link options (not in the scope of this paper) are described elsewhere [Saxena et al 89b]. An example of an object description in DKRL is given in section 4.

ii) **Collection of Knowledge Sources** : KSs are organised along the tripartite structure : **trigger - condition - action** and are rule based. In this structure, only the condition part is allowed to access data from other LMs. The action part can send data to other LMs to manipulate their database. The trigger is restricted to the entries of the local database. The KSs held within a LM may engage in indirect communication with other LMs via Communication Control System (CCS). The knowledge sources are defined as follows :

```
( DEFINE-KS ( :NAME name-of-ks ) ["Documentation"]
[ ( :AUTHOR  name-of-author ) ]
 ( :INPUT-LEVEL  name-of-input-level )
 ( :OUTPUT-LEVEL name-of-output-level )
 ( :TRIGGER  list-of-triggers )
[ ( :EFFICIENCY  default-value ) ]
[ ( :RELIABILITY default-value ) ]
 ( :RULES {( IF condition THEN action )}+))
```

DEFINE-KS creates a new knowledge source. The knowledge source monitors a sub-board indicated by :INPUT-LEVEL for events/triggers listed in argument list of :TRIGGER to occur. :OUTPUT-LEVEL indicates the sub-board where the knowledge source can record its contribution as given in the action part of the RULE. :EFFICIENCY and :RELIABILITY arguments indicate the efficiency and the reliability of KS in obtaining the solution. These values are used by scheduler in deciding which KS to schedule next for execution.

iii) **Local Scheduler:** Each LM is considered to be an autonomous module with local control. Local control is effected by the local scheduler which operates on instances of the KSs belonging to the LM in which it resides.

iv) **Control Database**: The control database contains information useful to the local scheduler in making control decisions. This is private to the LM in which it resides, but may contain information with a more global extent.

v) **Matcher and Action Interpreter**: These are responsible for matching preconditions of KSs and for executing actions. The presence of separate matchers and action interpreters allow different LMs to use different knowledge representations (like frame, semantic nets etc.) if the problem domain so requires.

vi) **Communication Control System**: It has its own database to handle the communication for each LM. Each site has a Communication Level Manager responsible for message transfer between two sites. It controls the physical ports of the computer and uses heuristics to take care of communication link failure and congestion control.

The LMs exist within envelopes which are concerned with implementation of the basic **match-schedule-execute** loop.

The communication system is based on atomic multicast protocols similar to those proposed in [Birman and Joseph 87] and [Chang and Maxenchule 84] to provide virtually synchronous environment. The protocol provides for general message passing capabilities and ensures that all of its operational destinations receive the message unless the sender

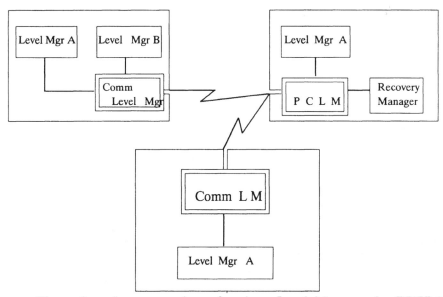

Figure -2   Interconnection of various Level Managers in DISPROS

fails, in which case either all destinations receive it or none does so. Moreover, all recipients see the same message delivery ordering. It provides a fault-tolerant environment for building distributed problem-solvers [Saxena et al 89c].

There are two distinct types of messages provided for by the architecture : problem solving and control messages. As there is no restriction of linear hierarchy of blackboard levels; LMs may be arbitrarily related with the connections being realised by inter LM channels. As shown in Figure-2 the LMs are distributed over a network with no particular hierarchy. If needed the hierarchy can be established at the time of definition of BB.Note that this not only removes constraints imposed by the linear hierarchy requirements of monolithic blackboard, but also offers added modularity and flexibility to the architecture.

The most important aspect of the architecture is its control model. The control is divided into local and global control. Each LM has a representation of its local state and can make control decisions based upon it. The independent scheduling decision maximises strategic flexibility and potential for opportunism. The global control is implemented by message-passing. This results in a completely distributed system with no centralized control.

4 DKRL - Knowledge Representation Scheme for DISPROS

DISPROS does not strictly adhere to the structuring technique followed by most of the BB systems. It allows the BB to be partitioned into sub-boards, which are further partitioned into levels. This represents hierarchy of abstraction in the solution space. The levels are contained in an autonomous entity the Level Manager. Each LM is an independent process and executes entirely asynchronously. Within a LM the representation is like that of some frame systems, with slot and fillers, providing a **Class** mechanism with user defined classes and compile-time and run-time inheritance. A slot may be initialized at the definition time only or it can be filled with a value as a result of events which are recorded on BB in real-time.

The KSs are triggered as a result of events recorded on the BB. From the triggered KS one rule for which the condition part is true is selected for execution. The evaluation of condition part of a rule is done in the order in which they are listed in a knowledge source.

In order to create a description of a situation that is more specific than a given one, it is only necessary to mention those attributes being modified or added, one does not have to copy all of the attributes of the general situation. Besides conserving memory storage, this feature also facilitates in maintaining consistancy.

The link mechanism in DKRL is quite powerful as it can explicitly associate user defined property inheritance. It has a number of system defined relationships, such as

- Is a
- Is an Instance of
- Is a neighbour of

- Is a subclass of, and
- Is predecessor of.

The user can also define arbitrary relationship between nodes. Additionally, the procedures can also be attached to particular operations that need to be performed. They are attached to the classes of objects and it is possible for sub-classes to inherit procedures as well as data from their associated super-class. This helps in defining generic operations whose implementation details can be defined differently for different classes of objects.

By default, properties and/or procedures are inherited from an included object. However, event-inheritance-keywords in DKRL allow the user to have some control. All event-inheritance-keywords have the form { :NO-DEFAULT-INHERITANCE |
(event-name :NEVER-INHERIT) |
(event-name :ALWAYS-INHERIT) } *

Specifying :NO-DEFAULT-INHERITANCE disables the normal inheritance from the included object. Specifying (event-name :ALWAYS-INHERIT) indicates that the specified event should always be inherited to any object that include this object, even if those objects specify :NO-DEFAULT-INHERITANCE. Specifying (event-name :NEVER-INHERIT) indicates that the specified event should never be inherited to this object from its included object.

With the structured inheritance network provided by DKRL it is possible to express necessary distinctions. For example, it is possible to maintain subtle distinctions as those among "Walk", "Run", "Amble", "Drive" and "Fly" and at the same time not to overlook the commonality between these specific concepts and the general concept "Move". Also as the new distinctions become important, they can be introduced by refining or modifying existing concepts, and is always possible to introduce more general concepts that abstract details from more specific concepts.

DKRL allows the assimilation of arbitrary new information in a very natural way. Objects can be added at any point of time during problem solving process by issuing

(ADD-OBJECT object-definition)

Instances of an already existing object can be created by

(CREATE-OBJECT object-specification)

To define a plane on runway, we can consider RUNWAY as an abstract level of the blackboard with FLIGHT as an object on it. The representation in DKRL for this object will be as follows

```
(DEFINE-OBJECT (FLIGHT  :CONSTRUCTOR  RUNWAY
                        :CREATION_EVENTS  ARRIVAL
                        :DELETION-EVENTS  DEPARTURE
                "It represents the flight on runway"
                (:SLOTS  (ARRIVAL-TIME)
                         (AIRCRAFT-TYPE   :TYPE 'r')
                         (FLIGHT-NO)
                         (DEPARTURE-TIME)
                         (FLIGHT-TYPE     :TYPE 'r')
                         (STATUS     :TYPE 'r')
                )
            )
    )
```

To create an instance for the arrival of flight AI127 which is WIDE-BODY the code in DKRL will be as follows

```
BEGIN
      CREATE-OBJECT (RUNWAY.FLIGHT) ;
         MODIFY-SLOT(RUNWAY.FLIGHT.FLIGHT-NO,"AI127") ;
         MODIFY-SLOT(RUNWAY.FLIGHT.FLIGHT-TYPE, ="WIDE-BODY");
END
```

5 Conclusion

As argued above, DKRL generalizes the notion of abstract data types to the level of abstraction, inheritance, and expressive adequacy for distributed blackboard systems. It has advantage of flexibility and extensibility. It allows one to combine independently developed systems to produce integrated systems more powerful than the mere union of their parts.

References

[Aiello 86]

Aiello Nelleke, The Cage User's Manual, Technical Report KSL-86-23, C.S.Dept., Standford University, 1986.

[Birman and Joseph 87]

Birman K. and Joseph T., Reliable Communication in the Presence of Failures, ACM Transactions on Computer Systems, Vol 5 , No.1, Feb 1987.

[Chang and Maxemchule 84]

Chang J. and Maxemchule N., Reliable Broadcast Protocols, ACM Transations on Computer System, Vol 2, No.3, Aug 1984.

[Corkill 88]

Corkill Daniel D., Design Alternatives for Parallel and Distributed Blackboard Systems, COINS Technical Report 88-38, Univ of Massachusetts, Amherst, Aug 1988.

[Erman et al 80]

Erman Lee D, Hayes-Roth, Victor Lesser and D. Raj Reddy, The Hearsay - II Speech Understanding System : Intergrating Knowledge to Resolve Uncertainity, ACM Computing Surveys, Vol 12, June 1980.

[Hayes-Roth 83]

Hayes-Roth B., the Blackboard arctructure : A General Framework for problem solving ?, Report no. HPP 83-30, Stanford University, May 1983.

[Nii 86]

Nii H.P., Blackboard Systems Part Two: Blackboard Application Systems, Artificial Intelligence Magazine, Vol 7, No.3, PP 82-106, 1986.

[Saxena et al 89a]

Saxena M.K., Biswas K.K. and Bhatt P.C.P., DISPROS - Distributed Blackboard Architecture - An Overview, Internal Report, C.S.E.Dept., I.I.T Delhi, April 1989.

[Saxena et al 89b]

Saxena M.K., Biswas K.K. and Bhatt P.C.P., DKRL - Knowledge Representation Language for DISPROS, Internal Report, C.S.E.Dept, I.I.T. Delhi, May 1989.

[Saxena et al 89c]

Saxena M.K., Biswas K.K. and Bhatt P.C.P., DISPROS - A Distributed Blackboard Architecture for Expert System, Proceedings of IEEE TENCON'89, Nov 1989.

Logic Programming

IMPROVING PROLOG PERFORMANCE BY

INDUCTIVE PROOF GENERALIZATIONS

Milind Gandhe   G Venkatesh
Department of Computer Science and Engineeing
Indian Institute of Technology
Bombay 400076
uunetlshaktilbetaallcselgv

ABSTRACT

This paper investigates the possibility of improving PROLOG performance by using the history of search for previous queries to guide the search for subsequent queries. First, the notion of a *proof plan* is introduced, and it is shown how a given logic program can be translated into a *plan version* of it. The plan version allows search to be guided by a proof plan. A specific plan version called the *uninformed* plan version allows proofs to be generated from the search performed for any query.

Proof plans can be obtained by a generalization from the collection of proofs obtained earlier. A notion dual to most general unification called most special generalization (msg) is introduced for this purpose. The uniqueness of the msg is shown and an algorithm similar to the unification algorithm is given for computing the msg of two proofs. The soundness of guiding a logic program with a proof plan obtained by such a generalization is then shown.

The soundness breaks down, however, for PROLOG programs that use cut. A method based on multiple plan inference is introduced for such programs and its soundness is proved.

1. INTRODUCTION

The user of a PROLOG program does not usually ask random queries but has a certain purpose behind asking them. Thus, it is often found that the different searches made in one session of use of a PROLOG program have a fair amount of similarity in structure. It should therefore be possible to improve the search performance by using the history of the searches performed earlier to guide the proof search for subsequent queries.

In this paper, a method for achieving this is described. The method is based on the notion of a proof plan which is essentially a plan for carrying out the proof of a given query.

The notion of a "proof plan" is discussed in [Milner,87] as an object necessary for interactive proof checking. There, it is called a "tactical". A tactical breaks the assertion to be proved into simpler assertions which can then be proved. Thus, tacticals are hints about how to prove a assertion. There is thus a close relationship between searching for proofs and proof checking. In fact, proof checking is nothing but searching for a proof with a complete plan.

Further insight was gained into the relationship between proofs and the assertions they prove when the notion of propositions-as-types was introduced in type theory [Hindley and Seldin86]. Once the correspondence between terms and proofs on one hand and types and propositions on the other was set up, type checking algorithms in programming languages [Gordon et al.,79][Aho et al.,86]could be applied for the purpose of proof checking. Thus, by making a systematic translation of logic programs into a suitable system of constructive logic or type theory, it should be possible to build a sound theory for proof plans.

In [Gandhe,88], such a method is given for Horn clause programs which works by translating them into the Martin-Lof type theory [Martin-Lof,80]. For Horn clause programs, however, it is fairly easy to directly present the notion of proof plans and its use for guiding proofs without involving type theory and that is how we present the material in this paper. The use of type theory may, however, be necessary for applying the method discussed in this paper to other kinds of logic programs such as non-Horn or higher order logic programs.

In section 2, we present the motivation for our work. Section 3 introduces the notion of a proof plan and plan versions of a program. In section 4, the possibility of generalization is discussed with the help of the concept of most special generalization. The system for plan inference is presented in section 5 and its soundness is demonstrated. In sections 6 and 7, we discuss the problems of extending the system to handle "assert" and "cut" and present some solutions.

2. MOTIVATION

Consider a family tree database that gives parent-child relationships. the facts are in the form "parent(a,b)" where "parent(a,b)" reads as "a is the parent of b". The following rules define "ancestor" and "relation":

(r1) ancestor(X,Y) :- parent(X,Y).

(r2) ancestor(X,Y) :- parent(X,Z), ancestor(Z,Y).

(r3) relation(X,Y) :- ancestor(W,X), ancestor(W,Y).

Assume the facts in the database are such that most of the relations of any individual turn out to be uncles, aunts, brothers, sisters or cousins. Then the search for relations will be substantially speeded up if we can first check for these special cases and try the special rules only if these fail.

Can we get the system to infer these special case rules automatically from the search performed for previous queries?

Example 2.1 Consider the following facts.

(f11)   parent(a1, b1).

(f12)   parent(a1,c1).

(f13)   parent(b1,d1).

(f21)   parent(a2,b2).

(f22)   parent(a2,c2).

(f23)   parent(b2,d2).

It is easy to see that the queries ?-relation(d1,c1) and ?-relation(d2,c2) will have similar proof paths, as shown in figure 2.1 (for i= 1,2).

	L
:-relation(di,ci).	
:-ancestor(W,di), ancestor(W,ci).	r3(M,N)
:-parent(W,Z), ancestor(Z,di), ancestor(W,ci).	r3(r2(P,Q),N)
:-ancestor(bi,di),ancestor(ai,ci).	r3(r2(fi1,Q),N)
:-parent(bi,di),ancestor(ai,ci).	r3(r2(fi1,r1(R)),N)
:-ancestor(ai,ci).	r3(r2(fi1,r1(fi3)),r1(O))
:-parent(ai,ci).	r3(r2(fi1,r1(fi3)),r1(fi2))

PROOF OF THE QUERY ?-relation(di,ci)
FIGURE2.1

The proof has been represented by the proof term on the right. As the proof builds up, the term gets filled in. Initially it is just a variable. When we apply rule r3, it becomes a tree with r3 at the root and two children(as the body of r3 has two goals) and is written as r3(M,N), where M and N are variables that get filled in later. Thus when the proof is complete we get r3(r2(fi1,r1(R)),r1(fi2))

Now suppose we have the means of generalizing the proof trees r3(r2(f11,r1(f13)),r1(f12)) and r3(r2(f21,r1(f23)),r1(f22)) to get r3(r2(O,r1(R)),r1(P)), then the resulting generalization can be used to guide the search for a similar query later. We therefore , need the following devices -

• A method to guide logic programs with proof plans.

• A method to generate proofs from search.

• A method to generalize from proofs to obtain proof plans.

<u>Note</u> Through out this paper we assume the PROLOG computation rule,i.e.leftmost subgoal first.However the results hold irrespective of the choice of the computation rule[Lloyd,84],[Apt and Van Emden,82].

3. PROOF PLANS AND PLAN VERSIONS

We assume a set Lc of proof labels and a set Lv, of proof variables. We use f, r ,nr with or without subscripts to stand for proof labels and L,M,N... with or without subscripts to stand for proof variables.

Definition 3.1 *Proof Trees* are defined inductively as follows :

(i). If f is a proof label, f is a proof tree.

(ii). If L is a proof variable, then L is a proof tree.

(iii).If r is a proof label and T1,...,Tn are proof trees then r(T1,...,Tn) is a proof tree.

We use T with or without subscripts to stand for proof trees.

Definition 3.2 The *plan version* of a n-ary predicate q is a (n+1)-ary predicate pq where the first n arguments are the same as those of q and the n+1th argument is a proof tree called the *proof plan* of pq.

Definition 3.3 The *plan version* of a *rule*

q(t1,..,tn) :- q1(t11,..,t1n1),..qk(tkk,..,tknk)   is a rule

pq(t1,..,tn,r(L1,...,Lk)):- pq1(t11,..,t1n1,L1),...,pqk(tkk,..,tknk,Lk).

The proof label r is called the label of the rule.

Definition 3.4 The *plan version* of a fact q(t1,..,tn) is a fact pq(t1,..,tn,f).

The proof label f is called the label of the fact.

The plan version of a fact is the plan version of its predicate with only a proof label as the plan.

Note that different plan versions of a clause differ essentially only in the labels given to the clause.

Definition 3.5 The *uninformed plan version* of a *Horn clause program* is the conjunction of the plan versions of each fact and rule in the program such that the labels of clauses having the same head predicate are distinct i.e.if C1 and C2 have the same head predicate, then the labels of C1 and C2 are distinct.

Definition 3.6 The *plan version* of a *query* ?-q(t1,..,tn) is the query ?-pq(t1,..,tn,L), i.e. the proof plan is a proof variable.

Example 3.1 Consider the program 3.1.

PROGRAM 3.1

ancestor(X,Y) :- parent(X,Y).

ancestor(X,Y) :- parent(X,Z), ancestor(Z,Y).

relation(X,Y) :- ancestor(W,X), ancestor(W,Y).

parent(a1,b1).

parent(a1,c1).

parent(b1,d1).

An uninformed plan version of program 3.1 is given in program 3.2.

PROGRAM 3.2

ancestor(X,Y,r1(L)) :- parent(X,Y,L).

ancestor(X,Y,r2(L,M)) :- parent(X,Z,L), ancestor(Z,Y,M).

relation(X,Y,r3(L,M)):-ancestor(W,X,L), ancestor(W,Y,M).

parent(a1,b1,f1).

parent(a1,c1,f2).

parent(b1,d1,f3).

Now consider the execution of the planned version of the query ?-relation(di,ci,L) in figure 3.1.

:-relation(di,ci,L).	L = L
:-ancestor(W,di,M),ancestor(W,ci,N)	L = r3(M,N)
:-parent(W,Z,P),ancestor(Z,di,Q),ancestor(W,ci ,N).	L = r3(r2(P,Q),N)
:- ancestor(bi,di,Q),ancestor(ai,ci,N).	L = r3(r2(fi1,Q),N)
:-parent(bi,di,R),ancestor(ai,ci,N).	L = r3(r2(fi1,r1(R)),N)
:-ancestor(ai,ci,N).	L = r3(r2(fi1,r1(fi3)),r1(O))
:-parent(ai,ci,O).	L = r3(r2(fi1,r1(fi3)),r1(fi2))

PROOF OF THE QUERY ?-relation(di,ci,L)
FIGURE3.1

Then consider an execution of the query ?-relation(di,ci,r3(r2(f11,r1(f13)),r1(f12))) which essentially checks the proof returned above. If we follow the execution in detail, we see that it is the same as in figure 3.1.

Thus proof checking is the same as a completely planned proof search.

Lemma 3.1 A plan version of a Horn clause program generates a unique proof tree T as the result of a execution of a planned query pq(t1,..,tn,L) if the plan L is a variable.
[]

Lemma 3.2 If the same planned query is repeated with T as a plan instead of L,the execution in Lemma 3.1 is retraced.

<u>Proof</u> follows trivially from the fact that clause labels are unique and therefore at any instance at most one rule can succeed.   []

A partial plan is a proof tree with variables. A planned query with a partial plan(also known as an informed query) does proof checking initially and later does detailed goal search and is consequently much faster than an uninformed search.

4. GENERALIZATIONS FROM PROOF PLANS

Recall example 2.1. There we said that we wanted to generalize from the terms r3(r2(f11,r1(f13)),r1(f12)) and r3(r2(f21,r1(f23)),r1(f22)) to get r3(r2(O,r1(R)),r1(P)). We notice that a proof tree is generalized if a subtree of it is replaced by a variable. However, we want to generalize to the least possible extent i.e.we must find the smallest subtrees that must be pruned so that the resulting tree is the generalization of both the trees.

Definition 4.1 The most special generalization (msg) of two terms t1 and t2 is a term t such that $t\theta1 = t1$ and $t\theta2 = t2$ and for all t' such that $t'\theta1 = t1$ and $t'\theta2 = t2$, there exists a θ' such that $t'\theta' = t$.

Algorithm 4.1 The msg of two terms t1 and t2 is generated by the following procedure.

```
procedure match(t1,t2,t)
if   root(t1) =  root(t2)  and  the number of children of root(t1) =  number of children
of root(t2)
then
        let t1 =  r(t11,..,t1n);
        let t2 =  r(t21,..,t2n);
        for i =  1 to n do
                match(t1i,t2i,t0i);
        let t =  r(t01,..,t0n);
        return(t);
else
return (new variable)
```

Theorem 4.1 The msg of two terms is unique and is given by Algorithm 4.1.

<u>Proof</u> From Algorithm 4.1, it is obvious that there exist t, $\theta1, \theta2$ such that $t\theta1 = t1$ and $t\theta2 = t2$.

Note that we have cut out all and only those subtrees that do not match. So for any G1, G2 such that tG1 unifies with t1 and tG2 unifies with t2, tG1 and tG2 cannot be unified.   []

5. PLAN INFERENCE

Definition 5.1 A *planning clause* is a clause of form

pq(t1,..,tn,nr(L)) :- pq(t1,..,tn,T)

where L is a proof variable, T is a proof tree and nr is a new label called the label of the clause.

A planning clause thus allows an uninformed query to pick up a proof plan. The idea is to use a search rule that matches the planning clause first and then tries the rest of the program.

Definition 5.2 An *informed plan version* of a Horn clause program is the conjunction of its uninformed plan version with one or more planning clauses.

We now propose a plan inference strategy. Let P be a Horn clause program without asserts or cuts. Let pq(t11,..,t1n,L1) and pq(t21,..,t2n,L2) be two queries proved earlier which returned the proof trees T1 and T2 respectively. From them we propose to infer the planning clause

(C):   pq(t1,..,tn,nr(L)) :- pq(t1,..,tn,T)

where T is the msg of T1 and T2 and ti is the msg of t1i and t2i for i = 1 to n.

Theorem 5.1. (Soundness Theorem). Let P' be the informed version of P obtained by asserting C at the top of P. Then P' is correct with respect to P in the sense that whenever a query pq can be proved in P',it can be proved in P.

Proof. Every execution in P' either goes through C or avoids it. If it does not go through C, then it is a valid execution of P. So suppose it does not.

In this case the program first proof checks the plan in P(since T is proof tree in P). After this it searches in P for the goals corresponding to the variables in T.These searches are valid in P by the lifting lemma [Llyod,84]. Then by induction, we can show that the entire search is valid in P.   []

Example 5.1. Thus the planning clause that searches for uncles and aunts is

relation(X,Y,nr(L)):-relation(X,Y,r3(r2(O,r1(R)),r1(P)))

Similarly we can verify the clause

relation(X,Y,nr(L)):- relation(X,Y,r3(r1(M),r2(P)))

stands for the rule that all your parents' dessendants are related to you.

It is important to note that only some and not all generalizations give planning clauses that speed up search substantially. It is essential to have good heuristics to know when to infer a planning clause. In the system we have implemented, the choice of when to infer is left to the user.

5.1 SIMPLIFICATION PROCEDURE

Suppose that in example 3.1 we infer the planning clause

relation(X,Y,nr(L)):-relation(X,Y,r3(r2(O,r1(R)),r1(P)))

Then we see that as a result of the execution of nr, the following goals will be searched for

:-parent(U,V,M), parent(V,X,N), parent(U,Y,O).

Thus the planning clause nr is equivalent to the following clause nr'

relation(X,Y,nr'(M,N,O)):-parent(U,V,M), parent(V,X,N), parent(U,Y,O).

In essence what we have done is unfolded the planning clause. So we may infer nr' instead of nr, i. e. we may do the unfolding once and for all instead of doing it every time.

6. PROLOG PROGRAMS WITH ASSERT

Suppose we make a series of queries, infers and then follow them by an assert, is the program still correct?

Note Throughout this section and the next, we assume a depth first search strategy.

Lemma 6.1 Let P' be a correct informed version of P. Let Q and Q' be the programs obtained by asserting a new clause C at the top of P and P' respectively. Then Q' is correct with respect to Q.

Proof is trivial since the presence of a new clause does not obstruct the proof of Theorem 5.1 which still goes through.   []

Let us now see what happens if we allow asserts in the body of a rule.

Lemma 6.2 If asserts are allowed in the body of a rule, then the inference strategy in section 5 may give incorrect programs.

Proof If we are allowed to use assert, we can count the number of ways in which a query was satisfied by putting the goal count at the end of every rule whose head matches the query. The code for count is

```
count :- is_count(X),
     X1 is X + 1,
     asserta(is_count(X1).
count :- asserta(is_count(1)).
```

Now obviously P' will succeed once more than P(through C)and so they will both give different results on the query is_count(X). QED []

It is also interesting to note that P' may, in case of multiple answers, give answers in a different order than P. This difference will not be seen in the answers being returned unless you use asserts to accumulate the answers in a list.

7. PROLOG PROGRAMS WITH CUTS

We showed our strategy to be correct for Horn clause programs in section 5. PROLOG however has many non-declarative (procedural) features like the cut [Clocksin and Mellish,81].

Lemma 7.1 Let P be a PROLOG program with cuts. Then the inference strategy of section 5 gives incorrect inferences on P.

Proof Consider program 7.1.

a(X,r1(M,N)) :- even(X,M), !, b(X,N).
a(X,r2(M)) :- c(X,M).
c(X,r3(M)) :-d(M).
Program 7.1

If we did queries a(1) and a(3), we would get the following planning clause

a(X,nr(L)) :- a(X,r2(r3(M))).

at the top of the program.

Now if we execute a(2,L), we would execute d(M) which would never have been executed in program 7.1.   []

The problem, as is easy to see, occurs when we try to guide the search past the rule r2 before trying rule r1 which has a cut in its body.

Definition 7.1 A predicate pq is *procedural* if there is a cut in the body of a rule that has pq as the head.

We will not attempt to guide the search past a procedural goal. The following machinery is needed to ensure this.

Definition 7.2 A *clause* is said to be *procedural* if its head predicate is procedural.

Definition 7.3 A *proof label* is said to be *procedural* if it is the label of a procedural rule.

Definition 7.4 A *proof tree* is *procedural* if its root is procedural.

We decide to prune out all procedural proper subtrees of the msg and call the resulting tree *declarative msg(dmsg)*. We also notice that the meanings of procedural rules change if we change their order.

252

Inference Strategy Let P be a PROLOG program with cuts. Let pq(t11,..,t1n,L1) and pq(t21,..,t2n,L2) be two previous queries that generated proof trees T1 and T2 respectively. Then we infer

(C)   pq(t1,..,tn,nr(L)):-pq(t1,..,tn,T)

(where ti = msg of t1i and t2i, i = 1 to n and T = dmsg of T1 and T2.)

assert it at the top of p if T is not a procedural proof tree. Otherwise we assert C just before the rule labeled by the root of T.

Theorem 7.1 Let P' be the program obtained as a result of infering a new rule C in P according to the new strategy. Then P' is correct with respect to P.

Proof If C is non procedural then the strategy is similar to that of section 5 and a proof similar to that of theorem 5.1 can be given. We only need to note that the dmsg unifies with msg.

Suppose C is procedural. Let the root of the plan T in C be r. Now if C is tried in P', all rules before it must have failed. That means that in P, the rule labeled r would have been tried. Thus the execution in P' is guided through r by C only if r would have been tried in P. The remaining part of the guided search is in the declarative fragment of P and is hence correct as shown earlier. Thus every valid execution in P' is a valid execution in P.   QED []

We lose a lot of information when we prune msgs to get dmsgs. This information can be used if the pruned subtrees are used as plans. Thus from a msg, we can get multiple dmsgs and hence infer more than one clauses.

Example 7.1 Consider the program fragment 7.2.
a(X,r1(L,M)) :- b(X,Y,L), c(Y,M).
b(X,Y,r2(L)) :- d(X,Y,L).
c(Y,r3(L,M)) :- e(Y,L), !, f(M).
c(Y,r4(L)) :- g(Y,L).
g(Y,r5(L)) :- h(L).

r3 and r4 are procedural labels. Suppose the strategy in section 5 resulted in the predicate a(X,r1(r2(L),r4(r5(M))))

If we do single inference, then we can only infer

(C)   a(X,nr(L)) :- a(X,r1(r2(L),M))

where we throw away the subtree r4(r5(M)). However if we did multiple inferences then we could also have inferred

(C1)   c(Y,nr(L)) :- c(Y,r4(r5(M))).

and asserted it between r3 and r4. C1 will be tried only if r3 fails, i.e. if r4 was tried in program 7.2.

8. CONCLUSIONS

We have presented a method by which the search for PROLOG queries can be substantially speeded up by using proof plans obtained by generalizing earlier searches.

A prototype implementation in PROLOG has been made which consists of a preprocessor that translates PROLOG programs into their plan versions and a runtime environment which accepts queries and makes plan inferences. If plan inferences are made carefully then the method works very well. Further investigation needs to be done to identify suitable criteria for automatic plan inference. The ratio of the size of the generalized plan to the size of the original proof may be used as one such criterion.

The use of history to modify a given propositional logic program was studied from a complexity point of view in [Lowen,88]. A similar study of complexity improvements for restricted versions of Horn clause programs needs to be done.

Another direction for future study is to use type theory to extend the suggested method to other kinds of logic programs.

References

[Aho et.al.,86]   Aho,A.V., Sethi Ravi and Ullman, J.D. Compilers; Principles, Techniques and Tools, Reading, Addison-Wesley, 1986.

[Apt and van Emden,82]   Apt, K.R. and van Emden, M.H., Contributions to the Theory of Logic Programming, JACM, 29(3), pp.841-862, 1982.

[Clocksin and Mellish,81]   Clocksin, W.F. and Mellish, C.S., Programming in Prolog, Springer Verlag, 1981.

[Gandhe,88]   Gandhe, M., Studies in Intuitionistic Type Theory, Internal Report, Department of COmputer Science and Engineering, I.I.T. Bombay, 1988.

[Gordon et.al.,79]   Gordon, M., Milner, R. and Wadsworth, C. Edinburgh LCF, LNCS vol.78, Springer Verlag, 1979.

[Hindley and Seldin,86]   Hindley, J.R. and Seldin, J.P., Introduction to Combinators and Lambda Calculus, London Mathematical Society Student Texts #1, Cambridge University Press, 1986.

[Lloyd,84]   Lloyd, J.W., Foundations of Logic Programming, Springer Verlag, 1984.

[Lowen,88]   Lowen,U., Optimization Aspects of Logical Formulas in Proceedings of the First Workshop on Computer Science Logic CSL'87, eds. Borger, E, Kleine Buning, H. and Richter, M.M., LNCS vol 329, Springer Verlag, pp. 173-187, 1988.

[MartinLof,80]   Martin-Lof, P., Constructive Mathematics and Logic Programming in Logic, Methodology and Philosophy of Science, vol 6, North Holland, pp.153-175, 1980.

[Milner,87]   Milner, R, Dialogue with a Proof System, Proceedings of TAPSOFT'87, LNCS vol 249, Springer Verlag, 1987.

A Unified Framework for Characterising Logic Program Executions

E Ravindran and SL Mehndiratta
Department of Computer Science and Engg.,
Indian Institute of Technology,
Bombay, 400 076, India.

Abstract

This paper presents a unified framework for characterising execution models for logic programs. The *framework* consists of two basic entities, viz., *objects* and *actions*. Objects are abstractions of data values, program encodings, variable bindings etc., whereas actions represent events like application of a function to its arguments, unification, solving a conjunction,etc. The relationship between objects and actions are specified as rules, within an *execution model*. These rules govern the behaviour of an execution model. Within the *framework*, it is shown how to characterise the salient properties of dataflow model of logic programs, as well as execution models of concurrent logic languages. This enables us to understand better the relationships between the execution models of logic programs.

1 Introduction

In this paper, we present a framework for characterising logic program executions. By a *framework* [1] we mean a collection of entities called *objects* and *actions*, together with the object categories. Objects are abstractions of data values, program encodings, variable bindings etc., whereas actions represent events such as application of a function to its arguments, unification, solving a conjunction,etc. The *framework* gives rise to the definition of an execution model. By an execution model, we mean a way of characterising computations, generated either by the standard interpreter for a language, or one obtained by applying a model of concurrency to a computational paradigm. Thus, execution models for concurrent logic languages, as well as dataflow models for logic programs, belong to the class of execution models. In this paper, we illustrate how a proper definition of *framework* and *execution model* can capture the behaviour of execution models of logic programs.

---

[1]Throughout this paper, the words *framework* and *execution model* written in italics, refer to their respective definitions

It may be noted that the motivation for our *framework*, and *execution model*, is based on the following observations.

- Execution models for logic programs can be compared, contrasted and their relationships amongst them brought out within a unified framework.

- Execution models can be combined to yield new execution models within our framework.

- Although a rigorous and formal setting as in [Saraswath, 1987], can capture the operational behaviour of *concurrent logic languages* it is not directly applicable for capturing the behaviours of execution models.

A *framework* assigns an interpretation to objects, and object categories. Thus, a logic programming framework equates the encodings of logic programs as objects, and the syntactic categories of logic programs as the object categories. An *execution model*, based on a *framework*, assigns an interpretation to actions. The behaviour of an execution model is governed by the relationships between objects and actions. These relationships are captured by *rules*, which tell how the objects in an *execution model* interact. These rules can be combined or modified to reflect the differences in the behaviours of execution models. Moreover, we can show that some of the existing execution models of logic programs are *instances* of the the abstract definition of an *execution model*.

The organisation of the paper is as follows. Section 2 presents the *framework*. The execution models based on the *framework*, are presented in Section 3. Section 4 provides instances of various execution models. In Section 5, we outline how concurrent logic programming models are captured within our *framework*. The paper ends with a section on conclusion.

2 The Framework

The two major components of the *framework* are the collection of *Objects* and *Actions*. Objects are produced and consumed by actions. Objects have a finite number of attributes and actions fixed arities. Objects have an interpretation depending on the *framework* chosen. In a dataflow framework, objects are interpreted as data values, whereas in a logic programming framework, they are interpreted as 'encodings' of logic programs. Moreover, objects could be structured, with 'types' associated with each structure/sub-structure. The collection of all such types constitutes the 'Object category'. A *framework* also specifies the mapping which associates each object in the *framework* to an element in the Object category. Actions model *events* that occur during the executions in any execution model. Unlike objects, actions are given interpretations only within an execution model and not within the *framework*.

Thus we arrive at the following definition of a *framework*.

256

Definition 2.1 (Framework) *A framework F is a 4-tuple $F = (O, A, OC, Type)$ where*

> *O   Collection of* objects *, each object having a finite number of attributes.*
>
> *A   Collection of* actions, *each action having a fixed arity. For $a \in A$, $In(a)$ and $Out(a)$ give the input and output arities of 'a' respectively.*
>
> *OC   Collection of syntactic categories of objects.*
>
> *Type   The function $Type : O \to OC$ assigning to each object its object category.*

It may be noted that what is 'common' among all execution models based on a *framework*, is the interpretation to objects, object categories, and the Type function whereas what distinguishes one execution model from another is the 'behaviour' which depends on the interpretation to actions and the relationship between objects and actions.

3   Execution Models

An *execution model* is based on a *framework*. An essential component of any *execution model* is the collection of 'events' and the association of actions to events. Events are the semantic counterparts of actions. They specify functions/relations on the domain of objects. The 'occurrence' of events causes a change in the 'state' of the system whose behaviour is being captured by the *execution model*.

Another important component is the association between objects and actions. This is given by the *Flow relation* $\to$. Intuitively, $(o \to a)$ is interpreted to mean that object o is *input* to action a. Conversely, $(a \to o)$ is interpreted to mean that object o is *output* from action a. (ie., produced by action a as a result of execution). For an action a with input arity m, the flow relation is generalised to $(o \to_i a)$ and is interpreted as follows — object o is input to the ith port of action $a(i \leq m)$. A similar remark applies to objects being output by actions with arity greater than 1.

The effects of the occurrence of events, in an *execution model E*, are reflected as changes of *configurations* of E. A *configuration* is a *finite* subset of the flow relation. (finite, because it models a situation when finite occurrences of events have taken place, starting from an initial configuration). An execution model specifies the configurations it permits. This is the collection $\{C_i\}$ In any configuration, the objects and actions in it must satisfy certain *restrictions* (to be explained shortly). Moreover, if a configuration C_i transits to configuration C_j through the occurrence of an event modelled by an action a, then a must belong to the set of *visible Actions* — VA, which is another component of E. In other words, VA is the set of all actions through which a configuration in E can change itself. The occurrence of an event whose action is not visible can still change the configuration; but such a configuration will not be visible to the E (by being not present in the set of permissible configurations)

The behaviour of any execution model E is governed by its 'rules'. This is captured through the set of *Restrictions* of E. These are first-order logic formulae which define the relationship between objects and actions of any configuration of E. There are two types of restrictions. (i) Rules which every (object,action) or (action,object) pair has to satisfy in any configuration of E. (ii) Rules which govern how configurations progress after each occurrence of an event. These are first-order logic formulae of the type $P \Rightarrow Q$. Each such rule will be indexed by a member of the set of Visible Actions. Operationally, this is to be viewed as a *rewrite rule* for configurations.

The interpretation associated to a rule of type (ii) is that whenever a configuration C_i satisfies P, the occurrence of an event (modelled by a visible action which indexes the rule) transforms the configuration C_i to a configuration C_j which satisfies Q and *does not* satisfy P. The analogy with the rewrite rule is because the relationship between objects and actions within a configuration can be viewed as being rewritten upon the occurrence of an event. This leads us to the following definition of an execution model.

Definition 3.1 (Execution Model) *An Execution Model E based on a framework* $F = (O, A, OC, Type)$ *is a 6-tuple* $E = (\mathcal{E}, I, VA, \rightarrow, \{C_i\}_{i \in \mathcal{I}}, R)$ *where*

$\mathcal{E}$ *Set of events*

$I : A \rightarrow \mathcal{E}$ *Interpretation function for actions.*

$VA \subseteq A$ *Set of Visible Actions*

$\rightarrow$ *Flow relation* $\subseteq (O \times A) \cup (A \times O)$

$\{C_i\}_{i \in \mathcal{I}}$ *Collection of configurations, where C_i is a finite subset of $\rightarrow$ and*

$\vdash \subseteq \{C_i\}_{i \in \mathcal{I}} \times VA \times \{C_i\}_{i \in \mathcal{I}}$ *is the Transition relation*

R *Set of Restrictions.*

4 Instances

As instances of the *framework* and *execution model* we will describe in this section, the execution model for dataflow, the logic programming execution model and the dataflow execution of logic programs. In each of the above cases, we give a description of the execution model, followed by the definitions which capture the above behaviour.

4.1 Dataflow model

Here, the computation is modelled on an underlying graph called a dataflow graph [Arvind and Culler, 1986][Davis and Keller, 1982]. The nodes of the graph represent instructions and the directed edges represent data paths along which data flows in the form of *tokens*. The *firing* of a node takes place upon arrival of tokens at all its incoming edges. This causes all the incoming tokens which participate in the firing of a node to disappear from the incoming edges, and new tokens to appear at all its outgoing edges. The token that is produced as a result of firing of a node depends only on those that are responsible for the firing of that node — the firing of any other node in the graph cannot possibly affect its outcome, thus ensuring total freedom from side-effects. A *snapshot* in a dataflow computation corresponds to a distribution of tokens across the edges of the dataflow graph. Executions progress as a series of snapshots, until we reach one in which no more nodes can fire.

The collection of Objects, for a *dataflow framework*, is the collection of all *data values*. Objects have only *one* attribute., viz., the value of the data itself. The collection of all *instructions* constitutes the set of Actions. The arities of actions are fixed by the number of input operands an instruction requires and the number of operands it emits after the execution of the instruction. As regards the Object category, there is only one category, to which any data value belongs— that is, the collection of all data values itself. Thus, we arrive at the following definition.

Definition 4.1 (Dataflow framework) *A dataflow framework is a framework* $F = (O, A, OC, Type)$ *where*

   O Collection of data values.

   A Collection of instructions

   OC The category of all data values.

   Type The constant function which maps every data value to the above category.

A dataflow execution model based on the above *framework* can be derived once we impose the 'control structure' of a dataflow graph on the definition of an execution model. This is necessary because an execution model defines only the relationships between *objects and actions* (through the flow relation) or amongst *objects and objects* (objects are permitted to be structured entities) but *not* between actions and actions (which defines the structure of a graph, since actions are analogous to nodes). It may be noted that the relationship amongst actions is not independent of the others. Restrictions allow us to impose this control structure through rules which constrain the relationship between objects and actions.

Snapshots of a dataflow model are identical with configurations of an execution model. The firing rule of a node in a dataflow graph is directly translated into a rewrite rule among configurations. The events are equated with computation of functions on data values. All actions are 'visible' in a dataflow computation model. This is a consequence of the fact that none of the nodes in a dataflow graph is 'hidden' from the structure of the graph. In fact, computations on a dataflow graph with an *encapsulation* property (a node in a graph represents a subgraph) may be modelled effectively with the set of Visible Actions.

Definition 4.2 (Dataflow execution Model) *A dataflow execution model based on the dataflow framework is an execution model* $E = (\mathcal{E}, I, VA, \rightarrow, \{C_i\}_{i \in \mathcal{I}}, R)$ *where*

   $\mathcal{E}$ *Set of functions computed by instructions.*

$I \to \mathcal{E}$ *The mapping associating instructions to functions.*

VA *The entire set of actions, ie., instructions.*

$\to \&\{C_i\}_{i \in \mathcal{I}}$ *Satisfying the Restrictions R.*

R *As listed below*

Restrictions[2].

(Rule 1: Defining the underlying graph)

$\forall a_1 a_2 \in A \forall o_1 o_2 \in O : ((a_1 \to_i o_1) \wedge (a_1 \to_i o_2) \wedge (o_1 \to_j a_2)) \implies (o_2 \to_j a_2)$

(Rule 2: Defining the firing rule)

$$\forall a \in A \forall o_{m_r} \in O : \bigwedge_{r=1}^{In(a)} (o_{m_r} \to_r a) \implies \bigwedge_{s=1}^{Out(a)} (a \to_s o_k)$$

where $o_k = f_a(o_{m_1}, o_{m_2}, \ldots, o_{m_{In(a)}})$.

It may be noted that rule 1 applies to all configurations, ie., these relationships between objects and actions must be satisfied by all configurations. Rule 2 is the rewrite rule for configurations. This is indexed by the action a, which models the occurrence of the an event that changes the configuration. f_a in rule 2 is the function computed by the event associated with a.

4.2   Logic program executions

Logic programs are Horn clauses of the form $A \leftarrow B_1, B_2, \ldots, B_n$[Kowalski, 1979]. The procedural interpretation of logic programs and in particular its AND-OR process model description is well known and can be found in [Conery, 1983]. In this interpretation, two phases of execution can be identified. In the *forward* phase, AND(OR) processes are set up to solve conjunctive(disjunctive) queries, whereas in the *backward* phase, the conjunction(disjunction) on the solutions is performed.

In order to relate the above form of computation to the *framework*, the collection of program encodings of a given logic program can be thought of as the collection of objects, where each object is assumed to have an attribute, viz. the value of the encoding itself. Each object can be viewed to be a structured one, and can be represented in terms of its sub-structures.(for example, an object representing a program encoding has objects which represent clause encodings as its sub-structures) We shall employ the notation $o = (o_1, \ldots, o_k)$ for an object o whose sub-structures are $o_1, \ldots, o_k$. Thus,

Definition 4.3 (Logic programming framework) *A logic programming framework is a framework $F = (O, A, OC, Type)$ where*

O *Encodings of logic programs, each encoding has a single attribute.*

A *Actions are entities modelling interpreting procedures.*

---

[2]Throughout this paper, o with possible subscripts/primes will denote objects, and a, with possible subscripts/primes will denote actions.

OC Syntactic categories of logic programs, viz., {Program, Clause, Unit-clause, Literal, Term, Query}

Type Association of an encoding to its syntactic category.

In any execution model of logic programs, actions are interpreted to be the *steps* involved in a computation . For example, in a top-down interpretation of logic programs involving AND and OR processes, these steps would be *solving a conjunctive set* (SOLVE-AND) or performing the conjunction of solutions of a set of processes (AND) etc. We shall consider an execution model in which the set of *events* comprises of SOLVE-AND, SOLVE-OR, AND, OR and UNIFY. UNIFY is a function among encodings of logic programs, and outputs a unifier of the encodings. The states of such an execution model yield information regarding evaluation of program encodings (for example, whether the corresponding SOLVE-AND and SOLVE-OR have executed or not). Even within such an execution model, we can hide some state information, by taking the set of visible actions as a subset of the given set of actions. In fact, for logic programs, SOLVE-AND, SOLVE-OR and UNIFY need be visible always — a larger set of visible actions gives rise to a more fine-grained execution model. Such an execution model for logic programs is characterised thus.

Definition 4.4 (Logic programming execution model) *A logic programming execution model based on the logic programming framework is defined as*
$E = (\mathcal{E}, I, VA, \rightarrow, \{C_i\}_{i \in \mathcal{I}}, R)$ *where*

$\mathcal{E}$ *{SOLVE-AND, SOLVE-OR, UNIFY, SOLVE-UNIT, AND, OR}*

I *Association an action with its event.*

$\rightarrow$ *Relationship between program encodings and the interpreting actions.*

VA *Actions whose events belong to {SOLVE-AND, SOLVE-OR, UNIFY}*

$\{C_i\}$ *States of the interpreter that are visible.*

Restrictions

$$((o \rightarrow a) \wedge (a \rightarrow o') \wedge (I(a) = \text{SOLVE} - \text{AND}) \wedge (o = (o_1, \ldots, o_k)) \Longrightarrow$$
$$\bigwedge_{i=1}^{k} (o_i \rightarrow a_i) \wedge (I(a_i) = \text{SOLVE} - \text{OR}) \wedge \bigwedge_{i=1}^{k} (a_i \rightarrow o'_i) \wedge (o'_i \rightarrow a') \wedge (I(a') = \text{AND}) \wedge (a' \rightarrow o')$$

(Whenever a structured object is to be solved conjunctively, split the structure into its individual components, solve the components disjunctively, and then take the conjunction of all such solutions).

$$((o \rightarrow a) \wedge (a \rightarrow o') \wedge (I(a) = \text{SOLVE} - \text{OR}) \wedge (o = (o_1, \ldots, o_k)) \Longrightarrow$$
$$(\bigvee_{i=1}^{k} (o_i \rightarrow a_i) \wedge (I(a_i) = \text{SOLVE} - \text{AND}) \vee (I(a_i = \text{SOLVE} - \text{UNIT})) \wedge$$

$$\bigvee_{i=1}^{k} a_i \rightarrow o'_i) \wedge (o'_i \rightarrow a') \wedge (I(a') = \text{SOLVE} - \text{OR}) \wedge (a' \rightarrow o')$$

(Similar to the above)

$(Type(o) = Clause \vee Term \vee Query \vee Program) \wedge (o \rightarrow a) \implies (I(a) = \text{SOLVE} - \text{AND})$

$(Type(o) = Literal \wedge (o \rightarrow a)) \implies I(a) = \text{SOLVE} - \text{OR}$

$(Type(o) = Unit - clause \wedge (o \rightarrow a)) \implies I(a) = \text{SOLVE} - \text{UNIT}$

(An object which is of type Clause, Term, Query or Program can only be solved conjunctively. A Literal object can only be solved disjunctively and a unit clause all by itself)

$(o_1 \rightarrow a_1) \wedge Type(o_1) = Literal \wedge (o_2 \rightarrow a_2) \wedge Type(o_2) = Unit - clause \wedge$

$(a_1 \rightarrow o_3) \wedge I(a_2) = \text{SOLVE} - \text{UNIT} \wedge I(a_1) = \text{SOLVE} - \text{OR}) \implies o_3 = \text{UNIFY}(o_1 o_2)$

(Whenever a Literal object and a Unit-clause object have unified, the result object is the unifier of the two)

$(o_1 \rightarrow a_1) \wedge Type(o_1) = Literal \wedge (o_2 \rightarrow a_2) \wedge Type(o_2) = Clause \wedge$

$o_2 = (o_{21}, \ldots, o_{2k}) \wedge (a_1 \rightarrow o_3) \wedge I(a_2) = \text{SOLVE} - \text{AND} \wedge I(a_1) = \text{SOLVE} - \text{OR} \implies$

$(o_1' = \text{UNIFY}(o_1, o_{21})) \wedge (I(a) = \text{SOLVE} - \text{AND}) \wedge o_2' = (o_1', o_{22}, \ldots, o_{2k}) \wedge (o_2' \rightarrow a)$

(Whenever a Literal object is to solved in association with a clause, then unify the literal with the 'head' of the clause, and solve conjunctively the new object formed by appending the body of the clause to this unifier)

$\exists! o : ((o \rightarrow a) \vee (a \rightarrow o)) \wedge Type(o) = Query$

(Any configuration can contain exactly one query)

4.3 Dataflow model for logic programs

A dataflow model of computation views computations as being generated by events triggered by the availability of data. At a very coarse level, the program encodings of the logic programming framework could themselves be viewed as data, the events being those identified by any logic programming execution model. We argue that in *any dataflow model for logic programs*, the events occurring in the 'forward' phase (initiating procedures for solving conjunction and disjunctions) as well as the 'backward' phase (collecting together the solutions by these procedures) must be made *visible*. This is on account of the fact that the 'data' in a logic programming computation is present in the 'bindings' of variables, which are *generated* and *propagated* in the backward phase. The events in the forward phase must be described because they govern the inter-relationships between the various events that occur during the backward phase.

Moreover, the main feature of dataflow is its ability to capture *pipelined parallelism*. For this, the control structure of the dataflow graph becomes important. Since the execution model does not have an explicit notion of a graph, the restrictions which define the dataflow graph must be *included in a dataflow execution model of logic programs*.

Thus, the logic program execution model (Definition 4.4) becomes *a dataflow execution model for logic programs* by (i) Defining the set of Visible Actions as those which are interpreted over {SOLVE-AND, SOLVE-OR, AND, OR, UNIFY} and (ii) Adding the following rule to the set of Restrictions.

$(a_1 \rightarrow o_1) \wedge (o_1 \rightarrow a_2) \wedge (a_1 \rightarrow o_2) \implies (o_2 \rightarrow a_2)$

(This expresses the control structure of a dataflow graph)

The above definition leads to the following proposition.

Proposition 4.1 *Both Halim's data driven model [Halim, 1986] and Wise's Epilog model [Wise, 1986] are* dataflow execution models of logic programs.

The proposition can be established[Ravindran and Mehndiratta, 1989] by relating the dataflow primitives in both the above models to the actions in the above definition, the tokens/dframes to the objects, and showing that the relationships between objects and actions as specified by the definition, are properties of the above models.

The granularity of an execution model is captured through the notion of *refinement*.

Definition 4.5 (Refinement) *An execution model E_A is a refinement of an execution model E_B iff $C_i^A \vdash_a C_j^A \iff$*
$\exists C_{i_0}^B, \ldots, C_{i_k}^B : C_i^A = C_{i_0}^B, \vdash_{b_1} C_{i_1}^B, \vdash_{b_2} C_{i_2}^B, \ldots, \vdash_{b_k} C_{i_k}^B = C_j^A$ where C_i^A belong to the set of configurations of E_A and C_j^B belong to the set of configurations of E_B.

The intuitive notion in the definition of refinement is that there exists a series of steps in the execution model that is refined for every step that is taken in the execution model that is *coarse*, while transiting between *equal* configurations. The equality between configurations is a *syntactic equality* if the two execution models are based on the same *framework*. If not, the equality among execution models will have to be a *semantic* one, being defined across *frameworks*. The following propositions are consequences of the definition of refinement.

Proposition 4.2 *Let execution models E_A and E_B be based on the same* framework *and have identical set of restrictions. Then E_A is more refined than E_B whenever the set of Visible Actions of A subsumes the set of Visible Actions of B.*

Proposition 4.3 *Halim's data driven model is a refinement of Wise's Epilog model.*

5 Concurrent Logic Programming Models

In this section, we outline how the behaviours of concurrent logic programming execution models are captured within our framework. One of the features of concurrent logic programming execution models is the *controlled sharing* of information across the literals or clauses. Literals share variables and therefore the bindings of variables shared across literals within the same clause will have to *agree*. Clauses share information with regard to their success when invoked by the same literal. Sharing of information amongst objects within an object category, is captured through a *dependency relation $\mathcal{R}$*. The agreement amongst objects is captured through an *agreement relation $\mathcal{M}$* on objects.

Definition 5.1 (Shared Execution Model) *Let E be the logic programming execution model (Definition 4.4), based on framework $F = (O, A, OC, Type)$. E is a shared execution model if there exists a family of dependency relations $\mathcal{R}_k$ defined on every subset O_k of O, where $O_k = \{o \in O | Type(o) = k, k \in OC\}$*

Definition 5.2 (Unishared execution model) *A Unishared execution model is a shared execution model in which the family of dependency relations $\{\mathcal{R}_k\}$ is a singleton, ie., the dependency relation $\mathcal{R}_k$ is non-empty for exactly one object category.*

A shared execution model is said to be a multi-shared *execution model if it is not unishared.*

Definition 5.3 (Stream based execution model) *A stream based execution model is a shared execution model E with the following rule added to the set of restrictions of E.*

$$(o_1 \rightarrow a) \wedge (o_1 \mathcal{R}_k o_2) \Longrightarrow (o_2 \rightarrow a)$$

Definition 5.4 (Execution model with suspension) *Let E be a shared execution model based on $F = (O, A, OC, Type)$ with dependency relations $\mathcal{R}_k$ defined on O. Let $\mathcal{M}$ be the* agreement *relation* on objects. *E is* an *execution model with suspension if the following rule is added to the Restrictions of E.*

$(o_1 \mathcal{R}_k o_2) \vee \neg(o_1 \mathcal{M} o_2) \Longrightarrow (o_1 \rightarrow a) \wedge (o_2 \rightarrow a)$ *where the event associated to action a is to* cause suspension *of o_1 or o_2, but* not both.

Definition 5.5 (Eager sharing) *Let E be a shared execution model based on $F = (O, A, OC, Type)$ with dependency relations $\mathcal{R}_k$ defined on O. Let $\mathcal{M}$ be the* agreement relation *defined on objects. Let $o_1, o_2, \ldots, o_m, o$ belong to O_k, and let $o'_1, o'_2, \ldots, o'_n, o'$ belong to O_r, where $o \mathcal{M} o'$. E is said to exhibit eager sharing if the following rule is added to the set of restrictions of E.*

$$\bigwedge_{i=1}^{m}(o \rightarrow o_i) \wedge (o_i \rightarrow a) \Longrightarrow \bigwedge_{j=1}^{n}(a \rightarrow o'_j)$$ *where the event associated with action a is the transfer of information from the objects o_i to the objects o'_j.*

The above definitions help us to relate the various properties of execution models of concurrent logic languages. Some of these relationships are stated in terms of propositions given below; their details can be found in [Ravindran and Mehndiratta, 1989].

Proposition 5.1 *A sequential logic programming model is a* multi-shared *execution model. An* OR-parallel *(AND-parallel) logic programming model is a* unishared *execution model.*

Proposition 5.2 *A logic programming execution model with stream parallelism [Gregory, 1987] is a* stream based *execution model.*

Proposition 5.3 *Both* PARLOG *[Gregory, 1987] and Concurrent Prolog [Shapiro, 1983] execution models are* execution models with suspension.

Proposition 5.4 *The execution models of Saraswath's CP [Saraswath, 1986] family of languages exhibit* eager sharing.

6 Conclusion

We have presented a unified framework for characterising logic program executions to understand the commonalities, differences and relationships amongst the various execution models of logic programs. Some of these relationships are captured through propositions. The basic definition of *framework*, and *execution model* can be augmented to support non-trivial control strategies adopted by other logic programming interpreters[Bruynooghe and Pereira, 1984]. It remains to be seen whether the framework discussed in this paper can be adopted to capture the details of various OR-parallel implementations as outlined in [Lusk et al., 1988]. Attempts are also under way to apply the framework to model dataflow interpreters for concurrent logic languages.

References

[Arvind and Culler, 1986]
> Arvind and Culler DE. *Dataflow architectures*. Annual Reviews in Computer science I, pp 225-253, 1986.

[Bruynooghe and Pereira, 1984]
> Bruynooghe M and Pereira LM. *Deduction revision by intelligent backtracking*, Implementations of Prolog, J.A.Campbell(ed.), Ellis Horwood, pp 194-215, 1984.

[Conery, 1983]
> Conery JS. *The AND-OR process model of parallel interpretation of logic programs*. Technical report 1204, University of California at Irvine, 1983.

[Davis and Keller, 1982]
> Davis AL and Keller RM. *Dataflow program graphs*, IEEE Computer, pp 26-41, February 1982.

[Gregory, 1987]
> Gregory S. *Parallel logic programming in PARLOG*. Addison Wesley, 1987.

[Halim, 1986]
> Halim Z. *A Data driven machine for OR-parallel evaluation of logic programs*. New Generation Computing, 4, pp 5-33, 1986.

[Kowalski, 1979]
> Kowalski R. *Logic for problem solving*. Elsevier North Holland, 1979.

[Lusk et al., 1988]
> Lusk E. Warren DHD. Haridi S. et al. *The AURORA OR-parallel PROLOG system*. Proceedings of the Intl. Conf. on FGCS, pp 819-830, 1988.

[Ravindran and Mehndiratta, 1989]
Ravindran E and Mehndiratta SL. *A unified framework for characterising logic program executions.* Technical Report, TR-003-89, I.I.T Bombay, October 1989.

[Saraswath, 1986]
Saraswath V. *Problems with Concurrent Prolog.* Technical Report, CMU-CS-86-100, Carnegie-Mellon University, 1986.

[Saraswath, 1987]
Saraswath V. *The Concurrent logic programming language CP: Definition and operational semantics.* Proceedings of the ACM Symposium on Principles of Programming Languages, pp 49-62, 1987.

[Shapiro, 1983]
Shapiro EY. *A subset of Concurrent Prolog and its interpreter.* Technical Report, TR-003, Weizmann Institute of Science, Israel, 1983.

[Wise, 1986]
Wise MJ. *Prolog Multiprocessors.* Prentice-Hall 1986.

An Abstract Machine for the Reduce-OR Process Model for Parallel Prolog*

Balkrishna Ramkumar   Laxmikant V. Kalé

ramkumar@cs.uiuc.edu   kale@cs.uiuc.edu

Dept. of Computer Science

University Of Illinois at Urbana–Champaign

Urbana, Illinois 61801

Abstract

We discuss the design of an abstract machine for the Reduce-OR process model (ROPM) for the AND and OR parallel execution of Prolog programs. It differs from the WAM in many respects, and some of these differences are elaborated upon in this paper. Some of the significant differences are related to the binding environment which has been designed to support AND and OR parallel execution of logic programs on both shared and nonshared memory machines, the process model, and the handling of solutions for AND parallel branches in the *Data Join Graph* (DJG[1]) that is used to represent data dependencies in a Prolog clause. An emulator for the abstract machine has been implemented and is targeted for both shared and nonshared memory machines.

1 Introduction

Much research has been conducted recently on efficient schemes for the parallel execution of logic programs with promising results. The schemes proposed include those that exploit AND parallelism [DeGroot 1984, Hermenegildo 1986, Lin and Kumar 1988], and OR parallelism [Hausman et al 1987, Lusk et al 1988]. These process models are suitable mainly for shared memory machines. Other models that support both AND and OR parallelism [Biswas et al 1988, Conery 1987, Kergommeaux and Robert 1988, Gupta and Jayaraman 1989] have been proposed. Of these, the model proposed in [Gupta and Jayaraman 1989] is designed specifically for shared memory machines. The others are designed to be suitable for a distributed environment. The work described in this paper also supports both AND and OR parallelism and is designed to run on all general purpose MIMD machines.

The distinction between shared and nonshared memory machines is getting increasingly blurred. A recent paper [Mudambi 1989] describes the performance of the Aurora OR-parallel system on the Butterfly GP1000 shared memory system, where non-local memory references are shown to affect performance significantly. We believe, therefore, that the real challenge is in designing a parallel Prolog compiler that makes no assumptions about the underlying machine, but can optimise execution on shared memory systems.

---

*This work is supported in part by a National Science Foundation grant NSF CCR-87-00988

[1]The difference is that in DJGs arcs represent literals and nodes represent the joining points for the data produced by literals on its incoming arcs.

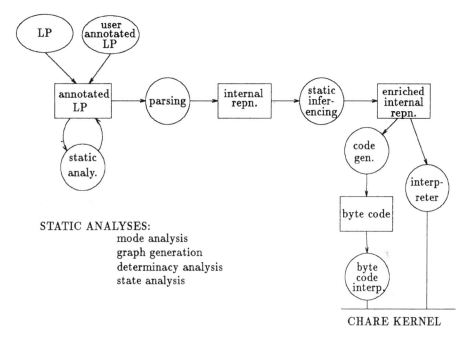

Figure 1: A top level view of the Parallel Prolog program development system

The Reduce-OR process model (ROPM) [Kale 1987b] for parallel logic programs exploits both AND and OR parallelism in logic programs and handles their interaction. Like the other AND and OR parallel process models mentioned above, for efficiency reasons, only independent AND parallelism is exploited in our implementation of ROPM. It supports full OR parallelism, including a form of OR parallelism called *consumer instance* parallelism (see [Kale 1987a]) where different instances of a literal in a clause can be evaluated in parallel.

We have also proposed a binding environment that is suitable for AND and OR parallel execution of logic programs on both shared and nonshared memory machines [Kale et al 1988]. The binding environment has been optimised considerably for a compiled environment. The main differences between the abstract machine for the Reduce-OR process model and the WAM stem from the binding environment, the process model and the join operation on solutions for AND parallel branches in the DJG. We discuss each of these differences in Section 4. We first give a top view of our project in Section 2, following which we describe the underlying execution model of the compiler.

2   The Parallel Prolog Environment

Figure 1 gives a top level view of the parallel Prolog development system. A Prolog program is supplied by the user as input. A static analysis module would then perform mode analysis on the program and use the results for graph generation. The graph generation phase of static analysis would involve detecting independent AND parallelism in clauses and annotating the program appropriately (see example in Figure 2). This annotated program can now be used to perform determinacy and state analyses: this information is also represented using annotations.

After all the static analysis has been performed, the result is a set of heavily annotated Prolog clauses. A parser reads in these annotated clauses and produces an internal representation of the program. A *static inferencing* module deduces further information that is of use during run time. Currently, this module computes common ancestor information for each clause in the program. This information is used during run time to perform the optimised join algorithm (see Section 4.3). In general, for each clause, this module computes any information that can help optimise code generation for faster compiled execution, or facilitate more efficient interpreted execution, of the Prolog program. We refer to the output from this phase as an *enriched* internal representation of the program.

The enriched internal representation can now be used either by a interpreter for Prolog, or by a code generator that generates byte code for the Prolog program. The byte code is then interpreted by an abstract machine emulator. The Prolog interpreter and the abstract machine emulator are both application programs written on top of the *Chare Kernel* (see Section 3). They are therefore machine *independent* and can be easily ported to both shared and nonshared memory machines.

The above framework also permits the user to provide additional information about the program regarding determinism, mutually exclusive clauses for a procedure, grain size control etc. via compiler directives and program annotations. The user supplied information can permit bypassing some of the static analysis phases. The static analysis module would then simply check the annotations for consistency and perform determinacy and state analyses to see if any more information about the program can be deduced. This has several advantages. First, it permits development of a code generator for compiled execution without being hampered by the lack of availability of a sophisticated static analysis module. The information provided via hand-annotations can be used to generate optimised code. Such a system can be used as a test bed for research on static analysis techniques, since the code generator is already in a position to exploit additional information available through such analyses. Third, it enables the user to convey his knowledge about the program to the system. Using current static analysis techniques, this information may be very difficult (or impossible) to deduce from an unannotated Prolog program. Finally, it makes it quite easy to incorporate any new developments in static analysis into the system, since (a) the framework for storing this information for use during optimised code generation is already in place, and (b) optimised code can be generated in advance for hand-annotated programs which supply results of such developments. In the latter case, it is only necessary to plug in the newly developed static analysis module and let it annotate the program instead of the user.

3 The Execution Model

An objective of our research was to develop the Prolog system as an application on top of the *Chare Kernel* [Kale and Shu 1988], a run time support system for machine *independent* parallel programming. The *Chare Kernel* support includes memory management, load balancing and queue management, all of which is *invisible* to the application. It therefore provides a clean separation between decomposition of a computation into parallel parts and the allocation of parallel actions to processors.

Conceptually, the *Chare Kernel* maintains a pool of *messages* created by the abstract machine emulator and is responsible for supplying work to the processors from this pool. A message may be a seed for a small grained process (called a *chare*) or a *response* to a (parent) *chare*. For brevity, we will call the former a *new-chare* message. A *new-chare* message results in the creation of a new chare whereas a *response* message wakes up an existing sleeping chare. Each message has an entry point associated with it in the application code. A message is first supplied to the application by jumping into a predefined entrypoint in the application. The application program begins processing the message by jumping to the entry point associated with it and executing the chare until it voluntarily suspends itself. Hence, after processing a *new-chare* or a *response* message, the chare in question always voluntarily suspends itself and relinquishes the processor, returning control to the *Chare Kernel*.

When a *new-chare* message is deposited into the message pool at a processor P (on a nonshared memory machine), the *Chare Kernel* may decide that the load on P is sufficiently high according to some load balancing criteria and decide to "ship" the message off to another node. Also, a *chare* that has already been processed may be waiting for responses from its children. So, when a response message is deposited into the pool, it has to be "shipped" to the node on which its parent *chare* resides.

4 The Abstract Machine

One of the main features of the abstract machine for ROPM is that it uses structure sharing as opposed to structure copying. This has some significant advantages when executing logic programs on nonshared memory machines. First, in a nonshared memory environment, structure sharing permits the "pure code" (i.e. the skeletal code of the program) to be broadcast to all the processors initially, and all references to "pure code" can be shipped between processors as indices during the rest of the execution. This can save a considerable amount of overhead in "shipping" goals between processors. This is especially significant for programs involving large amounts of input data that are static, but are referenced frequently throughout the execution. Second, the structure sharing approach permits the optimisations in term representation and unification described in [Kale et al 1988] to be used during compiled execution. Finally, the use of structure sharing imposes no unequivocal overhead over structure copying schemes barring the extra memory required to store the pure code (in addition to the generated byte code). In terms of execution time, the cost of constructing the terms during unification offsets the cost of indirect references to "pure code" and the associated "current" binding tuple.

4.1 The Process Model Instructions

Every message has an entry point associated with it. A *new-chare* message represents a goal to be solved. For a goal G, upon entry all the clauses in the procedure for G are tried in succession (see Figure 2: lines 1-29 for a simple example). The *new-chare* message results in the creation of a chare K which creates a query Q_i for every clause C_i that matches the goal G. For each clause C_i, the corresponding chare K creates *new-chare* messages for all its subgoals that can be started in parallel based on the DJG for C_i. If C_i

```
p([elem(a,b)|B],C,C,D).
p(A, B, C, D) :- ((q(A , B) // r(A ,C)), null) //  s(A, D).
```

```
--> 1      GetFactEnv     <ptr>, 3              /* set up fact env. (3 vars)  */
    /* AllocateBlock  2 */                      /* for structs, nest level 2  */
    2      UnifyStrct     <ptr>, nextArg=9, fail=13  /* unify: [              */
    3      UnifyStrct     <ptr>, nextArg=7, fail=13  /*         elem(         */
    4      UnifyAtom      a, fail=13            /*                   a,       */
    5      UnifyAtom      b, fail=13            /*                   b        */
    6      PopStack       Molecule Stack        /*                 ) |        */
    7      Unify1stVar    $1,fail=13            /*            B               */
    8      PopStack       Molecule Stack        /*            ],              */
    9      Unify1stVar    $2,fail=13            /*            C,              */
    10     UnifyVar       $2,fail=13            /*            C,              */
    11     Unify1stVar    $3,fail=13            /*            D               */
    12     SendFactResp                         /* send solution as response  */
    13     GetClauseEnv   <ptr>, 4              /* setup clause env- 4 vbls    */
           :                                    /* code for unification        */
    23     CreateNewQuery nodes=3, arcs=4       /* create data struct. for DJG */
    24     FireArc        0, 0, goalE=62,respE=30,q(...)
    25     FireArc        1, 0, goalE=68,respE=43,r(...)  /* fire subgoals    */
    26     FireArc        3, 0, goalE=74,respE=56,s(...)
           :
    29     Suspend
--> 30     CheckResponse                        /* response R recd. for q()   */
    31     SetUpJoin      <common ancestor info>, fail=42
    32     JoinTuples                           /* join R with solns. for r() */
    33     CopyBackPtr                          /* to carry backptrs to common
                                                   ancestors for later join   */
    34     Nop                                  /* for the null arc            */
    35     PushStack Join Stack                 /* save outer join environment */
    36     SetUpJoin      <common ancestor info>, fail=40
    37     JoinTuples                           /* inner join                  */
    38     SendClauseResp                       /* solution for clause available */
    39     NextTuple   37                       /* join with next soln. of s() */
    40     PopStack    Join Stack               /* inner join complete - restore
                                                   outer join environment     */
    41     NextTuple   32                       /* join R with next soln. of q() */
    42     Suspend
--> 43     CheckResponse                        /* response R recd. for r()   */
           :
    55     Suspend
--> 56     CheckResponse                        /* response R recd. for s()   */
    61     Suspend
           :
```

Figure 2: Fragment of code generated for a toy program used to illustrate the various features of the generated code. The arrows indicate entry points into the byte code.

is a fact and unification is successful, then a *SendFactResp* instruction sends the resulting bindings in a *response* message to G's parent. When all these clauses have been tried, all the chares created are suspended awaiting *response* messages from any chares they may have spawned.

A *response* message bound for a chare K (representing clauses C_i) constitutes a solution S for a subgoal of one of the C_is (say C_k). The availability of S may permit the creation of *new-chare* messages for subgoals in the body of C_k that were dependent on the availability of S. If S is a solution of an AND parallel branch, it may be necessary to join it with solutions from other AND parallel branches (see Figure 2). If S represents a set of bindings that satisfy all the subgoals in the body of C_k, a solution is computed and sent to K's parent, i.e. the chare representing the clause that spawned the goal G.

Initially, a *new-chare* message is created for the top level goal (query) and put in the work pool. The entry point for the top level goal is supplied in the code in a predetermined location. One of two instructions – *GetFactEnv* and *GetClauseEnv*, sets up the parent and child environment registers for unification with the corresponding fact or clause head respectively. This also involves creating a tuple of the required length for the clause bindings. Upon successful unification, a *CreateNewQuery* instruction, creates the necessary run time data structures that represent the DJG for the clause, and subgoals in the body of the clause may be fired using *FireArc* instructions. This is done by creating *new-chare* messages to solve the subgoals. The *FireArc* instruction supplies each *new-chare* message with a goal entry point - the entry point in the code for the newly created *chare*, and a response entry point - i.e. the entry point for one or more *responses* from the newly created subgoal. The *FireArc* instruction is similar to the *call* instruction in the WAM. However, unlike the WAM, no *put* instructions need to be generated prior to a *FireArc* (due to structure sharing). All parallel arcs emanating from the "current" node are fired, following which the *chare* suspends via a *Suspend* instruction and returns control to the *Chare Kernel*.

Code is generated to execute builtin predicates (we consider only deterministic and small grained builtin predicates here) in-line, since the overhead of creating *chares* and processing responses for such small granules of work is clearly unwarranted. Thus, the DJG is traversed, executing builtin predicates in-line successively, until a 'nonbuiltin' is encountered. Upon successful unification, code for the builtins is generated in-line, and a later node (i.e. not necessarily in the 1st node of a DJG) may possibly generate a *FireArc* for a nonbuiltin. Also, all builtins invoked before the first *FireArc* for that query have the same fail address associated with them as for failed head unification Should any of these builtins fail, the query is considered to have failed. This provides an efficient way of using a conjunct of builtin predicates as a *guard* in the body of a clause. Builtin predicates occurring later in the query (i.e. have a *FireArc* preceding it) have to be treated differently. Should they fail, one simply throws away the current partial solution.

4.2 Unification

The unification algorithm described in [Kale et al 1988] was specialised for compiled execution. For forward unification, instructions are generated for unification of the subterms of the head of the clause, much the same way as in the WAM except that the terms do not have to be constructed as in the structure copying scheme. However, once unification succeeds, for non-facts, instructions need to be generated for *closing* the variables in the child tuple. This is in keeping with the second phase of unification described in [Kale et al 1988]. Also, once a solution tuple for a query is generated, the parent (reference) tuple needs to be closed with the solution tuple to create a response. This is done in the *SendFactResp* and *SendClauseResp* instructions respectively.

As with the WAM, separate instructions are generated for constants, variables and structures. However, due to structure sharing, structures are handled differently. It is possible that subterms within a structure may be referenced via *molecules*. This would mean that subterms may refer to tuples different from the current tuple. As a consequence, a stack of current tuples needs to be maintained while accessing a structure and its subterms. This poses no problem since the stack can only be as deep as the structure itself and the depth is known at compile time. Therefore, an instruction is generated to allocate space for a stack (*AllocateBlock*) before unification for structures is carried out. Every *UnifyStruct* instruction pushes the current binding tuple address onto the stack. The "current" binding tuple can thus be different for subterms of the structure. Upon stepping out from depth d to a subterm at depth $d-1$ in the structure, an explicit *PopStack* instruction restores the binding tuple for depth $d-1$. The code in Figure 2 also illustrates the code generated for structures. In practice, for efficiency reasons, a preallocated stack is used for the binding tuple. Since the depth of terms is known at compile time, an *AllocateBlock* instruction is only generated if the required size exceeds the preallocated size.

During unification, compilation permits other optimisations that are not possible in interpretive execution. Registers can be used to represent the two binding tuples being unified. The cost of allocation and deallocation of memory is saved for failed unification. The close operation may involve extending the child tuple: this can be done in place. Also, it is only necessary to close the variables occurring in the head of the clause. Closing *all* clause variables is inevitable in the interpretive framework as it was not known which variables were "head" variables and which were not without additional bookkeeping at run-time.

4.3   Joining Solutions on AND parallel Branches

The support, by the abstract machine, of the *join* operation of AND parallel branches in a DJG is the point of significant departure from the WAM and WAM-like abstract machines for the other process models mentioned in Section 1. When (partial) solutions for all the AND parallel branches incident on a node in a DJG are available, it is necessary to perform a relational join of these solutions. The solutions can be combined incrementally as and when they are created (an *incremental* join), or a *full-relational* join can be done once all the solutions have arrived in all the AND parallel branches. The abstract machine supports an incremental join operation on solution tuples from AND parallel branches. Besides our abstract machine, an incremental join is also used in the PEPSys approach by the ECRC group [Kergommeaux and Robert 1988]. Gupta and Jayaraman [Gupta and Jayaraman 1989] use *cross-product* nodes similar to PEPSys' *join-cells* to implement the join of solutions from AND parallel branches in their model for shared memory machines. For reasons of brevity, we do not describe the join algorithm here. A description of it can be found in [Kale 1987b].

In Figure 2 we provide the a code fragment for a nested join operation. Assume that a solution tuple $T_{A,B}$ has arrived as a solution for $q(A,B)$. It is first inserted in the arc relation $R_{A,B}$ for q. The parameters for the *SetUpJoin* instruction (Figure 2: line 31) enable the extraction of the the common ancestor for the join and the the arc relation $R_{A,C}$ for r (containing all solution tuples $T_{A,C}$ for r already received) that share a common ancestor with $T_{A,B}$. The *JoinTuples* instruction performs the join of the tuple $T_{A,B}$ with the next tuple $T_{A,C}$ in $R_{A,C}$ to create a *joined* tuple J. J now needs to be joined with relevant solution tuples for $s(A,D)$ that have already been received. Since only tuples sharing the same common ancestor need to be joined, the back pointer to the common ancestor needs to be copied into J (line 33). Also, the context of the "outer level" join already performed (the common ancestor for q and r, the tuples in $R_{A,C}$ not yet considered, etc.) needs to be saved before an "inner" level join can be initiated (line 35). It is necessary to use a stack for this purpose, since the nesting of the joins can be arbitrarily deep. The inner level join (lines 36 – 39) is now performed between J and all the tuples in the relation $R_{A,D}$ that share the same common ancestor with J. In this example, each of these joins produces a solution for p (line 38). The context of the outer level join can now be restored (line 40) to permit $T_{A,B}$ to be joined with the next tuple in $R_{A,C}$.

Although the joins can be arbitrarily deep, the depth of the nesting is known when the code is generated. As was the case for unification of structures, a single preallocated stack is used for this purpose. If however, the depth is seen to exceed the size of this stack, instructions to explicitly allocate (and subsequently free) a larger stack are generated by the compiler.

4.4 Special Purpose Registers

In this section, we briefly describe some of the special purpose registers used by the abstract machine emulator for efficient interpretation of byte code instructions.

C registers These registers are used to store the child tuple during unification. Should unification fail, the cost of allocating and subsequent freeing of memory is not paid. Also, during the second phase of unification (*Close*), the child tuple is extended *in place* by *importing* variables from the parent.

P registers These registers store the parent tuple (PT) during unification.

PTerm is used to refer to the parent term during unification.

CTerm is used to refer to the child term during unification.

Ctuple is used for any partial solution tuples that may be received as solutions to subgoals in the DJG. During unification with the clause head, it points to the C registers.

MStack is called the Molecule stack. The maximum depth of the stack is known at compile time: it cannot exceed the depth of the *child* term being unified. See Section 4.2 for its use. *TOPMstack* maintains the top of the Molecule stack.

JStack is called the Join stack. This stack is needed in the presence of nested joins. Its use is discussed in detail in Section 4.3. *TOPJstack* is used to maintain the top of the Join stack.

ptrGS is a pointer to a data area used to store the "goal status" for the currently active subgoal G in the system. It maintains a reference (ptrQ) to the clause C the subgoal occurs in, some completion detection information for G, and a reference to a context tuple if the subgoal being evaluated corresponds to a join arc in the DJG for C.

ptrQ (pointer to Query.) is used to refer to the data area used to maintain the status of the clause C currently being evaluated. One such data area is allocated for each active clause in the system. It maintains completion detection information for C, a reference to the goal status (ptrGS) of the (parent) subgoal S that matched C's clause head, and a copy of the parent tuple *after* successful head-unification between S and C.

In addition to these special purpose registers, several general purpose registers are used to compute and store temporary results during run time.

5   Current Status and Future Work

A emulator for the abstract machine has been developed as an application running on top of the *Chare Kernel*, thereby making it machine independent. It has been ported to a variety of machines, both shared and nonshared (including the Encore Multimax, the Alliant FX/8, the Sequent Symmetry and the Intel iPSC/2 hypercube). The implementation exploits full OR parallelism and independent AND parallelism in logic programs.

Annotations are used in the Prolog programs to supply information about the data dependencies in a clause, for example, which subgoals are independent and may be solved in AND parallel. We plan on availing of current advances in static and state analysis to optimise the code generated by the compiler. The programmer will be allowed to give information about the program like calling patterns, grainsize control, determinacy information, mutual exclusion in clauses etc. via compiler directives. This information can also be provided by a static-analysis front end instead. We hope that our system will provide a framework for developing and testing static analysis techniques for other researchers.

Preliminary results are quite promising; the emulator runs at about half the speed of the SB-Prolog compiler on a sequential processor and its performance scales up linearly with the number of processors. We discuss the performance of the emulator on a variety of benchmarks in more detail in [Ramkumar and Kale 1989].

Several improvements and optimisations are being looked into. One problem with the process model is that when a *chare* C spawns child *chares*, all solutions generated by the child *chares* are sent to the parent C. If a large number of solutions is generated, these solutions have to be processed sequentially by C, thereby creating a bottleneck. Ways to split up a parent *chare* after it spawns all its children are being explored.

References

[Biswas et al 1988] Biswas P., Su S.C. and Yun D. Y. *A Scalable Abstract Machine Model to Support Limited-OR/Restricted-AND Parallelism in Logic Programs*. In Proceedings of ICLP, Seattle, August 1988.

[Conery 1987] Conery J.S. *Binding Environments for Parallel Logic Programs in Nonshared Memory Multiprocessors.* In Proceedings of SLP, San Francisco, September 1987.

[Kergommeaux and Robert 1988] de Kergommeaux J.C. and Robert P. *An Abstract Machine to implement efficiently OR-AND Parallel Prolog,* In Proceedings of ICLP, Seattle, August 1988.

[DeGroot 1984] DeGroot D. *Restricted AND Parallelism.* In Proceedings of the International Conference on FGCS, November 1984.

[Gregory 1987] Gregory S. *Parallel Programming in Parlog, the Language and its Implementation.* Addison Wesley, 1987.

[Gupta and Jayaraman 1989] Gupta G. and Jayaraman B. *Combined AND-OR Parallelism on Shared Memory Multiprocessors.* In Proceedings of NACLP, Cleveland, October 1989.

[Hausman et al 1987] Hausman. B., Ciepielewski A. and Haridi S. *OR-Parallel Prolog Made Efficient on Shared Memory Multiprocessors.* In Proceedings of SLP, San Francisco, September 1987.

[Hermenegildo 1986] Hermenegildo M.V. *An Abstract Machine based Execution Model for Computer Architecture Design and Efficient Implementation of Logic Programs in Parallel.* Ph.D. thesis, Dept. of Computer Science, University of Texas at Austin, 1986.

[Kale 1987a] Kale L.V. *'Completeness' and 'Full Parallelism' of Parallel Logic Programming Schemes.* In Proceedings of SLP, San Francisco, September 1987.

[Kale 1987b] Kale L.V. *Parallel Execution of Logic Programs: The Reduce-OR Process Model.* In Proceedings of ICLP, Melbourne, May 1987.

[Kale and Shu 1988] Kale L.V. and Shu W. *The Chare Kernel Language for Parallel Programming: A Perspective.* Technical Report UIUCDCS-R-88-1451, Dept. of Computer Science, University of Illinois at Urbana-Champaign, August 1988.

[Kale et al 1988] Kale L.V., Ramkumar B. and Shu W. *A Memory Organization Independent Binding Environment for AND and OR Parallel Execution of Logic Programs.* In Proceedings of ICLP, Seattle, August 1988.

[Lin and Kumar 1988] Lin Y-J. and Kumar V. *Performance of AND Parallel Execution of Logic Programs on a Shared Memory Multiprocessor.* In Proceedings of International Conference of FGCS, Tokyo, November 1988.

[Lusk et al 1988] Lusk et. al. *The Aurora OR-Parallel Prolog System.* In Proceedings of International Conference of FGCS, Tokyo, November 1988.

[Mudambi 1989] Mudambi S. *Performance of Aurora on a Switch-Based Multiprocessor.* In Proceedings of NACLP, Cleveland, October 1989.

[Ramkumar and Kale 1989] Ramkumar B. and Kale L.V. *Compiled Execution of the Reduce-OR Process Model on Multiprocessors.* In Proceedings of NACLP, Cleveland, October 1989.

[Taylor et al 1986] Taylor S., Safra S. and Shapiro E. *A Parallel Implementation of Flat Concurrent Prolog.* Technical Report CS87-04, Weizmann Institute of Science, October 1986.

Believability in Default Logic Entails Logical Consequence from Circumscription (Sometimes)

Atsushi TOGASHI   Ben-Hui HOU   Shoichi NOGUCHI

Research Institute of Electrical Communication
Tohoku University, 2-1-1, Katahira, Aoba, Sendai 980, Japan
togashi@heart.riec.tohoku.ac.jp

Abstract

There have been a number of efforts, recently, towards developing default logic and circumscription, two important formalisms for non-monotonic reasoning. In this paper, we shall propose a partial translation of default logic to circumscription. We limit ourselves to an open default of the form, $\alpha(x):M\beta(x)/\gamma(x)$, whose justification $\beta(x)$ contains no positive occurrences of a predicate. We show, under certain conditions, for a given default theory, any consistent extension is a logical consequence of the resulting circumscription.

1. Introduction

Default logic [Reiter, 1980] and *circumscription* [McCarthy, 1980; McCarthy, 1986; Lifschitz, 1985] have been proposed to formalize *non-monotonic reasoning* in the absence of complete knowledge. Default logic formalizes the reasoning pattern of the form - in the absence of any information to the contrary, assume $\cdots$. Circumscription attempts to characterize a rule of conjecture - the objects that can be shown to have a certain property are all objects that have this property. While both systems attempt to capture a similar phenomena, very little has been done to explore the relationship between them. A natural question is " how the two approaches are related each other ".

Imielinski [Imielinski, 1987] has introduced a *modular translation* from defaults to circumscription. He gave the negative result which showed that even *normal* defaults (with prerequisites) could not be modularly translated to circumscription. He proved that only *simple semi-normal* defaults without prerequisites (*e.g.*, a default of the form $:M\beta\wedge\gamma/\gamma$) were modularly translatable to circumscription. Following Imielinski, Etherington [Etherington, 1987] has attempted to translate circumscription to default theory. For particular classes of first order theories, he has provided a translation from circumscription to default logic. This translation applies only to theories with *domain-closure axioms*, and then only when the circumscriptive theory specifies all predicates as parameters.

Both of them are motivated by the wish to present an equivalent translation. Different from them, in this paper, we shall work on a partial translation of default theories to circumscription. Our approach can apply to a larger class of defaults whose justifications contain no positive description. Under certain conditions, we prove that for a given default theory, any consistent extension is a logical consequence of the resulting circumscription.

2. Default Logic and Circumscription

To begin with, in this section, several basic concepts will be recalled about default logic [Reiter, 1980] and circumscription [McCarthy, 1980; Lifschitz, 1985].

2.1 Default Logic

A *default* δ is a logical expression of the form $a(x):M\beta(x)/\gamma(x)$, where $a(x)$, $\beta(x)$ and $\gamma(x)$ are (*well formed*) *formulas* in first order logic whose free variables are in $x = \{x_1, \cdots, x_n\}$. $a(x)$ is called the *prerequisite*, $\beta(x)$ the *justification*, and $\gamma(x)$ the *consequent* of δ. For a set D of defaults, let JUST(D) denote the set of all predicate symbols appearing in the justifications of defaults in D. The default δ is called *closed* if none of $a(x)$, $\beta(x)$ and $\gamma(x)$ contain free variables, usually represented as $a:M\beta/\gamma$. Otherwise, it is called *open*. The default δ is said to be *quantifier-free* if none of $a(x)$, $\beta(x)$ and $\gamma(x)$ contain quantifiers. A default $a(x): M\beta(x)/\gamma(x)$ is roughly explained as: for all free variables in x if the prerequisite $a(x)$ is believable, and the justification $\beta(x)$ is not unbelievable, then the consequent $\gamma(x)$ can be assumed.

A *default theory* Δ is defined as a pair (D, W), where D is a set of defaults and W a set of formulas. Δ is *closed* when every default in D is closed and every formula in W is closed. Otherwise, it is *open*. Δ is *quantifier-free* if every default in D is quantifier-free and every formula in W is quantifier-free. A closed quantifier-free default theory is called a *ground* default theory.

In this paper, we will focus our attention on open default theories. One reason is that genuinely interesting cases involve open defaults. As an example, the *Closed World Assumption* CWA, see [Reiter, 1978], can be described naturally as an open defaults theory $\Delta_{CWA} = (D_{CWA}, W)$, where D_{CWA} is the set of defaults of the form $:M\neg p(x)/\neg p(x)$, for all predicate symbols p appearing in W. For a closed default $a:M\beta/\gamma$, as there are no common free variables among a, β and γ three components are mutually independent. In the almost application of default logic, those components are usually connected by some common free variables, such as the open default $bird(x):Mfly(x)/fly(x)$. Another reason is that a closed default is the special form of an open default without free variables.

As we know, any open default theory Δ can be changed into a closed *Skolemized* default theory by instantiating all free variables in Δ with ground terms in the expanded language. The extension of Δ is defined as that of the resulting default theory [Reiter, 1980]. If a default theory is quantifier-free, we do not need any Skolem function to convert it into a closed default theory. Thus, we can treat transformation in the fixed first order language. We assume a *first order language*, consisting of a finite set of *predicate symbols* and a finite set of *function symbols* (including *constant symbols*), and fix it throughout this paper. For the above reasons, we will confine ourselves to open quantifier-free default theories in this paper. Accordingly, by a formula we mean a quantifier-free formula unless stated otherwise. For that reason, the following definitions about extensions of default theories and generation defaults, originally introduced by Reiter in [Reiter, 1980], are modified to adapt our intended default theories.

Definition 1. Let $\Delta = (D, W)$ be an open quantifier-free default theory and E a set of quantifier-free ground formulas. Define

(1) $E^{(0)} = \text{INST}(W)$;
(2) $E^{(i+1)} = \text{Th}(E^{(i)}) \cup \{ \gamma \mid \alpha: \mathbf{M}\beta/\gamma \in \text{INST}(D), \text{ where } \alpha \in E^{(i)} \text{ and } \neg\beta \notin E \}$.

E is an *extension* for Δ *iff* $E = \bigcup_{i \geq 0} E^{(i)}$. $\square$

In the above definition, $\text{INST}(W)$ and $\text{INST}(D)$ are used to denote the results of instantiating every free variable in W and D with a ground term, respectively. $\text{Th}(E^{(i)})$ denotes the set of all logical consequences from $E^{(i)}$. A formula is said to be *believable* in a default theory if it is contained in some extension of the default theory. It is clear that any extension of an open quantifier-free default theory is a set of ground formulas.

Definition 2. Let $\Delta = (D, W)$ be an open quantifier-free default theory and E an extension for Δ. $\text{GD}(E)$ is the set of *generation defaults wrt E*, defined by

$$\text{GD}(E) = \{ \delta \mid \delta = \alpha: \mathbf{M}\beta/\gamma \in \text{INST}(D), \text{ where } \alpha \in E \text{ and } \neg\beta \notin E \}.$$

We call $\Delta' = (\text{GD}(E), \text{INST}(D))$ is the *generation default theory wrt E*. $\square$

By definition, every default in $\text{GD}(E)$ is a ground default, *i.e.*, a closed quantifier-free default.

2.2 Circumscription and Minimal Models

Let $P = \{p_1, \cdots, p_n\}$ be a finite set of predicate symbols, and $Z = \{z_1, \cdots, z_m\}$ a finite set of predicate symbols disjoint from P. Suppose $T(P, Z)$ is a quantifier-free first order theory containing predicate symbols in P and Z.

Definition 3. The *circumscription* of P in $T(P, Z)$ with parameter Z is the following statement, denoted by $\text{Circum}(T; P; Z)$, this is not a formula, it can be specified as a second order formula if $T(P, Z)$ is finite:

$T(P, Z)$ and for every P', Z' [if $T(P', Z')$ and $P' \Rightarrow P$, then $P \Rightarrow P'$],

where $P' = \{p_1', \cdots, p_n'\}$ and $Z' = \{z_1', \cdots, z_m'\}$ are disjoint sets of predicate variables similar to P and Z, respectively. $T(P', Z')$ is the result of $T(P, Z)$ substituting p_i' and z_j' for each occurrence of p_i and z_j, respectively. $P' \Rightarrow P$ stands for $\forall x_i.[p_i'(x_i) \supset p_i(x_i)]$, for every i, where x_i is the tuple of object variables corresponding to p_i. $\square$

This statement means that predicate symbols in P have minimal possible extensions under the assumption that $T(P, Z)$ holds and extensions of predicate symbols in Z are allowed to vary in the process of minimalization.

In the following, we assume that the reader is familiar with the notions of *structures, Herbrand structures, models, logical consequence,* and so on. See [Chang and Lee, 1973], for instance. Note that a Herbrand structure can simply be represented as a set S of ground atoms. Since we are concerned with quantifier-free formulas it is reasonable to consider Herbrand structures as structures. Thus, unless noted otherwise, by a structure we mean a Herbrand structure.

Definition 4. Let M and N be structures, P *and* Z disjoint set of predicate symbols. M is a *substructure* of N wrt $\leq_{P;Z}$, written as $M \leq_{P;Z} N$, iff $|M| = |N|$; $M[q] = N[q]$, for any symbol $q \notin P \cup Z$; and $M[p^+] \subseteq N[p^+]$, for any $p \in P$. Here, $|M|$ denotes the domain of M, $M[q]$ is the interpretation of q in M, and $M[q^+] = \{a \in |M|^n \mid M[q](a) = \text{True}\}$. $\square$

Thus, $M \leq_{P;Z} N$ if M and N differ only in how they interpret the predicate symbols in P and Z, and the extension $M[p^+]$ of each $p \in P$ in M is a subset of its extension $N[p^+]$ in N. A structure M is *minimal* in a class S of structures if $M \in S$ and there is no structure $M' \in S$ such that $M' <_{P;Z} M$. We write $M <_{P;Z} N$ if $M \leq_{P;Z} N$ but not $N \leq_{P;Z} M$. If M is minimal in the class of models for a theory T, we simply say that M is a *model of T minimal with respect to* $\leq_{P;Z}$, denoted by $M \vDash_{P;Z} T$. $T \vDash_{P;Z} F$ indicates that a formula F is true in very model of a theory T minimal *wrt* $\leq_{P;Z}$. In this case, F is said to be *minimally entailed* by T wrt $\leq_{P;Z}$.

The models of a circumscriptive description can be characterized now as follows.

Theorem 1. [McCarthy, 1980; Lifschitz, 1985] *Let T be a theory, P and Z disjoint sets of predicate symbols. A structure M is a model of* Circum$(T; P; Z)$ *iff M is a model of T minimal wrt* $\leq_{P;Z}$. $\square$

3. Translation of Default Logic to Circumscription

Given a default $a(x): M\beta(x)/\gamma(x)$, we attempt to enlarge the domain, on which $\beta(x)$ holds. If the justification $\beta(x)$ contains only negative description, such as $\neg p(x)$, enlarging the domain of $\beta(x)$ is equivalent to minimizing the extension of p. The properties of extensions generated by such defaults could be characterized by minimality of p's. On this basis, we shall concentrate on the defaults whose justifications contain no positive description.

Given a default theory $\Delta = (D, W)$ of our restricted form, we translate it into a first-order theory by replacing each default $\delta = \alpha(x): \mathbf{M}\beta(x) / \gamma(x)$ in D with a formula $\alpha(x) \wedge \beta(x) \supset \gamma(x)$. Intuitively, any believable formula in Δ could be expected to be a logical consequence of the circumscription in this translated theory. What predicate symbols should be circumscribed and what predicate symbols should be allowed to vary? An intuitive observation may lead us to circumscribe every predicate symbol in the justification $\beta(x)$ and to allow every predicate symbol in the consequent $\gamma(x)$ to vary. However, in this manner, the expected result cannot be definitely obtained. This will be illustrated in *Example* 1.

Example 1. Let consider the default theory $\Delta = (\{ bird(x) :\mathbf{M} \neg ab(x) / fly(x) \}$, $\{penguin(x) \supset bird(x), penguin(x) \supset ab(x), bird(A) \})$. Δ has a unique extension $E = \text{Th}(\text{INST}(W) \cup \{ fly(A) \})$. Trans($\Delta'$) (defined later) is the theory of INST(W) along with the translated formula $bird(A) \wedge \neg ab(A) \supset fly(A)$ from the singleton GD(E). Let us take $AB = \{ab\}$ and $FLY = \{fly\}$. Consider Circum(Trans(Δ'); AB; FLY). We shall enumerate all minimal models of Trans(Δ') *wrt* $\leqq_{AB;FLY}$.

$M_1 = \{ bird(A), fly(A) \}$
$M_2 = \{ bird(A), penguin(A), ab(A) \}$
$M_3 = \{ bird(A), penguin(A), ab(A), fly(A) \}$

The extension E of Δ is not true in M_2, thus, Circum(Trans(Δ'); AB; FLY) E. The problem lies in selection of parameters. Let us take $Z = \{ penguin, bird, fly \}$ as parameter. Consider Circum(Trans(Δ'); AB; Z). Neither M_2 nor M_3 is a minimal model of Trans(Δ') *wrt* $\leqq_{AB;Z}$. M_1 is the only minimal model of Trans(Δ') *wrt* $\leqq_{AB;Z}$. Thus, Circum(Trans(Δ'); AB; Z) $\vDash E$. This is what we are expecting and looking for. The formal discussions about what to be taken as parameters will be carried out below. $\square$

For the circumscription in the translated theory from a given default theory, any predicate symbol in the justification of the default will be circumscribed. It is necessary to determine what should be taken as parameter. The choice for parameter in circumscription relies mainly on the dependencies of predicate symbols. As has been mentioned in *Example* 1, by the formula $bird(A) \wedge \neg ab(A) \supset fly(A)$, ab is related to $bird$ and fly. In order to make this formula hold for the object A in a structure M such that $Mab(A)$, we have alternative choices. One is to suggest this object is not a bird. Another is to suggest A can fly. In other words, the interpretations for $bird$ and fly vary with the one for ab. As we want to circumscribe ab, it is reasonable to take $bird$ and fly as parameters. Such dependencies among predicate symbols will be formally described below.

By $F[p^+; q^-]$, we mean F is a quantifier-free formula containing some *positive occurrences* of atomic formulas on p and some *negative occurrences* of atomic formulas on q. Similarly, we use the notations $F[p^+; q^+]$, $F[p^-; q^+]$, and $F[p^-; q^-]$. To determine parameters, *oriented* predicate symbols $p \downarrow$ and $p \uparrow$ are introduced for all predicate symbols p. $p \downarrow$ is read as reducing the extension of p; $p \uparrow$ as enlarging the extension of p.

Definition 5. Let T be a quantifier-free theory, *i.e.*, a set of quantifier-free formulas, and P a set of predicate symbols. Define a set $\mathbf{R}(T; P)$ of oriented predicate symbols as the least set satisfying the following rules:

(0) $p\downarrow \in \mathbf{R}(T; P)$, for every $p \in P$;

(1) $r\downarrow \in \mathbf{R}(T; P)$, if there is either a formula $F[q^+; r^-]$ in T for some $q\downarrow \in \mathbf{R}(T; P)$; or $F[q^-; r^-]$ in T for some $q\uparrow \in \mathbf{R}(T; P)$;

(2) $r\uparrow \in \mathbf{R}(T; P)$, if there is either a formula $F[q^+; r^+]$ in T for some $q\downarrow \in \mathbf{R}(T; P)$; or $F[q^-; r^+]$ in T for some $q\uparrow \in \mathbf{R}(T; P)$.

Define the set $Z(T; P)$ of predicate symbols.

$$Z(T; P) = \{\, q \mid q \notin P \text{ and } q\downarrow \in \mathbf{R}(T; P) \text{ (or } q\uparrow \in \mathbf{R}(T; P))\,\} \quad \square$$

$Z(T; P)$ is actually the set of all predicate symbols whose extensions will be affected when the extensions of all predicate symbols in P are reduced. $Z(T; P)$ will be taken as parameter when we want to circumscribe P.

Now, let us make an investigation on *Example 1*. According to *Definition 5*, we have $\mathbf{R}(\text{Trans}(\Delta'); AB) = \{ab\downarrow, penguin\downarrow, bird\downarrow, fly\uparrow\}$, $Z(\text{Trans}(\Delta'); AB) = \{\, penguin, bird, fly \,\}$, where $AB = \{\, ab \,\}$. As we want to circumscribe AB, those in the set of $Z(\text{Trans}(\Delta'); AB)$ will be taken as parameters.

Definition 6. Let T be a quantifier-free theory and P a set of predicate symbols. T is *directional wrt* P *iff* there is no predicate symbol q such that both $q\downarrow$ and $q\uparrow$ are in $\mathbf{R}(T; P)$. $\square$

Before proceeding further, we need several terminologies in first order logic. Refer to [Chang and Lee, 1973], for a full description. A *positive literal* is an atomic formula. A *negative literal* is the negation of an atomic formula. A *literal* is defined as a positive literal or a negative literal. A *clause* is a disjunction of literals. Every variable appearing in a clause is implicitly quantified by the universal quantifier $\forall$. A *clausal theory* is a set of clauses. As well known, any formulas is equivalently transformed into a clausal theory by introducing *Skolem functions*. The resulting set is called the *clausal form* of the set of formulas. If every formula is quantifier-free, we obtain the clausal form without Skolem functions.

Lemma 1. *Let T be a quantifier-free theory and P a set of predicate symbols. If T is directional wrt P, then the clausal form of T is directional wrt P.* $\square$

The partial translation for default theories, discussed in the last subsection, will be precisely given in the following definition.

Definition 7. Let $\Delta = (D, W)$ be a (an open) quantifier-free default theory. The *translation* of Δ is defined as a quantifier-free theory $\text{Trans}(\Delta)$, where

$$\text{Trans}(\Delta) = W \cup \{\, \alpha(x) \wedge \beta(x) \supset \gamma(x) \mid \alpha(x) : M\beta(x) / \gamma(x) \in D \,\}. \quad \square$$

Recall that a ground default theory is a closed quantifier-free default theory. If E is an extension of a quantifier-free default theory $\Delta = (D, W)$, the resulting generation default theory $\Delta' = (\text{GD}(E), \text{INST}(W))$ *wrt* E is a ground default theory. So that, the translation $\text{Trans}(\Delta')$ of Δ' is a set of ground formulas.

Lemma 2. *Let $\Delta = (D, W)$ be an open quantifier-free default theory. For any consistent extension E of Δ, we have $E \models \text{Trans}(\Delta')$, where $\Delta' = (\text{GD}(E), \text{INST}(W))$ is the generation default theory wrt E. Hence, $\text{Trans}(\Delta')$ is consistent.*

Proof. To prove the lemma, we show $E \models F$ for any formula F in $\text{Trans}(\Delta')$. If $F \in \text{INST}(W)$, since $\text{INST}(W) \subseteq E$, then $E \models F$. Otherwise, suppose $F = \alpha \wedge \beta \supset \gamma$ with respect to a default $\alpha : M\beta / \gamma$ in $\text{GD}(E)$. Since $\gamma \in E$, then $E \cup \{\alpha \wedge \beta\} \models \gamma$, hence, $E \models \alpha \wedge \beta \supset \gamma$. **Q.E.D.**

Now, we are in a position to show the key lemma which plays the essential role to prove the main result. In the following proof, to avoid confusion, t (possibly with subscripts) will be used to denote the tuple of ground terms. Recall a clausal theory is a set of clauses.

Lemma 3. *Let T be a, possibly infinite, consistent clausal theory, P a set of predicate symbols, and M any minimal model of T wrt $\leq_{P;Z}$, where $Z = Z(T; P)$. If T is directional wrt P, then $M \models p(t)$ iff $T \models p(t)$, for every ground atom $p(t)$ on $p \in P$.*

Proof. (*outline*) Let M be any minimal model of T wrt $\leq_{P;Z}$. Since the *if-half* is trivial, we will show the *only-if-half*. Let $\text{INST}(T)$ denote the set of all ground instances of clauses in T. Since function symbols in first order language are assumed to be finite, $\text{INST}(T)$ is enumerable. Let $C_1, \cdots, C_n, \cdots$ be an enumeration of $\text{INST}(T)$. Suppose $M \models p(t_0)$, for some p-atom $p(t_0)$, where $p \in P$. Let us construct a tree Π of structures, and show the following statements:

(a) $p(t_0) \in \text{Del}(N)$;
(b) $r\downarrow \in \mathbf{R}(T; P)$, for every atom $r(t) \in \text{Del}(N)$;
(c) $r\uparrow \in \mathbf{R}(T; P)$, for every atom $r(t) \in \text{Add}(N)$;
(d) $\text{Del}(N) \subset M$; $\text{Add}(N) \cap M = \varnothing$; $N = (M - \text{Del}(N)) \cup \text{Add}(N)$

for all nodes (structures) N in Π by structural induction.

Induction Basis: The root node is $M_0 = M - \{p(t_0)\}$. Let $\text{Del}(M_0) = \{p(t_0)\}$, and $\text{Add}(M_0) = \varnothing$. $p(t_0)$ is called the *deleted atom* at the node M_0. Intuitively, for any node N in the tree Π, $\text{Del}(N)$ ($\text{Add}(N)$) denotes the set of ground atoms deleted from (added to) M along the path from M_0 to N. From the construction of M_0, we can easily show the statements (a) $\sim$ (d), for M_0.

Induction Step: Let N be any leaf node of the tree so far constructed by deleting $q(t)$ from (or, adding $q(t)$ to) its predecessor N' (When $N = M_0$, $p(t_0)$ is the deleted atom from M). If the deleted atom $q(t)$ or the negation $\neg q(t)$ of the added atom $q(t)$ at the node N is a logical consequence of T, N has no successors. Otherwise, N has successors. As *induction hypothesis* we assume that the statements (a) $\sim$ (d) are satisfied by N. By induction hypothesis and directionality of T wrt P, we have $N <_{P;Z} M$. Thus, N is not a model of T. Let C be the first ground clause in the enumeration of $\text{INST}(T)$ which is not satisfied by N. C must be of the form:

$$\neg q_1(t_1) \vee \cdots \vee \neg q_n(t_n) \vee q_{n+1}(t_{n+1}) \vee \cdots \vee q_{n+m}(t_{n+m}) \vee l,$$

where we have, immediately,

(1) $l = q(t)$ for some $q(t) \in Del(N)$, or $l = \neg q(t)$ for some $q(t) \in Add(N)$;
(2) $n + m \neq 0$;
(3) $q_i \downarrow \in \mathbf{R}(T; P)$ and $q_i(t_i) \in M \cap N$, for any $i, 1 \leq i \leq n$;
(4) $q_{n+j} \uparrow \in \mathbf{R}(T; P)$ and $q_{n+j}(t_{n+j}) \notin N \cup Del(N)$, for any $j, 1 \leq j \leq m$.

In this case, N has $n + m$ successors $N_1, \cdots, N_n, N_{n+1}, \cdots, N_{n+m}$, where

$N_i = N - \{q_i(t_i)\}$;
$Del(N_i) = Del(N) \cup \{q_i(t_i)\}$;
$Add(N_i) = Add(N)$, for any $i, 1 \leq i \leq n$, and

$N_{n+j} = N \cup \{q_{n+j}(t_{n+j})\}$;
$Del(N_{n+j}) = Del(N)$;
$Add(N_{n+j}) = Add(N) \cup \{q_{n+j}(t_{n+j})\}$, for any $j, 1 \leq j \leq m$.

$q_i(t_i)$ is the deleted atom at N_i $(1 \leq i \leq n)$, and $q_{n+j}(t_{n+j})$ is the added atom at N_{n+j} $(1 \leq j \leq m)$. For each successor N_k of N, $1 \leq k \leq n + m$, we can show the statements (a) ~ (d). Notice that C is true in every successor N_k of N. We call C the clause *associated with* the node N.

As for the tree Π, we have:

Claim Π is finite.(Outline of the proof is shown at the appendix.)

Now, we shall prove $p(t_0)$ is a logical consequence of T by induction on the number k of nodes in Π. Base case is clear. Let $k > 1$. Assume $p(t_0)$ is a logical consequence of T if the number of nodes in Π is less than k. Let Π be a tree with k nodes. Suppose N is a non-leaf node all of whose successors are leaf nodes. We assume that it has $n + m > 0$ leaf nodes, $N_1, \cdots, N_n, N_{n+1}, \cdots, N_{n+m}$, and the clause (not satisfied by N) associated with N is of the form,

$$\neg q_1(t_1) \vee \ldots \vee \neg q_n(t_n) \vee q_{n+1}(t_{n+1}) \vee \ldots \vee q_{n+m}(t_{n+m}) \vee l.$$

Since $q_i(t_i)$ $(q_{n+j}(t_{n+j}))$ is the deleted (added) atom at the leaf node N_i (N_{n+j}), we have $T \vDash q_i(t_i)$ and $T \vDash \neg q_{n+j}(t_{n+j})$, for any $i, j, 1 \leq i \leq n, 1 \leq j \leq m$. Thus $T \vDash l$. Since l is a logical consequence of T and is equal to the deleted atom $q(t)$ or the negation of the added atom $\neg q(t)$ at N (or its ancestor N'), the subtree with the root N (or N') is reduced to N (or N'). Thus Π collapses to a tree with at most $k - (n + m) < k$ nodes. By induction hypothesis, $p(t_0)$ is a logical consequence of T. **Q.E.D.**

Corollary 1. *Let T be a consistent quantifier-free theory, P a set of predicate symbols, and M any minimal model of T wrt $\leq_{P;Z}$, where $Z = Z(T; P)$. If T is directional wrt P, then $M \vDash p(t)$ iff $T \vDash p(t)$, for every ground atom $p(t)$, where $p \in P$.*

Proof. By *Lemma 1* and *Lemma 3*. **Q.E.D.**

Theorem 2. *Let $\Delta = (D, W)$ be a (an open) quantifier-free default theory and E a consistent extension for Δ. Let $\Delta' = (GD(E), INST(W))$ and $Z = Z(\mathrm{Trans}(\Delta');$ $\mathrm{JUST}(GD(E)))$. If every default in $GD(E)$ contains only negative occurrences of predicate symbols in its justification and $\mathrm{Trans}(\Delta')$ is directional wrt $\mathrm{JUST}(GD(E))$, then $\mathrm{Circum}(\mathrm{Trans}(\Delta'); \mathrm{JUST}(GD(E)); Z) \vDash E$.*

Proof. It is sufficient to show E is true in every minimal model of Trans(Δ') *wrt* $\leq_{\text{JUST(GD}(E)); Z}$. Suppose M is such a model. We show $M \models E^{(i)}$ for any $i \geq 0$, by induction on i.

Base case is clear. Let $i \geq 0$. We assume $M \models E^{(i)}$. Now, we shall prove $M \models E^{(i+1)}$. That is, for any ground default $\alpha : \text{M}\beta / \gamma \in \text{INST}(D)$, we show $M \models \gamma$ if $\alpha \in E^{(i)}$, and $\neg\beta \notin E$. By induction hypothesis, we have $M \models \alpha$. We will show $M \models \beta$ by refutation. Suppose $M \not\models \beta$. By the conditions, β must be a negative ground literal on some $p \in \text{JUST(GD}(E))$. Then we assume $\beta = \neg p(t)$. Since $M \not\models \beta$, $M \models p(t)$. Hence, Trans(Δ') $\models p(t)$ by *Corollary* 1. By *Lemma* 2, we have $E \models \text{Trans}(\Delta')$, hence, $p(t) \in E$. Because every logical consequence of E belongs to E. This contradicts $\neg\beta \notin E$. Therefore $M \models \beta$. Since $M \models \text{Trans}(\Delta')$ and $\alpha \wedge \beta \supset \gamma \in \text{Trans}(\Delta')$, $M \models \gamma$ follows.

Q.E.D.

Corollary 2. *Let* $\Delta = (D, W)$ *be a (an open) quantifier-free default theory and* E *a consistent extension for* Δ. *If every default in* D *contains only negative occurrences of predicate symbols in its justification and* Trans(Δ) *is directional wrt* JUST(D), *then* $Circum(\text{Trans}(\Delta'); \text{JUST(GE}(E)); Z) \models E$, *where* $\Delta' = (\text{GD}(E), \text{INST}(W))$ *and* $Z = Z(\text{Trans}(\Delta'); \text{JUST(GD}(E)))$. $\square$

Theorem 2 is proved under a condition that the translation of the generation default theory $\Delta' = (\text{GD}(E), \text{INST}(W))$ is directional *wrt* JUST(GD(E)). This is absolutely essential to *Theorem* 2.

Example 2. Let consider the default theory $\Delta = (\{:\text{M}\neg p(a) / p(b)\}, \varnothing)$. Δ has a unique extension $E = \{p(b)\}$. The translation of Δ, Trans(Δ) = $\{p(a) \vee p(b)\}$, is not directional *wrt* JUST(GD(E)) = $\{p\}$. Trans(Δ) has two minimal models $M_1 = \{p(a)\}$ and $M_2 = \{p(b)\}$ *wrt* $\leq_{\{p\}; \varnothing}$. E is not true in M_1. $\square$

4. Conclusions

In this paper, to relate default logic and circumscription, we have proposed a partial translation of default theory to circumscription. Under certain conditions, we have proven that, any consistent extension is a logical consequence of the resulting circumscription.

Appendix

Claim Π is finite.

Proof. *(outline)* Suppose Π is infinite, then Π must have at least a path of infinite length. Let $N_0 (= M_0), N_1, \cdots, N_n, \cdots$ be such a path. Let us define a structure N in the following manner:

$N[q] = \bigcap_{i \geq 0} N_i[q]$, if $q \downarrow \in R(T; P)$;
$N[q] = \bigcup_{i \geq 0} N_i[q]$, if $q \uparrow \in R(T; P)$;
$N[z] = M[z]$, otherwise.

The structure N is well defined because of the directionality of T. Let $Del(N) = \bigcup_{i \geq 0} Del(N_i)$ and $Add(N) = \bigcup_{i \geq 0} Add(N_i)$.

Now, we shall show that N is a model of T. Suppose T is false in N, then C is not satisfied by N, for some clause $C \in INST(T)$. C must be eventually selected as an associated clause in the construction process of N. Assume C is of the form,

$$\neg q_1(t_1) \vee \cdots \vee \neg q_n(t_n) \vee q_{n+1}(t_{n+1}) \vee \cdots \vee q_{n+m}(t_{n+m}) \vee l,$$

and C is selected at N_k. Then, $q(t) \in Add(N_k)$ when $l = \neg q(t)$, or $q(t) \in Del(N_k)$ when $l = q(t)$. By the construction of Π, $q_i(t_i) \in Del(N_{k+1})$ or $q_{n+j}(t_{n+j}) \in Add(N_{k+1})$ for some i, j, $1 \leq i \leq n$, $1 \leq j \leq m$. In both cases, we have $N \models C$. This contradicts the assumption that N C. Thus $N \models C$ for any C in $INST(T)$. Therefore, $N \models T$. Since $N <_{P;Z} M$, $N \models T$ contradicts the minimality of M in the class of models of T. Thus Π must be finite.. **Q.E.D.**

References

[Chang and Lee, 1973]
  Chang, C.L., and Lee, R.C.T., *Symbolic Logic and Mechanical Theorem Proving*, Academic Press, New York, 1973.

[Etherington, 1987]
  Etherington, D.M., *Relating Default Logic and Circumscription*, Proc. 10th-IJCAI87, pp 489-494, 1987.

[Imielinski, 1987]
  Imielinski, T., *Results on Translating Defaults to Circumscription*, Artificial Intelligence, 32, pp 131-146, 1987.

[Lifschitz, 1985]
  Lifschitz, V., *Computing Circumscription*, Proc. 9th IJCAI, Los Angeles, CA pp 121-127, 1985.

[McCarthy, 1980]
  McCarthy, J., *Circumscription - A Form of Non-Monotonic Reasoning*, Artificial Intelligence, 13, pp 27-39, 1980.

[McCarthy, 1986]
  McCarthy, J., *Applications of Circumscription to Formalizing Common Sense Knowledge*, Artificial Intelligence, 28, pp 89-116, 1986.

[Reiter, 1978]
  Reiter, R., *On Closed World Data Bases*, in: Logic and Databases, H. Gallaire and J. Minker, Eds., Plenum, New York, pp 56-76, 1978.

[Reiter, 1980]
  Reiter, R., *A Logic for Default Reasoning*, Artificial Intelligence, 13, pp 81-132, 1980.

Generalized Predicate Completion

Atsushi TOGASHI   Ben-Hui HOU   Shoichi NOGUCHI

Research Institute of Electrical Communication
Tohoku University, 2-1-1, Katahira, Aoba, Sendai 980, Japan
togashi@heart.riec.tohoku.ac.jp

Abstract

Circumscription, proposed by McCarthy, is a formalism of non-monotonic reasoning. Predicate completion is an approach, proposed by Clark, to closed world reasoning which assumes that given sufficient conditions on a predicate are also necessary. Reiter has shown that for clausal sentences which are Horn in a predicate p, the circumscription of p logically subsumes the predicate completion of p. In this paper, we present a *generalized completion* of a predicate p, which is appropriate for clausal sentences which are not Horn in p. The main results of this paper are: (1) for *non-overlapping* clausal sentences (which may not necessarily be Horn in the predicate p), the circumscription of p logically subsumes the generalized completion of p; (2) for *non-overlapping* clausal sentences which are *collapsible wrt* (with respect to) the predicate p, the generalized completion of p is even logically equivalent to the circumscription of p.

1. Introduction

Non-monotonic reasoning is an area of growing significance to artificial intelligence [Clark, 1978; McCarthy, 1980; McCarthy, 1986; Lifschitz, 1985; Reiter, 1978; Reiter, 1980]. Especially, McCarthy's *circumscription* [McCarthy, 1980; McCarthy, 1986; Lifschitz, 1985] turns out to be an influential formalism which attempts to characterize a rule of conjecture - the objects that can be shown to have a certain property from certain facts are only those that satisfy this property. Prior to McCarthy's circumscription, Reiter has proposed the *closed world assumption* (CWA) [Reiter, 1978], which says that the implicit representation of negative facts presumes total knowledge. Circumscription is very similar to CWA in terms of "minimal entailment" and "minimal inference" which captures some characters of human plausible reasoning. As we consider clausal sentences, CWA can efficiently be implemented via Clark's *negation as failure* [Clark, 1978]. Furthermore, that can be proved with negation as failure inference rule from a clausal sentence is a logical consequence of the predicate completion of this sentence [Clark, 1978]. Predicate completion simply states that the given sufficient conditions on a predicate are also necessary.

Since both predicate completion and circumscription attempt to capture some similar phenomena in the aspect of non-monotonic character, it is therefore important to achieve better understanding of the relationship between them. Recently, Reiter has shown that for clausal sentences which are Horn in a predicate p, Clark's predicate completion is implied by McCarthy's circumscription [Reiter, 1982]. Clearly, the completion is a non-trivial logical consequence of circumscription. That predicate completion is subsumed by circumscription for a wide class of clausal sentences is of some theoretical and computational interests. From these points of view, we shall enlarge the class of first-order clausal sentences for which predicate completion can be subsumed by circumscription. In this paper, we shall present a *generalized completion* of a predicate p, which refines on the definition of Clark's predicate completion. The generalized predicate completion is appropriate for clausal sentences which are not Horn in p. Clark's predicate completion and Reiter's result mentioned above are covered by our generalized predicate completion and results. Our main results of this paper are: (1) for *non-overlapping* clausal sentences (which may not necessarily be Horn in the predicate p), the circumscription of p subsumes the generalized completion of p; (2) for non-overlapping clausal sentences which are *collapsible wrt* (with respect to) the predicate p, the generalized completion of p is even logically equivalent to the circumscription of p.

This paper is organized as follows. In *Section* 2 we recall the definition of McCarthy's circumscription and some of its useful characterizations; In *Section* 3 we recall the definition of Clark's predicate completion and Reiter's result; In *Section* 4 we make some investigation on Clark's predicate completion, propose a generalized predicate completion and show our results. This paper is concluded in *Section* 5.

2. Circumscription and Minimal Entailment

Circumscription [McCarthy, 1980; McCarthy, 1986; Lifschitz, 1985] is an approach to the problem of non-monotonic reasoning, which augments formulas with a refinement of minimal inference. In this paper, we are particularly interested in clausal sentences. A *clausal sentence* is a conjunction of clauses (equivalently, a finite set of clauses). A *clause* is a universally quantified disjunction of literals, written as $l_1 \vee \cdots \vee l_n$, which is logically identified with $\forall x. (l_1 \vee \cdots \vee l_n)$, where x is the tuple of variables appearing in the clause and l_i is a *literal* (an *atom* or the negation of an atom) for i, $1 \leq i \leq n$.

Definition 1. Let T be a clausal sentence, p and z distinct predicate symbols. The *circumscription* of p in T with parameter z, denoted by Circum($T; p; z$), is defined as the second-order formula:

$$T \wedge \forall p', z'. [\, T(p', z') \wedge \forall x. (\, p'(x) \supset p(x)\,) \supset \forall x. (\, p(x) \supset p'(x)\,)\,],$$

where p' and z' are predicate variables of the same arity as p and z, $T(p', z')$ is the result of T substituting p' and z' for each occurrence of p and z, and x is the tuple of variables. □

This formula states that p has a minimal possible *extension* under the assumption that $T(p, z)$ holds and the extension of z is allowed to vary in the process of minimalization. If no z will be involved, Circum$(T; p)$ is used for Circum$(T; p; z)$.

In the following, we assume that the reader is familiar with the notions of *structures, Herbrand structures, models, logical consequence,* and so on. See [Chang and Lee, 1973], for instance. Note that a Herbrand structure can simply be represented as a set S of ground atoms. Since we are concerned with clausal sentences it is reasonable to consider Herbrand structures as structures. Thus, unless noted otherwise, by a structure we mean a Herbrand structure.

Definition 2. Let M and N be structures, p and z distinct predicate symbols. M is a *substructure* of N wrt $\leq_{p; z}$, written as $M \leq_{p; z} N$, iff $|M| = |N|$; $M[q] = N[q]$ for any symbol $q \notin \{p, z\}$; and $M[p^+] \subseteq N[p^+]$, where $|M|$ denotes the *domain* of M, $M[q]$ is the *interpretation* of q in M, and $M[q^+] = \{ a \in |M|^n \mid M[q](a) = \text{True} \}$. □

Thus, $M \leq_{p;z} N$ if M and N differ only in how they interpret the predicate symbols p and z, and the extension $M[p^+]$ of p in M is a subset of its extension $N[p^+]$ in N. A structure M is *minimal* in a class S of structures if $M \in S$ and there is no structure $M' \in S$ such that $M' <_{p;z} M$. We write $M <_{p;z} N$ if $M \leq_{p;z} N$ but not $N \leq_{p;z} M$. If M is minimal in the class of all models for a clausal sentence T, we simply say that M is a *model of T minimal wrt* $\leq_{p;z}$, denoted by $M \vDash_{p;z} T$. $T \vDash_{p;z} C$ indicates that a clause C is true in very model of T minimal wrt $\leq_{p;z}$. In this case, C is said to be *minimally entailed* by T wrt $\leq_{p;z}$. If no z will be involved, $\leq_p$ and $\vDash_p$ are used for $\leq_{p; z}$ and $\vDash_{p; z}$, respectively.

Theorem 1. [McCarthy, 1980; Lifschitz, 1985] *Let T be a sentence, p and z distinct predicate symbols, and M any structure. M is a model of* Circum$(T; p; z)$ *iff M is a model of T minimal wrt* $\leq_{p; z}$. □

3. Predicate Completion

Predicate completion is an approach, proposed by Clark [Clark, 1978; Lloyd, 1984], to closed world reasoning which assumes that given sufficient conditions on a predicate are also necessary. Let p be a distinguished predicate symbol. According to Clark's definition, a clause written of the following implication form is called a clause *about p*

$$l_1 \wedge \cdots \wedge l_m \supset p(t_1, \cdots, t_n), \tag{3.1}$$

where $l_1, \cdots, l_m$ are literals and $t_1, \cdots, t_n$ are terms. Let $x_1, \cdots, x_n$ be variables not appearing in the clause (3.1) and L be $l_1 \wedge \cdots \wedge l_m$. The clause (3.1) can then be equivalently transformed into the clause

$$x_1 = t_1 \wedge \cdots \wedge x_n = t_n \wedge L \supset p(x_1, \cdots, x_n).$$

Finally, if $y_1, \cdots, y_r$ are the variables in (3.1), the clause (3.1) is itself equivalent to

$$\exists y_1, \cdots, y_r. [x_1 = t_1 \wedge \cdots \wedge x_n = t_n \wedge L] \supset p(x_1, \cdots, x_n). \qquad (3.2)$$

We call (3.2) the *general form* of the clause (3.1). Suppose there are exactly $k \geq 0$ clauses about the predicate symbol p. Let

$$E_1 \supset p(x_1, \cdots, x_n)$$
$$\cdots \cdots \qquad\qquad\qquad\qquad\qquad (3.3)$$
$$E_k \supset p(x_1, \cdots, x_n)$$

be k general forms of these clauses. Each E_i will be an existentially quantified conjunction of literals as the left hand side of (3.2), The *completed definition of* p, implicitly given by those k clauses, is

$$\forall x_1, \cdots, x_n. [E_1 \vee E_2 \vee \cdots \vee E_k \equiv p(x_1, \cdots, x_n)]. \qquad (3.4)$$

When there is no clause about p, i.e., $k=0$, the completed definition of p is

$$\forall x_1, \cdots, x_n. [\mathsf{False} \equiv p(x_1, \cdots, x_n)].$$

Let T be a clausal sentence. The *completion* of p in T, denoted by Comp$(T; p)$, is the sentence T along with the completed definition of p and the *equality axioms* (E1)~(E8) by Clark in [Clark, 1978; Lloyd, 1984].

$$\mathrm{Comp}(T; p) \equiv T \wedge \forall x_1, \cdots, x_n. [E_1 \vee E_2 \vee \cdots \vee E_k \equiv p(x_1, \cdots, x_n)]$$
$$\wedge (E1) \wedge \cdots \wedge (E8) \qquad\qquad (3.5)$$

A clause is said to be *Horn* in a predicate p *iff* it contains at most one positive literal on p. A clausal sentence T is said to be Horn in p *iff* every clause in T is Horn in p.

Theorem 2. [Reiter, 1982] *Let T be a clausal sentence Horn in a predicate symbol p. Then* Circum$(T; p) \models$ Comp$(T; p)$, *i.e., the completion of p in T is implied by the circumscription of p in T.* □

4. Generalized Predicate Completion

As discussed previously, we know that for clausal sentences Horn in p, the completion of p is implied by the circumscription of p. By the investigation below, we understand this is not always the case for clausal sentences.

4.1 Investigation on Predicate Completion

Example 1. Let T be a sentence consisting of the single clause (4.1).

$$\neg p(a) \supset p(b) \qquad\qquad\qquad\qquad\qquad (4.1)$$

We have the following completed definition of p in T.

$$\forall x.\, [\, x = b \wedge \neg p(a) \equiv p(x)\,] \tag{4.2}$$

Let $M_1 = \{\, p(a)\, \}$. M_1 is a model of T minimal $wrt \leq_p$. Since $M_1 \vDash p(a)$, the *only-if-half* of the expression (4.2) is not true in M_1, hence M_1 Comp$(T;\, p)$. Therefore, Circum$(T;\, p)$ Comp$(T;\, p)$. $\square$

Proposition 1. *The predicate completion is not always implied by the circumscription for any clausal sentence.* $\square$

In this example, the predicate designated by p is actually defined by the clauses $\neg p(a) \supset p(b)$ and $\neg p(b) \supset p(a)$, while Comp$(T;\, p)$ specifies only one part of the definition given by $\neg p(a) \supset p(b)$. Thus the minimal model M_1 of T, which satisfies the part of the definition given by $\neg p(b) \supset p(a)$, does not satisfy Comp$(T;\, p)$. We attempt to compensate for the loss of the partial definition given by $\neg p(b) \supset p(a)$. To illustrate how to refine on the completion of p, let us continue observing this example.

Let split T into the two parts.

$$\neg p(a) \supset p(b) \tag{4.1}$$
$$\neg p(b) \supset p(a) \tag{4.3}$$

Note that (4.3) is logically identical with (4.1). Then Comp$(T;\, p)$ is the expression (4.4) and the equality axioms (E1)~(E8).

$$\forall x.\, [\, (x = b \wedge \neg p(a)) \vee (x = a \wedge \neg p(b)) \equiv p(x)\,] \tag{4.4}$$

All models of T minimal $wrt \leq_p$ are $M_1 = \{\, p(a)\, \}$ and $M_2 = \{\, p(b)\, \}$. Hence, Circum$(T;\, p) \vDash$ Comp$(T;\, p)$.

4.2 Generalized Predicate Completion

In [Clark, 1978], Clark pays attention upon only one positive literal on p. Therefore, he has imposed the condition that a given clausal sentence is Horn in p to get the completed definition on p. Here we shall focus on each positive literal on p respectively. Therefore we write a clause about p in the form of (4.5), which puts all positive literals on p explicitly on the right hand side of $\supset$. Suppose that

$$l_1 \wedge \cdots \wedge l_m \supset p(t_{11}, \cdots, t_{1n}) \vee \cdots \vee p(t_{h1}, \cdots, t_{hn}) \tag{4.5}$$

is a clause about p, where l_i is any literal which is not negative one on p for any i, $1 \leq i \leq m$. The tuple $(t_{j1}, \cdots, t_{jn})$ is simply denoted by t_j, for j, $1 \leq j \leq h$, and the conjunction $l_1 \wedge \cdots \wedge l_m$ by L. Then the clause (4.5) can be equivalently transformed into each of the following h clauses about a predicate p.

$$L \wedge \neg p(t_2) \wedge \cdots \wedge \neg p(t_h) \supset p(t_1)$$
$$\cdots \cdots \cdots$$
$$L \wedge \neg p(t_1) \wedge \cdots \wedge \neg p(t_{j-1}) \wedge \neg p(t_{j+1}) \wedge \cdots \wedge \neg p(t_h) \supset p(t_j)$$

$$\cdots \cdots$$
$$L \wedge \neg p(t_1) \wedge \cdots \wedge \neg p(t_{h-1}) \supset p(t_h)$$

Let $x_1, \cdots, x_n$ be variables not appearing in (4.5), simply denoted by x. Then the above clauses are equivalent to the following ones, respectively.

$$x = t_1 \wedge L \wedge \neg p(t_2) \wedge \cdots \wedge \neg p(t_h) \supset p(x)$$
$$\cdots \cdots$$
$$x = t_j \wedge L \wedge \neg p(t_1) \wedge \cdots \wedge \neg p(t_{j-1}) \wedge \neg p(t_{j+1}) \wedge \cdots \wedge \neg p(t_h) \supset p(x)$$
$$\cdots \cdots$$
$$x = t_h \wedge L \wedge \neg p(t_1) \wedge \cdots \wedge \neg p(t_{h-1}) \supset p(x)$$

If $y_1, \cdots, y_r$ are all variables appearing in (4.5), simply denoted by y, those clauses can be equivalently transformed into the follows.

$$\exists y. [x = t_1 \wedge L \wedge \neg p(t_2) \wedge \cdots \wedge \neg p(t_h)] \supset p(x)$$
$$\cdots \cdots$$
$$\exists y. [x = t_j \wedge L \wedge \neg p(t_1) \wedge \cdots \wedge \neg p(t_{j-1}) \wedge \neg p(t_{j+1}) \wedge \cdots \wedge \neg p(t_h)] \supset p(x) \tag{4.6}$$
$$\cdots \cdots$$
$$\exists y. [x = t_h \wedge L \wedge \neg p(t_1) \wedge \cdots \wedge \neg p(t_{h-1})] \supset p(x)$$

We call (4.6) the *general forms* of the clause (4.5).

Let T be a clausal sentence. Suppose there are exactly $k \geq 0$ clauses in T about the predicate p. Let

$$E_{11} \supset p(x)$$
$$\cdots \cdots$$
$$E_{1h_1} \supset p(x)$$
$$\cdots \cdots \tag{4.7}$$
$$E_{k1} \supset p(x)$$
$$\cdots \cdots$$
$$E_{kh_k} \supset p(x)$$

be $h_1 + h_2 + \cdots + h_k$ general forms of these k clauses. Each E_{ij} will be an existentially quantified conjunction of literals.

$$\exists y_i. [x = t_{ij} \wedge L_i \wedge \neg p(t_{i1}) \wedge \cdots \wedge \neg p(t_{ij-1}) \wedge \neg p(t_{ij+1}) \wedge \cdots \wedge \neg p(t_{ih_i})]$$

The *generalized completed definition* of p in T is the expression (4.8).

$$\forall x. [E_{11} \vee \cdots \vee E_{1h_1} \vee \cdots \vee E_{k1} \vee \cdots \vee E_{kh_k} \equiv p(x)] \tag{4.8}$$

When there is no clause about p, $k = 0$, the generalized completed definition of p is

$$\forall x. [\text{false} \equiv p(x)].$$

The *generalized completion* of p in T, $\text{Comp}_G(T; p)$, is the sentence T along with the generalized completed definition of p in T and the equality axioms (E1)$\sim$(E8).

$$\text{Comp}_G(T; p) \equiv T \wedge \forall x. [E_{11} \vee \cdots \vee E_{1h_1} \vee \cdots \vee E_{k1} \vee \cdots \vee E_{kh_k} \equiv p(x)]$$
$$\wedge (\text{E1}) \wedge \cdots \wedge (\text{E8})$$

For a clause not Horn in a predicate p, Clark's predicate completion gives only one component of the completed definition of p. Different from his, for each positive literal P on p in the clause we give the completed definition of p and group them. The grouped completed definition of p is the generalized completed definition of p. If a clausal sentence is Horn in p the generalized completion of p is apparently identical with Clark's completion.

Proposition 2. *Let T be a clausal sentence and p a predicate symbol. If T is Horn in p, then* $\mathrm{Comp}_G(T; p) = \mathrm{Comp}(T; p)$. □

4.3 Circumscription implies Generalized Predicate Completion (Sometimes)

The generalized predicate completion is not always a logical consequence of the circumscription. Let us consider the clause

$$p(a, y) \lor p(x, y). \tag{4.9}$$

We know $p(a, y)$ is an instance of $p(x, y)$, and the clause (4.9) is logically equivalent to $p(x, y)$, where x and y are variables and a is a constant. The generalized completed definition of p is

$$\forall x_1, x_2. [\exists x, y. (x_1 = x \land x_2 = y \land \neg p(a, y)) \lor$$
$$\exists x, y. (x_1 = a \land x_2 = y \land \neg p(x, y)) \equiv p(x_1, x_2)]. \tag{4.10}$$

Let consider the structure $M = \{ p(a, a) \}$ with its domain $\{ a \}$, which is a model of (4.9) minimal *wrt* $\leqq_p$. Let $x_1 = a$ and $x_2 = a$. Then

$$[\exists x, y. (a = x \land a = y \land \neg p(a, y)) \lor \exists x, y. (a = y \land \neg p(x, y)) \equiv p(a, a)] \tag{4.11}$$

will be induced from (4.10). Since there is only a single individual a in the domain, (4.11) is always false in M. Hence, M is not a model of the generalized completed definition of p in T (4.10). Note that the distinct positive literals on p in the clause are unifiable.

Proposition 3. *The generalized predicate completion is not always implied by the circumscription for any clausal sentence.* □

Lemma 3.1 *Let F be a formula without positive occurrences of p. If F is true in a structure M then it is true in every substructure of M wrt $\leqq_p$.* □

Lemma 3.2 *Let F be a formula without negative occurrences of p and M a structure. If F is true in some substructure of M wrt $\leqq_p$, then F is true in M.* □

Definition 3. Let C be a clause and p a predicate symbol. C is *non-overlapping wrt p* iff for any distinct positive literals P and P' on p in C, P is not unifiable with P'. If every clause in a clausal sentence T is non-overlapping *wrt p*, T is said to be *non-overlapping wrt p*. □

Theorem 3. *Let T be a clausal sentence and p a predicate symbol. If T is non-overlapping wrt p then* $\mathrm{Circum}(T; p) \models \mathrm{Comp_G}(T; p)$, *i.e., the generalized completion of p in T is implied by the circumscription of p in T.*

Proof. It is sufficient to show the the *only if* half (4.12) of the generalized completed definition of p in T is true in every model of T minimal *wrt* $\leqq_p$.

$$\forall x. [\, p(x) \supset E_{11} \vee \cdots \vee E_{kh_k} \,] \tag{4.12}$$

Here, x is the tuple of variables and each E_{ij} is the expression of the form

$$\exists y_i. [x = t_{ij} \wedge L_i \wedge \neg p(t_{i1}) \wedge \cdots \wedge \neg p(t_{ij-1}) \wedge \neg p(t_{ij+1}) \wedge \cdots \wedge \neg p(t_{ih_i})] \tag{4.13}$$

Let M be any model of T minimal *wrt* $\leqq_p$. Suppose (4.12) is false in M. Then there is at least a ground substitution θ such that $p(x)\theta$ is true in M but

$$(E_{11} \vee \cdots \vee E_{kh_k})\theta \tag{4.14}$$

is false in M. Assume $p(x)\theta = p(t)$, where t is the tuple of ground terms. Construct a proper substructure M_0 of M *wrt* $\leqq_p$ in the following way:

$$M_0[q] = M[q] \quad \text{if } q \neq p, \text{ and}$$
$$M_0[p^+] = M[p^+] - \{ t \}.$$

Now, we shall prove $M_0 \models T$. By *Lemma 3.1*, every clause in T without positive occurrences of p is true in M_0 since M is a model of T. Then it is sufficient to show the *if* half (4.15) of the generalized completed definition of p in T is true in M_0.

$$\forall x. [\, E_{11} \vee \cdots \vee E_{kh_k} \supset p(x) \,] \tag{4.15}$$

It is clear from the construction of M_0 that $(E_{11} \vee \cdots \vee E_{kh_k} \supset p(x))\sigma$ is true in M_0 for every ground substitution $\sigma \neq \theta$. Thus, it remains to show that

$$(E_{11} \vee \cdots \vee E_{kh_k} \supset p(x))\theta \tag{4.16}$$

is true in M_0. Note that $p(x)\theta$ is false in M_0. Suppose $M_0 \models E_{ij}\theta$, for some i, j. That is,

$$[t = t_{ij} \wedge L_i \wedge \neg p(t_{i1}) \wedge \cdots \wedge \neg p(t_{ij-1}) \wedge \neg p(t_{ij+1}) \wedge \cdots \wedge \neg p(t_{ih_i})]\sigma \tag{4.17}$$

is true in M_0 for some ground substitution σ which replaces variables in y_i by ground terms. $L_i\sigma$ is true in M by *Lemma 3.2*. Because there is no negative occurrences of p in L_i. $t = t_{ij}\sigma$ must be true in M since it is true in M_0. Since T is non-overlapping, $t = t_{ij}\sigma \neq t_{ij'}\sigma$, for very $j' \neq j$. Hence, $[\neg p(t_{i1}) \wedge \cdots \wedge \neg p(t_{ij-1}) \wedge \neg p(t_{ij+1}) \wedge \cdots \wedge \neg p(t_{ih_i})]\sigma$ is true in M since it is true in M_0. Thus, (4.17) is true in M. This means that $E_{ij}\theta$ is true in M, which contradicts that (4.14) is false in M. Therefore, $M_0 \nvDash E_{ij}\theta$, for every i, j. Hence, (4.16) is true in M_0.

Hence, we can conclude $M_0 \models T$. Since M_0 is a proper substructure of M *wrt* $\leqq_p$, $M_0 \models T$ contradicts the minimality of M. Thus, (4.12) is true in M. **Q.E.D.**

Corollary 3.1 *Let T be a clausal sentence non-overlapping wrt a predicate symbol p. Then* $\mathrm{Th}(T) \subseteq \mathrm{Th}(\mathrm{Comp_G}(T; p)) \subseteq \mathrm{Th}(\mathrm{Circum}(T; p))$, *where* $\mathrm{Th}(T)$ *denotes the set of all logical consequences form T.* $\square$

294

By *Proposition* 2, *Theorem* 2 is apparently covered by *Theorem* 3. *Theorem* 3 can also be easily extended to the circumscription with parameter.

Corollary 3.2 *Let T be a clausal sentence, p and z distinct predicate symbols. If T is non-overlapping wrt p then* $\text{Circum}(T; p; z) \models \text{Comp}_G(T; p)$, *i.e., the generalized completion of p in T is implied by the circumscription of p in T with parameter z.*

Proof. Because every minimal model of T wrt $\leqq_{p; z}$ is also minimal wrt $\leqq_p$.

$$\text{Q.E.D.}$$

It is clear that the converse of *Theorem* 3 is not always true. Now we shall figure out the cases in which the converse of *Theorem* 3 is true.

Definition 4. Let T be a clausal sentence and p a predicate symbol. T is *collapsible wrt p* if it consists of clauses containing no positive occurrences of p or clauses containing no negative occurrences of p. $\square$

Theorem 4. *Let T be a clausal sentence and p a predicate symbol. If T is non-overlapping and collapsible wrt p, then the generalized completion of p in T is logically equivalent to the circumscription of p in T.*

Proof. It is sufficient to show that any model of $\text{Comp}_G(T; p)$ is a minimal model of T wrt $\leqq_p$. Let M be a model of $\text{Comp}_G(T; p)$. We shall prove M is a minimal model of T wrt $\leqq_p$. It is clear $M \models T$. Let M_0 be any model of T such that $M_0 \leqq_p M$. Since T is collapsible wrt p, then E_{ij} in (4.8) contains no positive occurrences of p for any i, j, $1 \leqq i \leqq k$, $1 \leqq j \leqq h_i$. For any $t \in M[p+]$, *i.e.*, t such that $p(t)$ is true in M,

$$(E_{11} \vee \cdots \vee E_{kh_k})\sigma \tag{4.18}$$

is also true in M, for σ such that $p(x)\sigma = p(t)$ since $M \models \text{Comp}_G(T; p)$. Then (4.18) is true in M_0 by *Lemma* 3.1. Hence, $M_0 \models p(t)$, *i.e.*, $t \in M_0[p+]$. Otherwise M_0 T. Therefore $M[p+] \subseteq M_0[p+]$. Since $M_0 \leqq_p M$, then $M_0[p+] \subseteq M[p+]$, hence $M[p+] = M_0[p+]$. Thus M must be a minimal model of T wrt $\leqq_p$. **Q.E.D.**

Corollary 4.1 *Let T be a clausal sentence and p a predicate symbol. If T is Horn in p and collapsible wrt p, then the predicate completion of p in T is logically equivalent to the circumscription of p in T.* $\square$

5. Conclusion

In this paper, we have presented a generalized completion of a predicate p, which is appropriate for clausal sentences not Horn in p. It is clear that the generalized predicate completion presented in this paper is exactly same as the predicate completion proposed by Clark, if the relative sentence is Horn in the predicate p. The class of clausal sentences whose generalized predicate completion can be subsumed by the circumscription is obviously wider than the class of clausal sentences which are Horn in p. The result obtained by Reiter could be covered by *Theorem* 3. In some cases the generalized predicate completion is rather close to the circumscription. As shown in *Theorem* 4 and *Corollary* 4.1, sometimes both are completely logically equivalent. As the generalized predicate completion can be constructed in a heuristic way, it may be an effective approach to circumscription within the framework of first-order logic before invoking the full power of the circumscription.

References

[Chang and Lee, 1973]
Chang, C.L., and Lee, R.C.T., *Symbolic Logic and Mechanical Theorem Proving*, Academic Press, New York and London, 1973.

[Clark, 1978]
Clark, K.L., *Negation as Failure*, in Logic and Databases, Gallaire, H. and Minker, J., Eds., Plenum Press, New York, pp. 293-322, 1978.

[Hou et al, 1988]
Hou, B.H., Togashi, A. and Noguchi, S., *On the Reducibility of Circumscription*, Preprint WGAI, IPSJ, Vol.88, No.44, pp. 27-35, 1988.

[Lifschitz, 1985]
Lifschitz, V., *Computing Circumscription*, Proc. Ninth International Joint Conference on Artificial Intelligence, Los Angeles, CA, pp. 121-127, 1985.

[Lloyd, 1984]
Lloyd, J.W., *Foundations of Logic Programming*, Springer, 1984.

[McCarthy, 1980]
McCarthy, J., *Circumscription - A Form of Non-Monotonic Reasoning*, Artificial Intelligence, Vol. 13, pp. 27-39, 1980.

[McCarthy, 1986]
McCarthy, J., *Applications of Circumscription to Formalizing Common Sense Knowledge*, Artificial Intelligence, Vol. 28, pp. 89-116, 1986.

[Rabinov, 1989]
Rabinov, A., *A Generalization of Collapsible Cases of Circumscription*, Artificial Intelligence, Vol.38, pp. 111-117, 1989.

[Reiter, 1978]
Reiter, R., *On Closed World Data Bases*, in: Logic and Databases, Gallaire, H. and Minker, J., Eds., Plenum, New York, pp. 56-76, 1978.

[Reiter, 1980]
Reiter, R., *A Logic for Default Reasoning*, Artificial Intelligence, Vol. 13, pp. 81-132, 1980.

[Reiter, 1982]
Reiter, R., *Circumscription Implies Predicate Completion (Sometimes).*, Proc. AAAI-82, pp. 418-420, 1982.

On the Completeness of Narrowing for E-Unification

Jia-Huai You

Department of Computing Science
University of Alberta
Edmonton, Alberta, Canada, T6G 2H1

P.A. Subrahmanyam

AT&T Bell Laboratories
Holmdel, NJ 07733

Abstract

The *narrowing* mechanism has been a major tool in designing complete *E-unification* procedures for classes of equational theories in the last few years. Meanwhile, it has also been noticed that it is sometimes difficult to build complete procedures using only the narrowing mechanism. This paper analyzes several examples encountered by the authors in the course of research, which show that in certain situations narrowing fails to yield a complete *E*-unification procedure. Furthermore, we augment the narrowing mechanism with a restricted form of the paramodulation rule. This yields a complete *E*-unification procedure for all the equational theories that can be described by a confluent term rewriting system. We then present a new procedure in which paramodulation is eliminated by using a set of pre-constructed terms, called *cover set*, which is a substantially reduced set of terms of certain complexity. This provides a degree of completeness, called *relative* completeness, which is measured by complexity of terms.

1. Introduction

The general problem of unification in the presence of an equational theory E, called E-unification, is known to be an important, albeit a difficult problem [Siekmann, 1984].

Many unification procedures for individual equational theories have been invented since the milestone paper [Plotkin, 1972]. While the proposed methods for these individual theories seem to be quite different, a complete procedure for the class of equational theories that possess a canonical (confluent and noetherian) term rewriting systems has been obtained by Fay [Fay, 1979], and improved by Hullot [Hullot, 1980]. These results were later extended to a class of nonterminating term rewriting systems in [You and Subrahmanyam, 1986]. The central idea in these procedures is the use of the narrowing process, combined with term rewriting techniques.

It is well-known that the narrowing mechanism is essentially a special form of paramodulation [Robinson and Wos, 1969]. One of the major differences is that narrowing substitutes into nonvariable terms using *directed* equations, while paramodulation can substitute into variable terms using two-way equations and an additional set of functionally reflexive axioms. The practical impact of this difference is so significant that narrowing can avoid countless (often infinite) search branches. A natural question arises: when does narrowing yield a complete unification procedure? i.e., what is the power of narrowing? Although narrowing has been shown to be complete for the class of canonical term rewriting systems, the generality and limitations of narrowing do not seem to have been fully understood.

The question of completeness of paramodulation without the functionally reflexive axioms have been tackled by several researchers. Robinson and Wos conjectured that the completeness would only require the axiom $x = x$. The modification method given by Brand [Brand, 1975] provided an indirect proof of this claim. A direct proof was given by Peterson [Peterson, 1983], which is based on a simplification ordering, order isomorphic to ω on ground terms. Hsiang and Rusinowitch [Hsiang and Rusinowitch, 1986] later improved the results by using a more general ordering that is only required to be *total* on ground terms. One common assumption in all of the above approaches is that equations are either used symmetrically or oriented by an ordering employed in the method. Recently, systems of another type have been extensively used for computational purposes, such as those described in [Dershowitz, 1985; Fribourg, 1985b; O'Donnell, 1977; Reddy, 1985; You, 1989], where the orientation of an equation is pre-determined by the user; i.e., the user writes a set of directed equations, called rewrite rules, which may bear certain computational purposes. Fribourg [Fribourg, 1984] defined an oriented form of the paramodulation rule, which requires the functionally reflexive axioms (and therefore substitution into variables), and gave the completeness results. We show in this paper that, unlike the previous results based on two-way equations or system-oriented equations, the completeness of user-oriented equational systems indeed relies on the functionally reflexive axioms, even in the case that the system is a confluent term rewriting system.

In this paper, we first analyze two examples to show that narrowing sometimes fails to yield a complete unification procedure. We also present a unification procedure, complete for all of the confluent term rewriting systems. The procedure uses narrowing, augmented with a restricted form of paramodulation, i.e., *substitution into variables* using a set of functionally reflexive rules. As it is well-known that oriented paramodulation is complete, the main result of this procedure is that in the context of E-unification for confluent term rewriting systems, the full use of paramodulation is unnecessary. That is, substitution into variables using rules other than functionally reflexive rules is redundant in order to preserve the completeness, and thus can be ignored. Furthermore, the set of functionally reflexive rules can be *totally* separated from the given term rewriting system R; i.e., only R is required to be confluent. This improves Fribourg's results on oriented paramodulation [Fribourg, 1985a].

Although the proposed procedure can cut off many redundant derivations, it is still far less efficient than desired. The difficulty for narrowing to be complete stems from the need of some "miracle" terms in the course of narrowing derivations. Enumerating all of the terms is unrealistic. To alleviate this problem, we present another procedure that uses a term enumeration process, up to certain complexity of terms, before the narrowing process is engaged. The method is incomplete in general. It however, provides a degree of completeness, which is measured by complexities of terms. A term is said to be of complexity n if it contains n function symbols. A substitution is said to be of complexity n if its most complex substituting term is of complexity n. If the term construction process generates all of the terms whose complexities are less than or equal to n, then for any E-unifier σ, whose complexity is less than or equal to n, narrowing can generate an E-unifier more general than σ. We call this *relative completeness* with respect to n. We also show that to be relatively complete, one does not need the set of all terms up to certain complexity; a substantially reduced set of it, called *cover set*, is sufficient. The major advantage of this method is that cover sets of different complexities can be constructed in advance and can be stored for repeated use, thus eliminating the time spent on the process of substitution into variables during the course of narrowing. In addition, the user has direct control over the sets to be used, and even over when they should be used; this gives an extra amount of flexibility over the tradeoff between efficiency and completeness. Thus, the resulting procedure performs well for solving equations involving a small number of variables, whose solutions consist of less complex substituting terms and for which the underlying term rewriting systems possess a small set of function symbols.

The next section provides notations used in this paper. Examples are presented and analyzed in Section 3 to show that narrowing fails to yield a complete unification procedure. A unification procedure augmenting narrowing with a restricted form of paramodulation is presented in Section 4, which is shown to be complete for all of the confluent term rewriting systems. Section 5 discusses the realization of the procedure using a term construction process.

2. Notations

Given a set of function symbols F and an enumerable set of variables V, the *free algebra* over V, denoted by $T(F,V)$ contains the set of all terms constructed from the function symbols in F and the variables in V. Terms are viewed as *labeled trees* in the following way: a term A is a partial function from the set of sequences of positive integers to $T(F,V)$ such that its domain satisfies: (i) $\varepsilon \in D(A)$, and (ii) $u \in D(t_i)$ iff $i.u \in D(f(t_1, ..., t_i, ..., t_n))$ $1 \leq i \leq n$. $D(A)$ is called a set of *occurrences* of A; $O(A)$ denotes the nonvariable subset of $D(A)$. The set of occurrences is partially ordered: $u \leq v$ iff $\exists w\ u.w = v$ and $u < v$ iff $u \leq v$ & $u \neq v$. We use $V(A)$ to denote the set of variables occurring in A, and use x, y, z as variables. We define $A[u \leftarrow B]$ as the term A, in which the subterm at occurrence u has been replaced by the term B.

A term A is said to be of *complexity n*, denoted by $Complexity(A)$, if A contains n number of function symbols. A term A is said *linear* if no variable in A occurs more than once.

A *substitution* is a mapping σ from V to $T(F,V)$, extended to an endomorphism of $T(F,V)$. We denote by S, the set of all substitutions. If $\sigma \in S$ and $A \in T(F,V)$, we write σA for the application of σ to A. The domain of a substitution σ, denoted by $D(\sigma)$, contains the variables that are not mapped to themselves. A substitution σ is said to be of *complexity n*, denoted by $Complexity(\sigma)$, if its most complex substituting term is of complexity n. A substitution is said *variable-pure* iff all the substituting terms therein are variables.

The set of *introduced* variables by a substitution σ is defined as $I(\sigma) = \cup\ V(\sigma x)$ for all x in $D(\sigma)$. The composition of substitutions σ and θ is defined as a mapping: $(\sigma \cdot \theta)x = \sigma(\theta x)$. We denote by $\sigma_{|W}$ the *restriction* of the substitution σ to the subset W of V.

An *equation* $A = B$ is a pair of terms separated by the symbol $=$. An *equational theory* is a set E of equations. We define *E-equality* $=_E$ as the finest congruence containing E and closed under replacement and instantiation.

The notion of *E-equality* is extended to substitutions as follows: $\sigma =_E \theta$ iff $\forall x \in V\ \sigma x =_E \theta x$. We will write, for a subset W of V: $\sigma =_E \theta\ [W]$ iff $\forall x \in W\ \sigma x =_E \theta x$. In the same way, σ is more general than θ under the equational theory E over W: $\sigma \leq_E \theta\ [W]$ iff $\exists \eta\ \eta \cdot \sigma =_E \theta\ [W]$.

Two terms A and B are said to be *E-unifiable* iff there exists σ in S, such that $\sigma A =_E \sigma B$. We denote by $U_E(A,B)$ the set of all *E-unifiers* for A and B. Let W be a finite set of variables containing $V = V(A) \cup V(B)$. We say that a set of substitutions Σ is a *relatively* complete set, with respect to an integer n, of unifiers for A and B away from W iff:

(i) $\forall \sigma \in \Sigma\ D(\sigma) \subseteq V\ \&\ I(\sigma) \cap W = \varnothing$ (protection of W)

(ii) $\Sigma \subseteq U_E(A,B)$ (correctness)

(iii) $\forall \sigma \in U_E(A,B)\ \&\ Complexity(\sigma) \leq n\ \ \exists \theta \in \Sigma\ \ \theta \leq_E \sigma\ [V]$ (completeness)

Completeness is similarly defined by removing the requirement $Complexity(\sigma) \leq n$.

An E-unification procedure is complete if it generates a complete set of E-unifiers away from W for all E-unifiable input terms. An E-unification procedure is relatively complete with respect to n if it generates a relatively complete set of E-unifiers, with respect ot n, away from W for all E-unifiable input terms.

A *term rewriting system* R is a set of pairs of terms $\{\alpha_i \to \beta_i \mid i \in I\}$ such that $V(\beta_i) \subseteq V(\alpha_i)$ for all i. We say that a term A reduces at occurrence u to a term B using the rule $\alpha_k \to \beta_k$ and write $A \to_{[u,k]} B$, if there exists a match η from α_k to A/u and $B = A[u \leftarrow \eta(\beta_k)]$. We may sometimes write $A \to B$ or $A \to_u B$. $\to$ is called the *reduction relation* on $T(F,V)$. We denote by $\overset{*}{\to}$ the reflexive, transitive closure of $\to$.

We say that a term A is in *normal form* iff there does not exist a term B such that $A \to B$. A term that has a normal form is said to be *normalizable*. A substitution is said to be *normalized* if each term therein is in normal form.

A term rewriting system R is said to be *canonical* iff:

(i) $\overset{*}{\to}$ is noetherian, i.e., there does not exist any infinite derivation sequence: $A_0 \to A_1 \to \dots$

(ii) $\overset{*}{\to}$ is confluent, i.e., $\forall A, B, C$ $(A \overset{*}{\to} B \ \& \ A \overset{*}{\to} C) \Rightarrow (\exists D \ B \overset{*}{\to} D \ \& \ C \overset{*}{\to} D)$.

Let $\alpha_i \to \beta_i$ and $\alpha_j \to \beta_j$ be two rewrite rules in R with variables properly renamed so that α_i and α_j share no variables. We say that the pair $\langle \sigma(\alpha_i[u \leftarrow \beta_j]), \sigma(\alpha_j) \rangle$ is *critical* in R, if $u \in O(\alpha_i)$ and σ is the most general unifier for α_i/u and α_j.

Given a term rewriting system R, a term P *narrows* to a term Q at occurrence u, $u \in O(P)$, denoted by $P \sim>_{[u,k,\rho]} Q$, iff there exists a rewrite rule $\alpha_k \to \beta_k \in R$ and ρ is the most general unifier of P/u and α_k away from $V(P) \cup V(\alpha_k)$, and $Q = \rho(P[u \leftarrow \rho\beta_k]) = \rho(P[u \leftarrow \beta_k])$. We may abbreviate $\sim>_{[u,k,\rho]}$ by $\sim>_\rho$. We denote by $\overset{*}{\sim>}$ the reflexive, transitive closure of $\sim>$.

2.1. Unification Procedures Based on Narrowing

Given a term rewriting system R, a term P *narrows* to a term Q at occurrence u, $u \in O(P)$, denoted by $P \sim>_{[u,k,\rho]} Q$, iff there exists a rewrite rule $\alpha_k \to \beta_k \in R$ and ρ is the most general unifier of P/u and α_k away from $V(P) \cup V(\alpha_k)$, and $Q = \rho(P[u \leftarrow \rho\beta_k]) = \rho(P[u \leftarrow \beta_k])$. We may abbreviate $\sim>_{[u,k,\rho]}$ by $\sim>_\rho$. We denote by $\overset{*}{\sim>}$ the reflexive, transitive closure of $\sim>$.

The relationship between reduction sequences and narrowing sequences was formally established by Hullot [Hullot, 1980], as described below.

Theorem 1. (Hullot 80) Let A and B be two terms and H be a function symbol not in F. Let $C - H(A,B)$. Let also W be a finite set of variables containing $V = V(C)$, and θ be any *normalized* unifier for A and B. For any reduction sequence issuing from $\theta(C)$:

(i) $\theta(C) = A_0 \to_{[u_0, k_0]} \dots \to_{[u_{n-1}, k_{n-1}]} A_n = H(M, M)$

there exists a narrowing sequence issuing from C:

(ii) $C = B_0 \sim>_{[u_0, k_0, \rho_0]} \dots \sim>_{[u_{n-1}, k_{n-1}, \rho_{n-1}]} B_n = H(P_n, Q_n)$,

such that P_n and Q_n are unifiable with the minimum unifier μ, $\sigma = \mu \cdot \rho_{n-1} \cdot \dots \cdot \rho_0|_V$ is an E-unifier for P and Q, away from W, and $\sigma \leq_E \theta [V]$.

Conversely, for any narrowing sequence (ii) issuing from C and the generated substitution σ, there exists a reduction sequence (i) issuing from $\sigma(C)$. $\square$

2.2. Paramodulation

We briefly review the terminology that will be used in defining paramodulation. A *sentence* is a conjunction of clauses. A *clause* is a disjunction of literals, conveniently rewritten as a set of literals. A *literal* is an atomic formula or the negation of an atomic formula. An *atomic formula* is of the form $P(t_1,...,t_n)$, where P is a predicate symbol and t_i are terms with all the variables implicitly universally quantified. Paramodulation is an inference rule used in resolution proof procedures and is defined as follows (see [Loveland, 1978] for details).

Let C_1 and C_2 be two clauses (called parent clauses) with no variables in common. Let $L[t]$ denote the literal L containing the term t. If C_1 is $\{L[t]\} \cup D_1$, and C_2 is $\{t_1 = t_2\} \cup D_2$, where D_1 and D_2 are clauses, and if t and t_1 (or t and t_2, respectively) are unifiable with the minimum unifier σ, then infer $\{\sigma L[t_1 \leftarrow \sigma t_2]\} \cup \sigma D_1 \cup \sigma D_2$. We say that C_2 is paramodulated into C_1.

When the term t in the literal L is a variable term, we say that the corresponding paramodulation is *paramodulation into variables*.

The completeness of paramodulation requires an additional set of functionally reflexive axioms, i.e., $S_{RF} = \{ f(x_1, ..., x_n) = f(x_1, ..., x_n) \} \cup \{x = x\}$ for all n-ary function symbols. It has also been shown that S_{RF} is absolutely needed for the set-of-support strategy [Loveland, 1978], and this is true even for unit equations [Henschen, 1985].

Narrowing can be viewed as a restricted form of paramodulation: it only substitutes into nonvariable terms and there is no need for functionally reflexive rules. Furthermore, narrowing uses rules directionally and is a goal-oriented (linear) strategy.

3. Limitations of Narrowing

It was shown in [Fay, 1979, Hullot, 1980] that narrowing provides a complete E-unification procedure for canonical term rewriting systems. Due to the attractiveness of narrowing, we would now like to know if there are other classes of term rewriting systems for which narrowing is complete. We assume that we would like to work only with rewrite rules, because the use of two-way equations can easily result in the generation of useless derivations and yield loops that cause non-termination.

Now, is narrowing complete for any confluent term rewriting system? The answer is no. The following example was originally provided by Henschen [Henschen, 1985] and is modified for the discussion here. Consider

$$R_1 = \{g(a, f(b), f(c)) \to g(b, f(b), f(c))$$
$$g(b, f(b), f(c)) \to g(a, f(b), f(c))$$
$$b \to c$$
$$c \to b\}.$$

It is easy to see that R_1 is confluent but not terminating. Now, we would like to unify $g(a, x, x)$ and $g(b, x, x)$. Although there exists an E-unifier $\sigma = \{x \leftarrow f(b)\}$, narrowing alone cannot generate any unifier. It appears that the problem with this example is that there are *critical pairs* in this term rewriting system [Knuth and Bendix, 1970]. From each critical pair, a new rewrite rule can be obtained by orienting the two elements to form a rule. This process is usually called *superposition* on R. By superposition, we can obtain two more rewrite rules (among others) from R_1:

$$g(a, f(c), f(c)) \to g(b, f(b), f(c)) \text{ and } g(b, f(c), f(c)) \to g(a, f(b), f(c)).$$

Narrowing on $g(a, x, x)$ and $g(b, x, x)$ now produces $\sigma' = \{x \leftarrow f(c)\}$, where $\sigma =_E \sigma'$.

The problem here lies in the fact that an equational theory can be represented by different term rewriting systems. Since superposition is a process which tries to represent an equational theory by different term rewriting systems, it might appear that superposition interleaved with narrowing can yield a complete E-unification procedure. Unfortunately, this is not true either. There are term rewriting systems with no critical pairs for which narrowing is not complete. Suppose we only have one rewrite rule:

$$R_2 = \{h(a,a) \to c(h(a,a))\}.$$

There is no critical pair here and superposition is not needed. We now try to unify the following two terms:

$$h(c(x), c(x)) \text{ and } h(c(y), c(c(y))).$$

There exists an E-unifier $\sigma = \{x \leftarrow h(a,a), y \leftarrow h(a,a)\}$, such that when σ is applied to both terms, we get

$$h(c(h(a,a)), c(h(a,a))) =_E h(c(h(a,a)), c(c(h(a,a)))),$$

because the lefthand side can be rewritten to yield the righthand side. Narrowing again cannot generate any unifier. Once again, the problem is that the variables x and y in the two terms to be unified need to be instantiated properly in order for narrowing to proceed.

For this example, we may well represent the equational theory by reversing the orientation of the rule, i.e., $\{c(h(a,a)) \to h(a,a)\}$, so why do we have to use a rewrite rule such as $h(a,a) \to c(h(a,a))\}$? Firstly, different orientations of rewrite rules may have different computational purposes. Secondly, as argued earlier, we would like to deal with rewrite rules rather than equations.

To see why narrowing is not general enough, let us go back to Theorem 1; the substitution θ is required to be normalized, and this is not always possible for nonterminating term rewriting systems. If the substitution θ were not normalized, then the correspondence between the reduction sequence (i) and the narrowing sequence (ii) would not always hold.

4. A Complete E-Unification Procedure

In this section we present a complete unification procedure for all confluent term rewriting systems, based on narrowing and a restricted form of paramodulation which is called *functionally reflexive demodulation*, or *demodulation* for abbreviation.

Given a term rewriting system R, let $S_{RF} = \{f(x_1, ..., x_n) \to f(x_1, ..., x_n) \mid \text{for all } n\text{-ary } f \in F\}$ be the set of functionally reflexive rules. A term P demodulates to Q at a *variable* occurrence u, denoted by $P \to_{[u,k,\rho]} Q$, iff $\alpha_k \to \alpha_k \in S_{RF}$, ρ is the most general unifier of P/u and α_k, away from $V(P) \cup V(\alpha_k)$, and $Q = \rho(\Gamma[u \leftarrow \rho\beta_k]) = \rho(P[u \leftarrow \beta_k])$. Note that since u represents a variable the substituting term is simply the term α_k with variables therein properly renamed. We may abbreviate $P \to_{u,k,\rho} Q$ by $P \to_{[\rho]} Q$, and denote by $\overset{*}{\to}$ the reflexive, transitive closure of $\to$.

We are now to establish the relationship between reduction sequences and narrowing/demodulation sequences. The proof is omitted.

Lemma 2. Given a term rewriting system R, let P and Q be two terms and H be a function symbol not in F. Let $C = H(P,Q)$. Let also W be a finite set of variables containing $V = V(C)$, and η be any unifier for P and Q. For any reduction sequence issuing from $\eta(C)$:

(i) $\eta(C) = B_0 \to_{[u_0, k_0]} B_1 \to_{[u_1, k_1]} \cdots \to_{[u_{n-1}, k_{n-1}]} B_n = H(M, M)$

there exists a narrowing/demodulation sequence from C:

(ii) $C = C_0 \overset{*}{\twoheadrightarrow}_{[v_0]} D_0 \to_{[u_0, k_0, \rho_0]} C_1 \overset{*}{\twoheadrightarrow}_{[v_1]} D_1 \to_{[u_1, k_1, \rho_1]} C_2 \cdots \to_{[u_{n-1}, k_{n-1}, \rho_{n-1}]} C_n = H(P_n, Q_n),$

such that P_n and Q_n are unifiable with the minimum unifier μ, $\sigma = \mu \cdot \rho_{n-1} \cdot \upsilon_{n-1} \cdot \ldots \cdot \rho_0 \cdot \upsilon_0|_V$ is an E-unifier for P and Q, away from W, and $\sigma \leq_E \eta \, [V]$.

Conversely, for any sequence of the form (ii) and generated substitution σ, there exists reduction sequence of the form (i), issuing from $\sigma(C)$. $\square$

Procedure 1. Enumerating all narrowing/demodulation sequences. $\square$

Theorem 3. Procedure 1 is complete for all confluent term rewriting systems.

5. Relative Completeness Based on Complexities of Terms

The process of demodulation is the main source of inefficiency of the procedure described in the last section. In this section we show that the process of demodulation is used essentially to construct terms during the narrowing process. The idea is to generate sets of terms up to certain complexity before applying the narrowing process. This is incomplete in general, but is relatively complete with respect to the given complexity. Furthermore, to be relatively complete with respect to n, it is not necessary to enumerate the set of all terms whose complexities are less than or equal to n; a subset, called *cover set* (which will be defined shortly), is sufficient. This approach has two main advantages. First of all, demodulation is completely eliminated from the reasoning process, and the work done by demodulation is pre-processed and can be exploited repeatedly for different applications. Secondly, the user has direct control over the set of terms to be used and even over when they should be used; these may be determined by domain knowledge, some heuristics and the tradeoff between efficiency and completeness. For example, if we totally ignore the use of the constructed terms, Theorem 1 tells us that the missed E-unifiers, if any, must be those involving nonterminating substituting terms.

Term Construction Process

1. There is a distinguished node, called the *root node*. There is a finite set of variables W to be protected.

2. For each n-ary function symbol f in F (including constant function symbols), a nonvariable term of the form $f(x_1, \ldots, x_n)$, where variables $x_1, \ldots, x_n$ are distinct, is created as a child of the root node. None of the introduced variables $x_1, \ldots, x_n$ should be in W.

3. Recursively, if A is a node in the tree and u is an occurrence such that $u(A)$ is a variable, then for each n-ary function symbol f in F, a node with the term $A[u \leftarrow f(x_1, \ldots, x_n)]$, where variables $x_1, \ldots, x_n$ are distinct, is created as a child of A. None of the introduced variables should be in W. The construction of the tree stops at the depth n. $\square$

We should notice one crucial (though technical) property of constructed terms: distinct terms have no variables in common. The set of all nodes in a tree of depth n contains all linear terms, up to variables renaming, whose complexities are less than or equal to n. This is described in the proposition below, whose proof is trivial.

Proposition 4. For any linear nonvariable term A, the term construction process generates a finite set of linear terms Ω such that A is in Ω, and for any linear nonvariable term B, we have

$$Complexity(B) \leq Complexity(A) \implies B \in \Omega,$$

up to variable renaming.

Furthermore, for any nonlinear term A' of complexity n, there exists a linear term A of the same complexity and a variable-pure substitution σ, such that $A' = \sigma(A)$. $\square$

We have already seen nonlinear terms are excluded from Ω. We now further reduce the size of Ω.

Definition: (Cover Sets of Complexity n)

Let Ω be a set of constructed terms of complexity n. Let Ω' be the *nonterminating* subset of Ω. Partition Ω', induced by $=_E$, into congruence classes. A cover set Π of complexity n is a set that contains exactly one element from each partitioned congruence class. $\square$

There can be more than one cover set for any given complexity; the choice might affect the preformance of the procedure described below. However, any cover set is theoretically sufficient for relative completeness with respect to complexity n.

Procedure 2.

Let R be a term rewriting system. Given two terms A and B to be unified, let $V = \{x_1, \ldots, x_n\}$ be the set of variables occurring in A and B, and W be a finite set of variables containing V that is being protected. Let also Π be a cover set of complexity n.

Enumerate all substitutions $\sigma = \{x_i \leftarrow t_i, \ldots, x_j \leftarrow t_j\}$ where $\{x_i, \ldots, x_j\} \subseteq V$ for all combinations of the terms $t_i, \ldots, t_j$ in Π. As a special case, σ may be an "empty" substitution, i.e., $\sigma = \{\}$ (a special case of identity substitution).

For each substitution σ so obtained, perform narrowing on the term $\sigma(H(A,B))$. If there is a narrowing sequence issuing from $B_0 = \sigma(H(A,B))$:

$$B_0 \sim>_{\rho_0} \cdots \sim>_{\rho_{n-1}} B_n = H(P_n, Q_n),$$

such that P_n and Q_n are unifiable with the minimum unifier μ, then output $\xi = \mu \cdot \rho_{n-1} \cdot \ldots \cdot \rho_0 \cdot \sigma_{|V}$. $\square$

For the rewrite system R_1, we have seen that narrowing alone fails to generate any unifier for $g(a,x,x)$ & $g(b,x,x)$. Now from the pre-processed cover set $\Pi = \{b, f(b)\}$, we can start narrowing from $\xi(g(a,x,x))$ & $\xi(g(b,x,x))$, where $\xi = \{x \leftarrow f(b)\}$.

$\xi H(g(a,x,x), g(b,x,x)) =$

$H(g(a,f(b),f(b)), g(b,f(b),f(b))) \sim> H(g(a,f(b),f(c)), g(b,f(b),f(b))) \sim>$

$H(g(b,f(b),f(c)), g(b,f(b),f(b))) \sim> H(g(b,f(b),f(c)), g(b,f(b),f(c))) = H(M,M)$

Theorem 5. Procedure 2 is relatively complete with respect to n for all of the confluent term rewriting systems, if the cover set used is of complexity n.

Proof: Let $\delta = \{y_1 \leftarrow s_1, \ldots, y_k \leftarrow s_k\}$ be an E-unifier for A and B such that $Complexity(\delta) \leq n$, i.e., $Max[complexity(s_1), \ldots, complexity(s_k)] \leq n$. We will first show the existence of another E-unifier, which is E-equivalent to δ, and then show the generation of a more general E-unifier by the procedure.

First of all, $\forall s_i, s_j, 1 \leq i, j \leq n$, if $s_i =_E s_j$ then replace the substitute $y_i \leftarrow s_i$ by $y_i \leftarrow s_j$. Thus, there exists an E-unifier $\theta = \{y_1 \leftarrow t_1, \ldots, y_k \leftarrow t_k\}$ for A & B, such that $\theta =_E \delta \ [V]$, $\forall t_i, t_j, t_i =_E t_j$ iff $t_i = t_j$, and $Complexity(\theta) \leq n$. For each substitute $y_i \leftarrow t_i$ in θ, we can decompose θ into composition of several substitutions, depending on the term t_i.

case a: t_i is normalizable.

In this case, let $\tau = \{y_i \leftarrow t_i\}$ and $\theta' = \theta - \{y_i \leftarrow t_i\}$. We then have $\tau \cdot \theta' =_E \theta \ [V]$.

case b: t_i is not normalizable.

From Proposition 4, for any term t_i, there exists a linear term t and a variable-pure substitution κ, restricted to $V(t)$, such that $\kappa(t) = t_i$. By the definition of cover sets, $\exists t' \in \Pi \ t' =_E t$, from which we have $t' =_E t \Rightarrow \kappa(t') =_E \kappa(t) \Rightarrow \kappa(t') =_E t_i$.

Let $\gamma = \{y_i \leftarrow t'\}$ and $\theta' = \theta - \{y_i \leftarrow t_i\}$. We then have $\theta' \cdot \kappa \cdot \gamma =_E \theta \ [V]$. After processing each substitute in θ this way, we will get $\theta =_E \tau_1 \cdot \ldots \cdot \tau_{k_1} \cdot \kappa_1 \cdot \gamma_1 \cdot \ldots \cdot \kappa_{k_2} \cdot \gamma_{k_2} \ [V]$, where $k_1 + k_2 = k$.

Notice that all the substituting terms in γ_i are in Π. From the Term Construction Process, no distinct substituting terms share common variables. That is, let t'_i be the substituting term in γ_i and

t'_j in γ_j, $I(\gamma_i) \cap I(\gamma_j) = \emptyset$ iff $t'_i \neq t'_j$, iff $t'_i \neq_E t'_j$. The last inequality was because all E-equivalent substituting terms in θ are identical and no two terms in Π are E-equivalent. Thus, $I(\gamma_i) \cap I(\gamma_j) \neq \emptyset$ iff $t'_i = t'_j$, iff $\kappa_i = \kappa_j$. Therefore, the composition can be rearranged as:

$$\theta =_E \tau_1 \bullet ... \bullet \tau_{k_1} \bullet \kappa_1 \bullet ... \bullet \kappa_{k_2} \bullet \gamma_1 \bullet ... \bullet \gamma_{k_3} \ [V].$$

Let $\xi_1 = \tau_1 \bullet ... \bullet \tau_{k_1} \bullet \kappa_1 \bullet ... \bullet \kappa_{k_2}$ and $\xi_2 = \gamma_1 \bullet ... \bullet \gamma_{k_3}$. Clearly, ξ_1 is normalizable. Let ξ'_1 be the normalized substitution of ξ_1. Up to this point, we have already had $\xi'_1 \bullet \xi_2 =_E \theta =_E \delta \ [V]$.

We now show that the procedure can generate an E-unifier, which is more general than $\xi'_1 \bullet \xi_2$, and therefore more general than δ, restricted to V.

The confluence property guarantees the existence of the following reduction sequence:

(i) $\xi'_1 \bullet \xi_2(H(A,B)) = A_0 \rightarrow_{[u_0, k_0]} \cdots \rightarrow_{[u_{n-1}, k_{n-1}]} A_n = H(M,M)$.

By Theorem 1, we have the following narrowing sequence:

(ii) $\xi_2(H(A,B)) = B_0 \sim\!\!>_{[u_0, k_0, \rho_0]} \cdots \sim\!\!>_{[u_{n-1}, k_{n-1}, \rho_{n-1}]} B_n = H(P_n, Q_n)$,

such that P_n and Q_n are unifiable with the minimum unifier μ. Therefore, $\mu \bullet \rho_{n-1} \bullet ... \bullet \rho_0$ is an E-unifier of $\xi_2(A)$ and $\xi_2(B)$; hence $\zeta = \mu \bullet \rho_{n-1} \bullet ... \bullet \rho_0 \bullet \xi_2$ is an E-unifier of A and B, and $\zeta \leq_E \xi'_1 \bullet \xi_2 =_E \delta \ [V]$, away from W.

From Theorem 1, for any generated substitution $\mu \bullet \rho_{n-1} \bullet ... \bullet \rho_0$, there exists a reduction sequence issuing from s $\mu \bullet \rho_{n-1} \bullet ... \bullet \rho_0 \bullet \xi_2(H(A,B))$, thus proving the correctness. $\square$

6. Final Remarks

We have shown there always exists a complete E-unification procedure for any confluent term rewriting system. We further demonstrated that relative completeness can be obtained by constructing a subset of nonterminating terms, up to certain complexity in advance before applying narrowing. It was shown that the need of construction of these "miracle" terms corresponds to the mystery of why the completeness of paramodulation relies on functionally reflexive axioms and the mechanism of substitution into variables. This demonstrates an advantage of using rewrite systems rather than two-way equations whenever a confluent rewrite system can be obtained; in equational systems, because of symmetric reasoning, every term is nonterminating. The two procedures presented in this paper, though still far from being satisfactory, are both more efficient than the unrestricted use of paramodulation.

A different approach has been considered by You [You, 1989] where for the purpose of equational logic programming the underlying notion of equality is modified slightly. It was shown that not only completeness can be restored for a class of equational theories, but by a special narrowing strategy complete and minimal sets of unifiers can be generated.

References

[Brand, 1975]

Brand, D., *Proving theorems by the modification method*. SIAM J. of Computing, Vol. 4, pp. 412-430, 1975.

[Dershowitz, 1985]

Dershowitz, H., *Computing with rewrite rules*. Information and Control, May/June, 65, 2/3, 1985.

[Fay, 1979]

Fay, M.J., *First-order unification in an equational theory*. in 4th Workshop on Automated Deduction, pp. 161-167, 1979.

[Fribourg, 1984]

Fribourg, L., *Oriented equational clauses as a programming language*. J. of Logic Programming, Vol 2, pp.165-177, 1984.

[Fribourg, 1985a]

Fribourg, L., *A superposition oriented theorem prover*. Theoretical Computer Science, Vol. 1, 1985.

[Fribourg, 1985b]

Fribourg, L., *SLOG: A logic programming language interpreter based on clausal superposition and rewriting*. Proc. Symposium on Logic Programming, pp. 172-184, Boston, Mass., July, 1985.

[Henschen, 1985]

Henschen, L., Private communication, 1985.

[Hsiang and Rusinowitch, 1986]

Hsiang J. and M. Rusinowitch, *A new method for establishing refutational completeness in theorem proving*. Proc. of 8th Conference on Automated Deduction, LNCS 230, pp. 141-152, 1986.

[Hullot, 1980]

Hullot, J.M., *Canonical forms and unification*. Proc. 5th Conference on Automated Deduction, pp. 318-334, 1980.

[Knuth and Bendix, 1970]

Knuth, D. and P. Bendix, *Simple word problems in universal algebras*. Computational problems in abstract algebra, ed. J. Leech, pp. 163-279, Pergamon Press, 1970.

[Loveland, 1978]

Loveland, D.W., *Automated theorem proving: a logical basis*, Norther-Holland, New York, 1978.

[O'Donnell, 1977]

O'Donnell, M., *Computing in systems described by equations*. LNCS 58, Springer-Verlag, New York, 1977.

[Peterson, 1983]

Peterson, G.E., *A technique for establishing completeness results in theorem proving with equality*. SIAM J. of Computing, Vol. 12, No. 1 pp.82-100, 1983.

[Plotkin, 1972]

Plotkin, G., *Building-in equational theories*. Machine Intelligence 7, pp. 73-90, Edinburgh University Press, 1972.

[Reddy, 1985]

Reddy, U., *Narrowing as the operational semantics of functional languages*. Proc. Symposium on Logic Programming, pp. 138-151, Boston, Mass., July, 1985.

[Robinson and Wos 1969]

Robinson, G. and L. Wos, *Paramodulation and theorem-proving in first order theories with equality*. Machine Intelligence 4, B. Meltzer and D. Michie, eds., Edinburgh University Press, Edinburgh, 1969, pp. 135-150.

[Siekmann, 1984]

Siekmann, J., *Universal unification*. Proc. 7th International Conference on Automated Deduction, pp. 1-42, Napa, California, May, 1984.

[You and Subrahmanyam, 1986]

You, J.-H. and P.A. Subrahmanyam, *A class of confluent term rewriting systems and unification*. J. Automated Reasoning Vol. 2, 391-418, 1986.

[You, 1989]

You, J.-H., *Unification Modulo an Equality Theory for Equational Logic Programming*. To appear in J. Computer and System Sciences.

Natural Language Understanding

Intelligent Categorization, Archival and Retrieval of Information

Abhay Bhandarkar, R Chandrasekar, S Ramani, Anurag Bhatnagar

National Centre for Software Technology
Gulmohar Cross Road No. 9, Juhu, Bombay 400 049, India
Email: {abhay,mickey,ramani,anurag}@shakti.uu.net

Abstract

This paper describes the problem of intelligent categorization, indexing, archival and retrieval of news stories. A solution to this problem is described. An implementation of these ideas is detailed, and performance analyses are presented.

1   Introduction

In today's world, information is a very valuable commodity. For such information to be usable, it is important that it be structured, and easily made available to potential users.

In [Chandrasekar and Ramani, 1988b], we have considered bibliographic information retrieval as a potential domain of application. In this paper, we will consider the categorization, archival and retrieval of news stories from a wire service agency. However, many of the ideas presented here transfer smoothly to other domains.

2   The Need for News Archival and Retrieval

A typical wire service agency in India distributes about 600 stories every day to its subscribers. A large number of these subscribers are newspapers with a relatively small circulation, and consequently have limited access to facilities such as in-house libraries, in-house research departments, etc. Clearly, newspapers can benefit a lot from such libraries and research departments.

News evolves with time. What looks like an item worth only six column cms on Page 8 today might well be headline quality material tomorrow. On the other hand, what is news today might pale into insignificance three days later. It is therefore essential that all news stories be properly indexed and archived for later use.

Part of a newspaper's task is to follow events, international, domestic and local, and to detect patterns in them. Editorials often follow from such studies. Investigative articles need the weight of precise dates and other facts. Economic trends can be studied only if we have the requisite information ready to be analysed. In all such cases, stories related to a particular topic or topics have to be located.

3   Approaches to Information Retrieval

There are many classical approaches to information storage and retrieval. However, most of them do not produce satisfactory results, for one reason or the other.

One standard method of retrieving news stories of interest involves the use of keywords. Typically, keyword entries would constitute a fraction, of the order of about 1%, of the length of the news story. In a keyword scheme, it is easy to miss out words which may be critically relevant for retrieval. For example, consider a story on an accident involving an aircraft carrying foreign aid for quake victims in Armenia. It may be indexed using the terms: *foreign aid, earthquake-victims, aircraft* and *accident*. But retrieval of such articles using a simple keyword search may be ineffective. If inappropriate keywords (say *Armenia* and *earthquake*) are specified in a query, hundreds of stories may be retrieved, which have nothing to do with the aircraft accident.

One alternative to this would be to scan news stories for the occurrence of keywords. This could be time-consuming, and error-prone.

4   Current Categorization Systems

One well known scheme for classifying news stories is the Keesing's index (see for example, [Keesing, 1985]). Keesing's index is a supplement to Keesing's Contemporary Archives, an international digest of news which many news agencies use. While Keesing's has excellent digests of world events, their categorization is inconsistent. The same class of stories is categorized under one heading one month, and in a (totally) different head at a later date.

The UNESCO Thesaurus [UNESCO, 1977] has top level categories such as *humanities & culture, education, social sciences* etc. and is perhaps better suited for bibliographic categorization, rather than for categorizing news items.

About 30 people are engaged full-time in the research bureau of one of India's best known dailies, in manually indexing and filing all items of news published in major national dailies, using a two-level categorization scheme. There is no formal training given to the indexing personnel; most of them learn 'on the job'. They are able to provide answers within a day to most of the queries that they get. However, since the system depends on the abilities of individual indexing personnel, it is at best ad-hoc.

Clearly, we need something better than the systems discussed above. After briefly surveying related work in information retrieval and categorization, we propose an alternative scheme to tackle this problem.

5 Related work in Information Retrieval

FRUMP [DeJong, 1982] was a system which correctly understood 10% of all the UPI wire service stories that were input to it. FRUMP used a database of 63 domain-specific *sketchy scripts*, which covered several common news categories. Its output was in terms of (partially) instantiated scripts. FRUMP is an example of a program which attempts to understand as much as possible of a news story, to answer questions about it.

The CONSTRUE project [Hayes et al, 1988] which uses the Text Categorization Shell (TCS) [Hayes et al, 1989] demonstrates categorization of text into a number of (possibly closely-related) conceptual categories. TCS is oriented more towards categorization rather than towards retrieval. TCS uses a *hand-crafted* rulebase, fine-tuned to a *specific* application domain, to achieve high accuracy information retrieval.

FERRET [Mauldin, 1989] parses its input documents by text skimming and stores their representations as case frames, called abstracts. Queries to the system are similarly converted to case frames, and matched against the stored abstracts. FERRET uses a rudimentary script learning component to go beyond the scripts that were used in the basic system.

[Lewis et al, 1989] describes ADRENAL (Augmented Document REtrieval using NAtural Language processing). In the final version of ADRENAL, a frame-based representation of a query will be used to retrieve documents which would be further filtered using a text skimmer, with the aid of some heuristics. The notion of document relevance will be decided in a dialogue with the user, and a final list of relevant documents presented.

RUBRIC [Tong et al, 1989] maintains descriptions of domain concepts, evidence for these concepts, and beliefs about concepts that can be sustained on the basis of the evidence, to provide a concept-based full-text retrieval system.

[Lewis et al, 1989] contains a good survey of previous work in this area.

6 Intelligent Retrieval of Information

The major idea in the proposed solution is to use Artificial Intelligence (AI) techniques in the proper categorization, indexing and retrieval of information.

In the retrieval system envisaged, users will specify a few sentences or phrases that are of interest to them. The system is expected to retrieve all the stories related to them. Concept clusters, significance ratings and canonical forms can be used to intelligently index and retrieve stories of interest to the user.

For each topic, there is a cluster of related ideas or phrases. Phrases such as *LTTE (Liberation Tigers)* and *IPKF (Indian Peace Keeping Force)* are related to the topic *Sri Lankan problem*; together they form a **concept cluster**. Such concept clusters can be extracted from a corpus of news stories using standard techniques, such as those described in [Salton and McGill, 1983; Section 3.5] or [Lewis, 1989]. If a query refers to some items from a concept cluster, all the stories relating to the items in the cluster should be retrieved.

News stories can be categorized using ideas of **significance ratings**, at lexical, sentential and story levels [Chandrasekar and Ramani, 1988a]. At the word level, for instance, *assassinated* or *crashed* would be more significant than *street* or *contrast*.

News stories can also be classified using the canonical versions of content words in the story. Content words are mapped onto their **canonical forms**, and the story can be indexed on these forms. For example, *kill* may be the canonical form of the word *assassination*, and a story about an assassination may be indexed using the word *kill*.

As an example, even if the user specifies just *aircraft accidents*, the system could retrieve stories which do not have this phrase in them, but have, for example, phrases such as *Fokker Friendship accident* or *Indian Airlines accidents*.

Thus, we envisage a system which will retrieve semantically related items. The items sought and those retrieved might not be identical, but will be related in a useful sense.

7   The Proposed Categorization & Retrieval Scheme

Considering the requirements listed above and related work in information retrieval, we propose a two-level categorization scheme. The top level consists of ten different categories, as shown in Table 1. The second level of categories is dependent on the top level. For example, the Political category is subdivided into three subcategories: National (news related only to India), Neighbouring (news related to neighbouring countries), and International. However, the sports category has as many subcategories as areas of sport (that is, swimming, hockey, etc.).

Agriculture	Environment	Non-Business Services
Business	Industry	Political
Disasters	Law and Order	Sports
Defence		

Table 1. List of top level categories

Note that we are providing a general framework for categorization, and hence *our work is essentially independent of the actual categories used*. Note also that as long as we are consistent in using the same categorization in archival and retrieval, it is not critical that these categories be universally accepted; it is enough that they are usable.

We will now describe the manner in which news stories are categorized, archived and retrieved in our system. The scheme that we use assumes a small number (say, less than 30) of top-level categories; it is not necessarily optimal for schemes where there are a large number of top-level categories, such as CONSTRUE [Hayes et al, 1988].

8 Categorization and Retrieval of News Stories

News stories are first categorized into one or more of the top level categories using weights derived in a training phase. The second level categorization is knowledge-based, and is heavily dependent on patterns that occur in news items of specific categories.

8.1 Initial Processing of News Stories

Before the news story is categorized, the text of the story is processed in the following manner:

1. All function words are removed from the text of the news story. Some special characters are also removed. Common phrases are converted to hyphenated items, for example *Prime-Minister* or *United-Nations*, and treated as one conceptual unit.

2. The words in the input text are subject to a morphological analysis, and converted to their stem forms. This will ensure that two stories with different forms of the same content words do not get categorized differently. The words that remain in the input text are now canonicalized. Ambiguous words are not altered.

3. A *signature* is derived for this processed input text. The system stores a signature for each story in the archive. This signature of a story is a bit-vector representation of the content words in the story. Each content word of the story sets a bit in the bit-vector using a hashing function. No attempt is made to resolve collisions. This signature will be used to speed up information retrieval. This scheme is similar to those used in [Tolani, 1975] and [Stanfill and Kahle, 1986].

After this processing, the input text is now sent for categorization.

8.2 Top-level Categorization

At this stage, we wish to categorize all news items into one of a set of predefined categories (such as the ones given in Table 1). To do this, we use essentially a statistical model, based on the notion of *usage-tuples*.

8.2.1 Deriving Usage-Tuples: The Training Phase

Usage-tuples are derived during a training phase, using a training set consisting of several processed stories which have been manually categorized. A program scans each word in every such hand-categorized story, and forms a usage-tuple for the word. This usage-tuple is an n-tuple, where n is the number of top-level categories. Each element in the n-tuple corresponds to a particular category.

Thus, if the usage-tuple for a word W is T_W, then:
$$T_W = (a_1, a_2, ...a_n)$$

Here a_j is the number of times that the word W occurs in stories of category j, when only the training set is considered. and appropriately normalized.

For example, the usage-tuples for a few words are given below: (the categories are in the same order as listed in Table 1):

$$\textbf{Arson } (0\ 0\ 0\ 0\ 0\ 5\ 0\ 0\ 0)$$
$$\textbf{Player } (0\ 0\ 0\ 0\ 0\ 0\ 0\ 0\ 15)$$
$$\textbf{Alleged } (5\ 0\ 2\ 1\ 2\ 2\ 13\ 0\ 20\ 1)$$

The word **Arson** is clearly in the Law & Order (seventh) category, while **Player** is in the Sports category. **Alleged** occurs all over, but more frequently in stories related to Law & Order and Political. Note that this usage-tuple is associated with the graphemic form of the word, and not with any particular sense of the word.

8.2.2 Scanning a Story

Once a knowledge base of usage-tuples is set up, we have a simple algorithm to categorize the input text at the topmost level. We scan the input text and vector sum the tuple values associated with each word to decide the category of the story. Thus, at the end, we will have a n-tuple (call it the text-tuple) associated with the whole story.

Text-tuple $= \sum_{W_i \in Words\ occurring\ in\ the\ text} Usage - tuple\ of\ W_i$

Each component of this text-tuple represents, in a sense, the probability that the story belongs to a particular category. For example, given the news story,

---

TOKYO PTF23
CANDIDATE
Socialist Party Withdraws Candidate who Took a Wrong Train:
From PTI Correspondent
Tokyo, July 19 (pti)- A Japanese Socialist Parliamentary candidate took a wrong train and rode straight out of the contest in blazing publicity last night.

The erring candidate, on the stump for days and nights and tired, boarded a Super-Express that would not stop where he had to get off for a campaign meeting to be addressed by his party boss Ms. Takako Doi. The only thing he could think of doing and did was plead with the conductor to bring the Bullet Train to an emergency halt.

However, the emergency solution saw him out of the Upper House election next Sunday so far as his party was concerned. Ms. Doi immediately withdrew him from her party slate and ordered him to apologize to the inconvenienced passengers and the railway staff.

The incident made top TV news throughout the nation last night and hit headlines this morning. Candidate Kijun Sakurai called a press conference to say "sorry" to the electorate.

Sakurai, however, remains a candidate on the ballot paper and may still be elected - to the embarrassment of the party that has disowned his candidacy.

The incident shows to what extreme the Socialists are prepared to go to avoid scandals in Japan's scandal-sodden politics. PTI CORR ANS
NNNN

---

we could get the text-tuple:

(1482 1664 1760 1448 1160 792 2940 1490 6425 1827)

Note that the highest value is for the 9th category, corresponding to the *Political* category. This text-tuple is interpreted to mean that this story is likely to be of category *Political* corresponding to the component of the tuple with the highest value. In case there is another high value, within a certain range of the highest value, the input story is deemed to fit into the second category as well. Thus a story may be categorized under more than one heading.

8.3 Second Level Categorization

Once the top level categorization is done, the story can be semantically bound to a certain category. We can use knowledge specific to that category to achieve a second level of categorization.

The knowledge base may store information as a set of associative pairs such as :

```
* Benazir    is-related-to  Pakistan
* Pakistan   is related-to  NEIGHBOUR
* Gandhi     is-related-to  INDIAN
* Sonia      is-related-to  Gandhi
* Zardari    is-related-to  Benazir
  . . .
```

where sub-category names are in capitals. By using transitive links, it is easy to show that Benazir and Zardari are also terms related to NEIGHBOUR, and Sonia is related to INDIAN. These terms are thus arranged in a forest of trees, the roots of which define the sub-categories of interest.

Thus, using a pattern-matching operation, we sub-categorize the story by applying transitive relations on an associative knowledge base. The major hurdle in this procedure is the formation of the knowledge base for each category. We are exploring ways to automate the generation of these knowledge-bases, for example by identifying words unique to one subcategory (such as Grandmaster in CHESS).

8.4 Archival of News Stories

Once a story is categorized and indexed, the original (unprocessed) version of the story is archived. Each sub-category has information about the stories that come within its purview. Given a particular story-id (unique to each story), the corresponding story can be retrieved.

9 Retrieval of News Stories

To frame queries about the archived news material, users specify a string of words which are related to the news stories of interest. Stories that are retrieved need not contain all the words that are specified. However, they will, in general, have at least a pre-specified number of words (or concepts) in common with the words in the query set.

Retrieval is achieved in two steps. In the first step, the words in the query set are analysed exactly as a news story is analysed (see Section 8.2), and the category(ies) and subcategory(ies) of relevance are identified. Alternately, the user may directly specify categories/subcategories of interest to him.

In the second step the signature of the query is computed, and pairwise multiplied (ANDed) with the signatures of the stories in the subcategory(ies) of interest. The resulting vector examined to locate items which contain at least a specified number of matching words or concepts. The corresponding stories are then retrieved for display to the user.

Instead of looking only into specific categories and sub-categories of the stories, one could have considered stories categorized under all categories and sub-categories. However, this would have been computationally inefficient, considering the size of the archive. By categorizing the query, the scope of the search is bounded. Of course, there is a risk that one's query may be wrongly categorized.

10   The Implementation of the System

The system described above has been implemented on a VAX2000 using Common LISP. By slight modifications to the user interface code, the system may be ported to any other machine running Common LISP.

10.1   Archival

All the stories for a day are stored in a single story-file. Each story-file has an index-file associated with it, where the story-id and starting record number for each story are stored. This allows for random access of stories. All the stories for a month are collected into a sub-directory, with one file directory for each year.

There is one signature directory for each category, and one signature file for each sub-category. The signature file has an entry for each story in the sub-category. Each entry contains a signature along with the date-stamp and story-id.

Each story is typically 1 KB long, and contains about 125 words, of which about 75 are content words. Currently, the length of the signature bit-array is 400 bits (50 bytes). Even at this level, with around 400 stories per day, it will require over 7 Mbytes (50*400*365) per year just for storing signatures.

10.2   Retrieval

Three processes are used to retrieve the stories, namely: the User Process, the Story Identification (SID) process and the Story Retrieval (SR) process. Several user processes may be executed in parallel. One SR process is created by each user process. However, only one SID process is required at any given time.

The user process accepts the query from the user, and passes it on to the SID process. The story identification process is created when the system is initialized. The SID process loads the signatures of all the stories that are archived already. This process accepts the query from the SR process, computes its signature, identifies the story/stories satisfying the query and passes these story-ids to the SR process.

The story-retrieval process accepts the story-id from the SID process, retrieves appropriate stories and sends them to the user process for display.

The main advantage of this design is that all the three processes can do the processing concurrently. Thus retrieval is considerably faster. The system is better structured, than if there had been only one process. On a multi-processor machine, these processes could execute on different processors, leading to speedier retrieval.

11 Performance Measures

A system such as this can be analysed in terms of its effectiveness in categorization, as well as in retrieval.

11.1 Categorization

A set of 1242 news stories was partitioned into a training set of 900 stories and a test set of 342 stories. The training set was processed on a VAX GPX-II with 13 MB of memory, running VAXLISP on VMS. Usage-tuples were derived for a lexicon of over 14,000 words.

Number of Stories: 342

Category	Stories in this category only	Properly classified	Improperly classified	Stories also in another category
Agriculture	1	0	0	7
Business	12	12	2	28
Disasters	1	1	0	10
Defence	2	2	0	13
Environment	18	18	0	25
Industries	2	2	0	6
Law&Order	38	38	0	49
Non-Business				
Services	4	4	5	23
Political	114	104	2	66
Sports	35	35	0	4
Total	227	216	11	230

Table 2. Analysis of Top-level Categorization

The test set of 342 stories was then categorized by the system, on the same machine. The system took an average of 15 seconds to categorize each story. The stories categorized by this system were then examined by a newsman to locate misclassifications. We define a missclassified story as one which the newsman felt had been classified by the system in the wrong category.

The statistics generated by the categorization program (for top-level categorization only) are given in Table 2.

Stories classified into only one category were first examined, to provide statistics in columns 2 to 4 of Table 2. A total of 216 correct categorizations (out of 227) were made in this single-category classification, which works out to a **95%** success rate. The percentage of misclassified stories is very small, in general, except in the non-business services category.

Stories which were classified into two categories were separately examined, giving the statistics reported in Table 3.

Both categories correctly identified	108
One category correctly identified	102
Neither category correctly identified	20
Total	230

Table 3. Analysis of stories classified into 2 categories

If we count each instance of each story as a unique story, the percentage of successful (two category) categorization is: $(108 * 2 + 102) * 100/(230 * 2)$, that is, **70%** . This success rate can be improved by modifications to the matching thresholds used in this system, and enhancing the morphological analysis and canonicalization modules.

11.2 Retrieval

The performance of a retrieval system is usually measured in terms of recall and precision. The average **recall** is the total number of stories retrieved as a fraction of all that should have been retrieved. The average **precision** is the number of stories correctly retrieved as a fraction of all that were retrieved

Category	Query Word Set	Number of stories correctly retrieved	Number of stories (total) retrieved	Number that should have been retrieved
Defence	afghan rebels kabul attacked jalalabad pakistan peshawar	7	9	10
Disaster	maharashtra storm raigad bombay nanded rained washed	4	5	6
Law-order	punjab terrorists shot gunned arms ammunition encounter hardcore	10	10	15
Political	Bofors Lok-sabha opposition walk-out CAG report parliament	27	31	31
Total		48	55	62

Table 4. Performance of retrieval system

A few sample queries were tried out, to get precision and recall figures for the system. The results are given in Table 4. In this experiment, a story is retrieved if at least N words in the query set are related to the story where $N = Max(2, one\text{-}third\ of\ the$ $number\ of\ words\ in\ the\ query)$

The average recall works out to: 48/62, that is **77 %**
The average precision works out to: 48/55, that is **87 %**

Conclusion

In this paper, we have shown that categorization and retrieval can be done efficiently using AI techniques. The performance of the system can be improved by enhancing the canonicalization and morphological analysis components. The user-interface of the system is being improved. Experiments in automatic cluster location are being carried out.

The system as described here can act as a stand-alone information retrieval system. However, there is another role envisaged for the categorization component. [Chandrasekar et al, 1989] describes a machine translation project, one component of which is meant to categorize a news story, to define its semantic context, and hence to help in word sense disambiguation. We expect the categorization component of this system to fit into that project as the topic analysis module.

Acknowledgements

We acknowledge our colleagues from Press Trust of India, Mr P Unnikrishnan, Mr GS Kundapur and Mr YS Upadhye, for useful discussions and comments. Comments from the members of KBCS group at NCST on drafts of this paper were invaluable. This paper has vastly benefited from the detailed comments of an anonymous referee.

References

[Chandrasekar and Ramani, 1988a]
Chandrasekar, R and Ramani, S. *An Intelligent Interface for Structuring Stories*, in *Information Technology in Indian Languages*, edited by Raghavan SV and Venkatasubramanian, S. Macmillan India, 1988.

[Chandrasekar and Ramani, 1988b]
Chandrasekar, R and Ramani, S. *Knowledge Representation and Information Retrieval*, Indo-US Workshop on Signals and Systems, Bangalore, January 1988.

[Chandrasekar et al, 1989]
Chandrasekar, R, Srikant, M and Ramani, S. *An Integrated Approach to News Story Analysis*, Workshop on Natural Language Processing, Roorkee, January 1989.

320

[DeJong, 1982]
DeJong, G. *An overview of the FRUMP system* in *Strategies for Natural Language Processing*, edited by Lehnert, WG and Ringle MH, Lawrence Erlbaum Associates, 1982, pp 149-176, Chapter 5.

[Hayes et al, 1988]
Hayes, PJ, Knecht, LE and Cellio, MJ. *A News Story Categorization System*. Proc ACL Conf on Applied Natural Language Processing, Austin,Texas, February 1988.

[Hayes et al, 1989]
Hayes, PJ, Anderson, PM, Nirenburg, IB and Schmandt, LM. *TCS: A Shell for Content-Based Categorization*. Submitted to IEEE Conf on AI Applications, September 1989.

[Keesing, 1985]
Keesing's Subject Index, Index No. S1/1985, published as a supplement to Volume XXXI No. 4 of Keesing's Contemporary Archives, Jan-March 1985.

[Lewis, 1989]
Lewis, DD. *Representation and Learning in Information Retrieval*. PhD dissertation, University of Massachusetts at Amherst, in preparation, 1989.

[Lewis et al, 1989]
Lewis, DL, Croft, WB, and Bhandaru, N. *Language-Oriented Information Retrieval*. Intnl Jnl of Intelligent Systems, Vol. 4, No. 3, pp 285-318, Fall 1989.

[Mauldin, 1989]
Mauldin, M. *Information Retrieval by Text Skimming*. Thesis Summary, School of Computer Science, Carnegie Mellon University, August 1989.

[Salton and McGill, 1983]
Salton, G and McGill, MJ. *Introduction to Modern Information Retrieval*. McGraw-Hill, 1983.

[Stanfill and Kahle, 1986]
Stanfill, C and Kahle, B. *Parallel Free-Text Search on the Connection Machine System*. Comm. of the ACM, Vol. 29, No. 12, December 1986.

[Tolani, 1975]
Tolani, R. *Automated Information Retrieval for Libraries*. B.Tech. dissertation, Dept of Electrical Engineering, Indian Institute of Technology, Bombay, 1975.

[Tong et al, 1989]
Tong, RM, Appelbaum, LA, and Askman, VN. *Knowledge representation for Conceptual Information Retrieval*. Intnl Jnl of Intelligent Systems, Vol. 4, No. 3, pp 259-283, Fall 1989.

[UNESCO, 1977]
UNESCO Thesaurus: A structured list of descriptors for indexing and retrieving literature in the fields of education, science, social science, culture and communication, UNESCO UK, 1977.

Representing Discursive Temporal Knowledge : A Computational Application of DRT

Myriam Bras

Institut de Recherche en Informatique de Toulouse
LSI, Université Paul Sabatier
118, route de Narbonne
31062 TOULOUSE cedex FRANCE
E-mail : bras@irit.fr

Abstract

In this paper, we present an approach to the representation of temporal knowledge described in Natural Language discourse. For this purpose, we chose the framework of Discourse Representation Theory (DRT), which can be used as a theory for knowledge representation. Basing our work on precise linguistic analysis of time expression in French, we propose an extension to DRT for the temporal reference calculus, that takes temporal adverbials into account.

We show the complete processing of a Natural Language text. This includes syntactic and semantic analysis in a single framework. We propose a computational model for the semantic representation of sentences, extending the Three Branched Quantified Tree formalism. We then introduce a formalism for discourse representation, which integrates sentence representations.

1 Introduction

Among the problems raised by Natural Language understanding, temporal semantics constitutes a crucial topic : temporal concepts are fundamental in natural reasoning, making it necessary to formalize temporal reasoning and to represent temporal knowledge. In this paper, we present an approach for the analysis of Natural Language texts and the representation of their temporal structure.

We chose the framework of a theory for Natural Language semantics, Discourse Representation Theory, introduced in [Kamp, 1981a]. This framework is particularly well adapted to represent the semantics of a text (or discourse), in particular the structure of events, states of affairs and temporal references which are described by the text. In order to express this temporal knowledge, we use DRT as a theory for the representation of knowledge, following [Günthner et al, 1986].

First, we present the formal framework provided by DRT for the representation of temporal knowledge in discourse by illustrating, using a few examples, the structures that DRT assigns to discourses (section 2).

We then show how the temporal information being extracted from different linguistic markers such as tenses, aspectual categories, or semantic features of temporal adverbials, is represented as the result of the sentence parsing process. For this purpose, we propose a computational formalism for the semantic representation of sentences, which can be directly and declaratively handled in Prolog, using the Extended Three Branched Quantified Tree formalism (section 3).

The semantic representations of isolated sentences are then processed in order to obtain discourse representations. We define an extension to DRT in order to take temporal adverbials into account. We show how temporal relations between sentences can be computed using a set of declarative rules. Finally, we explain how the semantic representations of discourses are translated into a computational formalism (section 4).

We would like to point out that our work concerns a subset of French with the aim of obtaining exhaustive linguistic analysis, thus providing the necessary elements for a very refined temporal reference calculus. We believe that the computational application of a semantic theory really needs a strong linguistic validation.

2 DRT as a framework for temporal knowledge representation

DRT was formulated by Hans Kamp [Kamp, 1981a], [Kamp, 1981b] to represent discourses, taking into account intersentential links such as pronominal anaphora, temporal anaphora, tense and quantification. Although DRT can be seen as a variant of first order logic, these links are rather difficult to formalize through the usual predicative scheme. DRT is however very general and needs to be specified in detail for each discourse phenomena.

DRT is a theory for Natural Language semantics which can be seen as a theory for knowledge representation as it defines a method for translating Natural Language discourses into logical forms. These logical forms are called Discourse Representation Structures (DRSs) and are the well-formed formulas of the DRS language. The DRS language is also given a well-defined formal semantics in order to link DRSs to the structure of the real world. DRSs can be evaluated within a model theoretic semantics [Kamp, 1981a], [Kamp, 1981b][1] , or in partial structures [Günthner et al, 1986][2] . Günthner et al also proposed a deductive theory for DRSs based on tableau calculus. The existence of a formal semantics and a deductive theory make it possible to consider DRT as a knowledge representation language.

A discourse is represented by a DRS, which is a pair <U,C> where U is a set of referent markers, also called the Universe of discourse, and C is a set of conditions on these referent markers. To introduce the DRS language informally, we give examples showing how simple discourses can be represented.

Thus *(1) the cosmonaut entered the space shuttle.* is represented by the following DRS:

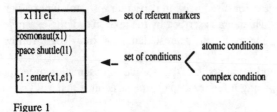

Figure 1

---

[1] In [Kamp, 1981b] a temporal version of DRT is presented, where events are the temporal primitive entities. DRSs evaluation models are based on event structures, see also [Kamp, 1979].

[2] This citation may also be referred to for a precise definition of DRS language syntax and semantics.

The set of referent markers can include :
- objectual markers such as x1 (individual) and l1 (place)
- temporal markers such as e1 (event marker). We could also have state markers (s), or time markers (temporal constants), as will be seen in the following sections.

The set of conditions on the referent markers is made up of :
- atomic conditions (here in predicative form, the arguments are referent markers)
- complex conditions : a temporal referent is associated to an atomic condition by the symbol ':'.

Now let us consider the following discourse fragment :

(1) The cosmonaut entered the space shuttle.

(2) Then, he went through the airlock.

we have the following DRS:

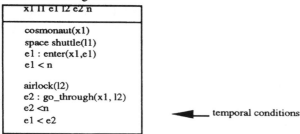

cosmonaut(x1)
space shuttle(l1)
e1 : enter(x1,e1)
e1 < n

airlock(l2)
e2 : go_through(x1, l2)
e2 <n
e1 < e2   ◀──── temporal conditions

Figure 2

Discursive relations linking sentences (1) and (2) are expressed in this DRS :
- a pronominal anaphora has been resolved, associating the pronoun with the referent of its anaphoric antecedent x1,
- a temporal relation between the two sentences (e1 < e2) has been introduced in the DRS.

The other temporal conditions will be described in the following sections. Let us simply mention that temporal relations between temporal referents are :

o (overlapping) and < (precedence), which are the basic relations of the event structures, from which ⊂ (temporal inclusion) and ≡ (temporal equivalence) can be defined.

3 From isolated sentences to their semantic representation

3.1 Defining the linguistic field

The linguistic field we work on is a fragment of French, as we have precise linguistic analysis available. For the sake of simplicity, we will take examples of a restricted linguistic field defined by a limited lexicon in the spatial domain :
- individuals nouns : *cosmonaute* (cosmonaut), *robot* (robot), ...,
- place nouns : *navette* (space shuttle), *sas* (airlock), *soute* (hold), ...,
- localization verbs : *se trouver, être placé, être dans*, ...(to be situated, to stand, to be in),
- motion verbs : *entrer, sortir, traverser*,... (to go in, to go out , to go through),
- place adverbials : *dans* (in) + place noun, *hors de* (out of) + place noun,
- temporal adverbials : *à X heures* (at X o'clock), *à ce moment-là* (at that moment), *trois minutes après* (three minutes later), *puis* (then)...

We also use simple syntactic structures for declarative sentences and the past tenses of French: Passé Simple (ps), Imparfait (imp).

3.2 A formalism for the sentence semantic representation

To represent isolated sentences as well as discourses, we extend the Three Branched Quantified Tree formalism (hereafter 3BQT), initially introduced in [Colmerauer, 1982]. As a result of the parsing, we get the semantic representation of each sentence, consisting of a 3BQT augmented with a temporal component. We shall not focus here on the parser [Saint-Dizier, 1989], which is based on a computational model of Government and Binding theory.

Roughly speaking, the 3BQT formalism organizes sentence representation around determiners. Thus giving the following representation to sentence (3) :

(3) le cosmonaute entre dans la navette . (the cosmonaut enters the space shuttle)

le (x1, cosmonaute(x1), la (l1, navette(l1), entrer_dans(x1, l1)))

In order to build the text temporal structure, we need to extract the temporal and aspectual information from different linguistic markers in the sentence. This information acts as a sentence modifier; therefore it is represented separately in a temporal component, which extends the representation given above :

temporal_comp (Tv, Cv, Et, adverbial (feat (F1, F2, F3), Fla, Cta))

Tv is the verb tense, its value is directly given by the parser,

Cv is the aspectual category of the verb or verb phrase (in our simple examples, we only have. stative (stat) or motion (mot) verbs, that information is encoded in the lexicon. In most cases though, we have to compute the aspectual category of the verb phrase from the verb category and the verb complement category),

Et is the temporal entity being associated with the sentence. It is either an event marker, or a state marker. Its value depends on the tense and the verb phrase aspectual category (cf 3.4.),

feat(F1,F2,F3) is a set of semantic features characterizing the temporal adverbial (cf 3.3)

Fla is the adverbial logical form,

Cta is the temporal constant associated to the adverbial logical form.

3.3 A description of temporal adverbial semantics

In order to illustrate the necessity of precise linguistic analysis to compute the temporal reference, we give the semantic elements used to describe the temporal adverbials (following [Borillo A, 1983] and [Molinès, 1988]). In the set of semantic features associated to the temporal adverbial (feat(F1, F2, F3)), **F1** and **F2** express the adverbial reference function.

F1 can have the value :

- deictic (the adverbial sets a relation with the enunciation) : *en ce moment* (at the moment/now), *hier (yesterday), la semaine prochaine* (next week)

- anaphoric (the adverbial sets a relation with an antecedent already introduced by the discourse) : *puis* (then), *la veille* (the day before), *trois minutes après* (three minutes later)

- polyvalent (the adverbial behaves like a deictic or like an anaphoric): *à cinq heures* (at five)

- autonomous (sets an absolute reference) : *le 14 juillet 1989* (July 14th 1989)

F2 characterizes the relation that links the reference induced by the adverbial and the anaphoric antecedent or the enonciation time. For anaphoric adverbials, it takes the values :

- Id (substitutive anaphora) : *à ce moment-là, pendant ce temps* (at that moment, meanwhile)

- Post (posteriority) : *ensuite (then), trois minutes après* (three minutes later)

- Ant (Anteriority) : *une heure avant* (one hour before), *la veille* , (the day before)

F3 concerns the reference interval description which is done by the adverbial.

For localization adverbials it can be <u>punctual</u> (*à ce moment là,* (at that moment)), or <u>inclusive</u> (*ce jour-là, dans la journée.* (that day, in the day)).

For duration adverbials it takes the <u>durative</u> value : *pendant trois heures* (during three hours)

In some cases, the semantic features do not completely express the adverbial semantics. Such adverbials are represented in addition by a logical form (Fla). For that purpose we define a simple formal language based on predicates associating different elements of the adverbial semantics. For example, we will use the following predicates:

- <u>loc(N,U)</u> expresses a localization on the temporal axis, N being a quantity, U a measure unit. E.g :*à trois heures* (at three o'clock) is represented by : feat(aut,0,pct), loc(3,h). (It is considered as an autonomous adverb within a day interval : F1=aut. It induces a punctual localization : F3=pct. loc(3,h) conveys the quantitative information that has to be localized on the temporal axis)

- <u>dist(R,N,U,O)</u> expresses a distance between an antecedent and the reference introduced by the adverbial. E.g :*trois minutes après* (three minutes later) is represented by : feat(anaph,post,pct) dist(R,3,mn,'+') (it is an anaphorical adverbial F1=anaph, inducing a posteriority relation : F2=post, it localizes a punctual reference: F3=pct, located 3 minutes after the antecedent reference R, thus we have dist(R,3,mn,'+'))

The value of semantic features and logical forms are compositionally computed during the adverbial phrase parsing process. In a well-defined subset of adverbials, it is possible to associate semantic features with lexical items. Thus the semantic features of an adverbial depend on the lexical items included in the adverbial.

3.4 Illustration

As an illustration, we give the complete semantic representation of a sentence (figure 3), and simple parsing rules, in DCG form, designed to analyse this sentence and produce its semantic representation (figure 4).

(4) A trois heures, le cosmonaute entra dans la navette.
(At three o'clock, the cosmonaut entered the space shuttle.)

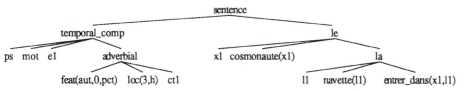

Figure 3

$s(sentence(temporal\_comp(Tv,Cv,Et,Adv),P)) \rightarrow tc(Adv), ss(P,Tv,Cv), \{temp\_entity(Et,Cv,Tv)\}.$
$ss(P,Tv,Cv) \rightarrow np(G,N,Sem\_t,X,P1,P),vp(G,N,t(Tv,Cv),X,P1).$
$np(G,N,Sem\_t,X,P1,P) \rightarrow det(G,N,X,P2,P1,P), noun(G,N,X,P2).$
$vp(G,N,t(Tv,Cv),X,P1) \rightarrow verb(G,N,t(Tv,Cv),X,Y,L\text{-}cpt), prep(Prep), np(G1,N1,Sem\_t,Y,P2,P1),$
$\{mb\_of([Prep,Sem\_t,P2],L\_cpt)\}.$

Figure 4

326

The *s* rule produces the sentence semantic representation. The *tc* rule stands for temporal complement analysis (here only the adverbial is concerned). The *ss* rule stands for simple sentence analysis and produces the right branch of the representation (*P*).

Notice the Prolog call *{temp_entity(Et,Cv,Tv)}* expressing constraints on variables. Here it states an equation to compute the value of *Et* , temporal entity associated to the sentence (see 4.1).

In the last three rules noun phrases (*np*), verb phrases (*vp*), determiners (*det*), prepositions (*prep*) and nouns and verbs are analysed. The variables *X, Y, P1,P2* are used to construct the logical representation P. G,N stand for gender and number. *{mb_of([Prep,Sem_t,P2],L_cpt)}* is a control for the adequacy of prepositions and semantic types.

4 Representing the temporal structure of discourses

Our aim is now to describe the way we process the information stored in the semantic representation of each isolated sentence, in order to build the semantic representation of a text (DRS). The referent markers are generated during the parsing process thus producing the set U of referent markers. Then the set C of conditions on referent markers has to be built. As we saw in section 2, the DRS conditions express, on the one hand, the semantics of sentences and on the other hand, the relations between sentences.

The first kind of conditions, which we call **sentence local conditions**, are formed from isolated sentences. All the information required for local conditions is available in the sentence semantic representation. Thus for sentence (4), whose semantic representation is given in figure 3, we have the incomplete DRS (figure 5). (In this DRS, the logical form loc(3,h) is associated to a temporal constant ct1. Ct1 can be seen as a marker on the time axis.)

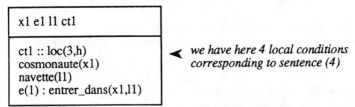

> x1 e1 l1 ct1
>
> ct1 :: loc(3,h)
> cosmonaute(x1)
> navette(l1)
> e(1) : entrer_dans(x1,l1)

◄ *we have here 4 local conditions corresponding to sentence (4)*

Figure 5

The second kind of conditions, which we call **intersentential conditions** represent discursive level as they express the relations between sentences. In our case, they mainly deal with anaphorical links, either temporal or pronominal anaphora.

Before coming to the main point - temporal relations between sentences - let us see the parser's results for the three sentence text :

(4) A trois heures, le cosmonaute entra dans la navette.
  (At three o'clock, the cosmonaut entered the space shuttle.)
(5) Puis, il traversa le sas. (Then he went through the airlock.)
(6) Trois minutes après, il entra dans la cabine .(Three minutes later, he entered the cabin.)

Parser's output :
(4) : see Figure 3

327

(5):

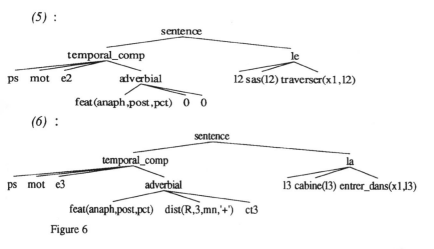

Figure 6

4.1 DRSs construction rules for temporal conditions

In the DRT framework, rules are defined to express discursive temporal relations. In particular the construction rules for past tenses are based on the anaphoric or deictic function of tenses and on the concept of reference point. This is illustrated by the contrast between Passé Simple and Imparfait in French narrative texts [Kamp, 1981b], which can be roughly viewed in terms of punctuality vs durativity or perfectivity vs imperfectivity (recent works on the anaphoric approach for the semantics of tenses in DRT can be found in [Eberle and Kasper, 1989]).

Based on linguistic observations, we state the following rules on the temporal entity to be associated to a sentence:

- a motion verb conjugated in the Passé Simple introduces a new event (e) in the DRS.
- a stative verb conjugated in the Imparfait introduces a new state (s) in the DRS.

The notion of reference point is essential in the construction of the temporal structure of a discourse. It was first introduced by Reichenbach [Reichenbach, 1947], who claimed that a three element system (Event time, Speech time, Reference Time) was necessary to model the semantics of tenses (the reference point being used by the speaker to locate the event he talks about). Reichenbach's system was the starting point for many works in linguistics and recently in Artificial Intelligence [Borillo et al, 1989]. In [Kamp and Rohrer, 1983], the notion of reference point is taken up with the statement that the reference time is established by context, and very often by the previous part of the discourse. It is formalized as a kind of variable, moving with the DRS construction.

The rules for the DRSs construction are the following [Kamp and Rohrer, 1983]:

- the last event introduced in the DRSs is marked as Reference point Rt
- if the new introduced entity is an event e, the following conditions will be produced:

$Rt < e$ (the new event is temporally preceded by Rt)

$e < n$ (the event took place before the moment of speech)

$Rt \leftarrow e$ (e becomes the new reference time)

- if the new introduced entity is a state s, the following condition is produced:

$Rt \subset s(i)$ (the new state completely overlaps the reference point)

These rules mainly take tenses into account and are valid only for the sentences which are not modified by a temporal adverbial. In order to represent sentences including temporal adverbials, the rules must take temporal adverbial information into account so as to link times, events and states. This leads to a more detailed set of rules, resulting from linguistic analysis. Examples of such rules are given in figure 7. In these rules the temporal information described in section 3 is taken into account in order to produce the temporal conditions to be introduced in the DRS. The reference time Rt is used to compute the temporal conditions.

rule	sentential temporal data					conditions to be introduced in the DRS	New Reference Time (Rt)
	Feat	Fla	Cta	Tv	Et		
1	0	0	0	ps	e	Rt < e e < n	e
2	0	0	0	imp	s	Rt ⊂ s	-
3	aut,0,pct	loc(N,U)	ct	ps	e	ct = e e < n	e
4	aut,0,pct	loc(N,U)	ct	imp	s	ct ⊂ s	ct
5	anaph,post,pct	0	0	ps	e	Rt < e e < n	e
6	anaph,id,pct	0	0	ps	e	Rt O e e < n	e
7	anaph,id,pct	0	0	imp	s	Rt ⊂ s	-
8	anaph,post,pct	dist(Rt,N,U,'+')	ct	ps	e	ct = e Rt < e e < n	e
9	anaph,post,pct	dist(Rt,N,U,'+')	ct	imp	s	ct⊂ s	ct

Figure 7

To illustrate the use of these rules, we give, in figure 8, the DRS corresponding to the text:

(4) *A trois heures le cosmonaute entra dans la navette.*(At 3 o'clock, the cosmonaut entered the shuttle)
(5) *Puis, il traversa le sas.* (Then, he went through the airlock.)
(6) *Trois minutes après, il entra dans la cabine.*   (Three minutes later, he entered the cabin.)
(7) *A ce moment-là, le robot se trouvait dans la soute.* (At that time, the robot was in the hold.)

4.2 Implementing the DRSs construction

For the purposes of computation, we have defined a computational formalism to represent discourse. The schematic recursive description of a discourse is the following :
    discourse (Sent, Relations, Discourse)
    Sent is the semantic representation of a sentence, **Relations** stand for the relations of the sentence with the antecedent discourse and **Discourse** is the representation of the following part of discourse.

The results presented in figure 7 are coded under the form of modular and declarative rules. We give for example the rules 3 and 5:
    temporal_relations(feat(aut,0,pct),loc(N,U),Ct,ps,Et,rel(equiv(Ct,Et),bef(Et,n))):-
        asserta(reference(Et)), event(Et).
    temporal_relations(feat(anaph,post,pct),0,0,ps,Et,rel(bef(Rt,Et),bef(Et,n))) :-
        reference(Rt), asserta(reference(Et)), event(Et).

As an illustration we give in figure 9 a part of the representation of the discourse dealt with in 4.1.

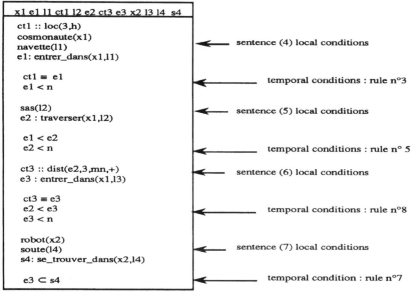

```
┌─────────────────────────────────────────┐
│  x1 e1 l1 ct1 l2 e2 ct3 e3 x2 l3 l4  s4  │
├─────────────────────────────────────────┤
│  ct1 :: loc(3,h)                          │
│  cosmonaute(x1)                           │
│  navette(l1)                              │
│  e1: entrer_dans(x1,l1)                   │
│                                           │
│  ct1 ≡ e1                                 │
│  e1 < n                                   │
│                                           │
│  sas(l2)                                  │
│  e2 : traverser(x1,l2)                    │
│                                           │
│  e1 < e2                                  │
│  e2 < n                                   │
│                                           │
│  ct3 :: dist(e2,3,mn,+)                   │
│  e3 : entrer_dans(x1,l3)                  │
│                                           │
│  ct3 ≡ e3                                 │
│  e2 < e3                                  │
│  e3 < n                                   │
│                                           │
│  robot(x2)                                │
│  soute(l4)                                │
│  s4: se_trouver_dans(x2,l4)               │
│                                           │
│  e3 ⊂ s4                                  │
└─────────────────────────────────────────┘
```

← sentence (4) local conditions

← temporal conditions : rule n°3

← sentence (5) local conditions

← temporal conditions : rule n° 5

← sentence (6) local conditions

← temporal conditions : rule n°8

← sentence (7) local conditions

← temporal condition : rule n°7

Figure 8

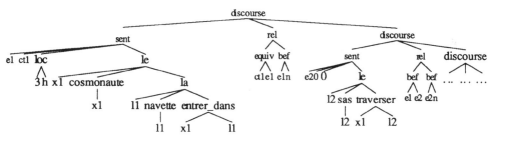

Figure 9

5 Conclusion

In this paper, we have presented an extension for the temporal reference calculus in DRT , in a well defined linguistic field of French, taking the semantics of temporal adverbials into account. We have based our work on precise and exhaustive linguistic analysis. We have proposed an articulation with a syntactic component, which is a computational model of Government and Binding theory. In order to represent knowledge from Natural Language discourses, we have proposed a computational modeling. Therefore we have extended the Three Branched Quantified Tree formalism for the semantic representation of isolated sentences. We have also introduced a computational formalism for discourse representation. The complete model is implemented in Prolog.

Our aim is now to extend this approach to other linguistic phenomena in the temporal domain. In particular, we intend to take complex sentences into account, since they include temporal connectors such as *quand (when)* or *après que (after)*. These connectors induce temporal relations which we have already studied at the sentence level [Borillo et al 1989]. We also aim at enriching the text temporal structure with new temporal informations that could be obtained deductively, such as, for example, deducing spatial relations (state : to_be_in(x,y)) from events (enter(x,y)). For this purpose, we will use a deductive module such as Event Calculus [Kowalski and Sergot, 1986]. We also intend to integrate more general works in lexical semantics in order to have a more uniform representation of all lexical data and to integrate our work on the semantics of spatial relations.

Acknowledgements

I wish to thank A.Borillo, M.Borillo, F. Molinès, P. Saint-Dizier, Co.Vet and anonymous referees for their helpful comments on earlier versions of this work.

References

[Borillo A, 1983]
  Borillo, A. Les adverbes de référence temporelle dans la phrase et dans le texte, *Revue du DRLAV* 29, pp. 109-131, 1983.
[Borillo et al, 1989]
  Borillo, M., Borillo, A., Bras, M. A temporal reasoning cognitive approach, *Semiotica*, forthcoming
[Colmerauer, 1982]
  An interesting subset of Natural Language, in *Logic Programming*, K. Clark and S.Tarnlund Eds., Academic Press, 1982.
[Eberle and Kasper, 1989]
  Eberle, K., Kasper, W. Tenses as anaphora, Proc. ACL Manchester, pp. 43-50, 1989.
[Günthner et al, 1986]
  Günthner, F., Lehmann, H., Schoenfeld, W. A theory for the Representation of Knowledge, *IBM Journal* 30(1), pp. 39-56, 1986.
[Kamp, 1979]
  Kamp, H. Events, Instants and Temporal reference, in Bauerle, Egli, Von Stechow (eds) *Semantics from different points of view*, pp. 376-417, Berlin: de Gruyter, 1979.
[Kamp, 1981a]
  Kamp, H. A Theory of Truth and Semantic Representation, in Gronendijk, Janssen, Stockof (eds) *Formal methods in the study of language*, 136, pp. 277-322, Amsterdam: Mathematical Centre Tracts, 1981.
[Kamp, 1981b]
  Kamp, H. Evénements, représentations discursives et référence temporelle. *Langages*, 64, pp.34-64, 1981.
[Kamp and Rohrer, 1983]
  Kamp, H., Rohrer, C. Tense in texts, In Bauerle, R., Schwarze, C. and von Stechow, A. (eds) *Meaning, Use and Interpretation of Language*, pp.250-269. Berlin: de Gruyter, 1983.
[Kowalski and Sergot, 1986]
  Kowalski, R., Sergot, M. A logic-based calculus of events, *New Generation Computing*, 4, pp. 67-95, 1986.
[Molinès, 1988]
  Molinès, F. Adverbes de localisation temporelle à base de noms de temps, M.A Thesis, Université Toulouse Le Mirail, 1988.
[Reichenbach, 1947]
  Reichenbach, H. Elements of Symbolic Logic, Mac Millan:New York, 1947.
[Saint-Dizier, 1989]
  Saint-Dizier, P. Programming in Logic with Constraints for Natural Language Processing, Proc. ACL Manchester, pp 87-94, 1989.

Novel Terms and Cooperation
in a Natural Language Interface

Paul McFetridge

Chris Groeneboer

Centre for Systems Science
Simon Fraser University
Burnaby, British Columbia
Canada V5A 1S6
mcfet@css.sfu.ca

Centre for Systems Science
Simon Fraser University
Burnaby, British Columbia
Canada V5A 1S6
groen@css.sfu.ca

Abstract

An approach for dealing with novel terms in input to a natural language interface to databases is presented. Traditionally terms not found in the lexicon are assumed to be database values. It is thus taken for granted that customization is complete, i.e., the lexicon contains all synonyms for all attributes. The problem then becomes one of determining the attribute of which the novel term is a value. The present approach entertains the possibility that the novel term is either a database value or a structural term. We argue that there are linguistic phenomena which in conjunction with the usual methods of defining database values can be used to distinguish between values and structural terms. Novel terms are treated as ambiguous, and the interface attempts to constrain the set of candidate interpretations using certain heuristics. If these methods fail to disambiguate the term, a focussed, informative response is generated for the set of interpretations. When appropriate, the user is solicited for information which the interface uses to create a lexical entry for the previously novel term.

Keywords: Natural language interface, relational database, knowledge acquisition, cooperative response.

1. Introduction

One of the problems with which a natural language understanding system must cope is the presence of undefined words in the input, words which have not been entered in the system's lexicon but which users reasonably expect the system to comprehend. The problem is particularly acute for natural language interfaces to databases as they are designed to be 'portable'; they are to be attached to different application domains, each with a unique semantic model. A natural language interface must be provided with the semantic model underlying a new application domain and with the means of anchoring terms present in requests and queries to this semantic model. Providing a natural language interface with this knowledge is generally known as the 'customization problem'.

332

In the early life of a natural language interface in a new application domain, it is unlikely that customization will be complete. To be complete, all possible lexical expressions for referring to entities described in the database must be anticipated. For example, if the database describes a university and includes descriptions of students, not only must the word *student* be anchored to the semantic model, but also *pupil, scholar, graduate, undergraduate, co-ed, man, woman, freshman*, as well as others which may occur to the reader. If the customization process is incomplete the interface will be 'brittle', it will be unable to interpret requests and queries which contain terms that have not been entered in the lexicon.

We follow Kaplan [1984, pg. 15] in distinguishing among 'general', 'structural' and 'volatile' lexical entries. General entries are applicable to any application domain and form a permanent lexicon which travels with the interface. This permanent lexicon contains verbs and auxiliaries such as *have* and *be*, prepositions such as *in, to* and *from*, relative pronouns, quantifiers, *etc*. We assume, with all other researchers, that this permanent lexicon is comprehensive, so that it will not be considered as a source of error.

Structural entries make reference to aspects of the structure of the application domain. For example,*student* and *pupil* refer to the records in the table which describes students; *major* and *age* refer to columns in this table.

Volatile entries refer to values in the database. As their name suggests, the lexical entries for database values are unstable. Each time the database is updated, the set of lexical entries required by the interface potentially changes. If values are deleted from the database, lexical entries corresponding to the terms used to refer to them are no longer required; if values are added to the database, the lexicon must also be updated.

The focus of research on the acquisition of the semantics of undefined terms by natural language interfaces to databases has been on volatile entries, on recognizing database values in the input rather than requiring that each value in the database also be defined in the semantic lexicon of the natural language interface. A benefit to recognizing database values rather than explicitly defining them is that the contents of the database are not duplicated in the lexicon of the natural language interface, thereby saving significant memory allocation. However, recognition of structural entries has been largely ignored. For example, Johnson [1984] discusses how the undefined string *1982* is recognized by general classifier rules in the query

Who has extension 1982?

but does not discuss how the query would be processed if *extension* was undefined. Similarly, Kaplan [1984] discusses how *Nasa Headquarters* and *oceanography*, both values in a database for the National Center for Atmospheric Research, are recognized in the query

Which projects in oceanography does Nasa Headquarters sponsor?

but does not consider the problems encountered with the same query when the word *projects* is undefined.

The reasons for this focus are pragmatic. The set of structural entries is significantly smaller than the set of volatile entries; consequently, users are less likely to use undefined structural terms than to use undefined references to database values. Moreover, it is reasonable to expect that in the fullness of time all possible structural terms will be defined. The same could not be expected of a set of volatile terms, which by definition will require updates concurrent with the database updates. Indeed, it is even possible to query the presence of a value in the database; if the value is not entered in the database, the query is uninterpretable by an interface which requires explicit definition, though it is intelligible to the user.

Although recognition of database values is important in a robust natural language interface, it is in fact part of a taxonomy of problems which a truly robust natural language interface must consider (see figure 1). A natural language interface may fail to find a lexical entry for a word in an input sentence either because it is misspelled — the user has made an error — or because the word is truly novel — it is a legitimate word but has yet to be entered in the lexicon. Determining whether a word is misspelled or novel is difficult, sometimes even for humans, and a working assumption that all input is correct is useful in investigations of acquisition of the semantics of undefined terms.

A second assumption implicit in the focus on recognition of database values is that customization of the structural entries is exhaustive, and consequently only database values remain undefined. The possibility that an undefined term may refer to a structural characteristic of the database is never entertained. This assumption is made despite the observation that the greatest effort in customizing a natural language interface for a new application domain is providing lexical entries for structural terms [Kaplan, 1984, pg. 14].

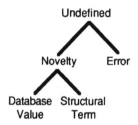

Figure 1. A Taxonomy of Undefined Terms

In this paper, we present a contrasting approach to novelty. Rather than assume that a word for which no lexical entry can be found is a database value, we take as a working assumption that such a word is not an error, but is novel and may be either a database value or a structural term. We argue that there are linguistic phenomena which in conjunction with the usual methods of defining database values can be used to distinguish between values and structural terms. We show that, where these methods fail, it is possible to both provide an informative response and, when appropriate, solicit information from the user, information which the interface uses to create a lexical entry for the previously undefined term.

2. Techniques for Defining Database Values

Natural language systems have employed various solutions to the problem of recognizing references to database values in queries. Such techniques include what we will call *search, restricted input, propositional frames*, and *semantic relatedness*. LUNAR [Woods, et al., 1972] and ROBOT/INTELLECT [Harris, 1978; Harris, 1980] are examples of systems which use search. The LUNAR system stores database values in the lexicon. This approach is fine for small domains but admits duplication and its associated problems in volatile databases when values are updated. ROBOT, and later INTELLECT, incorporate a view of the database contents as an extension of the lexicon. This means a huge search space for large databases, so newer versions of INTELLECT constrain search to indexed fields only. However, as is noted by Kaplan [1984] well-formed queries may contain references to valid values not currently in the lexicon or in the database.

Ladder [Hendrix, et al., 1978], TQA [Damerau, 1988], and NLMENU [Thompson, 1984] restrict user input language so that references to values are easily recognizable to the system. Ladder and TQA require that references to certain values have a particular shape for which recognition rules can be written based on a description of the shape. For example, course names (e.g., MATH100) are comprised of four alphabetic characters followed by three digits. An advantage to this approach is that the definition of the recognition rules can be automated [Damerau, 1988]. However, not all values have such a regular physical shape that they can be defined in this manner. The NLMENU system restricts the user to menu-based queries. Successive menus guide the user through construction of a query thus constraining queries to a subset of English without requiring that the user learn and remember the subset. Thus unrecognizable values are not an issue. The disadvantages of this approach are (1) the system does not get the opportunity to learn, an irreconcilable inconsistency with our view of a dynamic, evolving natural language system, and (2) it is cumbersome in the extreme in very large databases where the user may be forced to search through hundreds or thousands of values for the intended value.

The propositional frames technique involves construction of schemata which describe selectional restrictions on noun and verb phrases. Such schemata are variously referred to as argument structures for nouns and verbs [Damerau, 1988], predictors in CO-OP [Kaplan, 1984], and IRULES in IRUS [Moser, 1984]. CO-OP also contains predictors for prepositions. An example of a propositional frame for the verb teaches might be:

> teach ((subject faculty-name)
> (object course-name)
> (d-object student-name)).

A second technique used in the CO-OP system is semantic relatedness. Kaplan proposes that "unknown terms" (references to database values) be handled by the same mechanisms that handle semantic ambiguity. CO-OP uses two heuristics to disambiguate words which can refer to more than one entity in the database: predictors and semantic relatedness.

The assumption underlying the second heuristic is that semantically related terms tend to be near each other in the database schema. This assumption has been given explicit definition by Hall [1987] and has been implemented as Pathfinder [Hall, et al., 1988]. The Pathfinder system is a subcomponent of SystemX [McFetridge, et al., 1988b], a natural language interface to relational databases developed at Simon Fraser University. Pathfinder is used to discover navigation paths through the database among the columns implicit in the query as well as to assist in creating propositional frames for novel verbs and structural terms as they are encountered in queries [McFetridge, et al., 1988a].

The techniques of *search, propositional frames* and *semantic relatedness* are not always definitive. Search is effective, if time-consuming, when the value is located in the database. However, the technique fails when the reference is to a possible value which does not exist in the database. The propositional frame and semantic relatedness techniques build a set of candidate columns to which the unknown term could refer. If this set is singular, its member is assumed to be the correct referent. However, it is possible that neither technique can produce an unambiguous analysis.

The problem of ambiguous analyses is evident in an example from Kaplan [1984].

> Query: Which F-5s carry strut curve radar?
> Paraphrase: (I am assuming that "F-5s" is a SHIP NAME.) (I am
> assuming that "strut curve" is a RADAR NAME.) Which F-5s
> carry strut curve radar?

The predictors associated with the notion of *carry radar* do not distinguish among ships, aircraft or submarines. Instead, the system relies on defaults and in this case incorrectly translates *F-5* as the name of a ship rather than a type of aircraft.

The lessons from current research on recognizing and defining database values in input queries and commands are two. First, since the methods developed to date are not always definitive the possibility that the system may not be able to fully disambiguate a query or define a new word is always present. The Kaplan example demonstrates that reliance on default interpretations to handle this event is unsatisfactory. Instead, it is necessary to interact with the user, providing him/her with the means to supply the system with the necessary information to define novel terms. This should not be a surprising result as in any situation where commands are given interaction between the participants is usual when the command is ambiguous or is not understood by the participant expected to execute the command.

Research from the problem of handling ill-formed input, i.e. queries and commands which contain errors, has demonstrated that this interaction should be *focussed* (see esp. [Carbonell and

Hayes, 1987]); the system should both identify the source of the error and the type of error. In the case of undefined terms, it is insufficient to simply inform the user that a term is unknown to the system expecting the user to supply a semantic representation, as this type of information may be arcane to the naive user. Rather, the system must supply the user with a small set of forced choices which are presented in a way which the naive user can understand.

The second lesson is that the set of heuristics which a system uses when confronted with novelty should be as rich as possible. It has been noted [Kaplan, 1983] that there exist clues within the query which indicate the structure and contents of the database presupposed by the user. Clues like those noted by Kaplan may be subtle and infrequent; nonetheless, the system should be equipped to recognize them and use them to define novel words. The richness of a system of heuristics is a function of both the number of heuristics which the system has at its disposal and the degree to which they have been integrated. For example, both the search and propositional frame heuristics are useful, but their efficiency increases when the propositional frame can constrain the search space by restricting it to a small set of candidate columns in the database.

In the following, we expand the set of heuristics used to recognize and define database values, and show that it is possible to use the expanded set in the recognition and definition of structural terms as well database values, and to use it to focus interactions with the user so that the response of the system confronted with undefined terms is cooperative both in requesting information from the user and providing information to the user about the results of the query.

3. Responses to Novel Terms

We assume that during the customization of a natural language interface, the system is provided with at least the heuristics outlined above. These function both in the normal operation of the system to disambiguate and process queries as well as when the system is presented with a query which contains novel terms. In addition, each column in the database which will be directly referenced will be provided with at least one synonym. For example, a table which contained the columns *student#, name, age, sex* and *major* may have associated with the *student#* column the synonym *student*, although other synonyms may be added in time.

Among the columns in a table, it is necessary to distinguish between *key* and *nonkey* columns. Nonkey attributes are *dependent* on key attributes in the sense that the value of the key attribute determines the value of the nonkey attributes [Wiederhold, 1983]. Although it is possible for the key of a table to comprise more than one attribute, tables with multiple keys are restricted to those which describe relationships among other objects in the database. Since we are concerned only with tables which will be referenced by terms, that is tables which model entities not relationships, we need not consider tables with multiple keys.

Given this distinction, a natural language interface confronted with an unknown term must entertain the following possible ways of defining it (see figure 2). If the novel term is a database value, it is either a value of a key attribute or a nonkey attribute. If the novel term is a structural term, it refers either to a key attribute or a nonkey attribute.

The import of the distinction between key and nonkey attributes is that the value of a key attribute uniquely determines the tuple (or tuples if the dependency is multivalued) in which it appears. In this respect, the key is much like a proper name. A proper name, when used as such and not as a common noun,[1] uniquely identifies the individual named. It is certainly possible for individuals to share proper names, but common discourse treats them as uniquely referring expressions.

Identifying this semantic correspondence between a value of a key attribute, which uniquely identifies a tuple in a table, and a proper name, which uniquely identifies an individual, is

Database Value	Key	Nonkey
Structural Term	Key	Nonkey

Figure 2. Possible Definitions of Unknown Terms

important as the syntactic behaviour of proper names is distinguished from count nouns and this distinction can be used to recognize terms which refer to values of key attributes.

Proper names, when used as uniquely referring expressions, do not undergo quantification. They do not appear with quantifiers such as *all, every* or *most*, not with the determiners *a* and *the*. It is occasionally argued that proper names may appear with *the* as in *The Hague* and *The Gambia*. An alternative analysis has *The* as part of the name and thereby retains the observation that proper names are not quantifiable. Since proper names identify a single individual, they appear only in the singular. In usual discourse, proper names are not modified by adjectives, prepositional phrases or relative clauses. Modification with adjectives has a literary tone—e.g. *A happy and contented Mary drifted down the stairs*—and is not likely to be encountered in a query to a database. Restricted relative clauses function to further distinguish the referent of the noun phrase from other possible referents. Since a proper name is a uniquely referring expression, it does not take restricted relatives.

These observations amount to the grammatical restriction that proper names in normal discourse appear in the singular without quantification or modification. This grammatical restriction is not shared by count nouns, although it is by mass nouns and by count nouns when used in a mass noun sense. Count nouns, when used as count nouns, must be either plural or grammatically quantified. Thus, the statement *Cat is mammal* is ungrammatical, but *Cats are mammals* is not.

Database Value	Key	Nonkey
Structural Term	Key	Nonkey

Figure 3. Definition of Singular Terms

The semantic correlation of values of key attributes with proper names is paralleled by similar restrictions on the grammatical behaviour of values of key attributes. For example, if the word *math344* in the query

Who received the highest grade in math344?

is undefined it can nonetheless be identified as a value of a key attribute, because it is neither plural nor quantified. A propositional frame or semantic predictor associated with the verb *receive* will identify the table referred to by *math344*. That *math344* is singular and unquantified is sufficient to eliminate three possible interpretations within that table and identify it as a value of the key attribute (figure 3).

Database Value	Key	Nonkey
Structural Term	Key	Nonkey

Figure 4. Possible Definition of Plural Terms

Just as the syntactic behaviour of a word can conclusively identify it as a database value, so too can its syntactic behaviour conclusively rule out the possibility that it is a database value. If it appears in the plural and/or is quantified, it cannot be a value of a key attribute. It is either a value of a nonkey attribute or a structural term referring to a key or nonkey attribute (figure 4.

Even this small amount of information from a plural noun can be useful, as can be demonstrated by Kaplan's example

Which F-5s carry strut curve radar?

where *F-5s* is incorrectly identified by CO-OP with *ship name*. Unfortunately, Kaplan does not present a database schema so the following observations are tentative. If the database were implemented as a relational database then, because ship names are unique, they can serve as keys. So *F-5* a value of a non-key attribute, say *aircraft--type*. That it is not the value of a key attribute such as *ship name* can be ruled out because it is used in the plural.The mistake made by CO-OP is avoidable.

The situation we have arrived at may be described as follows. Propositional frames or semantic predictors associated with verbs can identify possible tables and even columns within those tables which may be referenced by a term for which the system has no semantic definition. If the term is grammatically singular and unquantified, it can only be a value of the key attribute of the table identified by the propositional frames.

If the unknown term is grammatically plural and/or quantified it may be either a value of a nonkey attribute or a structural term. A search of the values of nonkey attributes is conclusive if the term is found. However, if the term is not found the term may nonetheless have been intended as a value and this possibility must still be entertained.

At this point, the system has exhausted its list of heuristics and must begin interaction with the user. As previously mentioned, the interaction should be focussed and informative, requesting information which a user ignorant of the structure of the database can be expected to control and in a way which a naive user can understand. The interaction must also be constrained so that the user supplies only information which the system can understand and so that the system supplies information which is informative to the user.

The most effective way of constraining information supplied by the user is to request it using yes/no questions, those which accept only affirmation or denial as possible answers. Thus, to determine if an undefined term X is a structural term referring to nonkey attribute, it is only necessary to pose the query

Is X synonymous with Y?

where Y is the synonym associated with the attribute during customization. If the answer is *yes*, the previously undefined term can be added to the list of synonyms associated with the attribute. If the answer is *no*, the undefined term is either a value of a nonkey attribute or a structural term referring to the key attribute 5.

Database Value	Key	Nonkey
Structural Term	Key	Nonkey

Figure 5. Metonymic relation between values and key

This configuration of possible meanings of an unknown term is of considerable interest because it is indicative of the ways in which sets and subsets of objects are frequently referenced in normal discourse. A set may be referenced by using the term designating the set or by naming a property which all members of the set share. The latter method is known as *metonymy*, less commonly as *synechdoche*. Examples of metonymical use are:

We need new *blood* in this department.

He is reading *Plato.* (i.e. the works of Plato)

Using a nonkey database value to designate a set of tuples which contain that value is metonymical. To return to Kaplan's example

Which F-5s carry strut curve radar?

the term *F-5* is metonymical for *aircraft which are of type F-5.*

Metonymy is prevalent in normal discourse and should also be expected in natural language queries to databases. This frequency suggests that when a natural language interface to a relational database is confronted with an unknown term which is not a value of the key attribute, it will either be a value of a nonkey attribute or a structural term referring to the key attribute.

More importantly, if the system is able to reduce the possibilities to those illustrated in figure 5it will be able to provide a cooperative response. This reduction may be effected either by querying the user as suggested or by the assumption that customization is complete and that therefore an unknown term cannot be a synonym of a nonkey attribute.

If the system has not previously searched the database for the unknown term, then it now generates a database query with the unknown term as a value of the nonkey attribute predicted by propositional frames associated with the verb. Since the unknown term is plural, the possibility that it is a value of a key is eliminated from the set of possible frames. In the example, the query will search for tuples which have *F-5* as the value of *aircraft type* and *strut curve radar* as the value of *radar name.* A nonNULL answer to the query is an indication that the unknown term was in fact a database value.

A NULL response to a database query is the least informative answer, largely because the reasons for obtaining a NULL response are many [Kao, et al., 1988]. Recognition of the metonymy relation between a database value and the structural term referring to the key attribute provides a method for reacting to a NULL response by providing further information, information which the user may use to reframe the query to better suit his or her purposes.

To generate a cooperative response to NULL, the database query is reformulated interpreting the unknown term as a structural term referring to the key attribute. In the example, this will be a search for tuples which have *strut curve radar* as the value of *radar name.* The term *F-5* is effectively ignored because it is not interpreted as a database value. The result of both queries are then presented to the user according to the interpretation of the unknown term using the synonyms associated with the appropriate attributes. This may be illustrated with Kaplan's example, assuming that *F-5* is not entered in the database.

Query: Which F-5s carry strut curve radar?
Response: If *F-5* is an *aircraft-type,* the answer is NULL, but the
aircraft which carry strut curve radar are ...

The last resort to undefined terms need not be failure or default interpretations. The metonymy relation between a nonkey value and the key attribute of a table provides a mechanism for providing an informative response.

4. Conclusion

We have presented an approach for dealing with novel terms in a natural language interface which is based upon the integration of domain-independent knowledge, domain-dependent knowledge, a learning capability, and a cooperative response generator. This approach extends the traditional methods by correlating the semantic and syntactic properties of key attribute values with those of proper names. It relies on the correlation between database structure and the linguistic phenomena of proper names and metonymy.

The advantages of the approach are many: (1) it is based on the linguistic behaviour of proper nouns and the correlated behaviour of references to key database values, (2) the set of candidate interpretations is extended to include synonyms for attributes, (3) it does not default to one, possibly incorrect, interpretation when the heuristics fail to disambiguate a novel term, (4) the system can acquire the semantics of new structural terms, (5) responses are focussed and cooperative, and (6) the system integrates linguistic knowledge, knowledge of the structure of the database, acquisition of synonyms, and cooperative response generation.

It would be supercilious not to admit that the approach which we are proposing has its drawbacks. Because it depends upon a good database design, i.e., a normalized relational database, successful use with a nonnormalized database cannot be guaranteed. It has also been argued by Shwartz [1982] that domain-independent heuristics cannot guarantee correct interpretations, that conceptual domain-specific knowledge is essential to achieve an acceptable level of performance even though that means a decrease in portability to new application domains. Our position is that domain-independent semantics using the heuristics we have proposed is the default semantics for a natural language interface to databases and that the interface must also be able to incorporate conceptual domain-specific knowledge which overrides the default semantics when appropriate.

Acknowledgements

We are pleased to acknowledge the financial support of the Natural Sciences and Engineering Research Council of Canada and the contribution of equipment and space by Simon Fraser University.

Notes

1 It is possible, though unusual, to use proper names as count nouns. For example, *There are two Bills in this room.*

References

[Carbonell, J. G. and Hayes, P. J., 1987]
 Carbonell, J. G. and Hayes, P. J. "Robust parsing using multiple construction-specific strategies." *Natural Language Parsing Systems.* Ed. L. Bolc. Berlin: Springer, 1987.
[Damerau, F., 1988]
 Damerau, F. "Prospects for knowledge-based customization of natural language query systems." Vol. 24: pp. 651–664, 1988.
[Hall, G., 1987]
 Hall, G. Querying Cyclic Databases in Natural Language. Simon Fraser University CMPT TR 87-4, 1987.

340

[Hall, G., Luk, W. S., Cercone, N. and McFetridge, P., 1988]
Hall, G., Luk, W. S., Cercone, N. and McFetridge, P. "A solution to the MAPP problem in natural language interface construction." *Proceedings of International Computer Science Conference '88, Hong Kong.* Pp. 351–359, 1988.

[Harris, L. R., 1978]
Harris, L. R. "The ROBOT system: natural language processing applied to database query." *Proceedings of Annual Conference of the ACM, Washington, D.C.* Pp. 165–172, 1978.

[Harris, L. R., 1980]
Harris, L. R. "Prospects for practical natural language systems." *Proceedings of 18th ACL, Philadelphia, Pa.* 1980.

[Hendrix, G., Sacerdoti, D., Sagalowicz, D. and Slocum, J., 1978]
Hendrix, G., Sacerdoti, D., Sagalowicz, D. and Slocum, J. "Developing a natural language interface to complex data." *ACM Transactions of Database Systems.* Vol. 3: pp. 1978.

[Johnson, D. E., 1984]
Johnson, D. E. Design of a robust, portable natural language interface grammar. IBM Thomas Watson Research Center RC 10867, 1984.

[Kao, M., Cercone, N. and Luk, W. S., 1988]
Kao, M., Cercone, N. and Luk, W. S. "Providing quality responses with natural language interfaces: the null value problem." *IEEE Transactions on Software Engineering.* Vol. 14: pp. 959–984, 1988.

[Kaplan, S. J., 1983]
Kaplan, S. J. "Cooperative responses from a portable natural language database query system." *Computational Models of Discourse.* Ed. M. Brady and R. C. Berwick. Cambridge, Ma.: MIT Press, 1983.

[Kaplan, S. J., 1984]
Kaplan, S. J. "Designing a portable natural language database query system." *ACM Transactions on Database Systems.* Vol. 9: pp. 1–19, 1984.

[McFetridge, P., Hall, G., Cercone, N. and Luk, W.-S., 1988a]
McFetridge, P., Hall, G., Cercone, N. and Luk, W.-S. "Knowledge Acquisition in SystemX: A Natural Language Interface to Relational Databases." *Proceedings of International Computer Science Conference '88, Hong Kong.* Pp. 604–610, 1988a.

[McFetridge, P., Hall, G., Cercone, N. and Luk, W.-S., 1988b]
McFetridge, P., Hall, G., Cercone, N. and Luk, W.-S. "System X: A Portable Natural Language Interface." *Proceedings of 7th Biennial Conference of the CSCSI, Edmonton, Alberta.* Pp. 30–38, 1988b.

[Moser, M. G., 1984]
Moser, M. G. "Domain dependent semantic acquistion." Proceedings of First Conference on Artificial Intelligence Applications, Denver, Co. Pp. 13–18, 1984.

[Shwartz, S. P., 1982]
Shwartz, S. P. "Problems with domain-independent natural languages datbase access systems." *Proceedings of ACL 20th Annual Meeting,* Pp. 60–62, 1982.

[Thompson, C. W., 1984]
Thompson, C. W. "Recognizing values in queries or commands in a natural language interface to databases." *Proceedings of First Conference on Artificial Intelligence, Denver, Co.* Pp. 25–30, 1984.

[Wiederhold, G., 1983]
Wiederhold, G. *Database Design.* New York: McGraw-Hill Book Company, 1983.

[Woods, W. A., Kaplan, R. M. and Nash-Webber, B., 1972]
Woods, W. A., Kaplan, R. M. and Nash-Webber, B. *The Lunar Sciences Information System: Final Report. Bbn Rep. 2378.* Cambridge,, Mass.: Bolt, Beranek and Newman, 1972.

Representing and Using Protosemantic Information in Generating Bus Route Descriptions

T. Pattabhiraman and Nick Cercone

Centre for Systems Science
Simon Fraser University
Burnaby, B.C., CANADA V5A 1S6
patta@cs.sfu.ca and *nick@cs.sfu.ca*

Abstract

In this paper we examine the domain of route communication, and propose a representation for the bus route map of a city and an effective route finding procedure for use in the context of generating bus route descriptions in natural language. We present a concise analysis of bus route descriptions from the perspective of their information structure. We have noted that route descriptions involve information of different degrees of granularity, and that in the case of bus route descriptions, the activation of coarse-grained information can be separated from that of finer-grained information. Accordingly, we represent the map mainly as a collection of routes. We use simple set operations at the core of our route finding procedure. We have adapted these operations to extract relevant annotations from the knowledge base for generating text plans. We briefly discuss how the spatial problem of route finding can be treated as a search problem in the context of giving bus route directions. Finally, we consider bus route description generation as a candidate problem domain for knowledge based systems. We have implemented our knowledge base design and the route finding procedure in a prototype system that finds bus route directions in Vancouver, Canada.

1 Introduction

In this paper we report our recent research on generating bus route directions in English, from a given source to an intended destination within a city. When viewed as pure problem-solving, the task is to find a path from a source to a destination on a city-map, by a series of one or more bus journeys. From the perspective of natural language generation, the task consists in producing route directions in natural language, by selecting relevant information from the knowledge base, expanding the selected information, ordering it sequentially and expressing it in the form of coherent multisentential text.

Research described in this paper is part of a continuing investigation into the connection between domain-level tasks and text planning tasks in monological multisentential language generation. We follow the modularization of natural language generation into a set of processes concerned with non-linguistic preliminaries, collectively termed *planning* [Appelt, 1985] or *conceptualization* [Levelt, 1989; Kempen and Hoenkamp, 1987], and a set of processes concerned with rendering the planned discourse in linguistic form, collectively termed *realization* [Hovy, 1988; McDonald, 1983], or *formulation* [Levelt, 1989; Kempen and Hoenkamp, 1987]. Our investigation focusses on a class of descriptive tasks in which a *protosemantic* knowledge base provides the primary raw material for information expressed in multisentential text. (The term *protosemantic* refers to the initial knowledge structures from which semantic structures are built. Protosemantic information is in principle language- and discourse-independent, and may also be expressed non-verbally. [van Dijk and Kintsch, 1983] term this *episodic* information.) We have analyzed various kinds of route directions as candidate domains of discourse, concentrating, in particular, on the problem of generating bus route directions.

The major considerations for generating bus route directions include: (1) the design of a knowledge base for storing the map, (2) the design of an effective procedure for finding appropriate bus routes and (3) integrating the problem-solving aspect of route-finding with the language production process of generating text plans. Our work has exposed a variety of interesting issues pertinent to bus route finding as an instance of knowledge-based problem solving. This paper is devoted primarily to the first two considerations listed above. A detailed discussion of how text plans are produced will be presented in a separate document. Our current effort is accompanied by an implementation in CProlog of a prototype system that finds bus route directions in Vancouver, Canada.

The purpose of this paper is to describe the domain of route communication, to present the protosemantic knowledge base and the route finding procedure designed for use with our bus route description planner and to present route finding as a candidate problem for knowledge based systems. In section 2 we describe the domain of route directions in general and bus route directions in particular. Our representation of bus route information is developed and presented in section 3. In section 4 we outline the procedure for route finding. In the concluding section we discuss our results and suggest directions for future work.

2 Domain: Route Communication and Route Description

The co-operative verbal action that consists of requesting route directions and giving them is termed *route communication* [Klein, 1982]. Route communication can commonly take place in a variety of settings: face-to-face interaction, telephone conversation, written communication and so on. Most of the research material available to date on route communication is the result of psycholinguistic and cognitive studies. [Klein, 1982] presents a linguistic analysis of route communications that occurred naturally on the streets of Frankfurt, West Germany. In particular, Klein deals with the relation between the *cognitive task* of route finding and the *linguistic task* of generating a route description as manifested in the choice of local deictic referential terms like *here*, *there*, *right* and *left*. [Wunderlich and Reinelt, 1982] noted in their study that the complete discourse emerging in route communication dialogues may be divided into four phases performed sequentially: (1) *initiation* by the questioner, (2) *route description* by the informant, (3) an optional *securing* phase in which crucial parts of the route description are recapitulated or paraphrased and (4) *closure*, which is typically an expression of gratitude. Although full route communication represents a dialogue, the roles of the participants are not symmetric as they would be, say, in a casual conversation or an argument.

The works of [Klein, 1982] and [Wunderlich and Reinelt, 1982] are empirical in nature, and as such, are not cast in terms of computational procedures and representations. They do not assume or adduce a proof of the universal use of a single representation or route finding procedure in route communications. Nor do they concern themselves with the mutual influence of the cognitive representation of the map and the cognitive task of route finding. In our research on generating bus route directions we emulated their methods to gather and analyze natural text. However, we use our analysis to motivate the design of the knowledge base and the route finding procedure implemented in our prototype system.

We concentrate on *route description*, where the informant's role is dominant. We neglect interruptions by the questioner that may occur amidst this phase, and treat the text emerging during this phase as a monologue. The initiation by the questioner consists in specifying a starting point and a final destination of travel, and inclines the informant to find a route and to generate a route description.

Route descriptions are often given graphically, as when a route map is sketched. There are interesting parallels between route maps and verbal route descriptions as bearers of information. While route maps are two-dimensional sketches, route descriptions in natural language are sequential (linear). (*Readings* of a route map, however, are sequential.) A one-to-one correspondence may be observed between features of a route map and certain verbal devices in route descriptions. However, the use of some mechanisms such as connectives, pronominals and deictic words in route descriptions is associated exclusively with the use of natural language as the medium of description.

Two tasks may be distinguished in generating a route description:
- the *problem-solving* task of planning a route, given the end-points of travel. This is essentially a *cognitive* task, consisting in activating a cognitive map of the relevant spatial area, identifying within the map the end-points of travel and planning a route between these points. The map is part of the protosemantic knowledge-base which remains invariant during route communication.
- the *natural language generation* task of planning and realizing a concise, informative route description. The text planner selects, expands and orders information, and outputs a sequence of semantic units, or *text plans*. These text plans form the main input to the realization module, which generates surface forms from the text plans using linguistic and contextual (pragmatic) knowledge.

2.1 Spatial Information in Route Descriptions

All varieties of route communication involve activating parts of maps. However, the nature of information selected from the knowledge base, and in particular, the kind of spatial information included in the route description depend on such factors as the mode of transportation used, whether the questioner will be navigating or whether he will be using a public transportation system, etc.

For example, a set of directions given to someone who will be driving to his destination by car is likely to include information on change of orientation and location of landmarks in terms of local deictics like *left* and *right*, or global deictics like *north* and *south*. Distance information may be expressed in terms of number of blocks or number of traffic lights to be encountered, as in the following illustration, excerpted from Riesbeck's study on the *interpretation* of route directions by their users [Riesbeck, 1980]:

Rosecrans exit- get over to the far left- and it will be about the third
stoplight that's the midway drive intersection ... Be in the left-hand
only lane. And turn left on Midway Drive. About two or three long blocks
down on the right is the main post office...

In contrast, a set of directions given for getting around in a subway system consists mainly of a sequence of instructions for boarding and disembarking trains. Spatial expressions involving distance and orientation are relatively scant. In this case, route finding can be treated as a problem of graph search.

2.2 Bus Route Descriptions

Our primary linguistic data consist of about 40 bus route descriptions to various destinations in Vancouver, and include written (printed) descriptions as well as transcriptions of spoken descriptions. In analyzing the spoken route communications, we transcribed the relatively monological route description phase, and neglected features such as false starts, speed of speech and durations of pauses which are psycholinguistically significant.

The following spoken text describes how to get from *Lougheed Mall* to *Grouse Mountain* in Vancouver. The "..."s correspond to pauses or confirmatory expressions like *ok* or *yeah* by the questioner.

from Lougheed Mall? ... ok, you could catch a 151 or a 152 called
Vancouver ... get off at Hastings and Kootenay right by the Kootenay Loop ...
on Hastings in front of the loop transfer to bus number 28 called
Phibbs Exchange ... will cross Second Narrows Bridge to Phibbs Exchange
on the other side ... and that's where you could catch
the 232 Grouse Mountain bus ... and it goes right up to Grouse Mountain.

The information conveyed by this text could also be expressed graphically as illustrated in figure 1.

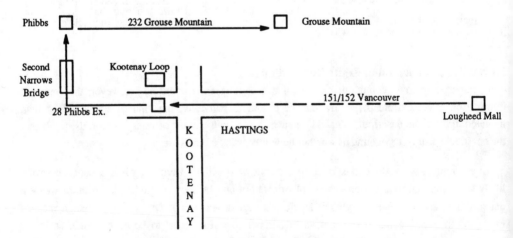

Figure 1: From *Lougheed Mall* to *Grouse Mountain*

The skeletal information in bus route descriptions consists of a series of one or more units, each specifying a single bus ride, in terms of the bus label and where to board and disembark the bus. In figure 1, the skeletal information is the connected sequence of arrows, marked with the bus labels. The extremities of the arrows are labelled with the end-points of bus journeys. This information is extracted from the map by the route-finding procedure, and is expanded by the text planner to include descriptions of landmarks (for example, *Second Narrows Bridge* in figure 1), location, orientation and so on.

When the full journey involves taking two or more buses, the connecting buses may be available at the point of disembarkation (from the previous bus) itself, or just across the street. But often, one may have to walk a fair distance before transferring from one bus to another. In such cases, the bus route description also includes walk-route information, as illustrated by the italicized portion of the following example:

> you want to catch bus number 106 called Metrotown ... take it down to the
> Edmonds skytrain station ... take the skytrain as far as Burrard station ...
> *and at Burrard station you want to walk north on Burrard one block ... as*
> *far as West Pender* ... and on West Pender going westbound it's bus number 19
> and it's called Stanley Park

Spatial Information in Bus Route Descriptions: The protosemantic knowledge base consists of bus routes laid out on a city map. As long as the end-points of travel lie along bus routes, and bus connections can be obtained without much walking, route descriptions have very little information on orientation and distance. However, when giving directions to the passenger to walk to the next intermediate (or final) destination, finer-grained spatial information involving distance, location and orientation is invoked. Thus, in the bus route domain,

- we need knowledge of different *granularities* in generating route descriptions; and
- the points at which the different levels of granularity assert themselves as relevant are clearly separated, and are evident in the route description.

We will use these observations to develop the representation for the map, as well as in the route finding procedure.

Spatial Reasoning in Bus Route Finding: The problem of route finding is essentially one of spatial reasoning. Given that knowledge of different granularities is used in giving bus route directions, we examined the following issues:

1. *Modularity in representation:* to what extent can we separate representation of explicit geographical (orientation and distance) information from geography-independent or implicit spatial information (sequence and adjacence) in the protosemantic knowledge base?
2. *Modularity in processing:* to what extent can we separate geography-dependent processing from geography-independent processing in the route finding procedure?

3 Protosemantic Knowledge Base

A typical bus route map of a city consists of bus routes prominently coloured and labelled, with the city map serving as the background. Analogously, in designing our knowledge base, we modularize bus route representations from street map representations. In this section we describe the salient features of our bus route representation. Our prototype system does not use street map representations at present. The routes encoded in our knowledge base as well as the examples used here have been drawn from the Transit Guide of the Vancouver Regional Transit System.

346

3.1 Representation of Bus Routes

We represent a bus route as a sequence of stages terminated by the source and destination of the bus. The stages are the streets that the bus traverses in sequence. Certain *points of interest*, which may serve as landmarks or which may be possible end-points of travel, are marked on the stages, in the order in which they are encountered during a journey on the given bus. Figure 2 is a simplified bus route, implemented in a schematic frame-like structure in Prolog.

```
route(routeid(kl133),
      source(junction(lougheed_mall)),
      stages([austin, north_road,
            cameron:[poi([],cameron_public_library)],
            east_lake:[poi(centaurus,pats_house)],
            lougheed, government, sperling,
            hastings:[poi(kensington,sylvia_barber_shop)]]),
      dest(junction(kootenay_loop))).
```

Figure 2:   Bus Route *kl133*

The location of a point of interest along a stage is indicated by the name of the nearest intersecting street. When the location is not known, we use an []. In figure 2, the point of interest *pats_house* is at the intersection of *east_lake* and *centaurus*, and *cameron_public_library* is *somewhere* on the *cameron* stage. The route is identified by an internal label (*kl133* in figure 2) which is associated with the name and the number of the bus in a separate, simple module, which, corresponding to the *kl133* route, contains: *id(kl133, 133, kootenay_loop)*. All routes are directional. Therefore, routes corresponding to return trips are represented separately. (The return route of a bus is not always the exact reverse of the outbound trip. The variation may be, for example, due to some stages' traversing one-way streets.)

Geometrically, we have a pair of labelled points (source and destination of the bus) at the extremities of a connected sequence of labelled directed line segments (stages) which possibly contain labelled points (points of interest). Our route representation is, in a sense, analogous to the bus route laid out on the city streets. The analogy is not thoroughgoing, in that the length of the stages and the place of the route in the global co-ordinate system are not included in our route representation.

3.2 Representing how Routes are Related

Of vital importance to our route finding procedure is the representation of how various routes are related. In a typical city bus system, a given route may be related to a number of other routes in several ways. A given street may form a stage of a number of bus routes. Should we represent explicitly all the relations among all the routes? On the one hand, everything that is relevant to giving bus route directions should be represented. On the other, given the multiplicity of route intersections and overlaps, representation of irrelevant information will lead to wasteful search. An analysis of the types of route relations has led to some useful design criteria. We present the salient aspects of our analysis below.

Types of Relations between Bus Routes : We note that two given bus routes may be related to each other in *one or more of* the following ways:

- Overlapping routes, having common stages.

- Intersecting routes, serving intersecting streets. These routes do not share a common stage. However, at (or near) the point of intersection of the streets, it is possible to transfer from one bus to the other.
- Routes having common termini:
    - Routes having a common source.
    - Routes having a common destination.
    - The destination of one route being the same as the source of the other.

Of the overlapping and intersecting routes, not all may be potential candidates for transfer. For example, consider two buses *r1* and *r2*, having a common destination *d* and a common last stage. Consider a passenger riding the bus *r1* from its source and intending to travel to *d*. It will not be necessary to advise the passenger to disembark *r1* before the last stage and to transfer to *r2* to cover the last stage, for he could reach *d* just as well by staying on *r1*. We analyzed the various types of intersections and overlaps to determine which of them are relevant for transfers, and chose to represent those overlaps and intersections which are potentially relevant in giving transfer information.

Implementation: In our prototype system, we associate intersecting and overlapping routes with bus stages, in a way similar to our representation of *points of interest*. The following representations of bus route stages illustrate the types of route relations:

- lougheed:[route([along],[van151,pqc151])]
  (The routes of *van151* and *pqc151* overlap all along the stage *lougheed*.)
- sperling:[route([halifax],[kl136])]
  (On the stage *sperling*, where it intersects *halifax*, one can transfer to *kl136*).
- lougheed:[route([underhill,brighton],[kl133,lm133])]
  (The routes of *kl133* and *lm133* overlap along *lougheed* between *underhill* and *brighton*.)

A bus route representation (like the one shown in figure 2) need not carry information about other routes sharing its termini, since such information can be easily computed by examining other route representations. However, we mark the presence of major bus junctions along the routes in the route representations, and associate the junctions with the labels of the buses serving the junctions, in a separate module in the knowledge base containing clauses such as

    exchange(lougheed_mall,[kl133,sfu145,nw147,van151,van152,pqc151]).
    exchange(sfu,[lm145,met144,kl135]).

This module is consulted by the route finding procedure when a junction is considered as a transfer point. A full example of a route representation, that of the bus *van151*, is given in figure 3, showing representations of points of interest as well as route intersections and overlaps. The bus *van151* passes through the junction *kootenay_loop* on stage *hastings*.

4 Bus Route Finding

As noted in section 2.1, the cognitive task of route finding is executed by activating a cognitive map, locating the end-points of travel in the map and planning a route between the end-points. In the instances where bus route directions are given without the aid of a map, the processes by which the end-points of the journey are located and irrelevant routes ignored are not directly evident, since the relevant information is recalled from memory. When we give route directions with the aid of a bus route map, visual processing aids greatly in *anchoring* ([Klein, 1982] calls this *localizing*) the end-points of travel and in ignoring irrelevant routes, by using geographical information effectively. By retaining the basic characteristics of the cognitive strategy and by systematically compensating for the

```
route(routeid(van151),
    source(junction(lougheed_mall)),
    stages([austin,
        lougheed:[route([underhill,brighton],[kl133,lm133]),
                 route([bainbridge],[kl133,lm133])],
        willingdon:[poi(lougheed,brentwood_mall),
                 route([along],[can120]),
                 route([along],[met130])],
        hastings:[junction(kootenay_loop),
                 route([renfrew],[h16]),
                 route([nanaimo],[h4]),
                 route([commercial],[vic21]),
                 route([main],[mai3,h8,h19,h22]),
                 poi(main,vancouver_public_library),
                 route([granville],[gra20])],
        burrard]),
    dest(hornby)).
```

Figure 3: Bus Route *van151*

absence of visual processing, intelligent procedures and representations that are cognitively relevant could be developed. In this section we describe the major steps of the bus route finding procedure as implemented in our prototype system.

4.1 Anchoring the End-Points of Travel

We start with the end-points of travel, *Source* and *Dest*, sufficiently well-specified. Anchoring the end-points of travel, to us, is tantamount to computing *Startlist*, the list of labels of buses proceeding out of *Source*, and *Endlist*, the list of labels of buses reaching *Dest*. The top-level call in our implementation is

```
rfind(Source,Dest) :-
    findstart(Source,Startlist),        /* localize Source */
    findend(Dest,Endlist),              /* localize Dest */
    rfind1(Source,Dest,Startlist,Endlist). /* further processing */
```

Startlist and *Endlist* are computed using a combination of methods. For important points of interest such as public parks, entertainment centres, hospitals, major shopping centres and the like, we maintain associated lists of buses departing from and arriving at these points. The information necessary for *Startlist* and *Endlist* computations is retrieved from this module.

In other cases, *Startlist* and *Endlist* are computed by examining the route representations and determining whether *Start* and *End* lie on the routes. We need to resort to this method particularly when the end-points of travel are not named points of interest, but are rather specified in terms of street names as, for example, in *Willingdon and Hastings*. The number of route representations examined is reduced by grouping routes into regions and requiring that the regions of *Start* and *Dest* be specified in the input, or be derivable from street map representations. Our prototype route finder, which has been implemented to serve as the nucleus of a text planning system, at present handles only simple *Sources* and *Dests* for which *Startlist* and *Endlist* can be computed easily. A complete knowledge-based system giving bus route directions, however, should handle arbitrary *Sources* and *Dests*, and compute *Startlist* and *Endlist* in a more sophisticated manner.

4.2 Journeys Involving a Single Bus Ride

After anchoring the end-points of travel, we compute *Intersectlist* as the set-theoretic intersection of *Startlist* and *Endlist*. If *Intersectlist* is non-empty, the elements of *Intersectlist* are the labels of the buses serving both *Source* and *Dest*. Among those elements, the buses one can take *from Source to Dest* are those in which *Source precedes Dest* in the route representation. An empty *Intersectlist* indicates that the buses in *Startlist* do not reach *Dest*. We then examine the route representations of the elements of *Startlist* to compute the list of buses that one may have to transfer to from a bus in *Startlist*. The clauses corresponding to this stage in our implementation are

```
rfind1(Source,Dest,Startlist,Endlist) :-
    intersection(Startlist,Endlist,Intersectlist),
    decide1(Source,Dest,Startlist,Endlist,Intersectlist).
decide1(Source,Dest,Slist,Elist,[]) :- rfind2(Source,Dest,Slist,Elist).
decide1(Source,Dest,Slist,Elist,Ilist) :- plantext1(Source,Dest,Ilist).
```

4.3 Journeys Involving Transfers

One Transfer: In section 3.2 we discussed how the relevant intersecting and overlapping routes are represented. We use this information in computing the list of (labels of) buses that one may transfer to (called *Transferlist*), given a starting point of travel *Source* and a starting bus route label *Sroute* selected from *Startlist*. For example, with reference to figure 3, if *Sroute* is *van151* and *Source* is *brentwood_mall*, then *Transferlist* will consist of *can120, met130*, the labels of the buses proceeding out of the junction *kootenay_loop, h16, h4, vic21, mai3, h8, h19, h22* and *gra20*.

We now compute the intersection (called *Ilist*) of *Transferlist* with *Endlist*. If *Ilist* is non-empty, its elements represent the buses to which one can transfer from *Sroute* in order to reach *Dest*. We do this in turn for every *Sroute* in *Startlist* until a non-empty *Ilist* is found, at which point the route finder passes on the relevant information to the text planner.

Two or More Transfers: When all the routes in *Startlist* have been examined and a non-empty *Ilist* still not found, we examine the route representations of the elements of *Transferlist* and compute the next level of potential bus transfers. The various *Transferlists* computed during the previous stage are saved on stack for possible examination at this stage, for a second transfer. Again, we perform the intersection of the newly computed list with *Endlist*. With a non-empty intersection, we obtain a path from *Source* to *Dest*. In principle this procedure is applicable to instances of three or more bus transfers, though, in practice, seldom will one have to take more than three buses to travel within a city.

5 Discussion and Further Research

Bus Route Finding as a Search Problem: Though route finding is essentially a spatial problem, a major part of the task in the domain of generating bus route directions consists in finding a sequence of bus labels, boarding points and disembarkation points. We have shown how the knowledge base and the route finding procedure could be designed so that the spatial problem of route finding could be treated as a search problem on bus labels, orientation information could be used to perform the search intelligently, and the search could be conducted by means of representation look-up and simple set operations. Figure 4 depicts how the search proceeds. The circles in figure 4 denote bus labels. The

350

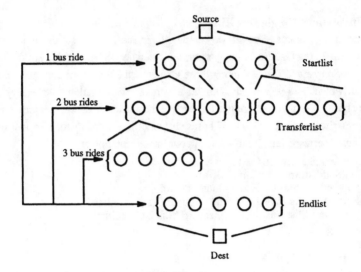

Figure 4: Bus Route Finding as a Search Problem

tree proliferates (breadth-first) when transfers from a bus are considered. The search succeeds and halts when a non-empty intersection of the newly-generated set of bus labels with *Endlist* is obtained. The route finding procedure does not generate *all* routes from *Source* to *Dest*, but is amenable to be modified easily to do so.

Route Preference and its Relation to Route Description Planning: The route finding procedure *prefers* a route with *fewer* bus rides. The preference is inherent in the design of the procedure. This preference can often be, but need not always be, the best from the traveller's perspective. For example, one may take a sequence of two buses instead of one straight bus in order to get to the destination *sooner*. The duration of travel, frequency of buses and ease of transfer are some of the factors that could call into question the optimality of the route preferred by our procedure.

However, our design has some implications for the speaker's perspective. We noted in section 2.3 that a unit of skeletal information in bus route descriptions specifies one bus ride. A route finding procedure that prefers fewer bus rides, when used in the context of route description generation, seeks to minimize the length of the description, *ceteris paribus*. (The description may increase in length if, for example, the chosen route necessitates communication of information on landmarks, orientation, etc.) A more concise route description could also be preferable from the listener's (traveller's) perspective, as it is likely to be more easily comprehensible. In their work on giving driving directions in northern New Jersey, [Elliott and Lesk, 1982] note that shortest-route prescriptions often had far too many turns, and were therefore rejected by their users. In general, routes that involve the fewest number of changes to the relevant variables of motion (turns, street crossings, transfers, etc) of the traveller are likely to be most concise in their description and most easily comprehensible. This accords well with the minimal effort principle derived in the experimental work of [Levelt, 1982]. (Everything else being equal, speakers will prefer to give descriptions which minimize the length of the description.)

In our research, the problem of route finding arises naturally in an instance of natural language generation. We are at present working on integrating the steps of route finding with the steps of text planning. In our prototype program, the set operations that extract bus labels from the knowledge base have been tailored to extract other relevant annotations for inclusion in text plans and later expression in bus route descriptions. For instance, when computing *Transferlist*, we also extract information pertaining to the point at which transfer should be taken. The skeletal information extracted by the route finder, that forms an input to the text planner, is illustrated by the following output of our prototype system. *kl133* is the return route of *lm133*, and *lm145*, that of *sfu145*.

```
yes
| ?- rfind(pats_house,sfu).

take(lm133) ^
board_at(pats_house) ^
get_off_at(dest(lougheed_mall))
and_then
take(sfu145) ^
board_at(lougheed_mall) ^
get_off_at(sfu)

yes
| ?-
```

```
yes
| ?- rfind(sfu,pats_house).

take(lm145) ^
board_at(sfu) ^
get_off_at(dest(lougheed_mall))
and_then
take(kl133) ^
board_at(lougheed_mall) ^
get_off_at(pats_house)

yes
| ?-
```

We present the details of our text planner in a separate paper.

Knowledge-Based Bus Route Finding: When all the contingencies affecting route finding are considered, giving bus route directions in a city emerges as a good candidate for knowledge based problem solving. There probably are no objective criteria for assessing what constitutes a *best route*. A flexible system would take into account schedule information, speed of buses (i.e., slow bus or express bus), length of routes, level of familiarity of the traveller with the area and so on. Some of the independent variables may conflict in their effect on the choice of the route. Suitable weights may be assigned to the independent variables, and the objective function (*best route*), maximized. Full geographical information is necessary to communicate route information effectively. Further research needs to be done on how the map of a city should be represented.

In our prototype, a relatively small knowledge base is used, and route preference is implicit in the route finding procedure. We haven't attended to all of the complex details of bus route finding, as our route finder is ancillary to our objectives of text generation research. However, by drawing from natural text and empirical psycholinguistic studies and by using a knowledge base comprising information from the real world, we have uncovered an interesting problem with potential practical application and have opened several avenues for further research.

Acknowledgments

This research has benefitted greatly from discussions with Dr. Romas Aleliunas, Dr. Bob Hadley and Dr. Ray Jennings, and to them our thanks are due. This work has been supported in part by a Simon Fraser University Graduate Research Fellowship, a British Columbia Advanced Systems Institute Graduate Student Scholarship and Natural Sciences and Engineering Research Council of Canada operating grant A-4309.

References

[Appelt, 1985]

Appelt, D.E. *Planning English Sentences*. Cambridge University Press, 1985.

[Elliott and Lesk, 1982]

Elliott, R.J. and Lesk, M.E. "Route Finding in Street Maps by Computers and People". In *Proceedings of AAAI' 82*,pages 258-261. 1982.

[Hovy, 1988]

Hovy, E.H. "Planning Coherent Multisentential Text". In *Proceedings, 26th Conference of the ACL, Buffalo*. 1988.

[Kempen and Hoenkamp, 1987]

Kempen, G. and Hoenkamp, E. "An Incremental Procedural Grammar for Sentence Formulation". *Cognitive Science* 11:201-258,1987.

[Klein, 1982]

Klein, W. "Local Deixis in Route Directions". *Speech, Place and Action, Jarvella, R.J. and Klein, W., Editors*. John Wiley & Sons Ltd, 1982, pages 161-182.

[Levelt, 1982]

Levelt, W.J.M. "Linearization in Describing Spatial Networks". *Processes, Beliefs, and Questions, Peters, S. and Saarinen, E., Editors*. Reidel, Dordrecht, 1982, pages 199-220.

[Levelt, 1989]

Levelt, W.J.M. *Speaking: From Intention to Articulation*. M.I.T.Press, 1989.

[McDonald, 1983]

McDonald, D.D. "Description Directed Control: Its Implications for Natural Language Generation". *Computers and Mathematics* 9(1):111-129,1983.

[Riesbeck, 1980]

Riesbeck, C.K. "You Can't Miss It!: Judging the Clarity of Directions". *Cognitive Science* 4:285-303,1980.

[van Dijk and Kintsch, 1983]

van Dijk, T.A. and Kintsch, W. *Strategies of Discourse Comprehension*. Academic Press, 1983.

[Wunderlich and Reinelt, 1982]

Wunderlich, D. and Reinelt, R. "How to Get There from Here". *Speech, Place and Action, Jarvella, R.J. and Klein, W., Editors*. John Wiley & Sons, Ltd., 1982, pages 183-201.

Parsing with Extended Unification Mechanisms

Patrick Saint-Dizier
LSI Université Paul Sabatier
118, route de Narbonne
31062 TOULOUSE FRANCE
stdizier@irisa.irisa.fr

Abstract

In this paper, we present an approach to parsing within Government and Binding theory and to representing lexical semantic knowledge based on logical types and on an extension to the usual unification mechanism. The work we present here is a first, exploratory step towards the specification of a logical feature system based on the idea of abstract data type which integrates a dynamic treatment of syntactic and semantic relations like taxonomies and meronomies. Our aim is to augment the unification mechanism so that it integrates the general laws of sentence construction.

1. Introduction

With the development of highly parameterized syntactic theories like Government and Binding theory and Head-Driven phrase structure grammars and with the development of theories where unification plays a central role, like Categorial grammars and Unification Grammars, there is an increasing need for more appropriate and more efficient feature systems.

Feature systems must be designed to preserve the adequacy, the expressiveness and the explanatory power of the linguistic system that one wants to model. They must also offer great freedom in the specification of features in grammar symbols and a significant modularity so that each linguistic aspect (morphological, categorial, ...) can be dealt with independently.

The work we present here is a first step towards modelling some aspects of Government and Binding theory which we thing appropriate for natural language processing. We believe that Government and Binding theory is of much interest to computational linguistics because of its high degree of generality, explicative power, conciseness and modularity. Furthermore, its constraint-based formulation of linguistic phenomena is particularly attractive for logic programmers. We will present here only the 'structural' aspect of GB, namely: *X-bar syntax, movement theory, bounding theory, trace theory and the structure preserving principle*. Moreover-, although the theory is particularly vague on lexical issues, we think that GB must be paired with a detailed lexicon to be adequate for natural language processing.

The work we present here is a first, exploratory step towards the specification of a logical representational feature system based on the idea of abstract data type construction which integrates a dynamic treatment of syntactic and semantic relations. Our goal is to augment the unification mechanism so that it integrates the general laws of sentence construction. Besides this augmented unifier, we have a set of parameter values specifying those general laws and a lexical knowledge base containing descriptions of words.

In this document, we first present Login [Aït Kaçi and Nasr 1986], which was the starting point of our work. We then propose extensions to Login for natural language parsing within the framework of Government and Binding Theory.

2. An overview of Login

Login [Aït-Kaçi and Nasr 1986], is an extension to Prolog in which first-order terms are replaced by a more general notion: ψ-terms. These terms allow the integration of taxonomies directly into the unification mechanism. This enhances the expressiveness of the language as well as the efficiency of the resolution-based inference mechanism of Prolog.

2.1 Motivations

Here is a simple, motivational example that we directly borrow from Aït-Kaçi and Nasr's paper. A student is a person; p1,.... , pn are persons; s1, ..., sm are students; pi and sj have the property prop. This can be represented in Prolog as:

```
person(X) :- student(X).
person(p1).      ......    person(pn).
student(s1).     ......    student(sm).
prop(pi).
prop(sj).
```
Asking for a person having property prop results in the following query:
```
?- person(X), prop(X).
```
In Prolog, finding solutions involves a state transition with context saving and variable binding. It would be more convenient to 'declare' that *student* can match *person,* for example by means of an *isa* (noted as <) relation:
```
student < person.  (student isa person)
{p1, ... , pn) < person.
{s1, ... , sm} < student.
```
the query becomes:
```
?- prop(X : person).
```
where X is a typed variable.

Unification becomes the computation of the greater lower bound (noted hereafter GLB) of two symbols relative to <. Then, the answer follows by unification rather than by resolution.

2.2 Partially ordered type structures

The syntactic representation of a structured term is called a ψ-term. It consists of:

(1) a *root symbol*, which is a type constructor and denotes a class of entities,

(2) *attribute labels*, which are record field symbols. Each attribute denotes a function in extenso, from the root to the attribute value.

(3) *coreference constraints* among paths of labels, which indicate that the corresponding attributes denote the same function. They are indicated by variables.

Here is an example:

```
person( id => name(first => string,  last => X: string),
         born => date(day => integer,  month => monthname,  year => integer),
         father => person( id => name(last => X ))).
```

The root symbol is *person; id, born* and *father* are three sub-ψ-terms. *X* indicates a coreference. All different type structures are tagged by different symbols. Notice also that in the latter field only relevant information about person is mentioned. Infinite structures can also be specified by coreference links.

The type signature Σ is a partially ordered set of symbols. It always has two elements: a greatest element (Τ) and a least element (⊥). Type symbols denote sets of objects and the partial order on Σ denotes set inclusion. In [Aït-Kaçi 1984], it is shown that Σ is such that GLBs (respectively LUBs) exist for all pairs of type symbols with respect to the signature ordering, then GLBs (LUBs) also exist for the extended well-formed term ordering.

3. Extending Login for parsing

Our linguistic basis for syntax is the theory of *Government and Binding* [Chomsky 1982], [Chomsky, 1986]. We first introduce its main characteristics and then present a computational model which uses principles of Login and extends them.

3.1 An introduction to Government and Binding theory

Government and Binding theory (hereafter GB), is a complete revision of the baroque set of rules and constraints of the Standard Transformational framework, achieving a much greater generality, expressive power and explanatory adequacy. GB theory is composed of a small base component, a single movement rule and a small set of general principles which control the power of the movement rule. We believe that GB is worth investigating for language analysis and generation, paired with other tools from computational linguistics and AI (to deal with, for example: the lexicon, lexical semantics, feature systems and logical form construction). GB has indeed several attractive computational properties:
- *conciseness and economy of means* (small number of rules and principles),
- *high degree of parameterisation* (abstract, general filtering principles, X-bar syntax),
- *modularity* (independence of filtering principles),
- *declarativity* (no order in the application of rules),
- *absence of intermediate structures* (no deep-structure, for example).

We have developed a quite extensive natural language parser and generator based on GB theory [Saint-Dizier 1987], [Saint-Dizier 1989b] (see other approaches in [Berwick and Weinberg 1986], [Johnson 1988], and in [Stabler 1987, 1988] for parsing and in [Brown et al.1988] for sentence generation).

3.2. Modeling GB theory

We have modeled the structural aspects of GB theory: X-bar syntax, movement theory, bounding theory, trace theory and the structure preserving principle. We now briefly summarize the main lines of our model, given in [St-Dizier 1987, 1989a].

356

The **base component** is based on a current version of **X-bar theory**. Rules are highly parameterized. Here are these rules for French:

$X^2 \to spec, X^1$.
$X^1 \to X^0, compl$.
$X^1 \to adjunct, X^1$.
$X^1 \to X^1, adjunct$.

X stands for the clausal categories COMP or INFL or for one of the lexical categories V (verb), N (noun), A (adjective) or P (preposition). The index, ranging from 0 to 2, indicates the bar level. The highest level is 2, it corresponds to the traditional phrase level. X is the head in a rule and controls syntactic and semantic features agreement. Each compl, spec and adjunct may be filled in with another X^2. As an example, the spec of an N is a determiner, the compl of an N is an A^2. The spec of a verb is an auxiliary and its compl is a direct object N^2.

These base rules are translated into Definite Clause grammar form. Specification of spec, compl and adjuncts is made via a small base of Prolog facts called mod:

```
xp(Cat,2,Features,Logic) -->            % rule X2 --> spec,  X1.
    {mod(spec,Cat,Cat1,Bar1)},          % call to the spec database
      xp(Cat1, Bar1, Features1, Logic1),   % specifier
      xp(Cat, 1, Features2, Logic2),       % head category
    {agreement(Features1, Features2, Cat, Cat1,F)}.
```

```
mod(spec,n,det,0).    % specifier database: det with bar level 0 is the spec of n
mod(spec,aux,v,0).    % aux with bar level 0 is the spec of v.
```
(logic is not dealt with here, for the sake of clarity).
We have the same type of rule and database for complements and adjuncts.

GB postulates a single movement rule **move-α** : *move any constituent α to any position,* which is controlled by general principles. Move-α and these principles are clearly too general and too abstract to be computationally tractable. Move-α needs to be somewhat instantiated without losing its generality and linguistic adequacy. Some principles like the **structure preserving principle** (a category C moves to a position of type C) are directly encoded in the movement rules.

We have modelled movement rules in **Dislog** [St-Dizier 1988], which is an extension to Prolog designed to express in a simple and declarative way long-distance relations and constraints. We now illustrate it by an example. A Dislog clause is of the form:

$\{ a \to a1, b \to b1, \ldots, n \to n1 \}$.

where a, b, n are non-terminal symbols, a1, b1 and n1 are a sequence of terminal and non-terminal symbols. This Dislog clause is an unordered set of Prolog clauses, it can be paraphrased by: *somewhere in the proof tree a is rewritten into a1, b into b1 , ..., and n into n1 with the same substitutions applied to all identical variables occuring in the Prolog rules.* Variable bindings permit, for example, to percolate feature values and logical forms.

A Dislog programme is a set of Dislog clauses. Here is now an example of a movement rule written in Dislog: the construction of a relative clause. The general annotated surface form of a relative clause is:

[COMP PRO_i .... [N2 trace_i] .....]   as in:
[COMP THAT_i John met [N2 trace_i] yesterday].
and we have the following Dislog rule:

{ xp(comp, 0, pro, _) --> xp(n,0,pro,I), xp(comp,0,_,I) ,
    xp(n, 2, F, I) --> [ ]. }

This rule means that if there is an N with feature pro (xp(n,0,pro,I)) (a pronoun) adjoined to a comp node, then somewhere else in the proof tree, an N with bar level 2 is derived into the empty string (or a trace). **Bounding theory** limits the domain in which this latter rule can be found, with respect to the first rule. Bounding nodes are declared in the Dislog programme and are managed by the Dislog compiler. Finally, the variable I is the co-indexation link, as postulated by **trace theory**. Relations between traces and indexes are here straightforward since, in a parse, each instance of a Dislog rule originates an index unified to a different value.

3.3 Type-based grammars

We now show how X-bar syntax and movement rules can be formulated in terms of types and hierarchical relations. In this approach, there is a high gain in the freedom of feature specification (features are specified when necessary and in any order), in linguistic adequacy and expressiveness and in modularity (relations between features representing the same phenomenon in different symbols are specified separately by means of unification rules).

The very regular format of grammar symbols allows us to define a simple type constructor *xp* for all grammar symbols. Each feature originates an attribute representation by a sub-ψ-term. Here are some examples of lexical entries. The operator := as in *a := T* permits us to bind constant *a* (a word) to the type specification T. In GB, this could be viewed as the lexical insertion operation (examples are given here for French):

```
la := xp(syn => category(cat => det, bar => 0 ),
         morph => flection(gender => fem, number => sing ),
         logic => la ).
programme := xp(syn => category(cat => n, bar => 0 ),
                morph => flection(gender => masc, number => sing ),
                sem => traits( proper => object, cpt => human),
                logic => f( X, programme(X)) ).
```

The semantic control on complements is made possible by the feature *sem* which, for example in usual simple natural language systems, introduces the semantics of the word itself (attribute *proper*) and its possible complements (attribute *cpt*, which can be a list of possible values). All words are structured by means of lexical relations; then all possible words dominated in a taxonomic relation by the attribute value of *cpt* are acceptable since it unifies with that attribute value.

As in unification grammars (see [Sheiber 86] for a general presentation), terminal values of ψ-terms can refer to types. This permits us to avoid redundancy: all information shared by several lexical entries can be extracted to form a type (also called a lexical template), which is then appropriately refered to in lexical entries.

We can now consider **grammatical relations**. The first one is the categorial relation (category and bar level). We can say that, for example, a determiner with bar level 0 together with a noun with bar level 1 (noted n,1) form a noun with bar level 2. We cannot say that a det,0 is an n,2: categorial relations cannot be expressed by taxonomic hierarchies, but rather by **meronomic hierarchies** which denote the part-whole relation [Cruse 1986]. A det,0 is a part of an n,2. Meronomies (as well as taxonomies) also introduce horizontal relations between sisters (called co-meronyms): a det,0 is a co-meronym of an n,1 to form an n,2.

Categorial relations are more restricted than pure meronomic relations since in a noun phrase we always want the determiner to appear before the noun. To express this ordering constraint, we introduce the notion of *left co-meronym* and *right co-meronym*:: det, 0 is the left co-meronym of n,1 and n,1 is the right co-meronym of det,0.

Contrary to the taxonomic relation in Login, we cannot introduce a relation *part_of* like:

adv, 2 part_of(left) v, 1

because it is ambiguous if there are several ways of building v,1's. We can only have rules where meronomic descriptions are compiled into a set of rules that directly specify unification. Let us consider the operator *with* where the type to the left of the operator is the left co-meronym of the type to the right of the operator.This operator is not commutative. The informal meaning of:

A with B unify C.

is that A and B unify to give C.   A, B and C are (partial) type specifications.

For example, we have the following rule for X-bar syntax:

```
xp(syn => category(cat => C1, bar => B ))      with       % X2 --> spec, X1.
   xp(syn => category(cat => C, bar => 1 ))    unify
   xp(syn => category(cat => C, bar =>2 )) :-    mod(spec,C,C1,B).
```

mod(_,_,_,_) refers to a small database of specifiers, complements and adjuncts.

Partial evaluation, by instantiating categories and bar levels, can be used to make the system more efficient.

We can at this level introduce the head feature representation. In X-bar syntax, X symbols are heads, thus we can add to the above categorial description the head feature. For the first rule we have:

```
xp(syn => category(cat => C1, bar => B ), head => 1)     with       % X2 --> spec, X1.
   xp(syn => category(cat => C, bar => 1 ))           unify
   xp(syn => category(cat => C, bar =>2 ) head => 1 ) :-     mod(spec,C,C1,B).
```

Let us now consider the description of **morphological agreement** and **inheritance of morphological features**. For example, we can say that the det,0 agrees in gender and number with the n,1 and that the result of unification is the flection of the noun. Contextual data like noun and determiner have to be taken into account. Feature inheritance between heads is expressed as follows:

```
xp(morph => X,  head => 1)    with
xp(head => 0)    unify
xp(morph => X).
```

This is directly the expression of the *Head Feature Convention* in GPSGs [Gazdar et al. 1985]. This rule permits us to block percolation (up or down) of morphological features from non-head categories. The rule above for feature control and inheritance permits the expression and the control of a limited form of transitivity in meronomies.

Our formulation of feature control and inheritance is more general than in current unification grammar systems since feature control and inheritance is not expressed in grammar rules but by means of a few general rules. Our approach is also more modular and avoids complex grammatical rules. The same approach is used for lexical subcategorization.

Finally, **semantic representation computation** is also modeled in a similar way. Here is the example of the composition of the logical form (here a logical form called a three-branched quantified tree) of a det,0 with an n,1:

```
xp(syn => category(cat=>det, bar => 0), logic => F1)     with
  xp(syn => category(cat=>n, bar => 1),   logic => f(X, F2))     unify
  xp(logic =>   f( X, quant([F1,X],F2,F3) )).
```

We have, in fact, a knowledge base of semantic composition rules called *f_logic*. Thus, we can have a more general formulation of semantic representation construction at the GLB rule level and a separate module with semantic rules.

The introduction of databases of modifiers and of semantic composition rules permits us to clearly separate the data from the construction rules. We then have a (small) set U of **general rules** (following, in a certain way, the idea of universal grammar in GB theory) and **a set of parameter values** (which can be complex terms, for example for semantic representation computation) which can be tuned up depending on the language considered. This idea is also central and to M. Johnson's work [Johnson 1988, 1989]. Furthemore, the set U of general rules could be integrated into a specialized unifier designed for natural language processing; the parameters are then the body of the natural language processing program.

3.4 Dealing with movements

Movement rules are expressed in Dislog (see section 3.2). Instead of having grammar rules in Dislog clauses, we have unification rules. Here is as an example the relativisation rule:

```
{ ( xp(syn => category(cat => n, bar => 2, pronoun => rel))     % first rule
    with
  xp(syn => category(cat => comp, bar => 2))     unify
  xp(syn => category(cat => comp, bar => 2), trace => I)   ),

  xp(empty => yes)     unify
  xp(syn=>category(cat=>n,bar=>2),trace => I, empty => yes ) }. % second rule
```

The informal meaning of this Dislog rule is that if one of the unification rules is used during the parse, then the other one must also be used with identical variable substitutions applied to identical variable identifiers. This is exactly the same treatment as we have for regular DCG rules in Dislog rules. The two unification rules are managed by the Dislog compiler in a way transparent to the grammar writer [Saint-Dizier 1987, 1988]. The second rule is a **promotion rule** of the empty category into an N^2.

3.5 Principles and Filters

In this paper, we mainly deal with the 'structural' aspect of GB theory (mainly: X-bar, more-α, bounding theory, trace theory and structure preserving principle). We believe however that GB should be considered as a whole and that principles and filters like binding theory, θ-theory and case theory in conjunction with government should also be taken into account. They could be viewed as constraints, either static or active (as in the Constrained Logic Programming framework) on type constructors.

We give here some elements on the way to deal with some of these constraints within our type-based approach. It turns out that constraints like case-marking (all overt, i.e. lexically induced, N^2 must be assigned one and only one case) and the θ-criterion (all N^2 must be assigned one and only one θ-role such as: agent, instrument, etc...) can be expressed in terms of well-formedness conditions on the types constructed from the unification rules given above.Those well-formedness conditions can be expressed by means of type-frames which must unify with any type instance constructed during the parsing process. If unification fails, the instance is ill-formed. Here is the constraint of the θ-criterion:

$$xp(\; syn => category(\; cat => n, \; bar => 2, \; lexical => yes \;),$$
$$case => C \;) \quad :- \; not(\; X = empty \;) \; ; \; not(\; X = [\_|\_] \;).$$

The constraint prevents case C for an N^2 from being either empty or a list of cases. Thus, the N^2 will be assigned one and only one θ-role. This constraint is checked as soon as an N^2 is produced. It could also be merged into the unification mechanism.

3.6 Parsing with type-based grammars

Parsing a sentence (or any phrasal structure) is essentially the computation of a type common to all the elements constituting that sentence. The result of the parse is thus a single xp. If several possible types exist, then the sentence is ambiguous relative to the rule system. This computation is performed in a bottom-up fashion: after lexical insertion, types corresponding to words or sentence structures are constructed from the unification rules. The process ends when no more types can be constructed.

The constraint on the computation of these types is that each type must always have at least three fields: category, morphology and logic. Unification rules are activated on one or two type specifications to produce partial types which are then merged to form a new type. This merging operation is straightforward since partial unification are independent from each other.

Our parsing system as well as our unification rule format can easily be extended so that n type specifications can be taken into account at the same time instead of just two.

3.7 Comparison with other logic-based grammars

Our approach has several advantages over other logic-based grammars.

The first advantage is the greater freedom of specifying only relevant features and in any order in lexical entries and in grammar symbols. More attention is also devoted to feature specification and to feature value percolation during the parse. This approach is the major advantage of Unification Grammars. Notice that, within the same range of ideas, [Johnson 1989] proposes to merge unification-based theories and frame structures of artificial intelligence using a quantifier-free first order theory with equality which overcomes difficult problems with negation and disjunctions.

Unification rules can deal with complex situations and can also block the percolation of features, as we have seen for morphological features. Our system is an extension to Unification Grammars, which use a more direct system of unification. We have indeed on the one hand general unification rules which can be integrated into a unifier and on the other hand a set of parameter values. Thus, instead of having three components like in Unification Grammars (unifier, rules and feature descriptions), we only have two components (augmented unifier and parameter values).

A greater linguistic adequacy is also attained by describing separately each linguistic aspect by rules: the categorial aspect, the morphological feature system, the computation of a semantic representation, etc...

Epilogue

In this document, we have shown how the approach initiated in Login can be fruitfully extended to express in a modular, declarative and transparent way feature systems for natural language processing by means of abstract data-type constructions.

This work is preliminary, but it clearly indicates that this approach is worth pursuing. It preserves the adequacy and the expressive and explanatory power of linguistic systems and offers a convenient and a well-founded computational framework.

Forthcoming work is twofold: exploring more in depth semantic and syntactic relations in linguistic systems and specifying the logical and computational aspects of the extended unification mechanism we have introduced in this document.

Acknowledgements

I thank Hassan Aït-Kaçi and Roger Nasr for their nice welcome and discussions during my visit at MCC, Austin. I also thank Enrico Maim for drawing our attention on Login. This work was supported by the PRC-CNRS Communication Homme-Machine.

References

[Aït-Kaçi, 1984]
Aït-Kaçi, H., A Lattice-Theoretic Approach to Computation Based on Calculus of Partially Orderd Type Structures, PhD. Thesis, Computer Science dept, University of Pennsylvania, Philadelphia, 1984.

[Aït-Kaçi and Nasr, 1986]
Aït-Kaçi, H., Nasr, R., LOGIN: A Logic Programming Language with Built-in Inheritance, *journal of Logic Programming*, vol. 3, pp 185-215, 1986.

[Berwick and Weinberg, 1986]
Berwick, R. and Weinberg, A., *The Grammatical Basis of Linguistic Performance*, MIT Press, 1986.

[Brown et al., 1988]
Brown, C., Pattabhiraman, T., Massicotte, P., Towards a Theory of Natural Language Generation: the Connection between Syntax and Semantics, in: *Natural Language Understanding and Logic Programming II*, V. Dahl and P. Saint-Dizier Edts, North Holland 1988.

[Chomsky, 1981]
Chomsky, N., *Lectures on Government and Binding*, Foris Pub., Dordrecht, 1981.

[Chomsky, 1986]
Chomsky, N., *Barriers*, Linguistic Inquiry monograph nb. 13, MIT Press 1986.

[Cruse, 1986]
Cruse, D.A., *Lexical Semantics*, Cambridge University Press, 1986.

[Gazdar et al., 1985]
Gazdar, G., Klein, E., Pullum, G., Sag, I., *Generalized Phrase Structure Grammar*, Harvard university Press, 1985.

362

[Johnson, 1988]
Johnson, M., Deductive Parsing with Multiple Levels of Representation, *proc of ACL '88*, Buffalo, 1988.

[Johnson, 1989]
Johnson, M., Features, Frames and Quantifier-Free Formulae, to appear in: *Logic and Logic Grammars for Language Processing*, P. Saint-Dizier and S. Szpakowicz edts, Ellis Horwood, 1989.

[Saint-Dizier, 1987]
Saint-Dizier, P., Contextual Discontinuous Grammars, 2nd NLULP, Vancouver 1987 and in: *Natural Language Understanding and Logic Programming II*, V. Dahl and P. Saint-Dizier Edts, North Holland, 1988.

[Saint-Dizier, 1988]
Saint-Dizier, P., Foundations of Dislog, programming in Logic with Discontinuities, in *proc. of FGCS'88*, Tokyo, 1988.

[Saint-Dizier, 1989a]
Saint-Dizier, P., Constrained Logic Programming for Natural Language Processing, *proc. ACL-89*, Manchester, 1989.

[Saint-Dizier, 1989b]
Saint-Dizier, P., A Generation Method Based on GB Principles, in proc. *2nd European Workshop on Natural Language Generation*, Edinburgh, 1989.

[Sheiber, 1986]
Sheiber, S., An Introduction to Unification-Based Approaches to Grammar, *CSLI lecture notes no 4*, Chicago University Press, 1986.

[Stabler, 1987]
Stabler, E., Restricting Logic Grammars with Government and Binding theory, in *Computational Linguistics*, vol. 13, 1-2, 1987.

[Stabler, 1988]
Stabler, E., Parsing with Explicit Representations of Syntactic Constraints, in: *Natural Language Understanding and Logic Programming II*, V. Dahl and P. Saint-Dizier Edts, North Holland, 1988.

Pattern Recognition and Vision

Shape Based Object Recognition

DK Banerjee*   SK Parui   D Dutta Majumder

(*National Centre for Knowledge Based Computing)
Electronics and Communication Sciences Unit
Indian Statistical Institute
Calcutta 700 035

Abstract

This paper examines the problem of shape based object recognition and proposes an approach to it based on certain characteristic planes of an object. It deals with a certain class of 3-D objects and their shapes. A shape distance for such objects is proposed on the basis of which shape discrimination between 3-D objects is possible. Two objects have the same shape if and only if one is a translation, dilation and rotation of the other. Thus, for shape matching, an object has to be normalized in terms of its position, size and orientation. Normalization of an object in terms of its position and size can easily be achieved. The main problem in shape matching involves normalization of orientation of an object. Here this problem is solved by using certain characteristic planes of an object. Thus, in order to compare shapes of two 3-D objects, first their position and volume are normalized. Then after normalizing their 3-dimensional orientation using the characteristic planes, they are superimposed on each other. The resulting volume of mismatch is taken to be a shape distance between the two objects. In the analog domain, this shape distance satisfies all the four metric properties.

1   Introduction

Object recognition is one of the most important aspects of visual perception. In computational vision, the problem of recognizing objects from visual input has met so far with limited success. We often recognize an object visually on the basis of its characteristic shape. We may also use visual, but non-shape, cues such as colour and texture. The recognition of a tree of a given type is based more on texture properties, branching pattern and colour than on precise shape. Similarly, various material types and different scenes such as mountain terrain can be recognized visually without relying on precise shape. Certain animals such as a tiger or a giraffe can sometimes be recognized on the basis of texture and colour pattern rather than shape.

Objects can also be recognized visually solely on the basis of their location relative to other objects. For example, a door knob may have a non standard shape, and still can be recognized immediately as a door knob on the basis of its size and location relative to the door. Yet another possibility is to recognize objects visually, on the basis of their characteristic motion, rather than specific shape. For example, a fly in the room may be perceived as a small dark blob, and still be recognized as a fly, on the basis of its characteristic erratic motion.

Below we review the main classes of approaches that have been proposed for object recognition and then present an approach that appears to offer a promising general strategy for a variety of object recognition problems on the basis of shape. The conclusions are given at the end.

1.1 Regularity Problem and Alignment Approach

As propounded by Ullman [1984] the process of object recognition requires the inversion of a complicated one-to-many mapping. The image cast by a single object will change when the object translates or rotates in space. It will also change with the illumination conditions. Formally, one can think of a mapping M that maps a given object O to one in a large set of possible views $(V_1, V_2, ...V_k)$. Given a single view of the object, the problem is in a sense to invert M and recover the original object O.

The recognition problem is difficult because the set of possible views of a given object is large and because different views of the same object can be widely dissimilar. This dissimilarity problem may have a solution if we can define an appropriate similarity measure between objects views. We may therefore try to define a similarity measure that would render all different views of the same object as closely similar to one another and still assign a large measure of dissimilarity to views belonging to different objects. In fact, the entire process of object recognition can be thought of as providing such a similarity measure.

The conclusion is that finding regularities in the set of views that belong to a single object (or class of objects) is the key to visual object recognition. Ullman refers to this problem as the "regularity problem" in object recognition. His "alignment approach" [Ullman,1986] is a solution to this regularity problem where the recognition process is divided into two stages. The first determines the transformation in space that is necessary to bring the viewed object into alignment with possible object models. This stage can proceed on the basis of minimal information such as the object's dominant orientation or a small number of corresponding feature points in the object and the model. The second stage determines the model that best matches the viewed object.

1.2 Invariant Properties and Feature Spaces

A common approach to object recognition has been to assume that objects have certain invariant properties that are common to all of their views. Formally, a property of this type can be defined as a function from the set of object views to the real numbers. In an invariant properties scheme the overall recognition process is thus broken down into the extraction of a number of different properties followed by a final decision based on these properties, where each of these stages is relatively simple to compute.

In some cases, a property defined for a given object (or a class of objects) is not expected to remain entirely invariant, but to lie within a certain range. Property of different objects may have partially overlapping ranges, but by defining a number of different properties, it is possible to define each object (or class) uniquely. This concept of "feature spaces" has been extensively used in pattern recognition. If n different properties are measured, each viewed object can be looked upon as a point in the n-dimensional Euclidean space $\mathcal{R}^n$. The set of all the views induced by a given object defines in this manner a subspace of $\mathcal{R}^n$. This representation can be useful for identifying and classifying objects, provided that the subspaces have simple shapes.

Another approach that belongs to the general category of invariant properties theory is Gibson's theory of high-order invariances [Gibson, 1979]. Gibson suggests that invariant properties of objects may be reflected in so called "higher order" invariances in the optic array. Such invariances may be based for example on spatial and temporal gradient texture density. A set of invariances are then used to characterize object and object classes.

In summary, the invariant properties approach offers one possible solution to the regularity problem of object recognition. The weakness of this approach is that in visual object recognition there is no particular reason to assume the existence of relatively simple properties that are preserved across the transformations that an object may undergo.

1.3   Object Decomposition

A third general approach to object recognition is based on the decomposition of objects into their constituent parts. These parts are found first and then the recognition of the entire object could use the identified parts. The approach assumes that each object can be decomposed into a small set of generic components. The components are 'generic' in the sense that all objects can be described as different combinations of these components. The decomposition must also be stable, that is, preserved across views. The crucial point in this approach is that the many to one mapping implied by object recognition begins at the component level. Following the initial classification of the individual components, a final classification can then be performed on the basis of these components and their relations.

An example of structural decomposition recognition scheme is Biderman's [1985] theory of recognition by components. According to this scheme, objects are described in terms of a small set of primitive parts called 'geons'. These primitives are similar to the generalized cylinders used by Marr and Nishihara [1978], Brooks [1981] amd others. They include simple 3-D shapes such as boxes, cylinders and wedges. More complex objects are described by decomposing them into their constitutent geons together with a description of the spatial relation between components. In Biderman's scheme certain nonaccidental relationships between contours in the image are used to determine the part decomposition. These relations include, the collinearity of points or line, symmetry and skew symmetry and parallelism of curve segments.

Another scheme employing part-decomposition is the 'codon' scheme proposed by Hoffman and Richards [1986] for the description and recognition of contours. Contours are segmented at curvature minima. The resulting parts are then described in terms of a small 'vocabulary' of shape primitives termed 'codons'. The geon and the codon schemes are complementary to each other. The codon scheme concentrates on the initial stages of analyzing image contours whereas Biderman's geon scheme assumes that certain analysis of image contours has already been performed and then consider the description of the complete object.

Attempts have been made recently in combining these two levels of analysis into working systems that would actually recognize objects from their projections. A scheme by Connel [1985] starts at the level of analyzing image contour in terms of constituent parts and properties, using a representation scheme developed by Asada and Brady [1986]. It has a graph structure in which the nodes represent components and labelled arcs represent relations between parts. Recognition can be achieved by matching such graphs generated from the image with already known graph structures.

Though the notion of part decomposition appears to be natural and it is also argued by Biderman [1985] and Hoffman [1983] that human observers sometimes find it easy to identify the parts of an object even when the object is unfamiliar, the use of structural decomposition has at least two severe limitations. The first problem is that the decomposition into generic parts often falls considerably short of characterizing the object in question. A second limitation of the structural description approach is that many objects do not decompose naturally into the union of clearly distinct parts.

2 Shape Based Object Recognition

Most common objects can be recognized in isolation, without the use of context and expectations. For the purpose of our present discussion we will focus on the recognition of individual objects only on the basis of their shape.

In our approach a volumetric representation for 3-D solids is used on the basis of 3-D spatial information in the form of a 3-D array or matrix whose elements, called voxels, can have two values 0 or 1. Techniques for obtaining such a representation from 3-D solids are already available in the literature [Srihari, 1981; Chien and Aggarwal, 1986]. It can be seen that this representation gives an approximation to the actual 3-D objects as cavities etc. cannot be captured by 3 orthogonal projections. We propose here a method for quantifying shape distance for 3-D objects using this representation. The approach taken here to shape distance quantification is an extension of an earlier work on 2-dimensional shape discrimination [Parui, 1984; Parui and Dutta Majumder, 1984]. In the analog case a 3-D object is looked upon as a subset of the 3-dimensional Euclidean space $\mathcal{R}^3$. Two objects have the same shape if and only if one is a translation, dilation and rotation of the other. Now, for matching, an object often has to be normalized in terms of position, size and orientation. The normalization of an object with respect to position and size can easily be achieved if its centre of gravity and volume are considered. The main problem in that case involves the normalization of orientation of an object. Here, this problem is solved by using certain characteristic planes of an object [Parui and Banerjee, 1987]. In what follows, the shape of 3-dimensional objects is defined and a shape distance for such objects is proposed which involves infinitely many rotations. In order to solve this problem of rotations, an alternative shape distance is proposed which needs only 5 rotations. Certain characteristic planes are defined for a 3-D object on the basis of which the second shape distance is constructed. The techniques to compute this shape distance for 3-D objects are also provided.

2.1 Shape Distance for 3-D Objects

A subset A of $\mathcal{R}^3$ is called an *object* if (i) A is compact, (ii) Interior(A) is non-empty and (iii) Closure(Interior(A)) $= A$. Since shape is independent of the position and size of an object, we consider only those objects which have the centre of gravity at the origin $(0,0,0)$ and the volume unity. Let C be the class of all such objects.

Now, any rotation of an object in $\mathcal{R}^3$ about the origin is determined by the corresponding rotation of the system of axes which is in turn specified by three angles θ, ϕ and φ in $[0,2\pi)$ where θ is the angle between the new and old x-axes, ϕ is the angle between the new and old y-axes and φ is the angle between the new and old z-axes. Let $A_{\theta,\phi,\varphi}$ be the rotation of an object A in C where θ, ϕ and φ determine the new system of axes. It is clear that $A_{\theta,\phi,\varphi}$ also is in C.

Rotation defines an equivalence relation on C. This equivalence relation is denoted by R. The *shape* of an object is defined as an equivalence class generated by R in C. $\mathcal{F}$ is the family of all such equivalence classes, that is, of all shapes.

D_1 is a distance function on C such that for A, B in C,

$$D_1(A, B) = m_3[(A - B) \cup (B - A)]$$

where m_3 is the Lebesgue measure in $\mathcal{R}^3$. Note that D_1 defines a metric on C and $0 \le D_1 \le 2$.

D_2 is a distance function on C such that for A, B in C,

$$D_2(A, B) = \inf_{\theta,\phi,\varphi} D_1(A, B_{\theta,\phi,\varphi}).$$

D_2 defines a metric on $\mathcal{F}$. That is, for A, B and C in C,
(i) $D_2(A, B) \ge 0$
(ii) $D_2(A, B) = 0$ if and only if $A = B_{\theta,\phi,\varphi}$ for some θ, ϕ and φ
(iii) $D_2(A, B) = D_2(B, A)$
(iv) $D_2(A, B) + D_2(B, C) \ge D_2(A, C)$

2.2 Major and Minor Planes

For an object in C, its position and size are already normalized. In order to normalize its orientation certain planes of the object are considered as follows.

The *major plane* of an object is the one which minimizes the integral of the square of the perpendicular distance of the object points to the plane. The *minor plane* is the one which maximizes the above integral of the square of the perpendicular distance. The above two planes, it can be seen, pass through the centre of gravity of the object.

The equation of a plane in 3 dimensions may be given by $x\cos\alpha + y\cos\beta + z\cos\gamma - p = 0$ where $\cos\alpha$, $\cos\beta$, $\cos\gamma$ are the direction cosines of the normal to the plane from the origin and p is the length of that normal. The perpendicular distance from an arbitrary point (x, y, z) to the above plane is given by $|x\cos\alpha + y\cos\beta + z\cos\gamma - p|$.

The integral of the square of the perpendicular distance of the points in the object A to the plane is given by $\int_A (x\cos\alpha + y\cos\beta + z\cos\gamma - p)^2 da.$ .... (1)

We would like to find a plane (characterized by $\cos\alpha$, $\cos\beta$, $\cos\gamma$, p) which will minimize the above integral of the square of the perpendicular distance. It can be seen that the optimum p will be $\bar{x}\cos\alpha + \bar{y}\cos\beta + \bar{z}\cos\gamma$ where $(\bar{x}, \bar{y}, \bar{z})$ is the centre of gravity of A.

Let λ be the Lagrange's multiplier and $s_{xx} = \int_A (x - \bar{x})^2 da$, $s_{xy} = \int_A (x - \bar{x})(y - \bar{y}) da$ and so on. The optimum direction cosines are given by $[S + \lambda I]\underline{e} = \underline{0}$, where I is the identity matrix of order three,

$$S, \text{ the scatter matrix } = \begin{bmatrix} s_{xx} & s_{xy} & s_{xz} \\ s_{xy} & s_{yy} & s_{yz} \\ s_{xz} & s_{yz} & s_{zz} \end{bmatrix}$$

$$\underline{e} = \begin{bmatrix} \cos\alpha \\ \cos\beta \\ \cos\gamma \end{bmatrix} \quad \text{and} \quad \underline{0} = \begin{bmatrix} 0 \\ 0 \\ 0 \end{bmatrix}.$$

It can be seen that if $\lambda_1 \geq \lambda_2 \geq \lambda_3$ are the three eigen values of S and e_1, e_2, e_3 are the corresponding eigen vectors respectively, then (λ_1, e_1) will minimise (1) and (λ_3, e_3) will maximise (1). The former is the major plane which is the 3-D equivalent of the principal axis in the 2-D case. In other words, it is the plane of least inertia in 3 dimensions. An eigen value indicates the amount of scatter in the direction of the corresponding eigen vector.

If an object is rotated by some angles in 3 dimensions, then each of the major and minor planes of the object is rotated by the same angles in 3 dimensions [Parui and Banerjee, 1987].

2.3   Shape Distance Using Major and Minor Planes

The distance function $D_2(A, B)$ considers all possible rotations of the object B keeping the orientation of A unchanged. The computation to find the value of D_2 in this case will be costly in terms of computing time. So we propose another definition of shape distance D_3 on the basis of the major and minor planes.

The 3-dimensional orientation of an object is said to be *normalized* if its major plane coincides with the xy plane and its minor plane with the yz plane. It can be seen that this normalized orientation is always possible since the major and minor planes are perpendicular to each other. But it is not unique. Now, suppose A is an arbitrary object and A_1 is a rotation of A so that the orientation of A_1 is normalized. Suppose, E_1 is the rotation matrix which rotates an object about the z-axis by 180 degrees. E_2 and E_3 are the similar rotation matrices about the y-axis and x-axis respectively. It can be seen that $E_i E_j = E_k$ for all distinct i, j, k and $E_i E_i = I$, the identity matrix, for all i. Note that, for all i, the major and minor planes of $E_i A_1$, say A_{i+1}, are the xy and yz planes respectively, that is, the orientations of $E_i A_1$ are also normalized. In fact, there is no other rotation of A_1 which is normalized. Now, suppose B is another arbitrary object and B_1 is a rotation of B so that the orientation of B_1 is normalized. In the same way as above, B_2, B_3 and B_4 are defined.

For A and B in $\mathcal{C}$, i.e., for A and B having their centres of gravity at the origin and having unit volumes, we construct a shape distance function $D_3(A, B)$ as follows :

$$D_3(A, B) = \min_{i,j} D_1(A_i, B_j)$$

Now, since $D_1(A_i, B_j) = D_1(E_k A_i, E_k B_j)$ for all i, j, k, we can write

$$D_3(A, B) = \min_j D_1(A_1, B_j)$$

so that the minimum among four rather than sixteen values is to be computed to get the value of D_3. Like D_2, D_3 also defines a metric on shapes in $\mathcal{F}$.

2.4 Computational Techniques

Here the volumetric representation of a 3-D object is given by a 3-D binary matrix $M(i, j, k)$. That is, $M(i, j, k)$ is either 0 or 1. The volume of the object is computed as $a =$ the number of 1-voxels in the image matrix M. The centre of gravity is computed as $(\bar{i}, \bar{j}, \bar{k})$ where

$$\bar{i} = \left(\sum_{M(i,j,k)=1} i\right)/a, \qquad \bar{j} = \left(\sum_{M(i,j,k)=1} j\right)/a, \qquad \bar{k} = \left(\sum_{M(i,j,k)=1} k\right)/a.$$

The details of the algorithms used here for dilation and rotation of 3-D binary matrices (i.e. objects) are available elsewhere [Parui and Banerjee, 1988]. The factor for this dilation algorithm is arbitrary in the sense that it need not be an integer but can be any rational number so that an object with any volume can be dilated to any higher volume. Also, the dilation factor along each of the three axes is the same so that the shape of the object remains undisturbed through dilation. The rotation algorithm deals not only with angles that are multiples of 45 degrees but with any arbitrary angles in 3 dimensions and also preserves the shape of 3-D objects.

Suppose A and B are two 3-D objects whose shape distance D_3 is to be computed. Let A and B have the image matrices M and N respectively and volumes a and b respectively. Without loss of generality, suppose $a > b$. So, B is dilated to B_1 such that the volume of B_1 also is approximately equal to a. Due to the digital nature of the images involved, there will be small errors in the output image in general and in the output volume in particular. The error usually varies upto 5 per cent. Let the volume of B_1 be a'.

Then A and B_1 are translated to A_1 and B_2 respectively so that they have centres of gravity at $(0,0,0)$. Now A_1 and B_2 are rotated to A_2 and B_3 respectively such that the major planes of A_2 and B_3 coincide with the xy plane and their minor planes with the yz plane. Let $B_4 = E_1 B_3$, $B_5 = E_2 B_3$, $B_6 = E_1 E_2 B_3$. For two binary matrices $M(i,j,k)$ and $N(i,j,k)$, define $d'(M,N)$ as the number of voxels (i,j,k) such that $M(i,j,k)$ is not equal to $N(i,j,k)$. Suppose, M_1, N_1, N_2, N_3, N_4 are the binary matrices corresponding to A_2, B_3, B_4, B_5 and B_6 respectively.

Let $$d(A,B) = min[d'(M_1,N_1), d'(M_1,N_2), d'(M_1,N_3), d'(M_1,N_4)]/a''$$

where $a'' = (a + a')/2$ and division by a'' is for normalization. Note that d is the discrete form of D_3.

3 Conclusions

As described above, the characteristic planes have been used to normalize the orientation of an object. In some cases, this approach has certain shortcomings. For example, the regular objects, such as spheres, cubes and other regular polyhedrons, do not have unique characteristic planes, and hence the shape distance D_3 cannot be defined for them. Nearly regular objects also pose a problem. Slight distortions in such a shape may drastically change the characteristic planes, and consequently, two nearly same shapes may have a high value of D_3. Thus, it is not appropiate to use D_3 as a shape distance for regular or nearly regular objects. The shape distance D_1 can be useful for symmetry analysis of 3-D objects. Note that if an object is symmetric about a plane P then P coincides with one of the characteristic planes of the object. Suppose the reflections of an object A about its three characteristic planes are A_1, A_2 and A_3. Then $dev(A) = min[D_1(A,A_1), D_1(A,A_2), D_1(A,A_3)]$ gives a measure of deviation from symmetry. Clearly, $dev(A) = 0$ for symmetric A. Also, for a nearly symmetric object A, if $dev(A) = D_1(A,A_i)$, then the characteristic plane corresponding to A_i gives an approximate plane of symmetry of A.

So far we have considered shape to be invariant under translation, dilation and rotation. The definition of shape can be extended by making shape invariant under reflection also. In fact,

$$D_4(A,B) = min[D_3(A,B), D_3(A, refl(B))]$$

is a shape distance which is invariant under reflection, where A and B are any two 3-D objects and $refl(B)$ is the reflection of B around any plane.

As described earlier in the paper, the derivations of the characteristic planes involve computations of second order statistics. These computations involve all the voxels of the object and hence are of order n^3, where n is the side length of the object along each of the three axes. These computations can possibly be reduced by considering only the surface voxels instead of all the voxels of the object. The order of complexity in this case is $O(n^2)$. But finding the characteristic planes of an object on the basis of only the surface voxels has a drawback. These planes are quite sensitive to noise that may be present on the surface of the object while the characteristic planes computed on the basis of all the voxels of the object are less so.

It is possible to compute D_1 between two objects belonging to C on the basis of their octree representation. This can be done by making the centre of the octrees coincide with the centre of gravity of the objects and by considering the octree leaves which do not match in the two images. Let $dev_1(O_1, O_2)$ denote the number of voxels of mismatch between two octrees O_1 and O_2. Here, we are essentially making the octree representation independent of the position of the object. But, for the purpose of computing D_3 between two objects from C, their octree representations have to be independent of orientation also. Earlier in the paper, we have proposed a method of normalizing the orientation of an object on the basis of its characteristic planes where four different orientations of an object satisfy the normalizing condition. Let these four orientations of an object B have the octree representations O_1, O_2, O_3 and O_4, and let another object A have the octree representation O in any of the normalized orientations. Then

$$dev_2(A, B) = min[dev_1(O, O_1), dev_1(O, O_2), dev_1(O, O_3), dev_1(O, O_4)]$$

is the same as $D_3(A, B)$. Now, note that the derivations of all the four octree representations $O_i, i = 1, .., 4$, directly from the image is not necessary. There is a definite relationship among the O_i's of a given object. So we can first compute only one of the four octrees directly from the image and then find the other three from the first octree.

References

[Asada, 1985]
Asada H and Brady M. *The curvature primal sketch.* IEEE PAMI, 8(1), pp.2-14, 1986.

[Biderman, 1985]
Biderman I. *Human image understanding : Recent research and a theory.* Comp. Vision, Graphics and Image Processing, 32, pp.29-73, 1985.

[Brooks, 1981]
Brooks R. *Symbolic reasoning among 3-dimensional models and 2-dimensional images.* Art. Int., 17, pp.285-349, 1981.

[Chien and Aggarwal, 1986]
Chien CH and Aggarwal JK. *Identification of 3-D objects from multiple silhouettes using quadtrees/octrees.* Comp. Vision, Graphics and Image Processing, 36, pp.256-273, 1986.

[Connel, 1985]
Connel JH. *Learning Shape descriptions : Generating and generalizing models of visual objects*. MIT AI Tech. Report 853, 1985.

[Gibson, 1979]
Gibson JJ. *The Ecological Approach To Visual Perception*. Boston , Houghton Mifflin, 1979.

[Hoffman, 1983]
Hoffman D. *The interpretation of visual illusions*. Scientific American, 249(6), pp.154-162, 1983.

[Hoffman and Richards, 1986]
Hoffman JJ and Richards W. *Parts of recognition*. In : A.P. Pentland(ed), From Pixels to Predicates, Norwood N.J. : Ablex Publishing Corp., 1986.

[Marr and Nishihara, 1978]
Marr D and Nishihara HK. *Representation and recognition of three dimensional shapes*. Proc. Roy. Soc. B., 200, pp.269-291, 1978.

[Parui, 1984]
Parui SK, *Some Studies in Analysis and Recognition of 2-Dimensional Shapes*. Ph.D. Thesis, Indian Statistical Institute, Calcutta, 1984.

[Parui and Dutta Majumder, 1984]
Parui SK and Dutta Majumder D. *How to quantify shape distance for 2-dimensional regions*. Proc. 7th Int. Conf. on Pattern Recognition, Montreal, pp.72-74, 1984.

[Parui and Banerjee, 1987]
Parui SK and Banerjee DK. *A shape distance for 3-D objects*. Tech. Report, ECSU, ISI, 1987.

[Parui and Banerjee, 1988]
Parui SK and Banerjee DK. *Some operations on 3-D binary images for shape matching*. Proc. IEEE Int. Conf. on Systems, Man and Cybernetics, Shenyang and Beijing, 1988.

[Srihari, 1981]
Srihari SN. *Representation of 3-D digital images*. ACM Comp. Surveys, 13, pp.399-424, 1981.

[Ullman, 1984]
Ullman S. *Visual routines*. Cognition, 18, pp.97-159, 1984.

[Ullman, 1986]
Ullman S. *An approach to object recognition : Aligning pictorial descriptions*. MIT AI Memo No.931, 1986.

NEWSPAPER IMAGE UNDERSTANDING [1]

Venu Govindaraju, Stephen W. Lam, Debashish Niyogi,
David B. Sher, Rohini Srihari, Sargur N. Srihari, and Dacheng Wang

Department of Computer Science
State University of New York at Buffalo
226 Bell Hall
Buffalo, NY 14260, USA
srihari@cs.buffalo.edu

Abstract

Understanding printed documents such as newspapers is a common intelligent activity of humans. Making a computer perform the task of analyzing a newspaper image and derive useful high-level representations requires the development and integration of techniques in several areas, including pattern recognition, computer vision, language understanding and artificial intelligence. We describe the organization and several components of a newspaper image undertanding system that begins with digitized images of newspaper pages and produces symbolic representations at several different levels. Such representations include: the visual sketch (connected components extracted from the background), physical layout (spatial extents of blocks corresponding to text, half-tones, graphics), logical layout (organization of story components), block primitives (e.g., recognized characters and words in text blocks, lines in graphics, faces in photographs, etc.), and semantic nets corresponding to photographic and textual blocks (individually, as well as grouped together as stories). We describe algorithms for deriving several of the representations and describe the interaction of different modules.

1 Introduction

Paper documents continue to be the most common medium of information transmission in society. Understanding messages conveyed by printed documents such as newspapers is a common intelligent activity of humans. Making a computer perform the task of analyzing and understanding a newspaper is a challenging one. It requires the development and integration of techniques in several areas including pattern recognition, computer vision, language understanding and artificial intelligence.

Newspaper pages are a particularly good domain to study issues in document image understanding. They pose a challenge at the visual level since, their structure tends to

---

[1]This work was supported by the National Science Foundation grant IRI-86-13361 and by a grant from the Eastman Kodak Company.

involve several forms of information representation: textual, pictorial, and their combinations. They are large and yield poorer quality images than most office documents. On the other hand, at the level of understanding newspaper narrative, the task is considerably simplified due to the presence of headlines, which can evoke appropriate contextual frames.

We have divided the task into a set of conceptual levels: *document image analysis*, *document image recognition* and *document understanding*. Within these levels there are several interacting modules as follows: image acquistion, binarization, block segmentation, block classification, logical block grouping, character and word recognition, picture processing and analysis, graphics analysis, picture understanding, text understanding, and graphics understanding. The interactions between these processes are shown in Fig. 1. The following sections describe our work in developing some of the modules mentioned.

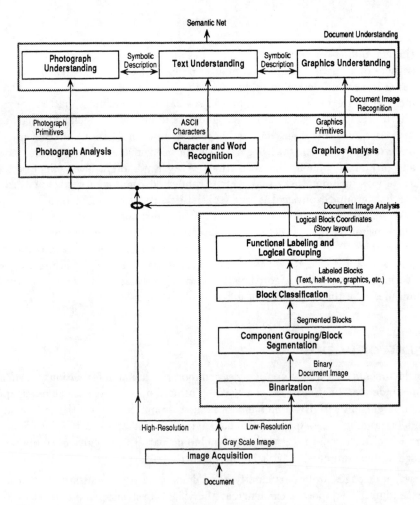

Figure 1: *Data flow between levels in document image understanding*

2 Block Segmentation and Classification

A newspaper page is first optically scanned with image resolution of 100 pixels per inch. A grey-scale image is obtained and then converted into a binary-valued image. This binary-valued image is the input data to the block segmentation and classification system. Fig. 2(a) shows a digitized newspaper page in binarized form.

The standard X-Y cuts technique as described in [Nagy *et al.*, 1985] is inadequate for documents with complicated layout structure like newspapers. In newspapers, articles are not always enclosed in standard rectangles, photographs and/or graphics may appear within the rectangle bounding an article, and often explicit lines demarcate the boundaries of some articles. We adopt a method that combines the connected component analysis and merging techniques. This works in three different stages consisting of connected component extraction, big component filtering, and text line merging.

All eight-connected black pixels are grouped together to form a single component and enclosed in a bounding rectangle. Features like coordinates, centroids, dimensional ratios, area of bounding rectangle, and black pixel density are computed for each component. Most of the components in a newspaper are character components which have different font and point size with small area. Photographs, graphics, boundary lines, and close bounding lines form the non-character components. The components corresponding to photographs or graphics have large area; dimensional ratio of boundary lines is very large (small); closed bounding lines have large area but small black pixel density. These attributes help filter the various components. If the dimensional ratio of a component is greater than a threshold then it is a line; if its area is greater than some threshold then it is a non-character component; if the black pixel density is less than a threshold then it is a close bounding line; else it is a photograph or a graphic. Character components are merged into individual text lines. If the edge-to-edge distance of every connected component with its lateral neighbors is less than some threshold then the components are merged (different thresholds are chosen for the different point sizes).

Characters in newspapers are classified as large point (head-line), medium-point (title), and small-point (story) using texture analysis [Wang and Srihari, 1989] based on the gray-level run length technique [Galloway, 1975]. Two new matrices have been designed: the black-white pair run length matrix and the black-white-black combination run length matrix. Three features are extracted from these matrices and the feature spaces created by these statistical measures are effectively used in classifying blocks into various predetermined categories. Fig. 2(b) shows the blocks generated by this system. The black rectangular blocks are classified as photographs or graphics; the dark grey blocks are the large point text, the light grey blocks are the medium point text, and the white blocks are the samll point text.

3 Functional Labelling and Logical Grouping

The process of deriving the logical structure of a document from the physical structure uses concepts from the field of *Office Automation Systems*. A detailed analysis of the process is as follows : After initial segmentation and block classification have been performed on a document image, we have a list of the different physical printed blocks in the image

378

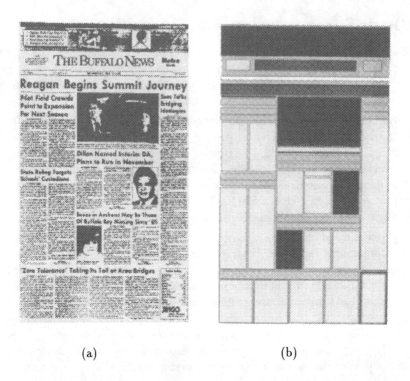

(a)   (b)

Figure 2: *(a) A binarized newspaper page image. (b) The result after the block segmentation and classification have been performed.*

with their positions on the document page as well as their class (photograph, line drawing, small-text, medium-text or large-text). This is the *physical* representation of the document page. For semantic understanding of a document image, we need to transform this physical representation into a *logical* representation that groups the logically related parts of the document together so that the document image can be further analyzed in terms of its logical component units rather than its physical component units. This task uses domain knowledge about document structure (e.g., in a newspaper, whether a "small-text" block is actually a photo caption or a regular story block). This involves representation of the physical layout of the document and inferring the spatial relations between the various printed blocks. The blocks are then labelled using this information and grouped into meaningful logical units (e.g. newspaper stories).

The assumption underlying the operation of this system is that a sufficient number of characteristics about each block in the image can be derived from the block segmentation and classification operations so that these blocks can be labelled and grouped without reading the text contained in any of these blocks, using knowledge about standard document layout conventions.

4 Character Recognition

The task of text recognition is to recognize a sequence of character patterns and to generate a string of plausible words for this sequence. The characters are machine printed and can appear in various fonts and point sizes. The image resolution is 200 pixels per inch. The character classifier is based on the structural and statistical approaches described in [Baird, 1988]. The classification process can be divided into two stages: *feature analysis* and *statistical feature classification*. The feature extractor looks for five types of features from a character: *stroke, hole, arc, and cross point*. A line Adjacency Graph(LAG) whose nodes represent dark segments in the run length code is used to represent a character. The LAG is transformed into a *compressed* LAG (c-LAG, [Pavlidis, 1986]) by grouping segments to form a path. The features can be detected by examining the path in the c-LAG and the relationships between the paths which belong to the same junction. For example, a path can be classified as a vertical or horizontal stroke based on its height-to-width ratio; a cross point is detected when a horizontal stroke is found between two vertical strokes. Fig. 3 shows the features extracted from a character "A". Each of the features extracted from a character is then normalized with respect

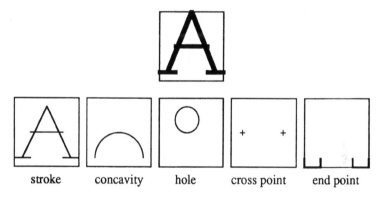

stroke   concavity   hole   cross point   end point

Figure 3: *Features extracted from a character "A".*

to the character size and is mapped onto a feature space. A feature mapping function extracts information from a feature and maps it onto a parameter space. Each feature class has its own feature mapping function and parameter space. The parameter spaces may have different dimensions depending on the amount of information needed from a feature for classification. Characters in the same class have features which tend to map closely together in the parameter space.

A binary feature vector is created from each parameter space by partitioning the dimensions of the parameter space into 5 equal-sized intervals and obtaining a cross product of these intervals. The five feature vectors are concatenated to form a global feature vector used by the Bayesian classifier [Duda and Hart, 1972]. The classifier is trained and tested with newspaper character images. The training and testing sets are different. It has about 98.5% accuracy if the testing characters are among the top three selected classes.

5 Photo Analysis

Any attempt to understand newspapers in their entirety must include a method of processing the photographs that appear in almost every newspaper page. As a first step towards this goal, we have focused on locating people in photographs. We have developed a model-based system to locate human faces in newspaper photographs [Govindaraju *et al.*, 1989]. Input to the system are scenes from newspaper photographs, parameters derived from the accompanying caption (expected number of faces, their sizes, ages etc.) and a model of a prototypical human face. The system returns the hypothesized location of human faces in the photograph (see Fig. 4).

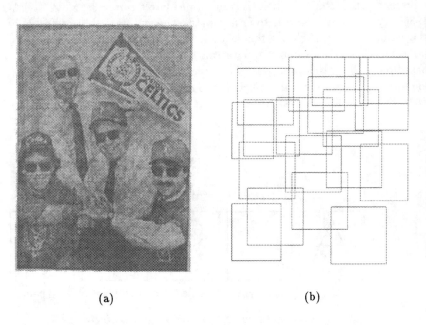

(a)   (b)

Figure 4: *(a) Grey scale image of a photograph with caption "Wearing their new Celtics sunglasses are Joseph Crowley, standing with penant, and seated from left, Paul Cotter, John Webb and David Buck". (b) Candidate regions generated by the image-processing modules.*

The algorithm is based on a hypothesis generation and testing paradigm. The candidate generation stage has three phases: feature selection, feature detection and grouping. Although most human faces have a definite shape, the contour is not analytical. Considering the points of discontinuities in curvature, we perceive the shape of the face as four *parts* [Hoffman and Richards]: the hair-line arc, the chin-line arc, and the two sides of face. Fig. 5 illustrates the model of the human face considered with the precise proportions of the various features. The *scale* (R) of the arcs is taken as the radius of the circular arc that best approximates the contour of the face. The size of the faces is thus derived in real-time from the image and it proves to be an important parameter to make qualitative descriptions of the people in the photograph.

Each feature of the face-contour is parametrically represented and extracted by adopt-

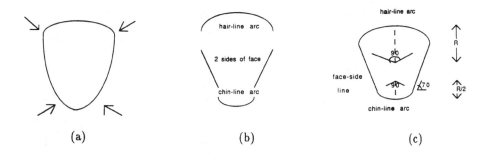

Figure 5: *The model of a human face: (a) The four features considered are the hair-line arc. (b) The chin-line arc. (c) The two sides of the face.*

ing Hough transform techniques. First the edge-image is obtained by a statistical edge-detector which has high sensitivity to orientation. Since, the next stage (Hough transform) is sensitive to the vertical lines and arcs (plausible parts of a face contour) it is useful to have accurate orientations to work with. A first-level Hough transform [Duda and Hart, 1972] detects the arcs and collinear edges in the image. A line-finder then uses back-projection from the accumulator array into the original image to extract line-segments. The curves and line segments are grouped together by a modified Hough transform to generate candidate regions for faces.

The next stage is to rank the candidates by their "facedness". We filter out some of the non-faces using measures like symmetry and black-pixel density. The remaining candidates are searched for face specific features like eyes and mouth. Proper spatial relations between these features verifies the candidates as faces.

6 Caption-Aided Picture Understanding

This section describes the implementation of a system which uses caption information to locate and identify human faces in newspaper photographs [Srihari and Rapaport, 1989]. Captions must be informative and serve to identify the faces in the picture as well as provide some contextual information such as time, place etc. It will be demonstrated that in many cases, caption information along with some heuristics derived from photo-journalism are sufficient to label faces, thus eliminating the need for a costly model-matching technique. Input to the system is a digitized image of a newspaper photograph with a caption, as in Fig. 4a. The system returns a labeling of parts of the image corresponding to the faces of the people mentioned in the caption, as in Figs. 6a and b. SNePS [Shapiro and Rapaport, 1987], a fully intensional, propositional semantic network processing system, is used to represent both language and pictorial information. A three-stage process is employed in order to identify human faces in the newspaper photograph.

The first stage extracts from the caption all information pertaining to the picture. An ATN grammar is used in order to parse the caption. Factual information present in the caption is recovered along with information about the structure of the picture which can be derived from the caption. There are three classes of heuristics used in order to recover

382

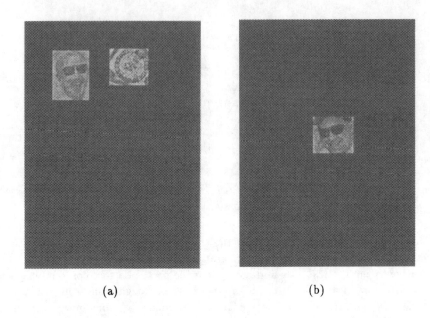

(a) (b)

Figure 6: *(a) output of system when asked to display Joseph Crowley (b) output of system when asked to display John Webb.*

this information: (a) those which predict the presence of human faces, (b) those which predict specific configurations of humans and (c) those which predict spatial relationships between faces. Sentence structure, specifically the position of noun-phrases and the use of certain verb phrases such as "greeting", "shaking hands" etc. is used in determining which people actually appear in the picture. Information such as "sitting", "standing", is translated into the appropriate spatial constraints and used in the identification stage. Finally, in cases where spatial constraints are not explicitly provided by the caption (e.g. centre, left), we have heuristics which derive them. The most commonly used rule is the implicit ordering of people in the picture which reflects their order of mention in the caption. This heuristic tends to be unreliable in the cases of well-known people or male-female pairs.

Fig. 7 illustrates the partial output of the parser on the caption of Fig. 4. It postulates that four humans, namely Joseph Crowley, Paul Cotter, John Webb and David Buck are present in the picture (nodes m38, m42, m46 and m50). Furthermore, it postulates that Joseph Crowley appears above the other three in the picture (since he is "standing") as represented by nodes m51, m52 and m53. The left to right ordering of the remaining three members is represented by the "left-of" relationship in nodes m54 and m55. A node such as m37 provides the link between the visual model of an object and the proper name it is associated with (in this case Paul Cotter).

The second stage in the face identification process consists of using the information in

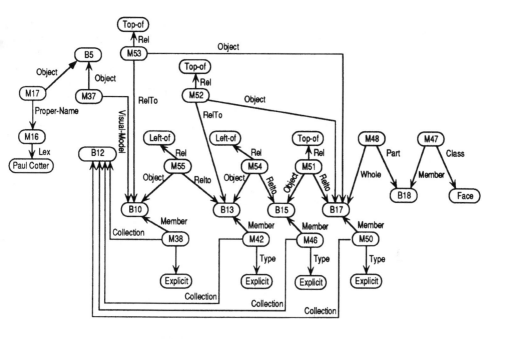

Figure 7: *Partial output of the parser on caption of Fig. 4(a)*

the hypothesised structure to find faces in the picture (described in a previous section). The third stage consists of further refinement of existing face candidates followed by labeling. Spatial constraints are first applied to the candidates generated by the face-locator in an attempt to produce all possible bindings of *model nodes* (SNePS nodes representing people predicted to be in the picture) and face candidates. Since we typically have more than one possible binding, it is necessary to evaluate the bindings and select the best binding(s). Refinement rules are used to prune out bad face candidates whereas identification rules are used for labeling. There are three classes of rules: (a) those which update the confidence of a candidate being a face (irrespective of who the face belongs to), (b) those which update the confidence of a *match* (an assignment of a face candidate to a model node) and (c) those which update the confidence of an entire binding. The final weight associated with a binding is computed using the above three types of confidences. In cases where the system cannot uniquely identify faces, all possible candidates for each person appearing in the caption are recorded as in Fig. 6a.

7 Conclusion

We have described several components of a knowledge based document image understanding system. Starting with a digitized newspaper image, we analyze the whole image in some instances and specific parts of the image, e.g., text blocks, photographs etc., in other instances. Each component uses local domain knowledge, and some of the components also contain extensive global domain knowledge about the document and include local control structures that guide their actions. A global control strategy to guide the entire document image understanding process is one of the components that is being developed, and will have access to a comprehensive base of domain and control knowledge.

The results obtained so far have been encouraging, and several interesting intermediate results have been obtained. Thus the prospects of significant results in the future are encouraging.

Acknowledgement

The authors would like to thank *The Buffalo News* for permission to use their pages in our research.

References

[Baird, 1988] H. Baird. Feature identification for hybrid structural/statistical pattern classification. *Computer Vision Graphics, and Image Processing*, 42:318–333, 1988.

[Duda and Hart, 1972] R.O. Duda and P.E. Hart. Use of the Hough transform to detect lines and curves in pictures. *Communications of the ACM*, 15:11–15, 1972.

[Galloway, 1975] M.M. Galloway. Texture Analysis Using Gray Level Run Lengths. *Computer Graphics and Image Processing*, 4:172–179, 1975.

[Govindaraju *et al.*, 1989] V. Govindaraju, D.B. Sher, R.K. Srihari, , and S.N. Srihari. Locating Human Faces in Newspaper Photographs. In *IEEE conference on Computer Vision and Pattern Recognition*, pages 549–555, 1989.

[Hoffman and Richards] D. Hoffman and W. Richards. *Parts of Recognition*, pages 268–293. Ablex Publishing Corporation.

[Nagy *et al.*, 1985] G. Nagy, S.C. Seth, and S.D. Stoddard. Document analysis with an expert system. In *Proceedings of Pattern Recognition in Practice II*, Amsterdam, 1985.

[Pavlidis, 1986] T. Pavlidis. A vectorizer and feature extractor for document recognition. *Computer Vision, Graphics, and Image Processing*, 35:111–127, 1986.

[Shapiro and Rapaport, 1987] S.C. Shapiro and W.J. Rapaport. Sneps Considered as a Fully Intensional Propositional Semantic Network. In Nick Cercone and Gordon McCalla, editors, *The Knowledge Frontier, Essays in the Representation of Knowledge*, Springer-Verlag, New York, 1987.

[Srihari and Rapaport, 1989] R.K. Srihari and W.J. Rapaport. Extracting Visual Information From Text: Using Caption to Label Human Faces in Newspaper Photographs. In *Proceedings of the 11th Annual Conference of the Cognitive Science Society*, pages 364–371, Ann Arbor, MI, 1989.

[Wang and Srihari, 1989] D. Wang and S.N. Srihari. Classification of Newspaper Blocks Using Texture Analysis. *Computer Vison, Graphics, and Image Processing*, 47:327–352, 1989.

Reasoning

Reasoning using Inheritance from a Mixture of Knowledge and Beliefs

Afzal Ballim,[α] Sylvia Candelaria de Ram,[β] & Dan Fass[γ]

[α]Institut Dalle Molle pour les   [β]Computing Research Lab   [γ]Centre for Systems Science
Etudes Semantiques & Cognitives New Mexico State University Simon Fraser University
Route des Acacias, 54   Las Cruces, NM   Burnaby, British Columbia
1227 Geneva, Switzerland   88003, USA   Canada V5A 1S6
afzal@divsun.unige.ch   *sylvia@nmsu.edu*   *fass@cs.sfu.ca*

Abstract

Certain inadequacies of homogeneous inheritance systems have caused an interest in *heterogeneous inheritance systems*. Heterogeneous representations allow for mixing of *'known'* relations (inherited through 'strict' links) and what is *'believed'* (inherits through 'defeasible' links). However, few well-founded systems have been proposed and heterogeneous systems have been considered to be not yet well understood. This paper presents a theory and implementation of a heterogeneous inheritance system. The principles of the system are that (i) *rules of composition* allow paths to be considered as single links (effective relationships), and (ii) *rules of comparison* allow selection of those effective relationships which state the most definite, specific information. These rules are enumerated and discussed, then an implementation of the theory is shown. An example of the operation of the system is explained in detail. Related recent work is noted.

1 Introduction

Inheritance systems have long been considered an important aspect of knowledge representation [Brachman, 1977; Fahlman, 1979; Fox, 1979; Carbonell, 1981]. Until recently, interest was focussed on *homogeneous inheritance systems with exceptions,* so called because they use one type of connection which expresses a relationship that can have exceptions, and (possibly) its negation. However, there are problems associated with these systems (see [Touretzky, Horty, & Thomason, 1987]), and any rich domain of knowledge often involves complex mixing of strict information (non-defeasible) and information that is defeasible. However, few such systems have been proposed.

This paper describes a heterogeneous inheritance system (a system that can contain both strict and defeasible information) in which reasoning is based on two groups of rules, (i) rules to generate the *effective relationship* stated by a chain of relationships (a path) between two objects, and (ii) and rules to compare effective relationships with the objective of selecting the most definite, specific effective relationship between the given objects. The system presented here is part of a more complex heterogeneous inheritance system which is described elsewhere [Ballim, Candelaria de Ram, & Fass, 1988a, 1988b].

A number of people have previously proposed heterogeneous inheritance systems. [Etherington 1987] has proposed using default logic to model inheritance reasoning. He suggests encoding defeasible links as default rules. However there is a problem with this approach in that a simple distinction is made between default and non-default derived statements, and this is insufficient for more complex cases of inheritance reasoning (see example in Section 3).

388

[Bacchus 1987] employs separate theories to explain strict and defeasible links. In those theories, strict links are grounded in the notion of set inclusion while defeasible links are viewed as statements about probability, so "P defeasibly IS-A Q" means that "greater than 50% of P's are Q's" [Bacchus 1987, p. 5]. Bacchus' theory has two main limitations. First, the theory specifies that a valid path may contain only one defeasible link, but valid paths with several defeasible links occur and must be treated. For example, birds are (defeasibly) flying things, and flying things are (defeasibly) things with wings (consider penguins and helicopters!). Second, probability is not a good basis for inheritance reasoning (cf. [Nutter 1987]). Many generalisations are not probabilistic (cf. [Rosch & Mervis, 1975]). Also, probability presupposes notions of sample spaces and ability to quantify actual probabilities. Even the use of Dempster-Shafer methods involves this [Shafer, 1976]; however, providing such probabilities is generally not possible (see [Nutter, 1987]). These problems with probability also apply to the use of probability in the approaches to reasoning developed by [Shastri and Feldman 1985] and by [Geffner and Pearle 1987].

The theory behind our system is described in Section 2, with its implementation being described in Section 3. Section 4 discusses some important issues and summarises the paper. In particular, it compares and contrasts our system with work recently first reported [Horty & Thomason, 1988], and which is similar to this work.

2 Path Precedence: A Heterogeneous Inheritance Theory

The theory presented here is called *path precedence theory* because it gives rules for assigning a precedence to the information expressed by some paths (chains of relationships) over other paths between the same two objects. There are two components to this theory: a representation and a process.

The Representation: The representation consists of objects divided into two types (individuals and classes), and of a set of relationship types. A relationship between an individual and a class is referred to as a *member* (m) relationship, while a relationship between a class and another class is referred to as an *inclusion* (i) relationship.

For flexibility, we put qualifications on the relationships, to be able to say if a given relationship is positive or negative, strict or defeasible. Although this gives eight combinations, only six of these are of interest to us. The two that are not are:

$$[d,+]m(I,C) \qquad\qquad [d,-]m(I,C)$$

which state, respectively, that some individual I is/is not defeasibly a member of a class C. The reason for (currently) disregarding these two combinations is that the meaning of "defeasible" for them is clearly different from the meaning of "defeasible" as applied to inclusion relationships and described by others (cf. Touretzky, 1986). What does "defeasible" mean as applied to inclusion relationships?

It has variously been taken to mean (i) there may be exceptions to the expressed relationship, (ii) the relationship holds for the typical case, (iii) in general the relationship holds, (iv) by default the relationship holds for a specific case unless known not to hold. We will tend towards taking the third interpretation in this paper, although without giving a formal definition of "in general."

We impose a further, important qualification on relationships. This is a comparative measure which enables us to give precedence to one effective relationship over another by indicating which we are more inclined towards accepting. This *inclination* qualifier (or, *leaning*, written as $\mathbb{L}^i, i \geq 0$, where lower index value indicates a greater inclination towards accepting the relationship) is similar to certainty levels of [Moore & Hutchins 1981], and the approaches of [Rescher 1968] and [Halpern & Rabin 1986] to likelihood reasoning.

The qualifier forms part of the *qualification tuple* of a relationship, and so relationships have one of the following forms:

$$[\mathbb{L}^i, s, +]i(C_0, C_1) \qquad [\mathbb{L}^i, d, +]i(C_0, C_1) \qquad [\mathbb{L}^i, s, +]m(I_0, C_0)$$
$$[\mathbb{L}^i, s, -]i(C_0, C_1) \qquad [\mathbb{L}^i, d, -]i(C_0, C_1) \qquad [\mathbb{L}^i, s, -]m(I_0, C_0)$$

The Process: The reasoning process is comprised of: (i) *rules of composition* which allow one to see a chain of relationships as an effective relationship (ER[1]) between the first and last object in the chain, and (ii) *rules of comparison* to select the "best" ER from a set of ERs, and to determine when one ER invalidates another.

(i) Rules of Composition: These rules allow a chain of relationships to be seen as an ER between the first and last object in the chain, if it is possible (not every chain has an ER). Each rule determines how a pair of relationships can be seen as a single ER. A chain of relationships is thus reduced to an ER by repeatedly applying these rules. The rules are given in tabular form below (Table 1[2]), where $\perp$ indicates that there is no effective relationship that can be drawn from the given pair.

$n_0 \to n_1 \to n_2$	$[{}^l, s, +]i(n_1, n_2)$	$[{}^l, s, -]i(n_1, n_2)$	$[{}^l, d, +]i(n_1, n_2)$	$[{}^l, d, -]i(n_1, n_2)$
$[{}^k, s, +]i(n_0, n_1)$	$[\mathbb{L}^{max(l,k)}, s, +]i(n_0, n_2)$	$[\mathbb{L}^{max(l,k)}, s, -]i(n_0, n_2)$	$[\mathbb{L}^{1+max(l,k)}, d, +]i(n_0, n_2)$	$[\mathbb{L}^{1+max(l,k)}, d, -]i(n_0, n_2)$
$[{}^k, s, -]i(n_0, n_1)$	$\perp$	$\perp$	$\perp$	$\perp$
$[{}^k, d, +]i(n_0, n_1)$	$[\mathbb{L}^{max(l,k)}, d, +]i(n_0, n_2)$	$[\mathbb{L}^{max(l,k)}, d, -]i(n_0, n_2)$	$[\mathbb{L}^{2+max(l,k)}, d, +]i(n_0, n_2)$	$[\mathbb{L}^{2+max(l,k)}, d, -]i(n_0, n_2)$
$[{}^k, d, -]i(n_0, n_1)$	$\perp$	$\perp$	$\perp$	$\perp$
$[{}^k, s, +]m(n_0, n_1)$	$[\mathbb{L}^{max(l,k)}, s, +]m(n_0, n_2)$	$[\mathbb{L}^{max(l,k)}, s, -]m(n_0, n_2)$	$[\mathbb{L}^{1+max(l,k)}, s, +]m(n_0, n_2)$	$[\mathbb{L}^{1+max(l,k)}, s, -]m(n_0, n_2)$
$[{}^k, s, -]m(n_0, n_1)$	$\perp$	$\perp$	$\perp$	$\perp$

Table 1. Rules of Composition.

The rules of composition in this table are inference rules. Each item from the left column and each item from the top row are antecedents, with the consequent being the item in the place where the row and column meet. They can be written separately in rule form. For instance,

$$\frac{[\mathbb{L}^k, s, +]i(n_0, n_1), [\mathbb{L}^l, s, +]i(n_1, n_2)}{[\mathbb{L}^{max(l,k)}, s, +]i(n_0, n_2)}$$

Much of the flexibility of these rules lies in the production of an inclination index for the consequent. The chosen function is to take the maximum index of the antecedents, and then to possibly add a constant to it. Remember, the lower the index, the more inclined we are to accept that the relationship holds. So, the "max" function encodes a maxim that can be phrased as *"the inclination towards a consequent can never be stronger than the weakest inclination towards any of its antecedents,"* i.e., a weakest link principle. In addition, the constants a categorisation of rules, in terms of the relative definiteness of their consequents. So, the rule for drawing an ER from two positive strict ERs gives a "stronger" consequent than the rule for drawing an ER from two positive defeasible ERs. An interesting point to note is that the above rules treat the following two chains differently:

---

[1] A relationship can be made into an effective relationship by giving it an inclination index of zero.

[2] The two columns not shown in this table are those where the second ER is a "member" type ER, and they are not shown because in every case no ER can be drawn from the pair.

$(c1)$ $[\ cj^0,d,+]i(A,B),[\mathbb{L}^0,s,+]i(B,C)$

$(c2)$ $[\ cj^0,s,+]i(A,B),[\mathbb{L}^0,d,+]i(B,C)$

The reason for this is our interpretation of "defeasible" as generally. In c1, all B's are C's, so all A's that are B's are also C's. Since generally A's are B's, then generally A's are C's. In c2, all A's are B's, and B's are generally C's. However, there is no guarantee that A's are not precisely the exception to B's being C's. So, the conclusion here is weaker than for c1. We will return to this in section 4.

(ii) Rules of Comparison: These rules are used to rank ERs against each other (for selection purposes) and to determine when one ER invalidates another. The rules are divided into four groups, named: *specialisation rules, conflict rules, invalidation rules,* and *precedence rules.*

Specialisation rules are used to derive that one effective relationship is stating information which is a specialisation of another effective relationship, e.g., saying that ALL elephants are mammals is a specialisation of saying that some elephants are mammals. If an effective relationship (ER1) is a specialisation of another (ER2), then this is written as "*ER*1 ⊣ *ER*2."

Conflict rules are used to derive that two effective relationships state contrary relationships between the objects, e.g., saying that all elephants are gray is contrary to saying that some elephants are not gray. If ER1 and ER2 are two effective relationships that conflict with each other, then this is written as "*ER*1 ⊗ *ER*2." Table 2 presents specialisation and conflict rules in a compacted form.[3]

$n_0 \rightarrow n_1$	$[\mathbb{L}^l s,+]i$	$[\mathbb{L}^l s,-]i$	$[\mathbb{L}^l d,+]i$	$[\mathbb{L}^l d,-]i$	$[\mathbb{L}^l s,+]m$	$[\mathbb{L}^l s,-]m$
$[\mathbb{L}^k s,+]i$	⊥	⊗	⊣ ,if $k \leq l$	⊗	⊗	⊗
$[\mathbb{L}^k s,-]i$	⊗	⊥	⊗	⊣ ,if $k \leq l$	⊗	⊗
$[\mathbb{L}^k d,+]i$	⊥	⊗	⊥	⊗	⊗	⊗
$[\mathbb{L}^k d,-]i$	⊗	⊥	⊗	⊥	⊗	⊗
$[\mathbb{L}^k s,+]m$	⊗	⊗	⊗	⊗	⊥	⊗
$[\mathbb{L}^k s,-]m$	⊗	⊗	⊗	⊗	⊗	⊥

Table 2. Rules of Comparison: conflict ⊗ and specialisation ⊣.

Invalidation rules determine when one ER makes another ER invalid. E.g., one relationship states that all elephants are gray, but another (which we are more inclined towards) states that some elephants are not gray, hence, invalidating the first. If ER1 invalidates ER2, then this is written as "*ER*1 # *ER*2," and we can say that ER2 is invalidated with respect to ER2 (written as "〖(*ER*1, *ER*2)"). We provide the following rules.

Invalidation Rule. *An ER is* invalid *there is a valid ER, which conflicts with, and is more inclined towards than the first.*

Validation Rule. *An ER is* valid *iff it is not invalidated by any valid ER, and iff all subchains of the chain of relationships from which it is derived are valid.*

Since every simple relationship is valid (simple relationships have inclination index zero, so cannot be invalid) it is possible to determine for any ER whether or not it is valid.

Precedence rules are used in selecting between competing relationships between two objects. I.e., they allow for a ranking of ERs. If ER1 takes precedence over ER2 then this is written as *ER*1/*ER*2. They precedence rules are given in schematic form below, where

---

[3] Both ERs must be between the same two objects, e.g., $[\mathbb{L}^k,s,+]i(A,B)$ and $[\mathbb{L}^k,s,-]i(A,B)$.

X_h is one of $\{s,d\}$, Y_i is one of $\{+,-\}$, and Z_j is one of $\{i,m\}$:

$$\frac{[\mathbb{L}^k,X_0,Y_0]Z_0(n_0,n_1),[\mathbb{L}^l,X_1,Y_1]Z_1(n_0,n_1),\ k<l}{[\mathbb{L}^k,X_0,Y_0]Z_0(n_0,n_1)/[\mathbb{L}^l,X_1,Y_1]Z_1(n_0,n_1)} \quad (P1)$$

$$\frac{[\mathbb{L}^k,X_0,Y_0]Z_0(n_0,n_1)\dashv[\mathbb{L}^l,X_1,Y_1]Z_1(n_0,n_1)}{[\mathbb{L}^k,X_0,Y_0]Z_0(n_0,n_1)/[\mathbb{L}^l,X_1,Y_1]Z_1(n_0,n_1)} \quad (P2)$$

We can now determine how a particular query of the form *"inherit(A,B)?"* should be answered:

- Let $T(A,B)$ be the set of valid effective relationships between objects A and B that can be derived.
- Define the precedence set of effective relationships between A and B as

$$P(A,B) = \{R_i \in T(A,B)\mid \text{there is no } R_j \in T(A,B) \text{ such that } R_j / R_i\}.$$

Now, responses to the query "inherit(A,B) ?" can be given according to the following:

(1a) answer "ambiguous"
 if for some $R_i \in P(A,B)$ there is $R_j \in P(A,B)$ such that $R_i \otimes R_j$,
(1b) answer "inconsistent"
 if conditions as for 1a, and inclination index of R_i and R_j is 0,
otherwise,

(2) answer "yes"
 if either
  $[\mathbb{L}^k,s,+]i(A,B) \in P(A,B)$,
  $[\mathbb{L}^l,d,+]i(A,B) \in P(A,B)$,
  or, $[\mathbb{L}^m,s,+]m(A,B) \in P(A,B)$,
(4) answer "no known relationship"
 if $P(A,B) = \varnothing$.

(3) answer "no"
 if either
  $[\mathbb{L}^k,s,-]i(A,B) \in P(A,B)$,
  $[\mathbb{L}^l,d,-]i(A,B) \in P(A,B)$,
  or, $[\mathbb{L}^m,s,-]m(A,B) \in P(A,B)$.

We now consider an implementation of this theory.

3 HETIS: A Path Precedence Inheritance Reasoner

HETIS is a program written in Quintus Prolog$^{(TM)}$ which implements the theory presented in Section 2. As an example, consider the network in Figure 1.

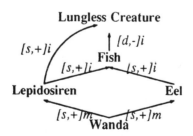

Figure 1. An inheritance network (Note heterogeneous link types s, d.)

Now, suppose we wish to determine whether "Wanda" can inherit the attributes of a "Lungless Creature," i.e., the query *inherit(Wanda,Lungless Creature)?* The program operates by iteratively searching out from the object "Wanda" to determine the set $P(Wanda,Lungless\ Creature)$. It does this by expanding only those partial chains (chains that have not yet ended at the "goal" object) that have precedence. This guarantees that the entire precedence set of ERs between the "source"(s) and "goal"(g) object have been found, even though the set $T(s,g)$ is not generated in its entirety.

At each intermediate stage in the processing, the program will have generated a number of partial chains (PCs). At stage i, the set of generated PCs is named $PC_i(s,g)$. Some of these PCs need not be considered further, because they cannot affect the final outcome. These are PCs that yield no effective relationship, invalid PCs, and PCs that end at an object that belongs to no superclasses (called a *leaf object*). Such PCs are called *discardable* and we name the set of these $DC_i(s,g)$. In addition, some chains may be valid, and yield an effective relationship between source and goal. The set of such *goal-complete* chains found up through stage i is $G_i(s,g)$.

The set of PCs which need to be considered further is named $T_i(s,g)$. Of these, those with precedence form the *precedence* set $P_i(s,g)$ and will be "expanded" for the next stage, while the remainder form the *leftover* set $L_i(s,g)$. At stage zero the situation is:

$$PC_0(s,g) = \{<[\mathbb{L}^0,s,+]bs\,(source,source),<[s,+]bs\,(source,source)>>\}$$
$$G_0(s,g) = \varnothing$$
$$DC_0(s,g) = \varnothing$$
$$T_0(s,g) = \{<[\mathbb{L}^0,s,+]bs\,(source,source),<[s,+]bs\,(source,source)>>\}$$
$$P_0(s,g) = \{<[\mathbb{L}^0,s,+]bs\,(source,source),<[s,+]bs\,(source,source)>>\}$$
$$L_0(s,g) = \varnothing$$
$$V_0(s,g) = \{<[\mathbb{L}^0,s,+]bs\,(source,source),<[s,+]bs\,(source,source)>>\},$$
$$\text{the set of valid ERs found to here}$$

where $<[\mathbb{L}^0,s,+]bs\,(source,source),<[s,+]bs\,(source,source)>>$ is a dummy effective relationship[4] used as a "boot-strap" for the process, and extra rules are employed to yield effective relationships from this. Now, inductively at stage $i+1$ the following is the situation:

$$PC_{i+1}(s,g) = \nabla\,P_i(s,g)\,\cup\,L_i(s,g)$$
$$G_{i+1}(s,g) = \{x\,|\,x\in PC_{i+1}(s,g),\,is\,valid\,and\,is\,of\,form\,ER(s,g)\}\,\cup\,G_i(s,g)$$
$$DC_{i+1}(s,g) = \{x\,|\,x\in (PC_{i+1}(s,g)-G_{i+1}(s,g))\,and\,is\,discardable\}$$
$$T_{i+1}(s,g) = PC_{i+1}(s,g)-G_{i+1}(s,g)-DC_{i+1}(s,g)$$
$$P_{i+1}(s,g) = \{x\,|\,x\in T_{i+1}(s,g),\,and\,there\,is\,no\,y\in P_{i+1}(s,g)\,such\,that\,y\,/\,x$$
$$nor\,such\,that\,y\,is\,more\,inclined\,towards\,than\,x\}$$
$$L_{i+1}(s,g) = T_{i+1}(s,g)-P_{i+1}(s,g)$$
$$V_{i+1}(s,g) = V_i(s,g)\,\cup\,\{x\,|\,x\in PC_{i+1}(s,g)\,and\,x\,is\,valid\}$$

Where $\nabla\,P_i(s,g)$ is an "expansion" of a set of partial chains, i.e., another set of partial chains. This expansion is defined as $\nabla\,P = \bigcup\limits_{x\in P} F(x)$, where $F(x)$ is the set of ERs formed as follows: say $x = ER(s,n_\alpha)$, and that there is a set of simple relationships $(R_{\alpha,*})$ such that all elements of it are of the form $SR(n_\alpha,n_{\beta_\lambda})$. Then, $F(x)$ is the set of effective relationships formed by applying rules of composition to each pair $ER(s,n_\alpha),SR(n_\alpha,n_{\beta_\lambda})$.

Members of $PC_{i+1}(s,g)$ can be validated as follows: (a) mark those that are invalidated by members of $V_i(s,g)$, (b) order the remainder according to increasing inclination index and beginning with lowest index eliminate those that they invalidate. This process terminates when either $P_i(s,g) = \varnothing$ for some i, or when every $R_{i,g}\in G_i(s,g)$ is more inclined towards than every $R_{i,p}\in P_i(s,g)$. At that stage, $G_i(s,g) = P(s,g)$, and the response can be generated according to the rules at the end of Section 2.

---

[4] An ER is a 2-tuple consisting of the ACTUAL ER, and the chain of simple relationships from which it is composed. The rules of composition and comparison are applied to the actual ERs.

So, for the query *inherit (Wanda ,Lungless Creature)?* the process works as follows (note: we abbreviate Wanda to "w", Lungless Creature to "lc", Lepidosiren to "l", Eel to "e", and Fish to "f").

$$G_0(W,LC) = DC_0(w,lc) = L_0(w,lc) = \varnothing \qquad \text{(stage 0)}$$
$$PC_0(w,lc) = T_0(w,lc) = P_0(w,lc) = V_0(w,lc)$$
$$= \{<[\mathbb{L}^0,s,+]bs(w,w),<[s,+]bs(w,w)>>\}$$

Now, expanding the ERs in the set $P_0(w,lc)$ yields:

$$PC_1(w,lc) = \{<[\mathbb{L}^0,s,+]m(w,l),<[s,+]bs(w,w),[s,+]m(w,l)>>,$$
$$<[\mathbb{L}^0,s,+]m(w,e),<[s,+]bs(w,w),[s,+]m(w,e)>>\}$$
$$G_1(w,lc) = \varnothing$$
$$DC_1(w,lc) = \varnothing$$
$$T_1(w,ls) = PC_1(w,lc) \qquad \text{(stage 1)}$$
$$P_1(w,lc) = PC_1(w,lc)$$
$$L_1(w,lc) = \varnothing$$
$$V_1(w,lc) = V_0(w,lc) \cup PC_1(w,lc)$$

Next, $P_1(w,lc)$ is expanded.

$$PC_2(w,lc) = \{<[\mathbb{L}^0,s,+]m(w,lc),<[s,+]bs(w,w),[s,+]m(w,l),[s,+]i(l,lc)>>,$$
$$< [\mathbb{L}^0,s,+]m(w,f),<[s,+]bs(w,w),[s,+]m(w,l),[s,+]i(l,f)>>,$$
$$< [\mathbb{L}^0,s,+]m(w,f),<[s,+]bs(w,w),[s,+]m(w,e),[s,+]i(e,f)>>\}$$
$$G_2(w,lc) = \{<[\mathbb{L}^0,s,+]m(w,lc),<[s,+]bs(w,w),[s,+]m(w,l),[s,+]i(l,lc)>>\}$$
$$DC_2(w,lc) = \varnothing \qquad \text{(stage 2)}$$
$$T_2(w,ls) = PC_2(w,lc)-G_2(w,lc)$$
$$P_2(w,lc) = T_2(w,lc)$$
$$L_2(w,lc) = \varnothing$$
$$V_2(w,lc) = V_1(w,lc) \cup PC_2(w,lc)$$

Although at stage two an ER has been found between "Wanda" and 'Lungless Creature," we continue processing because we could still come across ERs which conflict with the ER that has been found.

$$PC_3(w,lc) = \{<[\mathbb{L}^1,s,-]m(w,lc),$$
$$<[s,+]bs(w,w),[s,+]m(w,l),[s,+]i(l,f),[d,-]i(f,lc)>>,$$
$$< [\mathbb{L}^1,s,-]m(w,lc),$$
$$<[s,+]bs(w,w),[s,+]m(w,e),[s,+]i(e,f),[d,-]i(f,lc)>>\}$$
$$G_3(w,lc) = G_2(w,lc)$$
$$DC_3(w,lc) = PC_3(w,lc) \qquad \text{(stage 3)}$$
$$T_3(w,ls) = \varnothing$$
$$P_3(w,lc) = \varnothing$$
$$L_3(w,lc) = \varnothing \quad raboveV_3(w,lc) = V_2(w,lc)$$

While this stage yields two more ERs between "Wanda" and "Lungless Creature," they are both invalidated by the ER found at stage 2 because they conflict with it, but are less inclined-towards than it is. Now, $P_3(w,lc)$ is null, so we have reached a termination point and can examine the set of ERs between "Wanda" and "Lungless Creature." Doing so, we find there is only one ER, and that it states that "Wanda" is a "Lungless Creature"; hence the answer "yes" is returned.

4 Discussion

An alternative approach might be to, instead of regarding a path as a compound link by simply applying rules of composition (as in Table 1), construct some kind of path-weakening measure. This approach is not radically different, and can still provide a "well-defined and intuitively attractive theory of inheritance for IS-A hierarchies containing strict and defeasible link types mixed together", as its developers note [Horty and Thomason, 1988, p. 427]. An advantage of the uniformity of effective-link formation using composition rules as here is their ready extensibility. Any number of link types can be covered by adding each new type to the tables. (The same method is used, enlarging truth tables for connectives, to define newer, expanded logics.) In addition, the simplicity of tabular rules, which can be directly implemented as we have shown, permits optimizing any table entry by selecting a nicely behaved definition after straightforward experimentation using variants on interesting nets. Both the compound or effective link approach and a "complexity measure" approach for mixed link-type paths demonstrate the practicality of the heterogeneous net: Clearly, inheritance systems can be built as these are to accommodate both defeasibility and strictness of information nicely. They show that on the one hand the effect of strictness (representing 'knowledge', either positive unconditional connection or negation) is uniform in its categorical behavior. Defeasibility, on the other hand, is not categorical but cumulative in its effect. Chaining through the weaker links successively weakens the conclusiveness of what might be reached as a goal. This property of defeasibility does not necessarily require probabilistic quantification to describe variable link strengths or inclinations. The heterogeneous net as defined in our work contains homogeneous nets (links all strict or all defeasible, for example), as special cases. Neither is as potentially interesting as the many patterns of heterogeneity that are expressible with the more general system of representing of inheritable relations of knowledge *and* belief.

In summary, a theory of hetereogeneous inheritance and its implementation have been described. This theory is based on rules which allow chains of relationships to be considered as a single effective relationship. Hence the theory allows for comparison between chains without recourse to probabilistic measures. In addition, it is relatively easy to consider the effects of adding new relationship types.

References

[Bacchus 1987]

Bacchus, F. *A Heterogeneous Inheritance System Based on Probabilities.* Tech. Report 87-03, Alberta Center for Machine Intelligence and Robotics, Dept. of Computer Science, Univ. of Alberta

[Ballim et al, 1988a, b]

Ballim, A., D. Fass, and S. Candelaria de Ram. Resolving a clash of intuitions: Utilizing strict and defeasible information in inheritance systems. Memoranda in Computer and Cognitive Science, MCCS-88-119, Computing Research Laboratory, New Mexico State University, Las Cruces, NM 88003, USA.

Ballim, A., S. Candelaria de Ram, and D. Fass. *Some Foundations for Inheritance Systems.* ISSCO working paper 55, ISSCO, 54 Rte des Acacias, Geneva, Suisse.

[Brachman, 1977]

Brachman, Ronald J. *What's in a Concept: Structural Foundations for Semantic Networks.* International Journal for Man-Machine Studies 9: 127-152.

[Brachman, 1979]

Brachman, Ronald J. *On the Epistemological Status of Semantic Networks,* p. 3-50 in Associative Networks: Representation and Use of Knowledge by Computers (Nicholas V. Findler, ed.). Academic Press, New York.

[Brachman, 1983]

Brachman, Ronald J. *What ISA Is and Isn't: An Analysis of Taxonomic Links in Semantic Networks.* IEEE Computer 16(10): 30-36.

[Brachman, 1985]

Brachman, R. J. *I Lied About the Trees (or, Defaults and Definitions in Knowledge Representation).* AI Magazine 6(3): 80-93.

[Candelaria de Ram, 1982]

Candelaria de Ram, S. *Utilizing Fuzziness: Toward a Model of Language Dynamics,* invited applications paper, First North American Workshop on Fuzzy Information Processing, Ogden, Utah.

[Carbonell, 1981]

Carbonell, Jaime C. *Default Reasoning and Inheritance Mechanisms on Type Hierarchies.* SIGPLAN Notices 16(1): 107-109.

[Etherington and Reiter, 1983]

Etherington, D. W. and R. Reiter. *On Inheritance Hierarchies with Exceptions.* Proceedings of AAAI-83: 104-108, Washington, D.C.

[Etherington, 1987a, b, c, d]

Etherington, D. W. *Formalizing Nonmonotonic Reasoning Systems.* Artificial Intelligence 31: 41-85.

Etherington, D. W. 1987. *Relating Default Logic and Circumscription.* Proceedings of the 10th International Joint Conference on Artificial Intelligence: 489-494, Milan.

Etherington, D. W. *A Semantics for Default Logic.* Proceedings of the 10th International Joint Conference on Artificial Intelligence: 495-498, Milan.

Etherington, D. W. *More on Inheritance Hierarchies with Exceptions: Default Theories and Inferential Distance.* Proceedings of AAAI '87: 352-357, Seattle.

[Fahlman, 1979]

Fahlman, Scott E. *NETL: A System for Representing and Using Real-World Knowledge.* MIT Press, Cambridge, Massachusetts.

[Falkenhainer et al, 1986]

Falkenhainer, B., K. Forbus, and D. Gentner. *The Structure-Mapping Engine.* Proceedings of the Fifth National Conference on Artificial Intelligence: 272-277, Philadelphia.

[Fass, 1987]

Fass, Dan C. *Semantic Relations, Metonymy, and Lexical Ambiguity Resolution: A Coherence-Based Account.* Proceedings of the 9th Annual Cognitive Science Society Conference: 575-586. University of Washington, Seattle.

[Findler, 1979]

Findler, N. V. *Associative Networks: Representation and Use of Knowledge by Computers* (Nicholas V. Findler, ed.). Academic Press, New York.

[Fox, 1979]

Fox, M. S. 1979. *On Inheritance in Knowledge Representation.* Proceedings of the 6th International Joint Conference on Artificial Intelligence (IJCAI-79): 282-284, Tokyo, Japan.

[Geffner and Pearle, 1987]

Geffner, H., and J. Pearle. *Sound defeasible inference.* Technical report TR CSD870058, Cognitive Systems Lab, UCLA, Los Angeles, CA 90024-1596.

[Halpern and Rabin, 1987]

Halpern, J. Y. and M. O. Rabin. *A Logic to Reason about Likelihood.* Artificial Intelligence 32: 379-405.

[Horty and Thomason, 1988]

Horty, J. F. and R. H. Thomason. *Mixing Strict and Defeasible Inheritance*. Proceedings of the 7th National Conference on Artificial Intelligence (AAAI-88): 427-432, St. Paul, Minnesota.

[Horty et al, 1987]

Horty, J. F., R. H. Thomason, and D. S. Touretzky. *A Skeptical Theory of Inheritance in Nonmonotonic Semantic Networks*. Proceedings of AAAI '87: 358-363, Seattle.

[Moore and Hutchins, 1981]

Moore, G. W. and G. M. Hutchins. *A Hintikka possible worlds model for certainty levels in medical decision making*. Synthese 48: 87-119.

[Nado and Fikes, 1987]

Nado, R. and R. Fikes. *Semantically Sound Inheritance for a Formally Defined Frame Language with Defaults*. Proceedings of AAAI '87: 443-448, Seattle.

[Nutter, 1987a, b]

Nutter, J. T. *Uncertainty and Probability*. Proceedings of the 10th International Joint Conference on Artificial Intelligence, V. 1: 373-379, Milan.

Nutter, J. T. *Default Reasoning*. p. 840-848 in Encyclopedia of Artificial Intelligence (S. C. Shapiro, ed.). John Wiley, New York.

[Peters and Shapiro, 1987]

Peters, S. L. and S. C. Shapiro. *A Representation for Natural Category Systems*. Proceedings of the 10th International Joint Conference on Artificial Intelligence: 140-146, Milan.

[Rescher, 1968]

Rescher, N. *Topics in Philosophical Logic*. Reidel, Dordrecht.

[Rosch and Mervis, 1975]

Rosch, E., and C. Mervis. *Family resemblances: Studies in the internal structure of categories*. Cognitive Psychology 7: 573-605.

[Sandewall, 1986]

Sandewall, Eric. *Nonmonotonic Inference Rules for Multiple Inheritance with Exceptions*. Proceedings of IEEE V 74 (No. 10; October, 1986): 1345-1353.

[Shafer, 1976]

Shafer, G. *A mathematical theory of evidence*. Princeton University Press, Princeton, NJ.

[Shastri and Feldman, 1985]

Shastri, L. and J. A. Feldman. *Evidential Reasoning in Semantic Networks: A Formal Theory*. Proceedings of the 9th International Joint Conference On Artificial Intelligence: 465-474, Los Angeles.

[Touretzky, 1986]

Touretzky, D. S. *The Mathematics of Inheritance Systems*. Morgan Kaufman Publishers, Los Altos, California.

[Touretzky et al, 1987]

Touretzky, D. S., J. F. Horty, and R. H. Thomason. *A Clash of Intuitions: The Current State of Nonmonotonic Multiple Inheritance Systems*. Proceedings of the 10th International Joint Conference on Artificial Intelligence: 476-482, Milan.

Handling Multiple Inheritance with Exceptions : An Alternative Approach

Sanjay Bhansali   Mehdi T. Harandi
Dept. of Computer Science
Univ. of Illinois at Urbana-Champaign
1304 W. Springfield Av., Urbana, IL 61801
Email : bhansali@cs.uiuc.edu   harandi@cs.uiuc.edu

Abstract

The design of inheritance systems that allow multiple inheritance combined with exceptions poses some difficult problems. Any good theory of inheritance should meet two, sometimes complementary, goals: it should provide answers that correspond to human intuition, and it should be backed by a simple and rational reasoning process. We propose a method for reasoning with inheritance hierarchies that focuses on differences of nodes from a common ancestor in the hierarchy to derive the set of properties inherited by a node. We show the application of the algorithm to some of the classic examples in inheritance systems, compare their results with ours, and discuss the rationale behind our approach.

1   Introduction

The importance of organising knowledge in a hierarchical manner, using inheritance, has been known for a long time [Brachman et al, 1983], [Fahlman, 1979], [Touretsky, 1986]. Such systems enable information to be abstracted and stored as a general concept, from which specific concepts inherit properties. The two primary advantages to be gained by such a representational scheme is space and computational efficiency.

In AI research, the need for *multiple* inheritance systems has been emphasized, where a more specific concept may inherit information from more than one general concept. A practical requirement for both single and multiple inheritance systems is that they allow for *exceptions* . The classical example is that of the concept *ostrich,* which should inherit all the properties of the concept *bird* except certain ones, like the property of being able to fly.

Techniques for dealing with exceptions in single-inheritance systems and for dealing with multiple inheritance systems without exceptions are well known. However, dealing with multiple inheritance with exceptions is much more difficult. The challenge is to design systems that provide the correct answer in cases where humans are able to resolve an ambiguity easily, and to report an ambiguity when there is no intuitively clear answer.

In [Sandewall, 1986], Sandewall presents a collection of inheritance structure types and argues that these should be considered as the current definition of the semantics for inheritance systems. Any new theory for inheritance should be calibrated against that semantics to verify its soundness. In this paper, we present a method for reasoning with inheritance hierarchies that focuses on differences of nodes from a common ancestor to derive the set of properties inherited by a node. We describe how the algorithm can be applied to two different schemes of representing information in inheritance nets. We then consider each of the structure types in [Sandewall, 1986] and show how our algorithm handles them, and discuss the rationale behind our approach.

2 Notion of Types

There are two basic ways of representing information in an inheritance net. In systems like NETL[Fahlman, 1979] and TMOIS[Touretsky, 1986], each node in the net represents an abstraction and the edges between the node represent class relationships. Thus the fact that Clyde is an elephant with four legs and is colored gray, would be represented by creating an abstraction for four-legged things, gray things and elephants. A possible inheritance scheme for Clyde is shown in Fig. 1a. We call such nets Type A.

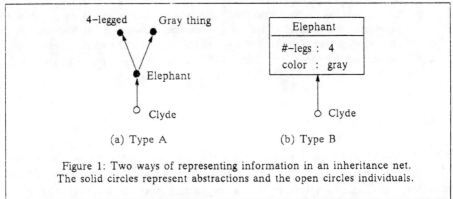

Figure 1: Two ways of representing information in an inheritance net. The solid circles represent abstractions and the open circles individuals.

Another way of structuring the inheritance net is to consider a type to be a collection of properties. Fig. 1b shows a possible inheritance scheme for Clyde in this scheme, which we call Type B. Such a view is adopted in FRL[Roberts and Goldstein, 1977] and in [Padgham, 1988], although in the latter the notion of a type is further refined to include two clusters of properties - the type *core* and the type *default*.

The representation of exceptions is different in the two types of nets. In Type A, exceptions are represented by a negative link, which is drawn as a hatched arrow from a node to the property that is to be cancelled. Thus, the fact that a royal elephant is not colored gray is represented by a negative link from *Royal elephant* to *Gr ay thing* as shown in Fig. 2a. The same information is represented in type B nets by overriding the color information in the node for royal elephant, as shown in fig. 2b. Clyde inherits the color property from the royal-elephant node and the other properties are inherited from the elephant node.

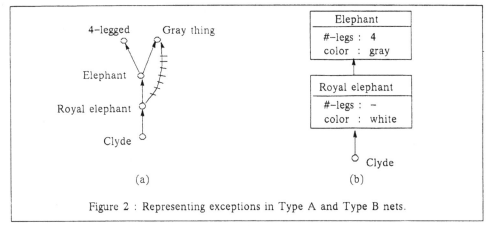

Figure 2 : Representing exceptions in Type A and Type B nets.

3   Reasoning in Type B Networks

We start with an example to give the intuition behind our algorithm. This example has been chosen from the domain of Unix programming, for which the algorithm was initially implemented.

The Unix operating system contains a set of commands that perform certain functions, like *ls* (listing directory contents), *grep* (searching patterns in a file), etc. Most of these commands have certain options associated with them, which extend the functionality of the commands in various ways. For example, the command *grep* produces a list of lines present in a file that contain a particular pattern. One of its options is *-n*; *grep -n* produces a list of lines as well the line number of each line in the file.

It is possible to combine different options to form a composite command. Thus *grep -vn* is a command that performs the functions of *grep -v* and *grep -n* (where-*v* is another option for *grep*). With n options there are 2^n potential commands obtained by taking various combinations of the options. In representing the knowledge of Unix commands in a knowledge base we would like to represent explicitly only the information about each individual option, and the functionality of commands which combine several options should be obtained automatically.

A partial description of how the *grep* command is represented in our system is shown in fig. 3. The description shows the functionality of each command together with certain relationships between the input and output arguments. Thus, *grep -v pat file* prints those lines in *file* that do not contain the pattern *pat*. The question we are interested in is: *what does* grep -vn *pat file do?*

This is a case of multiple inheritance with exception, because *grep -v* cancels the property *occurs(pat, line)*. So a simple union of the constraints will be inconsistent as it will contain both the clauses *occurs(pat, line)* and ¯*occurs(pat,line)*. The correct answer is obtained by using the following formula:

$$\text{Fn(Grep -vn)} = \{\text{Fn(grep -n) - Fn(grep)}\} \cup \{\text{Fn(grep -v) - Fn(grep)}\} \cup$$
$$\{\text{Fn(grep)} \cap \text{Fn(grep -n)} \cap \text{Fn(grep -v)}\}$$

where Fn(x) is the description of the command x and includes both the *Func* and

400

Constraints slot. The '-' is the set difference operator applied to the set of clauses comprising the *Func* and *Constraints* slot of the node. In the above example, this reduces to the two equations:

Func(grep -vn) = {list num} ∪ { } ∪ {list line} = {list num, list line}

Constraints(grep -vn) = {(= (line# line file) num)} ∪ {˜(occur pat line)} ∪

{(occur line file)}

= {(= (line# line file) num),˜(occur pat line), (occur line file)}

To understand how this formula works, notice that the first two terms isolate the extra functionality provided by the *grep -n* and *grep -v* commands. These in some sense reflect the reason for creating the two new commands. Therefore, it is reasonable to expect that any command that inherits directly from these commands should contain at least these functionalities. At the same time the new command should have the functionalities/properties that get inherited by both *grep -n* and *grep -v*, i.e. those functionalities which have not been cancelled during the paths from *grep* to *grep -v* and *grep* to *grep -n*. These common functionalities are obtained by the last term that takes the intersection of the three functionalities.

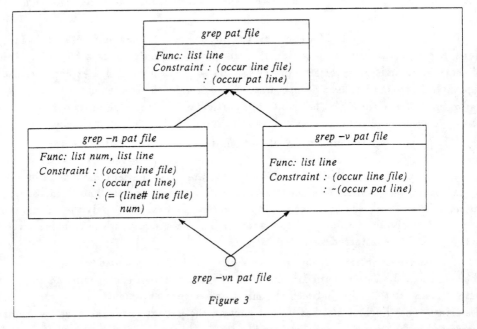

Figure 3

This idea can be generalized to the case when there are intermediate nodes in the path from the common ancestor and when a node inherits from more than two parents.

We first define a few terms. Let N denote the set of nodes in the inheritance net. The inheritance relation induces a partial order (N, ⊑) on the nodes in the inheritance graph such that $a \sqsubseteq b$ iff a ISA b. Let S be a subset of N. A node $u \in$ N is an upper bound of S if $s \sqsubseteq u$ for all $s \in$ S. u is said to be the *least upper bound* or the *lowest common ancestor* if u is the least element of the set of all upper bounds of S. The lowest common ancestor need not be unique. Therefore, we use the term *lowest common ancestor set* to denote the entire set of lowest common ancestors of the nodes.

The algorithm for multiple inheritance in type B networks is given below. (Note that we omit the case when a node has a single parent, for simplicity).

M-inherit-B(plist)

plist is a list of parent nodes $(P_1, P_2, ..., P_n)$ *from which a node inherits directly. In the following, we use the name of a node to denote the properties at that node too, relying on the context to distinguish between the two usages.*

1. For each pair $(P_i, P_j) 1 \leq i, j \leq n, i \neq j$, find their lowest common ancestor set LCA_{ij}. Let LCA denote the union of the properties of all LCA_{ij}. (It is possible that LCA contains contradictory clauses).

2. Compute
$$P'_i = \bigcup_{i=1,n} (P_i - LCA)$$
Let P' denote the union of all the P'_i.

3. Compute $LCA'_{ij} = P_i \cap P_j \cap LCA_{ij}$ we for i=1,n. Let LCA' denote the union of the properties of all LCA'_{ij}.

4. Compute $C = P' \cup LCA'$. If C contains contradictory literals report ambiguity, else return C. { *C is the set of properties inherited by the node.*}

A few comments need to be made about the algorithm. Step 2 is used to obtain those properties that are due to the parent nodes independent of a common ancestor. Step 3 is used to get those properties of a common ancestor that are inherited by the parent nodes. If these two sets of properties result in one or more contradictory properties to be inherited, the algorithm reports an ambiguity in step 4.

Figure 4 gives examples of two nets and the properties inherited by the node using this algorithm.

For Figure 4a, $plist = \{C, D, E\}$ and assume that $\{A\}$ and $\{B\}$ are the lowest common ancestor sets of $\{C, E\}$ and $\{D, E\}$ respectively:

$LCA = P_A \cup P_B = \{a, \tilde{a}, b, c\}$
$P' = \{d\} \cup \{c, e\} \cup \{g\} = \{c, d, e, g\}$
$LCA'_{CE} = \{b\}; LCA'_{DE} = \{a\}; LCA'_{CD} = \phi$
$LCA' = \{a, b\}$
$LCA'' = LCA$
$P(F) = \{c, d, e, g\} \cup \{a, b\} = \{a, b, \tilde{c}, d, e, g\}$

For Figure 4b, $plist = \{D, E\}$ and assume $\{A, B, C\}$ to be the lowest common ancestor set:

$LCA = P_A \cup P_B \cup P_C = \{a, b, c, d, \tilde{e}\}$
$P' = \{f\} \cup \{c, e, \tilde{f}\} = \{c, e, f, \tilde{f}\}$

402

$$LCA'_{DE} = \{a, b, d\} = LCA'$$
$$LCA" = LCA'$$
$$P_F = \{\tilde{c}, e, f, \tilde{f}\} \cup \{a, b, d\} = \{a, b, \tilde{c}, d, e, f, \tilde{f}\}$$

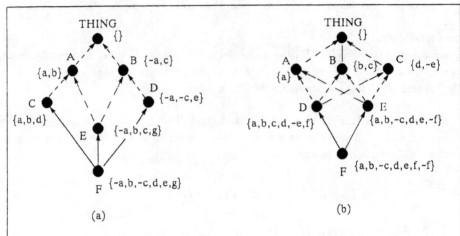

Figure 4. Two examples of multiple inheritance. The solid line indicates a direct link between two nodes, whereas the dashed line indicates a path containing 0 or more intermediate nodes.

A few interesting observations can be made from these examples. In example 4a, the parents of node F, have contradictory properties (~a and a , c and ~c). However some of these properties are present in their common ancestors whereas some of them are obtained due to cancellation of the properties of the parents at some point in the path from the common ancestor to the parent nodes (the path includes the parent node). According to our algorithm, differences in properties between the parent node and the common ancestor are important. Thus, in the case of a conflict between two contradictory literals, the literal that is derived from a parent node is preferred to a literal that is derived from the ancestor set.

To make this point clear, consider the example in Figure 5. X is a Trained-ostrich and a Caged-bird. Both Trained-ostriches and Caged-birds are Birds. However, the important difference between a Trained-ostrich and a Bird is that a Trained-ostrich has some ostrich-like features not found in typical birds, whereas the important difference between a Caged-bird and a Bird is that a Caged-bird cannot fly. Since these differences are assumed to be important, an individual that is both a Trained-ostrich and a Caged-bird should not be able to fly, which is the result obtained by our algorithm.

Figure 4b presents a case where there is an ambiguity. In this case contradictory feature {f, ~f} inherited from the parents cannot be resolved, because neither of these features is present in a common ancestor. Therefore, it is not clear which of these features should be considered more important. For the example in Figure 5, this would occur if the property {Can-fly} is removed from the node BIRD. Now, it is ambiguous whether X can fly or not.

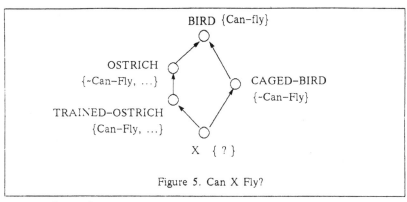

Figure 5. Can X Fly?

4 Reasoning in Type A Networks

We now consider type A networks and see how our algorithm can be applied to it. As has been mentioned earlier, such networks use a negative link from a node x to a node y to denote that x is not a (NISA) y. Such a link implies that x contradicts y in at least one property. However, unlike in type B networks, we cannot identify which property is to be cancelled. Therefore, the chain of reasoning cannot be carried further than one NISA link. For this reason, the paths allowed by [Touretsky, 1986], [Padgham, 1988], etc. are of the form:

$$< x_1, x_2, ... x_{n-1}, x_n >$$

where x_i ISA x_{i+1} for i=1,n-2, and only the last link may be a negative link, x_{n-1} NISA x_n. To reason with nets of this type we make the following two modifications:-

1. With each node N, create a dummy property n, which says that node N has the property of belonging to the class of objects of type N.

2. In following a path from a node to its ancestors whenever a negative link is obtained, mark the node at the head of the link as a terminal node.

The reason for the second step is that while ISA is transitive, NISA is not. Therefore if an object A NISA Y and B NISA A, then it does not follow that B NISA Y. Hence, all properties inherited by A are invalidated. This is accomplished by marking the node as a terminal node, which means that the node does not inherit any properties from a node above it.

With these transformations, the same algorithm given in section 3 can be used, with a minor modification: when a node inherits from another node through a NISA link the property that is inherited gets negated.

4.1 Examples

In figure 6 we give the results of applying this algorithm to the structure types given in [Sandewall, 1986].

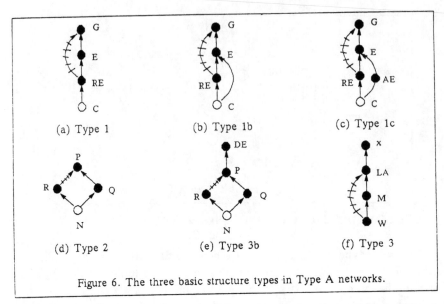

(a) Type 1   (b) Type 1b   (c) Type 1c

(d) Type 2   (e) Type 3b   (f) Type 3

Figure 6. The three basic structure types in Type A networks.

Figure 6a represents the facts - Clyde is a royal elephant, royal elephants are elephants but not gray, and elephants are gray. Using our algorithm, we get for the properties of Clyde:

$$P_{RE} = \{g, e, re\} = P_C$$

Thus Clyde is an elephant and a royal elephant, but is not gray.

Figure 6b is similar to figure 6a, with the redundant link Clyde ISA elephant added. The addition of such a link should not affect the conclusions about Clyde. Using our algorithm, we get the same result as before for RE:

$$P_{RE} = \{g, e, re\} = P_C$$

Thus, again Clyde has the same properties.

In figure 6c, an extra node, African elephant is inserted between Clyde and elephant. The properties inherited by C is given by:

$$P_C = \{g, e, re, ae\}$$

Thus, Clyde is a non-gray, African royal elephant.

Figure 6d is the *Nixon diamond* problem and represents the relations - Nixon is a Republican and a Quaker, Quakers are Pacifists, Republicans are not Pacifists. We need to determine whether Nixon is a Pacifist or not. Using the algorithm, we get:

$$P_N = \{p, r, q\}$$

Nixon is a republican, a quaker but NOT a Pacifist.

Figure 6e is similar to figure 6d, with the added link that Pacifists are draft-evaders. This link will not affect the outcome about Nixon, because we make P a terminal node and hence all nodes that lie above P are discounted. Therefore, we again get:

$$P_N = \{p, r, q\}$$

i.e., we cannot make any conclusion about whether Nixon is a draft-evader or not.

Figure 6f represents the relationship - Whales are mammals, mammals are land animals, land animals are x, and whales are not land animals. We want to determine if whales are x. Using the algorithm on node W, we get:

$$P_W = \{\bar{l}a, m\}$$

Thus, whales are mammals, but not land-animals, whereas we cannot conclude anything about their being x.

If we add a link from M to x to the example of figure 6e, then LCA, and LCA' remain the same. However, $P'_M = \{m, x\}$. Hence, $P_W = \{\bar{l}a, m, x\}$ Thus, in this case Whales would be x's. This seems intuitively correct because now there is an independent reason for drawing the conclusion that whales are x's which does not depend on their being a land animal.

5 Discussion of the Results

Most of the results obtained above offer no surprises and correspond to our intuition. For figures 6a, 6b, 6c, 6e and 6f the results agree with those in [Touretsky, 1986], [Sandewall, 1986],[Padgham, 1988]. However, for figure 6d, our results are different from those in the above works. According to those algorithms, the question of whether Nixon is a Pacifist or not cannot be answered unambiguously. Notice, that this is the same structure as the *grep -vn* example in Unix. Surprisingly enough, when people are shown the two structure and asked about the properties inherited, most people agree that the Nixon diamond is ambiguous, but have no trouble in arriving at the correct conclusion regarding the functionality of *grep -vn*. (In fact, the Unix manual simply states what the *-n* and *-v* option for grep do without specifying what the *-nv* option does).

A natural criticism of our work is that since the Nixon diamond is confusing, an algorithm that adopts a *credulous* or *skeptical* view ([Touretsky et. al., 1987]) and reports an ambiguity would be preferable. We point out that our algorithm *is* skeptical and reports an ambiguity, when it derives contradictory clauses (step 4 of the algorithm). It is simply that the intuition underlying our approach is different. In TMOIS and other systems the intuition underlying inheritance with exceptions is that claims about sub-classes are more specific and should be allowed to override superclasses. This intuition is captured by using a measure called *inferential distance ordering* in TMOIS.

Our intuition leads us to the assumption that *for a given context properties of a node that differ from its parents are more significant than the properties inherited*. The *context* is defined by the set of all the nodes from which a node directly or indirectly inherits properties. The justification for this assumption is that if a node were identical to one of its parents, there would be no reason to create it at all. The differences reflect, in a sense, the reason for creating a node as opposed to its parent. The reason the Nixon diamond is confusing is that it is being viewed without a context. In a realistic system one would not have an isolated structure as shown in fig. 6 d. (If we did, there is essentially no difference between a Quaker and a Pacifist and one would replace it by a direct link from Nixon to Pacifist. For such a structure our algorithm *does* report an ambiguity). There would be other properties of a Quaker, possibly inherited from other nodes. When compared against a Republican these properties become independent

properties of a Quaker and are considered more important than the inherited property
of being a Pacifist. For a Republican, however, the property of being a non-Pacifist is
quite significant and, infact, it is quite plausible that the Republican node has no other
properties and is simply a synonym for non-Pacifist. Therefore our algorithm concludes
that Nixon is not a Pacifist.

Finally, note that the assumption in TMOIS and other systems follows as a special
case of our assumption, an observation that is empirically validated by the examples of
figure 6a-c,6e and 6f.

6 Conclusions

We have presented an algorithm for multiple inheritance in acyclic graphs that focuses
on differences of nodes from a common ancestor, and identifies those properties that
seem 'intuitively' important, to determine the set of properties inherited by a node.
It can be used, with minor modifications, on nets in which a node represents an abstraction of some properties. The algorithm has been implemented for an automatic
programming system in the domain of Unix programming, where it is used to represent
and reason about the functionality of Unix commands. It has been tried on a representative sample of Unix commands and has produced answers that correspond to the
actual functionality of the commands.

References

[Brachman et al, 1983] Brachman, R.J., Fikes, R.E. and Levesque, H.J. KRYPTON:
A Functional Approach to Knowledge Representation, *IEEE Computer*, 16(10), 1983.
pp. 67-73.

[Fahlman, 1979] Fahlman, S.E., *NETL: A System for Representing and Using Real-
World Knowledge.* The MIT Press, Cambridge, MA, 1979.

[Padgham, 1988] Padgham, L. A Model and Representation for Type Information
and Its Use in Reasoning with Defaults, *Proceedings of AAAI-88*, Saint Paul, Minnesota,
1988, pp. 409-414.

[Roberts and Goldstein, 1977] Roberts, R.B. and Goldstein, I. P. The FRL Manual,
MIT AI Laboratory Memo 409, Cambridge, 1977.

[Sandewall, 1986] Sandewall, E. Non-monotonic Inference Rules for Multiple Inheritance with Exceptions. *Proceedings of the IEEE*, vol 74, 1986, pp. 1345-1353.

[Touretsky, 1986] Touretsky, D.S. *The Mathematics of Inheritance Systems.* Morgan
Kaufmann Publishers, Los Altos, CA, 1986.

[Touretsky et al, 1987] Touretsky, D.S., Horty, J.F., Thomason, R.H. A Clash of
Intuitions: The Current State of Nonmonotonic Multiple Inheritance Systems, *Proceedings of IJCAI 87*, Milan, August, 1987, vol 1, pp. 476-482.

From Utterance to Belief via Presupposition

Default Reasoning in User-Modelling

Andrew Csinger   David Poole
csinger@cs.ubc.ca   poole@.cs.ubc.ca
Department of Computer Science
University of British Columbia
Vancouver, Canada V6T 1W5

Abstract

This paper presents an approach to agent modelling using a logic of defaults in a natural language environment. We derive the agent's beliefs from his utterances using the minimal default reasoning framework **Theorist**. Following Gazdar [1979], we take the position that utterance meaning is more than just what is asserted, and derive implicatures and presuppositions through a theory of communications expressed within the logic. Immediate advantages of this approach are its representational clarity over other strategies, and its ease of implementation. Applications to user modelling are investigated, and a prototype is discussed with reference to related work.

1 From Utterance to Belief

The primary goal of this work is to explore the acquisition and representation of beliefs in intelligent agents engaged in "rational" communication.[1] With a logic of defaults, we achieve a normative theory more cohesive and of wider coverage than those of previous efforts. In addition, we present an implementation. We will treat the implementation as indistinguishable from the theory, and in fact, what the implementation produces as responses to queries is identical with what is derivable from the theory.

We begin in section 2 with a brief description of how this work fits into the context of user modelling. This discussion requires a short excursion into Gricean pragmatics.

Section 3 gives an overview of presuppositional phenomena as it relates to the current work. Previous efforts are introduced.

Section 4 describes how both the cooperative principles and the presupposition schemas of this theory have been implemented in **Theorist** [Poole, 1987], and how these play an important role in the derivation of an agent's beliefs from her utterances.

We conclude in section 5 with a summary of the key contributions of this paper.

---

[1]As in all normative studies, we assume rationality and do not explain it.

2   User Models

User modelling is the investigation of how assumptions about a user's background knowledge, plans and goals can be automatically created, represented, and exploited computationally in the course of interaction with the user. User modelling is a special case of *agent modelling*; we present an approach to agent modelling in a natural language environment which is based on a logic of defaults. Others have considered goals and plans of the user [Allen and Perrault, 1980], [Cohen and Perrault, 1979], [Carberry, 1988]; we restrict ourselves here to the user's *beliefs*.

The "old-fashioned" approach to user modelling in computer systems is to let the user do the modelling himself; some applications permit the user to modify variables in the environment which reflect user-proficiency parameters indirectly, while others query the user directly about preferences and capabilities. If user-modelling has come a long way since a user-determined 'help-level' first appeared on the menu of a popular word processing program, it has much farther to go before achieving the kind of flexibility we expect from our human interlocutors. User modelling is, arguably, what interactive systems will need to do to be responsive to the needs of the user.

Several studies (*e.g.* [Kass and Finin, 1988]) have pointed out that agents do not have access to "objective truth" about other agents and that it is therefore difficult to distinguish between *knowing* and *believing* a proposition. We do not concern ourselves here with this distinction, and will speak only in terms of the *beliefs* of an agent.

2.1   A Theory of Communication

If the goal of interaction via natural language is the transfer of knowledge or information between intelligent agents, then a simplifying and useful model of this interaction is that the *speaker* of the utterance and the *hearer* share the same world or common-sense knowledge, and that they have identical linguistic competences. Any realistic model would have to account for a wide variation in individual knowledge bases, but such efforts remain conjectural at best. A useful assumption that has been almost uniformly adopted is that the communication of an utterance is governed by a set of *cooperative principles*. Our theory also postulates a set of principles, where each element captures a normative aspect of communication. Taken together, the principles would completely describe the communicative process. As we do not currently know the extent of this set, any implementation should be considered partial.

$$principle_1 :\quad utt(\alpha,\omega) \Rightarrow bel(\alpha,B_{11}), bel(\alpha,B_{12}), \cdots, bel(\alpha,B_{1b_1}).$$
$$principle_2 :\quad utt(\alpha,\omega) \Rightarrow bel(\alpha,B_{21}), bel(\alpha,B_{22}), \cdots, bel(\alpha,B_{2b_2}).$$
$$\vdots$$
$$principle_m :\quad utt(\alpha,\omega) \Rightarrow bel(\alpha,B_{m1}), bel(\alpha,B_{m2}), \cdots, bel(\alpha,B_{mb_m})$$

This set of principles might be considered loosely isomorphic with early work [Grice, 1975], which advanced the following "Maxims of Cooperative Conversation."

Quantity: Make your contribution only as informative as is required.
Quality: Try to make your contribution one that is true.
Relation: Be relevant.
Manner: Be perspicuous.

2.2 Minimum Perversity: The Principles as Defaults

The cooperative principles capture what could be called *Assumption of Minimal Perversity*. This is the element of reasoning which eludes monotonic logics, and what non-monotonic systems attempt to capture.[2] In this study, minimal perversity manifests itself in that *given no indications to the contrary* the interlocutors assume that utterances adhere to the reasonable guidelines of the cooperative principles. Typically, such principles are applied from an extra-logical perspective, although various re-formulations are in use [Cohen and Perrault, 1979, Perrault, 1987]. Defeasibility is the prime motivation for turning to a representation with defaults. Neither the Gricean Maxims nor the principles discussed herein are rules that are followed unswervingly by speakers involved in a conversational exchange of information; they are more like helpful guidelines.

Quantity is the idea that a speaker should utter the most specific statement of what he wishes to communicate. A reasonable –but by no means exhaustive– formulation of this is that *when a speaker utters a disjunction, he does so because no other natural language connective is expressive of the 'tentativeness' of his belief in either of the disjuncts.* This rule thus sanctions the derivation of the clausal quantity implicatures as per Gazdar [1979] and Mercer [1987].

Quality is a sincerity condition. *A speaker believes his utterance.* We believe this naive formulation to be compatible with the Searlian account of Speech Acts expressed as follows [Searle and Vanderveken, 1985, p18]:

> It is always possible to express a psychological state that one does not have, and that is how sincerity and insincerity in speech acts are distinguished. An insincere speech act is one in which the speaker performs a speech act and thereby expresses a psychological state even though he does not have that state.

Relevance is tricky. We suggest that anyone who can completely formulate this in *any* kind of logic will have solved many –if not all– of the problems of Artificial Intelligence! Needless to say, we are still working on it, although as a first attempt, we might expect the speaker to *utter only what the speaker believes the hearer does not already know.*

Non-Standard principles: These maxims have no obvious analog in Grice's work, though they can perhaps be derived from them. For instance, a speaker is *sarcastic* when *the speaker 1) does not believe his utterance, 2) believes that the hearer does not believe the utterance, and 3) believes that the hearer believes that the speaker does not believe the utterance.* Other principles for *understatement, overstatement,* and *lying, etc.,* are similarly definable.

Perrault [1987] has described how multiple extension default theories are capable of representing alternate utterance interpretations. Our implementation also supports representations of utterances which are ambiguous between, for instance, sincere and sarcastic readings. As long as there is an *explanation* in the logic for an interpretation, it will be entertained (as possible) by the system.

---

[2]Elsewhere, we have noted the following definition of the Minimal Perversity *Factor:* the assumption that of the (possibly, or even likely) infinite number of clauses which might affect the reasoning process, only those whose truth value is known need be considered. This is analogous to the well-known *Closed World Assumption,* and to various circumscriptive devices, all suggestive of non-monotonicity.

3   Presupposition

Our project is to build a model of the speaker's beliefs based upon analysis of his utterances. We therefore wish to extract as much information as possible from the utterance. We recognize that much of what is communicated through an utterance is not captured by the propositional content alone. Gazdar [1979] and others have suggested that the *meaning* of an utterance should take stock of its associated *implicatures* and *presuppositions*. Maximizing the utility of a user interface has been expressed in terms of the bandwidth of the communications channel between the user and the application [Csinger *et al.*, 1987]; in these terms, we want the user-modelling subsystem to access the channel 'at its widest.' The non-propositional aspects of the utterance provide a means for increasing the bandwidth in this fashion. Presuppositions and implicatures are part of the information content of the utterance, and will thus play roles in the disambiguation of quantifier scoping, anaphora resolution, etc.

Although consensus on a linguistic definition of presupposition eludes us still, a relatively uncontroversial position is that simple, negated sentences presuppose, while their positive counterparts entail the same inferences. This criterion of linguistic ancestry has been called the *negation test*. For the presuppositional analysis that we implement and demonstrate, the following criteria suffice.

- Negated sentences presuppose those inferences which their unnegated counterparts entail. (The *negation test*.)

- Presuppositions are *implied* by the sentence, never stated in it.

- While entailments of a sentence are uncancellable, presuppositions can be defeated contextually, or by contradictory entailments.

3.1   Presuppositions and Non-monotonic Logic

The application of default logic to presupposition analysis is recent. Although Gazdar's notion of consistency is highly suggestive of a default logic approach [Gazdar, 1979], it predates that technology. Gazdar's work led to a new and more unified theory of entailment, implicature, and presupposition, although certain *ad-hoc* orderings remained unexplained [Mercer, 1987], [Whitelock, 1987].

Previous study of presuppositional phenomena has typically resorted to various non-standard logics to avoid certain difficulties. Truth-value gaps, multi-valued and higher dimensional logics have been proposed (See, e.g.: [McCawley, 1981, Burton-Roberts, 1989]). Mercer showed how default rules could be formulated to capture the presuppositions of various lexical environments, and did much to resolve the terminological ambiguity that has been rampant in the area [Lycan, 1984]. Certain features of presuppositions make them candidates for representation with a non-monotonic logic [Mercer, 1987]. In particular, the presupposition relation is *defeasible*. Presuppositions can be *blocked* by contradictory entailments, or *retracted* by later assertions in the conversation.

As with the cooperative principles, we propose a set of defaults, each element of which captures the behavior of a presuppositional environment. Here too, we are uncommitted as to the cardinality of the set; as many as thirty presupposition-carrying environments have been identified so far. This number is merely part of the historical record, and gives no real clues as to the value of p below:

$$presupposition_1 : \quad utt(\alpha, \omega) \qquad \Rightarrow pre(\alpha, \pi_{11}), pre(\alpha, \pi_{12}), \cdots, pre(\alpha, \pi_{1r_1})$$
$$presupposition_2 : \quad utt(\alpha, \omega) \qquad \Rightarrow pre(\alpha, \pi_{21}), pre(\alpha, \pi_{22}), \cdots, pre(\alpha, \pi_{2r_2})$$
$$\vdots$$
$$presupposition_p : \quad utt(\alpha, \omega) \qquad \Rightarrow pre(\alpha, \pi_{p1}), pre(\alpha, \pi_{p2}), \cdots, pre(\alpha, \pi_{pr_p})$$

3.1.1 No Problem with Projection

Both Gazdar and Mercer make use of (Gricean) clausal quantity implicatures to license the derivation of presuppositions in complex utterances. In our view, a problem with Mercer's formulation is the technique employed to introduce the implicatures into the default theory. In the present work, the implicatures are derived from the default representation of the maxim of quantity; unlike Mercer, we have had no need for recourse to a modal logic.

A side-effect of the problem just alluded to is that Mercer is able to perform his derivations using default theories with single-extensions; this is not the case in our formulation, nor is it desireable. Although debate continues over what the interpretation of an extension should be, we propose that for the matter at hand, they can be considered as operative components of a theory of presupposition without entering into more involved ontological commitments. In the current theory, contextually-consistent presuppositions of utterances are those which are in all extensions. There is a strong parallel between Gazdar's description of potential presuppositions (what he called *pre-suppositions*) and the interpretation in this work of presuppositions which are in some but not in all extensions.[3]

4 Implementation

A subsidiary purpose of this paper is to urge the use of non-monotonic logic in the area of user-modelling. The 'rules,' –if they can be called that– of this enterprise are characterized by their defeasibility, and by the incompletely specified context in which they apply. These are the very reasons why logicians turned to default reasoning in the first place. We argue here that defaults are a natural vehicle for the representation of the cooperative principles, and of the utterance meaning including its presuppositions.

A formulation for default reasoning exists which lends itself particularly well to implementation in a logic programming environment [Poole, 1987]. **Theorist** embodies a a mechanism for defeasible rules of inference, and is implemented using a non-clausal first-order theorem-prover, making it a likely candidate for implementing both the principles of cooperative communication, and the rules for presuppositional inference. The strategy in all of what follows is to abstract away from the temporal linearity of discourse that would lead into truth-maintenance considerations, and to assume instead that the entire

---

[3]cf. Gazdar's remarks concerning *pre-suppositions:* "... are entities whose only role is a technical one in the process of assigning actual presuppositions to utterances. No ontological claims are made in respect of them." [Gazdar, 1979, p124]

discourse is available for analysis. The problem is then one of achieving a *consistent explanation* of the discourse.

4.1 Implementation of the Principles

A subset of the principles governing cooperative communication have been implemented as default rules. In particular, we have rules which are similar in intent to the Gricean maxims of *Quantity,* and *Quality,* other rules cover for interpretations of utterances which are lies, understatement, and so on.

Space does not permit a discussion here; the remainder of this paper will focus instead on the implementation of the presuppositional schemas.

4.2 Presuppositional Schemas as Defaults

The presupposition relation is naturally expressed as a defeasible rule of inference in a non-monotonic logic [Mercer, 1987]. One of the goals of the present work is to implement a system to derive the valid presuppositions of a class of natural language utterance. The resulting system has been tested on most of Mercer's examples with the desired results. Examples in this paper are extracted directly from the **Theorist** implementation. Mercer demonstrated default-logic schemas which captured the presuppositions of numerous lexical environments; these schemas are not much altered in our work, although we employ Poole's framework for default reasoning, rather than Reiter's logic, mainly for the (good) reason that there is a useable implementation. We have also reified over properties to allow for a first order representation. We now introduce briefly the default rules representing a few of the presuppositional environments that have been analysed.

Criterial Properties: This rule of inference is "a type of lexical presupposition which is based on the deciding criterion of a negated lexeme's meaning." [Mercer, 1987, p76]. Given the utterance *My cousin is not a bachelor,* the following presuppositions can be derived: *1) The speaker's cousin is male, 2) The speaker's cousin is adult.*

The non-criterial presupposition schema has been implemented as the following **Theorist** default rule, which might be paraphrased as *when a negated lexical item appears in an utterance, and it has non-criterial properties, then if it is consistent to do so, infer that the speaker believes the indicated presupposition.*[4]

```
% default rules to enable presuppositions under negation:
% noncriterial presupposition schema:
default pre_by_nonc(S, Object, LexItem, Presupposition) :
        utt(S, property(Object, not LexItem)) and
        nonc(LexItem, Presupposition)
        =>
        bel(S, property(Object, Presupposition)).
```

The non-criterial properties of the lexemes are simply provided as facts in **Theorist**. Given the utterance by andrew of *My cousin is not a bachelor,* represented by **fact**

---

[4]Note that what is of concern here to us is not whether the listener *actually* believes something, but whether the speaker believes he does [Horton, 1987].

utt(andrew,property(cousin,not bachelor)))., **Theorist** ascribes the following beliefs to andrew.[5]

```
Answer is believes(andrew,property(cousin,male))
Theory is [pre_by_nonc(andrew,cousin,bachelor,male)]

Answer is believes(andrew,property(cousin,adult))
Theory is [pre_by_nonc(andrew,cousin,bachelor,adult)]
```

Factive Verbs: Utterances with factive verbs imply the complement clause, whether the verb is negated or not. The utterance *John regrets that Mary came to the party* entails that Mary came to the party. The negated form *John does not regret that Mary came to the party* presupposes the same thing. It is with the latter relationship that this study is concerned.

The presuppositional aspects of the factive verb environment can be easily captured with defaults. The conversational model which underlies this formulation assumes that both speaker and hearer share enough world knowledge to allow these presuppositional contents to go unsaid, and the logic recaptures the latent information. The implementation strategy in **Theorist** is analogous to the non-criterial properties schema.

4.2.1 Example: Intrasentential Cancellation and Multiple Extensions

The analysis of a disjunctive utterance, or what Mercer calls *intrasentential cancellation* [Mercer, 1987, p93], provides a deeper example. Mercer includes a collection of *clausal implicatures* as part of the default theory for a disjunctive utterance. In our implementation, these implicatures are derived from the representation of the Quantity Maxim, described in section 2.2. In the current formulation, the disjunctive clauses generate conjectural presuppositions. In the case of intra-sentential cancellation, the mutually contradictory presuppositions belong to orthogonal extensions of the default theory. This leads to a re-interpretation of the projection problem, where only those (conjectural) presuppositions of a disjunctive utterance are 'inherited' which occur in all extensions.

When our speaker utters *My teacher is either a bachelor or a spinster,* **Theorist** infers the belief-set shown in figure 1. The system has provided (conjectural) explanations for the mutually contradictory presuppositions that the teacher is both male and female.[6] This is because *scenarios* exist which explain each of these presuppositions, although there is no scenario which explains both [Poole, 1987]. As in the discussion of interpretation in section 2.2, the current situation is not so much one of contradiction, but of ambiguity. Whereas earlier we were concerned with ambiguity of interpretation in the discourse, we are now considering ambiguity of the utterance presuppositions. Here too, this ambiguity is captured in terms of multiple extensions of the default theory, and any attempt at resolution will necessarily (naturally) address itself to the contents of these multiple extensions. Predictably, **Theorist** will deny that the property of the teacher's male-ness is

---

[5]Other beliefs are sanctioned as well, deriving from explanations of sincerity, sarcasm, etc., but they have been omitted in the interests of brevity and clarity.

[6]These propositions are contradictory in the assumed presence of a fact that expresses the binary feature of sexuality. Other facts that are equally obvious have been included in the the **Theorist** database, and will not be discussed here.

```
Answer is bel(andrew,property(teacher,male))
Theory is [pre_by_nonc(andrew,teacher,bachelor,male),
          clausal_imp(andrew,teacher,bachelor)]
Answer is bel(andrew,property(teacher,adult))
Theory is [pre_by_nonc(andrew,teacher,bachelor,adult),
          clausal_imp(andrew,teacher,bachelor)]
Answer is bel(andrew,property(teacher,female))
Theory is [pre_by_nonc(andrew,teacher,spinster,female),
          clausal_imp(andrew,teacher,spinster)]
Answer is bel(andrew,property(teacher,adult))
Theory is [pre_by_nonc(andrew,teacher,spinster,adult),
          clausal_imp(andrew,teacher,spinster)]
```

Figure 1: Contradictory Presuppositions in different extensions Generated by **Theorist**

in all extensions; likewise with the teacher's female-ness. **Theorist** will, however, assert that the teacher's adult-ness is in all extensions (viz. figure 2).

```
No, bel(andrew,property(teacher,male)) is not explainable from
        [clausal_imp(andrew,teacher,bachelor),
         pre_by_nonc(andrew,teacher,spinster,female),
         clausal_imp(andrew,teacher,spinster)].
No, bel(andrew,property(teacher,female)) is not explainable from
        [clausal_imp(andrew,teacher,spinster),
         pre_by_nonc(andrew,teacher,bachelor,male),
         clausal_imp(andrew,teacher,bachelor)].
Yes, bel(andrew,property(teacher,adult)) is in all extensions.
        Explanations are:
        1: [pre_by_nonc(andrew,teacher,spinster,adult),
            clausal_imp(andrew,teacher,spinster)].
        2: [pre_by_nonc(andrew,teacher,bachelor,adult),
            clausal_imp(andrew,teacher,bachelor)].
```

Figure 2: Sexual Ambiguity

4.2.2 Summary: Our Approach to Presupposition

Mercer gives the following proof-theoretic definition of natural language presupposition.

> If α is in the logical closure of the default consequents and is provable from the utterance, and all proofs require the invocation of a default rule and in the case of multiple extensions of default theories, α is in all extensions, then α is a presupposition of the utterance.

We concur with his definition, but point out that multiple extension theories occur in our formulation where Mercer claims he has only single-extensions. In particular, our approach to intra-sentential cancellation results in multiple extensions, where he claims it does not. This divergence is due to the handling of the clausal implicatures, which are derived in our system from the maxims of cooperation.

Mercer's approach to intrasentential cancellation makes use of the Gazdarian clausal-quantity implicatures to perform a case analysis, where the cases themselves can be single-extension default theories. Our approach involves multiple extensions within a single default theory. Our approach has the advantage that it is readily implementable, and that it falls under the aegis of a more general theoretical framework. Presuppositions which are finally sanctioned by the system are those which are in all extensions; this ensures that they are not mutually contradictory (thus answering to the so-called projection problem) and that they are consistent with context.

Significant economy of expression has been gained over Mercer's default-logic formulation, with a resulting increase in transparency. The case analysis required by his approach is performed transparently by **Theorist** when the given rules are employed.

To date, any implementation which has sought to make use of natural language presupposition has done so with the *ad-hoc* flavor that is characteristic of the early work in AI. Mercer's formulation brings the study of presupposition into the light of a formal theory of default reasoning, and this paper probes tentatively in the same direction.

Further work is necessary to determine how readily the implementation scales-up to a real domain, but it is at least arguable that a **Theorist**-like system will be suitable to the task of deriving presuppositions from natural-language utterances.

5 Conclusion

This paper does *not* propose to

- Solve the 'projection problem': strictly speaking –and as Mercer emphasized– there is no room for traditionally defined projection, let alone for a problem with it, in a default consistency-based pragmatic theory. The problem is then the familiar one of maintaining consistency.

- Postulate 'sentences in the head,' or commit to a propositional attitude psychology. This work is agnostic on the issue of psychological relevance, and takes the position that if something works, it should be used, regardless of its ontological status.

- Make a claim as to the **meaning** of an extension of a default theory: we merely interpret the behavior of extensions in a consistent and 'meaningful' manner, without deciding their ontological fate. This attitude mirrors Gazdar's treatment of *pre-suppositions* or *potential presuppositions* as objects within his theory of merely technical significance.

- Put forth the validity of one semantic (form) representation over another. This is another issue that we will leave for others to resolve.

This work advances the utility of a usable test-bench. **Theorist** as currently implemented is an effective tool for the testing of default theories. Theoretical advances do not necessarily follow from working systems, but such systems are often the keys to unexpected discoveries.

To recap the key contributions of this paper:

- We represent presuppositions of complex utterances with multiple extension default theories. This approach is arguably more principled than Mercer's treatment, which makes use of multiple default theories of single extension. It is unclear how to proceed with a principled implementation of Mercer's method.

- We demonstrate belief modelling in a logic with defaults (compare Perrault in [Perrault, 1987]).

- We formulate elements of a set of principles of cooperation *within a framework for default logic*, allowing us to capture ambiguity of interpretation, as well as the intuitive, actual presuppositions of complex utterances.

- We integrate presupposition-generation and the formulation of the cooperative principles with user-modelling.

- Finally, we present an implementation. Though the usual caveats surrounding an embryonic study apply, the implementation produces the intuitively correct presuppositions of a class of utterances.

References

[Allen and Perrault, 1980] James Allen and Raymond Perrault. Analyzing intention in utterances. *Artificial Intelligence*, 15:143–178, 1980.

[Burton-Roberts, 1989] Noel Burton-Roberts. *The Limits to Debate: A revised theory of semantic presupposition*. Cambridge University Press, 1989.

[Carberry, 1988] Sandra Carberry. Modelling the user's plans and goals. *Computational Linguistics*, 14(3):23, September 1988.

[Cohen and Perrault, 1979] Philip R. Cohen and Raymond Perrault. Elements of a plan-based theory of speech-acts. *Cognitive Science*, 3:177–212, 1979.

[Csinger et al., 1987] A. Csinger, H. da Costa, and B. Forghani. A general-purpose programmable command decoder. In *IEEE Proceedings, Conference Compint*, pages 139–41, November 1987.

[Gazdar, 1979] Gerald Gazdar. *Pragmatics: Implicature, Presupposition and Logical Form*. Academic Press, 1979.

[Grice, 1975] H.P. Grice. Logic and conversation. In P. Cole and J.L. Morgan, editors, *Syntax and Semantics: Speech Acts, vol 3*, pages 47–58. Academic Press, New York, 1975.

[Horton, 1987] Diane Horton. Incorporating agents' beliefs in a model of presupposition. Technical Report 201, University of Toronto, 1987.

[Kass and Finin, 1988] Robert Kass and Tim Finin. Modelling the user in natural language systems. *Computational Linguistics*, 14(3):5, September 1988.

[Lycan, 1984] William G. Lycan. *Logical Form in Natural Language*. MIT Press, (A Bradford Book), Cambridge, MA, 1984.

[McCawley, 1981] J. McCawley. *Everything Linguists Always Wanted to Know about Logic.* University of Chicago Press, 1981.

[Mercer, 1987] Robert Mercer. A default logic approach to the derivation of natural language presuppositions. Technical Report 35, University of British Columbia, October 1987.

[Perrault, 1987] C. Raymond Perrault. An application of default logic to speech act theory. CSLI 90, Center for the Study of Language and Information, Stanford, CA., 1987.

[Poole, 1987] David Poole. A logical framework for default reasoning. *Artificial Intelligence*, 36(1):27–47, 1987.

[Searle and Vanderveken, 1985] John R. Searle and Daniel Vanderveken. *Foundations of Illocutionary Logic.* Cambridge University Press, 1985.

[Whitelock, 1987] P. Whitelock. *Linguistic Theory and Computer Applications.* Academic Press, London, 1987.

Implementing Persistence of Derived Information in a Reason Maintenance System

Dattatraya H. Kulkarni   N Parameswaran

Artificial Intelligence and Robotics Laboratory

Department of Computer Science and Engineering

Indian Institute of Technology, Madras-600 036, India

E-mail uunet!shakti!shiva!parames

Abstract

Class of deductions where their conclusions persist even though some components of justification are no more valid, pose some difficulty in reasoning about change. A partial solution is found in the notion called *inessentiality* of a component of a justification to its conclusion. The frame axiom to deduce the persistence of a sentence using the notion of inessentiality is accommodated within the framework of *Reason Maintenance System (RMS)*, by modifying the definition of *IN*-ness of a node and its current-support.

1 INTRODUCTION

Reasoning about actions gives rise to three classical problems, viz. the *persistence*, the *ramification* and the *qualification* problems [Ginsberg and Smith,1988]. Persistence problem is the difficulty in inferring all those things that do not change after an action is performed or as time passes. In this paper we consider the actions to be noncontinuous.

Research in reasoning about change has concentrated on the persistence of base facts, thus neglecting the persistence of derived facts [Myers and Smith, 1988]. One of the ways of handling persistence of base facts is to provide a default frame axiom. This frame axiom states that facts persist across states in the absence of information to the contrary.

If derived information always ceases to exist when components of its justification cease to, then having a justification information and applying the frame axiom to the base facts will take care of the persistence of the derived facts as well. However there is a class of deductions wherein the causality is incidental, and components of the justification are required only to establish the consequent. Once the consequent is established, it continues to persist even though some components of its justification cease to. If this is not taken care of, it leads to unnecessary loss of derived information.

[Myers and Smith, 1988] identified this class of problems and suggested a frame axiom, considering the *inessentiality* of the components of a justification to the consequent, to circumvent this problem. The approach however is not satisfactory when there are multiple derivations for a fact.

Any system that is not sensitive to justification information will be incapable of handling the persistence of derived facts [Myers and Smith, 1988]. An RMS is sensitive to justification information and can easily yield to such requirements. In this paper we discuss how one can take into account inessentiality, when an RMS is an underlying system used for reasoning about change. We assume a suitable representation in an RMS, for changes due to an action.

In section 2 we briefly introduce definitions relevant to an RMS. Discussion of the problem and the notion of inessentiality appears in section 3. In section 4 we present the machinery required to implement inessentiality in an RMS. We conclude with some comments on the usefulness of inessentiality and future work.

2 REASON MAINTENANCE

An RMS, also called a *Truth Maintenance System* (TMS), is basically a cache for beliefs of a problem solver. An RMS consists of a dependency network and associated algorithms for revision, dependency directed backtracking etc. RMS has the ability to revise its beliefs so as to maintain a consistent context [Doyle, 1979] and is therefore used extensively in implementing non monotonic reasoning systems.

Definition 2.1: A dependency network is a pair
D = (NODES, JUSTS)
where NODES is a set of nodes and JUSTS a set of justifications. A justification is of the form
$r = (i_1, i_2, ..., i_m; o_1, o_2, ..., o_n \Rightarrow c)$
where $i_1, i_2, ..., i_m, o_1, o_2, ..., o_n$ and c are nodes NODES.

A node represents a ground instance of a predicate and a justification represents a reason for believing in the ground instance of the predicate. The nodes are only symbolic entities for RMS, the internals of nodes are of concern only to a problem solver.

Definition 2.2: Let r be a justification of the form

$r = (i_1, i_2, ..., i_m; o_1, o_2, ..., o_n => c)$.

Monotonic antecedents ma(r) of justification r is a set

$ma(r) = \{i_1, i_2, ..., i_m\}$,

non monotonic antecedents nma(r) of justification r is a set

$nma(r) = \{o_1, o_2 ..., o_n\}$

and the consequent conseq(r) of justification r is

conseq(r) = c.

Definition 2.3: We define functions

label: NODES -> {IN,OUT} and valid: JUSTS -> {TRUE, FALSE} as

label(n)=IN if j JUSTS   conseq(j)=n   valid(j); otherwise label(n)=OUT.

valid(j)=TRUE if Vm   ma(j) label(m)=IN   Vk   nma(j)   label(k)=OUT; otherwise valid(j)=FALSE.

The labeling rules sound circular but they are really not so. There are some distinguished nodes called *premises* that are always IN and give support to the rest of the network. Well-founded node label assures a non-circular argument for the node.

3 THE PROBLEM AND INESSENTIALITY

Discussion in this section is aimed at presenting the work in [Myers and Smith, 1988] on inessentiality. We use situation calculus through out the paper with only some syntactic modification, viz. p_t stands for HOLDS(p,t).

As a way of handling persistence of base facts we apply a default rule of the form

$$\frac{p_t : p_{t \cdot 1}}{p_{t \cdot 1}}$$

i.e. 'facts persist over situations provided they are consistent with the new state'. If this default is applied only to base facts, all derived facts have to be removed and if possible rederived in the new state. We can use RMS to avoid the overhead of rederiving facts that remain valid across states due to continued support. The dependency structure enables one to identify those that have supports after the deletion of the base facts by an action.

This is a conservative approach, as there is a class of deductions where conclusions continue to persist even after some of the facts it depends on are removed. Consider a scenario where we have a robot going about and picking things in a room. There are some facts and domain rules to describe the room. If the situation is,

ontable(X)$_t$ -> liftable(X)$_t$. and ontable(cup)$_t$.

that is, to start with all things on table are liftable, and there is a cup on the table. If the robot picks the cup and places it on the floor, *ontable(cup)* is no more consistent with the domain constraints (that an object can not be in two places at a time), and has to be removed and *onfloor(cup)* has to be added. If we used the conservative approach we mentioned, *liftable(cup)* does not have support any more and ceases to persist.

This argument is true, from a syntactic point of view. The rule just describes a situation, but does not carry the causal relationship. Considering the semantics of the relation between *ontable(cup)* and *liftable(cup)*, it is incidental that objects on table are liftable, but liftability itself is a physical property, that does not change by change in location. It is a helpless usage of implication. Perhaps there is another property, say empty(cup) that causes the cup to be liftable.

empty(X)$_t$ -> liftable(X)$_t$. and empty(cup)$_t$.

Probably filling up a cup makes it unliftable and *empty(cup)* is essential for the continued persistence of *liftable(cup)*. The above arguments lead us to conclude that there are two kinds of relations between premises and conclusions.

The location of cup is inessential for its liftability and

the emptiness of cup is essential for its liftability.

We define predicate Inessential(p,q) that is true if p is inessential for the persistence of q. If nothing else is mentioned about q and other predicates that justify q, it means that they are essential for q's persistence.

We also define a predicate justifies(J,p,t) that is true if J is the minimal set of fluents that form the reason to believe in p in situation t. A frame axiom that takes inessentiality factor into account can be given informally as, if

1) p is derived at t_0 and has persisted till now,

2) all components of its justification, either persited or are

    inessential from t_0 to new state, and

3) p does not introduce any inconsistency then p can continue to persist.

or formally as,

$$\frac{precond(p,t) : p_{t \cdot 1}}{p_{t \cdot 1}}$$

where predicate precond is defined by

$\exists j$ justifies(j,p,t_0)

$\forall t' \; t_0 \leqslant t' \leqslant t \quad p_t' \wedge$

$\forall t' \; t_0 \leqslant t' \leqslant t+1 \; \forall j' \in j \; (j'_t \; V \; inessential(j',p))$

4 INESSENTIALITY AND RMS

Situations are not represented explicitly and currently IN labeled nodes of RMS dependency network represents the current situation. Actions are treated as changes to RMS dependency network. Whenever a change occurs the RMS revision procedure relabels affected part of the dependency network.

The RMS algorithm needs some modification to incorporate inessentiality, especially the labeling of nodes and justifications.

4.1 Definitions

Definition 4.1.1 Components of a justification:

Consider a justification $r = (i_1,i_2,...,i_m;o_1,o_2,...,o_n =>c)$.

mi(r) is a set of all monotonic inessential components of r i.e. mi(r) = {n|n $\in$ ma(r) $\wedge$ inessential(n conseq(r))}

and me(r) is a set of all monotonic essential components of r me(r) = ma(r) \ mi(r).

Similarly non monotonic inessential and essential components are nmi(r) and nme(r).

Definition 4.1.2 Types of justifications:

If all antecedents of a justification r are inessential to the consequent then we call r an inessential justification, i.e.

if me(r)$\cup$nme(r) = ϕ or if $\forall n \in$ (ma(r)$\cup$ nma(r)) inessential(n,conseq(r)).

A justification r is an essential justification if there is atleast one antecedent of r that is not inessential to its consequent, i.e.

if $\exists n \in$ (ma(r)$\cup$ nma(r)) -inessential(n,conseq(r))

or simply if it is not an inessential justification.

Definition 4.1.3 Some predicates and functions:
We define predicate iness-just, that is true if its argument, a justification is an inessential justification, false otherwise. Functions just and old-just give the current and old justification for a node.

just and old-just : NODES -> JUSTS

Predicates old-just-iness is true if its argument, a node, had an inessential justification that is, if iness-just(old-just(c)) = True; Otherwise it is false.

Definition 4.1.4 Validity of a justification:
We define predicate valid, that is true if its argument, a justification is valid.

valid(j) = TRUE if

$$[(\text{-old-valid}(j) \wedge ma(j) \subseteq I_{k-1} \wedge nma(j) \subseteq O_{k-1}) \; V$$

$$(\text{old-valid}(j) \wedge (ma(j) \cup nma(j)) \subseteq (I_{k-1} \quad O_{k-1}) \wedge me(j) \subseteq Ik\text{-}1 \wedge nme(j) \subseteq Ok\text{-}1)]$$

else valid(j) = FALSE.

Predicate old-valid is true if the argument was valid in the previous situation, and false otherwise. I_{k-1} and O_{k-1} are sets of nodes that are already labeled IN and OUT respectively. Informally, a justification j is valid if it was invalid in the previous situation and all of j's monotonic antecedents are labeled IN, and all of j's non monotonic antecedents are labeled OUT. Justification j is also valid if it were valid in previous situation, and all of j's monotonic essential antecedents are labeled IN and non monotonic essential components are labeled OUT. We do not care about the label of inessential antecedents of j, however to avoid circular labelings, we require that they be labeled, either IN or OUT.

Definition 4.1.5 Label of a node:
Now we define function label: NODES -> {IN,OUT}, to get the label of a node in current situation. Function old-label returns the label its argument had in previous situation. The consistency of the node p in a new situation is assured by the domain constraints and dependency directed backtracking.

Suppose a node p has a single justification and that at some time t_0 all the monotonic components ma(j) of a justification j for node p are IN and non monotonic components nma(j) are OUT. When a transition takes place from some state t to t+1 we need to check whether the node p was IN at t and all previous states upto t_0. Obviously the lone justification j also will be valid from t_0 till now if the node is IN in those states. Its validity in t+1 is checked by the incremental labeling algorithm using the definition 4.1.4 above. Since the definition 4.1.4 takes care of the inessentiality of j's components based on its old-label it suffices if we label the node p IN if its justification is valid in the new state. If j is not valid in new state p is labeled OUT.

The single justification case is short from interesting. The treatment when a node has multiple justifications is not satisfactory in [Myers and Smith, 1988]. When there are multiple derivations available for a node it is not necessary that all justifications be valid. It is sufficient if atleast one of the justifications is valid. The only complication created by the nature of inessentiality is that, a node having support of an inessential justification loses its support, when any of the available essential justifications becomes invalid and an alternative valid essential justification is required to keep the node IN. This nature forces the definition of current support to change and contributes for computational overhead as described later. Also, the definition given in [Myers and Smith, 1988] assumes that all justifications for a node are available at t_0, but one might get few more valid justifications in later states or available justifications could become invalid. The modified informal rule to label a node is

a node can be labeled IN if

it was labeled OUT

  and has atleast one valid essential justification

or it was labeled IN

  and its old justification was inessential

    and all essential justification are valid

   or old justification was essential

    and there is a valid essential justification.

otherwise the node is labeled OUT.

Formally, label and old-label : NODES -> {IN, OUT} and the rule is

if

{[(old-label(c)=OUT) [($\exists$ j $\in$ JUSTS (conseq(j)=c) $\wedge$ -inees-just(j)$\wedge$ valid(j)) V

                (($\forall$j$\in$JUSTS (conseq(j)=c) -> iness-just(j))$\wedge$

                        $\exists$j$\in$JUSTS conseq(j)=c $\wedge$ valid(j))]] V

  [(old-label(c)=IN) [(-old-just-iness(c) $\wedge$

               ($\exists$ j $\in$ JUSTS (conseq(j)=c)$\wedge$ -iness-just(j)$\wedge$ valid(j))) V

          (old-just-iness(c)$\wedge$(($\forall$ j$\in$JUSTS (conseq(j)=c) -> valid(j)) V

           ($\exists$ j $\in$ JUSTS (conseq(j)=c)$\wedge$ -iness-just(j)$\wedge$ valid(j))))]]}

then label(c) = IN

else label(c) = OUT.

.2 Modified RMS Algorithm

Whenever a structural modification, due to the effects of an action, is made to the dependency network, the affected part of the dependency network is relabeled by revision procedure. Revision involves *unlabeling* of the affected part of the dependency network and *relabeling* it accommodating the modification or change.

To identify the portion of the network to be unlabeled, we need the concept of *current-support* of a node, which is list of nodes its label directly depends on. We identify for each invalid essential justification of an OUT labeled node, a node that invalidates it. It is either a monotonic antecedent that is OUT or a non monotonic antecedent that is IN. A list of such nodes forms the current-support of an OUT labeled node. For an IN node it is the list of all essential antecedents of the supporting justification, if it is an essential justification. On the other hand if the support is an inessential justification then it is the list of essential antecedents of all the essential justifications. Due to the modified definition of current-support, the unlabeled part is considerably more compared to the case when there is no inessentiality.

Unlabeling [Freitag, 1987] proceeds by starting at the location of modification and following up current-support links along the dependency network, and recursively copying the label and justification to old-label and old-just and setting label to undetermined. Let *unlabeled* be the set of all such affected nodes.

procedure unlabel:
$\quad$ i <- 0; U_0 <- *unlabeled*
repeat
$\quad$ i <- i+1;
$\quad$ U_i <- U_{i-1} $\quad$ {n | $\exists$ m $\in U_{i-1}$ $\quad$ m $\in$ current-support(n)}
until $U_i = U_{i-1}$

This unlabeled set of nodes, say U_k, is partitioned into strongly connected components, to facilitate incremental relabeling of the network without backtracking [Goodwin, 1982; Freitag, 1987]. These components are partially ordered, based on dependency. We relabel the unlabeled part U_k, by relabeling each of strongly connected components, smallest first.

The following relabel algorithm [Freitag, 1987; Goodwin, 1982] is for relabeling one strongly connected component. Let INS, OUTS and *unlabeled* be the sets of nodes that are already labeled IN, already labeled OUT, and unlabeled respectively.

We first propagate existing labels in the first inner loop. This is where the modified definitions for label and valid are used. The second inner loop checks for well-founded support hierarchy of possibly IN labelable nodes. Inessentiality does not come into picture here as checking for the well-foundedness based only on essential monotonic antecedents may lead to circularities. Those nodes that do not have well-founded support hierarchy are labeled OUT and these nodes are once again propagated. When there are no more nodes without well-founded support hierarchy, the remaining nodes are labeled by labeling a node OUT arbitrarily and propagating the labels (in procedure PARTITION). We skip the details of partition procedure.

procedure relabel
repeat
    $j \leftarrow 0$; $I_0 \leftarrow$ INS; $O_0 \leftarrow$ OUTS;
    repeat
        $j \leftarrow j+1$;
        $I_j \leftarrow I_{j-1}$ $\{n \mid n \in$ NODES and label(n) = IN$\}$
        $O_j \leftarrow O_{j-1}$ $\{n \mid n \in$ NODES and label(n) = OUT$\}$
    until $I_j = I_{j-1}$ and $O_j = O_{j-1}$;
    unlabeled $\leftarrow$ *unlabeled*\$(I_j \cup O_j)$;
    INS $\leftarrow I_j$; OUTS $\leftarrow O_j$; $k \leftarrow 0$; $F_0 \leftarrow \phi$;
    repeat
        $k \leftarrow k+1$;
        $F_k \leftarrow F_{k-1}$ $\{c \mid \exists j \in$ JUSTS and conseq(j) = c and
            $c \in$ *unlabeled* and $\forall i \in$ ma(j) $i \in F_{k-1}$ or $i \in$ INS$\}$
    until $F_k = F_{k-1}$;
    UNFOUNDED $\leftarrow$ *unlabeled*\ F_k;
    if UNFOUNDED $\neq \phi$ then
        OUTS $\leftarrow$ OUTS UNFOUNDED;
        unlabeled = F_k;
until UNFOUNDED = ϕ;
while $\exists n \in$ *unlabeled* do PARTITION(n, INS, OUTS);

5 REMARKS AND CONCLUSION

Epistemological problems arising due to the need to specify the inessentiality of predicates has to be studied. We have made another implicit assumption, that has not surfaced, due to a single consequent in the rules. It is intuitive to assume that an antecedent bears the same inessentiality relation with all the consequents. Also we assumed that in all the instances of a rule the same inessentiality relations old. One can perhaps mention inessentiality in the rules themselves e.g.

ontable(X)$_{(i)}$, dry(X) -> liftable(X)

that is, ontable is inessential for the persistence of liftable and dry is essential. The inadvertent usage of inessentiality can result in unpredictable behaviors. Consider the default rule that says 'if tweety is a bird and we can not prove that it can't fly, then it flies'.

ird(X), -fly(X)(OUT)$_{(i)}$ -> fly(X). and bird(tweety).

By default we can deduce that fly(tweety). If -fly(X) is inessential for fly(X) then f in future we get an evidence for -fly(tweety), we can't retract fly(tweety). This introduces inconsistency and worse still the system becomes 'prejudiced'!. Since non monotonic components are introduced as a means to revise beliefs in face of contradictions, it is a bad idea to think of an inessential non monotonic component.

We presented the modifications for the RMS algorithms to accommodate inessentiality. However, a formal analysis of the effect of inessentiality on the complexity has to be done. Because of the modified definition of the current-support or a node one can expect an increase in complexity. The effect of inessentiality on dependency directed backtracking has to be studied.

Acknowledgment

We are indebted to referees, Murali Krishna, S. Sharad and T.V.D Kumar for their useful comments. We thank R. Nagarajan for his encouragement.

REFERENCES

Doyle, 1979]

Doyle, Jon. *Truth Maintenance System*, Artificial Intelligence 12, pp 231-272, 1979.

Freitag, 1987]

Freitag H. *An Admissible extension Theory Based Reason Maintenance System*, Report INF2 ARM-2-87, SIEMENS AG, 1987.

Ginsberg and Smith,1988]

Ginsberg ML and Smith DE. *Reasoning about actions I: A possible worlds approach*, Artificial Intelligence 35, pp 165-195, 1988.

[Goodwin, 1982]

Goodwin J. *An Improved Algorithm for Non-Monotonic Dependency Net Update*, Research Report LiTH-MAT-R-82-23, University of Linkoping, Sweden, 1982.

[Myers and Smith, 1988]

Myer KL and Smith DE. *The Persistence of Derived In formation*, AAAI-88, pp 496-500, 1988.

New Techniques in Model-Based Diagnosis

SIEMENS AG, Otto-Hahn-Ring 6, D-8000 Munich 83

West Germany

e-mail: struss@ztivax.siemens.com

Abstract

For about a decade, model-based reasoning has been investigated by AI
research. In particular diagnosis of technical devices requires explicitly
representing principal knowledge about the structure and behavior of the
device to be diagnosed and its components. The *General Diagnostic Engine*
(GDE) introduced by J. de Kleer and B. Williams is probably the most
promising approach to model-based diagnosis. This paper discusses problems
emerging from case studies based on GDE carried out by the *Advanced
Reasoning Methods* group at SIEMENS. In particular, questions of handling
devices with many components, reasoning about device behavior over time,
exploiting multiple tests and knowledge about faults, and dealing with
uncertain measurements are raised. Based on extensions to GDE, at least
partial solutions to these problems have been achieved, making real
applications of this approach become more feasible.

1 Objectives of Model-Based Diagnosis

Diagnostic systems of the first "Expert Systems" generation are characterized by
exploiting the rule-based paradigm. Despite the considerable success of this
approach in experimental environments, its serious limitations became evident in
the early eighties (see [Davis 82]). Although adequate primarily for representing
empirical associations (which relate symptoms to the underlying malfunctions), it
fails to provide a foundation for modeling existing general theories about a domain
or a principled way of building diagnostic systems. It results in diagnostic systems
which often are

- dedicated to very narrow classes of devices or even to a single device,
- restricted to devices, symptoms, and faults about which empirical knowledge
  already exists,
- expensive to build and to maintain,
- difficult or impossible to extend and to generalize.

These serious drawbacks lead to a significant limitation of the industrial
production and application of knowledge-based diagnostic systems.

In particular in the case of man-made systems, we (or at least domain experts) do not rely solely on experience emerging from trial and error. We know something about the specific ways components are involved, and how they are meant to interact in order to achieve the functionality of the whole device. Model-based diagnostic systems reflect this fact by encorporating a description of subsystems and constitutive mechanisms and of the device structure, i.e. the interaction paths between them which enable them to jointly establish the behavior of the entire device.

This approach promises to overcome several deficiencies of rule-based diagnosis:

- There is an explicit representation of the device structure.
- This approach is constructive: a specialized diagnostic system for a particular device can be created by supplying a domain-independent diagnostic procedure with a description of the structure of this device in terms of components taken from a domain specific library.
- Thus, it is possible to cover large classes of devices built out of the same set of components.
- Diagnosis of new, unexperienced devices has received a basis.
- Treatment of new symptoms and faults also appears to be feasible.
- For many technical domains, the component-centered organization of the knowledge appears to be more adequate than the rule-oriented representation.

2   The General Diagnostic Engine (GDE)

2.1   The Basic GDE

How can a device model be used by a diagnostic system? One way is to compare **observations** of certain features of the device to be diagnosed to what the knowledge about the components (or combinations of them) **predicts** about these features (Fig. 1). If this inference process leads to a **discrepancy**, i.e. contradictory conclusions for the same system variable, this indicates that at least one of the models involved in the predictions does not match the actual behavior of the respective component as was assumed in the reasoning process. In order to determine the assumptions which together form such a **conflict set**, the system has to record the model assumptions the predictions are dependent on. This task, **dependency recording**, can be solved by using an Assumption-Based Truth-Maintenance-System (ATMS, see [de Kleer 86]).

430

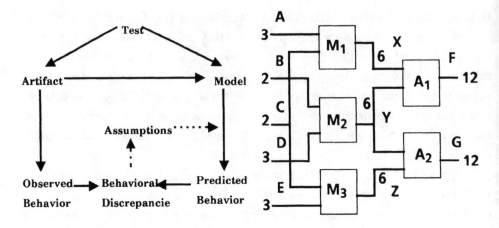

Figure 1   The principal idea of GDE   Fig. 2   Multipliers (M_i) and adders (A_i)

Based on these fundamental ideas, the General Diagnostic Engine (GDE) has been developed ([de Kleer-Williams 87]). The diagnostic task is performed by GDE in the following way: initial observations are entered, and predictions are made based on models of the correct behavior of all components. The ATMS returns the minimal conflicts detected so far. Any valid diagnosis has to resolve each conflict; hence, GDE constructs those sets of components that contain at least one element out of each conflict. These are the **candidates** for the diagnosis (Actually, only the minimal candidates are explicitly represented).

Using the standard example of a circuit containing adders (A_i) and multipliers (M_i) (Fig. 2), the mechanism can be demonstrated: Supplied with the input $A=3$, $B=2$, $C=2$, $D=3$ and $E=3$, the constraint system predicts output $F=12$ and $G=12$. For instance, $F=12$ depends on $\{A_1, M_1, M_2\}$ (where A_1 represents the assumption *"Adder A_1 works as expected"*). If we now measure $F=10$ and $G=12$ and enter these values as facts, $\{A_1, M_1, M_2\}$ is a conflict, and so is $\{A_1, A_2, M_1, M_3\}$. This set of assumptions is used to compute $G=10$ from $Z=6$ and $Y=F-X = 10-6 = 4$. The minimal candidates are $\{A_1\}$, $\{M_1\}$, $\{A_2, M_2\}$ and $\{M_2, M_3\}$. Each of them explains both conflicts.

Finally, GDE contains a module for **measurement proposal**. Based on the fault probability of each component and the existing candidates, the measurement of a variable is proposed which, on the average, promises the optimal gain in information. If the result of this measurement is entered as an observation, the cycle starts again until a candidate has achieved a probability significantly higher than any other.

2.2   Problems in Tackling Real Applications

In the *Advanced Reasoning Methods Group* at SIEMENS, we carried out a number of case studies which aimed at confronting the basic GDE with a number of problems which are likely to occur in realistic applications. Among others, the following issues were addressed:

- In real applications, we encounter hundreds or thousands of components (rather then about ten in the adder-multiplier circuit). Is this feasible for the model-based prediction module of GDE?
- The basic GDE assumes that the device and its components remain in one permanent (or reproducible) equilibrium state. But in many cases, the state of the device at hand changes over time.
- In particular, frequently a diagnosis is based on observing the device in different states, i.e. performing a series of tests.
- GDE uses models of correct, or intended, component behavior. Human diagnostic skills also use knowledge about faulted components.
- Since candidates in GDE are constructed from conflicts, correctly identifying inconsistencies among observations and predictions is crucial. A wrong observation causes wrong diagnoses.

In the following, these problems are discussed in more detail, the solutions achieved are outlined (and references are given), and an appreciation of their limitations and open problems is attempted. (A broader presentation is given in [Struss 89b]). The case studies performed included diagnosis of a circuit with thyristors used for rectifying and controlling the current through a DC motor provided by an AC voltage source, and diagnosis of the adder-multiplier circuit on the gate level. One main feature of the first example is obviously the need for modeling time-varying behavior, whereas the second one raises the problem of handling a device with many components (about 10^3 gates).

3   Diagnosis with Hierarchical Models

The obvious solution to the problem of diagnosing such a big system is to **hierachically structure the device model**, identify the faulty components at the higher level and recursively descend in the hierarchy until the fault is localized with the required grain size (this is, for instance, part of the troubleshooting system of [Hamscher 88]).

We have developed component-oriented modeling systems that allow for a hierarchical decomposition of the modules. For instance, the system of [Struss 87] provides a framework for executable component models that forms a basis for simulation and for the predictive mechanism in GDE. The components of a device can be organized in a part-of-hierarchy, and it is possible to create the refined level for each component independent of the others. Since component models can also be de-activated after their creation, it is possible to **focus** the predictive engine of GDE on the appropriate level of each interesting component.

The diagnostic process can be organized along this structure of the model. If a candidate has a significantly higher probability than the others, GDE is recursively applied to each suspected component in this candidate. For instance, the adder-multiplier example of Fig. 2 has been modelled at five levels, where, at the lowest level, the number of gates lies in the order of 10^3. Localizing a double fault (one in each adder) required only the instantiation of about 20 models on all levels with the recursive GDE.

This strategy, however, does not address some important issues. What we are ultimately aiming at is a global control mechanism which may also decide to step up in the hierarchy and to change the focus (for instance, if the fault cannot be localized at the lower level). Focusing completely on one suspected component as done in the recursive GDE assumes that the necessary observations can be made within this focus. However, often the components (in particular on lower levels) are not directly accessible and, hence, the focus of attention has to be larger than the focus of suspicion, though not necessarily at the same level of detail.

4   Diagnosis with Dynamic Models

You do not get much information about the thyristor circuit if you look only at a snapshot at one time point; the voltage supply changes continuously, and reasoning about the state changes of the thyristors is essential. There is another aspect of the problem: Even if the device is in an equilibrium state, it might be useful to shift it into a different state in order to obtain important information. For instance, we want to supply the adder-multiplier circuit with a different test vector.

Modeling component behavior can no longer be based on propagation of simple values by constraints. Each value has to receive a "time stamp" (a time point or an interval). [Williams 86] presents TCP, a constraint system that propagates episodes, i.e. value-time pairs, rather than mere values.

Episode propagation in a straightforward way may lead to considerable problems with complexity: if the same value combinations occur at different times, the same computation is performed several times. This fact motivated the implementation of a *Multiple Context Temporal Constraint Propagator*, MCTCP ([Dressler-Freitag 89]). MCTCP attaches a "temporal label" to the values. If the temporal extension of a value is changed, no new computation of values is required but only an update of the temporal labels along the dependency structure.

The temporal constraint systems described above have been used in the thyristor case study. Conflicts in this framework are indicated by contradictory values **with temporal overlap** . A candidate has to intersect all conflicts that are detected in the course of time.

The methods are applicable only to discrete values. This is natural for digital circuits. In the thyristor case, continuous functions had to be approximated by step functions. Using qualitative values is an alternative .

MCTCP provides only limited means for reasoning about temporal relations on a symbolic level. In particular, it does not perform symbolic reasoning about delay which would provide a basis for adequately handling feedback systems and detecting periodic behavior.

5   Diagnosis with Fault Models

The basic GDE depends on identifying inconsistencies between observations and predictions and their underlying correctness assumptions about components. It assumes that such an inconsistency can be removed by retracting any of the involved correctness assumptions and that, hence, the respective components are (a part of) a potential diagnosis. However, this does not imply that there exists a faulty behavior of this component which is consistent with the observations. This is why the basic GDE may work on candidates which are physically implausible.

Consider, for example, the circuit with a voltage source, S, six wires, W_i, and three light bulbs, B_i (Fig. 3). From the observation that B_3 is lit, while B_1 and B_2 are not, common sense tells us that these two bulbs are broken. The basic GDE, however, generates 22 minimal candidates, including e.g. $\{S, B_3\}$. The interpretation of this candidate is: *"The battery, S, is broken; it does not produce voltage. This is in accordance with B_1 and B_2 being off, but it contradicts the normal behavior of B_3 which implies the existence of a voltage when lit. B_3 is not working properly: It is lit without voltage."* Obviously, this is due to the lack of knowledge about the possible behaviors of broken bulbs.

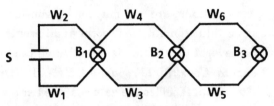

Figure 3 Circuit with 6 wires and 3 bulbs

This sort of knowledge and the required inferences can be exloited in GDE+ ([Struss 88b], [Struss-Dressler 89]). For each type of component a number of **fault models** may be entered which describe the possible ways of misbehavior. The basic inference that had to be added is that a component is working correctly, if none of its fault models applies.

For the thyristor circuit, exploiting fault models turned out to be crucial: any predicted value for the current depends on all thyristors. Hence, for the basic GDE, each of them could be responsible for a detected conflict. In contrast, GDE+ can pinpoint the faulty thyristor without further measurements since thyristors fail only in a few, well-specified ways. GDE+ depends on the assumption that a component fails in no other way than those specified in the fault models. In [Struss 88b, 89a] a way is shown to handle cases where components misbehave in an unknown mode (see also section 6).

With the use of fault models, predictions are no longer made on the basis of only one model. The combinatorial problem which lies in the existence of multiple models for each component requires tight control over the predictive engine, e.g. guided by a single fault heuristic. [Dressler-Farquhar 89] and [Farquhar 89] describe a technique that serves this purpose.

With the introduction of fault models, the scope of the diagnostic system is extended: it is no longer confined to identifying faulty components, but has the potential of determining their actual misbehavior. This idea of diagnosis as searching for a model of the device that is consistent with the observation has lead to the development of SHERLOCK ([de Kleer-Williams 89]). Fault models are also used in [Hamscher 88]. The idea of gathering information suitable for exonerating components, which is essential for the use of fault models, is also fundamental for the TRIAL system of [Raiman 89].

6   Diagnosis with Multiple Tests

Since a diagnosis has to account for all discrepancies regardless of the test that revealed them, candidates simply have to be constructed from the union of the sets of conflicts detected in different situations. This set is automatically collected by the ATMS over the various tests. All we need is a constraint system that is able to temporally index values and avoids combining values belonging to different tests. This is provided by systems mentioned in section 4.

Sometimes, not only the system's normal behavior may be dynamic but also a fault. A component works correctly for a while and exhibits a faulty behavior in other periods. Such intermittent faults are not a principal problem for the basic GDE: If observations are gathered at different times, some of them will produce conflicts, whereas others might be in accordance with the expected behavior and, hence, do not contribute information relevant for diagnosis. This means, candidates can still be constructed in the ordinary way from the set of conflicts, regardless of the potential intermittency of faults.

If we introduce inferences, however, that establish the correctness of components, as is the case for GDE $^+$ with its use of fault models, we run into trouble. We may no longer conclude the correctness of a component in general if each of its fault models was found to contradict the observations, since such a contradiction may be only temporary.

We are not completely lost, however, if we introduce an **unknown fault mode**. If all other fault models of the faulty component are ruled out based on observations during periods of correct behavior, the intermittent fault would be captured by the unknown fault (which is never ruled out because it makes no predictions).

This solution is not really satisfactory. It does not really make intermittency of faults an explicit concept in the diagnostic strategy, but rather "hides" it in the unknown fault. Thus, it prevents the diagnostic problem solver, for instance, from exploiting the fact that one fault model would be a perfect explanation for the observations made in exactly those test situations that produce conflicts. In other words, it is hard for the problem solver to decide whether the manifestation of the fault depends on the state (described by certain parameter values or test vectors) or on time (or, rather, accident). Different observations obtained for the same state (of the whole device or a single component) would provide evidence for the latter.

7 Discrepancy Detection

In real applications, we can not always trust the observations. They can suffer from inaccuracy of measurements. They could be supplied by sensors which themselves are malfunctioning. Or they may be based on the interpretation of a human (*"This curve is steeper than normal"*) or simply a typing error.

The basic GDE does not allow for a retraction of observations. As a straightforward extension, we no longer treat observations as facts but support them by an assumption (meaning *"The observation is correct"*) which is then recorded in dependencies just like the components' correctness assumptions are. [Struss 88a,b] shows how this change enables the system to retract observations and thus to avoid wrong diagnoses. Because the observation assumptions appear in conflicts, GDE can be extended also to "diagnose" the observations by applying the same diagnostic algorithm to both types of assumptions. An important special case of an observation assumption is one that supports treating two values as the same. This can be used to reflect the inaccuracy of measurements, e.g. by regarding a measurement $x = 15.25$ as a confirmation of the prediction $x = 15.0$.

Again, control knowledge is required in order to determine in which situation observations should be questioned.

8 Conclusions

In this paper, our starting point was the General Diagnostic Engine, which is meant to overcome limitations of traditional rule-based systems.

We presented a number of hard problems which could not be dealt with by the basic GDE. However, these problems have, to a certain extent, been solved by extending the basic framework in a principled, coherent way without violating its foundations. We are able to handle simple dynamic aspects, multiple tests, hierarchy, unreliable observations, and fault models. The generality of these solutions is still restricted. Further research is required, also w.r.t. other problems, which were not mentioned here, such as changing device structures, complex temporal behavior (e. g. feedback systems), and reasoning with approximate and qualitative models. But the research efforts have reached a point where it appears to be possible to apply these techniques to carefully chosen real applications with a good chance of success. Only applications can provide the empirical basis for progress in solving one of the most important open problems: control over the diagnostic process in general and over the use of the device model in particular [(see Struss 89a)]. Introducing richer, highly structured models will drown the principal power of this approach in an ocean of complexity if there is no tight navigation through the complex models. It is quite obvious that the necessary control knowledge contains algorithmic techniques and systematic reasoning about structure as well as empirical knowledge about a particular device or domain. In a sense, we are returning to exploiting heuristics and empirical associations. But this happens on a different foundation: a developing theory of diagnosis which reflects the "first principles" of our knowledge about devices.

Acknowledgements

For their contributions, comments, hints, discussions, and technical support, I would like to thank Johan de Kleer, Oskar Dressler, Adam Farquhar, Hartmut Freitag, Walter Hamscher, Claudia Johnson, Linda Pfefferl, Olivier Raiman, Michael Reinfrank, and Brian Williams. This research was supported in part by the German government (ITW 8506 E4).

References

[Davis 82]
Davis, R., *Expert Systems: Where Are We? And Where Do We Go From Here?*, The AI Magazine, Spring 1982
[de Kleer 86]
de Kleer, J., *An Assumption-Based TMS*, Artificial Intelligence 28(2), 1986
[de Kleer-Williams 87]
de Kleer, J., Williams, B.C., *Diagnosing Multiple Faults*, Artificial Intelligence 32(1), 1987
[de Kleer-Williams 89]
de Kleer, J., Williams, B.C., *Diagnosis with Behavioral Modes*, Proceedings IJCAI-89
[Dressler-Farquhar 89]
Dressler, O. , Farquhar, A., *Problem Solver Control over the ATMS*, Proceedings GWAI-89
[Dressler-Freitag 89]
Dressler, O., Freitag, H., *Propagation of Temporally Indexed Values in Multiple Contexts*, Proceedings GWAI-89
[Farquhar 89]
Farquhar, A., *Modifying Models during Diagnosis*, Proceedings GWAI-89
[Hamscher 88]
Hamscher, W., *Model-Based Troubleshooting of Digital Circuits*, MIT-TR 1074, 1988
[Raiman 89]
Raiman, O., *Diagnosis as a Trial: The Alibi Principle*, IBM Scientific Center, 1989
[Struss 87]
Struss, P., *Multiple Representation of Structure and Function*, in: J.Gero (ed.), Expert Systems in Computer-Aided Design, Amsterdam 1987
[Struss 88a]
Struss, P., *Extensions to ATMS-Based Diagnosis*, in: J.S. Gero (ed.), Artificial Intelligence in Engineering: Diagnosis and Learning, Southampton, 1988
[Struss 88b]
Struss, P., *A Framework for Model-Based Diagnosis*, Siemens Technical Report INF 2 ARM-10-88, Munich, 1988
[Struss 89a]
Struss, P., *Diagnosis as a Process*, Workshop on Model-Based Diagnosis, Paris, 1989
[Struss 89b]
Struss, P., Model-Based Diagnosis - Recent Advances and Perspectives, Siemens Technical Report INF 2 ARM-16-89, Munich, 1989
[Struss-Dressler 89]
Struss, P., Dressler, O., *"Physical Negation" - Integrating Fault Models into the General Diagnostic Engine*, Proceedings IJCAI-89
[Williams 86]
Williams, B., *Doing Time: Putting Qualitative Reasoning on Firmer Ground*, Proceedings AAAI-86

Network Search with Inadmissible Heuristics

A. Mahanti
Indian Institute of Management Calcutta
Post Box No. 16757, Alipore Post Office
Calcutta 700 027, India

K. Ray
Regional Computer Centre
Jadavpur University Campus
Calcutta 700 032, INDIA

Abstract

A new arc-marking algorithm, namely MarkC is presented. MarkC uses the run-time heuristic modification scheme (due to Mero), and the node selection criterion of AlgorithmC (due to Bagchi and Mahanti). AlgorithmC, based on the node expansion scheme, has some important properties under general inadmissible heuristics. AlgorithmC always finds a least costly solution path of V (an implicitly defined set of nodes) and makes $O(N^2)$ node expansions at the worst. It is shown that MarkC retains all the merits of C, yet it does not iterate more number of times than C. But there are examples where C can make some more iterations than MarkC. Finally, a comparative study is presented by summarizing the results on Algorithms MarkA, C, and MarkC.

1   Introduction

Heuristic search in networks have many important applications in problem solving and artificial intelligence. A variety of algorithms have been designed by several investigators. While the objective of such an algorithm is to find a minimal-cost solution path, finding a minimal-cost solution path often becomes very expensive in terms of the algorithm's execution time. Thus we want to have a trade-off between: (i) cost of solution path, and (ii) time taken to find a solution. We are interested in search algorithms that output optimal or near optimal solutions and do not take an inordinately long execution time.

Search algorithms in networks have been designed in three different approaches [Bagchi and Mahanti, 1985a]. In the first approach, [Nilsson, 1980], the idea is to choose a node for expansion from a list (called OPEN) for which a real valued function (called evaluation function) has the minimum value. In the second approach [Nilsson, 1980], a node that is expanded once is not expanded again; instead a "propagation" of values takes place. In the third approach [Martelli and Montanari, 1973, 1978] the notion of arc-marking is used. The algorithms in this approach do not maintain any list like OPEN, instead they generate explicit graphs during their executions. To identify the node to be expanded next some arcs of the explicit graph are marked.

To limit the execution time, algorithms are restricted to expand nodes from only a small set (implicitly defined), called V. In general arc-marking algorithms are considered to be efficient because :

   (a) only the nodes of V are selected for expansion and no node is expanded more than once, and

   (b) in each iteration, the node to be expanded is decided only by a bottom-up computation on the nodes in a part of the explicit graph.

When the heuristic function is admissible (h is a lower bound on h*) all existing search allgorithms output an optimal solution. But under inadmissible heuristics, none of the available marking algorithms can ensure the best possible solution from V. In this paper a new marking algorithm called MarkC is proposed. MarkC always outputs the best possible solution from V and its worst case running time is $O(N^2)$.

To show the power of heuristics Nilsson [Nilsson, 1980] has illustrated a heuristic function that fits very well in the case of 8-puzzle:

$$h(n) = P(n) + 3 * S(n),$$

where $P(n)$ is the Manhattan distance and $S(n)$ is a sequence score. It can be observed that h is inadmissible in this case. Where as $h(n) = P(n)$ is admissible, but not a good estimate of actual cost h*. Thus a good inadmissible heuristic function would be preferred over an ineffective admissible heuristic function.

To reduce the number of node expansions by algorithms a new method for run-time modification of heuristic estimate of nodes was presented in [Mero, 1984]. MarkC uses this method to determine the node to be expanded in each iteration.

AlgorithmC for network search was presented in [Bagchi and Mahanti, 1983]. It has some interesting properties. It always finds a least costly solution path of V and makes $O(N^2)$ node expansions at the worst. It is shown in this paper that the performance of MarkC, both in terms of quality of output, and execution time, is at least as good as or better than that of C. There are examples where C can take more execution time than MarkC.

In case of inadmissible heuristics the limitations of the existing arc-marking algorithms viz. HS [Martelli and Montanari, 1973, 1978] and MarkA [Bagchi and Mahanti, 1985a] (a modified version of HS) are :

(a) when a node is labelled solved no reevaluation is permitted at that node, and

(b) heuristic estimate at a node is used during its evaluation but not to guide the overall search to find a good (less costly) solution path.

MarkC tries to overcome these limitations and gives good performance in case of inadmissible heuristics. But when heuristic is admissible, in general, it may be still preferable to use MarkA, because of its simple node selection criterion.

2   Algorithm MarkC

Like other marking algorithms, MarkC runs on acyclic networks. During the execution of MarkC, at any iteration, below each node n in the explicit graph there is a path with root n having all its arcs marked. We call this the <u>marked path below n</u>. MarkC uses a TIP variable for every node n to identify the first node m on the marked path below n such that $TIP(m) = m$. At each iteration, it expands a node m with $TIP(m) = m$. We now present Alg. MarkC. It is assumed that the readers are familier with the notation and standard terminology as given in [Nilsson, 1980].

Algorithm MarkC

MarkC1   (Initially the explicit graph consists solely of the start node s.) Set $b(s) :=$ 0, $TIP(s) := s$.

MarkC2   Repeat the following steps until $TIP(s)$ is a terminal or nonterminal leaf node. If $TIP(s)$ is a terminal leaf node, exit with $b(s)$ as the solution cost; otherwise exit with failure.

MarkC2.1   Let n be the node $TIP(s)$. Expand n by generating all of its immediate successors, if any, and update the explicit graph.

(i) If an immediate successor n_i was not earlier present in the explicit graph and is now newly introduced then set $h(n_i) := \max \{ h(n_i), h(n) - c(n,n_i) \}$, $b(n_i) := 0$, and $TIP(n_i) := n_i$.

(ii) If an immediate successor n_i was earlier present in the explicit graph and $h(n) - c(n,n_i) > h(n_i)$ then set $h(n_i) := h(n) - c(n,n_i)$, $b(n_i) := 0$, and $TIP(n_i) := n_i$.

MarkC2.2   Create a set Z containing only node n. Then for each n_i, $1 \le i \le k$, such that n_i was earlier present in the explicit graph and its h-value has been just increased at step MarkC2.1(ii), add to Z all immediate marked predecessors of n_i (if any) in the explicit graph.

MarkC2.3   Repeat the following steps until Z is empty.

MarkC2.3.1   Remove from Z a node m such that no descendant of m in the explicit graph occurs in Z.

MarkC2.3.2   (i) If m has no successors set $h(m) := \infty$.
ii) a. Let m have immediate successors $m_1, m_2, ..., m_k$ in the explicit graph. Compute

$$e := \min_{1 \le i \le k} \{c(m,m_i) + h(m_i)\}.$$

b. If $h(m) > e$ then go to step MarkC2.3.3; Otherwise compute

$$w := \min_{1 \le i \le k} \{c(m,m_i) + b(m_i) \,|\, c(m,m_i) + h(m_i) = e\}.$$

Let this minimum occur for $i = i_o$ (resolve ties arbitrarily but always in favour of a node p, such that TIP(p) is a terminal leaf node). Mark the arc (m,m_{i_o}). Set $b(m) := w$, $h(m) := e$, and $TIP(m) := TIP(m_{i_o})$.

MarkC2.3.3: Add to Z every immediate predecessor of m along marked arcs, if it is not already present in Z [Ignore predecessors not connected to m by marked arcs.].

We analyze Algorithm MarkC using the formulation under inadmissible heuristics as suggested in [Bagchi and Mahanti,1983].

3   Definition

(a) At instant j in the explicit graph G_j, a node n is called a <u>bottom node</u> or <u>b-node</u> if $TIP(n) = n$ in G_j.

(b) A <u>maximal path</u> in G_j is a path from s to a tip node.

(c) G'_j is a subgraph of G_j consisting of all maximal paths starting from s and ending at a first available b-node. $P'_j(n)$ is the marked path below n in G'_j at instant j.

(d) $M_i = \underline{\text{pathmax}} (P_i) = \max_{n \in P_i} \{c (P_i, s, n) + h(n)\}$,

where $c(P_i,s,n)$ is the cost of path P_i from s to n.

(e) Define $Q = \min_{i \ge 1} \{M_i\}$

(f) $P_{i_1}, P_{i_2}, ..., P_{i_k}$ be the minimal cost solution paths in G.
Define $Q_{opt} = \min_{1 \le j \le k} \{M_{i_j}\}$.

(g) $s \in V$, and $n \in V$ if there is a path P from s to n such that $c(P) + h(n) \le Q$ and the immediate predecessor of n on P is in V. $N = |V|$.

(h) P is a Q path if pathmax $(P) = Q$. P is a Q_{min} path if it is a least costly Q path. C_{min} = cost of a Q_{min} path.

(i) h(n,j) is the modified h value of node n at instant j.

(j) By f_{MarkA}, f_{MarkC} and f_c we mean the output of Algs. MarkA, MarkC and C respectively.

We now illustrate the working of MarkC through examples.

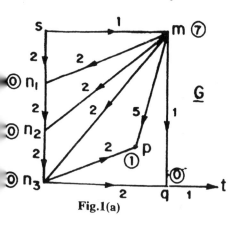

Fig.1(a)

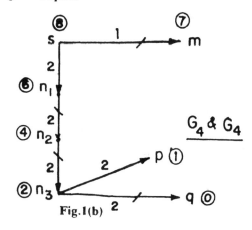

Fig.1(b)

4   Example

(a) In Figure 1(a), s and t are start and terminal leaf nodes; p is a non-terminal leaf node; m, q, n_1, n_2 and n_3 are other nodes. Heuristic estimates are encircled and arc costs are shown beside the arcs. Node m is expanded at instant 5. Nodes m, p and q are both b-nodes and tip nodes in G_4 and G'_4 shown in Figure 1(b). After expansion of m, G_5 will become as shown in Figure 1(c). After the bottom-up computation at instant 5, G_5 will be as shown in Figure 1(d). Note that n_2 was a b-node in Figure 1(c) but it is not a b-node in Figure 1(d). At the begining of instant 6, marked path below s is s, m, q and marked path below n_3 is n_3, q.

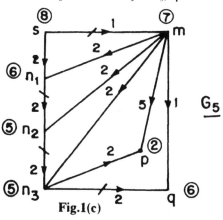

Fig.1(c)

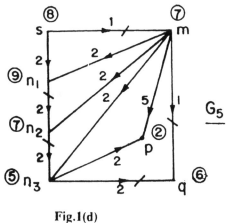

Fig.1(d)

446

(b) In Figure 2, the heuristic function h is admissible. $Q = Q_{opt} = h^*(s) = 6$; $V = \{s, n, m, p, t\}$; $N = 5$. MarkC expands nodes s,n,p,m. If we change the cost of arc (p,t) from 2 to 1, h becomes inadmissible, and then $Q = Q_{opt} = 6 > h^*(s) = 5$. But MarkC expands nodes in the same sequence and $f_{MarkC} = 5$.

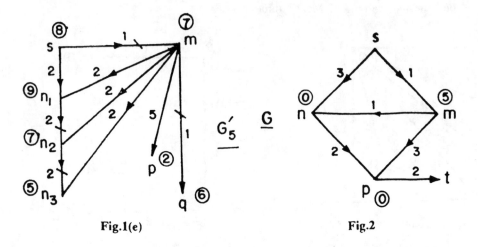

Fig.1(e)   Fig.2

(c) For network G in Figure 3, $Q_{opt} = 8 > Q = 7 > h^*(s) = 4$.
Solution paths are $P_1 = $ s,m,n,r,t; $P_2 = $ s,m,p,r,t; $P_3 = $ s,m,q,r,t. P_1 and P_2 are Q paths, and also P_1 is a Q_{min} path. Note that $f_{MarkA} = 6 > f_C = f_{MarkC} = C_{min} = 5$.

(d) Consider the network in Figure 4(a). If we compare Algs.C and MarkC here, we will find that both of them expand nodes in the sequence : $s, n_2, n_3, n_1, n_2, n_3, n_4$. It is interesting to observe that if we take the strictly increasing sequence of F values in C, and h(s) (modified) values in MarkC, these two sequences will be identical. In this example the sequence is 0,3,4,7. It can be observed that the explicit graphs of both the algorithms will be identical at these instants.

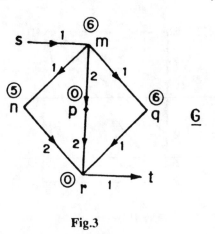

Fig.3

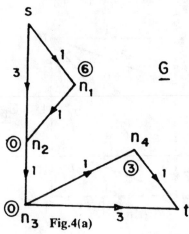

Fig.4(a)

(e) If we run Algs.C and MarkC on the network of Figure 4(b), node expansions will be as follows :

Alg.C : s, n_2, n_3, n_4, n_1, n_2, n_1, n_4;   **Alg.MarkC** : s, n_2, n_3, n_4, n_1.

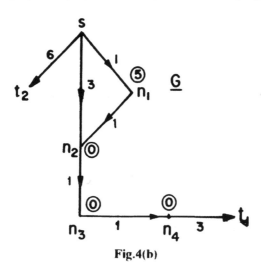

Fig.4(b)

5   Correctness proofs of Alg. MarkC

We give below a brief outline of proofs. Detailed proofs are omitted.

Theorem 5.1   At any instant j, $h(s,j) \leq Q$.

Proof   By double induction. First on instants and then at every instant j on the nodes of G'_j. At every instant j we show that for the leading node $n \in G'_j$ on a Q_{min} path P, $c(P,s,n) + h(n,j) \leq Q$.

Q.E.D.

Theorem 5.2   MarkC terminates.

Proof   It is easy to show that if G has a solution path, MarkC terminates successfully, otherwise it terminates with failure.

Q.E.D.

Theorem 5.3 $b(s,j) = c(P'_j) = \min \{c(P) + h(r,j) \mid c(P) + h(r,j) = h(s,j)\}$, where P is a path from s to any node r in G'_j.

Proof   Clear.

Q.E.D.

Theorem 5.4   If t is the terminal leaf node found by MarkC at instant j_0 then:

(i) $h(s,j_0) = c(P'_{j_0}) + h(t,j_0) = Q$, and

(ii) $b(s,j_o) = c(P'_{j_o}) \leq Q$.

Proof (i) Clear from Theorem 5.1.

(ii) Obvious.

Q.E.D.

Theorem 5.5 $b(s,j_o) = C_{min}$.

Proof By Theorem 5.4, $h(s,j_o) = Q$. Thus $b(s,j_o) = $ cost of a Q path $< C_{min}$. Suppose $b(s,j_o) > C_{min}$. If n be the leading node on a Q_{min} path P at j_o then
(a) $c(P,s,n) + h(n,j_o) \leq Q$ .... (as in Theorem 5.1)
(b) $h(s,j_o) = Q$ .... (by Theorem 5.2) and
(c) $b(s,j_o) > c(P) = C_{min} \geq c(P,s,n)$
    ... a contradiction by Theorem 5.3.

Q.E.D.

Remark : h admissible $=> Q = h(s)$.

Theorem 5.6 $b(s,j_o) = h^*(s)$ **iff** $Q = Q_{opt}$.

Proof $Q = Q_{opt} => C_{min} = h^*(s)$ and vice versa.

Q.E.D.

Theorem 5.7 MarkC makes $O(N^2)$ iterations of step MarkC2 at worst.

Proof $h(s)$ can increase maximum N times. Between two increasing $h(s)$ values $b(s)$ can be defined maximum N times by different b-nodes.

Q.E.D.

Theorem 5.8 The explicit graphs in Algs.C and MarkC are identical (i.e. having same nodes and arcs) at the time instants when F value in C and $h(s)$ value in MarkC increase.

Proof Omitted.

Q.E.D.

Theorem 5.9 For any acyclic network G, MarkC iterates step MarkC2 at most as many times as C makes node expansions.

Proof Use Theorem 5.8.

Q.E.D.

6   Conclusion

Finally we summarize the results in a table below giving properties of the algorithms discussed. In actual implementation, MarkC can keep track of expanded nodes and need not expand a node more than once. We quote here some results on Algs. C and MarkA from [Bagchi and Mahanti, 1985a]. We assume that the number of immediate successors of any node in G is bounded by a positive integer K.

Alg.	Storage requirement	Worst case run time	Quality of output		Remarks
			h admissible	h inadmissible	
MarkA	$O(N)$	$O(N^2)$	$f_{MarkA}=h^*(s)$	$f_{MarkA} \leq Q$	* $f_{MarkA} \geq C_{min}$ * No computation takes place below any solved node * At each iteration the node to be expanded is determined by following the marked path below s
C	$O(N)$	$O(N^2)$	$f_c=h^*(s)$	$f_c = C_{min}$	* Can expand nodes more than once * Can make more node expansions than MarkC
MarkC	$O(N)$	$O(N^2)$	$f_{MarkC}=h^*(s)$	$f_{MarkC}=C_{min}$	* No solve labelling procedure is used * At each iteration TIP(s) is expanded or reevaluated * Does not iterate more than C * Avoids using a large list like OPEN in C for node selection

Table 6.1

AND/OR graphs have important applications in Artificial Intelligence and Expert

Systems. It may be worthwhile to generalize Alg. MarkC for AND/OR graphs as well. Some results on AND/OR graphs are available in [Mahanti and Bagchi, 1985b] and [Martelli and Montanari, 1973].

7 References

[Bagchi and Mahanti, 1983]
Bagchi A and Mahanti A. *Search Algorithms Under Different Kinds of Heuristics - A Comparative Study*, JACM 30(1), pp.1-21, 1983.

[Bagchi and Mahanti, 1985a]
Bagchi A and Mahanti A. *Three Approaches to Heuristic Search in Networks*, JACM 32(1), pp.1-27, 1985.

[Mahanti and Bagchi, 1985b]
Mahanti A and Bagchi A. *AND/OR Graph Heuristic Search Methods*, JACM 32(1), pp.28-51, 1985.

[Martelli and Montanari, 1973]
Martelli A and Montanari U. *Additive AND/OR Graphs*, Proceedings of Third International Joint Conference on Artificial Intelligence, Stanford, California, pp. 1-11,1973.

[Martelli and Montanari, 1978]
Martelli A and Montanari U. *Optimising Decision Trees Through Heuristically Guided Search*, Comm. ACM, Vol.12, pp.1025-1039, 1978.

[Mero,1984]
Mero L. *A Heuristic Search Algorithm with Modifiable Estimate*, Artificial Intelligence, Vol.23, pp.13-27, 1984.

[Nilsson, 1980]
Nilsson NJ. *Principles of Artificial Intelligence*, Tiago, Palo Alto, California, 1980.

Pruning by Upperbounds in Heuristic Search: Use of Approximate Algorithms

UK Sarkar   PP Chakrabarti   S Ghose   SC DeSarkar

Department of Computer Science and Engineering
Indian Institute of Technology
Kharagpur - 721302
INDIA

Abstract

The use of approximate algorithms in aiding heuristic search is explored. Approximate algorithms are coupled with algorithm A* to generate an algorithm BFPR which maintains provably good quality of solutions. Experiments were performed with Euclidean Traveling Salesman problem and with the problem of Scheduling Independent Tasks. It is found that the algorithm expands considerably fewer number of nodes and yet very often produces optimal solutions.

1   Introduction

Admissible search strategies often restrict the use of heuristic functions to underestimates of the cost of the optimal solution, giving rise to the expansion of a large number of nodes. Attempts have already been made to reduce the number of nodes by using multiple heuristic functions [Chakrabarti et al, 1989; Pearl, 1984]. There are a number of excellent approximate algorithms available for many computationally intractable problems. A good approximate algorithm can provide a pessimistic but very good estimate and thus has the potential of assisting in heuristic search. This paper explores the possibility of exploiting the potential of approximate algorithms as an aid to branch and bound algorithms like A* [Nilsson, 1980] or its variants to improve its performance by node pruning and yet obtain good quality solutions.

Suppose there are r (r≥1) approximate algorithms A_i, i=1,2,..,r, available to solve a problem. Given r real constants ϵ_i, ($\epsilon_i \geq 0$, i=1,2,..,r) the approximate algorithms are coupled with algorithm A* to generate a parameterized algorithm BFPR($r,A_1,\epsilon_1,A_2,\epsilon_2, \ .. \ ,A_r,\epsilon_r$) (Best First Search with Pruning) which generates fewer nodes than A^*. The constants ϵ_i, i=1,2, .. ,r, control the balance between the quality of solution and node expansion. For large ϵ_i's, algorithm BFPR imitates A^*.

Some general characteristics of the algorithm BFPR() are established. It is proved that BFPR() always generates a solution which is no worse than the best solution achievable by any of the approximate algorithms used. Furthermore, there exists examples in which BFPR() finds the optimal solution and yet does not expand some node with a lower bound estimate which is less than the cost of the optimal cost solution. Experiments were performed with the Euclidean Traveling Salesman Problem (ETSP) and with the problem of Scheduling Independent Tasks. Results indicate that BFPR() often gives the optimal solution and the solution is obtained with the expansion of a very small number of nodes as compared to A^*.

2 The algorithm

2.1 Notation and definitions

s	:	start node,
n,m	:	nodes in the search graph,
t	:	goal node,
$h^*(n)$	:	cost of the minimal cost path from n to goal,
h(n)	:	estimate of $h^*(n)$, [$h \le h^*$],
g(n)	:	cost of the minimal cost path from s to n,
f(n)	:	g(n) + h(n),
P,X	:	solution paths from s to goal,
P^*	:	minimal cost path from s to goal,
cost(P)	:	cost of solution path P,
C^*	:	cost(P^*),
N^*	:	number of nodes expanded by A^*,
$A_1, A_2,...$	:	approximate algorithms,
PA^*	:	the best solution path generated by the approximate algorithms used,
CA^*	:	cost(PA^*),
$CA_i(n)$	:	cost of the path from n to goal, as generated by A_i applied at node n,
$FA_i(n)$	:	g(n) + $CA_i(n)$,
$M_i(P)$	:	max { $FA_i(n)$ }, $n \in P$,
B_i	:	$M_i(PA^*)$.

2.2 Algorithm BFPR

// Algorithm BFPR($p,A_1,\epsilon_1,A_2,\epsilon_2,...,A_p,\epsilon_p$). Modification of algorithm A^* [Nilsson, 1980] by the $p(p \ge 1)$ approximate algorithms A_i and constants ϵ_i ($\epsilon_i \ge 0$, i=1,2,...,p) //

step 0 : Use A_i, i=1,..,p to determine PA^* which is the best solution generated by A_i's. Calculate B_i for i=1,..,p.

step 1 : Put the start node s on OPEN.

step 2 : If OPEN is empty, exit with failure.

step 3 : Remove from OPEN and place on CLOSED a node n for which f(n) is minimum.

step 4 : If n is a goal node, exit with success with the solution corresponding to node n.

step 5 : Expand n, generating all its successors, and attach to them pointers back to n.
for every successor m of n do
  (i) If m is not already on OPEN or CLOSED then
      if ($\forall$ i $\in$ {1,..,p} (FA$_i$(m) $\leq$ B$_i$*(1+ϵ_i)))
      then calculate g(m), h(m), f(m); insert m in OPEN.
  (ii) If m is already on OPEN or CLOSED direct its pointers along the path yielding the lowest g(m).

step 6 : Goto step 2.

Note :

(i) h(n) used is an underestimate. We assume h to be monotone also, since an underestimate can always be made monotone[Pearl, 1984].

(ii) In the algorithm, if A$_k$ determines PA*, then B$_k$=cost(PA*).

Lemma 1 : The set S_r={ X | $\forall$ i $\in$ {1,..,r} (M$_i$(X) $\leq$ B$_i$)} is non-empty for any r, (1$\leq$r$\leq$p), where p is the number of approximate algorithms available.

Proof : M$_i$(PA*) $\leq$ B$_i$, for all i=1,2,..,p. Hence PA* $\in$ S$_r$. Thus, S$_r$ is non-empty.

Lemma 2 : At any time before BFPR(r,A$_1$,ϵ_1,.., A$_r$, ϵ_r) terminates, there exists an OPEN node n such that f(n) $\leq$ C$_{min}$ and $\forall$ i $\in$ {1,.. ,r} (FA$_i$(n) $\leq$ B$_i$*(1+ϵ_i)) , $\epsilon_i$$\geq$0, where C$_{min}$=min {cost(P)}, P$\in$S, and S={X | $\forall$ i $\in$ {1,..,r} (M$_i$(X) $\leq$ B$_i$*(1+ϵ_i))}.

Proof : Consider the solution path P$_{min}$ for which cost(P$_{min}$)=C$_{min}$. Let n be the shallowest OPEN node along P$_{min}$. It is obvious that there will be at least one node along P$_{min}$ in OPEN before BFPR() terminates as no node along P$_{min}$ is denied entry in OPEN by step 5 of BFPR().

For any i, (1$\leq$i$\leq$r), FA$_i$(n) $\leq$ M$_i$(P$_{min}$), since n $\in$ P$_{min}$.
                                 $\leq$ B$_i$*(1+ϵ_i), since P$_{min}$ $\in$ S.

Now, f(n) = g(n) + h(n) $\leq$ g(n) + h*(n),
                          $\leq$ C$_{min}$, since n $\in$ P$_{min}$.

Note : If cost(PA*) is finite and positive, then C$_{min}$ is also finite and positive.

Theorem 1 : If h is an underestimate, and $\epsilon_i \geq 0$ $\forall$ i $\in$ {1, 2,..,r}, then the algorithm BFPR(r,A_1,ϵ_1,.. , A_r,ϵ_r) terminates with cost= min {cost(P)}, P $\in$ S,
where S= { X | $\forall$ i $\in$ {1,.., r} (M_i(X) $\leq$ B_i*(1+ϵ_i)) }.

Proof : The proof that BFPR() terminates is similar to that of A^*, due to Nilsson [Nilsson, 1980]. From lemma 1, it follows that S is non-empty. The rest of the proof follows from lemma 2.

Corollary : The solution generated by BFPR(r,A_1,0, A_2,0,.. , A_r,0) for any r (1$\leq$r$\leq$p) is no worse than PA*.

Theorem 2 : No node n will be expanded by BFPR(r, A_1,ϵ_1, A_2,ϵ_2,.. , A_r,ϵ_r), ($\epsilon_i \geq 0$) if ($\exists$ i $\in$ {1,.., r} (FA_i(n) > B_i*(1+ϵ_i))) OR (f(n) > min {cost(P)}, P $\in$ S.

Proof : A node n for which there exists some i, (1$\leq$i$\leq$r), such that (FA_i(n) > B_i*(1+ϵ_i)) holds, will be denied entry in OPEN by step 5 of BFPR(), and hence it can not be expanded. The fact that no node n for which f(n)>min {cost(P)},P $\in$ S, holds is expanded by BFPR() follows from lemma 2 (since h(n) is an underestimate).

Theorem 3 :
(i) If $\epsilon_i' \geq \epsilon_i$, i=1,2, .. ,r, then the solution obtained by BFPR(r,A_1,ϵ_1', A_2,ϵ_2', .. , A_r,ϵ_r') is no worse (in terms of the cost of solution) than the solution obtained by BFPR(r,A_1,ϵ_1, A_2,ϵ_2, .. , A_r,ϵ_r).
(ii) If $\epsilon_i' \geq \epsilon_i$, $\forall$ i $\in$ {1,2,..,r}, and min {cost(P), P $\in$ S}, = min { cost(P), P $\in$ S' }, then nodes expanded by BFPR(r,A_1,ϵ_1,.. , A_r,ϵ_r) will be expanded by BFPR(r,A_1,ϵ_1', A_2,ϵ_2', .. , A_r,ϵ_r').

Proof :
(i) Let S = { P | $\forall$ i $\in$ {1,.., r} (M_i(P) $\leq$ B_i*(1+ϵ_i)) },
and S' = { P | $\forall$ i $\in$ {1,.., r} (M_i(P) $\leq$ B_i*(1+ϵ_i')) }.
clearly, S $\subseteq$ S'. Hence the proof follows from theorem 1.
(ii) Since both the algorithms terminate with the same solution, BFPR() with the bigger ϵ_i explores some extra nodes in the state space which are not explored by that with smaller ϵ_i. It may be noted that the anomalies due to the resolution of ties are not considered in the above analysis.

Corollary : If BFPR() finds an optimal solution, it does so by expanding no more nodes than A^*. This is because BFPR() with large ϵ 's imitates A^*.

It may be noted that there exist examples in which BFPR() does provide the optimal solution, and yet does not expand some node with f(n) < C^*.

2.3 Restriction on the use of approximate algorithms

For a given problem, the way in which the state space is generated by A^* and the approximate algorithms which can be tied together to generate algorithm BFPR() are closely related. An approximate algorithm A_k can be used in A^* to form BFPR() if $FA_k(n)$ is defined for each node n in the state space for A^*. This effectively means that, given any partial solution, A_k should be able to generate a complete solution without altering the partial solution.

However, in practice, this is not a serious restriction because a number of approximate algorithms are available to satisfy the requirement.

3 Experimental results

The state space and the approximate algorithms used in BFPR() are illustrated below with the problem of Euclidean Traveling Salesman (ETSP), and that of Scheduling Independent Tasks. For the ETSP, two different state spaces and two approximate algorithms for each are considered. For the Scheduling problem only one state space is considered.

3.1 Euclidean Traveling Salesman Problem

There are n points (cities), numbered 0 .. n-1 say, lying on an Euclidean plane. The problem is to find a Hamiltonian circuit of minimum length (all distances are Euclidean) of the underlying complete graph.

3.1.1 Method 1

state space : The root node is assumed to have visited city 0. Let P_n be the partial path corresponding to node n. n_1, n_2, .. ,n_k are the cities not yet visited by n, and n_* is the last city on P_n. Then n is expanded to have k children. Child i $(1 \leq i \leq k)$ extends P_n by adding to it the edge $<n_*,n_i>$.

A_1 : Nearest Neighbour Heuristic[Rosenkrantz et al, 1977]. $A_1(n)$ applies to node n to get a path from city n_* to city 0 passing through the cities n_1, n_2, .. ,n_k. This path, along with P_n clearly forms a Hamiltonian circuit.

A_2 : Double Spanning Tree Heuristic[Garey and Johnson, 1979]. $A_2(n)$ finds the minimum cost spanning tree of the complete graph having vertices as city 0, city n_*, and city n_i $(1 \leq i \leq k)$. A path from n_* to 0 is found through only (and all) the vertices of this tree whose cost is guaranteed to be within twice the cost of the spanning tree formed. Similarly, this path and P_n taken together forms a Hamiltonian circuit.

h(n) : Any admissible heuristic.

3.1.2   Method 2

State space : The root node is the partial tour formed by the boundary of the convex hull of the cities. Let $T_n = n_0$, n_1, $n_2, .., n_{k-1}$, n_0, be the partial tour corresponding to node n. Let v be some city not lying on T_n. Node n is expanded to have k children, where child i (0≤i<k) is obtained by inserting city v in between cities n_i and $n_{[(i+1) \mod k]}$ of T_n. This state space retains the optimal solution because it is known [Golden et al, 1980] that if the costs represent Euclidean distances and H is the convex hull of the points in two dimensional space, then the order in which the nodes on the boundary of H appear in the optimal tour will follow the order in which they appear in H. It may be noted that each node in the state space represents a partial tour, as opposed to a partial path in the state space mentioned under method 1.

A_1 : Farthest Insertion Heuristic [Rosenkrantz et al, 1977]. $A_1(n)$ applies to T_n, generating a complete tour.

A_2 : Convex Hull Heuristic [Golden et al, 1980]. $A_2(n)$, in a similar fashion, applies to T_n and generates a complete tour.

h(n)=0. Finding a non-trivial h() for a node in this state space is difficult. This example, however, highlights the fact that even with a poor h(), BFPR() works fine.

3.2 Scheduling Independent Tasks

Given a set $P = \{P_1, P_2, .. , P_m\}$ of m (m≥2) identical processors, and a finite set $T = \{T_1, T_2, .. , T_N\}$ of tasks, each task T_i (1≤i≤N) having an execution time $E(T_i) > 0$, to obtain a non-preemptive schedule for T and P which minimizes the overall finishing time.

State space : Rename the tasks such that $E(T_i) \geq E(T_{i+1})$, i=1,2,.. ,N-1. The root node assigns T_1 to P_1. While expanding node n, m children are generated. The i-th child (1≤i≤m) is generated by assigning task T_* to P_i, where T_* is the first task in the sequence T_1, T_2, .. ,T_N not yet assigned by the partial assignment corresponding to node n.

A_1 : Algorithm LPT [Horowitz and Sahni, 1984]. $A_1(n)$ generates a schedule for the yet unassigned tasks of node n. The current processor status corresponds to the assigned tasks at node n.

A_2 : Algorithm Multifit [Kunde and Steppat, 1987]. $A_2(n)$ applies Multifit strategy to node n to complete the schedule.

h(n) : Any admissible heuristic.

The data for the experimental results were generated in the following manner. For the Euclidean Traveling Salesman problem, the co-ordinates of the cities are taken from a uniform distribution over [0..100]. For a given number of cities, fifty problem instances are generated. For each instance, C^*, N^*, $CA_1(s)$, $CA_2(s)$, costs of solution and nodes expanded by $BFPR(1,A_1,\epsilon)$, $BFPR(1,A_2,\epsilon)$, $BFPR(2,A_1,\epsilon, A_2,\epsilon)$ are found for different ϵ. The ratio of costs obtained by the approximate algorithms and BFPR() to that of C^* are calculated, and their average for fifty problem instances are determined. Similarly, the average of the ratios of nodes expanded by BFPR() to that of N^* are calculated.

Table 1 summarizes the result when the approximate algorithms used are the Nearest Neighbour and the Double Spanning Tree Heuristics, discussed in section 3.1.1.

Results obtained by using the Convex Hull Heuristic, and Farthest Insertion Heuristic as approximate algorithms, as discussed in section 3.1.2, are noted in table 2.

For the problem of scheduling independent tasks, number of processors is taken to be 3, and the number of tasks are varied. The task times are taken at random from a uniform distribution over [0 .. 100]. Fifty different sets of task times are generated, and the averages of the ratios of cost and node expansions are noted in a fashion similar to that for the Euclidean Traveling Salesman Problem. Approximate algorithms considered are LPT, and Multifit, as discussed in section 3.2. Summary of the results appears in table 3.

It is interesting to note that even with $\epsilon=0$, BFPR() hardly misses the optimal solution, and the number of nodes expanded is significantly less than that of A^*. The reduction in node expansion becomes more significant as the problem size increases. Nodes expanded by BFPR() increases gradually with ϵ 's, while the quality of solution improves.

4 Conclusion

The algorithm BFPR() utilizes the heuristic information provided by approximate algorithms, in its attempt to improve the performance of A^* or its variants. A good approximate algorithm is used by BFPR() to detect the deviation of a partial solution path from the optimal/ near optimal path at an early stage, which enables it to control node expansions. Experimental results show that, even with a poor admissible h(), BFPR() reduces node expansions, and yet produces near optimal solutions. The parameters (ϵ_i, i=1,2, .. ,r) of BFPR() can be adjusted to utilize the trade-off of computation time and the quality of solution. For large values of ϵ 's,the algorithm reduces to A^* as a special case.

However, although the number of nodes expanded is usually taken to be the prime measure of computation time, complexity of heuristic calculation sometimes makes its effect felt. As BFPR() performs very well with one or two good approximate algorithms, burdening it with a larger number of approximate algorithms may not be cost-effective unless the process of node expansion proves to be very expensive.

We have shown how to use approximate algorithms in best first search only. It is quite evident that the same technique can be used in depth first branch and bound as well as other interesting variations like A_ϵ^* [Pearl, 1984] where a second heuristic is used for selection. Since the generalization is straightforward and the results achieved similar, we have not elaborated it.

Table 1 : Summary of result of BFPR() for solving ETSP with
A_1 : Nearest Neighbour Heuristic,
A_2 : Double Spanning Tree Heuristic.

No. of cities=8
No. of instances=50
Average of :
$CA_1(s)/C^* = 1.0640$
$CA_2(s)/C^* = 1.1298$

	$\epsilon=0$		$\epsilon=0.01$		$\epsilon=0.1$	
	Av. C/C^*	Av. N/N^*	Av. C/C^*	Av. N/N^*	Av. C/C^*	Av. N/N^*
BFPR($1,A_1,\epsilon$)	1.0062	.1057	1.0049	.1248	1.0006	.2838
BFPR($1,A_2,\epsilon$)	1.0000	.2672	1.0000	.3026	1.0000	.5840
BFPR($2,A_1,\epsilon,A_2,\epsilon$)	1.0071	.0903	1.0051	.1100	1.0006	.2726

(a)

No. of cities=10

Average of $CA_1(s)/C^*$ for 50 instances	Average of $CA_2(s)/C^*$ for 50 instances	BFPR($1,A_1,0$)		BFPR($1,A_2,0$)		BFPR($2,A_1,0,A_2,0$)	
		Av. C/C^*	Av. N/N^*	Av. C/C^*	Av. N/N^*	Av. C/C^*	Av. N/N^*
1.0865	1.1600	1.0032	.1021	1.0011	.2802	1.0055	.0737

(b)

Table 2 : Summary of result of BFPR() for solving ETSP with
A_1 : Convex Hull Heuristic,
A_2 : Farthest Insertion Heuristic.

No. of city = 15
No. of instances=50

	$\epsilon=0$		$\epsilon=0.01$		$\epsilon=0.1$	
Average of : $CA_1(s)/C^*=1.0026$ $CA_2(s)/C^*=1.0072$	Av. C/C^*	Av. N/N^*	Av. C/C^*	Av. N/N^*	Av. C/C^*	Av. N/N^*
$BFPR(1,A_1,\epsilon)$	1.0004	.2404	1.0000	.3336	1.0000	1.0000
$BFPR(1,A_2,\epsilon)$	1.0004	.2520	1.0000	.3544	1.0000	1.0000
$BFPR(2,A_1,\epsilon,A_2,\epsilon)$	1.0004	.2370	1.0000	.3336	1.0000	1.0000

(a)

No. of instances=50

No. of city	Av. of $\dfrac{CA_1(s)}{C^*}$	Av. of $\dfrac{CA_2(s)}{C^*}$	$BFPR(1,A_1,0)$		$BFPR(1,A_2,0)$		$BFPR(2,A_1,0,A_2,0)$	
			Av. C/C^*	Av. N/N^*	Av. C/C^*	Av. N/N^*	Av. C/C^*	Av. N/N^*
16	1.0076	1.0074	1.0000	.2248	1.0000	.3108	1.0000	.2084
17	1.0080	1.0128	1.0000	.1912	1.0000	.2424	1.0000	.1834
18	1.0098	1.0122	1.0002	.1616	1.0002	.2004	1.0002	.1556
19	1.0138	1.0192	1.0004	.1452	1.0002	.1764	1.0002	.1340
20	1.0158	1.0168	1.0002	.1310	1.0012	.1650	1.0002	.1102

(b)

Table 3 : Summary of result of BFPR() for Scheduling
Independent Tasks with :
A_1 : LPT Heuristic,
A_2 : Multifit Heuristic.

No. of processor=3 No. of task=10 No. of instances=50 Av. $CA_1(s)/C^*$=1.02 Av. $CA_2(s)/C^*$=1.02	$\epsilon=0$		$\epsilon=0.01$		$\epsilon=0.04$	
	Av. C/C^*	Av. N/N^*	Av. C/C^*	Av. N/N^*	Av. C/C^*	Av. N/N^*
BFPR($1,A_1,\epsilon$)	1.00	0.69	1.00	0.81	1.00	0.97
BFPR($1,A_2,\epsilon$)	1.00	0.44	1.00	0.66	1.00	0.91
BFPR($2,A_1,\epsilon,A_2,\epsilon$)	1.00	0.31	1.00	0.55	1.00	0.89

(a)

No. of processors=3 No. of tasks=15 No. of instances=50		**BFPR($1,A_1,0$)**		**BFPR($1,A_2,0$)**		**BFPR($2,A_1,0,A_2,0$)**	
Average $CA_1(s)/C^*$	Average $CA_2(s)/C^*$	Av. C/C^*	Av. N/N^*	Av. C/C^*	Av. N/N^*	Av. C/C^*	Av. N/N^*
1.0158	1.0074	1.0006	.4978	1.0018	.1354	1.0028	.0338

(b)

References

[Chakrabarti et al, 1989]
Chakrabarti PP, Ghose S, Pandey A, and DeSarkar SC. **Increasing search efficiency using multiple heuristics.** Information Processing Letters, 30, pp 33-36, 1989.

[Garey and Johnson, 1979]
Garey MR and Johnson DS. **Computers and Intractability, A guide to the theory of NP - completeness.** W. H. Freeman and Co., New York, 1979.

[Golden et al, 1980]
Golden B, Bodlin L, Doyle T, and Stewart W Jr. **Approximate traveling salesman algorithms.** Operations Research, Vol 28, No. 3, pp 694-711, May - June 1980.

[Horowitz and Sahni, 1980]
Horowitz E and Sahni S. **Fundamental of computer algorithms.** Galgotia, 1984.

[Kunde and Steppat, 1987]
Kunde M and Steppat H. **On the worst case ratio of a compound multiprocessor scheduling algorithm.** Information Processing Letters, 25, pp 389-396, 1987.

[Nilsson, 1980]
Nilsson NJ. **Principles of Artificial Intelligence.** Tioga, Palo Alto, CA, 1980.

[Pearl, 1984]
Pearl J. **HEURISTICS Intelligent Search Strategies for Computer Problem Solving.** Addison Wesley, 1984.

[Rosenkrantz et al, 1977]
Rosenkrantz DJ, Stearns RE, and Lewis PM. **An analysis of several heuristics for the traveling salesman problem.** SIAM Journal of Computing, Vol 6, No. 3, pp 563-581, September 1977.

Speech

A Probabilistic Training Scheme for the Time-Concentration Network

S Krishnan   P Poddar

Computer Systems and Communications Group
Tata Institute of Fundamental Research
Bombay, 400 005, INDIA
uunet!shakti!tifr!csc11

Abstract

The present paper studies the training aspect of the time-concentration neural network in the context of automatic speech recognition. The original model [Tank and Hopfield, 1987], uses constant connection weights to perform word-spotting from a input grapheme string. However, a more robust and automatic assignment of connection weights (i.e. training) is required for complex tasks such as speech recognition. A generalised training scheme based on probabilistic formulation has been proposed to enhance the performance of the network for a speech recognition experiment. Improvement of performance has been acheived using the proposed modification over the original formulation.

1 Introduction

Recognizing pattern sequences as a member of some pre-defined set of classes is important in human cognitive processes such as hearing or vision. Network structures have been used to study the regularity in temporal sequences of input symbols by [Kohonen, 1985], [Watrous, 1988], [Waibel et al, 1987]. The time-concentration model was proposed to recognize sequences that are distorted in time and form [Tank and Hopfield, 1987]. The primary requirement of networks recognizing a temporal sequence is to store the information of the whole sequence along with the temporal constraints present in it. In addition to this, such networks should be robust to (i) temporal misalignment, (ii) temporal distortion or warping and (iii) variability in the symbolic representations of different examples of the same class of sequence.

The present paper studies the time-concentration model proposed by Tank and Hopfield and offers generalisation to the model for performing complex cognitive tasks

466

such as speech recognition. The time-concentration model transforms the information present in the input sequence to evidences corresponding to the set of output classes to be recognized. This is done by a set of time delay filters and interconnection weights. A set of non-linear units called *neurons* receive the stimulus response through a set of delays and couplings of appropiate connection strength. The mutual interaction between these neurons as well as the symbols in the data stream drive the network in such a way that different neurons become activated strongly in response to different classes of sequences.

The original time-concentration model was successfully demonstrated for the task of word spotting on input grapheme sequences. The model per se does not perform as well in more complex tasks such as speech recognition. The reason is that, while the model has the inherent capability for handling the problem of temporal misalignment (endpointing problem) and time warping, it does not adequately account for the large amount of acoustic variability present in speech. A new scheme has been proposed here for assignment of the interconnection strengths to account for this variation.

Section 2 describes the structure and functioning of a time-concentration network, section 3 presents the training scheme, section 4 describes a speech recognition experiment using this scheme and section 5 presents the conclusions of this paper.

2 Time-concentration Neural Network Model

Let there be a symbol generation mechanism generating the probability vector $\mathbf{P}(t) = (p_1(t),\ldots,p_M(t))^T$ of a finite set of M symbols $X = \{x_1,\ldots,x_M\}$ at any time instant t (we assume discrete time throughout the discussion). Clearly, here $0 \leq p_i(t) \leq 1$ and $\sum_{i=1}^{M} p_i(t) = 1$. The vector $\mathbf{P}(t)$ is henceforth referred to as the *stimulus vector*. An array of detectors D_i, $i = 1,\ldots,M$ detects the probabilities $p_1(t), p_2(t)\ldots,p_M(t)$ associated with each of the M symbols. Each detector output is in turn connected to each of the neural units through a bank of K delay filters with impulse response $f_1,\ldots,f_K$ (refer Fig.1). The requirement on the impulse response of the delay filters is that, the impulse response of the k-th filter must build up and peak at $t = k$ and fall off for $t > k$. The actual nature of the impulse response function can be arbitrary. The following impulse response has been used in this paper,

$$f_k(t) = e^n \left(\frac{t}{k}\right)^n e^{-n(t/k)}$$

Here n in a parameter that can be chosen through experimentation. The coupling between the i-th symbol detector and the j-th neural unit through the k-th delay filter is called the *connection strength*, T_{ijk}.

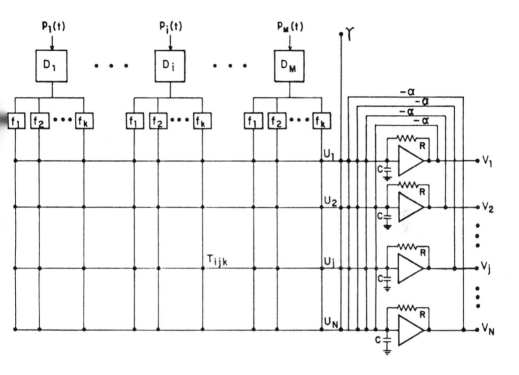

Figure 1: A block schematic of the time concentration neural network

The input to the network at any time instant comes from the stimulus vector through all possible delays with appropiate couplings. The response of the k-th delay filter to the i-th component of the stimulus vector is given by,

$$g_{ik}(t) = \sum_{l=1}^{t-1} p_i(l)f_k(t-l) \tag{1}$$

The total input to the j-th neuron at time t due to all the symbols through all the delays is given by,

$$C_j(t) = \sum_{i=1}^{M}\sum_{k=1}^{K} T_{ijk}g_{ik}(t) = \sum_{i=1}^{M}\sum_{k=1}^{K}\sum_{l=1}^{t-1} T_{ijk}\, p_i(l)f_k(t-l) \tag{2}$$

This term drives the j-th neuron whose dynamics is governed by the following equation,

$$\frac{du_j}{dt} = -\frac{u_i}{RC} - \alpha\sum_{i\neq j} V_i - \gamma + C_j(t) \tag{3}$$

where u_j and V_j are input and corresponding output of the j-th neuron. α is the measure of *mutual inhibition* and γ represents *global inhibition*. R and C are the input resistance and capacitance of the recognition neurons. The output V_j is any non-linear, monotonically increasing and asymptotically bounded function of the input u_j. A common choice is the sigmoid function, given by the following expression,

$$V_j = f(u_j) = \frac{1}{1 + \exp(-u_j)} \tag{4}$$

This function maps any real u_j between $[0, 1]$.

Now, a sequence of duration L is expressed as a sequence of M-dimensional stimulus vectors $\mathbf{P}(t)$ as, $\mathbf{S} = (\mathbf{P}(1) \ldots \mathbf{P}(L))$. Let there be N such reference sequences $\mathbf{S}^{(j)}$ for $j = 1, \ldots, N$ as representative of each of the N classes of sequences. The representative of the j-th class i.e. the reference sequence $\mathbf{S}^{(j)} = (\mathbf{P}_j(1) \ldots \mathbf{P}_j(L_j))$ is a sequence of vectors of length L_j. Here, $\mathbf{P}_j(t) = (p_1^{(j)}(t) \ldots p_M^{(j)}(t))^T$ and $p_i^{(j)}(k)$ is the probability of occurance of the symbol x_i at the k-th instant in the reference sequence $\mathbf{S}^{(j)}$.

Each of the N neurons corresponds to one of these reference sequences. The network dynamics is such that, given appropiate value of the parameters and a particular reference sequence or its variants as input, the response of the corresponding neuron will be much higher than the others at or near the end of the sequence. This behaviour of the network allows it to be used as a recognition device of a temporal sequence into several predefined class as defined by the set of reference sequences. The task of training can be defined as an assignment scheme of the connection weights T_{ijk} so that given a reference sequence $\mathbf{S}^{(j)}$ in the input data stream of the network, the output of the j-th neuron shows a sharp peak around the time of completion of the sequence while the other outputs remain at a low value. In the next section, we address the issue of training in this context.

3 Training of the Time-concentration Network

Tank and Hopfield in their original presentation of the time-concentration network [Tank and Hopfield, 1987] choose a simple training procedure. In their case, the detector array detected a single symbol at a time and the connection weights are assigned as follows:

$$T_{ijk} = 1/L_j \text{ if } x_i \text{ occurs at the } k-\text{th position from the end of the } j-\text{th sequence}$$
$$= -0.5/L_j \text{ otherwise} \tag{5}$$

This paper describes an alternative training scheme to enhance the performance of the network for speech recognition tasks. Here the symbol set consists of 100(or 200) VQ symbols unlike 26 alphabets. The variations in the examples of the same class is more than that encountered in the case of recognition of mis-spelt words [Gold and Lippmann, 1988]. In this scheme, the training rule is basically extended to work in the case where the symbol generation process is no longer deterministic and a confidence level of symbol occurance is obtained as the response of the symbol generator at a given instant of time. The assignment rule in this case is given as follows:

$$T_{ijk} = \epsilon_1 \, p_i^{(j)}(L_j - k) \quad \text{if } x_i \text{ is among the } m \text{ most probable symbols}$$
$$\text{in the stimulus vector } \mathbf{P}_j(L_j - k)$$
$$= -\epsilon_2 \qquad \text{otherwise} \tag{6}$$

Here ϵ_1 and ϵ_2 are constant numbers called *reward* and *penalty* respectively.

The connection weight T_{ijk} expresses the confidence level of the m-most likely symbols at the k-th instant from the end of the sequence $\mathbf{S}^{(j)}$. The rule can be modified slightly to learn from several examples of the same class. In this case, if there are J examples of $\mathbf{S}^{(j)}$ then the previous rule is applied repeatedly for each examples, noting that the duration L_j may be different in each case. The values of the connection strenght arrived at from different examples are added and scaled down by the number of examples.

4 Speech Recognition Experiment

A classification task is attempted to evaluate the potential of the model in the context of automatic recognition of spoken numerals. Speech is sampled with a 12-bit A/D convertor at 10KHz. A 10-th order LPC-Cepstral analysis is performed over 20 ms frames at the rate of 100 frames/s and the first 10 cepstral coefficients are used as the feature for each frame. An M $(= 100)$ level vector quantizer codebook is generated using phonetically balanced continuous speech of 60 second duration. Each frame is assigned m VQ-labels using this codebook. Each of these m labels is associated with a probabilty given by,

$$p_i = d_i^{-1} / \sum_{i=1}^{m} d_i^{-1}$$

for the i-th label. Here, d_i is the weighted Euclidean distance of the input frame from the i-th codevector.

The reference sequences are obtained by endpointing isolated utterance of each word and then translating each frame into its VQ transcription. Four utterances of each word constitute the training set and testing is done on a separate set of ten spoken digits. Two experiments have been performed to study the effectiveness of the proposed probabilistic training scheme. In the first experiment, the network is trained using eq.(5)

470

and Fig.2 shows the corresponding dynamic behaviour of the neurons in response to the test utterances.

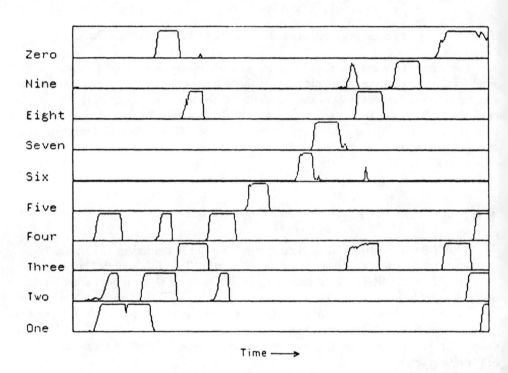

Figure 2 : Dynamics of neuron response in time with single VQ label
$(m=1)$. The value of the parameters: $\alpha=2\cdot0$, $\Gamma=5\cdot0$, $R=1\cdot0$,
$C=1\cdot0$, $\epsilon_1=0\cdot12$, $\epsilon_2=1\cdot0$.

Fig.3, on the other hand, illustrates the neuron response for the second experiment when the network is trained using eq.(6) with $m=3$. A simple decision circuit decides on the class of the utterance through a majority vote taken over the neuron responses. The second experiment gives a better recognition accuracy compared to the first one.

t can also be seen from the figures that the confusion in terms of spurious firings of the
wrong neural units is more pronounced in the first case.

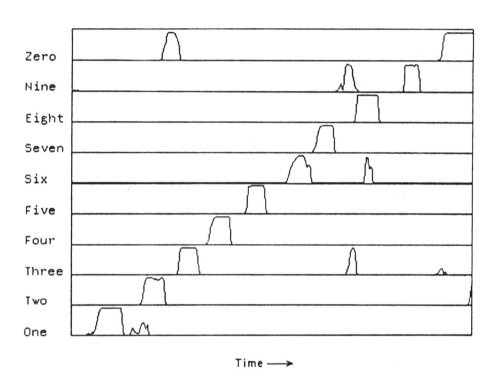

Time ⟶

Figure 3: Dynamics of neuron response in time with three VQ labels
(m = 3). The value of the parameters are the same as in Fig. 2.

5 Conclusion

The generalisation of the time-concentration model using a probabilistic formulation, presented in this paper, offers a better representation of complex temporal sequence
such as speech as is evident from the experiments described in the paper. Since this
model uses probabilistic evidences of the input symbols, and generates relative confidence levels about its output classes, the network can ideally fit into a hierarchical
recognition structure where the output of lower-level shorter time-scale events are difficult to ascertain. Another advantage of this model is that it can be used in recognition
of continuous speech without explicit segmentation. Only the decision circuit based on
majority voting needs to be modified to account for that task. It is felt that the performance of the proposed model can be further enhanced by proper choice of its various

parameters. An automatic training algorithm for selection of the network parameters, mainly the connection strengths, is currently being investigated.

References

[Tank and Hopfield, 1987]

Tank D.W. and Hopfield J.J., Neural Computation by concentrating information in time, Proc. of the National Academy of Sciences USA, vol. 84, pp. 1896-1900, April 1987.

[Kohonen, 1984]

Kohonen T. *Self-organization and associative memory.* pp. 16-20, Springer, Berlin, 1984.

[Watrous, 1988]

Watrous RL. *Speech Recognition using Connectionist Networks.* PhD Thesis, University of Pennsylvania, 1988.

[Waibel, 1987]

Waibel A, Hanazawa T, Hinton G, Shikano K, and Lang K. *Phoneme Recognition using Time-Delay Neural Networks.* Technical Report TR-1-0006, ATR Interpreting Telephony Research Laboratories, 1987.

[Gold and Lippmann, 1988]

Gold B and Lippmann RP. *A Neural Network for Isolated-Word Recognition.* Proceedings of International Conference of Acoustics, Speech and Signal Processing, pp. 44-47, 1988.

Activities at the
KBCS Nodal Centres

DOE NODAL CENTRE ACTIVITIES
DEVELOPMENT OF EXPERT SYSTEMS FOR GOVT. APPLICATIONS

K.K. BAJAJ
KBCS NODAL CENTRE, DEPARTMENT OF ELECTRONICS
LODI ROAD, A BLOCK, CGO COMPLEX, NEW DELHI
E-MAIL : +uunet!shakti!vikram!kbcs

ABSTRACT

The activities of the DOE Nodal Centre under the KBCS programme have been highlighted in this paper. The projects under development include : Expert System for Income Tax Assessment, Indian Import-Export Policies as a Logic Program, CCS Pension Rules as a Logic Program.

INTRODUCTION

DOE Nodal Centre of the KBCS Project has the responsibility for developing Artificial Intelligence (AI) applications in the government for decision support. Activities at this centre are directly in line with this responsibility. Because of the fact that this nodal centre is within the government, it is in a position to develop real applications for government.

The first appplication developed in this centre was an expert system for Income-tax Assessment using an expert system shell. This was presented as a paper in the KBCS conference held in Bangalore in 1988. This was followed by two large-scale systems implemented as logic programs, currently under-development. The first concerns Import Export Policy & Procedures as laid down by the office of the Chief Controller of Import & Export. The second concerns Central Civil Services Pension Rules. These Automated Legal Reasoning Systems are being developed with a view to assist the administration in its implementation and drafting of legislation. These systems are expected to clarify and simplify English language of the legislation. The two applications present diverse technical challenges - the first employs relatively simple but ambiguous English, contains a large database, requires a complex user interface, but comparatively shallow reasoning. The second employs more complex, but comparatively more precise, English language, and requires deeper reasoning including complex temporal inference. The applications demonstrate the suitability of logic programming for dealing with different legal domains. The first application has been presented in an International Conference on Expert Systems in Law at Florence, Italy in November'89. The second application on CCS Pension Rules as a Logic Program is being presented in this conference.

476

The   DOE Nodal Centre is presently discussing with   the
Centre   for Railway Information System for development   of a
plannning   and   scheduling system using   the   expert   system
techniques   for   the   wagons distribution   on   the   Railways
Network. The traditional operations research techniques have
been   found   to   be   inadequate   for   handling   such   large
scheduling   problems with a very large number of   parameters
and constraints such as in this case. The discussion is only
at a very preliminary stage at present.

We   will   briefly   describe these   projects   and   their
outcome in the following paragraphs.

2.   EXPERT SYSTEM FOR INCOME-TAX ASSESSMENT

The   Income-tax   assessment   problem   had   been   chosen
primarily   because it can have a significant impact   on   the
working   of   Income-tax   officials   in   the   Department   of
Revenue.   The assessment problem is a very complicated   one,
and   comprises a large number of rules and laws.   These have
been   set   out   in   the   Income-tax   manual   and   other
notifications   which   are   issued by the   Central   Board   of
Direct   Taxes from time to time.   Besides,   in certain   gray
areas,   which are not small in number, the officer is guided
by his experience.   For example,   in the case of perquisites
such   as conveyance and accommodation,   valuation is   highly
subjective.   This   necessitates the use of   heuristics.   The
expert   system   developed   by the DOE Nodal   Centre   ensures
uniformity in assessment (1).

Income-tax   payers   are primarily   divided   into   three
categories   :   salaried group,   proprietorship companies and
corporate sector.   Some of the other Income-tax payers   such
as non-resident Indian,   Hindu Undivided Families (UF) etc.,
can   be   fitted   into   these   categories   with   slight
modifications.   This   centre has taken up the development of
an   Expert   System   for   the   first   category   i.e.   salaried
individuals.   However, the system that has been designed can
be   readily upgraded to proprietorship companies,   and   HUF
with   minor   modifications.   The corporate sector problem   is
much more complex since it involves complicated legal issues
which   are   subject   to   interpretation.   Conflicting   court
rulings   also   prevail   in many cases.   The PC PLUS Expert
System Development Tool has been used for the development of
the   assessment   system,   on IBM PC/AT compatibles.   The
knowledge base is divided into frames, sub-frames and rules.
There   are   10-12   frames which   are   basically   related   to
salary,   house   property,   income from securities and   other
sources,   capital   gains and deductions.   There are over 264
rules,   the   largest   number of them (125) being   under   the
salary frames.

The   system accepts details from the income-tax   return
filed   by   an   individual   through   a   series   of   questions

numbering about 100 in the worst case. At every prompt, the information entered by the user is checked against the stored knowledge base. The system responds appropriately to each item of data entered. If an entry is not acceptable, the system states the reasons and specific rules (appropriate act of the income-tax manual is quoted) which do not allow its acceptance. Help is also available at any point of time. The system is very user friendly.

The system has been linked to the DBASE III package on the PC/AT. Once the return has been accepted, it can get filed in the DBASE system. The returns, therefore, filed with the expert system will end up forming an information system for future MIS needs in the Income-tax department. The system is expected to be very useful because of the sample scrutiny concept which has been introduced in the department, due to which 95% of the returns are allowed to go without any detailed scrutiny. Such a system will help in processing the cases not selected for sample scrutiny, as if Income-tax experts were examining them.

The Income-tax assessment problem is highly amenable to rule based analysis.Hence a rule based package such as PC PLUS has been chosen for this work. The knowledge sources include the Income Tax Act, Ready Reckoners, Notifications etc. Moreover, the experience of a practising consultant had been used in checking the veracity of knowledge gathered. The Expert System has been extensively tested.

The expert system has been demonstrated to the officials of Department of Income Tax. All the changes of the 1989 budget have been incorporated in the latest version of the system.

INDIAN IMPORT POLICY AS A LOGIC PROGRAM

The Handbook of Import And Export Policy and Procedures is brought out annually by the Government of India. The policy reflects the Government's management of the mixed Indian economy, which is at different stages of development in different industries. Depending upon indigenous capabilities, the policy allows the import of an item liberally under Open General Licence (OGL), restricts its imports, or bans it completely.

Depending upon the category of the item, the type of importer, and the purpose of the import, different policies are applicable, and different importation procedures are specified. The Hand Book is publised in two volumes, one dealing with Policy and the other with Procedures.

The Hand Book lays down policy for import of capital goods, raw materials, consumables, and components and spares. Individual items in these categories are listed in three categories : OGL, restricted, and banned. These are

long lists, which take up a large part of the volume on
Policy. So far the work has concentrated on the import of
capital goods, which is one of the most complex parts of
the Hand Book and deals with the largest number of items.

Capital goods are subdivided into such classes as
machinery equipment, instruments and samples/prototypes
Machinery equipment, for example, is further classified into
35 further subclasses. The total number of items classed as
machinery equipment is 1179 in the OGL category. and 144 in
the restricted category. The total number of items classed
as instruments is 30 in the restricted category. And the
total for samples/prototypes, which are mostly drugs or
medicines, is 277. Thus the representation of this
information requires the use of a relatively large database.

The number of rules is also large. Import policy of
capital goods is presented in 18 clauses, which are
subdivided into 38 clauses. Import procedures for capital
goods are presented in 55 clauses, which are subdivided into
85 subclauses.

By July 1989, a first implementation of capital goods
policy, some of the associated procedures, and all of the
associated database was completed and running on a personal
computer under PROLOG. This implementation mixed knowledge
representation of the legislation with data caputure from
the user. Because of the resulting complexity, neither the
knowledge representation nor the user interface performed as
well as required.

It was decided to reimplement the policy and
procedures, separating knowledge representation from user-
interaction, concentrating first on knowledge representation
using logic programming techniques. Several options for
adding user-interaction later were considered, including the
use of Apes. Eventually it was decided to explore a
different architecture, preceeding the knowledge
representation module (KR) by a user data interface module
(UDI), and following it with an explanation module (FX) (2).

By August, a second PROLOG implementation concentrating
on the knowledge representation aspects of capital goods
policy had been completed.

Our work so far has a knowledge representation in the
second implementation. The problem of choosing appropriate
predicates to represent policy statements has underlined the
need for undertaking the kind of analysis involved in
database design of identifying entities, attributes,
relationship and dependencies. The need for entity
relationship analysis along with propositional logic for
representing legislation is found to be very important. The
examples presented in (2) show that the current
identification of predicates for propositional logic depends

upon the entity relationship analysis. The second implementation in which pure logic programming for Knowledge Representation had been upper most in the design necessitated the development of a User Data Interface (UDI). The UDI performs data collection before execution of Knowledge Representation module, unlike APES architecture and other expert system shells where the data is captured interactively. The architecture proposed is menu-driven which captures the entire data before consultation begins and is a general architecture. Wherever possible the user is presented with the list of possible answers to questions. This includes presentation of the rather large lists of OGL and restricted capital goods. These lists are displayed in the form of chapters which the user can move forward and backward. Same approach has been followed in the case of CCS Pension Rules also. In the present application the UDI asks 24 questions in two stages about the item and the importer.

The explananation module displays the section numbers applicable. Knowledge Representation of the problem can display English lanuage in a more informative manner in addition to the verbatim text of the rules.

The work on refining the UDI and the explanation module is also under further development. Some of the other features in the import policy which provide fast track procedures for certain categories of imports under certain conditions need to be included in the Knowledge Representation module. We hope to complete this task in the next few months.

We have pointed out an alternative to the existing implementation. This is based on the fact that the UDI already contains much of the knowledge in the knowledge representation module. The questions are asked based on the conditions of the rules. Each possible path of questions and answers corresponds to conditions of all the rules that are applicable to a given case. The UDI can be extended into a decision tree by associating all knowledge in the form of appropriate conclusions with each path of conditions. The Knowledge Representation module would then become redundant. However, with the extended UDI, it becomes difficult to provide meaningful explanations.

CCS PENSION RULES AS A LOGIC PROGRAM

We have noted earlier that the CCS Pension Rules are more complex but use comparatively more precise English language and require deeper reasoning including temporal inferencing. This problem has been covered in detail separately in the form of a paper presented in this conference (3). Up to now, we have only represented the knowledge contained in the qualifying services rules. The rules contain a variety of interesting problems which can be handled rather nicely by logic programming. The negative conclusions in statements and the counterfactuals are represented without any difficulty. The first-order logic explicitly allows time as a parameter, thereby making temporal reasoning practical in a real life inferencing problem. These points have been illustrated in the paper presented separately in this conference.

The User Data Interface tries to capture the data at the initial stage itself through a series of forms which are displayed through a menu for the user to choose and fill the desired number. The forms ask for the requisite information from the user in the manner he would fill out a manual form. Unlike the previous application of Import Policy where the UDI is based on the rules themselves, the forms in this application are not based on the CCS Pension Rules. Hence, there is no possibility of extending UDI in the present case to a decision tree containing all the knowledge for CCS Pension rules.

Explanation module follows the same pattern as in the case of Import Policy. Rule numbers with the English text in rules as well English rules based on their knowledge representation can be displayed for conveying more meaningful information to the user.

Work is underway to complete the qualifying service rules and cover the other sections of the pension rules in order to provide a meaningful expert system

5. CONCLUSION

These examples of using logic programming in automated legal reasoning systems demonstrate the suitablity of logic programming for dealing with different legal domains. The knwowledge representation issues specific to the domain of law can be handled rather well and can result in the development of practical expert systems. Logic programming can help to disambiguate the rules. This can help in presenting the legislation in simple form to assist the policy makers in subsequent drafting.

We have an active user in the office of Chief Controller of Imports & Export, who are intersted in using the expert system for their day-to-day work as well as for drafting the future legislation. In the case of pension rules also we hope that the system can be put to practical use.

REFERENCES

- S.K. Srivastava, B.K. Murthy, K.K. Bajaj (1988),"Expert System for Income-Tax Assessment, Vivek, Vol. 1, No.2, April 1988.

- K.K. Bajaj, R.K. Dubash, A.S. Kamble, R. Kowalski, B.K. Murthy and D. Rajagopalan, "Indian Import Export Policy & Procedures", presented at International Conference on Expert System in Law at Florence, Italy, November, 1989.

- K.K. Bajaj, R.K. Dubash, R. Kowalski (1989),"Central Government Pension Rules As a Logic Program", presented at KBCS Annual Conference, Bombay in Dec.,1989

KBCS Activities at C-DAC

Vijay P. Bhatkar

KBCS Nodal Centre
Centre For Development Of Advanced Computing
Pune University Campus
Pune - 411 007. INDIA
uunet!shakti!parcom!bhatkar

Abstract

C-DAC is India's national initative in high-performance computing, covering both technology and applications development. Two main frontiers which are being addressed to are supercomputing and AI, based on parallel processing architectures. The KBCS Nodal Centre at C-DAC is pursuing research in development of graphics and intelligence based systems technology (GIST) for language processing. The basic technology has already been developed for uniform script processing for all living languages. This technology is being enhanced to cover raster image processors, OCRs, and speech input/output systems. Simultaneously, attention has been focussed on NLP for Indian languages. Sanskrit is being explored as a metalanguage for NLP. For this purpose symbolic language processing environments have been developed with Devanagari interface. A prototype tutoring system has been realized for Sanskrit in the Paninian Grammar framework. The ultimate objective is to provide comprehensive solution to language processing covering script, word and sentenace processing for all living languages, with immediate focus on Indian languages.

1. Motivation

Language forms the most fundamental medium for interaction amongst intelligent systems, be they humans or machines. The history of human civilisation is closely and deeply linked with the evolution of natural languages. There are presently over 4,000 living languages in the world, many of them are only spoken and do not have scripts. In India alone, there are over 14 major living languages and over 600 minor languages. Over 1,000 languages are spoken in Africa.

Linguists have grouped the living languages into eight main families. The Indo-European language family based on Sanskrit, Greek, Latin and German forms the basis for several Indian and European languages and over half the world's population speak a language from this family. Perso-Arabic is another dominant language family.

Language has two forms namely the speech and the script. The same language is spoken differently in different parts of the world. Both speech and scripts of a language have evolved over time. Several societies and cultures have given great emphasis on spoken form of the language. Sanskrit, for example, has been transmitted to successive generations through a disciplined and oral tradtion.

Different languages have different scripts. Most of the West-European languages use Latin or Roman alphabets and some of them add signs to the letters to show how they should be pronounced. While Indo-European lanugages are written from left to right, Perso-Arabic languages are written from right to left. Arabic is the second most widely used script. Chinese is a pictographic language. It is written in vertical columns as well as from left to right. Written Chinese has over 40,000 characters.

Most mature living lanugages of the world have formal, general structural models which capture as much as possible the regularities of language. Their models are in the form of their grammars. However, languages have a much deeper structure than expressed by syntactic grammar. Several issues such as phonetics, scripts, syntactics, semantics, pragmatics, logic, epistemology, cognitive psychology and philosophy are involved in understanding the natural language.

Language forms not only the basis for communication, natural between people, but also between humans and intelligent machines, as well as between the intelligent machines themselves. During the last two decades, several languages have been developed for encoding and decoding intelligence in machines. Major computer languages which are presently popular include Basic, Cobol, Fortran, ADA and symbolic languages like LISP, Prolog, etc. In recent years, in order to bring computers close to users and application developers, considerable work has been done in the area of functional languages, object oriented languages, and the so-called Fourth Generaltion Languages.

However, one of the greatest challenges for computer science in general, and Artificial Intelligence in particular is to provide: computers with the natural language interface; and the issues concerning Natural Language Processing (NLP), including natural language generation, natural language understanding, machine translation, etc. In order to provide human like interfaces to computers the research in speech input/output system has also been vigourously pursued. Many researchers believe that the major bottlenecks in bringing computer close to the people is essentially the slow progress in natural language interface development.

Since computers originated in Western Europe, and their technology developments and use has been initially in the UK and the USA, and the fact that much of the scientific work across the world is carried out in English, computer languages are essentially based on English word constructs. Also, computing technology in the form of word processors, and desk-top publishing remained available for several years only for English and European languages. Languages in the Indian subcontinent and particularly Perso-Arabic languages have suffered in the past due to non-availability of enabling computing technology in comparison to English and European languages.

Similarly, the work relating to natural language processing, natural language interfaces, speech input/output systems has largely remained confined to English language only. One of the main driving forces for the FGCS Project of Japan has been to provide Japanese language processing capability to computers. Significant progress has now been realised in Japan in bringing computing to Japanese language processing. However, this is not the case with other languages. Until recently even good word processors were not available to a large number of living languages. Whatever solutions that have been arrived at were ad-hoc and lacked standardization in terms of keyboards, codes, fonts, post-processors, etc. These ad-hoc solutions could not interface with the solutions available for English language and thus faced isolation and absence of growth paths.

Since computing has now permeated to all human endeavours, it is necessary that computing solutions are available uniformly for all lanugages. Absence of this enabling technology will have direct impact on the future usablity of the language itself. With the surging information technology revolution, many languages are likey to face virtual extinction in the coming decades. Since human civilization and cultures are deeply linked with the language, this is a serious political, social and cultural threat.

On the other hand, computers can bring significant enrichment to development of languages and their literature by providing technologies like desk-top publishing. It is also possible to create dictionaries, concordances, thesauruses, with the assistance of computers - the tasks which took several years, even decades, through manual methods. Computers can also effectively dissolve artificial barriers between languages by providing a medium whereby several languages can co-exist together. It is also possible to provide transliteration facilites within a family of languages. Moreover, researchers in computational linguistics can throw new lights on the language structure itself by providing the supportive computer technology to the language.

Thus there is a strong case for developing enabling computing technology for language processing. The enabling technology should encompass all technologies from script processing to natural language processing as well as technologies for speech analysis and synthesis. It would be most desirable to provide universal solutions for all living languages of the world. It is with this motivation that C-DAC KBCS Nodal Centre has taken up the development of language processing technology as its major mission, complimenting its parallel computing mission.

2. GIST Project

The project GIST acronymed from Graphics and Intelligence Based Systems Technology for Language Processing, attempts to provide universal solution to language processing. The initial focus is providing this technology to Indian languages. One of the first problems GIST addressed was standardization of the keyboard for Devnagri characters. The initial 8080 µp based GIST terminal in 1983 had a custom Devnagari keyboard. The subsequent 6800 µp based terminal was designed keeping in view the requirements of not only Devnagari but also of all Indian languages. The custom keyboard gave way to standard IBM PC keyboard in 1985. Finally, in 1986 DOE set up a keyboard standardization committee for Indian languages and this led to the developement of standrad Inscript keyboard for Indian languages. The keyboard committee standardized on the ISCII Code to match with Inscript keyboard. As different Indian scripts got implemented on GIST it became clear that for code compaction purpose it would be better to have separate character for nukta.

With the introduction of GIST card on IBM PC it became possible to transliterate and manage Devnagari and other Indian scripts efficiently. However, this necessitated development of PC Version of the ISCII code. The re-orientation of the ISCII code in 1988 for a separate nukta code facilitated a compatible usage on the PC. This way the ISCII code and the Inscript keyboard have been developed hand-in-hand for Indian scripts, by incorporating users' experience and latest technology, and by providing compatibility with international standards. Today GIST technology allows usage of Devnagari and other Indian Scripts on almost all computers. This is a major breakthrough in providing standard human-interface for Devnagari and other Indian scripts.

GIST Technology has now recently been extended to Perso-arabic scripts. There are 75 alphabets in Indian scripts. They can thus be easily accommodated in 8-bit extended ASCII character set (ISCII code). These alphabets can be overlayed on the three touch typable keys of a Qwerty keyboard (inscript keyboard). GIST has taken a phonetic approach to script processing. The approach yields faithful rendering of complex Indian script characters by providing high resolution fonts with 24 dot height. Script characters are displayed with proportional spacing. Syllable level composition from the basic alphabets can be done through display algorithms using character slice tasks.

Advantages of the phonetic approach adopted by GIST are as follows: Since the ISCII code is script independant, transliteration between scripts can be achieved by simply changing the display mode. ISCII alphabets are arranged such that Indian dictionary order is achieved through direct sorting. Unique spelling is achieved by choosing only the basic alphabets for composing a word. This unique word can be displayed in various forms, depending on the allowed alphabet combinations.

Because of phonetic nature of Indian script alphabets, they can be typed in phonetic order irrespective of the displayed forms.

The next task to be accomplished was to provide word processing technology to all Indian languages in addition to English, in a uniform way. C-DAC has developed such basic script porcessors that allow any compatible script attributes. They run on both IBM PC compatibles and UNIX systems. Today near print quality output from the script processors can be obtained on dot matrix printers, decibel printers and heavy duty line printers. This means that a comprehensive word processing capability is now available for Indian languages like that of English.

The script aspects of GIST can be combined with suitable publishing software approach. Application of DTP environment for Devanagari and other Indian scripts is possible in an elegant manner through a uniform single user interface. DTP can be accomplished from the normal script processor file. Already GIST manufacturers have interfaced the GIST card with well known publishing packages such as VENTURA publishing package of Xerox.

In order to bring DTP technology into widespread use it is necessary to design and develop Raster Image Processing (RIP) card which will sit along GIST card and allow direct driving of low cost laser printers. Not only will it be then a cost effective solution but would also allow proper Devnagari and other scripts handling techniques to be embedded in the RIP. This work has been presently undertaken. Enhanced postscript interpreter for RIP will allow high quality printing in Devnagari and other Indian scripts for the ISCII code. GIST terminal is also being used by leading typesetter companies for on-line data-entry in Indian scripts. Special typesetting packages have been developed for multiuser systems.

The character sets needed for high quality publishing has to be different from the basic alphabets contained on English keyboard today. The problem relates to graphic forms required for computerized character formation in order to have exchange of fonts between packages developed by different manufacturers. It is necessary to have a standardization of font designs. For this purpose a standrardization committee has been constituted of leading DTP manufacturers and font developers. The initial objective is standardization of a 192 character set for modern Devnagari, and other sets for remaining conjuncts required for Devnagari and other scripts. The standradised fonts after their practical evalutation would be brought into public domain for widespread usage.

The GIST terminal has also to satisfy the long term requirements of computerized libraries for displaying information about Indian language books. The automatic transliteration facility between Devnagari and any other Indian script would allow the user to view the information in the script he reads or he knows. It is even possible for a foreign reader to view the information in Roman script annotated with diacritical mark.

In order to enhance the word-processing and DTP compatibilites accomplished by GIST to a level of advanced text processing facilities, it is necessary to support this technology with standard lexicons, dictionaries and concordances. Word processing systems have not generally involved the use of linguistic theory, but these are surely areas in which they will depend on theory as they evolve further. An advanced processor in Devnagari can include spelling checkers and text critique facilities, by looking forward in stored dictionaries and concordances; such systems can point out and correct possible errors.

The development of standard dictionaries and concordances is of prime importance for Sanskrit language, where the contribution is expected to come from the linguists. The Deccan College in Pune, which has started a massive encyclopaedic Sanskrit dictionary based on historical principles of linguistics four decades back, is said to need another 60 years for its accomplishment. In fact, the project of this magnitude really needs use of computer and computational linguistics. Soon, however, the feasibility study would be carried out for employing computing technology for this project so that its implementation would be accelerated and scope widened. The project may require advanced computing platform based on parallel computing environment and intelligent interfaces based on knowledge based computer systems.

One of the major contributions of computer technology to Sanskrit and other Indian languages will be the preservation of its vast body of knowledge, available now only in the form of manuscripts in few libraries and individual collections. While microfilm/ microfiche storage system could be one alternative, preservation of this vast information on the optical disks is a better technological alternative. Ancient manuscripts could be preserved and made available on optical disks, which will become standard information storage and retrieval media in the coming years.

Since the task of data entry of original manuscripts is going to be massive and time consuming, it would be prudent to explore the possibilites of developing character/ word / text recognition system which can directly input the Sanskrit manuscripts into the computer for futher processing, annotation, classification, presentation, retrieval interface, and storage into magnetic or optical media. This technology is yet not perfected for the English language and will involve major development effort.

Development of speech processing technolofy for Sanskrit, covering both speech synthesis and speech recognition, is the next milestone to be achieved in bringing about synthesis of Sanskrit and advanced computing technology. At C-DAC, development project on text-to-speech conversion for various Indian languages supplementing the GIST card, is being worked upon.

The available sound synthesis systems are not directly suited for text-to-speech generation of Sanskrit or other Indian languages. Available speech synthesis VLSI's have varied numbers of English allophones stored. For e.g., GI SPP256-AL2 generates speech via 12 pole LPC using a suitable code for 59 stored allphones. It works in conjunction with a controller chip containing about 400 letter-to-allophone rules of English language. Similarly, Votrax SCOIA, Phillips MEA 8000 chips are suitable only for some European languages. More robust systems that can cater to more languages usually work on larger computers

In the development of speech synthesis hardware for Sanskrit and other Indian languages, detailed phonological and morphonemic rules of Sanskrit language will have to be made use of in designing the algorithms for converting the input text into corresponding allophones and then into various acoustic parameters.

The proposed text to speech system could be based on, for example, TMS 320C25, an A/D converter, an amplifier and a speaker. The input text would be first converted into necessary allophonic parameters by the ROM-resident text-to-allophone conversion program. On the GIST card these parameters could be sent to speech as-on board, where the TMS 320C25 chip could convert the incoming allophones into corresponding acoustic parameters.

Under the KBCS Project TIFR is pursuing the designe of Speech Recognition System for Indian languages including Sanskrit. In speech recognition the three broad approaches pursued simultaneouly are:

- acoustic sub-word unit based speech recognition

- hidden Markov Model (HMM) approach and

- rule based approach supported by direct phonetic feature analysis.

Ultimate aim is to develop a state-of-the-art speech recognition system in Indian languages by absorbing positive aspects of all these three approaches.

The goal of the project is the development of interactive input/output system for a computer with a facility for visual and voice feedback. Using primarily the speech mode, this will be an interactive facility with provisions for keyboard entry, voice output and visual display. Similar work on speech recognition is already underway at IIT Madras, CEERI Delhi, and IISc Bangalore. C-DAC Nodal Centre would be interacting with these institutes to engineer a speech synthesis system for Indian languages in general, and Sanskrit in particular.

The above hardware development for script porcessing would eventually lead to development of interfaces for OCR, RIP, and speech input / output; and would be built embedded into the silicon using C-MOS gate array or standrad cell technology, to realize language processing chip sets. C-DAC has already designed and fabricated a 6000 C-MOS gate-array chip for language processing. This chip called GIST 9000 is the first universal solution for script processing of all living languages of the world. PC-add-in cards are now being developed based on GIST 9000 which will be the new generation technology for language processing.

GIST technology is presently being widely applied in desk top publishing and government informatics. The national programme for computerisation of land records is being implemented in different states of India using the GIST Technology. Similar programmes are being launched for computerisation of legal systems and health-care systems.

3. Natural Language Processing for Indian Languages

Having provided universal solutions for scripts and word processing for Indian languages, the next frontier to be addressed is that of sentence processing, which forms the basis for Natural Language Processing.

Natural language communication with computers has been the major goal of Artificial Intelligence, both, for knowledge it has to give about intelligence in general, and its wide-scale utility in particular. Natural language processing has therefore attracted major attention in the field of Artificial Intelligence. Several approaches have been advanced for natural language processing which include context free grammars, phrase structure grammars, transformational grammars, augmented transition networks, expectations driven pars, word-expert parsing, conceptual dependency models, semantic networks, heuristics and scripts, etc. There have also been investigations carried out in Natural Language Processing from computational linguistic and cognitive psychology point of view. All the approaches have yielded partial successes, and Natural Language Processing remains still as a major challenge in computer science and technology. Perhaps, there is a need to look at Natural Language Processing in a fresh manner. It is particularly so while modelling Indian languages, as from Indian point of view, language is a holistic concept involving several dimensions.

All the Indian languages owe their origin to Sanskrit. Therefore, it is necessary to focus our attention to the study of Sanskrit from computational point of view. It is to be noted that the basic reason for natural language processing to be a hard problem is due to ambiguity of natural language. Sanskrit largely has circumvented this problem by being the most unambiguous language with a structure perfect in grammar, wherein all the complexities at conceptual, contextual, pragmatic, syntact, semantic, logical, symbolic and phonetic levels have been addressed to.

Sanskrit grammar is identified with Panini's Astadhyayi which is a great synthesis of the previous grammatical traditions coming down from Vedas, Aranyakas, Brahmanas, Upanishads, Shiksas and Pratishakhya literature and the subsequent works of several grammarians. In its holistic sense Sanskrit grammar besides that of Panini includes Katyayana and Patanjali. Last but not the least is the Vakyapadiya of Bhartrhari who brings out a grand synthesis not simply because he provides a firm philosophical foundation to Sanskrit grammar, but also because he represents a grand unification of all that marks universal grammar, linguistics, logic and epistemology. No wonder that, the celebrated Indologists in the past like Max Muller, Whitney, Bloomfield and others have acclaimed Panini's Sanskrit Grammar as the most mathematical formal grammar. And very recently, the computer scientists like Rick Briggs and Verboom have, after decades of search for computer language, felt that Sanskrit could be regarded as the model grammar for machine translation.

The broad features of Sanskrit grammar are:

- A semantic based phonetics, as is displayed in the Shivasturas and the scheme of letters (Varnamala) which in turn has a sound anatomical, physiological and psychological base.

- Semantic based syntax, word parsing

- Semantic based Sandhi rules (euphonic combination)

- Semantic based compound formation rules (synthesis and analysis)

- Semantic based nominal and verbal formations

- Semantic based tenses and moods, and voices, gender, number and persons.

- Semantic based Karaka theory affixes, suffixes

- Semantic based dictionaries, thesaurus and lexicons

- Semantic based logic and epistemology

According to Katyayana, the word, the meaning and their relation are siddha (natural, not sadhita - artificial, given as a fact), people have used them in that sense, therefore, rules of dharma (in a general sense) are formulated by the grammar. The second premise of Sanskrit grammar is that, the letter, the word or a sentence, as a speech is intentionally a sentence. The sentence therefore is a spoken phenomenon and marks the beginning of the grammar as a meaningful unit, with word as a sub-unit, with letters as their further sub-units. Sentence as a whole essentially has three units, the agent, the verb and the act (karta, karma, kriya). Their prominence decides the voice of the sentence - active or passive.

Semantics thus has been traced right from its source, the abstract level of the speech, brought down to the surface level, if needed even to the level of syllable as is the case with mantrasastra.

The next step is to decide semantically, the relationship of constituents, the words, through karaka theory, keeping pace with number, gender and the person of nominal and verbal terminals. Terminals are thus the last semantic units. This semantic relationship has also covered syntax, and has not only removed its positional rigidity but also circumvented ambiguity caused by it. This is one of the scientific landmarks that made Sanskrit grammar and Sanskrit itself a dynamic, perpetual, generative system. Only Sanskrit has bypassed the clutches of syntactic constraints. This is the natural semantic network of Sanskrit from top to bottom, a guiding principle throughout linguistic complexity.

The extension of the semantic relationship is found in formation of word, the lexicon, the dictionaries (both technical and literary) based on etymology, derivation that further brings grammatical unification of various literary and scientific disciplines. Simple and compound formations of words and sentences have further been guided by the sandhi rules. Semantic base has also been applied to logic for deciding the meaning of the word which itself is a complex dynamic aspect of the language.

The C-DAC KBCS Nodal Centre is carrying out explorations on Sanskrit for providing an alternative approach to natural language processing. The issues are being addressed to in step by step manner. The following projects have been taken up for immediate implementation.

4. NLP Projects Under Implementation

Symbolic Language Programming Environments in Devanagri:

In order to carry out exploration in computational linguistics, natural language processing, natural language generation, and natural language understanding in Sanskrit, it is necessary to create Devnagri script-based AI programming environments for computer scientists and Sanskrit experts. Towards this objective the Devnagri scripts based AI programming environments are being developed using the GIST Technology.

Devnagri Common LISP is being implemented using Golden Common LISP and GIST add-in card. This allows obvious use of Devnagri characters in string, but rest is manipulated by compiler. At some places Devnagri characters are not allowed. Some basic predicate functions of LISP like upper case - P, Alpha - P would have to be taken care once "ka,...,gnya" is added to list a-z and A-Z. Initial prototype implementation was completed in September, 1989, and it is currently being tested in various applications for Sanskrit grammar, such as Sandhi, Vigrah, etc.

Standard Prolog compiler is also being endowed with Devnagri scripts using the GIST add-in card. This allows rules from Sastras, experts on anicient Indian sciences, and sanskrit pandits to be fed directly into Sanskrit or any other Indian language. The Devnagri Prolog implementation is partially complete and is being tested for validation.

A spin-off of the above work is development of a Devnagri expert system shell called Visheshagya. Visheshagya would provide a programming environment to sanskrit pandits, domain experts in ancient Indian sciences, as well as common computer scientists for developing expert systems directly using Indian languages. This shell will be initially used to develop an Ayurvedic Health Diagnostic Expert System and on Yoga Health Advising System.

Language Processing Tools for Sanskrit:

Having made available the symbolic programming environments like LISP, Prolog and Expert System Shells in Devnagri, the next task to be accomplished is to develop tools and techniques for Sanskrit language processing in the Paninian Grammar Framework.

Panini has described Sanskrit in forms of the following three fundamental units: nominal stems (Pratipadika), verbal stems (Dhatu), and affixes (Partyay). Affixes are introduced after nominal / verbal stems to generate additional stems and finished words. Rules have been provided for generating the surface form of words from their deep structure and finally to generate sentences as units of communication. Further Sanskrit being a proper phonetic language, additional rules for phonetic combination of words have been provided to facilitate easy communication. Therefore, in the direction of Sanskrit Language Processing the following basic tools have been taken up for development:

- Sandhi Package
- Vigraha Package
- Shabda Roop Package

Predicates like NUMBERP, CONSP, LISTP etc are the basic testing functions for LISP language object. Similar predicates will have to be made avialble for Panini's grammar objects like "Sangya, Visheshan, Kriya", etc. This work has been taken up for providing Panini's grammar predicates in LISP and Prolog.

A prototype system has already been developed in COMON LISP that accepts sentences from user, checks for grammatical error in it and identifies the KARAKAS. The system uses a Sanskrit dictionary wherin relevant information concerning Sanskrit words is stored. The prototype system is part of the overall goal of developing a full-fledged Sanskrit understanding system.

KBCS ACTIVITIES AT I.I.T., MADRAS

H N Mahabala

Coordinator, KBCS Project
Department of Computer Science & Engineering
Indian Institute of Technology, Madras 600 036, India
uunet!shakti!shiva!mahabala

1. Introduction

The KBCS nodal center at the Department of Computer Science and Engineering, IIT, Madras has as its focus, promotion of Expert System Technology. The main objectives are:

* Development of Intelligent Information Systems for non-urban usage

* Development of Expert Systems for Engineering applications

* Development of Expert System tools

The following describes the completed prototypes and the projects in progress at our nodal center.

2. Development of a rule based shell in 'C' with a library of 'C' functions to implement variable control strategy

In this project, we are building a toolkit for expert systems. The important restriction imposed by commercial shells is that the shells provide certain fixed control strategies that are already built into the shell. The built in control strategies may not suit an application. Hence we are developing a library of C functions working on the rule base, goal stack and working storage using which the knowledge engineer can write different control strategies and generate custom inference engines which can be called by other C programs. For example one can generate an inference engine where after absorbing user given facts by forward chaining one can go to backward chaining, ordering the goals based on how 'hot' they are.

3. Intelligent Information Systems (IIS) for non-urban usage

Since nonurban centres are far away from urban communities where expertise is easily available, there is a need to build expert systems that capture the expert's knowledge and make the same available at each non-urban center.

The focus of attention, in IIS, is the area of health advice. We are concentrating on two specific aspects of the problem

a) Medical Diagnosis

b) Family health guide for common ailments and guide for Laboratory tests

c) Training of Medical Assistants

d) A Voice input enquiry system for recommending drugs from a relational database on drugs. The system includes side effects, suitability for a patient etc.

Specific expert systems have also been built:

a) 'Development of a Medical Diagnosis System' using a fuzzy decision table oriented methodology. This version is now being improved.

b) 'Expert System for family health care' has been built using Dr.Kapoor's family health guide. The system queries the user for symptoms of the patient and diagnoses the ailment. Treatment is suggested for the diagnosed ailment using commonly available drugs. For complicated ailments the user is requested to refer the patient to the nearest doctor. The system is implemented in C and it can currently diagnose 23 different kinds of ailments.

4. IITM blackboard expert system shell

Expert system for crane design using IITM blackboard shell.

Real world problems require experts in different fields to interact with each other. This project models such a problem solving behaviour. The experts interact with one another in two modes: a)Cooperating mode in which they share decisions. b)Criticising interaction in which an expert objects to the choice made by another expert. The rule based blackboard shell incorporates backstepping in case of objection using a timestamp technique and a dependency network.

The blackboard shell is used for crane design. In this design domain a mechanical, electrical and structural engineer interact with one another. Each expert maintains local decisions on a private working storage and uses the blackboard to post shared data.

5. Expert system shell for product formulation

We are developing a rule-based tool to build expert systems for formulation design problems. We use a task-oriented approach to enable clustering of pieces of design knowledge according to their role in problem solving. Control of problem solving is organized around a task-agenda. Design knowledge is represented using situation-action rules. There are different types of rule actions corresponding to different design methods. Our work is based on PFES - a demonstrator system of the Alvey project. We are developing our tool in COMMON LISP.

6. A Knowledge based process planning tool for cold forged fasteners

Process Planning is an important manufacturing activity. The problem solving issues for process planning in different domains are generic in nature. This project aims to develop a generic process planning system, PROPLAN. Knowledge based techniques are used to generate a process plan from the specifications of the target component. Apart from being able to list the 'best' manufacturing sequence and all possible sequences for a particular product's specification, the system operates in the 'manual' mode in which the system seeks the assistance of the user in the generation of complete manufacturing plans. The candidate domain for the testing of this system is cold forged fasteners. However the system can be adapted to other domains like machining, drawing etc.

The system uses rules to represent Planning knowledge and Constraints. 'Local Costs' may be associated with the actions prescribed by the Planning rules. The distinct feature of the system is the use of a constraint model that identifies two types of constraints, Hard and Soft. These constraints aid the modelling of the planning process and make the control strategy facile by providing for constraint relaxation. A Global Costing Function is used to guide the search procedure and helps produce globally optimal plans.

7. Intelligent Database system

A Database in real world systems is required to have enough knowledge about its application environment to reflect the real world system behaviour. In this project Database systems are endowed with reasoning capabilities. A production rule formalism is used to represent the knowledge. A rule interpreter works under the control of the database manager to provide reasoning capabilities. The system will be a tool for Semantic Integrity Management in databases and provide Decision Support.

8. Selection of Drill Tool for Process Planning

8.1 Objective

Choosing appropriate drills for drilling operations in the manufacture of components requires significant amount of judgmental knowledge acquired through experience. Conventionally, it is done by referring to a large number of charts and judgement is based largely on previous experience. As drilling is one of the most widely used processes in manufacturing, an effort in the direction of expert systems for process planning is being put in with the selection of drill tool as the starting point.

8.2 Description

An IF-THEN rule based expert system based on IITMRULE with nearly 350 rules has been developed. The system decides on the drill tool based on the following factors: a) Configuration of the surface b) Through hole or not c) Stepped or Uniform type of hole d) Solid or Cored form of component e) Diameter f) Material of the component to be drilled g) Hardness of the material h) Over travel i) Chip clearance etc.

The second phase of development is planned to extend the selection process to choose appropriate ancillaries like tool holding so that the expert system could be practically implemented on the factory floor.

9. Development of an Expert System for selection of tool inserts and revision based on failures

9.1 Approach

a) The first phase of this project is the selection of the insert code and the insert grade. This is now complete. Prolog was chosen for developing the system as it inherently supports backward chaining, rule representation of knowledge and relational databases.

Insert selection is accomplished in the following steps.

1) Determination of insert code (e.g. SNMG120408)
2) Determination of grade (e.g. TTR, TTS)
3) Determination of the cutting parameters
4) Determination of stock or availability with respect to the manufacturer and user.
5) Determination of the cost.

b) It is decided to enhance the system by building a front end process plan module and 'what if' module.

c) The second phase of the project involves the study of revising the insert selection upon failure. The personnel from Widia are being approached to provide the requisite knowledge to achieve this.

9.2 Impact of the work

This system was reviewed by the personnel from Widia India Limited, Bangalore and Hindustan Motors Limited. They were both very much satisfied with the tool and want extensions made. The following were their comments and recommendations.

- 70% of the work in insert selection has already been completed in the first phase of the project.

- A front end process plan module is necessary as the selection of inserts in real life takes place along with process planning. This would reduce the number of questions asked to the user and also produce better results.

- The parameter 'Feed' which is presently asked from the user could be decided by the system itself by using some thumb rules.

- A 'What if' module needed to allow the user to study the performance of the insert for different cutting conditions

- The credit and default values presently used by the system needs a thorough revision by the experts.

- The approach adopted to select tools is basically correct and needs no significant change.

- The system was also reviewed by a tool Expert from Hindustan Motors Ltd. He had indicated that 60% of the work is over and a 'what if' module for changing parameters would be greatly appreciated by the end user. A person from Hindustan Motors Limited is going to work on the extensions.

10 IITMRULE - An IF-THEN Rule based shell

IITMRULE is a shell for developing IF-THEN Rule based expert systems. It is written in Pascal and runs on IBM PC compatibles. Salient features of the system include an intelligent editor, forward and backward chaining inference engine, option for rerun (with modification of previous responses) and a compiler. Integer, real, string and boolean type of variables are permitted by the system with a rich set of operators. The shell also supports definition of mutual exclusion, Mycin type of confidence factors, user defined functions and relational database access. 'HOW' and 'WHY' explanations are provided by the shell.

On KBCS Approach In Image
Processing, Pattern Recognition and Computer Vision

(A report on activities at NCKBCST, ISI, Calcutta)

D. Dutta Majumder

National Center for Knowledge Based Computing
Electronics & Communication Sciences Unit
Indian Statistical Institute
Calcutta 700 035, INDIA

Abstract

The paper presents briefly the highlights of the projects undertaken at the NCKBCST at ISI, Calcutta on the application of knowledge based approach on some image processing, pattern recognition and computer vision problems in relation to some real life applications. Application areas are development of KBCS for structural and lithological discrimination and an aid to mineral location targetting in collaboration with GSI, an expert CAD system for industrial inspection and verification, and KBCS approach to the hydrocarbon exploration problems. Some of sub-problems on which results or partial results will be indicated are 3-D shape analysis, recognition and positioning of partially occluded 3-D objects, AI technique with fuzzy evaluation method for feature subset selection in automatic pattern recognition, fractal based criteria to evaluate the performance of digital image magnification techniques, binary contour coding using Bezier approximation, heuristic procedure for preparing geological classification from satellite MSS data, optimal thresholds for a class of learning algorithms, and an associative network for single object representation and recognition.

1. Introduction

Most of the application oriented topics reported in this paper are at the intersection of several disciplines or sub-disciplines, such as, artificial intelligence, pattern recognition, image processing, cognitive psychology and computer vision. The knowledge based approach to the interpretation of complex patterns, such as, satellite imagery, natural scene, industrial scene seismic patterns, speech signals or biomedical patterns is a complex task. By pattern interpretation we would like to mean the process of labelling the different parts of a pattern as instances of concept defined a-priori. The process involves many different types of knowledge gained in multiplicity of studies coming under different disciplines taking into account both local information in different parts of the pattern and global information, such as, the semantic constraints among the concepts.

In designing a system for the purposes mentioned above one has the experience that patterns acquired from the real world are characterised by a large variability from an instance to another due to almost infinite number of possible differences which can occur between the abstract description of an object and its physical existence. Moreover, noise in pattern acquisition and errors in signal contribute to make the classification task even more difficult. Probabilistic and possibilistic (fuzzy mathematical approaches) in recognising an inference making purposes are being experimented. In our work we have tried to focus our interest whenever possible to a simple but powerful approach which exploits patterns in the input data to select and trigger activities as pattern directed inference system (PDIS). Well known examples of PDISs are production system, grammatical inference system any in deductive or induction analytic or synthetic rule-based inference system that uses patterns or rules to guide the decision making process. Our objective is to develop as far as possible domain independent methodology for a knowledge based approach in systems for the interpretation of complex patterns, such as remotely sensed images of natural scenes for mineral location, targetting or hydrocarbon exploration or CAD system for industrial inspection and verification or even a rule-based system for medical diagnosis or fault diagnosis of a machine. All these require a unified approach in acquiring the ideas inherent in pattern recognition, image processing, computer vision and artificial intelligence [Dutta Majumder 1988], [Dutta Majumder 1986], [Moto-Oka et al. 1981]. In the subsequent sections we shall briefly present the initial goals, work status and in some cases results obtained in some of the problems and sub-problems undertaken at the NCKBCST at ISI, Calcutta.

2. KBCS Approach for Mineral Location Targetting

We have been working in this field in collaboration with the group of scientists at the Geological Survey of India for the last three years, particularly in the field of lithologic classification and structural analysis using band informations from landsat imagery. We have submitted our first report to the Government in this connection. We have tried to apply image processing and pattern recognition/classification technique seeking to use the computers' ability to extract and process statistical information to automatically assigned pixel to classes and produces classifications or thematic map. One of the important methodology developed and successfully applied in this report is feature reduction and change detection using principal components transformation. That maps image data into a new uncorrelated coordinate system or vector-space. In doing so it produces a space in which the data has most variance along with its first axis, the next largest variance along a second mutual orthogonal axis, and so on. In this principal component axes the data is uncorrelated, as a result of which regions of localised changes in MSS imagery gets enhanced by this data transforms. We have used seven features in this connection, namely, data of four bands and three band ratios to guide us for the development of prototypes. We have used supervised pattern classification technique in this work. By prototype we mean representative spectral signature for different rock type. In our experiment we consider six different rock types, namely, Monda granite, Romapahari granite, Bhuasani granite, Black phyllite, Alluvium and Quartz-quartzide along with vegetation and waterbody. For these classes training samples have been picked up from our area of interest ranging to 22° north to 22.15° north and from 86.30° east to 86.45° east. There was no problem in classifying vegetation and waterbody, but the gray level distribution for the different rocks are found to be highly overlapping which may be because of some natural effects. We have come to the conclusion that the work undertaken is extreme difficult, time consuming and required more manpower. The programme for the next phase have been worked out in several joint meetings of the scientists belonging to NCKBCST and Photo-Geology Division of GSI and a work is being oriented and the work programme is being redefined with the objective of developing a KBCS for structural and lithological discrimination and aid to mineral location targetting. The programme undertaken are as follows :

(a) designing of geological knowledge base; (b) development of methodologies for data representative; (c) development of inference mechanism for -

(i) lithologic discrimination; (ii) structural pattern recognition; (iii) mineral location targetting and (iv) system validation.

It is understood now that many qualitative information along with information obtained by us and the incorporation of knowledge of domain experts from several other domains, such as, Geo-chemistry, Geo-physics etc. will have to be incorporated [Tech.Report,ECSU,ISI,1989] .

3. Application of KBCS Project to the Hydrocarbon Exploration Problems

After several meetings between the representatives of ONGC and scientists of NCKBCST and ECSU, ISI, a project programme has been formulated and is awaiting final formal approval from the ONGC and ISI authorities. The topics decided upon may be briefly stated as

(1)   Different aspects and seismic data interpretations using pattern recognition and allied techniques;

(2)   Different well log data;

(3)   Available geological, geochemical and geothermal data;

(4)   Identification of source rock, reservoir rock traps, oil shells (traps are stratigraphic structural and combinational);

(5)   Entrapment conditions maturity data and possible paths of migration; and

(6)   Formulation of overall structure of knowledge-based system to be used in hydrocarbon exploration.

The development of relevant mathematical models and software packages apart from acquiring expert system building tools languages and environment for such a purpose and designing of the inference engine along with knowledge scheduler and knowledge interpreter is being envisaged in this project. ONGC has agreed to depute 3 of their scientists for a period of 3 years full time to this project to be carried out at NCKBCST, Calcutta.

4. Expert CAD Systems for Industrial Inspection and Verification

This section is a summary of the principal objectives, plans, time schedules and initial progress of a project which has just been initiated [Bose & Dutta Majumder 1989] . The role of expert systems in the area of industrial system development has been recently discussed [Dutta Majumder 1989]. In our present work, we hope to explore novel AI techniques for solving a broad class of computer-aided design (CAD) problems which are applicable to several key components in automated industrial design, inspection and verification systems.

4.1 Initial goals

The initial emphasis is on identifying and solving key generic sub-problems, which are applicable to a wide variety of CAD problems in an industrial setting. We briefly cite a couple of examples to illustrate the relationale behind our initial focus of research.

(a) Diagnosis Problems : Under this generic class of problems, several real-world problems in industrial inspection and verification as well as other domains can be justifiably handled. As an immediate application, we are considering the task of automated testing, functional verification and optimization of integrated circuit (IC) chips and boards as well as printed circuit boards (PCBs). Based on previous expertise, e.g., [Bose & Abraham 1982; [Bose 1988] , we have formulated a crisp, well-defined methodology for constructing an intelligent tool for structured logic design, test and simulation.

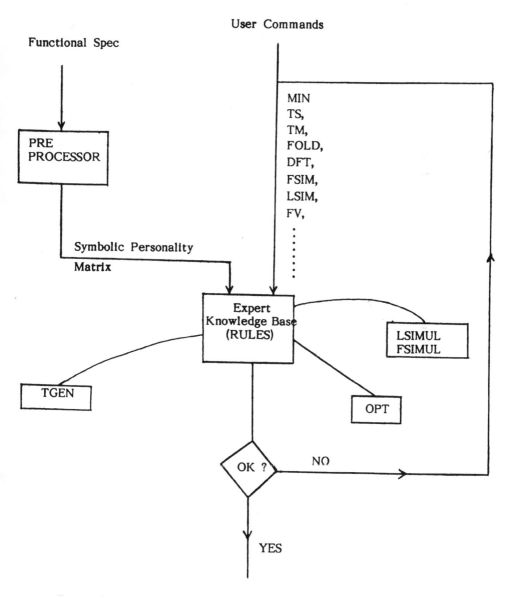

Figure 1. Functional block diagram of the iLOG system.

Figure 1 shows a functional block diagram of the proposed ILOG (intelligent logic designer and tester) presently under implementation. The end user provides input in the form of a high-level functional description of the logic to be implemented. The preprocessor converts this description into an internal symbolic personality matrix. The expert system knowledge base has rules which manipulate this symbolic matrix, in conjunction with conventional procedures (written in Pascal and C). The user has a number of commands available for guiding the expert system to his/her desired goal in an interactive fashion. The commands include minimization, test generation, design for testability, folding, functional verification and fault simulation. A generalized inspection-cum-verification job in this domain may consist in evaluating the functionality and space efficiency of a pre-wired IC-board. Usually, the output of such an inspection would include advice on correcting design errors, improving the design under given optimality criteria, etc.

(b) Placement Problems : The generic placement problem covers a wide range of applications, namely optimal location of plants, message switching centres, equipment on a manufacturing floor, cells on a VLSI chip, logic modules on a board, etc. The basic conventional algorithms for placement are directly applicable to the quadratic assignment problem [Hanan and Kurtzberg 1972]. For the purposes of this project, we focus on the problem of efficient placement and interconnection of logic modules on a board.

4.2 PLA Design and Test

We draw heavily upon existing knowledge of efficient synthesis and test generation heuristics. Here, we cite a simple example to illustrate how elegant heuristics and reformulations can result in intelligent, fast processing of algorithmically hard problems. We restrict ourselves to the crosspoint fault model used for PLAs, in which a single fault causes a programmed 0(1) in the input or output array to change to a 1(0). This physical fault model is equivalent to a logical fault model in which the product terms are subject to growth (G), shrinkage (S), disappearance (D) and appearance (A) faults. A PLA with n input variables, m product terms and p output functions, is referred to as a (n,m,p)-PLA. The area of this PLA is roughly proportional to $(2n+p)*m$.

Example : Generation of S-test set.

Generation of a minimal test set under any given physical fault model is generally accepted to be a NP-complete problem. However, in the context of PLA testing, the logical fault model enables us to use intelligent short-cuts which avoid the task of solving a minimal covering problem. The heuristic methods to generate a minimal S-test set for a (n,m,p)-PLA, using the "opposite-adjacent" method has been described earlier [Bose and Abraham 1982]. The conventional method would involve generation of all possible S-terms followed by selection of a set of minterms to (minimally) cover all the S-terms. However, by using a simple short-cut, a minimal S-test set may be derived in $0(m)$ time complexity, where m is the number of PLA product terms. It can be shown that in most cases, the upper bound on the number of S-tests for a product term of arbitrary size is usually only 2 or 3. Consider the example shown in Figure 2, in which we are interested in generating a S-test set for the product term $t = \bar{x}1$, represented as ixxx. First choose a free minterm t1=1100 (say). Choose a second minterm t2 by complementing the x-values chosen for t1. Thus, t2=1011, which is "opposite" to t1 within t. If t2 is also free then (t1, t2) forms the minimal S-test set for t (Figure 2a).

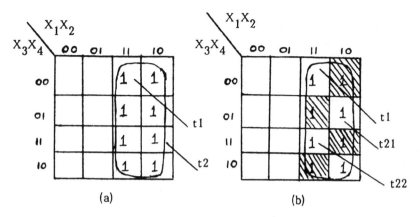

Figure 2. Illustration of "Opposite-Adjacent" Method.

If there is no free t1 for which a free t2 exists, then up to two free minterms "adjacent" to t2 (i.e., at unit binary distance from t2) must be chosen to cover the remaining shrinkages. This is illustrated in Figure 2b, where shaded positions indicate bound minterms of our example product term 1xxx. The theoretical upper bound of the number of test vectors needed to test all S-faults of a general, non-isolated product term can be proven to be as follows :

Lemma : The number of S-tests, Ns, needed for a general product term t is bounded as follows :

$$Ns \leqslant n - k + 1,$$

where, n = number of input variables, k = number of literals in t.

Usually, an S-test set for a given product term (generated using the "opposite-adjacent" method, say), will automatically test for most (if not all) the D- and A-faults of that product term. However, in certain cases, additional test vectors are required to cover all disappearances and appearances. Detailed analysis and discussion is omitted here. It should be clear that the initial choice of test vector for a S-test set must be made intelligently in order to reduce the overall PLA test set. The following two rules are among those designed to decide whether a candidate S-test vector t is a valid test vector, and if valid, whether it is a "good" starting choice for the Opposite-Adjacent method. Let c be the input cube (row) under consideration.

Rule 1.

IF SUBSUME (t:i.p, c':i.p) AND COVER (c':o.p, t:o.p) AND $(c' <> c)$ THEN t_is_INVALID = TRUE.

Rule 2.

IF SUBSUME (t:i.p, c':i.p) AND 1-DENSITY $(c':o.p) > 0.5$ THEN THERE IS 0.7 EVIDENCE THAT t_IS_A_GOOD_CHOICE = FALSE.

In the above rules, the qualifier i.p indicates the "input part" of the relevant cube. Rule 1 simply checks to see if t is covered by another product term of the PLA, in which case it would definitely be invalid. Rule 2, on the other hand, assigns a confidence factor of 0.7 to the assertion if the premise is true. (1-density of a bit vector denotes the fraction of bits which are 1). Note that SUBSUME, COVER and 1-DENSITY may be thought of as externally defined (Pascal) procedures accessed from the main knowledge base.

As enunciated in previous work [Bose and Abraham 1982], the heuristic methods of generating a complete test set Ts for a PLA are guaranteed to restrict Ts to a size less than the theoretical upper bound, as given by the following theorem :

Theorem : For a general (n,m,p)-PLA, the size of a Ts covering all single G, S, D and A faults is bounded as follows :

$$| \text{ Ts } | \leq m(n+p).$$

Thus, for PLA with 16 input variables, 48 product terms and 8 output functions, $| \text{ Ts } | \leq 1152$.

4.3 Placement and Verification

We follow Hanan and Kurtzberg [Hanan and Kurtzberg 1972] in explaining the basic concepts of the placement problem. In the context of electronic (computer) industry, designing a "card" or "board" involves positioning a set of computer modules into various slots in the board. The various circuit elements on the modules lead to connection pins located on the sides of the modules. On the basis of the given logic design, various subsets of these pins, termed signal sets must be interconnected to form nets. We speak of these pins as being electrically common. Since each module contains a number of connection pins, a module generally belongs to more than one distinct net. Furthermore, because of engineering considerations, some of the nets may be more critical than others, and thus the corresponding signal sets have greater "weight". The module placement problem consists of finding the optimal placement of modules in the board with respect to some norm defined on the interconnections, such as minimal weighted wire length.

In our work, we are interested in developing intelligent heuristics and search paradigms to speed up the solving of the placement problem for up to 100 logic modules on a board. The input data is assumed to be provided in the form of netlist, specifying the pin interconnections of given logic modules. In particular, we propose to investigate intelligent applications of simulated annealing and simulated evolution procedures.

In design verification, the problem is to verify the correctness or functionality of a logic or a wired logic board. In this domain, our ultimate aim is to devise a vision-based CAD methodology to achieve an automated industrial verification system.

4.4 Project outlook

Our immediate focus is on applying expert system technology for solving the logic design, test and verification tasks alluded to earlier. The theoretical framework for this phase of the project is quite firm, although some work is ongoing. We hope to finish the ILOG system within the next 6 months.

Overlapped with the above initial phase of research, we propose to initiate research on developing vision-based CAD algorithms. If the results are satisfactory, we propose to build a small prototype of the system after the vision laboratory with its SUN computing facility is ready. We hope to have a kernel set of vision-based algorithms within 4 months of the debugging of the ILOG systems. Within a time frame of a little over one year from the present time, we hope to set up a skeleton vision-based CAD toolkit, driven by our expert rule-base.

5. A few sub-problems related to PR, IP and CVS

In this section we shall present some results and partial results of some problems carried out in the last year or so by the scientists working at the NCKBCST, Calcutta.

5.1 A method for Shape Recognition and recovery

Several authors suggested distance measures for 2-D shape matching and under-standing in addition to the usual Fourier and other descriptors which are computationally complex. In the recent past, Dutta Majumder and Parui [Dutta Majumder & Parui 1982] suggested six new shape distance measures out of which five were information preserving and satisfies all metric properties (none of the previous shape distance measures satisfies all the metric properties). Two distance functions are for simple curves and four are for closed regions without holes.

This approach uses major axis in normalizing the orientation of a region in order to construct the shape distance functions explicitly as a result of which they can deal with almost any shape.

The directional codes used to construct some of the shape distances are also a generalization of Freeman's chain codes [Kundu, Choudhuri and Dutta Majumder 1985]. There have been several extensions to higher order chain codes. But here the codes are much more general in the sense that they can take any real value 0 and 8 which has not been used before.

In order to extend some of the shape definitions and algorithms to 3-D, continuous directional codes are defined in three dimensions. Some of the shape distances can be extended to 3-D cases in a straight forward manner. The 2-D shape distance based on shape vector can be extended to 3-D by considering concentric spheres instead of concentric circles. Similarly, other shape distances are also extendable - in some cases one has to consider skeletal voxels instead of pixels. Similarly, theoretically speaking, some of the definitions of measure of degree of symmetry and antisymmetry can also be extended. The approach of Dutta Majumder and Parui along with the approach of generalized cone/cylinder will lead to a more meaningful solution to the shape recognition problem [Dutta Majumder 1986] [Parui and Dutta Majumder 1983A] and [Parui & Dutta Majumder 1983].

Shape and Symmetry Understanding in 3-D

Shape of 3-D objects has been a very important problem in computer vision. The present section deals with the shape and symmetry of 3-dimensional objects and proposes methods for quantifying a shape distance or shape similarity and some degrees of symmetry for them. The quantified shape distance or shape similarity may be used for classifying the shape of a new object as one of several known shapes. The approach taken here to shape distance quantification is an extension of an earlier work on 2-dimensional shape discrimination. The techniques used for the distance quantification in turn employed to quantify various degrees of symmetry of 3-dimensional objects. A 3-D object is defined to be a subset in the 3-dimensional space. Two objects have the same shape if and only if one is a translation, dilation and rotation of the other. Now, for matching, an object has to be normalized in terms of position, size and orientation. Normalization of an object with respect to position and size can easily be achieved if its centre of gravity and volume are considered. The main problem in shape matching involves normalization of orientation of an object. Here, this problem is solved by using certain characteristic planes of an object. In the analogue domain, it is proved that the proposed distance has all the metric properties.

A shape distance for 3-D objects is defined on the basis of volume mismatch which involves infinitely many rotations of the 3-D objects. In order to solve this problem of rotations, another shape distance is proposed which needs at most 5 rotations. Here certain characteristic planes and axes are defined for a 3-D object on the basis of which the second shape distance is constructed. Three types of symmetry are dealt with, namely, symmetry around a plane, symmetry around an axis and symmetry around a point. Some relationship between a plane or axis of symmetry and the characteristic planes or axes are mentioned. A degree of symmetry for each of the three types of symmetry is proposed. Techniques to compute the second shape distance for 3-D objects are also provided. Here, 3-D objects are represented volumetrically, that is, in terms of 3-D binary matrices whose elements, called voxels, are either 0 to 1. Techniques to compute the three types of degree of symmetry also are provided [Parui, Banerjee and Dutta Majumder 1989].

5.2 Recognition and position of partially occluded 3-D objects

A new method has been proposed to recognize and locate partially occluded two-dimensional rigid objects [Ray and Dutta Majumder 1989] of a given scene. For this purpose we initially generate a set of local features of the shapes using the concept of differential geometry. Finally a computer vision scheme, based upon matching local features of the objects in a scene and the models which are considered as cognitive database, is described using hypothesis generation and verification of features for the best possible recognition.

A common task in computer vision is to recognize and locate an unknown object in a scene. The unknown object is usually assumed to be similar to one of a set of possible object models known as cognitive database of the vision system. The most straightforward way to recognize the objects would be to match models for each possible combination of identity, position and orientation to the image. But such an exhaustive search is computationally very cumbersome and proved to be hopeless for the case of three-dimensional objects [Knoll and Jain 1986] [Besl and Jain 1985]. Hence researchers have switched over to recognize occluded objects by their local features [Medioni and Yashmoto 1987].

The approach described here is based upon matching local descriptions of the scene and the models by a technique of hypotheses generation and verification coupled with an appropriate estimation of the model to scene transformations.

The proposed method is fast, accurate, robust to noise. It is general in the sense that it is basically independent of the kinds of primitives used to represent the two-dimensional shapes and in the sense that it can be extended without too much difficulty to the corresponding three-dimensional problem [Besl and Jain 1984].

The task of recognizing and positioning the partially occluded three dimensional (3-D) rigid objects of a given scene has been considered [Ray and Dutta Majumder 1989A]. The surfaces of 3-D objects may be planar or curved. The 3-D surface informations are captured through range data (depth map). For recognition we use the principal curvatures, mean curvature and Gaussian curvature as the local descriptions of the surfaces. These curvatures are the local invariant features of the surfaces. A computer vision schemes, based upon the matching between the local features of the 3-D objects in a scene and those of the models which are considered as knowledge database, is described. Finally, the hypothesis generation and verification scheme is considered for best possible reognition.

5.3 An application of AI technique to the problem of feature subset selection for Automatic Pattern Recognition System

One of the major problems in designing an automatic pattern recognition system is to select a proper subset of features in order to facilitate the performance of the classifier. All researches directed towards this goal fall under the following three categories :

i) use of linear and nonlinear transformation techniques to map the feature vectors to lower dimensional space in order to enhance the class separately.

ii) use of various feature selection criteria that bound the Bayes error probability and transformation that are optimum with respect to such criteria.

iii) use of search procedure for optimal selection of a subset from a given set of features.

One of our earlier works [Pal and Chakravorty 1986] falls under the category two where we have formulated a measure for evaluating features based on fuzzy set theoretic concept. The measure named 'Feature Evaluation Index' have been used earlier to rank the features independently. But the most annoying fact is that the set of 'k' individually best discriminating features is not necessarily the best discriminating feature set of size 'k' even for the case of independent features [Cover 1974].

So the problem of selection of best feature subset stands out to be the selection of the best subset of 'm' features from a large set of 'n' features by optimizing any criterion function over all subsets of size 'm'. Though exhaustive evaluation of all the subsets guarantees that the selected subset yields the globally best value, it is computationally prohibitive, as the number of subsets to be considered grows vary rapidly with the number of features. There are several subopotimal search techniques in AI which have been applied to feature selection problem. Branch and bound techniques are the most powerful combinatorial optimization tools and have been applied to feature evaluation problem by Narendra & Fukunaga [Narendra & Fukunaga 1977].

The method proposed by the above mentioned authors guaranteed the selection of an optimal feature subset if the monotonicity condition is satisfied which requires that the criterion function J used to evaluate feature subsets

508

change monotonically over a sequence of nested feature subsets $(F_1....F_k)$. They originally proposed to use probabilistic separability measures as criterion function. But it has a number of disadvantages. In this work [Chakraborty & Dutta Majumder 1989] we have used a fuzzy set theoretic measure based on Index of Fuzziness(nu) and entropy(H) as the criterion function for evaluating feature subsets. The measure named 'feature evaluation index' have been used earlier to rank the features independently [Cover 1974]. This criterion function used is free from any regorous mathematical computation unlike the probabilistic function. The algorithm has been implemented on a mango leaf dataset and is being implemented for other data sets such as Landsat, IRS and speech data.

5.4 Fractal based criteria to evaluate the performance of digital image magnification techniques

With the wide variety of techniques available for magnification of an image digitally, it is difficult to decide which technique is the most suitable. A simple and appealing way to decide the suitability of a particular technique is to visually compare the output images generated using the different techniques. However, this may not be suitable when image magnification is required as an intermediate step in image processing. We have to then ensure that the original radiometric values of the image are not tampered with to the extent that artifacts are introduced in the output images.

Leberl (1975) points out that any criteria used for comparing the performance of the different interpolation techniques must be data structure dependent when they are applied to image magnification problems. The mean square radiometric error is one such measure that has been used to compare the performance of the different digital magnification techniques [Simon 1975, Schlien1979, Park and Schowengerdt 1983]. In this context, a point that needs some investigation is, does a technique perform equally well at all scales of magnification ? In other words, is there a limiting scale up to which a particular technique is as good as any other ? Is there a quantitative measure of the image data structure by means of which one can decide to use a particular technique to magnify the image ? These points are important because it is possible that at a lower scale of magnification, a simple, computationally less intensive technique may perform as well as a more sophisticated, computationally intensive technique.

The present work [Lalitha and Dutta Majumder 1989] attempts to answer some of the above points using criteria based on the fractal dimensions of an image. Fractal dimension of an image apart from being a measure of the surface roughness is also invariant to scale changes of the original data [Pentland 1984]. Thus, the scale at which the fractal dimension of the magnified image differs from that of the original image can be ascertained to determine the limiting scale for any magnification technique.

5.5 Binary contour coding using Bezier approximation

Bezier approximation technique which uses Bernstein polynomials as the blending function provides a successful way to approximate an arc (not having any inflexion point) from a set of minimum three control points. The approximation scheme is simple and useful for its axis independence property. It is also found to be computationally efficient.

The present work [Biswas, Pal and Dutta Majumder 1988] attempts to formulate an algorithm for approximate coding of binary images based on Bezier approximation technique. A contour is first of all decomposed here into a set of arcs and line segments. For this, a set of key pixels are defined on the contour and the **vertices of Bezier characteristic triangles** corresponding to an arc are coded. Regeneration technique involves Bersenham's algorithm in addition to the Bezier method. During the regeneration process, key pixels one considered to be the guiding pixels and their locations are therefore in no way disturbed. In order to preserve them and to maintain the connectivity property some intermediate operations e.g. deletion and shifting of undesirable pixels generated by Bezier approximation, and insertion of new pixels are introduced in order to have better faithful reproduction.

Effectiveness of the algorithms is compared with two existing algorithms based on contour run length coding (CRLC) and discrete line segment coding (DLSC). The compression ratios of the proposed methods are found to be significantly improved without affecting the quality much when a set of images is considered as input. The compactness and the difference in area between the input and output versions keeping the locations of the key pixels the same are also computed to provide a measure of the error.

5.6 Optimum Thresholds for a Class of Learning Algorithms

The learning of the parameters of classifiers is an important aspect of pattern recognition. A large number of learning algorithms, based on different approaches, such as the Bayesian, the stochastic approximation and the maximum likelihood, are available to the PR scientist. The class of algorithms that this work refers to, learn recursively using stochastic approximation by first attempting to detect mislabeled and other unreliable training samples and removing them from the training set. These Generalised Guard-Zone Algorithms (GGAs) [Pathak & Pal 1986] and [Pal, pathak & Basu 1988] as they are called, allow only those samples to be used for learning which lie within the corresponding 'guard zone' (a closed ball with a specified radius, called the dimension of the guard zone, centered at the preceding estimate of the mean). Essentially, therefore, these algorithms use certain thresholds (the guard zone dimensions) to accept or reject samples, and are self-supervisory in nature. Those familiar with the theory of robust statistics will at once recognise this as one of the simplest strategies applied in that field for dealing with outliers. Therefore, it may be argued that robust techniques more sophisticated than the outlier-rejection used by us can be applied to solve our type of problem. However, so far there has not been much success in this area.

The present work [Pal 1989] attempts to estimate thresholds for the GGA automatically at every instant of learning, by minimizing the mean squared error (MSE). Explicit expressions for the MSE were first obtained for both the GGA and the non-GGA (our nomenclature for the usual unsupervised stochastic approximation learning algorithm) using Chittineni's model for mislabeled training samples. Then, under some simplifying assumptions, an approximation to the guard-zone dimension n for which the MSE of the GGA is smaller was found, using statistical large-sample theory.

5.7 Simulator for a Parallel and Distributed Processing System

In the course of the last decade, many new (and some regenerated) concepts have taken strong hold in the area of computer science. These concepts, loosely brought under the caption "Fifth Generation Computer System", are centered around two different foci: massive parallelization and knowledge-oriented computing. The first of these has resulted in VLSI based hardware research, as well as research in more abstract processing paradigms. Here, we investigate one such paradigms, namely Parallel and Distributed Processing proposed by Rumelhart and McCleland. Parallel and Distributed Processing is also generally referred to as a class of Neural Network.

A Network Definition Language (NDL) has been proposed [Gangadharan 1989] (unpublished report) to describe a highly Parallel and Distributed Processing (PDP) system. A simulator has also been implemented for the PDP system where an interpreter provides the input. The interpreter on the other hand receives the network description written in NDL as its input.

5.8 Semantic Network and Highlevel Computer Vision

Any knowledge representation scheme for high-level computer vision, it has long been recognized, must facilitate both feature directed and model directed searching needs. Logic programs, procedural methods, semantic nets, frames and production systems have been applied for object recognition and scene description with some degree of success. It has however been recognized that although a structured representation scheme is desirable for visual objects, no conventional scheme is completely sufficient to encompass this problem domain. What then are the considerations that are to be taken into account in order to represent visual objects such that both object modeling as well as object recognition ? In this report attempts have been made to address some of these.

The scope of this work [Sarkar 1989] (unpublished report) has been limited to unoccluded single objects primarily from the industrial domain. General scenes with more than one object are not taken into consideration. Here an associative network (semantic network) is developed to represent the model of visual object and then the same objects are recognized from a complete or incomplete input description which is assumed to be generated from a lower level image processing module. An associative network is chosen because in this form of representation (as opposed to say first order predicate calculus) the representation itself does not promote either top-down or bottom-up processing and the choice of matching objects given features or vice versa is controlled by some matching technique.

5.9 Procedural Knowledge and Logic Programming

For the last ten years. Logic Programming in general and in particular PROLOG, have gained substantial popularity as problem solving methodology. In a wide variety of application areas like database management, natural language processing, expert system design, compiler writing Logic Programming has proved its effectiveness. In any programming task, specification plays a major role with respect to reliable code generation. In the ordinary sense the most popular specification language till data is the natural language. But due to the semantic gap between the natural language and formal programming languages, programmers are directed towards more constrained but less imprecise structured algorithmic languages like Algol or Pascal. These languages are essentially imperative in nature and provides the programmer a precise way to formulate a 'recipe' for solving a particular problem. On the other hand one may use first order Predicate Logic as specification language, [Hogger 1981] , which may be converted into its near cousin Logic Programming language PROLOG without much difficulty. Even Logic Programming language as specification language is explored as a next step towards automatic programming and program verification. But till date technical literatures are rich with program specifications for various problems represented in algorithmic specification languages (ASL).

In this work [Basu & Dutta Majumder 1988] (unpublished) we shall try to develop a theory and method to synthesise Logic Programs from structured algorithmic specification programs. The basic intention is to develop machine independent Logic Programming synthesis algorithms based on the semantics of structured algorithmic language and that of standard PROLOG Emden 1976 The ASL resembles Pascal with some syntactical differences. To make Logic Programming Language independent of 'special features' of different PROLOG implementations, we have used only three built in system predicates which are available in almost all the PROLOG implementation, may be in different syntaxes. Primarily we have followed Edinburgh syntax of PROLOG. For a primary investigation we have taken a subset of the specification language, in which only simple input/output, assignment, conditional and loop statements are incorporated. For the time being arrays and more complicated data structures are kept out of its domain and all the variables are assumed to be scalar.

One important consequence of our investigation is that, using PARLOG, the parallel Logic Programming language rather than PROLOG as our target language, we may achieve parallelism from a sequential specification program. This enables the programmer to exploit the inherent parallelism in the algorithm without the tedious concurrency analysis.

References

[Dutta Majumder 1988]
Dutta Majumder D. "A Unified approach to artificial intelligence, pattern recognition, image processing, and computer vision in Fifth-Generation Computer Systems", Information Sciences 45, pp.391-431, 1988.

[Dutta Majumder 1986]
Dutta Majumder D. "Pattern recognition, image processing, artificial intelligence and computer vision in fifth generation computer systems", Sadhana, Proceedings of Indian Academy of Sciences, Bangalore 1986.

[Moto Oka et al, 1981]
Moto-Oka T et al. "Challenge for knowledge information processing systems (preliminary report on FGCS)", Proceedings of the International Conference on FGCS, pp.1-85, October 1981.

[Tech. Report, ECSU, 1989]
"Application of pattern recognition and image processing techniques to geological mapping and mineral detection", Tech. Report, Electronics & Communication Sciences Unit, ISI, Calcutta, March 1989.

[Bose and Dutta Majumder 1989]
Bose P and Dutta Majumder D. "Expert CAD systems for industrial inspection and verification", unpublished internal memo, ECSU, ISI, Calcutta, November 1989.

512

[Dutta Majumder 1989]
Dutta Majumder D. "Artificial intelligence and expert systems - its role in industrial system development", invited lecture, National Symposium on Electronics and Applications, September 1989.

[Bose and Abraham 1982]
Bose P and Abraham J.A. "Test generation for programmable logic arrays", Proceedings, 19th Design Automation Conference, Las Vegas, pp.574-580, June 1982.

[Bose 1988]
Bose P. "A novel technique for efficient parallel implementation of a classical logic/fault simulation problem", IEEE Trans. on Computers, December 1988.

[Hanan and Kurtzberg 1972]
Hanan M.A. and Kurtzberg J. "Placement techniques", Design Automation of Digital Systems : Theory and Techniques, Vol.1, Chap.5, Prentice-Hall N.J., pp.213-282, 1972.

[Dutta Majumder and Parui 1982]
Dutta Majumder D. and Parui S.K. "How to quantify shape distance for 2-D regions", Proceedings of 7th ICPR, 1982.

Parui S.K. and Dutta Majumder D. "A new definition of shape similarity", Pattern Recognition Letters, 1982.

[Kundu, Chowdhury and Dutta Majumder 1985]
Kundu M, Chowdhuri B.B. and Dutta Majumder D. "A generalized digital contour coding scheme", CVGIP, Vol.30, No.3, July 1985.

[Dutta Majumder 1986]
Dutta Majumder D. "Functional and Technical objectives of FGCS research", Institute of Engineers (India) Journal - Co., Vol.67, pp.1-10, September 1986.

[Parui and Dutta Majumder 1983A]
Parui S.K. and Dutta Majumder D. "Symmetry analysis by Computer", Pattern Recognition, Vol.16, 1983.

[Parui and Dutta Majumder 1983]
Parui S.K. and Dutta Majumder D. "Shape similarity measures for open curves", Pattern Recognition letters, Vol.1, 1983.

[Banerjee, Parui and Dutta Majumder 1989]
Banerjee D.K., Parui S.K. and Dutta Majumder D. "Shape-Based object recognition", Proceedings of KBCS 1989, Bombay.

[Ray and Dutta Majumder 1989]
Ray Kumar S. and Dutta Majumder D. "Application of differential geometry to recognize and locate partially occluded objects", PRL 9, pp.351-360, June 1989.

[Knoll and Jain 1986]
Knoll T.F. and Jain R.C. "Recognizing partially vision objects using feature indexed hypotheses" IEEE J. Robotics and Automation 2(1),3 13, 1986.

[Besl and Jain 1985]
Besl P.J. and Jain R.C. "Surface characterization for three-dimensional object recognition", RSD-TR-19-84, Center for Robotics and Integrated Manufacturing, Univ. of Michigan, Ann Arbor, December 1985.

[Medioni and Yasumoto 1987]
Medioni G. and Yasumoto Y. "Corner detection and curve representation using cubic B-splines", Computer Vision, Graphics and Image Processing 39, pp.267-278, 1987.

[Besl and Jain 1984]
Besl P.J. and Jain R.C. "An overview of three-dimensional object recognition", RSD-TR-19-84, Center for Robotics and Integrated Manufacturing, Univ. of Michigan, Ann Arbor, December 1984.

[Ray and Dutta Majumder 1989A]
Ray Kumar S. and Dutta Majumder D. "Recognition and positioning of partially occluded 3D-objects", Unpublished report, ECSU, ISI, Calcutta 1989.

[Pal and Chakraborty 1986]
Pal S.K. and Chakraborty B. "Fuzzy set theoretic measure for automatic feature evaluation", IEEE Trans. Syst. Man and Cybern, Vol.SMC-16, pp.754-760, 1986.

[Cover 1974]
Cover T.M. "The best two independent measurements are not the two best", IEEE Trans. Syst., Man and Cybern, 4, pp.116-117, 1974.

[Narendra and Fukunaga 1977]
Narendra P.M. and Fukunaga K. "A branch and bound algorithm for feature subset selection", IEEE Trans.Comput.Vol.C-26, pp.917-922, September 1977.

[Chakraborty and Dutta Majumder 1989]
Chakraborty B and Dutta Majumder D. "An application of A.I.Technique to the problem of feature subset selection for automatic pattern recognition system", National Conf. on Electronic Circuit and Systems, Roorkee, November 1989.

[Leberl 1975]
Leberl F. "Photogrammetic interpolation", Photogrametric Engg. and Remote Sensing 41, pp.603-612, 1975.

[Simon 1975]
Simon K.W. "Digital image reconstruction and resampling for geometric manipulation", Proc. IEEE Symp.on Machine Processing of Remotely Sensed Data, June 3-5, 3A-1-3A-11, 1975.

[Schlien 1979]
Schlien S. "Geometric correction, registration and resampling of Landsat imagery", Canad. J. Remote Sensing 5, 74-89, 1979.

[Park and Schowengerdt 1983]
Park S.K. and Schowengerdt R.A. "Image reconstruction by parametric cubic convolution", Comp.Vision, Graphics and Image Processing 23, pp.258-272, 1983.

[Lalitha and Dutta Majumder 1989]
Lalitha L. and Dutta Majumder D. "Fractal based criteria to evaluate
the performance of digital image magnification techniques", PRL 9 67
75, North-Holland, January 1989.

[Pentland 1984]
Pentland A.P. "Fractal based description of natural scenes", IEEE Trans.
Pattern Anal.Machine Intell., 6, pp.661-674, 1984.

[Biswas, Pal and Dutta Majumder 1988]
Biswas S.N., Pal S.K. and Dutta Majumder D. "Binary contour coding
using Bezier approximation", PRL 8, pp.237-249, North-Holland, November
1988.

[Pathak and Pal 1986]
Pathak A. and Pal S.K. "A generalized learning algorithm based on guard
zones", PRL 4, pp.63-69, 1986.

[Pal, Pathak and Basu 1988]
Pal S.K., Pathak A. and Basu C. "Dynamic guard zone for self-supervised
learning", PRL 7, pp.135-144, 1988.

[Pal 1989]
Pal A. "Optimum thresholds for a class of learning algorithms", National
Conf. on Electronic Circuit and Systems, Roorkee, November 1989.

[Gangadharan 1989]
Gangadharan K. "Simulator for a parallel and distributed processing system",
M.Tech. Dissertation, Computer Science, ISI, Calcutta, July 1989.

[Sarkar 1989]
Sarkar N. "Semantic network and highlevel computer vision", M.Tech.
dissertation, Computer Science, ISI, Calcutta 1989.

[Hogger 1981]
Hogger C.J. "Derivation of logic programs", JACM, Vol.28, No.2, April
1981.

[Basu and Dutta Majumder 1988]
Basu S. and Dutta Majumder D. "Procedural knowledge and logic
programming", Unpublished internal report, ECSU, ISI, Calcutta 1988.

KBCS Activities at NCST

S Ramani, R Chandrasekar and KSR Anjaneyulu

National Centre for Software Technology
Gulmohar Cross Road No. 9
Juhu, Bombay 400 049
Email: {ramani,mickey,anji}@shakti.uu.net

KBCS activities at NCST include work on intelligent information retrieval, early work for machine translation from English to Hindi, AI applications in education with a strong focus on intelligent testing, and intelligent scheduling of ships and aircraft. The other activities of NCST's KBCS group include running an AI quarterly, Vivek, conducting a Diploma Programme in KBCS, and the development of AI software such as an expert system shell, and a LISP interpreter.

Part I of this report broadly describes the goals of the group, and the areas of research. Part II is an overview of the technical work carried out by members of this group. The papers cited in the text give details of each active area.

Part I - The KBCS Project at NCST

1. Overall Goals

The overall goals of the KBCS project at NCST are:

* to develop prototype AI applications in Natural Language Understanding, Education and Rule Based Systems, and

* to develop AI software. This will include a logic programming system for parallel hardware, to be developed for possible use with the parallel machine being developed at the KBCS node at the Indian Institute of Science, Bangalore.

2. Areas of KBCS Research at NCST

2.1. Natural Language Understanding

Major advances in AI have brought exciting possibilities within reach. Objectives such as machine translation are likely to be realized within the next 10 years. R & D has to be carried out and prototypes built now.

We are working with machine readable text available on-line from news agencies, in cooperation with a national wire service agency. We aim at human aided processing by machine, instead of fully automatic processing. Our immediate focus is on intelligent information retrieval. We plan to have a prototype of a machine translation system (translating from English to Hindi) ready in 1991.

2.2. AI Applications in Education

Education and Training are important areas, and KBCS technology is expected to play a significant role in AI applications in these areas. Current technology is promising, but implementing viable applications requires pioneering work.

At NCST, we recognize the critical role that testing plays in education and pay special attention to testing in the overall context of Intelligent Tutoring Systems (ITS). The educational services offered by NCST are a good experimental test bed for many of the projects in the ITS area. Several testing tools and strategies have been tried out in courses run at NCST. We focus on areas of relevance to university level students, including areas which are prerequisites for university education.

We propose to implement an intelligent tutor to teach programming to novices. This system will assist novices to construct programs in LISP, using a graphical notation.

We also propose to implement an Intelligent Tutoring System covering subjects at the school (10th standard) level, for mathematics and English. This system will not be designed to cover the complete syllabus prescribed for that level. It will be a remedial system, covering only some of the topics, and will seek to enhance student performance. It will be a field-tested R&D prototype, but not a full production version.

We propose to implement a shell for building Intelligent Tutoring systems, and use it to create tutors in specific domains. Considering the magnitude of the problem being tackled, this work will not be completed during the KBCS project time-frame. However, we plan to take steps towards the creation of an intelligent tutor for 10th standard level school education. The proposed work will cover a part of the syllabus, but will deal with this part reasonably thoroughly.

2.3. Parallel Logic Programming

Logic Programming is an important paradigm to be understood and used. Parallel computing hardware is becoming widely available and at relatively low cost. However, though parallel symbolic computation is very promising for KBCS, it is in the early stages of R & D. There are major Indian efforts in progress to build parallel machines, and there are good opportunities for related software development.

We will use first create a sequential Prolog processor, and then go on to create an OR-Parallel implementation. We initially plan to work with a commercially available parallel computer system with a view to porting the software to parallel hardware being developed in India.

2.4. Software Tools for KBCS

Hundreds of students and young professionals in India need to get educated in the KBCS area. While the Indian computing industry is making hardware easily available, there has been relatively little effort so far in creating AI tools such as language processors and expert system shells.

We intend to work on inexpensive software which can be ported on to PCs and Unix computers, both of which are in use all over India. We will make the software widely available through the educational courses we offer, including our off-campus courses. We have done this already with our implementation of LISP, and our expert system shell Vidwan. After the software has been tried out by a large number of people in this mode, we plan to release these tools as low-priced software.

2.5. Rule Based Systems and Resource Scheduling

There is wide interest in India in Rule Based Systems. The tools we are developing, such as an expert system shell and a logic programming system, have to have convincing demonstration applications. A few major industrial groups interacting with NCST are interested in resource scheduling applications. We have developed a prototype of a major aircraft scheduling system using Prolog on a sequential machine. If possible, we will develop it further as a major demonstration application on a parallel computer.

A related application, ship scheduling, is in the advanced prototype stage.

Part II - Work Done

1. Applications in Natural Language Understanding

1.1. Comprehending English - A Prelude to Machine Translation

A limited vocabulary Machine Translation (MT) prototype, which will translate from English text to Hindi, is expected to be ready in 1991. As a prelude to developing an MT system, work is in progress to design systems that comprehend English text. A two-pronged effort is favoured, combining a top-down analysis of a news story with bottom-up sentential analysis. We have recently examined possible ways in which the top-down and the bottom-up mechanisms may exchange information of relevance, which could lead to more efficient analysis.

Publications: [Chandrasekar and Ramani, 1988a], [Chandrasekar et al, 1989a], [Srikant et al, 1988].

1.2. Intelligent Archival and Retrieval of Information

An intelligent information archival and retrieval system has been designed and implemented for use by a leading wire service agency. This will be used to archive and retrieve news stories distributed by this news agency. The system features automatic categorization of stories, and allows the user to retrieve news stories based on their content. Details are available in a paper in this volume.

This categorization system will form the basis of the topic analysis scheme which will be used in the machine translation system described above.

Publications: [Chandrasekar and Ramani, 1988b], [Bhandarkar et al, 1989].

2. Applications in Education

2.1. VEDA - A Generative Testing System

VEDA is a general purpose testing system which can be used to design and conduct on-line tests. The system accepts generative as well as non-generative questions. A generative question can be used to produce instances of a question given the structure of the question and constraints on variable elements. Non-generative questions can be either short answer or passage comprehension type questions.

VEDA provides tools for the designer of the test to create question generators. It allows the designer to classify questions into domains and specify the order in which questions will be generated from the different domains. It also allows the designer to specify other information, like the maximum time to be allowed for a question. The system provides tools for "item evaluation". These tools are used to determine statistical parameters (such as level of difficulty, and figure of merit) based on test scores. These parameters can be used to reclassify questions and to identify poor questions in the system.

VEDA provides a high degree of security. All text files are encrypted and decryption of questions takes place only at the time the questions are displayed. It is possible to restrict the usage of the system and also detect attempts to break into the system. VEDA was developed in the C programming language under Unix.

A mastery learning version of VEDA has been implemented and is in use. The system allows a candidate to take a given test a number of times, till he masters all the concepts covered in that test. Quizzes in Pascal, LISP, Expert Systems and UNIX have been developed using this system.

Publications: [Anjaneyulu et al, 1987], [VEDA, 1989]

2.2. A Knowledge Based Authoring System

A Knowledge Based Authoring System (KBAS) for VEDA is being implemented, and has recently been extended. VEDA, the generative testing system developed at NCST, uses question prototypes in the form of C programs. So knowledge of C was necessary to design questions for VEDA. Now KBAS allows a user to design test questions without having to program in C. KBAS also allows users to retrieve information from a knowledge base and use it in question prototype generation. KBAS considerably reduces the time taken to add new question prototypes, even for experienced programmers.

A frame based representation system has been added to KBAS. An interface between the knowledge base and the authoring system has been designed and partially implemented. This has also involved design of an authoring language which is compatible with the interactive specification system now in use. Several design issues related to a Knowledge Based Authoring System (KBAS) have been resolved, and a symbolic equation solver has been developed for KBAS.

Publication: [Srinivas et al, 1988]

2.3. SEQT - A Simultaneous Equation Tutor

A prototype of a tutor for teaching simultaneous equations was developed by staff members working with a visiting scientist, Dr. Elsom-Cook from the Open University of UK. The tutor uses production rules to model the problem solving strategies used by students. The system allows the student to type in the steps he uses to solve a given set of equations, and attempts to infer the method that the student is using to solve the equations. In case the student makes a mistake, the system attempts to diagnose his misconception. The system is implemented in Prolog.

2.4. DRLP: A Data flow Representation Language for LISP

A representation language called DRLP, which is a visual isomorph of LISP, has been designed and implemented for use by novice programmers. The attempt is to teach ideas of programming using such a representation. An experiment was conducted to test the relative merits of using DRLP compared to programming in LISP. For some classes of operations, DRLP was found to be better. This work was done at Carnegie-Mellon University, Pittsburgh, with Prof JR Anderson, by a member of the KBCS group during a fellowship visit.

2.5. A Tutor for Teaching Probability

A tutor for teaching basic concepts of probability has been designed and implemented on a Macintosh. The basis for the the tutor is a graphical representation which can be used to represent a subset of probability problems. The representation consists of a set of matrices corresponding to the different types of probability. The aim of the tutor is to make students understand the basic rules of probability and apply them where required. The problem solving process in probability has been split into different stages and students are required to go through each stage. The tutor allows students to ask for help and points out errors in their problem solving. This work was done at Carnegie Mellon University, Pittsburgh, with Prof JR Anderson, by a member of the KBCS group during a UNDP fellowship visit.

2.6. A Trigonometry Tutor

NCST has plans to develop several intelligent tutoring systems at the school leaving level. To start with, the prototype of an intelligent trigonometry tutor was designed, based on protocol analysis of students in the 9th and 10th standards. Details are available in a paper in this volume.

Publication: [Rajan et al, 1989].

3. Rule Based Systems for Resource Scheduling

3.1. Heuristic Scheduling

NCST has begun work on an intelligent airline scheduling system, working closely with a leading airline. The problem requires handling of a large number of constraints relating to the types of aircraft used, and conforming to national and international rules and guidelines etc. This makes an algorithmic approach to the problem impractical. A heuristic approach with manual monitoring and control has been therefore developed. A working prototype, which takes a large subset of the constraints into account, has been developed and demonstrated. Work on this system is progressing.

3.2. Product Tanker Scheduling System

Work is also in progress to develop a system to schedule tankers carrying petroleum products, covering the (coastal) movements of finished petroleum products to twelve ports all over India.

Some of these ports have refineries and hence produce different finished products. Those ports which do not have refineries are consumers. Ports which have refineries may themselves consume part of the products which have a local demand. Finished products have to be transported to ports, for consumption at that port and other neighbouring areas. In some cases, products from a refinery have to be picked up, either for distribution to other ports, or for export.

The task is to produce a schedule for the tankers, to distribute the finished products among the 12 ports, taking into account the supply and demand situation at each port. This distribution is to be achieved, keeping in mind objectives and constraints, and minimising the overall cost of the operation.

This problem is in some ways similar to the airline scheduling problem. We tackle both problems using the same methodology:

* tree search over a limited breadth and depth, for optimisation,

* rules to implement constraints, and to provide sophisticated heuristic functions, and

* a man-machine interface for allowing human control of the whole process.

A first prototype of this intelligent product tanker scheduling system has been designed and implemented. The product tanker scheduling system has been further extended to handle multiple products, and testing of this version is underway. Two prototypes have been developed, and a final system is expected to be ready by early 1990.

4. Parallel Logic Programming

NCST is interested in Parallel Logic Programming, and is working with the KBCS node at IISc (Bangalore) to develop an environment to support parallel logic programming on the multi-processor machine being developed there. As a first step, NCST has explored the use of Parlog.

4.1. A Compiler for Parlog

Parlog is a parallel logic programming language developed at the Imperial College, London. A compiler for Parlog was developed at Imperial College by a member of the KBCS Group, during a fellowship visit. The work was done jointly with the Parlog group at Imperial College. The compiler was written in Parlog itself. The target language was an abstract machine instruction set designed for implementing Parlog on shared memory multiprocessors such as Sequent and Multimax.

4.2. Additions to Aurora

Aurora, the or-parallel Prolog developed at the University of Bristol, was used to study available parallelism in a Civil Engineering application program. A dispatching scheduler for Aurora, an OR-parallel language for Prolog, was implemented. The work was carried out by a member of the KBCS group at NCST while he was on a fellowship visit to the Logic Programming Group in Bristol.

5. AI Software

5.1. NCLISP

An interpreter for a subset of Common LISP has been implemented at NCST. This package, named NCLISP, is used in NCST's educational programs. NCLISP is available on Unix, and on IBM PC-compatibles running DOS. NCLISP has recently been modified to allow much larger programs to be interpreted. Over a 100 copies of NCLISP are in use by participants of NCST's off-campus course on AI Programming.

Publication: [NCLISP, 1988].

5.2. Vidwan: An Expert System Shell

An Expert System shell named Vidwan has been developed for PC-compatible systems running DOS. Vidwan provides a backward chaining inference engine and an interactive editor for editing rulebases. Vidwan makes use of windows and cursor selection for providing a user-friendly interface. A version of Vidwan is also available under the Unix operating system.

Vidwan models uncertainity along the lines of the MYCIN system. Vidwan also provides explanation commands such as why, show rule, and facilities to inspect the system's reasoning process. Vidwan's functionality and user interface have been improved. More than 40 copies of Vidwan are in use by participants of NCST's off-campus course on Expert Systems.

Publications: [Sasikumar et al, 1988], [Vidwan, 1989].

6. Workshops and Courses

6.1. Advanced Courses

An Advanced Course on Applied Artificial Intelligence was conducted at NCST during Dec 8-19, 1986. The areas covered during the course were Intelligent Tutoring Systems, Natural Language Processing and Expert Systems.

A Workshop on AI Applications was held at NCST during December 14-23, 1987. Two major themes were covered in this workshop: Parallel Logic Programming (PLP) and Machine Translation (MT). The Logic Programming lectures were supplemented with practical work on Parlog, and many useful Parlog programs were developed by the participants in the workshop.

For both these events, there were a number of participants, from all over India, both from academic institutions and from industry.

Publication: [Anjaneyulu and Sasikumar, 1987].

6.2. Lecture Courses and Seminars

Dr Sergei Nirenburg, Senior Research Associate at the Center for Machine Translation, Carnegie-Mellon University, visited NCST for a week during December 1988 and delivered a series of lectures on Machine Translation, with special emphasis on Natural Language Generation.

Dr Mike Sharples, from the University of Sussex, UK visited NCST for a week in March 1989, and delivered lectures on Intelligent Tutoring Systems (ITS), and the use of Interactive Video in ITS.

NCST collaborated with the Department of Linguistics, University of Bombay, in organising the National Seminar on Problems in Translation, in Bombay during March 29-30, 1989.

6.3. Technical and Academic Affiliates

NCST has twelve technical affiliates, some of whom are major industrial organizations, keenly interested in the area of AI. The KBCS group at NCST has organized special programmes for such affiliates.

NCST has close academic cooperation with SNDT University, Bombay. A senior staff member of the Computer Science faculty at this University works closely with the KBCS group at NCST, and is working for a PhD in the area of ITS.

7. Vivek - A Quarterly in Artificial Intelligence

Vivek is a quarterly in Artificial Intelligence (AI) being published by NCST. Vivek includes technical articles, reviews and news items. Vivek also carries abstracts from various AI journals. Vivek is into its second volume this year, with over 200 individual and 60 institutional subscribers.

8. Educational Activities

8.1 Diploma in Knowledge Based Computer Systems

NCST launched a Post Graduate Diploma in KBCS about two years ago. This diploma is meant for people in the computer industry and related fields, who plan to specialize in KBCS. As a part of this diploma, a participant has to take 5 courses: one entrance course in AI programming, one core course on Knowledge Representation, two electives and a project. The entrance course is also offered in an off-campus version. Those who take this course get the prescribed books, a copy of NCLISP to run on their PCs and other course material. We also have an off-campus course on Expert Systems, which is based on the use of Vidwan (NCST's Expert System shell).

9. Conclusion

NCST has a KBCS group of ten professionals, working in the areas described above. Through its training activities, development of software, and technical and academic affiliations, this group operates with a significant number of professionals outside. Through Vivek, it contributes to the growth of the KBCS movement nation-wide. The publications of this group are listed below.

List of Publications

[Anjaneyulu et al, 1987]
Anjaneyulu, KSR, Chandrasekar, R and Ramani S (1987). Generative Testing at NCST, Proceedings of National Seminar on Information Technology and Non-formal Education, Hyderabad, 18-20 June, 1987, organised by the Computer Society of India.

[Anjaneyulu and Sasikumar, 1987]
Anjaneyulu, KSR and Sasikumar, M (Eds) (1987). Parlog Project Reports, NCST Bombay.

[Bhandarkar et al, 1989]
Bhandarkar, A, Chandrasekar, R, Ramani, S and Bhatnagar, A (1989). Intelligent Categorization, Archival and Retrieval of Information, in [Ramani et al, 1989].

[Chandrasekar and Ramani, 1987]
Chandrasekar, R and Ramani, S (1987). Issues in Machine Translation between English and Indian Languages. Proceedings of National Seminar on Computer Applications in Language Processing, New Delhi, 9-11 Sep, 1987.

[Chandrasekar and Ramani, 1988a]
Chandrasekar, R and Ramani, S (1988). An Intelligent Interface for Structuring Stories, Proceedings of CSI-88, the Annual Convention of the Computer Society of India, Madras, 6-9 Jan, 1988.

[Chandrasekar and Ramani, 1988b]
Chandrasekar, R and Ramani, S (1988). Knowledge Representation and Information Retrieval. Proceedings of Indo-US Workshop on Systems and Systems & Signal Processing, Bangalore, 8-12 Jan, 1988.

[Chandrasekar et al, 1989a]
Chandrasekar, R, Srikant, S and Ramani, S (1989). An Integrated Approach to Analysing News Stories, Proceedings of Workshop on Natural Language Processing for AI, Roorkee, January 14-15, 1989.

[Chandrasekar and Ramani, 1989b]
Chandrasekar, R and Ramani, S (1989). Interactive Communication of Sentential Structure and Content: An Alternative Approach to Man-machine Communication, International Journal of Man Machine Studies, Vol. 30, No. 2, February 1989.

[Chandrasekar and Ramani, 1989c]
Chandrasekar, R and Ramani, S (1989). Artificial Intelligence: a Developing Country Perspective, In Proceedings of Workshop on AI Technology Transfer to Developing Countries, IJCAI '89, Detroit, Aug 21-25, 1989.

[NCLISP, 1988]
NCLISP User Manual, NCST, Bombay, 1988.

[Rajan et al, 1989]
Rajan, P, Patil, P, Anjaneyulu, KSR and Srinivas, P. The Trigonometry Tutor, in [Ramani et al, 1989].

[Ramani and Chandrasekar, 1986]
Ramani, S and Chandrasekar, R (1986). Partitioning Computations and Parallel Processing, Sadhana, Vol. 9, Part 2, Sept 1986, pp. 121-137.

[Ramani et al, 1989]
Ramani, S, Chandrasekar, R and Anjaneyulu, KSR (1989). Knowledge Based Computer Systems, Proceedings of KBCS '89, Bombay, December 11-13, 1989, Narosa Publishing House, India and Springer-Verlag, Berlin.

[Sasikumar et al, 1988]
Sasikumar, M, Muthu Raman, S and Ramani, S (1988). Tools and Techniques for the Refinement of Rulebased Expert Systems. Proceedings of National Conference on Knowledge Based Computer Systems, Bangalore, 10-11 June, 1988.

[Srikant et al, 1988]
Srikant, M, Chandrasekar, R and Ramani, S (1988). An Interactive Analyzer for Natural Language Sentences. Proceedings of National Conference on Knowledge Based Computer Systems, Bangalore, 10-11 June, 1988.

[Srinivas et al, 1988]
Srinivas, P, Prakash, KN, Anjaneyulu, KSR and Ramani, S (1988). A Knowledge Based Authoring System for Test Creation, Proceedings of National Conference on Knowledge Based Computer Systems, Bangalore, 10-11 June, 1988.

[VEDA, 1989]
VEDA User Manual, NCST, Bombay, 1989.

[Vidwan, 1988]
Vidwan User Manual, NCST, Bombay, 1988.

Research and Development at KBCS Nodal Centre, IISc Bangalore

V. Rajaraman

Supercomputer Education and Research Centre

Indian Institute of Science

Bangalore 560 012 INDIA

uunet!shakti!turing!vidya!rajaram

Abstract

This paper gives a brief overview of research and development being carried out at KBCS nodal centre at Indian Institute of Science. The centre has now build three machines. The first machine is a multidimensional multilink system. Three variations of this system with four, eight and nine computing elements are built and are functional. The software environment for this machine provides a general purpose interface to any programming language. The second machine has been built using 16 CEs connected in a tree topology. This machine uses FIFO links for interprocessor communications. The third machine is a coarse grain data flow machine and has a dual token bus broadcast bus architecture. Besides this the centre has developed system software for PAR-C on VAX cluster.

1   Introduction

The KBCS nodal centre at Indian Institute of Science was set up in 1986 with the following goals.

- To design, develop and build a parallel processing architecture machine capable of executing logic programs.

- To offer courses in advanced computer architecture.

- To create the infrastructure and knowhow to design parallel processing architecture computers.

- To initiate and foster advanced reseach in computer architecture.

The main thrust of the development work at IISc Bangalore is to design and build parallel computers with different interconnection, communication and task assignment schemes. These prototype computers will provide test benches on which applications can be developed. Uniform methodology in terms of selection of processors and software environments for application development is planned so that all the teams work cooperatively and learn from each other.

At IISc nodal centre, three different architectures are being envisaged. Type of interconnection schemes that are being implemented on each of them is the special feature for each of these architectures. All the architectures are based on message passing paradigms. We believe that the message passing multicomputers scale better compared to the shared memory multiprocessor, as the number of CEs are increased.

Commercial computers are not available which use the architectural ideas being proposed. Our goal is to design systems which consist of two subsystems. The first subsystem is capable of executing programs and is called the computing elements (CEs). The other subsystem is responsible for the communication among CEs. Two subsystems are designed in a way that as better CEs become available, they can be used by just "plugging them in". Currently the designs are based on IBM PC motherboards with intel 8088 processor. We have experimented with 80386 based IBM PC/AT motherboards and found it to be working with the same communication subsystem. We are confident that any fast processor can be used for the design of a CE board provided it gives a standard IBM PC bus interface. Further, the use of commercially available motherboards with empty expansion slots to support boards will enable us to attach and use special purpose hardware accelerators, as the project progresses.

In the rest of the paper, we present the summary of work in progress at our nodal centre.

2 Multidimension Multilink System (MMS) Architecture

The MMS architecture is a general purpose architecture [Moona and Rajaraman, 1989b]. Here a number of CEs in multiple dimensions are connected through a fully connected network of CEs. The structure can be parameterized with two parameters [Moona, 1989]. The first parameter, **Drop** specifies the number of CEs that are connected through a fully connected network. The second parameter, **Dimension** specifies the number of fully connected networks to which a CE has access.

The communication links in this architecture provide 8 bit wide parallel data paths between a pair of CEs. The interface is developed such that two CEs can be kept at a distance of as much as 6 meters. Using this it is possible to provide a parallel computing environment by connecting a number of PCs kept in a laboratory.

We have developed three variations of this architecture. The first variation of this architecture is a one dimensional 4 drop MMS architecture with 4 CEs. The other system is a two dimensional 3 drop MMS architecture with 9 CEs. The third system is a three dimensional 2 drop MMS architecture with 8 CEs.

The architecture provides a very large communication bandwidth. the links operate at the processor to memory speeds. As the connectivity of the architecture is very rich, it is possible to emulate many other popular architectures like Hypercube, Ring, Mesh etc.

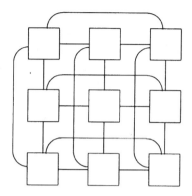

Figure 1: 9 CE Implementation of MMS Architecture

We have tried emulating some of these architectures on MMS architecture.

A programming language independent general purpose software environment has been developed for this architecture [Moona and Rajaraman, 1989c]. This allows a programmer to program the machine in any of the popular programming languages [Panwar et al, 1989] like Pascal, C, Fortran Prolog and Cobol. This environment provides system calls to create remote processes on other CEs, system calls to handle the communication among various CEs and many other support routines. We show the 9 CE implementation of this structure in Figure 1. Details of this system are presented in another paper by Moona and Rajaraman [Moona and Rajaraman, 1989a] in this conference.

3 Tree Architecture

In the tree architecture, a number of CEs are connected in a tree connected topology [Ghosal et al, 1988]. The architecture uses a FIFO interconnection scheme between CEs. A prototype is constructed with 16 CEs, each based on the IBM PC motherboards. The system provides a concurrent Pascal programming environment.

In the topology of 16 processor architecture, the root node is connected to three children. Each of these children is connected to 4 grandchildren as shown in Figure 2.

On this architecture many numerical applications like matrix operations, ODEs solutions [Ghosal, 1988] etc. are implementated and executed. Certain Diophontine Predicate Satisfiability problems also have been coded on it.

4 Coarse Grain Static Dataflow Multiprocessor

This architecture (Figure 3) uses a coarse grain static data flow oriented processing scheme with a dynamic scheduler. Simulation results have shown that if a program is partitioned with tasks having around 30 instructions then the proposed system will perform efficiently [Narayan and Rajaraman, 1989].

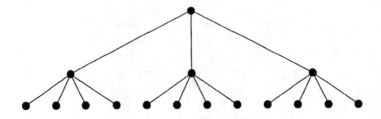

Figure 2: 16 CE Tree Architecture Implementation

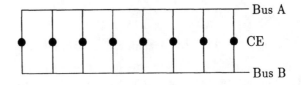

Figure 3: Broadcast Bus Architecture

A broadcast bus based parallel processing test bed system has been built. The broadcast bus provides 32 bit wide interconnection between CEs. The architecture supports point to point, multicast and broadcast communication with various arbitration schemes. Message packets of size upto 1KBytes can be exchanged between CEs. Communication hardware is interfaced to CEs through interrupt mecahnism, therefore, it is possible to implement various communication paradigms. The system is built as a test bed to experiment various concepts in scheduling and programming model. MARK I with IBM PC motherboards based on intel's 8088 processor is operational. An interprocessor communication library has been provided which can be called from any programming language. A second prototype uses 80386 based IBM PC/AT motherboards as CEs and is being tested.

5 Software Environment and Applications

The nodal centre is also developing system software and applications on a VAX cluster which uses the Ultrix operating system. This system software will eventually be ported to the multiprocessor systems. Programming language C has been extended to support "tasks" and a relavant runtime library X-Kernel, is provided so that user programs can be executed in a distributed LAN environment [Mohan and Annamalai]. A preprocessor called "PAR C" has also been developed that extends C language to support interprocessor communication between workstations connected to a LAN using TCP/IP [Sampath and Radhakrishnan, 1989].

On the VAX cluster, we have developed a small expert system for diagnosing chronic pulmonary disorders [Mohan, 1989]. The Quintus Prolog on VAX has been extended to support the usage of set operations. This is required for knowledge representations schema which is a part of the knowledge based retrieval system.

6 Advanced Courses on the Computer Architecture and Programming Languages

The centre has arranged two intensive courses during the last three years. The first course was given by Prof. Arvind and Prof. Nikhil of MIT USA during August 12-20 1987. This course was on dataflow architectures and programming languages and was attended by nearly 40 persons. The second course was given by Prof. Gary Lindstorm, University of Utah, USA. It emphasized implementation strategies of Functional and logic programming languages. This course was conducted during September 5-16, 1988 and was attended by around 30 persons from outside the institute and from the institute.

The centre also organized a workshop on parallel computing during October 30 to November 4. The emphasis in this workshop was on writing parallel programs on the parallel computers designed and working in our centre.

Besides this, the following three courses are planned. A course on implementation of functional programming languages for parallel computers is being organized from January 22 to February 2, 1990. This course will be given by Prof. Simon Peyton-Jones of University of Glasgow, UK. Another course on the use of custom design tools to design VLSI systems is being offered by Dr. van Leuken and Mr. De Graaf of Delft University, Netherlands, during February 5 to 16, 1990. Dr. Vivek Sarkar of IBM T.J. Watson Research Center, USA will be offering a course on compiling for parallelism during March 5 to 16, 1990.

7 Related Activities

The centre has co-sponsored the first national KBCS conference that was held in Bangalore during June 10-12, 1988. This conference was organized by the IISc nodal centre and Computer Society of India, Bangalore Chapter.

A workshop on "Issues in Parallel Computing" was cosponsored by IISc nodal centre which was held during January 19-21, 1981. This workshop was organized by CSI, Bangalore chapter.

8 Conclusion

The work at Indian Institute of Science nodal centre is advancing rapidly in the direction of achieving the project goals. Currently there are 8 full time project staff, one Ph.D. student, many undergraduate and graduate students involved in the project. Normally the technical manpower in these areas of research is not so easily available. We have a small but enthusiastic group at our nodal centre. We have implemented all the three architectures and explored the existing programming languages.

530

References

[Moona and Rajaraman, 1989a]
Rajat Moona, V. Rajaraman, "Design and Implementation of a Broadcast Cube Multiprocessor", *Proc. Second National Conference on Knowledge Based Computer Systems*, Bombay, Dec. 11- 13, 1989.

[Moona and Rajaraman, 1989b]
Rajat Moona, V. Rajaraman, "A Broadcast Cube Multiprocessor Architecture", *Proc. Int. Symp. on Computer Architecture and Digital Signal Processing*, Hong Kong, 1989.

[Moona and Rajaraman, 1989c]
Rajat Moona, V. Rajaraman, "A Software Environment for General Purpose MIMD Multiprocessors", *Proc. IEEE TENCON*, Bombay, 1989.

[Moona, 1989]
Rajat Moona, "Design and Implementation of a Multidimensional Multilink Multi-computer Hardware and Software", Ph.D. Thesis, Indian Institute of Science, Bangalore, India, 1989.

[Panwar et al, 1989]
R. B. Panwar, Rajat Moona, V. Rajaraman, "Application programming on Broadcast Cube Multiprocessor System", KBCS Tech. Rep., 1989.

[Ghosal et al, 1988]
S. K. Ghosal, S. Guha, S. M. Ariff, V. Rajaraman, "A Simple low-cost Multiprocessor using Message Passing FIFO links", KBCS Tech. Rep., 1988.

[Ghosal, 1988]
S. K. Ghosal, "The Numerical Integration of Ordinary Differential Equations on Multiprocessing Systems", KBCS Tech. Rep., 1988.

[Ghosal and Rajaraman, 1988a]
S. K. Ghosal, V. Rajaraman, "Comparing Parallel Methods for Solving ODEs", KBCS Tech. Rep., 1988.

[Ghosal and Rajaraman, 1988b]
S. K. Ghosal, V. Rajaraman, "A Parallel Digital Differential Analyzer", KBCS Tech. Rep., 1988.

[Narayan and Rajaraman, 1989]
Ranjani Narayan, V. Rajaraman, "Performance Analysis of a Multiprocessor Machine based on Dataflow Principles", KBCS Tech. Rep., 1989.

[Mohan and Annamalai]
T. S. Mohan, A. Annamalai, "Design and Implementation of a distributed kernel-X", KBCS Tech. Rep. under preparation.

[Mohan, 1989]

    T. S. Mohan, "Shushrutha - An Expert System for Diagnosing Chronic Pulmonary Disorders", KBCS Tech. Rep., 1989.

[Sampath and Radhakrishnan, 1989]

    D. Sampath, T. Radhakrishnan, "PAR C: An extension to the C language for Distributed Programming under Unix 4.2 BSD", KBCS Tech. Rep., 1989.

Speech Recognition for
Knowledge Based Computer Systems

PVS Rao   S Krishnan   P Poddar

V Ramasubramanian   K Samudravijaya   A Sen

Computer Systems and Communications Group
Tata Institute of Fundamental Research
Homi Bhabha Road
Bombay 400 005, INDIA
uunet!shakti!tifr!csc11

Abstract

The Knowledge Based Computer Systems project at the Tata Institute of Fundamental Research (TIFR) aims to make a concerted effort for research in the area of computer speech recognition in the context of Indian languages. For this, four approaches have been identified, namely the subword unit analysis, hidden Markov models, acoustic-phonetic feature analysis and artificial neural networks. This paper presents each of these approaches briefly and discusses the merits and demerits of each of these approaches. The activities related to the project as well as the work under way at TIFR in each of these approaches is also discussed. It is seen that the four approaches considered in this paper complement each other and may be used in conjunction with each other to improve the performance of speech recognition systems.

1 Introduction

One important feature visualized for fifth generation computers is the capability of interacting with the user in the speech mode. In other words, the computer should be able to accept information given to it as a spoken message as well as respond in speech mode; i.e., perform recognition and synthesis of speech. This requirement is important because speech is the fastest and most convenient means of communication among human beings and consequently interaction between humans and machines. The Voice Oriented Interactive Computing Environment being implemented at our nodal centre seeks to realise a speech input/output system.

The need for evolving speech recognition capabilities in Indian Languages cannot be overemphasized. The use of speech mode in one's own language for man-machine communication is important for fifth generation computers. As a first step in this direction, a system for recognition and synthesis of Hindi speech is being implemented. The strategy proposed is to work "at the frontier" and evolve suitable techniques and methodologies in addition to systematically examine existing approaches and to innovate and improve upon them to achieve the project objectives. This was chosen in preference to reverse engineering method of adopting a proven approach which has obvious limitations and disadvantages. This approach will help to advance the state of art and our understanding of speech, rather than merely yielding a working system.

At TIFR, several promising approaches are being considered in parallel for speech recognition. These are:

a) Subwords units

b) The hidden Markov model

c) The acoustic-phonetic analysis

d) Artificial neural networks

Recognition systems will be developed by integrating the results of all three approaches. These approaches can benefit from each other because they complement each other. In order to gain a better understanding of the merits and demerits of these approaches, it is planned to implement speech recognition systems based on different approaches in a practical task environment. The task vocabulary consists of 200 Hindi words used in making different kinds of enquiries in a railway station. The strategy is to build initially simple systems capable of recognizing words in a subset of full vocabulary and later expand the vocabulary of the system along with suitable refinements of the techniques.

This paper presents briefly basic philosophies and the implementation of the above mentioned approaches. Other activities related to speech recognition/synthesis being carried at the TIFR nodal centre are also mentioned.

2 The Approaches to Speech Recognition

2.1 Subword unit based speech recognition

Acoustic-phonetic and word-based approaches have been the main strategies employed in most automatic speech recognition systems. There are several distinctions between the two approaches which demarcate them clearly in terms of units of recognition, classification and decision procedure, training process and complexity. In terms of

534

performance, the acoustic-phonetic approach has yielded limited results, always requiring higher level information to resolve classification and segmentation errors. Word-based systems have achieved very good performances but face severe limitations as the vocabulary size increases. Training complexity and storage requirements increase proportionately with vocabulary; and the processing of whole-word prototypes thus become more difficult. Recognition accuracy also falls drastically because of higher scope for confusion between similar words. Most importantly, the two strategies have also "prototyped" the philosophy of machine recognition of speech, leaving little scope for improvements incorporating fresh evidence about the process of human recognition of speech. The primary difference between the two approaches is in the unit of recognition; and there is clearly a need for more flexible units which would allow the evolution of new approaches. One therefore looks for alternate representation schemes for multiple units which would a) be consistent in their definitions b) provide a manageable size of recognition primitives and c) could be made to correspond to a range of useful linguistic units from a phon to a word. These will offer the necessary flexibility to combine the existing strategies which operate at the two ends of the spectrum and free the user from their limitations.

Recent developments have opened up new techniques that exhibit considerable potential for the extraction and representation of consistent acoustic features termed as subword units. These are unsupervised clustering algorithms (such as vector quantization) combined with dynamic programming for handling segments as clusterable entities and stochastic-parametric modelling of spectral sequences in word utterances. The basic issues involved in the subword unit based approach for speech recognition are : a) automatic definition and extraction of subword segments b) segment clustering and/or statistical modeling for generating the subword unit inventory and c) generation of a word-lexicon in terms of the subword unit inventory for carrying out the recognition task [Wilpon et al, 1987].

The use of subword units for speech recognition involves study at various levels of the recognition scheme. Of particular importance is the development of procedures for segmentation, extraction and definition of subword units with particular emphasis on objective measures for defining these units. At the representational level, appropriate segmentation, clustering and statistical modeling techniques have to be developed for obtaining an inventory of subword unit representations from objectively defined subword segments. In view of the flexibilities offered by subword units over conventional word and phonetic units, development of new strategies which specifically exploit the properties of subword segment representations would be of considerable importance. The correspondence between the subword units and the linguistic units also needs to be established, in order to provide the link with speech recognition strategies using linguistically defined prototypes.

2.2 Hidden Markov Models

The motivation for this approach arises from the non-stationarity of the speech signal. A possible way of dealing with the non-stationarity is to divide the signal into a sequence of small time segments, where each segment is locally stationary. Representations of such segments can be obtained in any convenient form such as spectra derived using linear predictive analysis or using filter-bank analysis. In this framework, the global signal is considered to be a sequence of such locally stationary speech segments or their feature representations. The temporal relationship between these segments can be represented using Hidden Markov Models (HMM). In this form the states of the Markov chain represent the local segments and the actual features are problistic manifestations of these states. Thus, the process is doubly stochastic and the underlying process (which is hidden from direct observation) is a first order Markov chain. These models have been seen to provide a good parsimonious representation of the speech signal, by representing the acoustic as well as the temporal variability in the speech signal. Mathematically, HMM is a statistical 'parametric' model defined in terms of class conditional probabilities. It can be represented as $\lambda = \{\mathbf{A}, \mathbf{B}, \pi, \mathbf{D}\}$. Here $\mathbf{A}$ denotes the state transition matrix. In its most general form the model is ergodic, i.e., all states are connected. But a left to right temporal constraint is more meaningful in the context of speech. The topology of the state connections can be chosen to represent the temporal constraint of the speech segment to be represented. $\mathbf{B}$ represents the probability distribution of the actual feature vector observation associated with each state, or with each transition, depending on which is assumed to produce the observations. These can be probabilities of discrete symbols or probability densities of continuous observations. π denotes initial state distribution and $\mathbf{D}$ the explicit duration probabilities or probability densities of duration of state occupation. This is an important parameter for representing durational cues in speech. A comprehensive review of this approach is given in [Levinson 1985].

The speech recognition paradigm used is as follows : First represent each of the acoustic units (such as phonemes, context sensitive phonemes, other subword units or full words) by a HMM. Then using these representations the aposteriori probability $\mathbf{P}(\mathbf{W_i}/\mathbf{S})$ of different allowed word sequences $\mathbf{W_i}$ is computed given that the input feature sequence is $\mathbf{S}$. The word sequence getting the highest probabilistic score is decided to be the recognized sequence. In practice the liklihood measure $\mathbf{P}(\mathbf{S}/\mathbf{W_i})$ of a feature sequence being generated from word sequence is used as it can be computed easily from the HMM. The two probabilities are related by the Bayes rule as,

$$\mathbf{P}(\mathbf{W_i}/\mathbf{S}) = \frac{\mathbf{P}(\mathbf{S}/\mathbf{W_i})\mathbf{P}(\mathbf{W_i})}{\mathbf{P}(\mathbf{S})}$$

Here $\mathbf{P}(\mathbf{W_i})$ is the apriori probability of the word sequence and it is determined by the task and the grammatical constraints of the language. If this is not known all word sequences may be taken to be equally likely.

The speech recognition process consists of two phases : 1) Training and 2)Recognition. In the training phase the parameters of each HMM are estimated to best represent the corresponding acoustic unit using a the maximum liklihood criterion. This estimation procedure is fully automatic, being supervised only at the word or sentence level and is based on the maximization of the probabilistic measure. In the recognition phase the word sequence which maximizes the liklihood is taken to be the recognized sequence. The underlying state sequence obtained using the maximum liklihood criterion gives the implicit segmentation of the acoustic segment done by the HMM. It is therefore possible to use the meaningfulness of the segmentation to direct improvements in the representation.

HMM based isolated word recognizers have been built for recognizing English digits and a 40 word subset of the 200 word railway enquiry task in Hindi. Both these systems give more than 98 % recognition accuracy, for multiple speakers in normal acoustic environment. The models are word based. At present a tied training program is being developed to train phoneme based HMMs using training sentences. The training sentence can be directly fed to the program without any need for phonetic segmentation. The system relies on the implicit segmentation capability of HMM. This training approach is expected to give greater flexibility with respect to the nature of speech, i.e., isolated utterances or continuous speech and with respect to the vocabulary size as the models are phoneme based. A demonstration speech recognition system for handling the 200 word railway enquiry task in Hindi will be developed using this approach.

2.3 Acoustic-phonetic Feature Analysis

In Speech recognition, an acoustic signal is transformed into a sequence of linguistic labels such as phonemes, syllables, or words which carry the message the speaker wishes to convey. Since speech is highly encoded, it is difficult to recognize speech using acoustic information alone. Although spoken utterances can be represented as strings of phonetic units, a one-to-one correspondence does not exist at the segmental level. This difficulty is complicated by the ambiguity due to noise, phonological variations, articulatory laxity, speaking rate fluctuations, inter-speaker differences etc. Unambiguous extraction of the verbal message requires use of higher level knowledge sources such as syntax, semantics and pragmatics in addition to the acoustic information.

Human experts can quite accurately determine the phonetic identity of unknown utterances by visual inspection of a spectrogram, a three-dimensional time-frequency-intensity representation of the signal. Spectrogram reading involves interpreting the acoustic patterns in the image to determine the spoken utterance. One must selectively attend to many different acoustic cues, interpret their significance in the light of other evidence, and make inferences based on information from multiple sources. Spectrogram readers locate acoustic-phonetic features in the spectrogram and try to infer the presence (or absence) of groups of sounds based on a global look at the spectrogram. Thence, they look for other cues which will help them to refine their hypotheses. This approach captures in a transparent way the correspondence between articulatory processes and their manifestations at the acoustic level. Many of the conclusions drawn are closely associated with the knowledge of the phonological variation of sounds, the lexicon, the legally allowable combination of phonemes, words etc. Spectrogram readers also use knowledge about the context in which the utterance was spoken for disambiguation. By this means, expert spectrogram readers are able to recognize speech with high degree of accuracy (97% for continuous speech and 100% for isolated words) [Zue, 1985].

The scheme of using acoustic-phonetic features for speech recognition was implemented in a system for recognising ten digits of Hindi (0-9). This has been formulated more in the form of a pilot study to establish the general feasibility of the approach and to acquire an appreciation of the problems of rule-based recognition approach in general and of this approach for the Hindi language in particular. The strategy adopted here is similar to that employed by expert spectrogram readers. The first step is to perform some general analysis and detect features which reliably indicate either the presence of certain types of sounds or absence of some other group of phones, thereby pruning the list of candidate words. The 'correct' word is chosen out of this list after invoking special procedures which compute one or more features which will discriminate between the members of a group of sounds.

The unknown utterance was transcribed into a sequence of labels, each label being one of the following: *[silence, voiced, unvoiced]*. In the voiced region, the formant values were obtained from linear prediction spectra and the formants were tracked based on nearest neighbour criterion. Vowels in the voiced region are identified by the formant values in the steady state region of formant tracks. The fricatives were identified by their spectral shapes. Whenever there was lack of sufficient information to uniquely classify a segment, special tests designed to distinguish a given pair of candidate phonemes were conducted. The performance of the recognition system was tested on a set of 100 random numbers. 99% of spoken digits were recognised correctly by the system. Currently, the vocabulary of the system is being increased to 40, a subset of a 200 word railway enquiry task.

2.4 Neural Networks

The application of connectionist models or neural networks in speech recognition stems from two main objectives. Firstly, from the viewpoint of pattern recognition, speech recognition can be seen as a pattern classification problem in a high-dimensional space of large confusability. It has been shown that such networks of densely interconnected processing elements have the ability to generate arbitrarily complex discriminant boundaries and hence provides a paradigm for speech recognition task. Secondly, speech recognition can be viewed as a constraint satisfaction optimization problem in a high-dimensional space i.e. various hypotheses about the test symbol is pursued in parallel so that a pre-defined error function is minimized [Rumelhart et al, 1986] Neural networks through the inteconnection weights between its units or *neurons* directly implement a non-linear optimization under non-linear set of constraints.

There are various type of neural net architecture defined by the constraint on interconnection between their elementary units. A multilayer network with one hidden layer is used for our study. A task of isolated digit recognition is attempted to gain an understanding of the basic mechanism of learning and classification in these networks.

The word utterances of different speakers are sampled at 10KHz and the speech portion is separated from the silence by an automatic boundary detection technique based on local energy and zero-crossing rate. Each word duration is segmented into four regions depending on the energy profile over the duration of that word. An 8-channel filter-bank analysis is performed on each region and the resultant vectors from each region is appended to form the pattern vector of that word. There are 10 utterances of each digit for each of the ten speakers. The back-propagation learning algorithm is used to train the network. The recognition accuracy for speaker-dependent and independent cases outside training set is 92% and 86% respectively.

The present work addresses the problem of continuous speech recognition where no explicit boundary detection is necessary. Time-concentration neural network model proposed by Hopfield and Tank achieves this by concentrating information about a word near the completion of its utterance through a set of delay filters. We have modified the model so that it is able to accept probabilistic input rather than a single deterministic input token at every instant [Krishnan and Poddar, 1989]. A single-speaker digit recognizer has also been developed using this probabilistic model and it shows 100% accuracy. Recently, an automatic training rule using a mutual discrimination criterion has been used successfully [Unnikrishnan, 1989]. We are investigating to derive an training algorithm to learn the connection strengths of this network following an approach similar to back-propagation technique.

3 Other Activities

3.1 Analysis of the Acoustic Correlates of Speech Sounds of Indian Languages

Detailed information about the acoustic features of the various speech sounds of Indian languages is essential for both high quality text-to-speech systems and acoustic phonetic based speech recognition systems. The phonetic information is based on two factors: features which are inherent to a particular category of sounds and features which are phonologically controlled by the language system.

Although there exists several similarities among Indian languages, there are many differences in their phonologies. For instance, voiced aspirates have significant position in Hindi language whereas Tamil, in general, does not contain voiced aspirated sounds. Similarly, specific phonemes such as voiced retroflex approximant and the alveolar trill are available in Malayalam but absent in the Indo-Aryan languages. However, the differences among the various languages of the country are not overwhelming as compared to the common elements in their phonologies. Hence a systematic study of the phonetic features of Indian languages is a feasible and crucial project that is essential for fruitful speech I/O for systems through these languages.

A study to analyse four affricate sounds of Indian languages was undertaken. Characteristics of the sounds were analysed and comparative studies of a) voiced/unvoiced b) aspirated/unaspirated and c) affricate/sibilant categories were done. The features studied included Various durations (e.g. total duration, duration of transient, duration of frication, duration of aspiration), presence/absence of voicing, rate of rise of energy at onset, energy of various frequency bands. While sum of the durations of frication and aspiration was found to be the most important feature for aspirated/unaspirated categorization, presence/absence of voicing was the corresponding feature for voiced/unvoiced categorization.Features such as total duration, rate of rise of energy at onset and energy of various bands are useful to differentiate fricatives and affricates.

In April 1989, a pilot project was started to study some of acoustic correlates of the voiceless retroflex stops of Hindi language. This work was undertaken in collaboration with the Department of Linguistics, Deccan College, Pune. Several features such as energy of the burst, voice onset time (VOT) lag, energy in various frequency bands of release spectrum were studied as to their usefulness in distinguishing dental stops from retroflex stops. The results of this work indicated that VOT lag seems to be the most crucial feature for distinguishing these two sounds; the retroflexes have a very short VOT lag when compared to the dentals.

Encouraged by the outcome the above mentioned pilot project, it was decided to undertake a project to study the acoustic correlates of speech sounds of Indian Languages in general with a view to apply the knowledge gained to speech recognition/synthesis systems. The first phase of the project to study acoustic correlates of Hindi plosive sounds has already started.

3.2 Acoustic-Phonetic Data Base for spoken Indian Languages

An important requirement of research in the area of Human-machine interaction through voice is the study of acoustic-phonetic and prosodic aspects of speech and a comprehensive data base spoken Indian Languages. A project to prepare a data base of spoken Hindi is proposed as a first step in this direction. This project will be conducted in collaboration with Central Electronics Engineering Research Institute New Delhi and Aligarh Muslim University. The speech database will contain words of a restricted vocabulary spoken in isolation as well as in continuous speech by many speakers. A pilot project to create a database of 40 words, a subset of 200 word vocabulary railway enquiry task, is underway.

4 Discussion

The different approaches discussed in this paper represent different facets of speech recognition by machine. They lay emphasis on four different factors of automatic speech recognition, namely units of representation, the modeling of the process, the representation of speech-specific knowledge and appropriate structure for internal representation of auditory signal.

The subword and the HMM approaches are essentially statistical and require a large amount of speech data for preparing templates. These two methods do not assume any speech specific knowledge, but derive statistical properties directly from the speech data. HMM provides a representational toll for the units of recognition. Since HMM is parametric, it also requires that certain assumptions be made about the distribution of the data. These assumptions help in reducing the data requirements for training. HMM also has an additional advantage of begin compatible in representation with the probabilistic description of syntax. The subword unit, on the other hand, is essentially based on non-parametric analysis carried out in the statistical framework of HMM. The subwords however have the flexibility of being represented by HMM or by non-parametric clustering methods. Both these methods are automatic and do not require human intervention. However, both these methods suffer from the problem of word or unit boundary in the continuous speech recognition context, as the unit templates ignore the boundaries per se.

Speech recognition based on feature analysis using qualitative descriptors is essentially aimed at utilizing speech specific acoustic-phonetic knowledge. This incorporates the rules of articulation as gathered by phonetic experts as well as spectrogram readers. The main justification for this approach is that it is possible to identify quantitatively the systematic variability in speech due to articulatory constraints. A possible objection to this approach could be the loss of information which is otherwise present in the acoustic speech signal. A second limitation is that this requires exhaustively enumerating all the articulatory rules.

The speech recognition process can be viewed as a complex mapping from the input feature space of auditory signals to the output pattern space of word symbols. This complex mapping can be broken down to several simpler transformations using various stages of intermediate representations.The neurobiological data suggest that similar internal representations of the auditory input are present at various stages of the auditory processing in the brain. The artificial neural network architecture allows to form such internal representations. Specifically in the context of speech recognition it is possible to use speech specific information in the form of acoustic-phonetic knowledge and auditory representations along with neural networks. Here the neural network provide effective control structures where the interconection strengths between neurons capture correlations from various input features, thus forming an internal representation of the mapping in terms of the state of the neural activity in the intermediate layers. These interconnection strengths can be learned from examples. Preliminary experiments in phoneme recognition and word recognition show good internal representations and needs to be systematically investigated further.

5 Conclusion

In this paper, an overview of activities at the KBCS nodal centre for speech research is presented. Various approaches for automatic speech recognition being examined at this centre, their merits and demerits, activities related to speech research such as study of acoustic correlates of speech sounds of Indian languages, creation of speech database are summarized. An account of the current status of implementation of speech recognition systems by different approaches is given. The final speech recognition system is expected to be evolved on the basis of the experience gained through examination of different approaches and by the judicious integration of best features of all these. In this respect, each of the approaches discussed in the paper holds sufficient promise and that an appropriate integration of these would yield a viable and flexible speech recognition system.

References

[Krishnan and Poddar, 1989]
Krishnan S and Poddar P. *A probabilistic training scheme for the time concentration network.* Proc. of KBCS conference, Bombay, Dec. 1989.

[Levinson, 1985]
Levinson SE. *Structural methods in automatic speech recognition.* Proc. IEEE, **73**, pp.1625–1650, 1985.

[Rumelhart et al, 1986]
Rumelhart DE, McClelland JL and the PDP research group *Parallel Distributed Processing.* Explorations in the microstructure of cognition. MIT Press, 1986.

[Wilpon et al, 1987]
Wilpon JG, Juang BH and Rabiner LR. *An investigation on the use of acoustic sub-word units for automatic speech recognition.* Proc. ICASSP, 20.7.1–20.7.4, pp. 821–824, 1987.

[Unnikrishnan, 1989]
Unnikrishnan KP. Personal communication.

[Zue, 1985]
Zue VW. *The use of speech specific knowledge in automatic speech recognition.* Proc. IEEE **73**, pp. 1602–1615, 1985.

Referees

Arun Agarwal	Alan Lemmon	HV Sahasrabuddhe
Syed Ali	Sam Levine	P Saint-Dizier
KSR Anjaneyulu	David D Lewis	Rajeev Sangal
S Arunkumar	Rick Lewis	VVS Sarma
KK Bajaj	Garr Lystad	M Sasikumar
Tony Beaumont	HN Mahabala	C Ravi Shankar
R Bhaskar	CP Mariadassou	VVS Sharma
VP Bhatkar	Gord McCalla	B Shekar
Anurag Bhatnagar	Paul McFetridge	A Shrivastava
PCP Bhatt	Spiro Michaylov	SS Sian
P Bhattacharya	TS Mohan	RMK Sinha
Nick Cercone	G Nagaraja	J Spohrer
Vineet Chaitanya	BN Nair	M Srikant
AK Chandra	M Narasimhamurthy	P Srinivas
R Chandrasekar	Anil Nigam	SH Srinivasan
KC Chellamuthu	C Pandurangan	SM Sripada
Robert Cohn	N Parameswaran	RK Subramanian
Albert Corbett	T Pattabhiraman	Richard S Sutton
Alvah Davis	Fred Popowich	V Kripa Sundar
MP Diwakar	TV Prabhakar	Milind Tambe
P Eswar	Ravi Prakash	A Togashi
Dan Fass	BE Prasad	C Vasudevan
David Gilbert	Sanjay Raina	M Venkataramana
Jim Greer	Kanna Rajan	G Venkatesh
Chris Groeneboer	Parvati Rajan	YV Venkatesh
Gary Hall	V Rajaraman	Carl M Vogel
JR Isaac	V Rajasekar	Clive Williams
Gabriel Jakobson	RS Ramakrishna	Ralph Worrest
LV Kale	S Muthu Raman	B Yegnanarayana
H Karnick	S Ramani	S Yegneshwar
Deepak Khemani	E Ravindran	
Arun Lakhotia	AS Reddy	

Author Index

Lecture Notes in Computer Science